D1260376

Handbook of Multicultural Perspectives on Stress and Coping

International and Cultural Psychology Series

Series Editor: **Anthony Marsella,** *University of Hawaii, Honolulu, Hawaii*

A continuation Order Plan is available for this series. A continuation order will bring delivery of each new volume immediately upon publication. Volumes are billed only upon actual shipment. For further information please contact the publisher.

Handbook of Multicultural Perspectives on Stress and Coping

Edited by:

Paul T. P. Wong, Ph.D.
Lilian C. J. Wong, Ph.D.

Trinity Western University
Langley, British Columbia, Canada

Foreword by Walter J. Lonner

With 16 Figures

 Springer

Paul T.P. Wong
Graduate Program in Counselling
    Psychology
Trinity Western University
7600 Glover Road
Langley, British Columbia V2Y 1Y1
Canada
ptpwong@shaw.ca

Lilian C.J. Wong
Graduate Program in Counselling
    Psychology
Trinity Western University
7600 Glover Road
Langley, British Columbia V2Y 1Y1
Canada
lilian.wong@twu.ca

Library of Congress Control Number: 2005927415

ISBN-10: 0-387-26236-9   e-ISBN 0-387-26238-5
ISBN-13: 978-0387-26236-9

Printed on acid-free paper.

Printed in the United States of America.   (SPI/HAM)

9 8 7 6 5 4 3 2 1

springeronline.com

Foreword

The frontispiece of Geert Hofstede's influential book, *Culture's consequences: Comparing values, behaviors, institutions, and organizations across nations* (Hofstede, 2001) includes the following quote: "Vérité en-deça des pyrénées, erreur au-delà". Written about 350 years ago by the French mathematician and physicist Blaise Pascal and included in his *Pensées*, Hofstede's translation is "There are truths on this side of the Pyrenees that are falsehoods on the other." One can find hundreds of similar phrases in world literature. They are all variations of the axiom that what is true or valid in one's neighborhood, region or nation is not necessarily true or valid elsewhere. The quote, however, is not given here because it is clever or cute, or made more important because of the immense status of Pascal, but because it says something quite important about the seemingly eternal tendency of inquisitive humans to try and understand the differences in the psychological makeup among people, as well as to comprehend their similarities. Centuries earlier, Theophrastus, primarily a botanist and taxonomist, and apparently Aristotle's favorite student, was reported to have said the following in 319 B.C.:

> *I have often applied my thoughts to the perplexing question – which will probably puzzle me forever – why, while all Greece lies under the same sky and all Greeks are educated alike, we have different personalities. I have been a student of human nature for a long time, and have observed the different composition of men. I thought I would write a book about it.*

A century earlier, another Greek scholar by the name of Protagoras, said that "Man is the measure of all things: of things that are, that they are; of things that they are not, that they are not."

Fast forward to 1990 and we find a similar sentiment expressed by the cultural psychologist Richard Shweder:

> *(What) is truly true (beautiful, good) within one intentional world – is not necessarily true (beautiful, good) in every intentional world; and what is true (beautiful, good) in every intentional world may be truly true (beautiful, good) in this one or that one.*

Humans, in other words, have been curious about differences among and between people since the dawn of time. Indeed, these differences have led to any number of wars and have been the source of ridicule, prejudice, and many misunderstandings, both large and small. They have also been the source of fawning admiration, myths, and benign envies. Fortunately, however, many scholars throughout the ages have, like Theophrastus, sought to understand them by using various scientific methods and modes of inquiry. For many years, psychologists and other social scientists have shown considerable interest in the phenomenon of individual differences in a wide range of human characteristics. If one were to examine the psychological (and surely the anthropological) literature during the past 150 years, reams of material would be found in a quest to find and explain differences, and similarities, between human beings on all sorts of human capacities, qualities, abilities, beliefs, emotions, languages, and so forth.

Because this edited book has a focus on stress and coping, my brief comments will be limited to the field of psychology and, perhaps tangentially or by implication, to a few neighboring fields. Stress and coping, as well as numerous related concepts such as anxiety, emotionality, and adjustment, have been part of the psychological literature since psychology became a modern and respected field. The same concepts or constructs, when considered against the background of culture, have been heavily studied. This is also true of many other aspects of interest to psychologists. Thus, studying the various ways in which stress and coping come into play in different cultures or ethnic groups is not at all new. What is new, however, is the relatively recent emphasis that cross-cultural and cultural psychologists have placed on these areas in terms of intensity, sophistication, and international cooperation in scholarship and research. This Handbook is an example of this recent heightened interest. To explain, at least partially, how this came about requires a little background information.

It is generally agreed, among psychologists who identify themselves as cross-cultural psychologists, that the "modern movement" in cross-cultural psychology began in the mid-to-late 1960s. While this foreword is not the place to give the details about these beginnings, a small number of independent efforts converged to form the nucleus of a concerted and growing effort to understand, more than ever before, the nature and scope of human differences and similarities across cultures. The coalescing factors led, for instance, to the inauguration in 1972 of the International Association for Cross-Cultural Psychology. This effort spawned an ever-increasing sophistication of both scholarship, collegiality in sharing and designing studies, organization, and the dissemination of research findings in such publications as the *Journal of Cross-Cultural Psychology, Culture and Psychology, Transcultural Psychiatry,* and *the International Journal of Intercultural Relations.*

A critical factor, and one that is a clear measure of the growing sophistication of this area, has been the appearance of a small number of influential handbooks. Specifically, the seminal six-volume *Handbook of Cross-Cultural Psychology,* published in 1980, signaled that cross-cultural psychology had finally "come of age." Volume 6 in the *HCCP,* subtitled Psychopathology, included chapters of major concern to researchers who studied a wide range of phenomena within the context of other cultures. The *HCCP* was revised in 1997, but contained only three volumes (many of the previous chapters were archived). The revised Handbook contained several chapters of interest to those who study stress and coping. The *Handbook of Intercultural Training* appeared in 1996 and it contained some material relevant to the content of the present handbook. A related work, the *Handbook of International and Intercultural Communication* appeared in 2001. It, too, has chapters that are relevant in the understanding of stress and coping within and across cultures. Finally, the *Handbook of Culture and Psychology,* also published in 2001, contained several chapters of interest to those whose career orientations fall within the domain of stress, coping, and its various components. One chapter, concerned with the large area of research on acculturation, is especially relevant in this context.

And now we have a most welcome newcomer, the *Handbook of Multicultural Perspectives on Stress and Coping*. A sure sign of increasing interest in this important area, the HMPSC, as it will become known among the cognoscenti, will take its place among the growing collections of work that will contribute in numerous important ways to an understanding of the ways in which the complexities of culture interact with equally complex concepts of stress and coping. I congratulate Paul and Lilian Wong for their diligent efforts in this important project. To provide such a compendium of perspectives and challenges is a remarkable service to those who wish to contribute to an understanding of the various ways that culture interacts with stress and coping. They and the approximately 50 contributing authors merit applause for this effort. I am nearly certain the HMPSC will be revised within the next decade. The work that is done between now and then will inform an even better Handbook. The revision will likely be more expansive and more inclusive. Whatever shape it takes, those who are involved will have benefited greatly from the present energetic effort.

Walter J. Lonner
University of Washington

REFERENCE

Hofstede, G. H. (2001). Culture's Consequences: Comparing Values, Behaviors, Institutions, and Organizations Across Nations. Thousand Oaks, CA: Sage Publications.

Contents

CONCLUSION

Contributors

Naji Abi-Hashem is an independent scholar and an Associate with Venture International. He received the M.Div. (1985) from Golden Gate Theological Seminary; M.A. (1987) and Ph.D. (1992) from Rosemead Graduate School of Psychology, Biola University; Diplomate, American Board of Psychological Specialties (1998); and Diplomate, International Academy of Behavioral Medicine, Counseling, and Psychotherapy (2002). He is a Lebanese-American clinical and cultural psychologist (licensed in 1995), who is involved in international services, counseling, training, conference speaking, volunteer work, teaching, writing, editing, networking, and consultation. He is active in many professional organizations and serves on four boards of directors and is currently based in Seattle, Washington, USA. His special areas of interest are: grief, loss, and bereavement; spirituality and psychotherapy; pastoral care and counseling; Middle Eastern and cultural studies; peace and political psychology; existential philosophy; and contemplative faith and spirituality.

Kiyoshi Asakawa is Professor of Psychology, Faculty of Intercultural Communication, Hosei University, Japan. She received her Ph.D. in psychology (Human Development) from the University of Chicago in 1997. Major research interests include influences of the self-conceptions on daily experience and the study of flow experience and subjective well-being.

John Widdup Berry is Professor Emeritus of Psychology at Queen's University, Canada. He obtained his BA from Sir George Williams University (Montreal) in 1963, and his PhD at the University of Edinburgh in 1966. He was a Lecturer at the University of Sydney for three years (1966-1969), and worked as an Assistant to Associate to Full Professor at Queen's (1969-1999). He has been a Visiting Professor at a number of universities, including Nice, Geneva, Bergen, Helsinki, Oxford, Buenos Aires, Tartu, Baroda, Paris, Kwansei Gakuin, and Victoria University of Wellington. He is a Fellow of the Netherlands Institute for Advanced Study in the Humanities and Social Sciences, an Onassis Fellow, and a Fellow of the Canadian Psychological Association, the International Association for Cross-Cultural Psychology, and the International Academy of Intercultural Research. He has served as Secretary General, and President of the International Association for Cross-Cultural Psychology, is a member of the Board of Directors of the International Association of Applied Psychology, and sits on the Editorial boards of a number of journals. In 2001, he received Honorary Doctorates from the University of Athens, and Universite de Geneve. He has published over 30 books in the areas of cross-cultural, social and cognitive psychology.

Among these, he has co-authored (with Ype Poortinga, Marshall Segall, and Pierre Dasen) two textbooks in cross-cultural psychology: *Cross-Cultural Psychology: Research and Applications* (1992 and 2002), and *Human Behaviour in Global Perspective: An Introduction to Cross-Cultural Psychology* (1991 and 1999). He was the senior editor of the *Handbook of Cross-Cultural Psychology* (2nd edition, 1997), and is co-editor (with David Sam) of the *Cambridge Handbook of Acculturation Psychology* (2005). His main research interests are in the ecology of human behavior, and in acculturation and intercultural relations with an emphasis on applications to immigration, educational and health policy.

Noah E. Borrero was born in Boston, MA and raised in Hartford, CT. He attended Miami University in Oxford, OH, where he received two degrees: his Bachelor of Arts in Literature (1996) and his Master of Arts in Teaching (1997). After teaching high school English for four years in the San Francisco bay area, he entered a Ph.D. program in the Stanford University School of Education. He is currently conducting research in adolescent development within the Psychological Studies in Education Program. His research interests include school reform, the education of minority students, biculturalism, and ethnic identity in public schools.

Edward C. Chang is an Associate Professor of Clinical Psychology and a Faculty Associate in Asian/Pacific Islander American Studies at the University of Michigan, Ann Arbor. He received his B.A. in psychology and philosophy from the State University of New York at Buffalo, and his M.A. and Ph.D. degrees from the State University of New York at Stony Brook. He completed his APA-accredited clinical internship at Bellevue Hospital Center-New York University Medical Center. He serves as an Associate Editor of the Journal of Social and Clinical Psychology, and is on the editorial boards of several leading journals, including the *Journal of Personality and Social Psychology*, *Cognitive Therapy and Research*, and the *Asian Journal of Social Psychology*. He has published numerous works on optimism and pessimism, perfectionism, social problem solving, and cultural influences on behavior. Dr. Chang is the editor of *Optimism and Pessimism: Implications for Theory, Research, and Practice* (2001) and *Self-Criticism and Self-Enhancement: Theory, Research, and Clinical Implications* (2006), and is a co-editor of *Virtue, Vice, and Personality: The Complexity of Behavior* (2003) and *Social Problem Solving: Theory, Research, and Training* (2004). He is currently working on a book that takes a critical look at adaptive and maladaptive perfectionism (forthcoming, Oxford University Press).

Yu-Hsi Chen is Professor of the Department of Religious Studies, Fo Guang University, Taiwan. He was an East-West Center grantee and received his Ph.D. in political science from University of Hawaii in the early 1980s. His research interests cover several areas in the social sciences and humanities, and his academic works on politico-economic analysis have won wide recognition for his in-depth original thinking. In recent years, his interests have shifted to psychology of religion, with a focus on the psychological re-interpretations of the Buddhist doctrines. He also has a long-standing history of practicing Yoga and Buddhist meditation. Experience and insights gained in inner work serve as a strong basis for his writings in this particular area.

Chi-Ah Chun is an assistant professor in the Department of Psychology at California State University, Long Beach. She received her Ph.D. in Clinical Psychology from

University of California, Los Angeles, and her postdoctoral training at the Center for Health Care Evaluation with the VA Palo Alto Health Care System and Stanford University Medical School. Her research programs broadly examine Asian American mental health issues with specific focus on the role of culture in stress and coping, cultural idioms of distress, and prevalence of mental disorders (psychiatric epidemiology) in Asian Americans.

Lucian Gideon Conway, III received his Ph.D. from the University of British Columbia in 2001 and is currently an Assistant Professor of Psychology at the University of Montana. His primary research interests lie in political and social psychology; he is the author of 22 articles, commentaries, and book chapters in these areas. In particular, his interests revolve around the causes of complex (as opposed to simple) thinking and the subsequent consequences on decision-making in political arenas and mental health. He studies other sociopolitical issues as well, including how shared cultural beliefs (for example, stereotypes) emerge and persist.

Cary L. Cooper is Professor of Organizational Psychology and Health, Lancaster University Management School and Pro Vice Chancellor (External Relations) at Lancaster University. He is the author of over 100 books (on occupational stress, women at work and industrial and organizational psychology), has written over 400 scholarly articles for academic journals, and is a frequent contributor to national newspapers, TV, and radio. He is currently Founding Editor of the *Journal of Organizational Behavior* and Co-Editor of the medical journal *Stress & Health* (formerly *Stress Medicine*). He is a Fellow of the British Psychological Society, The Royal Society of Arts, The Royal Society of Medicine, The Royal Society of Health, and an Academician of the Academy for the Social Sciences. Professor Cooper is the President of the British Academy of Management, is a Companion of the Chartered Management Institute and one of the first UK-based Fellows of the (American) Academy of Management (having also won the 1998 Distinguished Service Award for his contribution to management science from the Academy of Management). In 2001, Cary was awarded a CBE in the Queen's Birthday Honours List for his contribution to organizational health. He holds Honorary Doctorates from Aston University (DSc), Heriot-Watt University (DLitt), Middlesex University (Doc. Univ) and Wolverhampton University (DBA). Professor Cooper is the Editor (jointly with Professor Chris Argyris of Harvard Business School) of the international scholarly *Blackwell Encyclopedia of Management* (12-volume set); and the Editor of *Who's Who in the Management Sciences*. He has been an adviser to two UN agencies: the World Health Organisation and ILO; published a major report for the EU's European Foundation for the Improvement of Living and Work Conditions on "Stress Prevention in the Workplace"; and is a special adviser to the Defence Committee of the House of Commons on their Duty of Care enquiry. Professor Cooper is also the President of the Institute of Welfare Officers, Vice President of the British Association of Counselling, an Ambassador of The Samaritans, and Patron of the National Phobic Society.

Ruth C. Cronkite received her doctorate in Sociology from Stanford University and an M.S. in Statistics, also from Stanford University. She is currently a Research Health Scientist at the Center for Health Care Evaluation, Veterans Affairs Palo Alto Health Care System, and a Consulting Associate Professor, Department of Sociology, Stanford University. Her research interests include: the long-term course of psychiatric disorders; mental health services research; the interrelationships among stress, social support, and coping; program evaluation, continuity of care, and gender differences.

Jera N. Cunningham Virginia Commonwealth University, Richmond, Virginia, USA

Anita DeLongis is an associate professor in the Department of Psychology at the University of British Columbia. She has published numerous articles and chapters on stress, coping, and social support. Her work examines the effects of stress across several contexts, including family stress and living with chronic illness. Her current research examines stress within stepfamilies and among those with rheumatoid arthritis.

John E. Fife, Ph.D., postdoctoral fellow at Virginia Commonwealth University, Richmond, Virginia, USA. He has expertise in the areas of stress, race and parenting.

Richard H. Harvey received his MA in psychology at San Francisco State University, and is currently completing his Ph.D. at the University of California, Irvine. At the latter school, he has run the Biofeedback and Stress Management Program in the Counseling Center, and taught undergraduate courses on hardiness training. He has also been supported by NIH fellowship to study research and community collaborations in reducing teenage tobacco use. He has published 10 papers on hardiness, stress, and scientific collaboration, and will join the faculty of San Francisco State University in 2005.

Satoko Hirayama is a Ph.D. candidate in Developmental Psychology at Ochanomizu University, Tokyo, Japan. She is also a staff researcher at the Culture and Emotion Research Laboratory at San Francisco State University. She earned her M.A. in Developmental and Clinical Psychology from Ochanomizu University in 1999 and a second M.A. in Psychology from California State University, Sacramento in 2003. Her major research interest focuses on the role of emotion regulation in adolescent mental health. She has also studied intercultural adjustment, Japanese cultural change, cultural display rules, and family relationships.

Kathleen M. Ingram, J.D., Ph.D., Associate Professor, Department of Psychology, Virginia Commonwealth University, Richmond, Virginia, USA

Susan James is an assistant professor at the University of British Columbia, Vancouver, Canada in the Counselling Psychology department. She is dedicated to improving the health care of Portuguese immigrants in Canada and the United States. Her research has led to a better conceptual understanding of *agonias,* a culture-specific phenomenon exhibited by this population. Her numerous articles, conference presentations, and training workshops have improved care and minimized misdiagnosis of immigrants. Dr. James integrates anthropology, philosophy, and theology with cultural psychology, which allows for a complex understanding of the person and his or her lived experience.

Derrick W. Klaassen, M.A., C.C.C. was the Assistant Director in the Graduate Program in Counselling Psychology at Trinity Western University and the Executive Director of the International Network on Personal Meaning. For the past two years, he served as the Executive Director for the International Society for Existential Psychology and

Psychotherapy and Managing Editor of the International Journal of Existential Psychology and Psychotherapy. He is a member of the Canadian Counselling Association and the Austrian Society for Logotherapy and Existential Analysis. His clinical and research interests include existential psychology and psychotherapy, cultural psychology and the role of spirituality and religion in mental health. In addition he works part-time in psychotherapy and psychological assessments for Professional Psychological Assessments in Coquitlam, BC. As of September 2005, he will be working on his PhD in Counselling Psychology at the University of British Columbia.

Agnes Kwong Arora Ed.M. is a doctoral student in the Counseling Psychology Program at the Steinhardt School of Education, New York University. She received her Masters in Education and Arts from Teachers College, Columbia University. Her research and clinical interests include Asian North American mental health, biculturalism, ethnic identity, coping, and multicultural competence. She has published in the areas of coping, self, and cultural adjustment.

Hong Seock Lee received his M.D. and Ph.D. degrees from Korea University, Seoul, Korea. He has worked at the Korean Board of Psychiatry, Department of Psychiatry, Korea University, College of Medicine, and Chuncheon National Mental Hospital. He spent two years (2002-2004) as a Visiting Scholar at the Graduate Program of Counselling Psychology of Trinity Western University. At present, he is Assistant Professor of Department of Psychiatry at St. Mary's Hospital of the Catholic University in South Korea, where he is Director of the Adult Posttraumatic Stress Disorder Clinic. He has authored and coauthored 19 articles and several chapters; many of these publications focused on PTSD and molecular studies. Currently his research is based on several key questions in traumatology: How does the personality system work in response to traumatic stress? How does the personality system reorganize as a way of coping with traumas? How is the personality system's reorganization related to the current psychiatry's diagnostic system? He attempts to bridge the gap between biological psychiatry and positive psychology. His chapter in this book is the theoretical foundation for his future work.

Frederick T.L. Leong is Professor of Psychology and Director of the Counseling Psychology Program at the University of Tennessee at Knoxville. Prior to UTK, he was on the faculty at Southern Illinois University (1988-1991) and the Ohio State University (1991-2003). He obtained his Ph.D. from the University of Maryland with a double specialty in Counseling and Industrial/Organizational Psychology. He has authored or co-authored over 100 articles in various counseling and psychology journals, 45 book chapters, and also edited or co-edited 6 books. Dr. Leong is a Fellow of the American Psychological Association (Divisions 1, 2, 17, 45, and 52) and the recipient of the 1998 Distinguished Contributions Award from the Asian American Psychological Association and the 1999 John Holland Award from the APA Division of Counseling Psychology. His major research interests are in vocational psychology (career development of ethnic minorities), cross-cultural psychology (particularly culture and mental health and cross-cultural psychotherapy), and organizational behavior. Currently, he is the President of both the Asian American Psychological Association and the Division of Counseling Psychology of the International Association of Applied Psychology.

Jeffrey A. LeRoux received his doctorate in Psychology from the University of California at Berkeley in 1987. He has taught at Scripps College, the University of Hawai'i at Hilo, Mills College, California State University at Hayward as well as at San Francisco State University for the last sixteen years. Dr. LeRoux is the President of the Graduate School of Human Behavior and the author of numerous articles in Psychology.

Bonita C. Long is professor of counselling psychology at the University of British Columbia. Her main areas of research and publication focus on the influence of personality and contextual factors on the health of individuals who experience chronic psychosocial stress (e.g., work stress, chronic illness). Her work examines conceptual and theoretical aspects of stress and coping processes, as well as person-environment interactions. She has published numerous journal articles and book chapters. Among her publications is the book *Women, Work, and Coping*. Professor Long is a Fellow in the Canadian Psychological Association.

Walter J. Lonner received his Ph.D. from the University of Minnesota in 1967. He is Professor Emeritus of Psychology of Western Washington University in Bellingham, Washington. He is also co-founder of Western Washington University's Center for Cross-Cultural Research, and has served for more than 15 years as its director. He had a full-year sabbatical in Germany (1984-85) as a Fulbright scholar. More recently, he had visiting scholar appointments to New Zealand (Waikato University in 1996 and Victoria University of Wellington in 2004). He is interested in a wide range of topics in cross-cultural psychology, both conceptually and methodologically, he is particularly interested in the history and development of psychology's involvement with the study of culture as well as issues and perspectives in teaching about psychology and culture at the university level.

He has been active in the area of cross-cultural psychology for nearly forty years. He is Founding and Special Issues Editor of the *Journal of Cross-Cultural Psychology*. Dr. Lonner is a charter member of the International Association for Cross-Cultural Psychology (IACCP) and has served as president (1986-88) and is an Honorary Fellow (1994). As author or editor, Lonner has been involved with more than 40 books in cross-cultural psychology, including the seminal six-volume *Handbook of cross-cultural psychology* (1980), *Cross-cultural research methods* (1973), *Field methods in cross-cultural research* (1985), and *Counseling across cultures* (five editions, with the sixth edition in preparation). His most recent book, co-edited with three colleagues, is *Ongoing themes in psychology and culture (2004)*. His most recent book chapter, published in the *German Encyclopedia of Psychology,* is titled "Das Aufkommen und die fortdauernde Bedeutung der Kulturvergleichenden Psychologie" (The Advent and Continuing Importance of Cross-Cultural Psychology).

Salvatore R. Maddi obtained his doctorate in clinical psychology from Harvard University in 1960. He then taught at the University of Chicago for 26 years, and is now a professor at the University of California, Irvine. His early work was on creativity and the motivation for new experiences. He began developing the hardiness and resilience approach in 1975, and founded the Hardiness Institute in 1984. Among other things, these research and conceptual activities have led to assessment and training procedures for hardiness. The author of more than 100 papers and six books, he is internationally recognized as a leader in psychology, and continues to win prestigious awards for his hardiness-based research and consulting work. The most recent of these prizes is the Henry A. Murray

Award, conferred on him by the American Psychological Association in 2004. An international survey in 1986 named him among the top 175 psychologists in the world.

David Matsumoto is an internationally acclaimed author and psychologist. He received his B.A. from the University of Michigan in 1981 with High Honors in two fields – Psychology and Japanese. He subsequently earned his M.A. (1983) and Ph.D. (1986) in psychology from the University of California at Berkeley. He is currently Professor of Psychology and Director of the Culture and Emotion Research Laboratory at San Francisco State University, where he has been since 1989. He has studied culture, emotion, and social interaction and communication for 20 years, and has written over 250 works in these areas. His books include well-known titles such as *Culture and Psychology: People Around the World* (Wadsworth; translated into Dutch and Japanese), *The Intercultural Adjustment Potential of Japanese* (Nihonjin no Kokusai Tekiouryoku) (Hon no Tomosha), and *The Handbook of Culture and Psychology* (Oxford University Press; translated into Russian). His newest book, *The New Japan* (Intercultural Press), has received national and international acclaim, and its Japanese translation was published in 2003 (Bungeishunju). He is the recipient of many awards and honors in the field of psychology, including being named a G. Stanley Hall lecturer by the American Psychological Association. He gives speeches to audiences all around the world and serves as a consultant to many international businesses, especially those dealing with intercultural training.

Rod McCormick received his Ph.D. in Counselling Psychology at the University of British Columbia. He is a status Indian of the Mohawk Nation, and works as an Associate Professor of Counselling Psychology at the University of British Columbia. Dr. McCormick is also a mental health consultant to numerous Aboriginal and government agencies.

Micah Lenard McCreary received his Ph.D. in Counseling Psychology at Virginia Commonwealth University. At present, he is Associate Professor, Assistant Vice-Provost for Diversity at the Virginia Commonwealth University. He is also Executive Director of IMPACT Family Programs, developed by Dr. McCreary and Staff and funded by Department of Health and Human Services. The IMPACT programs are culturally based and culturally sensitive educational, training and motivational programs, which teach families to nurture and develop one another. His current research foci are in the areas of family and multicultural psychology; equity, diversity and social justice in higher education; and student retention and engagement. His numerous publications encompass multicultural counseling and Black issues in psychology and pastoral care. He was recipient of the Elske V. P. Smith Distinguished Teaching Award at the Virginia Commonwealth University in 2000.

Marvin J. McDonald Ph.D., is Director of the MA program in Counselling Psychology at Trinity Western University. He is married to Darlys Carlson McDonald and joins her in parenting their two sons, Nathan and Christopher. He publishes in the areas of theoretical psychology, spirituality and health, and professional issues in counselling. He is co-author, with D. W. Klaassen & M. D. Graham, of "Constructivist stances for promoting justice in spirituality research." In J. Raskin & S. Bridges (Eds.), Studies in meaning 2: Bridging the Personal and Social in Constructivist Psychology (pp. 239-263). New York: Pace University Press. He is involved with the International Network on Personal Meaning, www.meaning.ca, and participates in interfaith dialogue activities in his community.

Rudolf H. Moos Ph.D., completed his undergraduate and graduate work in Psychology at the University of California at Berkeley. He then took a Postdoctoral Fellowship in Biobehavioral Sciences at the University of California School of Medicine in San Francisco. He joined Stanford University and currently is a Professor in the Department of Psychiatry and Behavioral Sciences at Stanford and a Senior Research Career Scientist at the Department of Veterans Affairs Health Care System in Palo Alto, California. Dr. Moos' research has focused on four main areas: (1) formulation of standard measures of the social climate of community settings, such as families, the workplace, and social and task-oriented groups; (2) development of indices of the quality of mental health treatment and specification of their relationship to treatment outcome; (3) conceptualization and assessment of approach and avoidance coping skills; and (4) clarification of the role of social context factors and coping strategies in personal growth and well-being, especially in relation to the outcomes of intervention programs for individuals with substance use and depressive disorders.

Amado M. Padilla was born and raised in Albuquerque, New Mexico. He received his Ph.D. in experimental psychology from the University of New Mexico and has taught at the State University of New York, UC Santa Barbara, UCLA, and is currently Professor of Psychological Studies in Education at Stanford University. He is a Fellow of the American Association for the Advancement of Science and the American Psychological Association. The APA, the American Educational Research Association, and the Modern Language Association have recognized Professor Padilla for his research. He has published many articles and chapters on a wide variety of topics including acculturative stress and Latinos. His books include *Latino Mental Health* (1973), *Crossing Cultures in Therapy* (1980), *Acculturation* (1980), *Chicano Ethnicity* (1987), *Foreign Language Education* (1991), *Bilingual Education* (1991), and *Hispanic Psychology* (1995). He is the founding editor of the *Hispanic Journal of Behavioral Sciences* (Sage Publications) that is currently in its 27th year.

Edward J. Peacock received his Ph.D. in personality and social psychology from the University of Toronto, where his dissertation on coping with anticipatory stress was supervised by Paul Wong. Currently, he is a licensed psychologist with the Correctional Service of Canada and is the director of a prison-based treatment program for sexual offenders. In addition to his long-standing interest in stress, appraisal, and coping, his current research interests include a number of issues related to the assessment and treatment of sexual offenders.

Paul B. Pedersen is a Visiting Professor in the Department of Psychology at the University of Hawaii. He has taught at various universities in the U.S., Taiwan, Malaysia and Indonesia. He was also on the Summer School Faculty at Harvard University, 1984-1988 and the University of Pittsburgh -Semester at Sea voyage around the world, Spring, 1992. He received a Senior Fulbright award teaching at National Taiwan University 1999-2000. He has authored, co-authored or edited 40 books, 99 articles and 72 chapters on aspects of multicultural counseling and international communication. He is a Fellow in Divisions 9, 17, 45 and 52 of the American Psychological Association. Research activities include: Co-Director of Research for an intercultural communication laboratory; National Science Foundation 6 year grant to study the re-entry adjustment of engineers returning to Taiwan after study abroad; and a National Institute of Education grant to develop a measure of cross-cultural counseling skill. Professional activities have included 3 years Presidency of the 1,800 member Society for Intercultural Education Training and

Research (SIETAR); Senior Editor for Multicultural Aspects of Counseling (MAC) Series, SAGE; Advising Editor for Education and for Psychology, Greenwood Press book series; and election to The Committee for International Relations in Psychology (CIRP) of The American Psychological Association.

Tan Phan Ph.D. started her career as a counselor with special emphasis on cross-cultural understandings. She has over time evolved to embrace issues of gender and sexuality; in the process, she has become a strong advocate for multicultural approaches to learning theories, stress and coping, risk and resilience. Her recent publication, *"Story telling to promote academic resilience: Vietnamese parents in America"* exhorts educators to consider multiple sites of learning particularly in relation to children raised by first generation immigrant parents. Although such parents often find the school alien and fail to show up for teacher conferences, it does not mean that they are not participating in their children's education or that they do not care. Instead, they have devised their own ways of educating their children using the genres available to them. This explains the high academic performance and resiliency for the children in Dr. Phan's study.

Gary T. Reker Ph.D., is a full professor in the Department of Psychology, Trent University, Peterborough, Ontario, Canada. As a life-span developmental psychologist, his research interests have focused on the aging process, particularly the role of personal meaning, optimism, subjective well-being, death attitudes, and creative coping in the promotion of successful aging. His recent research focuses on the conceptualization and measurement of existential regret, spirituality, and existential intelligence. He co-edited *Exploring Existential Meaning: Optimizing Human Development across the Life Span* and has published in *Ageing International, Canadian Journal of Behavioural Science, Canadian Journal on Aging, Journal of Clinical Psychology, The Gerontologist, Journal of Gerontology, Journal of the Gerontological Nursing Association, International Forum for Logotherapy, Omega*, and *Personality and Individual Differences*, among others.

Juan I. Sanchez is Professor of Management and International Business and College of Business Administration's Research Scholar at Florida International University. He earned his Masters' and Ph.D. from the University of South Florida, Tampa. His research has received awards from the International Personnel Management Association and the National Society for Performance and Instruction. He has published in referred journals such as the *Academy of Management Journal*, the *Academy of Management Executive*, the *Journal of Applied Psychology*, the *Journal of Organizational Behavior*, *Personnel Psychology*, the *Journal of Occupational and Organizational Psychology*, *Group and Organization Management*, the *Journal of Vocational Behavior*, the *Journal of Applied Social Psychology*, the *Journal of Quality Management*, the *Journal of Business and Psychology*, *Educational and Psychological Measurement*, and *Human Resources Management Review*, among others. He is a Consulting Editor of the *Journal of Applied Psychology*, and serves on the editorial boards of *Personnel Psychology* and the *International Journal of Selection and Assessment*. He currently serves in the executive committee of the Academy of Management's Human Resources Division. Professor Sanchez occasionally serves as an expert witness in cases involving human resource management disputes. He has consulted with multiple organizations in the U.S., Latin America, and Europe. He has also consulted with government agencies such as the

Federal Aviation Administration (FAA), the U.S. Army, the U.S. Department of Labor, and the Veterans Administration.

Carolyn Scott received her Bachelor of Arts degree in 1987 from Dalhousie University in Halifax, N.S. In 1999, she graduated from the Counselling Psychology program at Trinity Western University in Langley, B.C. Her Masters thesis is entitled *Empowerment of the Dually Diagnosed: Effective Social Networks*. Since graduating, she has worked in a treatment facility for women as well as a treatment center for dually diagnosed men. Currently, she is employed by the Correctional Service of Canada where she provides psychological services for incarcerated women.

Paul E. Spector attended the University of South Florida (USF) in Tampa from 1968 to 1975, receiving a BA in psychology and a MA and Ph.D. in industrial/organizational (I/O) psychology. He is a professor of I/O psychology and the I/O doctoral program director at the University of South Florida. His research interests include both the content and methodology of the field. Content areas concern the impact of jobs on the behavior and well-being of employees, including counterproductive behavior, job satisfaction, cross-cultural job stress, and withdrawal behavior, all of which are aspects of Occupational Health Psychology. Methodological areas are complex statistics and psychological measurement.

His work has appeared in many journals, including *Academy of Management Journal, Journal of Applied Psychology, Journal of Management, Journal of Organizational Behavior, Journal of Occupational and Organizational Psychology, Journal of Vocational Behavior, Organizational Behavior and Human Decision Processes, Personnel Psychology,* and *Psychological Bulletin*. At present he is an associate editor for *Journal of Occupational Health Psychology*, the Point/Counterpoint editor for *Journal of Organizational Behavior*, and is on the editorial boards of *Journal of Occupational and Organizational Psychology, Organizational Research Methods,* and *Personnel Psychology*. In 1991 the Institute For Scientific Information listed him as one of the 50 highest impact contemporary researchers (out of over 102,000) in psychology worldwide.

Yoshiyuki Takano is a registered clinical counsellor in B.C. He is currently working as an international student advisor at Douglas College to provide support for international students from various cultural backgrounds. He is also a facilitator for the Relationship Violence Treatment Program for the court mandated treatment program in B.C. for male offenders against their female partners. He is also facilitating the Japanese Men's Support Group in Vancouver in his own private practice. He has earned his M.A. from Trinity Western University and has been presenting his research actively in various conferences including in Japan. He is an active member of B.C. Association of Clinical Counsellors, Canadian Psychological Association, International Association for Cross-Cultural Psychology, International Network on Personal Meaning, and an associate member of American Psychological Association. He is also a member of the Japanese Society of Studies on Addictive Behaviors and a board member of the Japanese Society of Existential Therapy.

Dwight Tolliver is a graduate student in the Counseling Psychology Program at the University of Tennessee at Knoxville. He earned his master's degree in counseling with a concentration in school counseling at the University of Tennessee at Knoxville in 2001. Following his master's degree, his counseling and clinical experiences were as a school counselor at a public high school (2001-2003) and as a crisis counselor for children and adolescents (2003-2004). This is his first year in the Counseling Psychology Program at the University of Tennessee. His research interests include, primarily, cross-cultural psychology and the counseling process, and, secondarily, family psychology. He works under the tutelage of Dr. Frederick Leong.

Michele M. Tugade earned her Ph.D. in Social Psychology from the University of Michigan. After earning her doctorate, she then completed a National Research Service Award (NRSA) Postdoctoral Research Fellowship (from NIMH) in the Emotional Experience Laboratory of Boston College. She currently teaches in the Department of Psychology at Vassar College. Dr. Tugade's research focuses on positive emotions, emotional experience, and emotion regulation. She investigates the function of positive emotions in the coping process and the mechanisms by which people use positive emotions to achieve resilience in the face of negative emotional situations. Her research also examines the structure and dynamics of emotional experience and emotion regulation. Her program of research incorporates multiple research methodologies, including laboratory-based experiments, experience-sampling methodology, and psychophysiological measurement procedures.

Roger G. Tweed received his Ph.D. in psychology from the University of British Columbia and is now an assistant professor of psychology at Kwantlen University College in Surrey, British Columbia, Canada. His main cross-cultural research interests involve coping strategies, learning strategies, and cultural change within geographic regions over time.

Lilian C. J. Wong received her B.Sc. (Toronto), M.A. (Educational Psychology, University of Texas at Austin), and Ph.D. in Counselling Psychology at the University of British Columbia. She also completed courses in Special Education and Psychopathology from the University of California at Los Angeles. She is an Associate Professor and Coordinator of School Counselling of the Graduate Program in Counselling Psychology, at Trinity Western University, BC, Canada. She had held positions as Psychoeducational Consultant with the Peterborough County Board of Education, Ontario, and School Psychologist and Area Counsellor with the Vancouver School Board. Her primary research area is multicultural supervision competencies. Her Multicultural Supervision Competencies Questionnaire (developed with Paul Wong) has contributed to the conceptualization and measurement of multicultural supervision competencies. She has taken an active part in the Roundtable Discussions in Exploring Psychotherapy Supervision and Training, at APA Annual Conventions for the last few years. Her other research interests include cross-cultural assessment and counseling, emotional and social intelligence, and moral development. She has presented internationally workshops in play therapy and grieving in children and adolescents. She is currently on the Education Committee of BC Association for Play Therapy and on the board of the International Network on Personal Meaning. She is the editor of "A Journey of Courage" (a Commemorative Publication, Trinity Western University). She also is Vice-President of The Meaning-Centered Counselling Institute, Inc.

Paul T. P. Wong received his Ph.D. in Psychology at the University of Toronto. He has held professorial positions at the University of Texas at Austin, York University, Trent University, and the University of Toronto, and has spent one year as a Visiting Scientist at the University of California at Los Angeles.

He moved to Vancouver from Toronto in 1994 to assume the position of Director of Graduate Program in Counselling Psychology of Trinity Western University, where he currently holds the position of Research Director and Professor. He is the founding President of the International Network on Personal Meaning (www.meaning.ca), the International Society for Existential Psychology and Psychotherapy (www.existentialpsychology.org), and the Meaning-Centered Counselling Institute. With more than 120 published articles and book chapters reflecting his many research interests, he has focused on the roles of meaning, appraisal, and culture in the stress and coping process. The *Stress Appraisal Measure* developed by Edward Peacock and P. T.P. Wong has been widely used. His *resource-congruence model* is one of the early coping theories that emphasize the importance of cultural context. As well, he is a pioneer in research on stress and coping in the Chinese elderly. His edited volume (with Prem Fry as co-editor) on *The Human Quest for Meaning* (Lawrence Erlbaum Associates, Publishers) has contributed to the current interest in meaning research.

Katherine A. Wu M.A., Ed.M., is Counseling Coordinator and Instructor in the Freshman Year Experience program at Kingsborough Community College in Brooklyn, NY. She received her B.A. from Swarthmore College in Biology and Education and her M.A. and Ed.M. from Teachers College in counseling psychology. Her current research focuses on the development of multiculturally-competent counseling and teaching approaches that address academic, career, and personal needs of an urban community college student. She also is interested in the roles of racial and ethnic identity in the formation and stability of self-esteem and the acculturative stress experienced by recent Asian immigrants.

Christine Yeh is an Associate Professor of Psychology and Education in the Counseling Psychology Program, at Teachers College, Columbia University. She received her Masters in Education from Harvard University and her Ph.D. in Counseling Psychology from Stanford University School of Education. She was also a Postdoctoral Fellow at the Stanford University Center on Adolescence. Her research examines paradigms and methodologies for understanding cultural identity and addresses the influence of indigenous cultural values on mental health, coping, assessment, and help-seeking. She is currently the Principal Investigator of a 5-year NIMH grant (Mentored Research Scientist Award-KO1) investigating Asian immigrant cultural adjustment and mental health in a New York City public school. She has published in the areas of ethnic identity, self, online applications of counseling/counselor training, and coping. She has served on four Editorial Boards including, *The Counseling Psychologist, Journal of Counseling and Development, Journal of Multicultural Counseling and Development*, and *Ethnic Minority and Cultural Diversity Psychology Journal*. In 2001, she received the Early Career Award for Distinguished Contributions from the Asian American Psychological Association.

Dan Zhang Ph.D., M.Sci., M.D., was born and grew up in China. Dan obtained her MD from Capital Medicine University in Beijing. As a physician, she worked for 15 years (includes 10 years in inner Mongolia) before immigrated to Canada. In Canada, Dan obtained her master of science degree in clinical psychology and received her doctorate degree in counselling psychology from the University of British Columbia. Dan provides counseling services at the Vancouver Community College. She teaches psychology at Kwantlen University College and also works as an adjunct professor at a number of universities in China. Her area of research and publication focus on cross-cultural and health psychology (e.g., cultural values and stress coping, depression). She is also interested in cross-cultural career development. Beside her teaching and clinical practice, Dan volunteers her time with the Mental Health Association in Vancouver and in Richmond, BC.

Introduction

1

BEYOND STRESS AND COPING:
The Positive Psychology of Transformation

Paul T. P. Wong, Lilian C. J. Wong, and Carolyn Scott

1. INTRODUCTION

Often, it is easier to study a subject than to define it. Anyone foolish enough to attempt a comprehensive and universally acceptable definition of human culture would be like a blind person trying to describe an elephant. A similar difficulty exists in defining the psychology of stress and coping. Nevertheless, we cannot simply run away from these challenges; we still need to clarify and differentiate some of the key concepts, such as multiculturalism, stress, and coping in order to synthesize the vast and complex subject matter of this edited volume.

It is our hope that this book will inspire scholars and professionals to develop new visions of the human drama of surviving and flourishing in an ever-changing cultural context. We want to challenge our readers to venture out from their familiar territories of well-defined and rigorous research paradigms and consider larger but more abstruse issues of human existence. It is through integrating and transcending the various fragmented research paradigms that we can gain greater understanding of both the universal and culture-specific adaptive process of human beings.

2. WHAT IS CULTURE?

In our everyday conversations, the word "culture" is typically used to connote the customary practices and language associated with a particular racial or ethnic group. Culture is also commonly conceived as a way of perceiving the world based upon a shared set of social beliefs and values. However, at a deeper level, culture is a much more complex construct. Cultures are human creations, socially constructed and transmitted through language, conventions, socialization, and social institutions.

Paul T. P. Wong and Lilian C. J. Wong, Trinity Western University; Carolyn Scott, Correctional Service of Canada

Cultures are created not only to enhance human beings' physical survival and creature comforts, but also to meet their deeper psychological needs for meaning and significance through shared cultural metaphors and symbols. According to Brislin (1990), "culture refers to widely shared ideals, values, formation, and uses of categories, assumptions about life, and goal-directed activities that become unconsciously or subconsciously accepted as right and correct by people who identify themselves as members of a society" (p. 11).

In many important ways, cultures are the expressions of human nature in all its complexity and duality – fears and hopes, cravings and aspirations, selfishness and generosity, cruelty and compassion. Cultures are also manifestations of the human capacity for imagination, creativity, intellection, and adaptation. Cultural differences exist because each culture is shaped by its unique set of physical environments, historical context, political events, and dominant religions and philosophies. These differences may gradually diminish, when the hegemony of one culture dominates the global village.

We cannot overstate the importance of culture. Pedersen (1991, 1999) has emphasized that all behaviors are shaped by culture. Even when behaviors are largely genetically determined, their manifestations are still subject to cultural influences. At the same time, we also shape and create the culture in which we live. Various chapters in the first Section of this book clearly document that culture influences every aspect of our existence and prescribes ways for living. Segall, Lonner, and Berry (1998) are absolutely correct, when they write that "human behavior is meaningful *only* when viewed in the sociocultural context in which it occurs", but psychology has nonetheless "long ignored culture as a source on human behavior and still takes little account of theories or data from other than Euro-American cultures" (p. 1101).

All cultures are fluid and dynamic, subject to the impact from epochal events in the world and from frequent encounters with other cultures. To the extent a culture is resistant to change, its likelihood for survival is reduced. However, cultural changes need not follow the path of least resistance; both leaders and ordinary citizens of every nation have the responsibility to safe-guard their cultural treasures and protect their civilization from pathological elements. This kind of awareness and vigilance is necessary, because culture is a powerful change agent, both for good and evil.

Ho (1995) proposes the concept of internalized culture that describes the psychological process of enculturation rather than culture as a reality external to the person. He suggests that internalized culture functions as a cognitive map for our social world and influences the formation of our worldviews. Ho also writes: "human beings are both the products and creators of culture" (p. 19), and that "the relation between individual behavior and culture is best conceived as one of continuous interaction" (p. 19). Chun, Moos and Cronkite (Chapter 2) also emphasize the constant interplay between culture and individuals.

Because of the interactive nature of culture, psychologists need to study not only how culture impacts cognitive and behavioral processes, but also how human and social factors impact emerging cultures. The greatest challenge facing psychologists is to understand what contributes to the development of toxic, pathological cultures of tyranny, terrorism, and despair, and what contributes to healthy and salugenic cultures of freedom, compassion, and optimism.

3. THE POSITIVE PSYCHOLOGY OF TRANSFORMATION

When we apply the challenge of transforming culture, different kinds of questions arise in studying stress and coping. Instead of simply asking how people in different cultures cope with stress differently, we need to ask more fundamental questions, such as: What are the toxic and healthy elements in any particular culture? What are the social-economical, political, and behavioral factors contributing to a high level of stress or psychopathology? What can be done to transform a toxic culture? Some theorizing and research have been done about the positive psychology of cultural transformation at the organizational or corporate level (Wong, 2002; Wong & Gupta, 2004), but to our knowledge, little has been done regarding positive cultural transformation at the national level.

Different from situational coping, cultural transformation is a meta-coping strategy, which requires a variety of leadership skills, such as team work, shared vision, transparency, and treating people with dignity. It may include multicultural competencies (Sue & Sue, 2003). Cultural transformation may also be conceptualized as a form of macro-stress management, because it is aimed at a complete overhaul of the total environment rather than the solution of specific problems.

In some communities with pervasive, chronic conditions of poverty, terror, and suffering (Naji, Chapter 20), nothing short of regime-change and culture-transformation can provide some relief to the suffering people. However, it may take more than one generation to transform a society from a culture of oppression and terror to a culture of freedom and love. The important lesson is that for many pervasive societal stressors (Wong, 1993), it requires national/communal leadership and cultural transformation, and demands much more than what an individual could offer. The entire area of cultural transformation as a way of coping with societal or organizational stress remains under-researched.

Another challenge to psychologists is to discover the potential of personal transformation. This mode of coping refers to the strategy of changing one's personal meaning-value system, worldview, lifestyle, and some aspects of one's personality as a result of enlightenment (Chen, Chapters 4 and 5), spiritual conversion (Klaassen, McDonald, & James, Chapter 6), transcendence and duality (Lee, Chapter 8), personal growth and restructuring (Wong, Reker, & Peacock, Chapter 11). Personal transformation is developed and practised mostly in Asia and has received only scant attention in Euro-American psychology.

The relevance of personal transformation is self-evident, when the stressful situation is chronic and beyond personal control. In such situations, at best one can do is to transform oneself so that the stress would become less threatening and the pain more bearable. In some cases, such as a Zen Master or a Catholic Saint, personal transformation can attain such a high level that everyday hassles and even major life events become passing vapour that hardly stirs a ripple in the calm water.

Different from cognitive reframing, personal transformation is proactive rather than reactive. Cognitive reframing typically occurs in an encounter with a specific problematic situation, while personal transformation is typically an ongoing, holistic change process. It would be instructive to carefully examine the different types of personal transformation in Chapters 4, 5, 8, 11, and 20.

The positive psychology of transformation is beyond stress and coping because it takes us to a point in time prior to a stressful encounter, and to a space much larger and deeper than the actual stressful transaction. Transformation can take place in the deepest recesses of the human spirit. It can also take place in the political arena or boardroom. Transformation is more effective than coping, because when it is successful, it can eliminate most of the stress, whatever it maybe, and makes coping unnecessary in many situations.

4. MULTICULTURAL PERSPECTIVES

What makes this volume unique among stress-and-coping books is that it not only highlights the positive psychology of transformation, but also emphasizes the cross-cultural psychology of stress and coping. A word of explanation is needed to clarify the relationship between multiculturalism and cross-cultural psychology.

According to Leong and Wong (2003), multiculturalism, as a social movement in North America, is an important part of the larger, global human rights movement. As a social-political policy, multiculturalism endorses diversity, inclusiveness, and equality while recognizing the legitimacy and value of ethnic differences and cultural heritage. Multicultural counseling stems directly from this social movement. Leong and Wong (2003) make the point that technically, multicultural counseling should be called cross-cultural counseling, because it involves counseling across culturally different clients. However, multicultural counseling connotes a policy of embracing diversity, and challenging domination of "majority" values and worldviews.

Ibrahim (1991) emphasizes the importance for counselors to be aware of other people's worldviews. She believes that "the multicultural encounter is to a large extent dependent on ethnicity, cultures, and sociopolitical histories of the parties involved" (p. 17). It is through the multicultural perspective that we can gain a deeper understanding of individual differences. Ho (1995) makes the further distinction between ethnicity and culture because an individual may belong to a particular ethnic or racial group, but may have internalized one or more cultures from other ethnic backgrounds.

Cross-cultural psychology grows out of cultural psychology. It refers to the study of different cultures and nations in order to arrive at a fuller understanding of a psychological phenomenon – both its *etic* (universalist) and *emic* (culture-specific) aspects. Leong and Wong (2003) point out that the major flaw in Euro-American psychology is not that it is Eurocentric, but that it fails to recognize that it is Eurocentric. It is noteworthy that even the Euro-American brand of cross-cultural psychology is often Eurocentric, because it attempts to apply Euro-American psychological research to cultures that are very different. Segall, Lonner & Berry (1998) have pointed out the problems associated with the application of Euro-American theories and instruments to conduct research in other cultural settings. To impose our own culture's values and theoretical constructs as the standard to study and understand behaviors in other culture groups would not only be ethnocentric but also "bad science".

Therefore, we have chosen "multicultural perspectives" as part of the book title to signal that, much like counseling and education, the cross-cultural psychology of stress and coping needs to assume a multicultural stance as an antidote to the pervasive, insidious ethnocentric tendency. In other words, any theoretical model, any empirical finding, and any claim of truth must be examined through the lens of multiculturalism. It is only through multicultural perspectives that cross-cultural research can break away from the mindsets of Euro-American psychology and encompass the richness and complexity of indigenous psychology in diverse cultures.

If anything, this edited volume has provided ample evidence that our conceptions and understanding of stress and coping have been enlarged by learning from how people in other cultures cope with the demands of life. It has also documented the inadequacy of Euro-American psychology of stress and coping when it is applied to cultures with a very different history and dynamics. The future of psychology must take on multicultural and international perspectives, not only for the sake of scientific progress, but also for the practical benefits of learning to understand and get along with each other in multicultural global village.

5. CROSS-CULTURAL PSYCHOLOGY OF STRESS AND COPING

One of the most frequent complaints of Euro-American stress research is about decontextualization or acontextualization. For example, Moos and Swindle (1990) have pointed out that the ongoing context in which stressful events occur is typically ignored. Stress must be viewed in context, both cultural and situational. However, recent reviews of stress and coping (Lazarus, 1999; Folkman & Moskowitz, 2004; Snyder, 1999; Somerfield and McCrae, 2000) have shown a clear lack of research in cultural contexts. There are indeed a number of studies on ethnic/cultural differences in coping (Bjorck, Cuthbertson, Thurman & Lee, 2001; Chang, Tugade, & Asakawa, Chapter 19; Cross, 1995; Lam & Zane, 2004; Wong & Reker, 1985), but the comparisons are based on concepts and instruments rooted in Euro-American psychology.

Snyder (1999) asks a rhetorical but important question: "To what extent are our coping ideas a by-product of our Western society?" (p. 331). He further points out that "most researchers merely have borrowed from the prevailing research paradigms that form the zeitgeist in clinical, social, and personality psychology more generally. This status quo mentality about our methods, however, will not suffice as we address the complex and grand coping questions in the twenty-first century" (p. 327).

The lack of progress in stress and coping research has been attributed to theoretical and methodological limitations (Coyne & Gottlieb, 1996; Somerfield & McCrae, 2000; Snyder, 1999; Tennen, Affleck, Armeli, & Carney, 2000). However, we believe that the hegemony of Euro-American psychology is not necessarily healthy for the field, especially when it is dominated by a single paradigm. The supremacy of Lazarus and Folkman's (1984) model has remained uncontested for two decades and is clearly evident in this volume.

According to this model, coping is defined as the dynamic efforts, which involve "the thoughts and behaviors used to manage the internal and external demands of situations that are appraised as stressful" (Folkman & Moskowitz, 2004, p. 745). Many of the existing coping questionnaires focus on problem-focused and emotion-focused coping behaviors (e.g., Lazarus & Folkman, 1984) rather than on culturally specific coping strategies and resources. One of the major findings from coping research is that problem-focused or action-oriented coping is strongly related to positive psychological outcomes, while emotion-focused coping, such as avoidance, tends to be associated with poorer mental health (e.g., Endler & Parker, 2000; Folkman, Lazarus, Gruen, & DeLongis, 1986b; Lazarus & Folkman, 1984). This cannot be the last word on coping. We really need to venture beyond the confines of Euro-American psychology and explore other coping strategies in different cultures. For example, research on the adaptive functions of personal transformation can greatly expand the knowledge of coping.

Although the importance of culture has been recognized (i.e., Slavin, Rainer, McCreary, & Gowda, 1991; Wong, 1993), we still do not have well developed constructs, methodologies, and paradigms that facilitate cross-cultural research. Stevan Hobfoll's (1989, 1998) ecological emphasis is a promising start. He focuses on resources which are an inherent part of every culture. He also addresses the importance of congruence and proposes that it is the fit or lack of fit between demands and coping resources that determines the occurrence of stress and the ability of an individual to successfully meet the challenge.

Similarly, Wong's (1993) resource-congruence model posits "coping is effective to the extent that appropriate resources are available and congruent coping strategies are employed" (p. 51). Wong and his associates (Peacock, Wong, & Reker, 1993; Wong, Reker, & Peacock, Chapter 11) have proposed a two-stage model of appraisal. Primary proposal is the initial appraisal of the potential stressfulness of the situation. Secondary appraisal is an assessment of coping options according to one's coping schema of what works in what situation. Coping schema is based on cultural knowledge, because it represents the accumulated and crystallized coping knowledge in a particular cultural context. Research on coping schemas and implicit theories of coping are promising future directions for cross-cultural research. We need to move beyond testing the generalizability of Euro-American theories and findings to other cultural contexts. For example, Wong and Ujimoto (1998) have advocated the methodology of developing theoretical models and planning research that involve partners from other cultures and indigenous psychologists. Tweed and DeLongis (Chapter 10) have proposed a similar strategy of combining *emic* and *etic* research procedures. A good example of this research strategy is Wong's multinational research program on personal meaning (e.g., Takano & Wong, 2004; Kim, Lee, & Wong, 2005).

Since every aspect of the stress process is affected by culture (Chun, Moos, & Cronkite, Chapter 2), we need to develop a cross-cultural psychology of stress. It is through research from multicultural perspectives that we can narrow the gap between theory and application, and make research more relevant to the everyday struggles of individuals in different cultural contexts.

6. CULTURAL VALUES AND CONSTRUCT EQUIVALENCE

One clear message from this volume is the need to pay more attention to construct equivalence, because theoretical constructs reflect our cultural values, worldviews, and hidden ideologies. For example, liberal democracy that emphasizes individual rights and freedoms is one of the most widely held ideologies by Euro-American psychologists, and this is clearly reflected in the popularity of such constructs as self-efficacy, internal locus of control, optimism, and the pursuit of happiness in Euro-American psychological research. Therefore, we need to examine the values and assumptions of different cultures in the cross-cultural psychology of stress and coping.

Cross-cultural psychology has a long and venerable tradition of emphasizing differences in national or cultural differences (Hofstede, 1980; Kluckhohn & Strodtbeck, 1961; Rokeach, 1973; Triandis, 1995). In most of these studies, values refer to attributes and preferences at the national rather than individual level. It is clear from the present edited volume that the most researched cultural values are individualism versus collectivism (Hofstede, 1980; Triandis, 1995). However, there are other values that also deserve research attention, especially with regards to stress and coping.

According to Kluckhohn and Strodtbeck (1961), cultural values can be inferred from how people in every society answer five crucial human questions: (a) What is the basic nature of people? (b) What is the proper relationship to nature? (c) What is the proper focus in terms of the temporal dimension of life? (d) What is the proper mode of human activity? (e) What is the proper way of relating to one another?

Within each culture, responses to these questions naturally vary from person to person, but there is always a dominant response in any society. These value-orientations incorporate normative cognitive (thoughts about life), conative (inclinations towards a particular course of action), and affective (feelings about what is desirable or preferable) elements. This model deserves our attention, because it addresses basic existential assumptions and worldviews of different cultures. Furthermore, according to Zavalloni (1980), "The existential or general beliefs were seen as influencing concrete choices in everyday life" (p. 84).

6.1. Human nature orientation

There are three types of responses to the question of human nature: Evil, Good, or Both Good-and-Evil. To believe that human nature is evil is to believe that people are basically bad, and they need to be controlled by some form of authority, whether institutional, ecclesiastical, or political. This assumption may have contributed to hierarchical, authoritarian states in the Middle East (Naji, Chapter 20) and collectivistic cultures (Yeh, Kwong Arora, & Wu, Chapter 3), in which individual freedoms and rights are subservient to the needs and desires of the group and its leader.

The belief that people are born good and that most people are basically good at heart is more consistent with individualistic cultures emphasizing individuals' freedom and ability to make good choices and lead successful lives. In the psychological and therapeutic culture of contemporary America, people have lost the sense of evil (Delbanco, 1996). In a curious way, personal responsibility has been replaced by victimhood in a culture that emphasizes empathy and the basic goodness of people. Individuals who commit horrendous evil deeds are viewed as victims of upbringing and circumstances. Thus, value orientations do have many practical implications.

The belief that people are capable of both good and evil justifies cultures that protect individual human rights and individual freedoms, but at the same time emphasize the role of government to protect society from criminal elements; this orientation favors strong central governments. The so-called "Asian values" of having a strong man running a democratic capitalist society, as exemplified by the Singapore style of government, also reflect this value orientation.

6.2. Man-nature orientation

The three dominant responses are: Subjugation-to-Nature, Harmony-with-Nature, and Master-over-Nature. Subjugation-to-Nature represents the belief that life is determined by forces beyond one's control. This is the preferred response in primitive or poor societies, which feel powerless to protect themselves from the ravages of nature. Harmony with nature stresses oneness among people and union with nature. This orientation is consistent with Taoism (Chen, Chapter 5) and the general attitudes of North American Indians (McCormick & Wong, Chapter 22).

Taoism teaches non-action and subjugation to nature. Instead of fighting against circumstances, one should go with the flow. The best way to live is simple, spontaneous, and harmonious with nature, yielding continually to the changing life process. *I Ching* or the *Doctrine of Change* has this to say about the ideal life:

> *"The great man is he who is in harmony: in his attributes, with heaven and earth; in his brightness, with the sun and the moon; in his orderly procedure, with the four seasons... He may precede heaven, and heaven will not act in opposition to him; he may follow heaven, but will act only as heaven would at that time" (Liu, 1979, p. 131).*

Mastery-over-Nature orientation is consistent with individualistic cultures; it is the preferred orientation in North America and Western Europe. The attitude of mastery and domination over nature is responsible for the technological progress and the accumulation of wealth in Euro-American societies, but it has also resulted in problems of environmental pollutions.

6.3. Time orientation

The temporal focus of human life can be logically broken down to Past, Present, and Future. Clearly, every society and every individual must deal with all three aspects of the temporal dimensions; however, they may differ in terms of their preferences. Past orientation refers to an emphasis on traditional customs and cultural heritage. It is associated with traditionalism and conservatism. Traditional Chinese culture has a past orientation, because of its emphasis on ancestral worship, respect for traditions, and the elders; it also values classical writings by Confucius and other sages as the foundation for personal and society development. Aboriginal cultures also value traditions and learning from the elders (McCormick & Wong, Chapter 22).

Americans tend to favor the Future orientation – they are willing to work hard and make sacrifices in order to realize a better future. The future orientation of producing products that are faster, bigger, and better, is part of the impetus to material progress in a consumer society. However, material success is often achieved at the expense of character development. Thus, moral failure and decadence often follow the steps of material success.

In ancient China, Confucius pursued a very different kind of future orientation. He preached the gospel of social order and world peace through personal development and serving others. "Confucius said: Wanting to develop themselves, they also develop others; wanting to achieve things themselves, they also allow others to achieve what they want. This is the direction humanity takes: to use what is close to oneself as an analogy to be extended to others" (Sommer, 1995, p. 44). This emphasis also has its down side. An education that only emphasized propriety and moral virtues failed to prepare China militarily against the invading Western imperial powers.

A future orientation offers the best promise of successful adaptation, because it capitalizes on the human capacity for imagination, projection, and planning. Proactive or anticipatory coping is possible because of this orientation. The lesson learned from history is that the future must not be narrowly focused; the future must be expanded to include the large picture of other people and humanity.

The Present orientation emphasizes the here and now as being most important. The lifestyle of drug addicts is present oriented, because their all-consuming desire is to relieve their cravings and achieve an instant "high". An emphasis on the here and now would value the "flow" experience. The Present focus can indeed enrich our enjoyment of life, and make us more appreciative of the fleeting moments of joy. The Present orientation is also important in teaching us to value what we do have rather than regret what we have lost in the past or worry about what we may not attain in the future. However, a culture that only values the present is unlikely to develop its full adaptive potential and meet the challenges of societal changes.

6.4. Activity orientation

This has to do with the preferred mode of self-expression or modality of activity. The Being orientation focuses on the release of one's desires and spontaneous expression of one's emotions, impulses, and personality. Fiesta activities in Mexico are examples of this orientation. "Being" may be related to the present orientation.

In contrast, Being-in-Becoming orientation focuses on personal development. "The idea of development, so little stressed in the Being orientation, is paramount in the Being-in-Becoming one" (Kluckhohn & Strodtbeck, 1961, p. 16). The primary goal of Being-in-Becoming is aimed at the development and integration of personality through self-control. This Orientation would favor the coping strategy of personal transformation.

The Doing orientation is prominent in American society. It focuses on "the kind of activity which results in accomplishments that are measurable by standards conceived to be external to the acting individual" (Kluckhohn & Strodtbeck, 1961, p. 17). It is illustrated by such expressions as "Let's do it" or "Let's get it done." However, an instrumental orientation may not be adaptive in situations which are totally beyond one's control (Wong, 1993).

6.5. Relational orientation

This is concerned with how we relate to each other as human beings. This orientation is again sub-divided into three alternatives: the Lineal, the Collateral, and the Individualistic. The individualistic orientation values individual autonomy and personal agenda more than group needs. The material successes of capitalistic, individualistic societies are self-evident. It stands to reason that a culture that emphasizes self-efficacy, competition, and winner-takes-all economy, will lead to greater prosperity, especially for the "winners". However, an individualistic culture may lead to dehumanization and the weakening of human bonding.

Collaterality emphasizes individuals as part of a social group. The prototype of collaterality is biologically related sibling relationships. To further expand the circle, collaterality would encompass the extended family, neighborhood, community, and nation. It involves the expansion of the self to include many others in one's consciousness, concerns as well as concrete interactions. A Collateral orientation naturally leads to a collectivistic culture and collective coping (Yeh et al., Chapter 3; Zhang & Long, Chapter 24).

Lineality emphasizes that "individuals are biologically and culturally related to each other through time. There is, in other words, always a Lineal principle in relationships which is derived both from the biological givens of age and generational differences and from the fact of cultural continuity" (Kluckhohn & Strodtbeck, 1961, p. 18). When the Lineal principle is dominant, the continuity of group goals through time and succession of leadership positions become more important than individual performance. A Lineally oriented group tends to favor a clear and continuous line of authority. Its emphasis on cultural continuity makes it resistant to change. Examples of Lineality include the aristocracy of England and the caste system in India.

The Kluckhohn and Strodtbeck model may be criticized for including only a very limited set of cultural characteristics (Carter, 1991). For example, cultural anthropology has found people in every culture seek answers regarding spiritual or existential questions. Therefore, we propose to include two foundational questions regarding religion and the meaning of human existence.

6.6. Religious orientation

Religious orientation is concerned with questions such as: Where is God? What is God like? How can I know Him? What does God want from me? Bond's (2004) research on social axioms has identified religion as a major component of human life across cultures (e.g., "Belief in a religion helps one understand the meaning of life," p. 557), although cultures differ in their tendency to assert this belief.

There are three basic types of answers: Atheistic, Agnostic, and Theistic. A predominantly secular culture or a strongly communist society would advocate an atheistic orientation. A highly educated and technologically advanced nation may favor the agnostic alternative. According to this position, the existence of God cannot be proved or disproved; therefore, we should not take the God-concept seriously, nor should we place our trust in God even in extreme situations.

The theistic alternative assumes that God exists, although conceptions of the deity differ. These may range from the Hindu belief in pantheism, the Christian belief in one God, and some aboriginal people's belief in the presence of a divine spirit in nature. There are also cultural differences in beliefs regarding God's role in human lives. In America, according to Gallup polls, it is not uncommon for people to believe in a personal God, who answers prayers. Klaassen, et al. (Chapter 6) has documented a wide range of ways in which religious beliefs serve an adaptive function.

6.7. Existential orientation

Existential orientation is concerned with the assumptions regarding the nature and purpose of human existence. This human quest for meaning seems universal, and it is probably one of the oldest, most persistent philosophical concerns. We are all familiar with questions such as: What is the meaning of life? Why am I here? What is life all about? There are again three alternative responses to this existential question: (a) There is no meaning in life; (b) there is no inherent meaning in life, but one can create meaning through one's own efforts; and (c) there is inherent and ultimate meaning to be discovered.

For nations as well as individuals, denying the possibility of meaning would likely lead to hedonism or nihilism. If life has no meaning, then let's eat and drink and have fun, because tomorrow we die. An existence totally devoid of meaning can be self-handicapping and self-destructive. Generally, a lack of meaning has found to be related to substance abuse and suicidal ideation (Harlow, Newcomb & Bentler, 1986). Meaninglessness is also linked to psychopathology (Yalom, 1981). At the national level, the absence of a clearly articulated national purpose may also lead to stagnation, decay, and internal strife, because it is difficult to unite and mobilize the people without a shared vision or a national goal.

For those who believe that they can create meaning in this life through achieving personal goals, they are likely to live a very productive life (Baumeister, 1991; Reker & Wong, 1988; Wong & Fry, 1998). However, there are also limits to self-efforts in creating meanings. For example, what do people do when they can no longer fully function because of health problems? Self-efficacy and instrumental activities, powerful as they may be, cannot be always depended on as the royal roads to meaning.

The third alternative response seems to be the most adaptive in adverse or even catastrophic circumstances, which shatter our assumptions and overwhelm our abilities to cope. To survive such situations, it takes a heroic attitude to affirm the intrinsic meaning and value of human existence. To affirm that meaning can be discovered even in the worst possible situations has enabled Dr. Viktor Frankl and many others to endure horrific suffering and loss with dignity and optimism (Frankl, 1984, 1986; Wong, 1999, 2002, 2005).

The belief in intrinsic and ultimate meaning is often associated with the religious faith in God and in an afterlife. Research has shown that affirmation in faith and meaning enables people to adjust to traumas and tragedies (Wong & McDonald, 2002). The existential orientation is important because questions about meaning of existence have to do with the basic assumptions about life and go to the very heart of what each culture cherishes as its core values.

A contingency model of cultural competence (Leong & Wong, 2003) predicts that adaptation is likely to be successful if it takes into account the various preferred values in different cultures and the unique demands of different life situations. Stress and coping models based on Euro-American values do not always work in other cultures, which have vastly different preferred values and very different kinds of pressing circumstances. The main challenge to cross-cultural psychology of stress and coping is to develop constructs and instruments that reflect the preferred values of other cultures. The main problem of the current Euro-American approach to cross-cultural research is the lack of construct equivalence.

6.8. The challenge of construct equivalence

In view of the cultural differences in values and beliefs, it has become increasingly clear that cross-cultural research cannot simply generalize Euro-American constructs to other cultures. Sanchez, Spector, and Cooper (Chapter 9) point out that translation of an instrument could perfectly capture the same linguistic meaning and scale value, but that instrument may reflect different constructs. Furthermore, the same construct might manifest itself differently across cultures, so that different items describing the same construct need to be added (Brislin, 1990). Thus, Tweed and DeLongis (Chapter 10) emphasize the need to research indigenous coping constructs in order to include constructs and values that are important in other cultures. Such research would need to be based on the accumulated evidence on cultural differences in values and beliefs systems (Tweed and Conway, Chapter 7).

This volume has shown that construct nonequivalence has received far less attention than measurement nonequivalence in cross-cultural research and this neglect has hindered the progress of cross-cultural psychology. Without a good empirical base of cultural differences in values and constructs, it would be difficult for us to draw any valid inference about the similarities and differences across cultures.

7. FROM STRESS TO SUFFERING

Stress is a dynamic and multidimenional construct, thus posing a serious challenge for psychologists (Wong, 1990). Stress originally is an engineering concept referring to the amount of external pressure, such as weight or force, acting upon a certain structural material. In Euro-American psychology, stress is generally defined as "external and/or internal demands that are appraised as taxing or exceeding the resources of the person" (Lazarus & Folkman, 1984, p. 52). More recently, Folkman and Moskowitz (2004) define the coping process as "the thoughts and behaviors used to manage the internal and external demands of situations that are appraised as stressful" (p. 745). Here, stress is more clearly conceptualized as originating from external situations, such as major life events or everyday hassles.

Antonovsky (1990) comments that stress research often fails to recognize that stressful events are more commonplace than daily hassles and major events; there are also chronic life strain and frustrations. He proposes that a stressor may be defined as "a stimulus which poses a demand to which one has no ready-made, immediately available and adequate response" (p. 74). Wong (1993) also defines stress as a "problematic internal or external condition that creates tension/upset in the individual and calls for some form of coping" (p. 55). In all these definitions, the stress process begins with cognitive appraisal of a specific situation or condition.

However, existential psychologists (i.e., Yalom, 1981; Wong, 2005) have long recognized that sources of anxieties and stress can stem from our inner awareness of the vulnerable, impermanent, and unfulfilling nature of the human condition, in the absence of any immediate stressful situation. For example, even when one is living very well materially, the realization that we can never fulfill some of our fondest aspirations because death will put an abrupt and definitive end to all our pursuits; this will result in existential angst. The concept of stress does not quite capture the essence of such inner agony.

When we first approached Professor Chen to contribute something on the Buddhist and Taoist ways of coping with stress (Chapters 4 and 5), he was puzzled as to why we asked him to write about coping with stress rather than coping with suffering, for the two concepts were different to him. In one of his emails, he offered the following comments:

In Chinese, suffering is "shou ku" (literally, experiencing bitterness). As you know, "ku" has many meanings, such as pain, hardship, adversity, difficult times, etc.; these are all externally oriented. As the sage Meng-tzu says, when Heaven is going to assign a great mission to a person, it always inflicts "ku" on his mind and will. Ku in this context means hardships, pain, adversities and difficulties, etc. "Shou Ku" means experiencing these things, but it also means "suffering" in the western sense. In Buddhist psychology, "ku" (suffering) is always connected with the defense mechanism of clinging and rejection, craving and aversion, or greed and hatred, along with the primordial ignorance that gives rise to this mechanism. Therefore, to end suffering is to end ignorance and gain liberating insight. The Chinese concept of stress, on the other hand, is "tension and pressure," which can be relieved by relaxation of mind and body, and has little to do with suffering. I wish to know why suffering is not accepted by American academic psychology, and how suffering can be mixed up with stress.

We have no ready answer to Professor Chen's question, except that Euro-American psychology, in its endeavors to develop psychology as a scientific discipline, prefers the stress concept, because it can be objectively manipulated and measured. However, from a cross-cultural standpoint, there is clearly a lack of construct equivalence between stress and suffering. According to Chen (Chapter 4), Buddhism locates the primary source of stress and suffering within individuals. "It is the psychological mechanism of craving and aversion and the ignorance about its workings that are responsible for most of our troubles and difficulties in life." The first Noble Truth of *dukkha* (suffering) has a very existential flavor. Keown (1996) points out that "*dukkha* has a more abstract and pervasive sense: it suggests that even when life is not painful it can be unsatisfactory and unfulfilling. In this and many other contexts 'unsatisfactoriness' captures the meaning of *dukkha* better than 'suffering.'" (p. 47)

Naji Abi-Hashem (Chapter 20) focuses on the agony, silent grief, and deep frustration of many communities in the Middle East. The prolonged ethnopolitical conflicts and wars, the danger and brutality of terrorisms, coupled with poverty, multiple losses, and the depletion of coping resources, have created a great deal of mental and physical suffering to the people in that region. The concept of stress seems to minimize the horrors of the living conditions of these people caught in the midst of endless cycles of violence and terrorism. Perhaps, the cross-cultural psychology of stress and coping needs to include "suffering" as a distinct construct. Suffering, as different from stress and physical pain, may be defined as a condition of prolonged and often intense psyche pain as a result of traumas, catastrophes, existential crises, and prolonged deprivation.

8. COLLECTIVISTIC AND COLLECTIVE COPING

Recently, Lazarus (2000) emphasizes the "relational meaning" in the stress process and there has been some research on what may be called the relation-focused coping (Lyons, Mickelson, Sullivan, & Coyne, 1998; O'Brien and DeLongis, 1996). This new addition to the problem-focused and emotion-focused coping is a welcome development, because it recognizes that coping cannot be completely based on solo efforts.

This volume has extended relation-focused coping to collective and collectivistic coping. Chun et al. (Chapter 2) maintain the need to distinguish "*collective coping strategies* (i.e., mobilizing group resources) from *collectivistic coping style* (i.e., normative coping style of collectivistic individuals)". Yeh et al. (Chapter 3) have developed a collectivistic coping scale (CCS) that is based on East Asian's collectivistic values. Their research on the CCS has revealed seven factors: *Respect for Authority* (the tendency to cope by relying on community elders or mentors); *Forbearance* (one's preference for enduring the problems quietly); *Social Activity* (utilizing social networks); *Intracultural Coping* (drawing support from networks with racially similar individuals); *Relational Universality* (seeking social support from those with shared experiences); *Fatalism* (accepting problems as predetermined); *and Family Support* (coping with help from family members). These coping strategies, prevalent in collectivistic cultures, rely primarily on social resources within one's family and ethnic-cultural community.

Zhang and Long (Chapter 24) have developed a collective coping scale based on such strategies as support seeking. This scale is also based on the values of collectivistic cultures. Collective coping depends on group members rallying behind the individual with the problem, as described by Ho and Chiu (1994) "one's business is also the business of the group; and friends should be concerned with each other's personal matters" (p. 139). Zhang and Long borrowed some items from O'Brien and DeLongi's (1996) relationship-focused coping scale that emphasizes empathic and social support from others.

However, Wong (1993) has differentiated between collective coping and social support. He noted, "collective is more than receiving social support, it means the concerted effort involving all members of a group to tackle the same problem" (p. 57). Thus, the family takes on a family member's problem as their own, and works together to find a solution. This is quite different from an individual who uses his or her own effort to garner social support based on personal relationships.

Liang and Bogat (1994) found that Chinese group had less functional social support than the Anglos. This is how they explained their results: "measures initially developed for Western populations are potentially biased and insensitive to Chinese support patterns because they may include items less germane to Chinese culture and/or exclude items that measure support qualities specific to Chinese" (p. 143). Taylor et al. (2004) also found that Asian Americans were less likely to utilize social support than European Americans. However, it is too simplistic to assume that individuals from collectivistic cultures are more likely to seek social support. Yeh et al. (Chapter 3) have made it very clear that Asians do not like to seek social support from professionals, colleagues or strangers; in fact, they are even reluctant to reveal their personal problems to outsiders. Their collective coping is primarily drawn from their in-groups.

Both collectivistic coping and collective coping reflect an interdependent self-construal rather than independent self-construal (Markus & Kitayama, 1991). It remains an interesting question whether collective coping is more advantageous than problem-focused coping in stressful situations that are beyond the coping capacity of any individual.

9. FROM SECONDARY CONTROL TO PERSONAL TRANSFORMATION

According to Rothbaum and colleagues (Rothbaum, Weisz, & Snyder, 1982), *primary control* is basically problem-focused coping, while *secondary control* includes changing one's own feelings, thoughts or behavior, when situational control is no longer applicable. Secondary control is used to restore a sense of primary control in an uncontrollable situation. Four types of secondary control have been identified: Vicarious control by aligning oneself with powerful others; illusionary control by believing that luck will bring about a positive outcome; predictive control by predicting what will happen in future situations;

and interpretative control by interpreting the situation in a way that will help restore certain sense of primary control.

Morling and Fiske's (1999) harmony control is similar to secondary control, because individuals try to align themselves with luck, fate or a higher being, when they are not able to have any power to change the environment. When comparing primary control coping to secondary control coping, studies indicate that individuals from Asian cultures are more likely to engage in secondary control coping than those from Western cultures (Yeh et al., Chapter 3).

The various types of secondary control strategies are all motivated by the desire to restore a sense of control. It is fascinating how far Euro-American psychologists are willing to go in order to maintain the centrality of control in their theorizing about the coping process. Wong (1992) has pointed out that control is a double-edged sword, because "control can cut both ways with respect to our well being. A great deal of research has been done on the beneficial effects of control; it is now time to pay more attention to its negative effects in all three areas of control research. I believe that psychology can make a lasting contribution to humanity, if it can make people aware of the insidious effects of control and helps prevent ambitious, unscrupulous individuals from gaining power" (Wong, 1992, p. 145). Moreover, a narrow perspective of control may have directed researchers' attention away from transformational coping, which is widely employed in Asia to cope with situations over which individuals have little or no control.

Chen (Chapter 4) presents the Buddhist transformational approach to coping with stress and suffering. It advocates the development of the pathway of enlightenment and mental disciplines – to build up one's inner resources such as wisdoms and compassion, so that one is able to face whatever life may throw at him or her with equanimity and compassion. Effective coping results in becoming free not only from the negative effects of stress, but also the source of suffering. Chen writes: "We can be freed from suffering by transforming our craving and aversion, or equivalently, by dispelling the dark clouds of ignorance and confusion with the light of liberating wisdom."

Buddhism appeals to the Chinese who have endured many hardships and adversities throughout history. Buddhism shows them the way to be free from the bondage of cravings and protects them from sufferings. Buddhist teaching and practice also give them an abiding sense of serenity even in the midst of incomprehensive and uncontrollable evils.

Taoism prescribes yet another pathway towards personal transformation (Chen, Chapter 5.). It emphasizes the way of the Tao – the authentic, spontaneous, and natural way. Paradoxically, through the Tao of "do nothing" (*wu wei* in Chinese), and letting go of our impulse to strive, we achieve serenity, wisdom and enlightenment (Lao-tzu, trans., 2000, chapter 16). Thus, the coping strategy of actively attacking the problem becomes superfluous. One learns to flow like water, going around the problem, and still achieve a goal of living an authentic and fulfilling life.

This is another example of coping through personal transformation. Taoist teaching enables the Chinese to accept the harsh realities of life, and transcend all their troubles with serenity and courage. The virtue of enduring in the face of adversity, and accepting one's fate (Marsella, 1993) has its origin in Taoism. Different from secondary control or cognitive reframing, Taoism, like Buddhism, actually prescribes a way of life or a philosophy of life that is relatively immune to the vicissitudes of fortunes.

Lee (Chapter 8) describes a bio-socio-existential model of posttraumatic response from the general systems perspective. He was able to demonstrate that the personality structure of a sample of Koreans without prior experience of trauma was consistent with the bipartite view of the psychobiological model (Cloninger, Svrakic, & Przybeck, 1993), however, for Koreans that had been traumatized, their personality structure was consistent with the bio-social-existential model. The subscales constituting the Existential Factor included: Self-transcendence (transcending our limitations as a human being), Sentimentality (mourning our loss and suffering), Self-acceptance (accepting the uncontrollable problems as the reality of life), Exploratory excitability (exploring new positive meanings in negative situations), Persistence (taking actions to pursue new possibilities in spite of setbacks). It is noteworthy that these subscales of the Existential Factor are very similar to the components of Wong's model of tragic optimism (Wong, 2005). Lee's findings of personality transformation can be viewed as a way of transformative coping.

Maddi and Harvey (Chapter 17) define hardiness as the existential courage to face stressful circumstances openly and directly and the motivation to cope with them constructively. Hardiness is also referred to as transformational coping (Maddi & Kobasa, 1984), because it involves the process of transforming the stressful circumstance into a solvable problem through commitment, control, and challenge. Conceptually, hardiness is rooted in existentialism (Maddi, 1978, 2002), which emphasizes that meaning can be achieved through the courage of making commitment and facing the challenge through one's own resourcefulness. Strictly speaking, hardiness is based on problem-focused instrumental coping, but the motivation to overcome uncertainty and obstacles may involve the existential courage to confront ontological anxiety (Tillich, 1952). The transformation is often limited to one's subjective reaction to the problematic situation, rather than a more fundamental change in one's attitudes, values or philosophy of life. However, with intentional hardiness training or unintentional life experience of having survived difficult situations, individuals may be transformed into hardy persons.

The various possibilities of transformative coping promise to be the new frontier for cross-cultural psychology of stress and coping. It is our hypothesis that transformational coping would be more effective than both primary and secondary control in chronic and uncontrollable situations.

10. RELIGIOUS, SPIRITUALITY, AND EXISTENTIAL COPING

Related to transformational coping are religious/spiritual and existential coping (Wong, Reker, & Peacock, Chapter 11), because they too can be transformational, and serve adaptive functions in traumatic or extremely difficult situations. The Frankl-Wong model of tragic optimism (Frankl, 1984; Wong, 2005; Wong & McDonald, 2002) is transformational, because it is predicated on hope and optimism through affirmation of meaning and faith in God and others.

10.1. The role of meaning in coping and survival

Frankl (1986) argued that the "Will to Meaning" is a universal human need or fundamental motive for survival. When life is full of pain and suffering, it is the will to meaning that enables one to endure with dignity and hope. Antonovsky (1990) proposes that a sense of coherence, whereby individuals experience an orientation to the world that is characterized as comprehensible, manageable, and meaningful, is a core variable in shaping coping responses and has a positive impact on health status.

10.2. The adaptive functions of religion and spirituality

Klaassen, McDonald, and James (Chapter 6) document the wide range of adaptive functions of religions and spirituality, which have received increasing research attention in recent years (Emmons & Paloutzian, 2003; Hill & Pargament, 2003; Folkman & Moskowitz, 2004). Pargament (1997) defines coping as "a search for significance in times of stress" (p. 90) and propose eight assumptions about the coping process: (1) people seek significance; (2) events are constructed in terms of their significance to people; (3) people bring an orienting system to the coping process; (4) people translate the orientation system into specific methods of coping; (5) people seek significance in coping through the mechanisms of conservation and transformation; (6) people cope in ways that are compelling to them; (7) coping is embedded in culture; and (8) the keys to good coping lie in the outcomes and the process. Note that most of these assumptions imply meaning-seeking, meaning-making, and resorting to an orientation system that often includes religious faith.

10.3. The existential and transformational functions of religion

It is important to note that religious coping can be both existential and transformational. Pargament, Koenig, & Perez (2000) proposed that religion serves five main functions, represented by the five dimensions of the *RCOPE* Questionnaire, namely: (1) Finding meaning in the face of unexplainable and often horrific circumstances. (2) Gaining control through religious means. (3) Gaining comfort from achieving closeness to God. (4) Seeking intimacy with others and closeness with God, and (5) Experiencing life transformation. Klaassen et al. (Chapter 6) cite numerous studies which demonstrated the existential function of religious/spiritual coping in facilitating the discovery of positive meaning and purpose in adverse circumstances, such as HIV-infection (Siegel & Schrimshaw, 2002) and breast cancer (Gall & Cornblat, 2002).

11. ACCULTURATIVE STRESS

Acculturative stress not only highlights the importance of a multicultural approach to study stress and coping, but also provides a neat paradigm to study cultural uprootedness and minority status as unique sources of stress not covered by the traditional stress and coping paradigms. Acculturation research is also unique in that instead of going to different countries to study cultural differences and similarities in stress and coping, we can study how different ethnic or cultural groups in the same host country adjust to the same acculturation stress. Differences in acculturation strategies and outcomes may shed some light on cultural differences in values, attitudes, and resilience. Given the ethnocultural populations in most countries (see Chun, Balls-Organista & Marin, 2003; Sam & Berry, 2005 for overviews), acculturation research can yield considerable practical as well as scientific benefits.

Berry (Chapter 12) emphasizes that from the perspective of cross-cultural psychology (Berry, Poortinga, Segall & Dasen, 2002), it is imperative that we study acculturation by examining its cultural contexts. We also need to link the acculturation of an ethnic group and the *psychological acculturation* of individuals in that group.

Berry further points out that long-term adaptation to cultural change is multifaceted. There is a distinction between psychological and sociocultural adaptation as initially proposed by Ward (1996). Psychological adaptation or adjustment involves one's psychological and physical well-being (Schmitz, 1992), while socio-cultural adaptation refers to how well an acculturating individual is able to manage daily life in the new cultural context. Both aspects of acculturation need to be taken into account in research on acculturative stress.

The effects of acculturative stress can be seen in several chapters in this volume. Padilla and Borrero (Chapter 13) show that the traditional values of the Hispanic family, such as clearly defined gender roles, intergenerational interdependence, and the importance of religion in the "sacred" family, are undermined by the individualistic culture of the host country, and its culture of divorce that supports marital dissolution through its no fault laws. The negative forces of acculturative stress include marriage and family conflicts resulting from different rates of acculturation among family members.

A similar kind of domestic problem is documented by Takano (Chapter 14) in his study of how Japanese-Canadian women cope with domestic violence. Being far away from their families, friends, and other supportive groups, Japanese women immigrated to Canada not only have to face a host of acculturative stressors, but also become vulnerable to abusive husbands.

Lilian Wong (Chapter 15) examined how visible minority students cope with the stress they experience in clinical supervision situations. Many of these visible minority students are either immigrants or sojourners. They often experience a triple-acculturative stress: the stress of adjusting to a host culture, the stress of adjusting to a new university, and the stress of having to cope with clinical supervisors who lack multicultural sensitivity. To compound their problems, these students' own cultural values often make them over-sensitive to certain stressful situations, and hinder their ability to cope. However, there is also evidence of resilience based on their traditional cultural values of endurance, persistence, and family support.

Tan Phan (Chapter 18) presents a more positive picture of resilience. She documents how some Vietnamese refugee women cope with uprootedness and acculturative stress. These women were motivated by a clear sense of meaning and purpose: all their sufferings were worth it, if their children would succeed and achieve a better future in Canada. This is a clear example of existential coping, even though they may not be able to articulate it this way. Another salient point is that these refugee women employed diverse ways of coping, which included collective coping of support from extended families, friends, and the Vietnamese ethno-cultural community. These refugee mothers supported each other, and cooperated among themselves to make it easier for them to achieve their goals and live a meaningful life under difficult circumstances.

McCormick and Wong (Chapter 22) report the adjustment and resilience of aboriginal people in Canada. Like other minority groups, they are able to draw strength and support from their own cultural heritage and their aboriginal community in a host society with a history of discriminating against aboriginal people. Spiritual and collective coping strategies play an important role in their resilience and optimism.

McCreary, Cunningham, Ingram, and Fife (Chapter 21) describe a culture-specific model of resilience and "The IMPACT Program", which is an applied program of acculturation and stress based on their model of resilience. The IMPACT program is a family-based psycho-educational intervention that capitalizes on African American parents' adaptive childrearing strategies in violent neighborhoods, such as restricting play, keeping children inside the home and relying on prayer, spirituality, and religious support. This chapter demonstrates the importance of multicultural perspectives on coping and resilience.

Matsumoto, Hirayama, and LeRoux (Chapter 16) developed and validated the Intercultural Adjustment Potential Scale (ICAPS). Different from other broader measures of acculturation, such as Berry's (1990) four acculturative strategies of integration, separation, assimilation, and marginalization, ICAPS seeks to identify the specific psychological skills related to successful intercultural adjustment. Their research program has identified four basic psychological skills – emotion regulation, openness, flexibility, and critical thinking; all of these skills have been described in the coping literature as being effective. These coping skills seem general enough, but they are still based on Euro-American individualistic models of coping, because they do not include collective and transformational coping skills, which are widely employed in Asia.

Although Leong and Tolliver (Chapter 23) focus on occupational stress among Asian Americans, they do have something important to say on more recent developments in acculturation research, including cross-cultural models of stress and coping, and culture-specific measurements of occupational stress. It is a substantive chapter with broad implications for cross-cultural research.

12. COPING EFFICACY AND OUTCOMES

One of the major issues in stress and coping research is what constitutes coping efficacy and positive outcomes. Tweed and Conway (Chapter 7) point out that "depending on which tradition one follows, the appropriate prescription for coping may be to adapt to the environment, bring the environment into submission, rely on a deity, eliminate personal desire, or seek self-improvement. These strategies are not all mutually exclusive, yet these differing ideals suggest possible continuing cultural differences in regions influenced by one or more of these or other traditions. Empirical research has the potential to clarify the extent of variation and consistency in coping around the world."

Chun at al. (Chapter 2) recognize individualistic bias in the Euro-American psychology of stress and coping: "Part of this problem stems from the prevailing assumption that approach coping is overt, constructive, and adaptive, whereas avoidance coping is covert, passive, and maladaptive because it connotes lack of motivation and effort". In a similar vein, Yeh et al. (Chapter 3) criticizes Seiffge-Krenke's (1993) model, which differentiates functional coping from dysfunctional coping. *Functioning coping* includes active coping and taking concrete actions, thus reflecting a bias in favor of Western individualistic cultures. *Dysfunctional coping* includes withdrawal, controlling feelings, and having a fatalistic attitude, thus reflecting a bias against Asian collectivistic cultures. Even empirical studies in support of Seiffge-Krenke's model can be questioned, because the instruments and samples are culturally biased.

As a way of contextualizing coping, Chun et al. (Chapter 2) have argued for the need of a broader set of evaluation criteria of coping efficacy, which should be derived from the individual's coping goals. These criteria should include an assessment of the goodness of person-environment fit (Lazarus & Folkman, 1984), congruence between coping behavior and nature of the stress (Wong, 1993), and the individual's cultural values (Leong & Wong, 2003) and the multiple coping goals (Somerfield & McCrae, 2000).

Chun et al. (Chapter 2) propose four coping goals which reflect an implicit conflict between individualism and collectivism: (1) focus on the needs of self vs. the needs of others; (2) assert autonomy and independence vs. reinforce relatedness and interdependence; (3) control external environment vs. internal self; and (4) maximize gain vs. minimize loss. When one chooses other-focused coping goals, it may result in an increase in personal sacrifice and stress for the benefit of groups. Thus, the coping is ineffective in terms of personal well-being, but effective in achieving group harmony.

Cheng (2003) conducted an interesting study demonstrating that the flexible strategy of using different coping responses in different situations was associated with better adjustment. This finding suggests that the advantages of a multicultural perspective in terms of possessing a large collection of coping tools from different cultures and having the cross-cultural competencies to know what coping responses are appropriate for which situations in what cultural context.

Leong and Wong's (2003) contingency model of cultural competencies and Wong's (1993) resource-congruence model may have the heuristic value of studying coping effectiveness from multicultural perspectives. According to these models, coping efficacy depends on (a) sufficient coping resources, (b) multicultural competencies of what works in what situations, and what coping goals are valued in which culture, and (c) the selection of coping goals and responses that are appropriate to the situation and the cultural context.

13. CONCLUDING DISCUSSION

Coping with stress is a universal process because human survival depends on adaptation to stress, regardless of one's culture. The recent South Asian tsunami disaster poses a profound challenge to the psychologists working in the stress and coping field, and puts the spot light on the importance of cultural context of resilience.

To date, more than 3500 scientific papers have been published on the subject of stress and coping (Snyder, 1999). The lack of progress in cross-cultural psychology of stress and coping is partially due to the ethnocentric bias of trying to generalize popular American models to other cultures. Asian countries are well acquainted with sufferings – flooding, draughts, earthquakes, typhoons, civil wars, poverty, invasions, and occupations by foreign powers. The most telling example is the recent Asian tsunami disaster. Most of the problems are beyond the control of individuals. Yet, through it all, they have survived for thousands of years. Surely, along the way, they have learned how to cope and survive. In this volume, we have invited a number of writers from Asian cultures. We believe that they have much to offer in expanding our understanding and broadening our perspectives of stress and coping.

Some of the new frontiers of stress and coping, delineated by Wong (1993) are clearly evident in several chapters in this volume. In conclusion, we have to highlight several of the new developments:

13.1. From reactive to proactive coping

Proactive coping involves developing the resources through the process of (1) learning from experience and research, such as developing more reliable warning systems of tsunami to prevent or reduce loss of lives and properties, (2) relating – making friends, networking, developing love relationship, building communities, helping others, and (3) increasing the inner resources, such as the vitality of the person's mental and spiritual health, so that one can better deal with the stress and strains of every day life.

There has been some research on anticipatory coping (Aspinwall & Taylor, 1997; Peacock & Wong 1996; Schwarzer & Knoll, 2003). However, proactive coping involves more than simply anticipating a problem and regulating one's behavior and emotions, because it also involves cultivating coping resources and personal transformation so that one can adjust to any circumstances.

13.2. From instrumental to transformational coping

The most widely used coping strategy in American psychology is instrumental coping, designed to solve the problem or change the stressful situation. However, when the problem is chronic, all pervasive, overwhelming, and uncontrollable as described by Naji (Chapter 20), instrumental coping is of limited value. Buddhist enlightenment (Chapter 4), Taoist way of nature (Chapter 5), spiritual transformation (Chapter 6), and existential coping (Chapters 11 and 17) are all examples of transformational coping. Aldwin's (1994) "transformational coping" indicates the concept of transformation has begun to attract some research attention.

13.3. From individual to collective coping

Collective coping is another welcome development. As long as we only focus on the solo coping efforts of individuals, we will not make much progress in understanding the coping patterns of collectivistic cultures. The history of human survival attests to the importance and power of collective coping. The global relief effort in dealing with the tsunami disaster is a good example of the power of collective coping. The tragedy has united the global community with different ethnic backgrounds and religions.

13.4. From cognitive to existential coping

Recently, psychologists have recognized meaning-based coping (Affleck & Tennen, 1996; Folkman & Moskowitz, 2004; Taylor, 1983). But their focus is still on the cognitive analysis, such causal attribution, or finding positive meaning of a stressful event. Existential coping also includes acceptance of what cannot be changed, and discovering meaning and purpose for one's existence. Existential coping often employs Frankl's three avenues to discover meaning (i.e., experiential, creative, and attitudinal avenues) and Wong's (1998) seven domains (i.e., achievement, relationship, self-transcendence, religion, intimacy, self-acceptance, and fair treatment).

13.5. From dichotomic to dualistic thinking

Another important point in the study of east and west is the dichotomous thinking of Euro-American psychology and the holistic, paradoxical, and dualistic thinking of the East. Thus, one can embrace both internal and external control (Wong & Sproule, 1984) and one can be both pessimistic and optimistic (Wong & McDonald, 2002). This fundamental difference in thinking demands new strategies in cross-cultural research comparing the east and west. For example, instead of using a unidimensional scale to measure locus of control, one needs to use separate and independent scales to measure internal and external beliefs simultaneously. The cognitive process of dualistic thinking also needs experimental investigation.

According to Buddhism, the reactive pattern of the mind implies one's refusal to accept both pain and pleasure as inevitable aspects of human existence. This failure to embrace life's experience in its entirety is at the root of suffering.

Dualistic thinking is also prominent in Taoism. One of the important insights of Taoism is that all things co-exist in opposites, making the existence of each other possible. Thus, goodness cannot exist without evil; hope cannot exist without despair. Suffering occurs when we identify with only the aspect of polarity. However, when we embrace the duality of opposites, we lead an integrated life.

From a general system's perspective, Lee (Chapter 8) emphasizes the importance of the dialectical, reciprocal process of converging opposite pairs into a dualistic union. Self-transcendence and personal transformation naturally occur in an open system of dialectics and duality. This union of opposites was independently discovered by Heraclitus and Lao-tzu, and later adopted by Hegel and Engels in their dialectic logics. The generation of psychic energy and the development of personality transformation depends on the union of opposites, which can be facilitated by traumatic events. Dualistic thinking necessarily embraces the paradox of contradictions. (There are cultural differences in the belief that contradiction is an indication of error, Peng & Nisbett, 1999).

Such dualistic thinking would lead to different kinds of theorizing, such as Wong's (2005) existential model of tragic optimism, and Wong's (1992) dual-dimensional model of locus of control. Wong (1992) argues that "a dual-dimensional view of control is a more accurate picture of the complex interactions between internal and external sources of control. In other words, internal control and external control should be viewed as two independent dimensions and individuals can freely occupy various spots in this two-dimensional space. A person can be simultaneously high or low in both perceived and desired control in any given situation. For example, farmers generally perceive that a good harvest depends equally on hard work and good weather conditions." Dualistic models are able to explain behaviors in cultures that are more holistic than linear. Thus, dualistic versus dichotic thinking represents another major cultural difference in cognitive processes that requires research attention.

These new developments reveal a more complete story of human drama of survival and flourishing in the midst of stress and suffering. The multicultural perspective and positive, transformational orientation may open up new windows of multicultural understanding. In his concluding synthesis, Pedersen (Chapter 25) has identified additional gaps in cross-cultural research and raised provocative questions. We hope that this edited volume will have a lasting impact on cross-cultural research of stress and coping.

REFERENCES

Affleck, G., & Tennen, H. (1996). Construing benefits from adversity: Adaptational significance and dispositional underpinnings. *Journal of Personality, 64*, 899-922.

Aldwin, C. M. (1994). Transformational coping. In C. M. Aldwin (Ed.), *Stress, coping, and development* (pp. 240-269). New York: Guilford.

Antonovsky, A. (1990). A somewhat personal odyssey in studying the stress process. *Stress Medicine, 6*, 71-80.

Aspinwall, L. G., & Taylor, S. E. (1997). A stitch in time: Self-regulation and proactive coping. *Psychological Bulletin, 121*, 417-436.

Baumeister, R. F. (1991). *Meaning of life*. New York: The Guildford Press.

Berry, J. W. (1990). Psychology of acculturation. In J. Berman (Ed.), *Cross-cultural perspectives: Nebraska symposium on motivation* (pp. 201-234). Lincoln: University of Nebraska Press.

Berry, J. W., Poortinga, Y. H., Segall, M. H., & Dasen, P. R. (Eds.) (2002). *Cross-Cultural Psychology: Research and Applications* (2nd ed.). New York, NY: Cambridge University Press.

Bjorck, J. P., Cuthbertson, W., Thurman, J. W., & Lee, Y. S. (2001). Ethnicity, coping, and distress among Korean Americans, Filipino Americans, and Caucasian Americans. *Journal of Social Psychology, 141(4)*, 421-442.

Bond, M. H. (2004). Culture-level dimensions of social axioms and their correlates across 41 cultures. *Journal of Cross-Cultural Psychology, 35*, 548-570.

Brislin, R. W. (Ed.) (1990). *Applied cross-cultural psychology*. Newbury Park, CA: Sage.

Carter, R. T. (1991). Cultural values: A review of empirical research and implications for counseling. *Journal of Counseling & Development, 70*, 164-173.

Cheng, C. (2003). Cognitive and motivational processes underlying coping flexibility: A dual-process model. *Journal of Personality and Social Psychology, 84*, 425-438.

Chun, K., Balls-Organista, P., & Marin, G. (Eds.) (2003). *Acculturation: Advances in theory, measurement and applied research*. Washington: APA Books.

Cloninger, C. R., Svrakic, D. M., & Przybeck, T. R. (1993). A Psychobiological Model of Temperament and Character. *Archive General Psychiatry, 50*, 977-991.

Coyne, J. C., and Gottlieb, B. H. (1996). The mismeasure of coping by checklist. *Journal of Personality, 64*, 959-991.

Cross, S. E. (1995). Self-construals, coping, and stress in cross-cultural adaptation. *Journal of Cross-Cultural Psychology, 26*, 673-697.

Delbanco, A. (1996). *The death of Satan: How Americans have lost the sense of evil*. New York: Noonday Press.

Endler, M. B., & Parker, J. D. A. (2000). Coping with Health Injuries and Problems (CHIP) manual. Multi-Health Systems, Toronto, Canada.

Emmons, R.A. & Paloutzian, R.F. (2003). The psychology of religion. *Annual Review of Psychology, 54*, 377-402.

Folkman, S., & Moskowitz, J. T. (2000). Positive affect and the other side of coping. *American Psychologist, 55(6)*, 647-654.

Folkman, S., & Moskowitz, J. T. (2004). Coping: Pitfalls and promise. *Annual Review of Psychology, 55*, 745-774.

Folkman, S., Lazarus, R. S., Gruen, R., and DeLongis, A. (1986b). Appraisal, coping, health status, and psychological symptoms. *Journal of Personality and Social Psychology, 50*, 571-579.

Frankl, V. E. (1984). *Man's search for meaning*. New York: Washington Square Press.

Frankl, V. E. (1986). *The doctor and the soul: From psychotherapy to logotherapy*. New York: Vintage Books.

Gall, T. L., & Cornblat, M. W. (2002). Breast cancer survivors give voice: A qualitative analysis of spiritual factors in long-term adjustment. *Psycho-Oncology, 11*, 524-535.

Harlow, L. L., Newcomb, M. D., & Bentler, P. M. (1986). Depression, self-derogation, substance abuse, and suicide ideation: Lack of purpose in life as a mediational factor. *Journal of Clinical Psychology, 42*, 5-21.

Ho, D. Y. F. (1995). Internalized culture, culturocentrism, and transcendence. *Counseling Psychologist, 23*, 4-24.

Ho, D. Y. F., & Chiu, C. Y. (1994). Component ideas of individualism, collectivism, and social organization: An application in the study of Chinese culture. In: U. Kim, H. C. Triandis, C. Kagitcibasi, S. C. Choi, & G. Yoon, (eds.), *Individualism and Collectivism*. Sage, Thousand Oaks, pp. 137-156.

Hobfoll, S. E. (1989). Conservation of resources: A new attempt at conceptualizing stress. *The American Psychologist, 44*, 513-524.

Hobfoll, S. E. (1998). *Stress, culture, and community: The psychology and philosophy of stress*. New York: Plenum.

Hofstede, G. H. (1980). *Culture's Consequences: International Differences in Work-related Values*. Beverly Hills, CA: Sage

Ibrahim, F. A. (1991). Contribution of cultural worldview to generic counseling and development. *Journal of Counseling and Development, 70,* 13-18.

Keown, D. (1996). *Buddhism: A Very Short Introduction*, Oxford University Press.

Kim, M., Lee, H. S., & Wong, P. T. P. (2005). *The meaning of life according to Korean: The Korean-Personal Meaning Profile*. Paper presented at the American Psychological Convention, Washington, August.

Kluckhohn, R. R., & Strodtbeck, F. L. (1961). *Variations in value orientations*. Evanston, IL: Row Paterson.

Lam, A. G., & Zane, N. W. S. (2004). Ethnic differences in coping with interpersonal stressors. *Journal of Cross-Cultural Psychology, 35,* 446-459.

Lao-tzu (2000). *Tao Te Ching* (translated into modern Chinese by Lin An-Wu), Ilan, Taiwan: Tu-Cheh Cultural Enterprise Co.

Lazarus, R.S. (1999). *Stress and emotion: A new synthesis*. New York: Springer.

Lazarus, R. S. (2000). Toward better research on stress and coping. *American Psychologist, 55,* 665-673.

Lazarus, R. S., & Folkman, S. (1984). *Stress, appraisal and coping*. New York: Springer.

Leong, F. T. L., & Wong, P. T. P. (2003). Optimal functioning from cross cultural perspectives. In W.B.Walsh (Ed.), *Counseling psychology and optimal human functioning*. (pp. 123-150). Mahwah, NJ: Lawrence Erlbaum Associates.

Liang, B., & Bogat, G. A. (1994). Culture, control, and coping: New perspectives on social support. *American Journal of Community Psychology, 22,* 123-147.

Liu, D. (1979). *The Tao and Chinese culture*. New York: Schocken Books.

Lyons, R. F., Mickelson, K., Sullivan, M. J. L., and Coyne, J. C. (1998). Coping as a communal process. *Journal of Social and Personal Relationships, 15,* 579-605.

Maddi, S. R. (1978). Existential and individual psychologies. *Journal of Individual Psychology, 34,* 182-191.

Maddi, S. R. (2002). The story of hardiness: Twenty years of theorizing, research, and practice. *Consulting Psychology Journal, 54,* 173-185.

Markus, H. R., & Kitayama, S. (1991). Culture and the self: Implications for cognition, emotion, and motivation. *Psychological Review, 98,* 224-253.

Marsella, A. (1993). Counseling and psychotherapy with Japanese Americans: Cross-cultural considerations. *American Journal of Orthopsychiatry, 63,* 200-208.

Moos, R. H., & Swindle, R. W. (1990). Stressful life circumstances: Concepts and measures. *Stress Medicine, 6,* 171-178.

Morling, B., & Fiske, S. T. (1999). Defining and measuring harmony control. *Journal of Research in Personality, 33,* 379-414.

O'Brien, T. B., & DeLongis, A. (1996). The interactional context of problem-, emotion-, and relationship-focused coping: The role of the big five personality factors. *Journal of Personality, 64,* 775-813.

Pargament, K. I. (1997). *The psychology of religion and coping*. New York: Guildford.

Pargament, K. I., Koenig, H. G., & Perez, L. M. (2000). The many methods of religious coping: Development and initial validation of the RCOPE. *Journal of Clinical Psychology, 56,* 519-543.

Peacock, E. J., & Wong, P. T. P. (1996). Anticipatory stress: The relation of locus of control, optimism, and control appraisals to coping. *Journal of Research in Personality, 30,* 204-222.

Peacock, E. J., Wong, P. T. P., & Reker, G. T. (1993). Relations between appraisals and coping schemas: A test of the congruence model. *Canadian Journal of Behavioural Science, 25,* 64-80.

Pedersen, P. (1991). Multiculturalism as a generic approach to counseling. *Journal of Counseling and Development, 70,* 6-12.

Pedersen, P. (1999). *Multiculturalism as a Fourth Force*. Washington, DC: Taylor and Frances.

Peng, K., & Nisbett, R. E. (1999). Culture, dialectics, and reasoning about contradiction. *American Psychologist, 54,* 741-754.

Reker, G. T., & Wong, P. T. P. (1988). Aging as an individual process: Towards a theory of personal meaning. In J. E. Birren & V. L. Benston (Eds.). *Emerging theories of aging* (pp. 214-246). New York: Springer.

Rokeach, M. (1973). *The nature of human values*. New York: Free Press.

Rothbaum, F., Weisz, J. R., & Snyder, S. S. (1982). Changing the world and changing the self: A two-process model of perceived control. *Journal of Personality & Social Psychology, 42*(1), 5-37.

Sam, D., & Berry, J. W. (Eds.) (2005). *Cambridge handbook of acculturation psychology*. Cambridge: Cambridge University Press.

Schwarzer, R., & Knoll, N. (2003). Positive coping: Mastering demands and searching for meaning. In S.J. Lopez & C. R. Snyder (Eds.). *Positive psychological assessment: A handbook of models and measures.* Washington, DC: American Psychological Association.

Schmitz, P. (1992). Acculturation styles and health. In S. Iwawaki, Y. Kashima, & K. Leung (Eds.), *Innovations in cross-cultural psychology* (pp. 360-370). Amsterdam: Swets and Zeitlinger.

Segall, M. H., Lonner, W. J., & Berry, J. W. (1998). Cross-cultural psychology as a scholarly discipline: On the flowering of culture in behavioral research. *American Psychologist, 53,* 1101-1110.

Seiffge-Krenke, I. (1993). Coping in normal and clinical samples: More similarities than differences? *Journal of Adolescence, 16,* 285-305.

Siegel, K., & Schrimshaw, E. W. (2002). The perceived benefits of religious and spiritual coping among older adults living with HIV/AIDS. *Journal for the Scientific Study of Religion, 41,* 91-102.

Slavin, L. A., Rainer, K. L., McCreary, M. L., & Gowda, K. K. (1991). Toward a multicultural model of the stress process. *Journal of Counseling & Development, 70,* 156-163.

Snyder, C. R. (1994). *The psychology of hope. You can get there from here.* New York: Free Press.

Somerfield, M. R., & McCrae, R. R. (2000). Stress and coping research: Methodological challenges, theoretical advances, and clinical applications. *American Psychologist, 55(6),* 620-625.

Sommer, D. (1995). *Chinese religion: An anthology of sources.* New York: Oxford University Press.

Sue, D. W., & Sue, D. (2003). *Counseling the Culturally Diverse: Theory and Practice* (4th ed.) New York: John Wiley & Sons, Inc.

Takano, Y., & Wong, P. T. P. (2004). *The meaning of life according to a Japanese sample.* Paper presented at the American Psychological Association Convention, Honolulu, August.

Taylor, S. E. (1983). Adjustment to threatening events: A theory of cognitive adaptation. *American Psychologist, 38,* 1161-1173.

Taylor, S. E., Sherman, D. K., Kim, H. S., Jarcho, J., Takagi, K., & Dunagan, M. S. (2004). Culture and social support: Who seeks it and why? *Journal of Personality & Social Psychology, 87(3),* 354-362.

Tennen, H., Affleck, G., Armeli, S., & Carney, M.A. (2000). A daily process approach to coping: Linking theory, research, and practice. *American Psychologist, 55,* 626-636.

Tillich, P. (1952). *The courage to be.* New Haven, CT: Yale University Press.

Triandis, H. C. (1995). *Individualism and Collectivism.* Boulder, CO: Westview

Ward, C. (1996). Acculturation. In D. Landis & R. Bhagat (Eds.), *Handbook of Intercultural Training* (2nd ed., pp. 124-147). Newbury Park: Sage.

Wong, P. T. P. (1990). Measuring life stress. *Stress Medicine, 6,* 69-70.

Wong, P. T. P. (1992). Control is a double-edged sword. *Canadian Journal of Behavioural Science, 24,* 143-146.

Wong, P. T. P. (1993). Effective management of life stress: The resource-congruence model. *Stress Medicine, 9,* 51-60.

Wong, P. T. P. (1998). Meaning-centered counselling. In P. T. P. Wong and P. S. Fry (Eds.), *The human quest for meaning: A handbook of psychological research and clinical applications* (pp. 395-435) Mahwah, NJ: Lawrence Erlbaum Associates.

Wong, P. T. P. (1999). Meaning of life and meaning of death in successful aging. In A. Tomer (Ed.), *Death attitudes and the older adults.* Bruner/Mazel Publisher.

Wong, P. T. P. (2002). Creating a positive, meaningful work place: New challenges in management and leadership. In B. Pattanayak & V. Gupta (Eds.). *Creating performing organizations* (pp. 74-129). New Delhi, India: Sage Publications.

Wong, P. T. P., & Sproule, C. F. (1984). Attributional analysis of locus of control and the Trent Attribution Profile (TAP). In H. M. Lefcourt (Ed.), *Research with locus of control construct*, Vol. 3: *Limitations and extension* (pp. 309-360). New York: Academic Press.

Wong, P. T. P., & Reker, G. T. (1985). Stress, coping, and well-being in Anglo and Chinese elderly. *Canadian Journal on Aging, 4(1),* 29-37.

Wong P. T. P., & Fry, P. S. (Eds.) (1998). *The human quest for meaning: A handbook of psychological research and clinical applications.* Mahwah, NJ: Lawrence Erlbaum Associates.

Wong, P. T. P., & Ujimoto, K. V. (1998). The elderly Asian Americans: Their stress, coping, and well-being. In L. C. Lee & N. W. S. Zane (Eds.), *Handbook of Asian American Psychology.* Thousand Oaks, CA: Sage Publications.

Wong, P. T. P., & McDonald, M. (2002). Tragic optimism and personal meaning in counselling victims of abuse. *Pastoral Sciences, 20,* 231-249.

Wong, P. T. P. & Gupta, V. (2004). The positive psychology of transformative organizations. In V. Gupta (2004). *Transformative Organizations* (pp. 341-360). New Delhi, India: Sage Publications.

Yalom, I. D. (1981). *Existential psychotherapy*. New York: Basic Books.

Zavalloni, M. (1980). Values. In H. C. Triandis & R. W. Brislin (Eds.) *Handbook of cross-cultural psychology* (pp.73-115). Boston, MA: Allyn & Bacon.

Section 1

Theoretical Issues

CULTURE: A Fundamental Context for the Stress and Coping Paradigm

Chi-Ah Chun, Rudolf H. Moos, and Ruth C. Cronkite

1. INTRODUCTION

The field of stress and coping emerged more than three decades ago from the recognition of the dynamic interaction between person and environment (Lazarus & Folkman, 1984; Moos, 2002). Over the years, researchers developed a system of objectifying and quantifying people's environment, such as counting the number of major life events or daily hassles that occurred in the past month. Unfortunately, this system of measuring the environment resulted in acontextualizing the stress and coping research paradigm as it does not give much consideration to the meaning of the events that occur in an idiosyncratic life context. In recent years, the field has been trying to introduce more realism to stress and coping research, as the acontextual research of the last two decades yielded few solid findings that made a difference in people's lives (Somerfield & McCrae, 2000). One of the most important neglected contexts is culture. We believe that culture is a fundamental context that helps to shape both the individual and the environment.

There have been growing efforts to examine cross-cultural variations in stress and coping, but these efforts are fragmented and primarily descriptive, and usually lack an overarching conceptual framework. The aim of our overview is to help shape future research to address the generalizability of current models of stress and coping across cultural and ethnic groups. Here we describe a conceptual framework based on Moos' transactional model (1984; 2002) that encompasses the role of culture in stress and coping. Using this conceptual framework, we illustrate how culture serves as a pervasive context for the stress and coping paradigm, and present some empirical evidence on this issue. We conclude by addressing several key issues and assumptions of the current stress and coping paradigm that may have contributed to conceptual confusion and slowed the progress of cross-cultural investigations, and we offer ways to solve these problems.

Chi-Ah Chun, California State University, Long Beach; Rudolf H. Moos, Ruth C. Cronkite, VA Palo Alto Health Care System & Stanford University School of Medicine

2. A CONCEPTUAL MODEL OF STRESS AND COPING

Stress and coping models have placed varying degrees of emphasis on the role of the contextual factors and transactions between person and environment (Lazarus & Folkman, 1984; McCrae, 1984; Pearlin & Schooler, 1978; Wong & Ujimoto, 1998). Moos' model (1984; 2002) places emphasis on both (see Figure 1). It depicts the transactions between the ongoing *environmental system* (Panel I) and the *personal system* (Panel II), and encompasses their joint influences on subsequent *transitory conditions* (Panel III), *cognitive appraisal and coping skills* (Panel IV), and the *health and well-being* (Panel V) of individuals.

More specifically, the environmental system consists of relatively enduring aspects of the environment, such as the social climate and ongoing stressors and resources that arise from settings in different life domains (e.g., family and work). The personal system is composed of individuals' personal characteristics and resources, such as their cognitive abilities, personality traits, social competence, and self-confidence. Transitory conditions include new acute life events and changes that occur in an individual's life; individuals appraise these conditions for their degree of threat or challenge and whether they are equipped with adequate personal and environmental resources to deal with the situation. In turn, appraisal influences the type of coping strategies that will be employed; these strategies can be characterized in terms of their focus (approach/avoidant) and method (cognitive/behavioral). The success of coping subsequently influences the individual's health and well-being.

Figure 1. A model of interplay between context, coping and adaptation.

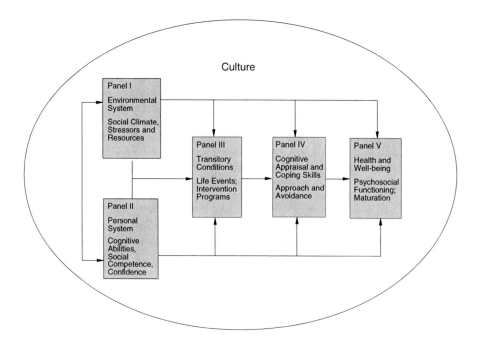

One of the key strengths of this model lies in its emphasis on the contextual factors in the stress and coping process. The model also depicts the transactional relationships among the five panels, as reflected by bi-directional arrows. For example, the bi-directional arrow between the environmental system and the personal system suggests that the social climate and personality characteristics can influence each other. The model also suggests that, together with the personal system, the ongoing environmental context influences the occurrences of transitional life events, as well as how individuals appraise and cope with the events and how they affect health and well-being.

Culture is one of the fundamental aspects of society that influence both the person and the environment. Although culture is part of the environmental system, it should be distinguished from the more proximal social climate of Panel I, which consists of specific settings (e.g., family, work, and neighborhood) and ongoing stressors and resources. Culture would be better conceptualized as a macro-social or ecological system that permeates the entire stress and coping process. Thus, culture influences all of the panels and serves as an overall context for the model, as depicted in Figure 1. In turn, at a macro-social level, the stress and coping process can also change culture. This role of the cultural system has not been explicitly articulated in most existing stress and coping models with the notable exception of Wong's Resource-Congruence Model (1993), which also emphasizes the influence of the cultural system on the stress and coping process.

2.1. The Role of Culture in the Stress and Coping Paradigm

Culture is best defined as a highly complex, continually changing system of meaning that is learned, shared, transmitted and altered from one generation to another (Triandis, 1995). This system of meaning encompasses the norms, beliefs, and values that provide prescriptions for behavior. While numerous cultural values have been proposed and identified to describe unique and shared elements of various cultures, individualism and collectivism are the most widely studied (see for review Oyserman, Coon, & Kemmelmeier, 2002). The theoretical and empirical utility of these concepts lies in the fact that they are able to meaningfully differentiate cultures (Hofstede, 1980; Oyserman et al., 2002; Triandis, 1995). In the following sections we illustrate how culture might influence each of the panels in our conceptual model of stress and coping, using the constructs of individualism and collectivism as examples.

2.2. Individualism and Collectivism

Individualism and collectivism consist of a set of values, attitudes, and behaviors that vary in the priority placed on the self versus the ingroup (Hofstede, 1980). In cultures oriented toward individualism, the self is a central unit of society. Consequently, individual rights, a concern for oneself and immediate family, and personal autonomy and self-fulfillment are emphasized. In contrast, in cultures oriented toward collectivism the ingroup forms the central unit of society and binds individuals to its needs, goals, and fate. Accordingly, duty and obligations to the ingroup, interdependence on other individuals within the group, and fulfillment of social roles are emphasized. These orientations have important ramifications for the environmental and personal systems, and for the extent to which context influences behavior.

While individualism and collectivism are often regarded as opposite poles of a single dimension, they would be better conceptualized as worldviews or orientations that place focus and emphasis on different issues (Kagitçibasi, 1997; Oyserman et al., 2002). Furthermore, as Hofstede (1980) suggested, these two orientations exist both at the individual and societal levels, and the two levels do not necessarily coincide.

Individualism and collectivism have been measured or manipulated in one of three different ways (Oyserman et al., 2002). The first method is based on Hofstede's landmark cross-national study on people who worked for a multinational corporation in 39 nations (Hoftstede, 1980). This study revealed country-level variations in individualism, with respondents in the United States being most individualistic, and respondents in Japan and other East Asian nations being much less individualistic. Subsequent studies have used Hofstede's ratings of country-level individualism as a proxy measure of individualism. Oyserman and colleagues' meta-analysis (2002) confirmed that, in general, people in the United States, especially Euro-Americans, tend to be more individualistic and less collectivistic than individuals of non-Western and/or developing nations.

The second method involves directly measuring the orientations at the individual level using standardized self-report instruments that consist of a list of statements that describe either individualistic or collectivistic attitudes, values, and behaviors (e.g., Matsumoto, Weissman, Preston, Brown, & Kupperbusch, 1997; Singelis, Triandis, Bhawuk, & Gelfand, 1995). One of the limitations of the direct assessment method is that it assesses only the explicit aspects of culture that individuals are aware of, and may not adequately capture subtle and implicit practices (Oyserman et al., 2002). The third method uses experimental priming techniques that manipulate the salience of either an individualistic or collectivistic schema or worldview by experimentally exposing individuals to certain cultural cues. The priming techniques are widely used in cognitive research that examines the role of culture in attention, perception, and memory.

Of the three methods, cross-cultural research on stress and coping tends to rely mostly on the ethnic or country level indices of individualism and collectivism. However, we need to keep in mind that Euro-Americans consist of individuals with very diverse cultural heritage from more than 40 different countries and distinct regions of the European continent, who vary significantly in their cultural beliefs, attitudes, and practices.

2.3. Culture and the Environmental System (Panel I)

Culture can set the tone for the characteristics of the environmental system and thus for dominant aspects of the social climate. In societies that are more individualistic, such as the United States, the social climate tends to value and protect individuals' rights to autonomy and independence. The social norm is to individuate from family at the end of adolescence; thus, cohesion with family and group may be played down. In contrast, the social climate of societies that are more collectivistic tends to promote social conformity and interdependence. Pursuit of individual autonomy is often viewed as selfish and a betrayal of the in-group. Instead, personal sacrifice for the larger community is regarded as an indication of maturity and strong character.

The environmental system partly determines the pressures and demands on individuals (ongoing stressors) and the social resources available to them. The cultural context shapes these ongoing stressors and social resources. More specifically, in individualistic societies, many of the ongoing stressors may stem from the pressure to be autonomous and independent. These pressures occur in early adulthood, when a person may not be ready to individuate or handle all responsibilities alone. The emphasis on independence and autonomy may also be associated with fewer available social resources. In contrast, in collectivistic societies, there is greater pressure to remain interdependent on the in-groups and to meet their demands, sometimes at the expense of the individual's own welfare. In fact, such patterns are easily observable in parent-child relationships. Asian American adolescents were found to be more sensitive to pleasing their parents than Euro-American adolescents (Pang, 1991). Also, in New Zealand parental pressure both motivated and hurt adolescents of Chinese descent when such was not the case for adolescents of European descent (Chung, Walkey, & Bemak, 1997).

Cultural context can also influence the social resources that are available to and accessed by individuals. In individualistic societies, the social network tends to consist of relatively loosely connected members, composed of the nuclear family and some relatives, friends, and acquaintances (Triandis, 1988). Because the distinction between ingroup and outgroup is not strong, social networks tend to be large and diverse, but weak. In collectivistic cultures, family networks include the extended family, but the boundary is often not clear because of its extensiveness. Thus, cross-cultural researchers often face difficulties in appropriately defining a family or household in Asian cultures, both in terms of memberships and residence (Knodel & Saengtienchai, 1999). The Asian household is often more fluid and co-residence among various family members is common and on a continuum. Such cultural differences are manifested in many different ways. For instance, young adults of Latin and Filipino American families tended to live with and contribute financially to the family and reported stronger sense of duty to family compared to their Euro-American counterparts (Fuligni & Pedersen, 2002). Young adults of Chinese- and Indo-Canadian families were also more likely than their British-Canadian counterparts to report a positive attitude towards sharing a home with an elderly parent (Mitchell, 2003).

Cultural differences in the dynamics within the nuclear family have implications for who can provide needed support and resources. Spousal presence was significantly more important for the well-being of American elders than of Japanese elders, whereas presence of children was important only for the Japanese elders (Sugisawa, Shibata, Hougham, Sugihara, & Liang, 2002). Older adults of other Asian cultures such as Cambodia (Zimmer & Kim, 2001), Indonesia (Beard & Kunharibowo, 2001), Korea (Kim & Rhee, 1997), and Thailand (Knodel & Saengtienchai, 1999) tend to live with their adult children or live close to them. The opposite is true for elders in the U.S. where the proportion of elderly living alone has dramatically increased over several decades. Specifically, in 1988 at least half of elders in Korea (65%), Japan (50%), and Taiwan (74%) lived with their adult children whereas only 10% of American elders and 5% of Danish elders lived with their adult children (Korea Gallup, 1990, Japanese Prime Minister's Office, 1990, and Jacobs, 1998; all cited in Kwon, 1999). The majority of elders in the U.S. (80%) and Denmark (90%) lived alone or with their spouse only. This is in part due to the rising income of older adults, but preferences and income levels of children also play an important role in why so many elders live alone (Kotlikoff & Morris, 1988).

In terms of adult sibling relationships, traditional cultures of Asia tend to foster close sibling relationships throughout their adulthood and these relationships tend to be obligatory compared to Western societies such as the U.S. and Australia where the adult sibling relationships tend to be discretionary (Cicirelli, 1994). It is important to note that discretionary relationships do not necessarily indicate lack of contact or closeness. In fact, adult sibling relationships in Western cultures tend to be very close when there is frequent contact.

2.4. Culture and the Personal System (Panel II)

Culture's influence on the personal system has been well-documented. Research has revealed culture-dependent variations in cognitive, behavioral, and emotional components of the personal system, including self-construal, personality traits, attribution, and motivation. These components are integral parts of the personal system in the stress and coping paradigm.

2.4.1. Self-construal and personality traits

According to Markus and Kitayama (1991), culture can influence the ways individuals define themselves in relation to their social context. For example, individualistic cultures tend to cultivate an independent self-construal that defines self as a separate and independent entity with well-defined boundaries and in terms of abstract and general traits. Collectivistic cultures tend to cultivate an interdependent self-construal that defines self in relation to other people with overlapping interpersonal boundaries and in terms of social roles and situations.

Recent studies on ethnic differences in self-descriptors have found that Euro-American college students used more personal trait descriptors and fewer social role descriptors than Asian-American and Korean college students (Rhee, Uleman, Lee, & Roman, 1995). In addition, Euro-American adolescents rated individualistic self-descriptors as more important than collectivistic self-descriptors and used fewer group-focused self-descriptors compared to Mexican-American adolescents (Dabul, Bernal, & Knight, 1995). Even within Euro-Americans, cultural orientation is associated with self-construals. Euro-American college students who scored low on collectivism used fewer social identities to describe themselves than did those who scored high on collectivism (Gaertner, Sedikides, & Graetz, 1999).

These differences in self-construals have implications for how individuals respond to and resist contextual influences. Markus and Kitayama (1991) proposed that individuals with interdependent self-construals are more attentive and sensitive to their social context compared to individuals with independent self-construals. This idea suggests that individuals who have more interdependent self-construals might be more socially competent in that they are more attuned to the social context. But at the same time, such individuals likely would be more field-dependent, have a more external locus of control, and be more affected by environmental demands. Indeed, compared to American college students, Hong Kong Chinese, Korean, and Japanese college students reported greater need for affiliation, nurturance, and sensitivity to social rejection (Hui & Villareal, 1989; Yamaguchi, Kuhlman, & Sugimori, 1995) and more inclinations to meet expectations of significant others, such as family and friends (Lay, Fairlie, Jackson, Ricci, Eisenberg, Sato, et al., 1998).

Locus of control is a very pertinent personality dimension to coping. Cross-cultural studies have revealed that individuals from individualistic cultures, such as Euro-Americans and New Zealanders, tend to have a stronger sense of internal locus of control than individuals from collectivistic cultures, such as the Japanese (Bond & Tornatzky, 1973; Mahler, 1974), the Chinese (Hamid, 1994), East Indians (Chandler, Shama, Wolf, & Planchard, 1981), and individuals from Zambia and Zimbabwe (Munro, 1979). Such cultural patterns in locus of control have also been found in children; Euro-American children scored higher on internal locus of control than Filipino and Brazilian children did (Paguio, Robinson, Skeen, & Deal, 1987). These results show that cultural values, such as individualism and collectivism, can shape perceptions of the extent of control over one's life and environment.

Rothbaum and colleagues (Rothbaum, Weisz, & Snyder, 1982; Weisz, Rothbaum, & Blackburn, 1984) took this idea of control one step further and proposed that the target of control can be the external environment or the individual. For individualistic persons with independent self-construals, the target of control is likely to lie outside of the person; thus, individualistic people are likely to exercise *primary* control by trying to control or change the external environment. For collectivistic persons with interdependent self-construals, however, the target of control likely will be the self, because the individual needs to fit into the group and protect it. Thus, these individuals are likely to exercise *secondary* control by trying to control or change their mind, emotions, thoughts, and behaviors. The idea of controlling one's self or environment has important implications for how one chooses to cope with stress.

2.4.2. Attribution

Attribution has a special place in the stress and coping paradigm, as it influences how individuals appraise an event or situation, and the specific coping strategies they employ. Because of the emphasis on the individual as an active agent, individualism should be associated with greater tendency to attribute causes of events to the self or other individuals. Collectivism, on the other hand, should be associated with a greater tendency for situational attribution because of its greater reliance on context for definition of motivation. Experimental findings support these hypotheses. In a very clever study on American (primarily Euro-American) and Chinese high school and graduate students, Morris and Peng (1994) demonstrated that American students used more dispositional attribution than situational attributions, especially on social reasoning tasks. Similar attributional differences were also found between Americans and individuals from other nations, such as Hindus (Miller, 1984, 1986; Shweder & Bourne, 1982) and Koreans (Choi & Nisbett, 1998).

Using the theoretical framework of locus of control, Kawanishi (1995) studied the role of culture in causal attribution. She found that Japanese college students were more likely than Euro-American students to make attribution to external chance factors. For example, they were more likely than Euro-American students to attribute successful coping to good luck, and attribute stress to bad luck. Kawanishi suggested that this attribution pattern was observed because of Japanese's common belief in luck, a type of external locus of control, which has been associated with collectivism (Bond & Tornatzky, 1973;

Mahler, 1974). These findings imply that how culture and personality traits, such as locus of control, can influence attribution style.

2.4.3. Motivation

Individuals' stable patterns of motivation have important implications for stress and coping. Many psychological theories are based on the premise of the pleasure principle, which postulates that individuals are motivated to maximize pleasure and minimize pain. Higgins' theory of *regulatory focus* (Higgins, 1997) proposes that there are two types of regulatory foci: *Promotion* and *prevention*. Promotion-focused self-regulation involves having *strong ideals* as desired end-states and working towards achieving these ideals. Promotion-focus leads to sensitivity to the presence (or absence) of positive outcomes and the use of approach as a strategic mean. Thus, people with promotion regulatory focus would be guided by what they would ideally like to do and work towards obtaining positive outcomes. Prevention-focused self-regulation involves having *strong oughts,* or being guided by obligations to oneself or significant others, and working towards meeting these obligations. A prevention-focus leads to sensitivity to negative outcomes and attempts to avoid them. People with prevention regulatory focus are guided by what they ought to do and work to avoid negative outcomes.

Higgins' theory was originally developed to explain individual differences in regulatory focus. However, this theory also has cultural implications because it emphasizes the role of socialization in how one might develop a particular regulatory focus. For example, Lee and Aaker (Aaker & Lee, 2001; Lee, Aaker, & Gardner, 2000) proposed that in a society that values individuals' right to pursue their own dreams and happiness, people would be more likely to be socialized to develop a promotion regulatory focus. On the other hand, in a society that values duty, responsibility, and maintaining stability of the group, people would be more likely to be socialized to develop a prevention regulatory focus. Culture can also shape whose ideals or whose oughts are internalized. As the theory of regulatory focus is meant to explain primarily individual differences, every society will have people with either type of regulatory focus. However, an individualistic person with a prevention focus is more likely to be concerned with minimizing the loss of the self, whereas a collectivistic person with the same prevention focus is more likely to be concerned with minimizing the loss of the in-group.

Using Higgins' regulatory focus theory, Lee and Aaker (Aaker & Lee, 2001; Lee et al., 2000) conducted a series of experiments examining the role of self-construals and cultural orientation in motivation and persuasion. They found that regulatory focus may differ as a function of self-construal. Specifically, college students with independent self-construals had a greater promotion focus and valued information regarding potential gain, whereas students with interdependent self-construals had a greater prevention focus and valued information regarding potential losses. The same relationship between self-construal and regulatory focus was obtained whether self-construal was assessed as individual differences using a self-report measure or as group differences using nationality (American vs. Chinese) as indicators of independence and interdependence. Furthermore, individuals seemed to be able to access both independent and interdependent self-construals through priming, and their regulatory focus shifted according to the dominant self-construal in the moment, demonstrating the relationship between self-construal and regulatory focus. These findings show that the immediate social context sometimes can transcend cultural differences.

The relationship between self-construal and motivation was also demonstrated in children. Iyengar and Lepper (1999) compared the effects of freedom of choice and choice by others on intrinsic motivation in Asian American and Euro-American children. They found that Euro-American children spent more time working on an anagram task when left alone and able to choose the type of anagram to work on compared to when the task was chosen by their mothers. In contrast, Asian American children spent more time on the anagram task when the task was chosen by their mothers than when they chose it themselves. The findings demonstrate that freedom of choice enhances intrinsic motivation in Euro-American children, whereas choice by a trusted authority figures (e.g., mother) enhances intrinsic motivation in Asian American children. The cross-cultural pattern of reliance on self or others for motivation appears to be consistent with that of locus of control. Individuals with independent self-construals tend to believe that the source of control lies within themselves, attempt to change external factors, and are more motivated to take action when they have a choice.

2.5. Culture and Transitory Conditions (Panel III)

Cultural and social factors have a pervasive influence on the occurrence and construal of life events, such as financial hardships, lack of employment, family-related stressors, physical and mental health problems, and discrimination. Cultural attitudes and values shape the types of events and conditions that are typical or common in a society and those that are regarded as stressful or challenging. As such, specific events or conditions are likely to be more common or stressful in individualistic versus collectivistic cultures. Earlier we described findings from cross-cultural research on living arrangement of the elderly. In collectivistic cultures of Asia the elderly tend to live with their adult children, customarily with their eldest son or in a complicated arrangement moving from one adult child's family to the next (Beard & Kunharibowo, 2001; Kim & Rhee, 1997; Knodel & Saengtienchai, 1999; Yoo & Sung, 1997; Zimmer & Kim, 2001), whereas in the U.S. the elderly tend to live alone (Kotlikoff & Morris, 1988). Such different types of normative family arrangements across cultures have implications for the kinds of stressful events that are more likely to occur in each culture.

In individualistic societies, the emphasis on independence and self-reliance can result in social stressors, such as isolation and loneliness in older age. The emphasis on freedom of choice can result in stressors associated with the inability to make choices, such as between following one vocation or another. On the other hand, in collectivistic societies, the emphasis on interdependence can result in an ongoing burden of caring for older or impaired family members. Situations of interpersonal conflict can also be significant stressors. In a collectivistic society, situations that precipitate changes in relationships, such as marriage, are more likely to be stressors due to the need to balance the separation from parents and forming bonds with a new family. In contrast, in an individualistic society, situations that precipitate dependence, such as an elderly person moving in with the family of an adult child, are more likely to be stressors.

Stressful events and conditions can also be categorized along two dimensions that may be differentially salient in individualistic and collectivistic cultures: (1) independent vs. interdependent stressors; and (2) change vs. constancy. First, certain events or conditions can threaten various aspects of the self, including its sense of independence from or interdependence with others. Heine and Lehman (1995) found that Japanese college students found interdependent events (e.g., "Sometimes in the future you will do something that will make your family ashamed of you.") more severe but more controllable than independent events (e.g., "After growing old, you will find out that you never realized your most important dreams."). The reverse was true for Euro-Canadian college students. Tafarodi and Smith (2001) made similar predictions regarding the differential sensitivity to life events. Their study revealed that collectivistic Malaysian students reported more dysphoria in response to negative social events compared to individualistic British students. These findings suggest that individuals may be more vulnerable to events or conditions that threaten the culturally salient aspects of the self.

Change and constancy are also culturally relevant dimensions of life events. In individualistic societies, which value progress, change is likely to be seen as a positive event because it can offer an opportunity for growth and improvement, whereas constancy may be seen as negative in that it threatens progress. In collectivistic societies, which value security, change can signal potential threat to stability and safety. Constancy is more likely to be viewed as a desirable condition because its predictability allows for better control and management of any given situation. Thus, cultural context can influence transient conditions (Panel III) by influencing the occurrence of specific types of events and by shaping the types of events that people will define as normative or as stressors, and intensifying or attenuating the severity of the threat of specific events.

2.6. Culture and Cognitive Appraisal and Coping Skills (Panel IV)

Panel IV addresses the heart of the coping process: What happens once an individual is faced with an event? This phase encompasses appraisal and coping. The individual first appraises the nature of the stressful event and available coping options. Then, based on the appraisal, coping responses are used to deal with the event. The cultural context can influence individuals' appraisals and their choice of coping strategies. Culture can also shape the goals individuals set for themselves, that is, what they hope to achieve through their coping efforts.

2.6.1. Cognitive Appraisal

Appraisal of a potential stressor is probably the most subjective part of the coping process. Potential stressors are evaluated for the type of negative impact they might have (primary appraisal) and what can be done to manage the situation with available personal and social resources (secondary appraisal). Primary appraisal of stressors includes appraisal for harm/loss, threat, or challenge (Lazarus & Folkman, 1984). Stressors are appraised as involving harm or loss when tangible damage to the person, whether it be physical, psychological, or both, has already occurred. Threat appraisal concerns anticipated harm or loss that might occur as a result of the stressor, or the potential for further impacts if actual harm/loss has already been sustained. On the other hand, challenge appraisal concerns anticipated positive growth or gains through the experience of the stressor. As in threat appraisal, challenge appraisal may take place even when harm or loss has already been sustained. The key difference between threat and challenge appraisals is their respective focus on potential loss versus gain.

This threat/challenge appraisal typology bears remarkable resemblance to the typology of prevention/promotion regulatory focus described in the discussion of Panel II. According to the theory of regulatory focus, individuals develop a stable regulatory pattern that shapes differential sensitivity to certain aspects of events or conditions (Higgins, 1997). A promotion-focused individual would be most sensitive to the potential "presence or absence of positive outcome" and see the situation as a challenge to attain the positive outcome. On the other hand, a prevention-focused individual is inclined to be most sensitive to the potential "absence or presence of negative outcomes" and see a situation as a threat to security. As noted earlier, Aaker and her colleagues' cross-cultural research (Aaker & Lee, 2001; Lee et al., 2000) demonstrated that Americans with dominant independent self-construal showed promotion-focused regulation, whereas Hong Kong Chinese with dominant interdependent self-construal engaged in prevention-focused regulation. Thus, we can hypothesize that individuals oriented towards individualism are more likely to appraise stressors as a challenge than as a threat, whereas those oriented towards collectivism are more likely to appraise stressors as a threat than as a challenge. In addition, collectivists are more likely than individualists to be sensitive to actual harms and losses incurred by stressors.

Bjork and colleagues (Bjork, Cuthbertson, Thurman, & Lee, 2001) tested similar cultural hypotheses by examining ethnic differences in stress appraisals in Euro-, Korean-, and Filipino-American college students. The students were asked to rate the most stressful situation they experienced in the past week on degree of threat, challenge, and loss. As predicted, Korean-American students appraised their stressors as involving greater losses than did Euro-American students. But contrary to expectation, Korean- and Filipino-American students also appraised stressors as more challenging than Euro-American students did. One explanation for these seemingly paradoxical findings is that Asian American students were more concerned about presenting themselves in a positive light to authority figures such as the researchers. An alternative explanation is the possible role of religiosity in appraisal for the Korean-American and Filipino-American students. Religiosity or spirituality may be an important personal factor influencing appraisal by enabling individuals to evaluate the event in a more positive and purposeful light (e.g., God has a special plan for me through this difficult experience) (Lazarus & Folkman, 1984). The strong religious affiliation and spirituality of these two Asian-American groups have been well-documented (Agbayani-Siewert & Revilla, 1995; Hurh & Kim, 1990). Consistent with this speculation, the Korean- and Filipino-American students in this study reported greater use of religious coping than their Euro-American counterparts. This study is a good reminder that cultural values are just one of the many determinants of the stress and coping process.

2.6.2. Coping Goals

Coping goals reflect the ultimate outcome that one hopes to achieve upon resolving the stressful situation (e.g., finding a new or better job, making up with a spouse after an argument, fixing a broken car). Coping goals are important to consider because they help to motivate and organize coping efforts, but they are rarely explicitly ascertained or examined in stress and coping research. In fact, ignoring individual and cultural variations in coping goals has contributed to the acontextualization of stress and coping research in the past. We propose that cultural values and beliefs influence coping goals, and there are four ways that coping goals might vary with individualism and collectivism: (a) focus on the needs of self vs. the needs of others; (b) assert autonomy and independence vs. reinforce relatedness and interdependence; (c) control external environment vs. internal self; and (d) maximize gain vs. minimize loss.

Past research on stress and coping has been based on the prevailing assumption that individuals set coping goals that primarily address their own needs, more specifically, the immediate reduction of their own psychological distress. This assumption reflects an individualistic value orientation where it is more common for people to place greater priority on goals focused on meeting the needs of the individual (self-focused coping goals) than on goals focused on meeting the needs of other people (other-focused coping goals). Unfortunately, such assumption ignores the fact that an immediate reduction of distress may not be the desired outcome for the individual nor an indication that one's coping goal has been met (Menaghan, 1983). Also, there are often multiple, competing goals within a situation (Austin & Vancouver, 1996), and coping goals may vary across situations and persons (Coyne & Racioppo, 2000). In fact, an individual can simultaneously have self-focused and other-focused coping goals; which type of goal becomes more salient or important will depend on the nature of the stressor and the characteristics of the individual. The primary goal of coping may lie in the improvement of other people's well-being or in the quality of interpersonal relationships as well as in the reduction of the individual's distress. For example, for people in nurturing roles, such as parents, caretakers, and clergy, the well-being of the person for whom they are caring may take a higher priority than their own well-being.

This is likely to be especially true for collectivistic individuals whose interdependent self-construal embraces other people as part of the self, making the welfare of the in-group an integral determinant of the welfare of the individual. When other-focused coping goals require some amount of self-sacrifice, this may result in an immediate increase in distress, rather than the decrease that researchers often use as evidence of effective coping. This may explain the frequent findings that Asians and Asian Americans tend to use seemingly ineffective coping strategies that do not reduce their psychological distress (Bjorck et al., 2001; Chang, 1996a, 1996b; Essau & Trommsdorff, 1996; Lee & Liu, 2001; Nakano, 1991; Radford, Mann, Ohta, & Nakane, 1993). The coping strategies known to be effective based on research that uses symptom relief as a measure of successful outcome may not necessarily be those that help achieve other types of desired coping goals.

Cross-cultural theories on interpersonal conflict resolution style have proposed similar cultural variations in coping goals specific to interpersonal stressors. Individualistic coping goals would assert the autonomy and independence of the self, whereas collectivistic coping goals would reinforce interdependence and relatedness between self and others. Markus and Lin (1999) proposed a cultural theory of conflictways, the meanings and practices of interpersonal conflict. Because of their different dominant self-construals Euro-Americans and Asian Americans attribute different meanings to interpersonal conflict and use different strategies to resolve conflict. For Euro-Americans with independent worldviews, interpersonal conflicts arise when there are constraints or restrictions placed on their individual freedom and rights, threatening the individual's sense of autonomy. Thus, the primary goal for conflict resolution is to remove the barrier to their desired outcome and to assert their individuality and autonomy. Compromise and accommodation are regarded as an undesirable conflict resolution strategy because they involve giving up part of one's needs or wishes.

For Asian-Americans with interdependent worldviews for whom self is a relational entity, interpersonal conflict indicates a disruption or disharmony in relationships between people that is an inevitable consequence of being interconnected with others. Thus, the goal for conflict resolution is not necessarily to remove the conflict (because it would be an impossible goal to achieve) but rather to manage the conflict, to "ride it out" without shaming anyone in the process so that the interdependence is reinforced and strengthened. Conflict resolution strategies are chosen with the long-term health of the relationship in mind. In this cultural context, compromise and accommodation are regarded as indication of maturity and tactfulness.

Coping goals also vary along the dimension of control. McCarty and her colleagues (1999) hypothesized that individualists with a more internal locus of control are likely to set *primary control coping goals* to modify or alter the environment to make it better fit their own personal agenda, whereas collectivists with a more external locus of control are likely to set *secondary control coping goals* to modify or alter themselves to fit environmental constraints. Thai children were more likely than American children to have coping goals that reflected secondary control for stressors, but only for stressors that threatened their interdependence with others such as separation from others (McCarty et al., 1999). In addition, compared to Nepali children, American children preferred to use primary control coping strategies that aimed at altering the situation (Cole, Bruschi, & Tamang, 2002).

Lastly, the theory of regulatory focus (Higgins, 1997) offers another way that coping goals might vary across cultures. According to the theory, individuals with promotion regulatory focus choose strategies and actions that maximize pleasure or gain, whereas individuals with prevention regulatory focus choose strategies and actions that minimize pain or loss. Thus, individuals' coping goals should be consistent with their regulatory focus. Individualism and collectivism, which have been found to covary with regulatory focus (Aaker & Lee, 2001; Lee et al., 2000), also have implications for whose gain or loss one tries to promote or prevent. For example, individualists with promotion focus might be most concerned with maximizing their own gains, while collectivists with prevention focus might be most concerned with minimizing the losses of their in-group.

In sum, coping goals can be shaped by culture in multiple ways. To take into account the role of cultural context in the choice of coping goals, researchers would need to assess the specific coping goals individuals set for themselves, widen the probe to include goals that address the needs of the self and relevant others, and evaluate self- and other-focused coping efforts in the larger interpersonal context of the individual's life.

2.6.3. Coping Strategies

Most cultural hypotheses of stress and coping concern cultural differences in normative coping strategies. Specifically, coping strategies that confront and modify external stressors (e.g., behavioral or approach-focused coping strategies) are expected to be more common in individualistic cultures, whereas coping strategies that avoid external stressors and instead modify internal psychological states (e.g., cognitive or avoidance-focused coping strategies) are expected to be more common in collectivistic cultures. These hypotheses were developed based on theorized and observed differences between the two cultures in personality, appraisal, motivation, and coping goals.

Individuals from individualistic cultures, compared to those from collectivistic cultures, have personality traits that reflect greater sense of internal locus of control (Bond & Tornatzky, 1973; Chandler et al., 1981; Hamid, 1994; Mahler, 1974; Paguio et al., 1987) and primary control (McCarty et al., 1999; Weisz et al., 1984), and cognitive styles oriented toward dispositional causal attribution, especially for stressors (Choi & Nisbett, 1998; Kawanishi, 1995; Morris & Peng, 1994). Accordingly, these individuals are expected to use more behavioral and approach-focused coping strategies that reflect their desire to influence the external environment to achieve their coping goals. On the other hand, individuals from collectivistic cultures, who have more external locus of control, greater secondary control, and greater tendency to attribute stressors to bad luck, are expected to rely more on cognitive and avoidance-focused coping strategies that reflect their greater desire to control their internal states to achieve their coping goals. To the extent that these individuals believe that they have control over outcome and are at the mercy of powerful forces or luck or fate, they will most likely feel helpless and thus reliant upon passive or avoidant coping strategies.

Individuals with a collectivistic orientation also may engage in more passive or avoidance coping because of their tendency to appraise stressors as a threat, whereas those with a more individualistic orientation are expected to engage in more active or approach coping because of their tendency to appraise stressors as a challenge. Although this hypothesis was only partially supported by Bjorck et al. (2001), they found that in general threat and loss appraisals were associated with greater escape-avoidance coping.

Differences in coping goals and motivation will also influence choices of coping strategies. For people with individualistic orientations, who place greater priority on meeting self-focused coping goals and more motivation to maximize pleasure (promotion regulatory focus), coping efforts are more likely to be directed at controlling the environment to suit their personal needs. Thus, they will be more likely to confront or approach the problem and try to solve it directly. For individuals with collectivistic orientations, who place greater priority on meeting other-focused coping goals and more motivation to minimize loss (prevention regulatory focus), coping efforts are more likely to be directed at protecting interpersonal relationships and other resources (Wong & Ujimoto, 1998).

In general, empirical investigations of normative coping strategies across cultures have yielded somewhat mixed evidence. However, overall there is more support for the association between a collectivistic orientation and the use of avoidance-focused coping than for the association between an individualistic orientation and the use of approach-focused coping. Specifically, adults and children of collectivistic cultures, such as Korean Americans, Malays, and Ghanaians were more likely to use passive coping (Bjorck et al., 2001; Essau & Trommsdorff, 1996), avoidant coping (Bjorck et al., 2001; Chang, 1996a, 1996b, 2001; Cheung, Lee, & Chan, 1983; Radford et al., 1993; Trubisky, Ting-Toomey, & Lin, 1991), emotion-focused coping (Eshun, Chang, & Owusu, 1998; Essau & Trommsdorff, 1996), and covert coping (McCarty et al., 1999), whereas adults and children of individualistic cultures, such as Euro-Americans and Germans, were more likely to use action-oriented and problem-focused coping (Cole et al., 2002; Essau & Trommsdorff, 1996; Radford et al., 1993).

Some studies examined the within-group variations in coping style with respect to acculturation. Using place of birth as a proxy for cultural orientation, Yoshihama (2002) compared coping of battered Japanese-American women born in the United States and in

Japan. As expected, the women born in the Unites States used more active coping and perceived it to be more effective than did the women born in Japan. Also, Taylor and colleagues (Taylor, Sherman, Kim, Jarcho, Takagi, & Dunagan, 2004) found that second generation Asian American college students (born in the United States) were in between the foreign-born Asian and Asian Americans students and the Euro-American students in how likely they were to seek family support to cope with stress.

Although less common, some studies found opposite patterns with individuals from more individualistic North American countries reporting greater use of certain emotion-focused coping strategies such as wishful thinking (Essau & Trommsdorff, 1996), and covert strategies when coping with physical injury (McCarty et al., 1999). There are also findings of no significant cultural differences in active or direct coping (Bjorck et al., 2001; Chang, 1996a; Lee & Liu, 2001) and in indirect coping (Lee & Liu, 2001). Overall, it is important to note that people rely on multiple coping strategies (Bjorck et al., 2001; Essau & Trommsdorff, 1996; Lee & Liu, 2001; Wong & Ujimoto, 1988) and that observed cultural (ethnic or national) differences are in terms of relative magnitude, not an absolute dichotomy. Furthermore, the contrary evidence is important as it can reveal the strong influence of changes due to acculturation and how individual and situational factors can at times override cultural influences.

Lastly, it is important to distinguish *collective coping strategies* (i.e., mobilizing group resources) from *collectivistic coping style* (i.e., normative coping style of collectivistic individuals). It is commonly hypothesized that collectivistic people, compared to individualistic people, would utilize more collective coping strategies such as support seeking because of their interconnectedness with the in-group. On the other hand, it has also been hypothesized that these individuals' desire to protect group harmony and not to become a burden on the group may discourage support seeking. Taylor and colleagues (2004) tested these two competing cultural hypotheses about collectivism and seeking social support. They found that Koreans, Asians, and Asian Americans were less likely to utilize social support than European Americans were; in addition, concern about their relationships with others (e.g., desire to protect group harmony and to save face and embarrassment) predicted lower likelihood of seeking support. These findings suggest that collectivistic individuals do not always engage in more collective coping. For collectivistic individuals under duress, choosing appropriate coping strategies appears to involve striking a delicate balance between taking care of the needs of the individual, maintaining the well-being of the in-group, and protecting the relationship between the individual and the group. This balance may result in the type of coping that appears to be individualistic, such as forbearance and self-reliance. Contextualized stress and coping research would investigate how personal and environmental factors together influence which coping strategies are utilized.

2.7. Culture and Health and Well-being (Panel V)

Culture has two important implications for this last panel of our stress and coping model, *Health and Well-being*. The primary issue deals with how coping outcome is defined and assessed. Traditional coping research has focused primarily on health outcomes with the assumption that individuals cope to enhance their own health and well-being. This assumption is problematic when the reduction of own distress is not the primary goal of coping, as it may be for individuals with collectivistic orientation who are likely to have other-focused coping goals. As a way of contextualizing coping, it has been argued that a broader set of evaluation criteria of coping effectiveness should be derived from the individual's coping goals (Folkman & Moskowitz, 2000). These criteria should include an assessment of the quality of person-environment fit reflected in the domains of physical, emotional, and social functioning (Lazarus & Folkman, 1984). There is also recognition that multiple coping goals might compete with each other, and that coping responses may be effective in achieving one goal (e.g., interpersonal harmony) at the expense of other goals (e.g., reduction of own distress) (Somerfield & McCrae, 2000).

Another issue is the question of how individuals experience and display health and well-being. Culture can shape socially acceptable and normative ways of experiencing and expressing distress. Thus, mental health outcomes should include cultural idioms of distress. For example, gender roles in the United States may partially account for the greater prevalence of depression in women and greater prevalence of alcohol use disorders in men (Robins, 1984). Similarly, cross-cultural and cross-ethnic investigations have revealed some culture-dependent variations in health outcomes, such as the greater tendency for reporting somatic symptoms in Asian, Latino, and African cultures compared to Western and Euro-American cultures (Brown, Schulberg, & Madonia, 1996; Chun, Enomoto & Sue, 1996; Farooq, Gahir, Okyere, & Sheikh, 1995; Oltjenbruns, 1998).

For certain cultural groups measures of somatization, such as neurasthenia, may be better indicators of psychological distress than traditional indicators such as depression. For example, in an epidemiologic study of Chinese Americans living in greater Los Angeles area, Takeuchi and his colleagues (Takeuchi, Chun, Gong, & Shen, 2002) found that stressors were associated with neurasthenia symptoms but not with depressive symptoms. The high prevalence of somatization and its stronger link to stressors in Asians and Asian Americans have been attributed to a cultural environment that encourages expression of somatic symptoms (Chun et al., 1996). In part, this is due to a holistic view of the mind and body, whereby psychological symptoms are regarded to have physical origin and thus can be alleviated by treating the physical organs. In addition, strong shame and stigma are associated with expressions of emotional distress because it is regarded as a sign of mental weakness and immaturity. Using a context-specific, multidimensional set of outcome criteria will help to address cultural variations in coping outcomes and to better assess the full impact of stressors on health and well-being.

3. FUTURE DIRECTIONS FOR CONTEXTUALIZING STRESS AND COPING RESEARCH

Thus far we have attempted to illustrate the role of culture as a fundamental context for the stress and coping paradigm. We have cited theories and empirical studies to depict how enduring and transient environmental conditions, internal personal make-up and resources, appraisal and coping, and health and coping outcomes can systematically vary by culture. We now conclude this chapter by examining some common misconceptions about the role of culture in stress and coping and offering suggestions for better grounding stress and coping research in cultural contexts.

3.1. Cultural Salience

In addressing culture, it is tempting to overemphasize the role of culture and assume that cultural differences in coping are large or ubiquitous. However, that is not necessarily the most parsimonious approach to examining individual differences in stress and coping. McCarty and her colleagues (1999) argued that the influence of culture would be most obvious when the essential cultural values and beliefs are "salient" in the stressful situation. "Cultural salience" is an important idea that can guide cross-cultural research to identify the conditions in which cultural differences are most relevant. In the context of coping, this idea suggests that the nature and extent of cultural differences in the use of various types of coping strategies should partly depend on the nature of the stressful situation. For example, the contrast between people who are more individualistic or collectivistic may be most observable when they are confronted with independent or interdependent stressors that threaten the most salient part of their self-construal.

Heine and Lehman (1995) compared the perceptions of independent and interdependent events in Euro-Canadian college students (known to have an independent self-construal) and Japanese College students (known to have an interdependent self-construal). They found that, within each group, Euro-Canadian college students rated independent events (e.g., "Sometimes in the future you will become an alcoholic.") to be more severe than interdependent events (e.g., "Sometime in the future you will do something that will make your family ashamed of you."). The opposite was true for the Japanese college students. When the two groups were compared to each other, the Japanese students rated the interdependent events to be more severe than the Euro-Canadian students, but the two groups rated independent events similarly. Furthermore, compared to the Euro-Canadian students, the Japanese students were more pessimistic about events that were threatening to interdependent selves.

In general, pessimism is associated with less problem solving; however, for Asian Americans pessimism is associated with more problem solving (Chang, 1996a). Chang explains that pessimism may be helpful in collectivistic cultures because anticipating negative interpersonal outcomes, such as shaming friends (an interdependent event), may help individuals take actions that prevent such negative outcomes from occurring. This view is consistent with the prevention-oriented self-regulation style observed in individuals from more collectivistic cultures, such as Asian Americans and Hong Kong Chinese (Aaker & Lee, 2001; Lee & et al., 2000). Recognizing such cultural tendencies of Asians and Asian Americans, Wong (1993) emphasized the role of proactive coping for anticipatory stressors. Identifying conditions in which cultural differences are likely to be salient could yield more fruitful knowledge about how people of all backgrounds cope with stressors.

3.2. Developing Culturally Sensitive Research Paradigm

Another way that stress and coping research can be contextualized is by addressing the lack of consensus in terminology and some underlying ethnocentric assumptions. The stress and coping literature is replete with dichotomous typologies of coping strategies. These typologies emphasize different characteristics of coping strategies, such as the movement of coping actions (direct vs. indirect) towards or away from problem (approach vs. avoidant), the primary focus of coping (problem vs. emotion), the intensity of coping efforts (active vs. passive), and the observability of coping responses (overt vs. covert). These terms are often used interchangeably, with the former category of each pair connoting more engaging and confrontative coping strategies and the latter category connoting more disengaging and avoidant coping strategies.

There are also some conceptual overlaps among these categories that create confusion for cross-cultural research on coping. For example, certain cognitive coping strategies, such as positive reframing (Yoshihama, 2002), have been categorized as a passive type of coping in some studies (Essau & Trommsdorff, 1996; McCarty et al., 1999; Yoshihama, 2002) and as an active type in others (Chang, 1996b; Lee & Liu, 2001). This type of conflicting or inconsistent categorization is partly due to the fact that many cross-cultural studies categorized coping strategies empirically using exploratory factor analytic methods and then labeled the factors/components by examining the factor solutions. More important, the inconsistent categorization may also be an indication that the current dichotomous categorization of coping strategies does not adequately capture the full complexity of cultural variations in coping.

Part of this problem stems from the prevailing assumption that approach coping is overt, constructive, and adaptive, whereas avoidance coping is covert, passive, and maladaptive because it connotes lack of motivation and effort. Empirical findings, mostly on American and European samples, support this view as approach coping strategies are usually associated with better physical and psychological outcomes than are avoidance coping strategies (e.g., Chung, Langenbucher, Labouvie, Panadina, & Moos, 2001; Hack & Degner, 2004; Holahan, Valentiner, & Moos, 1995; Penedo et al., 2003). However, when a stressor is uncontrollable or unavoidable, approach strategies may be ineffective.

Moreover, palliative or avoidance strategies may be more effective in some cultural contexts where the norm is to "fit in" with the social and physical environment. In the Eastern collectivistic cultures, the worldview is more holistic and the separation between person and environment is considered artificial and meaningless. When problems arise between the self and the environment, the cause is perceived to be neither within the person nor in the external world, and a "mature" person would take actions to control the self to make it fit better with the environment. Hence, coping strategies that focus on exercising secondary control, in other words, controlling one's own internal states and behaviors, are deemed desirable and may be more effective in achieving coping goals. Such coping efforts are neither passive nor avoidant; in reality they require intense effort and concentration on the target of control, the mind and behaviors of the self.

In fact, recent studies challenge the assumption that coping strategies that actively confront stressors are generally more adaptive than coping strategies that do not actively confront stressors. Chang (2001) examined the normative coping strategies of Euro-American and Asian-American college students and their relationships to positive and negative psychological outcomes. Compared to Euro-American students, Asian American students reported greater use of problem avoidance and social withdrawal. Consistent with past findings, the use of these avoidant strategies was associated with less life satisfaction and more depression in Euro-Americans. However, it was not associated with either of these outcomes in Asian Americans.

Similarly, Yoshihama (2002) found that the perceived effectiveness of passive coping strategies was associated with lower psychological distress in the more collectivistic

Japanese-American women born in Japan, whereas the perceived effectiveness of active coping strategies was associated with lower distress in their more individualistic counterparts born in the United States. Furthermore, active coping appeared to have deleterious effects on the psychological well-being of the Japan-born women. These studies suggest that for Asian Americans, higher usage and perceived effectiveness of avoidant and passive coping strategies may reflect the fact that Asian Americans do not have or perceive much control over their social reality. Avoidant strategies may be maladaptive only for people who have control but choose to avoid.

Another common assumption is that being more mindful of others and placing priority on their well-being leads to passive or indirect coping that demands quiet self-sacrifice and entails controlling or suppressing one's desire and needs. However, that is not necessarily true. If the in-group's welfare is challenged, it may lead to increased active and problem-focused coping on behalf of the in-group. In fact, a person with a collectivistic worldview may engage in *collective coping* aimed at primary control on behalf of the in-group (Wong & Ujimoto, 1998).

On the surface, collective coping appears to be very similar to utilizing social support, but that is not necessarily true as social support is only one of the many ways that collective coping can take place. In individual coping, individuals seek support to boost their ability and resources to cope with the stressor. In collective coping, the stressor *becomes* an in-group problem, and every member takes an active role in tackling the problem with a sense of responsibility that is different from providing emotional or instrumental support as a third party who is not directly affected by the stressor. In interpersonal conflict situations, it is often the responsibility of an in-group member to mediate the conflict. Thus, when coping is examined at the individual level, the individual may be engaging in seemingly passive and avoidant coping, but active mediation may be going on at the group level. Collectivistic individuals may take a more indirect or avoidant coping strategy for their own personal problems, but a more direct or approach coping strategy for in-group members' problems.

To expand the present typologies of coping strategies, we propose a distinction between coping that occurs at the individual level versus the collective level (see Figure 2). Within each level of coping (individual vs. collective), coping strategies can be categorized by (a) focus of coping action and (b) direction of coping effort. The focus of coping refers to whether coping is geared toward approaching or avoiding the stressor. The second dimension has to do with whether the coping efforts are directed toward the external environment or the self. Coping may be directed toward external circumstances that need to be managed to make them better fit the individual's agenda (assimilative coping) or toward managing the self to better fit the environment (accommodative coping). This distinction is similar to the distinction between primary and secondary coping (Rothbaum et al., 1982; Weisz et al., 1984), but we chose not to use these terms because of the embedded assumption that controlling the external environment is more basic and fundamental (primary) than controlling the inner self (secondary) (Azuma, 1984; Kojima, 1984).

Based on these two dimensions, coping strategies can be conceptualized with respect to four broad categories– inward and outward approach coping and inward and outward avoidance coping (see Table 2). At the individual level of coping, *inward approach* coping strategies attempt to deal with the stressor by controlling the self. Some strategies that would fall into this category, such as meditation, transcendental acceptance, and existential

Figure 2. Conceptual framework for contextualizing coping.

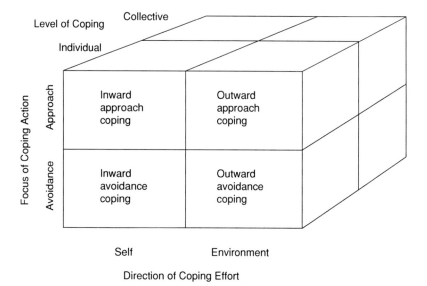

or spiritual coping, sometimes are miscategorized as avoidance coping. We believe that these strategies should be conceptualized as approach coping because they are active strategies targeted on controlling the self and trying to find meaning and peace in a troubling life situation. *Outward approach* coping strategies aim to deal with the stressor by reconstruing or controlling the external environment; problem solving and seeking social support would fall into this category.

Inward avoidance coping consists of strategies that are used to avoid dealing with the stressor by disengaging from the self. These strategies typically involve either denying reality or resigning oneself to being the victim of the stressor. *Outward avoidance* coping consists of strategies that are used to avoid dealing with the stressor by disengaging from the stressor, such as social withdrawal and venting affect.

At the collective level of coping, these categories can be applied in a similar fashion. But the focus is on how the in-group appraises the problem and chooses to cope with it. The family may engage in group denial of the individual's problematic situation by pretending there is no problem (inward avoidance coping) or alter it by helping the individual change the external situation that caused the problem (outward approach coping). Collective appraisal and coping may or may not be congruent with what happens at the individual level. Coping can occur at either or both levels in any cultural setting. Persons suffering from substance abuse may fail to cope with addiction problems on their own, and their family members may decide to intervene with or without their consent or knowledge. There is variation across cultures in the extent of collective coping efforts and how much weight or influence the individual or the society will allow for the collective efforts to complement or even supplant the individual coping efforts.

Culture's influence on what an individual does to obtain the desired outcome is most likely to be indirect by shaping the personal and environment systems. Our proposed framework attempts to resolve some of the existing conceptual problems in cross-cultural research on stress and coping and outline specific ways to integrate context into the stress and coping paradigm. But the framework is limited in the scope of the stress and coping process that it covers, as coping can occur in response to current stressors, in preparation of known upcoming stressors, and in anticipation of future potential stressors (Wong, 1993). People are dynamic and complex, often holding multiple realities shaped by different social contexts that might collide with one another. While certain individual traits and propensities prevail and surface consistently across situations, others are heavily determined by specific circumstances. Recognition of complex inter- and intra-personal realities allows for the possibilities that individuals conduct themselves in seemingly inconsistent and even paradoxical manners (Wong & Sproule, 1984). This is especially important to consider for individuals who tend to be collectivistic or field-dependent. Only when we place individuals in their full social contexts can we fully appreciate the complexity of human mind and behavior.

4. CONCLUSION

We have shown that culture provides a fundamental context for the stress and coping paradigm. Individualism and collectivism were used as examples of cultural constructs that can influence each component of stress and coping: the ongoing environmental and personal systems, transient life conditions, cognitive appraisal and coping, and health and well-being. We tried to base our discussion on available empirical findings. However, there is more extensive evidence on the role of culture in certain components, such as the personal system and appraisal and coping than in other components, such as the environmental systems and transient life conditions. Nevertheless, we believe that it is essential to evaluate the role of culture in stress and coping, especially when there is cultural salience. We also made some suggestions for developing more culturally sensitive research paradigms that can facilitate systematic and theory-driven investigations on the role of culture.

It is important to note that culture is not a static entity, but rather a dynamic system that evolves over time. This is especially true in modern times with instant world-wide communication in which events and opinions in one country can quickly influence attitudes and beliefs in other countries. Cultural changes also occur in many domains, with changes occurring faster and more dramatically in the political, educational, and economic systems, and slower and more gradually in family structures, religion, and some personal practices (Divale & Seda, 2001). As researchers who want to identify predictable patterns of behaviors, we need to continually examine and test our assumptions about people and the world, if our explanations of human behavior are to reflect current reality. Unfortunately, to illustrate the relevance of culture in stress and coping, we have simplified and treated culture as a static entity and emphasized cultural differences at the expense of cultural similarities. Also, as the primary focus of this chapter was to illustrate the influence of culture on human behavior, we have neglected ways in which coping, especially collective coping, can affect cultural attitudes and beliefs. From a historical perspective, we should recognize that culture and coping influence each other in an ever-evolving mutual relationship.

REFERENCES

Aaker, J. L., & Lee, A. Y. (2001). "I" seek pleasures and "we" avoid pains: The role of self-regulatory goals in information processing and persuasion. *Journal of Consumer Research, 28*(1), 33-49.

Agbayani-Siewert, P., & Revilla, L. (1995). Filipino Americans. In P. G. Min (Ed.), *Asian Americans: Contemporary trends and issues*. (pp. 134-168): Sage Publications, Inc.

Austin, J. T., & Vancouver, J. B. (1996). Goal constructs in psychology: Structure, process, and content. *Psychological Bulletin, 120*(3), 338-375.

Azuma, H. (1984). Secondary control as a heterogeneous category. *American Psychologist, 39*(9), 970-971.

Beard, V. A., & Kunharibowo, (2001). Living arrangements and support relationships among elderly Indonesians: case studies from Java and Sumatra. *International Journal of Population Geography, 7(1)*, 17-33.

Bjorck, J. P., Cuthbertson, W., Thurman, J. W., & Lee, Y. S. (2001). Ethnicity, coping, and distress among Korean Americans, Filipino Americans, and Caucasian Americans. *Journal of Social Psychology, 141(4)*, 421-442.

Bond, M. H., & Tornatzky, L. G. (1973). Locus of control in students from Japan and the United States: Dimensions and levels of response. *Psychologia: An International Journal of Psychology in the Orient, 16*(4), 209-213.

Brown, C., Schulberg, H. C., & Madonia, M. J. (1996). Clinical presentations of major depression by African Americans and whites in primary medical care practice. *Journal of Affective Disorders, 41, 181-191.*

Chandler, T. A., Shama, D. D., Wolf, F. M., & Planchard, S. K. (1981). Multiattributional causality: A five cross-national samples study. *Journal of Cross-Cultural Psychology, 12*(2), 207-221.

Chang, E. C. (1996a). Cultural differences in optimism, pessimism, and coping: Predictors of subsequent adjustment in Asian American and Caucasian American college students. *Journal of Counseling Psychology, 43*(1), 113-123.

Chang, E. C. (1996b). Evidence for the cultural specificity of pessimism in Asians vs Caucasians: A test of a general negativity hypothesis. *Personality & Individual Differences, 21*(5), 819-822.

Chang, E. C. (2001). A look at the coping strategies and styles of Asian Americans: Similar and different? In C. R. Snyder (Ed.), *Coping with stress: Effective people and processes* (pp. 222-239). London: Oxford University Press.

Cheung, F. M., Lee, S.-Y., & Chan, Y. Y. (1983). Variations in problem conceptualizations and intended solutions among Hong Kong students. *Culture, Medicine, & Psychiatry, 7(3)*, 263-278.

Choi, I., & Nisbett, R. E. (1998). Situational salience and cultural differences in the correspondence bias and actor-observer bias. *Personality & Social Psychology Bulletin, 24*(9), 949-960.

Chun, C.-A., Enomoto, K., & Sue, S. (1996). Health care issues among Asian Americans: Implications of somatization. In T. Mann (Ed.), *Handbook of diversity issues in health psychology* (pp. 347-365). New York, NY: Plenum Press.

Chung, R. C.-Y., Walkey, F. H., & Bemak, F. (1997). A comparison of achievement and aspirations of New Zealand Chinese and European Students. *Journal of Cross-Cultural Psychology, 28(4)*, 481-489.

Chung, T., Langenbucher, J., Labouvie, E., Panadina, R. J., & Moos, R. H. (2001). Changes in alcoholic patients' coping responses predict 12-month treatment outcomes. *Journal of Consulting & Clinical Psychology, 69*(1), 92-100.

Cicirelli, V. G. (1994). Sibling relationships in cross-cultural perspective. *Journal of Marriage and the Family, 56,* 7-20.

Cole, P. M., Bruschi, C. J., & Tamang, B. L. (2002). Cultural differences in children's emotional reactions to difficult situations. *Child Development, 73*(3), 983-996.

Coyne, J. C., & Racioppo, M. W. (2000). Never the twain shall meet? Closing the gap between coping research and clinical intervention research. *American Psychologist, 55*(6), 655-664.

Dabul, A. J., Bernal, M. E., & Knight, G. P. (1995). Allocentric and idiocentric self-description and academic achievement among Mexican American and Anglo American adolescents. *Journal of Social Psychology, 135*(5), 621-630.

Divale, W., & Seda, A. (2001). Modernization as changes in cultural complexity: New cross-cultural measurements. *Cross-Cultural Research, 35(2)*, 127-153.

Eshun, S., Chang, E. C., & Owusu, V. (1998). Cultural and gender differences in responses to depressive mood. A study of college students in Ghana and the U.S.A. *Personality & Individual Differences, 24*(4), 581-583.

Essau, C. A., & Trommsdorff, G. (1996). Coping with university-related problems: A cross-cultural comparison. *Journal of Cross-Cultural Psychology, 27*(3), 315-328.

Farooq, S., Gahir, M. S., Okyere, E., & Sheikh, A. J. (1995). Somatization: A transcultural study. *Journal of Psychosomatic Research, 39*, 883-888.

Folkman, S., & Moskowitz, J. T. (2000). Positive affect and the other side of coping. *American Psychologist, 55*(6), 647-654.

Fuligni, A. J., & Pederson, S. (2002). Family obligation and the transition to young adulthood. *Developmental Psychology, 38(5)*, 856-868.

Gaertner, L., Sedikides, C., & Graetz, K. (1999). In search of self-definition: Motivational primacy of the individual self, motivational primacy of the collective self, or contextual primacy? *Journal of Personality & Social Psychology, 76*(1), 5-18.

Hack, T., & Degner, L. F. (2004). Coping Responses Following breast cancer diagnosis predict psychological adjustment three years later. *Psycho-Oncology, 13*(4), 235-247.

Hamid, P. N. (1994). Self-monitoring, locus of control, and social encounters of Chinese and New Zealand students. *Journal of Cross-Cultural Psychology, 25*(3), 353-368.

Heine, S. J., & Lehman, D. R. (1995). Cultural variation in unrealistic optimism: Does the West feel more vulnerable than the East? *Journal of Personality & Social Psychology, 68*(4), 595-607.

Higgins, E. T. (1997). Beyond pleasure and pain. *American Psychologist, 52*(12), 1280-1300.

Hofstede, G. (1980). *Culture's consequences: Comparing values, behaviors, institutions and organizations across nations.* Beverly Hills, CA: Sage.

Holahan, C. J., Valentiner, D. P., & Moos, R. H. (1995). Parental support, coping strategies, and psychological adjustment: An integrative model with late adolescents. *Journal of Youth & Adolescence, 24*(6), 633-648.

Hui, C. H., & Villareal, M. J. (1989). Individualism collectivism and psychological needs: Their relationships in two cultures. *Journal of Cross-Cultural Psychology, 20*(3), 310-323.

Hurh, W. M., & Kim, K. C. (1990). Religious participation of Korean immigrants in the United States. *Journal for the Scientific Study of Religion, 29*(1), 19-34.

Iyengar, S. S., & Lepper, M. R. (1999). Rethinking the value of choice: A cultural perspective on intrinsic motivation. *Journal of Personality & Social Psychology, 76*(3), 349-366.

Jacobs, D. (1998). Social welfare systems in East Asia: A comparative analysis including private welfare (CASE paper 10). London: London School of Economics, Centre for Analysis of Social Exclusion.

Kagitçibasi, Ç. (1997). Whither multiculturalism? *Applied Psychology: An International Review, 46*(1), 44-49.

Kawanishi, Y. (1995). The effects of culture on beliefs about stress and coping: Causal attribution of Anglo-American and Japanese persons. *Journal of Contemporary Psychotherapy, 25*(1), 49-60.

Kim, C.-S., & Rhee, K.-O. (1997). Variations in preferred living arrangements among Korean elderly parents. *Journal of Cross-Cultural Gerontology, 12(2)*, 189-202.

Knodel, J., & Saengtienchai, C. (1999). Studying living arrangements of the elderly: Lessons from a quasi-qualitative case study approach in Thailand. *Journal of Cross-Cultural Gerontology, 14(3)*, 197-220.

Kojima, H. (1984). A significant stride toward the comparative study of control. *American Psychologist, 39*(9), 972-973.

Korea Survey (Gallup Poll) and Japanese Prime Minister's Office (1990). The quality of life of the elderly and their perception in Korea. Seoul: Korea survey.

Kotlikoff, L. J., & Morris, J. N. (1988, October). Why don't the elderly live with their children? A new look (NBER Working Paper No. W2734). Cambridge, MA: National Bureau of Economic Research.

Kwon, H.-J. (1999). Income transfers to the elderly in East Asia: Testing Asian values (CASEpaper 27). London: London School of Economics, Centre for Analysis of Social Exclusion

Lay, C., Fairlie, P., Jackson, S., Ricci, T., Eisenberg, J., Sato, T., et al. (1998). Domain-specific allocentrism-idiocentrism: A measure of family connectedness. *Journal of Cross-Cultural Psychology, 29*(3), 434-460.

Lazarus, R. S., & Folkman, S. (1984). *Stress, appraisal and coping.* New York: Springer.

Lee, A. Y., Aaker, J. L., & Gardner, W. L. (2000). The pleasures and pains of distinct self-construals: The role of interdependence in regulatory focus. *Journal of Personality & Social Psychology, 78*(6), 1122-1134.

Lee, R. M., & Liu, H.-T. T. (2001). Coping with intergenerational family conflict: Comparison of Asian American, Hispanic, and European American college students. *Journal of Counseling Psychology, 48(4)*, 410-419.

Mahler, I. (1974). A comparative study of locus of control. *Psychologia: An International Journal of Psychology in the Orient, 17*(3), 135-139.

Markus, H. R., & Kitayama, S. (1991). Culture and the self: Implications for cognition, emotion, and motivation. *Psychological Review, 98*(2), 224-253.

Markus, H. R., & Lin, L. R. (1999). Conflictways: Cultural diversity in the meanings and practices of conflict. In D. A. Prentice & D. T. Miller (Eds.), *Cultural divides: Understanding and overcoming group conflict.* (pp. 302-333). New York, NY, US: Russell Sage Foundation.

Matsumoto, D., Weissman, M. D., Preston, K., Brown, B. R., & Kupperbusch, C. (1997). Context-specific measurement of individualism-collectivism on the individual level: The Individualism-Collectivism Interpersonal Assessment Inventory. *Journal of Cross-Cultural Psychology, 28,* 743-767.

McCarty, C. A., Weisz, J. R., Wanitromanee, K., Eastman, K. L., Suwanlert, S., Chaiyasit, W., et al. (1999). Culture, coping, and context: Primary and secondary control among Thai and American youth. *Journal of Child Psychology & Psychiatry & Allied Disciplines, 40*(5), 809-818.

McCrae, R. R. (1984). Situational determinants of coping responses: Loss, threat, and challenge. *Journal of Personality & Social Psychology, 46*(4), 919-928.

Menaghan, E. G. (1983). *Individual Coping Efforts: Moderators of the Relationship between Life Stress and Mental Health Outcomes.* Unpublished manuscript.

Miller, J. G. (1984). Culture and the development of everyday social explanation. *Journal of Personality & Social Psychology, 46*(5), 961-978.

Miller, J. G. (1986). Early cross-cultural commonalities in social explanation. *Developmental Psychology, 22,* 514-520.

Mitchell, B. A. (2003). Would I share a home with an elderly parent? Exploring ethnocultural diversity and intergenerational support relations during young adulthood. *Canadian Journal on Aging, 22(1),* 69-82.

Moos, R. H. (1984). Context and coping: Toward a unifying conceptual framework. *American Journal of Community Psychology, 12*(1), 5-25.

Moos, R. H. (2002). 2001 INVITED ADDRESS: The mystery of human context and coping: An unraveling of clues. *American Journal of Community Psychology, 30*(1), 67-88.

Morris, M. W., & Peng, K. (1994). Culture and cause: American and Chinese attributions for social and physical events. *Journal of Personality & Social Psychology, 67*(6), 949-971.

Munro, D. (1979). Locus-of-control attribution: Factors among Blacks and Whites in Africa. *Journal of Cross-Cultural Psychology, 10*(2), 157-172.

Nakano, K. (1991). The role of coping strategies on psychological and physical well-being. *Japanese Psychological Research, 33*(4), 160-167.

Oltjenbruns, K. A. (1998). Ethnicity and the grief response: Mexican American versus Anglo American college students. *Death Studies, 22,* 141-155.

Oyserman, D., Coon, H. M., & Kemmelmeier, M. (2002). Rethinking individualism and collectivism: Evaluation of theoretical assumptions and meta-analyses. *Psychological Bulletin, 128*(1), 3-72.

Paguio, L. P., Robinson, B. E., Skeen, P., & Deal, J. E. (1987). Relationship between fathers' and mothers' socialization practices and children's locus of control in Brazil, the Philippines, and the United States. *Journal of Genetic Psychology, 148*(3), 303-313.

Pang, V. O. (1991). The relationship of test anxiety and math achievement to parental values in Asian-American and European-American middle school students. *Journal of Research & Development in Education, 24(4),* 1-10.

Pearlin, L. I., & Schooler, C. (1978). The structure of coping. *Journal of Health & Social Behavior, 19*(1), 2-21.

Penedo, F. J., Gonzalez, J. S., Davis, C., Dahn, J., Antoni, M. H., Ironson, G., et al. (2003). Coping and psychological distress among symptomatic HIV+ men who have sex with men. *Annals of Behavioral Medicine, 25*(3), 203-213.

Radford, M. H., Mann, L., Ohta, Y., & Nakane, Y. (1993). Differences between Australian and Japanese students in decisional self-esteem, decisional stress, and coping styles. *Journal of Cross-Cultural Psychology, 24*(3), 284-297.

Rhee, E., Uleman, J. S., Lee, H. K., & Roman, R. J. (1995). Spontaneous self-descriptions and ethnic identities in individualistic and collectivistic cultures. *Journal of Personality & Social Psychology, 69*(1), 142-152.

Robins, L. N. (1984). Lifetime prevalence of specific psychiatric disorders in three sites. *Archives of General Psychiatry, 41*(10), 949-958.

Rothbaum, F., Weisz, J. R., & Snyder, S. S. (1982). Changing the world and changing the self: A two-process model of perceived control. *Journal of Personality & Social Psychology, 42*(1), 5-37.

Shweder, R. A., & Bourne, E. J. (1982). Does the concept of the person vary cross culturally? In M. G. M. White (Ed.), *Cultural conceptions of mental health and therapy* (pp. 97-137). New York: Reidel.

Singelis, T. M., Triandis, H. C., Bhawuk, D., & Gelfand, M. J. (1995). Horizontal and vertical dimensions of individualism and collectivism: A theoretical and measurement refinement. *Cross-Cultural Research: The Journal of Comparative Social Science, 29,* 240-275.

Somerfield, M. R., & McCrae, R. R. (2000). Stress and coping research: Methodological challenges, theoretical advances, and clinical applications. *American Psychologist, 55(6),* 620-625.

Sugisawa, H., Shibata, H., Hougham, G. W., Sugihara, Y., & Liang, J. (2002). The impact of social ties on depressive symptoms in U.S. and Japanese elderly. *Journal of Social Issues, 58(4),* 785-804.

Tafarodi, R. W., & Smith, A. J. (2001). Individualism-collectivism and depressive sensitivity to life events: The case of Malaysian sojourners. *International Journal of Intercultural Relations, 25(1),* 73-88.

Takeuchi, D. T., Chun, C.-A., Gong, F., & Shen, H. (2002). Cultural expressions of distress. *Health: An Interdisciplinary Journal for the Social Study of Health, Illness & Medicine, 6(2),* 221-235.

Taylor, S. E., Sherman, D. K., Kim, H. S., Jarcho, J., Takagi, K., & Dunagan, M. S. (2004). Culture and social support: Who seeks it and why? *Journal of Personality & Social Psychology, 87(3),* 354-362.

Triandis, H. C. (1988). Collectivism and development. In D. Sinha & H. S. R. Kao (Eds.), *Social values and development: Asian perspectives.* (pp. 285-303). Thousand Oaks, CA, US: Sage Publications, Inc.

Triandis, H. C. (1995). *Individualism & collectivism.* Boulder, CO, US: Westview Press.

Trubisky, P., Ting-Toomey, S., & Lin, S.-l. (1991). The influence of individualism collectivism and self-monitoring on conflict styles. *International Journal of Intercultural Relations, 15(1),* 65-84.

Weisz, J. R., Rothbaum, F. M., & Blackburn, T. C. (1984). Standing out and standing in: The psychology of control in America and Japan. *American Psychologist, 39(9),* 955-969.

Wong, P. T. P. (1993). Effective management of life stress: The resource-congruence model. *Stress Medicine, 9,* 51-60.

Wong, P. T. P., & Sproule, C. F. (1984). Attributional analysis of locus of control and the Trent Attribution Profile (TAP). In H. M. Lefcourt (Ed.), *Research with locus of control construct,* Vol. 3: *Limitations and extension* (pp. 309-360). New York: Academic Press.

Wong, P. T. P., & Ujimoto, K. V. (1998). The elderly: Their stress, coping, and mental health. In N. W. S. Zane (Ed.), *Handbook of Asian American psychology* (pp. 165-209). Thousand Oaks, CA: Sage Publications, Inc.

Yamaguchi, S., Kuhlman, D. M., & Sugimori, S. (1995). Personality correlates of allocentric tendencies in individualist and collectivist cultures. *Journal of Cross-Cultural Psychology, 26(6),* 658-672.

Yoo, S. H., & Sung, K.-T. (1997). Elderly Koreans' tendency to live independently from their adult children: Adaptation to cultural differences in America. *Journal of Cross-Cultural Gerontology, 12(3),* 225-244.

Yoshihama, M. (2002). Battered women's coping strategies and psychological distress: Differences by immigration status. *American Journal of Community Psychology, 30(3),* 429-452.

Zimmer, Z., & Kim, S. K. (2001). Living arrangement and soci-demographic conditions of older adults in Cambodia. *Journal of Cross-Cultural Gerontology, 16(4),* 353-381.

A NEW THEORETICAL MODEL OF COLLECTIVISTIC COPING

Christine J. Yeh, Agnes Kwong Arora, and Katherine A. Wu

1. INTRODUCTION

According to the 2000 United States Census Bureau (U.S. Census Bureau, 2000) there are over 63 million racial and ethnic minorities, comprising almost 22 percent of the total population. In approximately two decades, racial and ethnic minority groups are expected to account for almost 40 percent of adults and 48 percent of children in the United States (U.S. Department of Health & Human Services, 2001). These rapid demographic changes underscore the need to recognize how cultural background and cultural orientation influence mental health. Many racial and cultural groups' ways of dealing with stress and mental health concerns may be different from current models of coping. In particular, we are interested in presenting a new theoretical perspective of coping from a collectivistic orientation.

2. COLLECTIVISM AND INDIVIDUALISM

The concepts of collectivism and individualism became especially popular in cross-cultural research since Hofstede's (1980) research that mapped 53 countries on four dimensions (individualism-collectivism, masculinity-femininity, power distance, and uncertainty avoidance). Over the last few decades, the collectivism-individualism dimension has been perhaps one of the most widely used constructs in cross-cultural psychology to explain differences between cultures. A critical characteristic of collectivistic cultures is that individuals may be encouraged to subordinate their personal goals to the goals of some collective, which is usually a stable ingroup, and life satisfaction is derived from carrying out social roles and obligations to this stable ingroup (Markus & Kitayama, 1991).

In individualistic cultures the behavior of individuals focuses on the attainment of personal goals (Markus & Kitayama, 1991; Oyserman, Coon, & Kemmelmeier, 2002). Triandis, Leung, Villareal, and Clark (1985) suggested the use of the terms *idiocentrism* and *allocentrism* to replace individualism and collectivism at the personality or individual level, respectively.

Christine J. Yeh, Teachers College, Columbia University; Agnes Kwong Arora, New York University; Katherine A. Wu, Teachers College, Columbia University

Similarly, Markus and Kitayama (1991), in describing one's view of the self, introduced the use of the terms *independent* and *interdependent* self-construal. Whereas the independent self-construal emphasizes the separateness, internal attributes, and uniqueness of individuals, the interdependent self-construal stresses connectedness, social context, and relationships (Singelis, 1994).

Collectivism has been associated with non-Western cultures such as those in Asia, Africa, South America, and the Pacific islands region (Singelis, 1994). Conversely, individualism has been associated with Western cultures, which include most northern and western regions of Europe, North America, and Australia (Singelis, 1994). Although individuals have both allocentric and idiocentric characteristics, there are differences in the extent to which individuals have these characteristics. For example, individuals in collectivistic cultures are assumed to be more allocentric or have a more interdependent self-construal, and the opposite is true of individuals in individualistic cultures.

Cultural orientation (collectivistic or individualistic), and on an individual level, self-construal (interdependent or independent), play a critical role in shaping one's cognition, emotion, and motivation (Markus & Kitayama, 1991). Accordingly, cultural orientation and self-construal have been found to influence individuals' coping behaviors (e.g., Bailey & Dua, 1999; Cross, 1995; Lam & Zane, 2004; Schaubroeck, Lam, & Xie, 2000; Zaff, Blount, Phillips, & Cohen, 2002). Lam and Zane (2004) examined the relationship between ethnicity and coping among Asian and White American students coping with interpersonal problems. Results indicated that Asian Americans were more oriented toward secondary control and less oriented towards primary control than white Americans and self-construal was found to mediate this relationship between ethnicity and coping. Cross (1995) found that individuals who placed more emphasis on the independent self-construal used more direct coping strategies than individuals with a more interdependent self-construal. Bailey and Dua (1999) found that the longer the Asian students in their study remained in the Western culture, the less they tended to use collectivistic coping styles. This suggests that coping styles were more related to cultural orientation, and perhaps acculturation, than they were related to race and ethnicity. Similarly, Zaff et al. (2002) found that although ethnicity was not associated with coping strategies, ethnic identity and self-construal were. In a study examining how cultural differences and efficacy perceptions influence the role of job control in coping with job demands of individuals from the United States and Hong Kong, Schaubroeck et al. (2000) found that individual attributes of idiocentrism and allocentrism influenced the participants' coping processes.

3. COPING

Coping behaviors and strategies have been traditionally dichotomized into categories, such as problem- versus emotion-focused, functional versus dysfunctional, approach versus avoidance, engagement versus disengagement, and primary versus secondary control coping (e.g., Lazarus & Folkman, 1984; Livneh, Livneh, Maron, & Kaplan, 1996; Rothbaum, Weisz, & Snyder, 1982; Scheier, Weintraub, & Carver, 1986; Seiffge-Krenke, 1993; Tobin, Holroyd, Reynolds, & Wigal, 1989). Lazarus and Folkman's (1984) method of categorizing coping behaviors into problem-focused or emotion-focused has been used extensively to study coping. Some behaviors, such as planful problem-solving can be labeled *problem-focused* and behaviors such as distancing, self-controlling, accepting responsibility, escape/avoidance, confrontive coping, and positive reappraisal can be categorized as *emotion-focused*. According to Lazarus and

Folkman, other behaviors such as seeking social support can be conceptualized as both problem- and emotion-focused. Comparable to the distinction between problem- versus emotion-focused coping, Seiffge-Krenke (1993) also differentiated functional coping from dysfunctional coping. *Functioning coping* includes active and internal coping and refers to attempts to deal with problems by seeking support, taking concrete action, or reflecting on possible solutions. *Dysfunctional coping* includes withdrawal and refers to denial or repression, controlling feelings, and having a fatalistic attitude.

Coping styles have also been dichotomized into primary versus secondary control coping (Rothbaum et al., 1982). According to Rothbaum et al., *primary control coping* involves changing the existing environment to fit the individual's needs and *secondary control coping* includes changing one's feelings and thoughts to adjust to the objective environment and it is the type of control that people use when they are unable to exert traditional primary control. Four types of secondary control have been identified: individuals may use secondary control to restore a sense of primary control by aligning with powerful others who might have primary control (vicarious), by aligning with luck to arrange a positive outcome (illusory), by predicting what will happen to them in future situations (predictive), or by interpreting some outcome in a way that restores their feeling of primary control (interpretive; Morling & Fiske, 1999). When comparing primary control coping to secondary control coping, studies indicate that individuals from Asian cultures engage in more secondary control coping than those from Western cultures (Flammer et al., 1995; Lam & Zane, 2004; McCarty et al., 1999; Oerter, Agostiani, Kim, & Wibowo, 1996; Seginer, Trommsdorff, & Essau, 1993; Trommsdorff & Friedlmeier, 1993).

Coping research has been criticized for basing much of its work on theories using an individualistic perspective or research that focuses primarily on White Americans (Bjorck, Cuthbertson, Thurman, & Lee, 2001; Dunahoo, Hobfoll, Moniier, Hulsizer, & Johnson, 1998; Sampson, 1983). One of the major findings from coping research is that action-oriented coping is strongly related to positive psychological outcomes, while avoidance and emotion-focused strategies tend to be associated with poorer mental health (e.g., Endler & Parker, 1990; Folkman, Lazarus, Gruen, & DeLongis, 1986; Lazarus & Folkman, 1984; Seiffge-Krenke, 1993; Stern & Zavon, 1990).

While coping behaviors such as developing and maintaining a sense of competence and self-esteem (i.e., use of skills, talents, and cognitive abilities to feel good about oneself) have been labeled positive coping strategies assumed to result in positive consequences, coping behaviors such as relieving tension through diversions (i.e., activities that provide ways of escape, denial, and sublimation), and avoiding confrontation and withdrawing (e.g., avoiding people, situations, or stimuli that are difficult, uncomfortable, or unpleasant) have been labeled negative strategies of coping which can be expected to result in negative consequences (e.g., Colomba, Santiago, & Rossello, 1999). Wong (1993) developed the resource-congruence model of coping which is based on first accumulating resources from a variety of personal, cultural, or environmental sources to aid one in the face of stress and then assessing the nature of the stressor (past life event, present everyday stress, future anticipated stress, intrapersonal interpretive or self-perpetuated stresses, and societal stress) in order to choose a rational coping strategy to logically resolve the stressful situation. In this model, rational and deliberate approaches are valued over instinctive responses in most situations in contemporary society, since the former is viewed as increasing the chances that stress is removed and a state of internal balance or congruence is regained. Indeed, coping research has been biased towards problem-focused coping and personal agency (Bandura, 1982; Dunahoo et al., 1998), which are both concepts highly valued and emphasized in individualistic cultures.

4. COPING AND CULTURE

There are cultural norms regarding coping so that in any particular culture, certain coping patterns and behaviors are encouraged, rewarded, and deemed appropriate while others are not (Lam & Zane, 2004; Lazarus & Folkman, 1984; Marsella & Dash-Scheuer, 1988). Individualistic cultures emphasize an independent self-construal that values independence and autonomy. Individuals with an independent self-construal may have a tendency to master and directly control their environment to fit their own personal needs and desires (Markus & Kityama, 1991) and may have a desire for self-expression and congruence between their behaviors and internal processes (Lam & Zane, 2004; Morling & Fiske, 1999; Weisz, Rothbaum, & Blackburn, 1984). Conversely, collectivistic cultures emphasize group cohesion. Individuals with an interdependent self-construal and connected sense of self have a desire for maintaining harmony and conforming to group norms (Chang, Chua, & Toh, 1997; Lam & Zane, 2004; Morling & Fiske, 1999; Weisz et al., 1984). Thus, in individualistic cultures, taking direct action, confronting others, or speaking up in order to defend oneself may be preferred and valued ways of coping with problems and stressors, but collectivistic cultures emphasize harmony with others so that interdependent individuals may attempt to adjust to social situations using coping processes that focus on changing the self rather than changing the situation (Cross, 1995; Weisz et al., 1984; Yang, 1986). As discussed earlier, these latter ways of coping have been thought of as indirect, avoidant, secondary, and dysfunctional.

According to Kluckhohn and Strodtbeck (1961; see Leong & Wong, 2003), cultural values are closely connected to how people answer five fundamental human questions, which correlates to five dimensions: (a) What is the basic nature of people? (b) What is the proper relationship to nature? (c) What is the proper focus in terms of the temporal dimension of life? (d) What is the proper mode of human activity? (e) What is the proper way of relating to one another? In each culture, there is a preferred way of answering these questions and the answers to these questions may inform one's coping strategies. For example, if a culture emphasizes oneness between people and nature as do many collectivistic cultures, coping strategies that only focus on the individual may not be effective. Also, traditional Chinese culture has a past orientation that focuses on ancestor worship and respect for traditions and elders (Leong & Wong, 2003). This focus on the past may imply that thinking about others who have undergone and overcome similar situations in the past could be a method of coping. Similarly individuals endorsing the cultural belief that self-control is the proper mode of human activity and self-expression may prefer to cope through forbearing one's problems rather than discussing it with numerous others. Regarding relational orientation, cultures may support a Lineal, Collateral, or Individualistic way of relating with each other (Leong & Wong, 2003). Individuals from collectivistic cultures emphasize Collaterality, which sees individuals as part of a social group and places the welfare of the group above that of the individual. This particular orientation has implications for how individuals cope with problems.

5. COLLECTIVISTIC COPING

Individuals from collectivistic cultures are socialized to cope in different ways in comparison to individuals from individualistic cultures. In light of the need for more research on coping that includes and takes into consideration coping methods used in collectivistic cultures, a growing number of researchers have attempted to examine the construct of coping beyond a Western cultural perspective. An extensive review of the literature revealed that collectivistic cultures emphasize ways of coping that are distinct from those encouraged in individualistic cultures. We present a new theoretical model for collectivistic coping, which includes the following dimensions: family support, respect for authority figures, intracultural coping, relational universality, forbearance, social activity, and fatalism.

5.1. Family Support

In collectivistic cultures, the interdependent self is intertwined with and inseparable from others in important relationships (Markus & Kitayama, 1991). Additionally, individuals from collectivistic cultures have fewer ingroups and when individuals have few ingroups, they become more dependent on them (Triandis, 1989). The family contributes strongly to the identity construal of a collectivistic person and serves a vital supportive and caring function for the members within (Yeh & Wang, 2000). Thus, interdependent individuals may prefer to seek help from their family members and solve their problems within the family system.

In particular, the family has been a major, if not central, source of ego strength for individuals in collectivistic cultures (Daly, Jennings, Beckett, & Leashore, 1995) and also serve as social support systems to buffer individuals against stressful events (Pierce, Sarason, & Sarason, 1992; Treharne, Lyons, & Tupling, 2001).The central role of the family to support and care for family members has been found across numerous cultures including African American, Arab American, Chinese, Korean, Japanese, Israeli-Arab, Taiwanese, and Thai (Ben-Ari & Lavee, 2004; Daly et al., 1995; Erickson & Al-Timimi, 2001; McCarty et al., 1999; Yeh & Wang, 2000).

Furthermore, in some collectivistic cultures such as certain Asian cultures, disclosing personal problems to others outside of the family is believed to bring shame and guilt to the entire family (Sue, 1994). For instance, in the highly collectivistic Japanese culture, engaging in family activities aids in coping with stress (Homma-True, 1997). Yeh and Wang (2000) found that Asian Americans tended to use coping sources and practices that emphasized talking with familial and social relations rather than professionals such as counselors. In Asian families, parents also serve as a coping resource because of filial piety, a Confucian behavioral norm that structures the unvarying intergenerational relationship where parents and elders are seen as wiser and more knowledgeable. Consistent with the literature, Lay et al., (1998) found that Asian Canadians had a more interdependent self-construal in relation to family members than European Canadian. Similarly, Li (2002) found that individuals in North America are more independent than those from China in terms of their connectedness with their family. In a study of Asian Americans who lost a family member in the World Trade Center Attacks in New York City in 2001, Yeh, Inman, Kim, and Okubo (2004a) found that all of the participants in the study coped with the loss by seeking support and comfort from family members including extended family members. In addition, Yeh, Inose, Kobori, and Chang (2001) found that amongst Japanese college students, collective identity was a significant predictor of seeking help from family members; this finding offers further evidence of the strong emphasis on family relations in collectivistic cultures (Homma-True, 1997).

For Mexican Americans and other Latin Americans, the importance of family support and togetherness is encapsulated in the notion of *familismo* (Castillo, Conoley, & Brossart, 2004; Kobus & Reyes, 2000). Seeking support from the family has also been found to be an important coping strategy for Mexican Americans who are undergoing stressful situations (Kobus & Reyes, 2000). Furthermore, in a study on sources of support and coping practices among Black and Latino college students, Chiang, Hunter, and Yeh (2004) found that these students tended to seek support from their parents when dealing with a mental health concern. Like in Asian American cultures, Hispanic Americans hold great respect for older family members; value saving face; and establish a lifelong reciprocal relationship of provision between parent and child (Sue & Sue, 2003).

Among African American families, collectivistic values are promoted which have provided the community with resilience against daily stressors and against the violence and oppression of slavery (Billingsley, 1992; Ho, 1987). The family has been referred to as a vital mechanism of survival in the African American community (Daly et al., 1995). African American family values include a strong sense of mutual sharing and responsibility, caring for each other, the sharing of material goods, and respect for elders (Billingsley, 1992; Ho, 1987); such family values make it more likely for African American individuals to consider family members as an important source of coping against daily stressors.

5.2. Respect for Authority Figures

Many collectivistic cultures have a strong cultural respect for elders or respected authority figures. Asian Americans have been found to seek advice from older members of the community (Atkinson, Ponterotto & Sanchez, 1984) and to deal with mental health problems by seeking help from parents and older relatives (Root, 1985; Suan & Tyler, 1990). Participants from a collectivistic background were found to use family and parents as a coping source (Yeh et al., 2001); this may be due not only to the fact that parents are within the family system but also because parents are elders and seen as wiser and more knowledgeable.

Yeh, Chang, Leong, Arora, Xin, and Kim, (2004b) found *Respect for Authority* to have a strong positive correlation with *Vertical Collectivism,* which refers to the degree to which an individual perceives him or herself as a part of a group, is willing to sacrifice his or her personal goals for the sake of the group goals, and is accepting inequalities within the group (Triandis, 1995). This is congruent with the literature that has found elders and authority figures in the communities of ethnic minorities to be highly respected and to serve as another source of intracultural coping for collectivistic persons (e.g. Atkinson et al., 1984; Daly et al., 1995; Root, 1985; Suan & Tyler, 1990). In collectivistic cultures, culturally congruent forms of counseling, such as indigenous healers, would involve an elder or authority figure that is known within the community and adhere to collectivistic norms (Sue & Sue, 2003). Indigenous healers, including shamans, santeria, folk healers, chi-gong, reiki, astrologers, and sangoma (Helms & Cook, 1999; Lee & Armstrong, 1995; Singh, 1999; Sue & Sue, 2003), are viewed as respected authority figures who possess special insight or healing powers. In contrast to Western forms of healing, these non-Western approaches view the body as made of and a part of nature as a whole (Yeh & Wang, 2000). Bemak and Chung (2000) describe how immigrants and refugees, who often come from collectivistic cultures, initially seek community elders or traditional healers and will utilize mainstream health care providers only when indigenous treatments are unsuccessful. Solberg, Choi, Ritsma, and Jolly (1994) reported that Asian Americans used nontraditional coping sources such as religious leaders, student organizations, and church groups to deal with daily stressors.

5.3. Intracultural Coping

Intracultural coping refers to the use of supportive networks comprised of racially similar individuals, such as one's family network or community-based social groups. Race, a cultural construction defined primarily on visible traits, offers unconscious guidelines and rules for daily interactions among racially diverse individuals (Smedley, 1993). Race influences how a member of a racial group identifies with a particular racial group, how this person processes information, uses language, creates thought patterns, and shapes one's psychological experiences (Carter, 1997). Wong (1993) also referred to intracultural coping in his resource-congruence coping model with the idea of *collective coping*, a form of coping extending beyond social support that encompasses the action of multiple group members to resolve a single problem.

Intracultural coping has been found to be positively correlated with one's feelings of importance to his or her identity (Yeh et al., 2004b), which reinforces the importance of race and racial identity to the interdependent self-construal since it is likely that one's group or social identity is highly salient to this self-construal. In particular, interdependent individuals tend to define in-group members more narrowly and with more overt impermeability than independent individuals (Hall, 2003; Triandis, 1989). Interdependent individuals maintain tighter and longer bonds with in-group members, that in turn, increases the distance between in-group and out-group members. Individuals from collectivistic cultures have been found to treat out-group members (e.g., racially or culturally dissimilar persons) differently, making it unlikely for them to understand the advantages and disadvantages of being interdependent (Markus & Kitayama, 1991). This occurrence may explain the inability of researchers, such as Coon and Kemmelmeier (2001) and Matsumoto, Weissman, Preston, Brown, and Kupperbusch (1997), to find evidence of idiocentric behaviors in collectivistic cultures, since they may have been considered out-group members.

In general, the behaviors, emotions, thoughts, and motivations of interdependent selves are seen as embedded in those of the group and closely connected with important others (Erez & Earley, 1993). Individuals from collectivistic cultures, including African American, Japanese, Mexican American, Turkish, and Asian American individuals, tend to avoid speaking about or formally reporting problems or difficulties since it is seen as burdening others in public (Hall, 2003; Heron, Jacobs, Twomey, & Kaslow, 1997; McCarty et al., 1999; Wasti & Cortina, 2002; Yeh et al., 2004a). Consequently, the Western tradition of seeking help from a stranger such as a counselor or a psychologist may be culturally inappropriate from a collectivistic perspective (Yeh & Wang, 2000).

5.4. Relational Universality

The interconnection of the elements comprising the interdependent self (e.g. self, other, environment) is related to the belief that individuals, when alienated from the larger social group cannot be fully understood (Markus & Kitayama, 1991). Rokach Bacanli, and Ramberan (2000) describe the "organic communities" comprised of interdependent persons as operating as though "the whole defines the individual, who could not exist without it. The individual greatly relies on the community for support, a sense of belonging, reciprocal sharing with others and a sense of identity" (p. 308). Because of this fundamental sense of interconnection, it follows that seeking support, advice, and guidance from people who have experienced or are experiencing similar problems may be an especially effective coping strategy.

In addition, having agency or the belief that one has control over events, an important belief in many Western and individualistic cultures, is de-emphasized in collectivistic cultures. Rather, this perception of control in interdependent persons is seen as residing in the environmental and social context (Morling & Fiske, 1999). Interdependent selves who find others in an overlapping space-time continuum consisting of the product of common environmental, social, or contextual experiences may find comfort in being connected to this interwoven fabric of human experience that extends toward other human experiences.

In a qualitative study of 18 powerful and highly-achieving African American women, Richie et al., (1997) found that having a strong sense of interconnectedness with their collective identity or shared experience with African American women enabled them to cope with the sexism and racism they encountered in their careers. Specifically, Richie and colleagues (1997) concluded that despite barriers that were attributed to various forms of oppression, these women revealed persistence and motivation. The effects of racism and sexism on the African American-Black women seemed to illuminate their collective identity. In fact, many of the African American-Black women understood themselves as part of their own history in their daily lives. Many of these women reported feeling empowered by other African Americans-Blacks as well as other women, even when they did not have direct encounters with them.

The sense of connection in these women's shared experiences of fighting oppression with other African American women imparted a sense of relational universality that enabled them to cope successfully with racist and sexist forces. While their common racial history and continued experience of racism increased their sense of interconnectedness, Richie et al., (1997) mention that the women also displayed individualistic traits in order to pursue their career goals. It appears, however, that having relational universality was a necessary motivating and empowering force that enabled them to cope with their hardships. It may be that these women's connection to an underlying fabric giving meaning and purpose to their lives served to buffer them from the daily encounters with racism and sexism.

An important goal for the interdependent self is to closely connect with others around common factors such as family, culture, religion, or life events. In terms of collectivistic coping, the idea that others have a shared experience with you is a way of establishing a close bond and validating the relational self. Yeh et al. (2004a) found that Asian Americans tended to cope with the death of a family member by seeking comfort and connection with other families who also lost a close relative.

5.5. Forbearance

In collectivistic cultures, the focus of attention in social relationships is on the other, and on the maintenance of social harmony between the involved parties (Markus & Kitayama, 1991). Thus, forbearing one's problems in order to minimize or avoid interpersonal conflict is a common way in which members of collectivistic cultures may deal with problems. As seen in a number of collectivistic cultures such as Arab Israeli, Chinese, Japanese, Thai, Vietnamese, and other Asian cultures, the desire to maintain harmony is prioritized over the desire to achieve or strive for personal gain or of embarrassing the other party (Ben-Ari & Lavee, 2004; Lee, 1997; McCarty et al., 1999; Wasti & Cortina, 2002). Maintaining control of one's inner desires, goals, and emotions "constitutes the core of the cultural ideal of becoming mature" (Markus & Kitayama, 1991, p. 227). Morling and Fiske (1999) suggested that collectivistic cultures, with their holistic worldviews and flexible movement between internal and external loci of control, utilize harmony control: "an active, intentional endeavor in which people recognize the agency in contextual, social, or spiritual forces and attempt to merge with these forces" (Morling & Fiske, 1999, p.382). In contrast to individualistic cultures, which emphasize a disconnected self and an internal locus of control, harmony control enables people to "serenely accept whatever outcomes emerge" (Morling & Fiske, 1999, p.384).

Collectivistic cultures promote *forbearance*, the withholding of one's opinions and emotions or the restraint shown in the face of provocation, as a means to maintain social harmony. Forbearance is accomplished by keeping problems and opinions to oneself, willingness to sacrifice to put the needs of others before one's own, enduring in the face of adversity, and accepting one's fate (Henkin, 1985; Marsella, 1993). Additionally, in contrast to independent individuals, interdependent selves may adjust themselves to the social context rather than changing the situation (Ben-Ari & Lavee, 2004; Morling & Fiske, 1999; Weisz et al., 1984; Yang, 1986).

Forbearance has emerged in numerous studies. Chinese culture values forbearance to the degree where it is viewed as a coping strategy that can foster a sense of enlightened awareness (Yue, 2001). Fukuhara (1989) found that students in Japan are reluctant to express their own problems to others and suggested that it may be because the students do not want to bother others or to disturb social harmony. In addition, Yeh and Inose (2002) found a trend for Asian students to keep their problems to themselves rather than to confront when they had problems. Similarly, almost a third of the Japanese college students reported that they preferred to keep problems to themselves (Yeh et al., 2001). Wasti and Cortina (2002) found that Turkish and Hispanic American women kept their problems to themselves more than the Anglo American women in their study. The authors attributed this finding to the Turkish and Hispanic American women's collectivistic cultural orientation, which was related to a heightened concern for harmony and disapproval of confrontation and conflict. Again, the maintenance of positive social relations is of utmost concern. In fact, Ohbuchi, Fukushima, and Tedeschi (1999) found that in conflict situations, interdependent individuals were primarily concerned with maintaining relationships rather than achieving justice, which was the main concern of independent individuals.

In examining the ability of one to forbear and forgive, McCullough, Fincham, and Tsang (2003) found that high empathy for the transgressor and weak responsibility attributed to the transgressor consistently led people to forbear transgressions. The existence of high empathy and a low internal locus of control or need to attach causal blame for the event is indicative of collectivistic cultures. These transgressions may also have been forborn in order for social harmony to be maintained between persons.

5.6. Social Activity

Due to the interconnectedness with others that shapes the interdependent sense of self, members from collectivistic cultures have been found to use social supports as an important means of coping (Conway, 1985; Daly et al., 1995; Houston, 1990; Liu, 1986; Mau & Jepsen, 1988; Solberg et al., 1994; Yeh & Inose, 2002; Yeh & Wang, 2000). For instance Yeh and Wang (2000) found that Asian Americans tended to endorse coping sources and practices that emphasized talking with social relations rather than professionals such as counselors. This trend was also found amongst Japanese college students (Yeh et al., 2001), Chinese, Japanese, and Korean immigrant adolescents (Yeh & Inose, 2002), and Asian Americans who lost a family member in the World Trade Center Attacks (Yeh et al. 2004a). In fact, collectivistic cultural groups, such as Latino/as and African Americans, have been found to use social support systems to a greater extent than White European Americans (Conway, 1985; Daly et al., 1995; Dunkel-Schetter, Gurung, Lobel, & Wadhura, 2001).

Culturally similar support systems, which extend outside the family, have also been found to aid the post-1960's immigrants who have largely come from collectivistic cultures (Roysircar-Sodowsky & Frey, 2003). Yeh and Inose (2002) reviewed the literature, which revealed the importance of maintaining a social support system that aids the welfare of international students, particularly from Asian, African, and Latin cultures, upon their arrival to the United States. Social connectedness and social support network satisfaction were both significant predictors of acculturative distress (Yeh & Inose, 2002). Acculturative stress has also been found to have the largest effect on reported mental health problems among Asian immigrants. Much of this is the result of experiencing cultural stress, such as being caught between two cultures, and having interpersonal conflicts with Whites. Finding comfort in peer and social interactions with culturally-similar others may help alleviate the distress. Kitayama and Markus (2000) described the use of "vicarious control" by Japanese women as a coping mechanism where one trusts and relies on one's peers to exert their influence on their behalf (p. 1534). In this instance, social assurance is a form of coping that has evolved from the expression of mutual empathy found in collectivistic cultures.

Dunkel-Schetter et al. (2001) found that social support benefited women from collectivistic American ethnic minority groups, such as Latinas and African Americans, more than White Americans, who typically embody the individualistic self-construal. Additionally, African Americans have been found to use more social support systems to cope with stressors than Caucasians (Conway, 1985; Daly et al., 1995). Similarly, Chiang et al., (in press) found that Black and Latino college students tended to deal with stress by seeking support from friends and social networks such as school organizations and clubs.

Daly et al. (1995) described the Africentric paradigm that has endured since its introduction by African priests who were taken to America as slaves. Similar to other collectivistic orientations, the Africentric paradigm values mutual responsibility, self-control, and shared concern that extends beyond one's blood family for the well-being of others. The church remains an important community and source of spiritual support for members (Daly et al., 1995; Koenig, George, & Siegler, 1988; Taylor, Chatters, Jakody, & Levin, 1996).

Japanese women prefer, and also may benefit from, a coping strategy that asserts that others will help them or exert influence on their behalf. Kitayama and Markus (2000) regarded this "vicarious control" as an expression of trust or a form of social assurance of receiving help from close others, including friends and family. Thus, social assurance is a form of coping that has evolved from the expression of mutual empathy found in collectivistic cultures.

5.7. Fatalism

A collectivistic orientation may contribute to a holistic worldview and a tendency to believe that control may lie in contextual or external forces (Morling & Fiske, 1999). Morling and Fiske (1999) distinguish between two kinds of coping strategies, secondary and harmony control. Secondary control, such as denial, avoidance, and the reinterpretation of events, is viewed as a strategy use when primary control cannot be exerted on a situation or problem. Whereas, harmony control refers to "an active, intentional endeavor in which people recognize the agency in contextual, social, or spiritual forces and attempt to merge with these forces" (Morling & Fiske, 1999, p. 382). When harmony control is used, individuals accept and adjust to their roles and to events just as they are. There is an acceptance of luck and fate and a higher being with no direct action on the environment. (Morling & Fiske,

1999, p. 382). Independent selves strive for autonomy and separateness (Markus & Kitayama, 1991; Triandis, 1989), and control of one's environment is critical to one's way of being. In contrast, interdependent selves are interconnected to the environment and relationships, are accepting of outcomes (Morling & Fiske, 1999, p. 384) and do not try to change their surrounding context.

The interconnectedness of interdependent selves not only includes close relationships, but a holistic view of the world, including a connection between mind, body, and spirit, nature, and a strong belief in fate. Randolph and Banks (1993) refer to spirituality as the belief of a force greater than oneself or the subjective experience of being connected with a higher power or a force that transcends the limitations of humanness. In this definition, spirituality is closely connected to fatalism or an acceptance of the power of the environment and social context. Individuals from collectivistic cultures, including many African cultures, have been found to use spirituality and religion as an important means of coping with daily stressors and problems (Daly et al., 1995; Koenig et al., 1998) more than those from individualistic cultures (Taylor et al., 1996). In a study of Asian Americans coping with the loss of a family member, Yeh et al. (2004a) found that many of the participants used fatalistic beliefs as a way of understanding their significant losses.

6. THE COLLECTIVISTIC COPING SCALE

This oversight of the coping literature on non-Western or non-individualistic self-construals reflects the continuing ethnocentric bias of psychological research that assumes perceived stressors and coping behaviors to be universal (Kagawa-Singer & Chung, 2002). Culture factors into every component of the stress process, including appraisal of events, coping options, and coping behaviors (Slavin, Rainer, McCreary, & Gowda, 1991). Lazarus (2000) emphasizes the "relational meaning" the person constructs as the product of the appraisals made about the social and physical environment, personal goals, beliefs about self and the world, and resources. Many of the existing coping questionnaires focus on problem-focused and emotion-focused coping behaviors (e.g., Folkman & Lazarus, 1988; Tobin et al., 1989) rather than on culturally specific coping practices, sources, and attitudes. A Collectivistic Coping Scale was developed (CCS; Yeh et al., 2004b) to begin to address the styles or ways of coping of persons with an interdependent self-construal.

Our work on the development of the CCS revealed seven factors accounting for 56.65% of the variance found in collectivistic coping: *Respect for Authority*, the tendency to cope by relying on the support of community elders or mentors (var. = 23.82%, α = .93), *Forbearance*, one's preference for refraining from sharing problems (var. = 11.94%, α = .89); *Social Activity*, an inclination to cope by utilizing social networks (var. = 6.41%, α = .90); *Intracultural Coping*, coping through supportive networks with racially similar individuals (var. = 5.00%, α = .94); *Relational Universality*, tendency to seek relationships with shared experiences (var.=3.51%, α = .91); *Fatalism*, tendency to see problems as predetermined (var. = 3.22%, α = .80); *Family Support*, preference for coping with help from family members (var. = 2.75%, α = .88). Intercorrelations among the seven factors ranged from .18 to .50 and strong alphas were reported for each of the seven factors. Confirmatory factor analysis of the seven-factor, first-order oblique model with a one-factor second order model determined that the first model was the strongest fit. This suggests that the use of an overall score is not appropriate and the seven factors should be treated as separate subscales.

7. IMPLICATIONS FOR COUNSELING RESEARCH AND PRACTICE

Most world cultures operate from a collectivistic standpoint where the individual is seen as an interconnected member of society and where the needs and desires of society trump those of the individual. It follows that coping behaviors will differ when individuals view themselves as inseparable and interconnected with their surrounding environment. Using past and current theory and research, we have presented a new theoretical model of collectivistic coping that highlights the importance of interconnection (with others and with external forces) and the maintenance of interpersonal harmony. We believe this model has critical implications for counseling, research, and practice.

7.1. Biculturalism and Collectivistic Coping

With the dramatic demographic increase of multiracial, bicultural, and immigrant youth and adults, it will be especially important to understand the use of individualistic and collectivistic coping methods as they relate to acculturation (Roysircar & Maestas, 2002), immigration, and interracial partnerships. For example, research indicates that even among third- and fourth-generation Asian Americans, although behaviors may have acculturated to the dominant American culture, cultural values and norms -including coping patterns- are still very much consistent with one's culture of origin (Hieshima & Shneider, 1994; Kim, Atkinson, & Yang, 1999; Sodowsky, Kwan, & Pannu, 1995).

Moreover, it would be necessary to examine if other cultural groups share this pattern with successive generations. It is important to examine the context in which collectivistic cultural values are used and observe the situations in which they arise. When are collectivistic and individualistic coping strategies more advantageous? Are these behaviors contextually determined or are they more stable and enduring? This research is critical since acculturation patterns remain in flux and intergenerational differences evolve and such cultural mechanisms should not be assumed to be universal (Kagawa-Singer & Chung, 2002).

7.2. Individualism and Collectivism

It is unlikely that individuals use only collectivistic or individualistic coping strategies just as people are not entirely interdependent or independent in their cultural orientation. Coon and Kemmelmeier (2001) found people with high individualism and collectivism or low individualism and collectivism. Hence, research needs to investigate coexisting individualistic and collectivistic coping behaviors that may be used when certain problems are encountered. Recent research has also evolved to conceptualize collectivism across vertical and horizontal dimensions (Triandis, 1995) and additional research is needed to understand how these dimensions interplay with coping strategies for individuals with varying degrees of individualism and collectivism.

7.3. Developing Collectivistic Coping Interventions

The new theoretical model for collectivistic coping has important implications for the development of interventions that integrate the role of culture and gender. One example may include the role of collectivistic coping among African American women. In discussing culturally competent interventions for suicidal women in abusive relationships, Heron et al. (1997) review the literature, which illustrates the power culture has on coping behaviors. Specifically, Black women are typically socialized that they should be strong and persevere through hardships in order to take care of their most important duty, the welfare of their family. African American culture socializes Black women with interdependent self-construals, where, for instance, racial preservation is valued above individual preservation. With the often-accurate perception that helping professionals are insensitive to their racial and cultural contexts or the belief that assistance will be ineffective, Black women do not seek assistance or enter shelters despite the high risk of violence. In addition, women are "likely to view battering as the African American male's displaced anger and aggression in response to racism and his constant struggle to assume or maintain economic and other social roles typically expected of males in America." (Daly et al. 1995, p. 243). Rather than convince a woman to leave her family, Heron et al. (1997) advocate for interventions that target the woman's relational nature as her strengths. Such relational strategies may include the collectivistic coping strategies outlined in this chapter.

8. CONCLUSION

Although there have been numerous studies documenting the use of "collectivistic" coping strategies (e.g. Chiang et al., in press; Yeh et al., 2001; Yeh, & Wang, 2000), an extensive review of the literature could not locate any formalized theoretical model describing the various dimensions of collectivistic coping. In addition, we were unable to find any instruments formally measuring the different aspects of collectivistic coping.

Our theoretical orientation on coping strategies departs from previous coping models and measures by its emphasis on the importance of analyzing the effectiveness of a coping behavior in relation to the underlying culturally-based beliefs, values, and orientations. In contrast to previous models and measure of coping, this one addresses coping behavior of an explicitly-stated cultural orientation of collectivism as defined by Hofstede (1980) and Markus and Kitayama (1991). Our measure does not attempt to bifurcate coping methods, where one form is invariably viewed more favorably than the other. This occurred after the widespread acceptance of the Lazarus and Folkman (1984) dualistic coping paradigm, despite the authors' emphasis that coping processes should not be seen as either good or bad but should be evaluated in regards to the cultural context of the behavior (Folkman & Moskowitz, 2004). For example, in Seiffge-Krenke's (1993) model, coping that is deemed "functional" reflects Western, individualistic behavioral norms of action-orientation and internal locus of control, while coping methods of emotional suppression (forbearance) and fatalism are categorized as "dysfunctional". While these labels may resonate with an idiocentric person with an independent self construal, they may not portray accurately the effectiveness of coping methods in an allocentric individual with an interdependent self construal. In Rothbaum et al.'s (1982) model on primary and secondary control coping, one may assume that a person naturally desires to alter one's environment to fit one's needs, and will rely on secondary forms of control only if the former is not possible. Yet someone who does not believe that it is possible that the environment can be adjusted to the individual would never seek this form of coping. It may be more fruitful to develop or expand upon effective secondary forms of coping instead of convincing one to adopt a primary form of coping.

In contrast to the models of coping mentioned above, Wong (1993) defines coping resources to include psychological, intellectual, spiritual, social, physical, financial, cultural, and environmental dimensions. This model does not bifurcate coping mechanisms. Instead, it posits that every coping method is potentially adaptive, but its effectiveness depends on being appropriate for the nature of the stressor, and congruent with culturally-based values and beliefs. Thus, both coping knowledge and cultural knowledge contribute to effective coping (Chapter 11).

We have described a new theoretical model for collectivistic coping, which includes the following dimensions: family support, respect for authority figures, intracultural coping, relational universality, forbearance, social activity, and fatalism. The newly developed Collectivistic Coping Scale enables these dimensions to be measured (Yeh et al., 2004b). Our theoretical model of Collectivistic Coping offers a framework for understanding future research and practice in the field of stress and coping among culturally diverse populations.

REFERENCES

Atkinson, D. R., Ponterotto, J. G., & Sanchez, A. R. (1984). Attitudes of Vietnamese and Anglo-American students toward counseling. *Journal of College Student Personnel, 25,* 448-452.

Bailey, F. J., & Dua, J. (1999). Individualism-collectivism, coping styles, and stress in international and Anglo-Australian students: A comparative study. *Australian Psychologist, 45,* 177-182.

Bandura, A. (1982). Self efficacy mechanism in human agency. *American Psychologist, 37,* 122-147.

Bemak, F., & Chung, R. C-Y. (2000). Psychological intervention with immigrant and refugees. In J. F. Aponte & J. Wohl (Eds.), *Psychological intervention and cultural diversity,* (2nd ed.) (pp. 200-213). Boston: Allyn and Bacon.

Ben-Ari, A., & Lavee, Y. (2004). Cultural orientation, ethnic affiliation, and negative daily occurrences: A multidimensional cross-cultural analysis. *American Journal of Orthopsychiatry, 74,* 102-111.

Billingsley, A. (1992). *Climbing Jacob's ladder: The enduring legacy of African American families.* New York: Simon & Schuster.

Bjorck, J. P., Cuthbertson, W., Thurman, J. W., Lee, Y. S. (2001). Ethnicity, coping, and distress among Korean Americans, Filipino Americans, Caucasian Americans. *The Journal of Social Psychology, 141,* 421-442.

Carter, R. T. (1997). Race and psychotherapy: The racially inclusive model. In C. E. Thompson & R. T. Carter (Eds.), *Racial Identity Theory: Applications to Individual, Group, and Organizational Interventions* (pp. 97-112). Mahwah, NJ: Lawrence Erlbaum Associates, Publishers.

Castillo, L. G., Conoley, C. W., & Brossart, D. F. (2004). Acculturation, white marginalization, and family support as predictors of perceived distress in Mexican American female college students. *Journal of Counseling Psychology, 51,* 151-157.

Chang, W. C., Chua, W. L., & Toh, Y. (1997). The concept of psychological control in the Asian context. In K. Leung, U. Kim, S. Yamaguschi, & Y. Kashima (Eds.), *Progress in Asian social psychology* (pp.95-118). New York: John Wiley.

Chiang, L., Hunter, C. D., & Yeh, C. J. (in press). Coping attitudes, sources, and practices among Black and Latino college students. *Adolescence.*

Colomba, M. V., Santiago, E. S., & Rossello, J. (1999). Coping strategies and depression in Puerto Rican adolescents: An exploratory study. *Cultural Diversity and Ethnic Minority Psychology, 5,* 65-75.

Conway, K. (1985). Coping with the stress of medical problems among Black and White elderly. *International Journal of aging and human development, 21,* 39-48.

Coon, H. M., & Kemmelemier, M. (2001). Cultural orientations in the United States: (Re)examining differences among ethnic groups. *Journal of Cross Cultural Psychology, 32,* 348-364.

Cross, S. E. (1995). Self-construals, coping, and stress in cross-cultural adaptation. *Journal of Cross-Cultural Psychology, 26,* 673-697.

Daly, A., Jennings, J., Beckett, J. O., & Leashore, B. R. (1995). Effective coping strategies of African Americans. *Social Work, 40,* 240-248.

Dunahoo, C. L., Hobfoll, S. E., Moniier, J., Hulsizer, M. R., & Johnson, R. (1998). There's more than rugged individualism in coping. Part 1: Even the Lone Ranger had Tonto. *Anxiety, Stress, and Coping, 11,* 137-165.

Dunkel-Schetter , C., Gurung, R. A. R., Lobel, M., & Wadhwa, P. D. (2001). Stress processes in pregnancy and birth: Psychological, biological, and sociocultural influences. In A. Baum, T. Revenson, & J. Singer (Eds.), *Handbook of health psychology* (pp. 495-518). Mahwah, NJ: Lawrence Erlbaum.

Endler, N. S., & Parker, J. D. A. (1990). Multidimensional assessment of coping: A critical evaluation. *Journal of Personality and Social Psychology, 58,* 844-854.

Erickson, C. D., & Al-Timimi, N. R. (2001). Providing mental health services to Arab Americans: Recommendations and considerations. *Cultural Diversity & Ethnic Minority Psychology, 7,* 308-327.

Erez, M., & Earley, P.C. (1993). *Culture, Self-identity, and Work.* Oxford University Press, NY.

Flammer, A., Ito, T., Luthi, R., Plaschy, N., Reber, R., Zurbriggen, L., & Sugimine, H. (1995). Coping with control-failure in Japanese and Swiss adolescents. *Swiss Journal of Psychology, 54,* 277-288.

Folkman, S., & Lazarus, R. S. (1988). *Ways of Coping Questionnaire sampler set manual, test booklet, scoring key.* Palo Alto, CA: Mind Garden.

Folkman, S., & Moskowitz, J. T. (2004). Coping: Pitfalls and promise. *Annual Review of Psychology, 55,* 745-774.

Folkman, S., Lazarus, R. S., Gruen, R. J., & DeLongis, A. (1986). Appraisal, coping, health status and psychological symptoms. *Journal of Personality and Social Psychology, 50,* 571-579.

Fukuhara, M. (1989). Counseling psychology in Japan. *Applied Psychology: An International Review, 38,* 409-422.

Hall, G. C. N. (2003). The self in context: Implications for psychopathology and psychotherapy. *Journal of Psychotherapy Integration, 13,* 66-82.

Helms, J. E., & Cook, D.A. (1999). *Using race and culture in counseling and psychotherapy: Theory and Process.* Needham Heights, MA: Allyn Bacon.

Henkin, W. A. (1985). Toward counseling the Japanese in America: A cross-cultural primer. *Journal of Counseling and Development, 63,* 500-503.

Heron, R. L., Jacobs, D. P., Twomey, H. B., & Kaslow, N. J. (1997). Culturally competent interventions for abused and suicidal African American women. *Psychotherapy, 34,* 410-424.

Hieshima, J. A., & Schneider, B. (1994). Intergenerational effects on the cultural and cognitive socialization of third and fourth-generation Japanese Americans. *Journal of Applied Developmental Psychology, 15,* 319-327.

Ho, M. K. (1987). *Family therapy with ethnic minorities.* Newbury Park, CA: Sage Publications.

Hofstede, G. (1980). *Culture's consequences.* Beverly Hills, CA: Sage.

Homma-True, R. (1997). Japanese American families. In E. Lee (Ed.), *Working with Asian Americans: A guide for clinicians* (pp. 114-124). New York: Guilford.

Houston, L. N. (1990). *Psychological principles and the black experience.* New York: University Press of America.

Kagawa-Singer, M., & Chung, R. C. (2002). Toward a new paradigm: A cultural systems approach. In K. S. Kurasaki, S. Okazaki, & S. Sue, (Eds.), *Asian American Mental Health: Assessment Theories and Methods* (pp. 47-66). New York, NY: Kluwer Academic/Plenum Publishers.

Kim, B. S. K., Atkinson, D. R., & Yang, P. H. (1999). The Asian values scale: Development, factor analysis, validation, and reliability. *Journal of Counseling Psychology, 46,* 342-352.

Kitayama, S., & Markus, H. R. (2000). The pursuit of happiness and the realization of sympathy: Cultural patterns of self, social relations, and well-being. In E. Diener & E. M. Suh (Eds.), *Culture and subjective well-being* (pp. 113-160). Cambridge, MA: MIT Press.

Kobus, K., & Reyes, O. (2000). A descriptive study of urban Mexican American adolescents' perceived stress and coping. *Hispanic Journal of Behavioral Sciences, 22,* 163-178.

Kluckhohn, R. R., & Strodtbeck, F. L. (1961). *Variations in value orientations.* Evanston, IL: Row Paterson

Koenig, H., George, L., & Siegler, I. (1998). The use of religion and other emotion-regulating coping strategies among older adults. *The Gerontologist, 28,* 303-310.

Lam, A. G., & Zane, N. W. S. (2004). Ethnic differences in coping with interpersonal stressors. *Journal of Cross-Cultural Psychology, 35,* 446-459.

Lay, C., Fairlie, P., Jackson, S., Ricci, T., Elsenberg, J., Sato, T., Teeaar, A., & Melamud, A. (1998). Domain-specific allocentrism-idiocentrism: A measure of Family Connectedness. *Journal of Cross-Cultural Psychology, 29,* 434-460.

Lazarus, R. S. (2000). Toward better research on stress and coping. *American Psychologist, 55,* 665-673.

Lazarus, R. S., & Folkman, S. (1984). *Stress, appraisal and coping.* New York: Springer.

Lee, E. (1997). Chinese American families. In E. Lee (Eds.), *Working with Asian Americans: A guide for clinicians* (pp. 46-78). New York: Guilford Press.

Lee, C. C., & Armstrong, K. L. (1995). Indigenous models of mental health interventions: Lessons from traditional healers. In J. G. Ponterotto, J. M. Casas, L. A. Suzuki, & C. M. Alexander (Eds.), *Handbook of Multicultural Counseling* (pp. 441-456). Thousand Oaks, CA: Sage.

Leong, F. T. L. & Wong, P. T. P. (2003). Optimal functioning from cross-cultural perspectives. In B. Walsh (Ed.). *Counseling psychology and optimal human functioning* (pp. 123-150). Mahwah, NJ: Lawrence Erlbaum

Li, H. Z. (2002). Culture, gender and self-close-other(s) connectedness in Canadian and Chinese samples. *European Journal of Social Psychology, 32,* 93-104.

Liu, W. T. (1986). Culture and social support. *Research on Aging, 8,* 57-83.

Livneh, H., Livneh, C. L., Maron, S., & Kaplan, J. (1996). A multidimensional approach to the study of the structure of coping with stress. *The Journal of Psychology, 130,* 501-512.

Markus, H. R., & Kitayama, S. (1991). Culture and the self: Implications for cognition, emotion, and motivation. *Psychological Review, 98,* 224-253.

Marsella, A. (1993). Counseling and psychotherapy with Japanese Americans: Cross-cultural considerations. *American Journal of Orthopsychiatry, 63,* 200-208.

Marsella, A. J., & Dash-Scheuer, A. (1988). Coping, culture, and healthy human development: A research and conceptual overview. In P. R. Dasen, J. W. Berry, & N. Sartorius (Eds.), *Health and cross-cultural psychology: Toward applications* (pp.162-178). Newbury Park, CA: Sage.

Matsumoto, D., Weissman, M. D., Preston, K., Brown, B. R., & Kupperbusch, C. (1997). Context-specific measurement of individualism-collectivism on the individual level: The Individualism-Collectivism Interpersonal Assessment Inventory. *Journal of Cross-Cultural Psychology, 28,* 743-767.

Mau, W-C., & Jepsen, D. A. (1988). Attitudes toward counselors and counseling processes: A comparison of Chinese and American graduate students. *Journal of Counseling and Development, 67,* 189-192.

McCarty, C. A., Weisz, J. R., Wanitromanee, K., Eastman, K., Suwanlert, S., Chaiyasit, W., & Band, E. B. (1999). Culture, coping, and context: Primary and secondary control among Thai and American youth. *Journal of Child Psychology and Psychiatry, 40,* 809-818.

McCullough, M. E., Fincham, F. D., & Tsang, J. (2003). Forgiveness, forbearance, and time: The temporal unfolding of transgression-related interpersonal motivations. *Journal of Personality and Social Psychology, 84,* 540–557.

Morling, B., & Fiske, S. T. (1999). Defining and measuring harmony control. *Journal of Research in Personality, 33,* 379-414.

Oerter, R., Oerter, R., Agostiani, H., Kim, H. O., & Wibowo, S. (1996). The concept of human nature in East Asia: Etic and emic characteristics. *Culture & Psychology, 2,* 9-51.

Ohbuchi, K., Fukushima, O, & Tedeschi, J. (1999). Cultural values in conflict management: Goal orientation, goal attainment, and tactical decision. *Journal of Cross-cultural Psychology, 30,* 51-71.

Oyserman, D., Coon, H. M., & Kemmelmeier, M. (2002). Rethinking individualism and collectivism: Evaluation of theoretical assumptions and meta-analyses. *Psychological Bulletin, 128,* 3-72.

Pierce, G. R., Sarason, B. R., & Sarason, I. G. (1992). General and specific support expectations and stress as predictors of perceived supportiveness: An experimental study. *Journal of Personality and Social Psychology, 63,* 297–307.

Randolph, S. M., & Banks, H. D. (1993). Making a way out of no way: The promise of Africentric approaches to HIV prevention. *Journal of Black Psychology, 19,* 204-214.

Richie, B. S., Fassinger, R. E., Linn, S. G., Johnson, J., Robinson, S., & Prosser, J. (1997). Persistence, connection, and passion: A qualitative study of the career development of highly achieving African American-Black and White women. *Journal of Counseling Psychology, 44,* 133-148.

Rokach, A., Bacanli, H., & Ramberan, G. (2000). Coping with loneliness: A cross-cultural comparison. *European Psychologist, 5,* 302-311.

Root, M. P. P. (1985). Guidelines for facilitation therapy with Asian American clients. *Psychotherapy, 22,* 349-356.

Rothbaum, F., Weisz, J. R., & Snyder, S. S. (1982). Changing the world and changing the self: A two-process model of perceived control. *Journal of Personality and Social Psychology, 42,* 5-37.

Roysircar, G., & Maestas, M. L. (2002). Assessing acculturation and cultural variables. In K. S. Kurasaki, S. Okazaki, & S. Sue, (Eds.), *Asian American Mental Health: Assessment Theories and Methods* (pp. 77-94). New York, NY: Kluwer Academic/Plenum Publishers.

Roysircar-Sodowsky, G., & Frey, L. L. (2003). Children of immigrants: Their worldviews value conflicts. In P. B. Pedersen & J. C. Corey (Eds.), *Multicultural counseling in schools: A practical handbook,* 2nd Ed (pp. 61-83). Boston: Peason Education, Inc.

Sampson, E. E. (1983). *Justice and the critique of pure psychology*. New York: Plenum Press.

Schaubroeck, J., Lam, S. S. K., & Xie, J. L. (2000). Collective efficacy versus self-efficacy incoping responses to stressors and control: A cross-cultural study. *Journal of Applied Psychology, 85,* 512-525.

Scheier, M., Weintraub, J., & Carver, C. (1986). Coping with stress: Divergent strategies of optimists and pessimists, *Journal of Personality and Social Psychology, 51,* 1257-1264.

Seginer, R., Trommsdorff, G., & Essau, C. (1993). Adolescent control beliefs: Cross-cultural variations of primary and secondary orientations. *International Journal of Behavioral Development, 16,* 243-260.

Seiffge-Krenke, I. (1993). Coping in normal and clinical samples: More similarities than differences? *Journal of Adolescence, 16,* 285-305.

Singelis, T. M. (1994). The measurement of independent and interdependent self-construals. *Personality and Social Psychology Bulletin, 20,* 580-591.

Singh, A. N. (1999). Shamans, healing, and mental health. *Journal of Child and family Studies, 8,* 131-134.

Slavin, L. A., Rainer, K. L., McCreary, M. L., & Gowda, K. K. (1991). Toward a multicultural model of the stress process. *Journal of Counseling & Development, 70,* 156-163.

Smedley, A. (1993). *Race in North America: Origin and Evolution of a Worldview.* Boulder, CO: Westview.

Sodowsky, G. R., Kwan, K. K., & Pannu, R. (1995). Ethnic identity of Asians in the United States. In J. G. Ponterotto, J. M. Casas, L. A. Suzuki, & C. M. Alexander (Eds.), *Handbook of multicultural counseling* (pp. 123-154). Thousand Oaks, CA: Sage.

Solberg, V. S., Choi., K-H., Ritsma., S., & Jolly., A. (1994). Asian-American college students: It is time to reach out. *Journal of College Student Development, 35,* 296-301.

Stern, M., & Zavon, M. (1990). Stress, coping, and family environment: The adolescent's response to naturally occurring stressors. *Journal of Adolescent Research, 5,* 290-305.

Suan, L. V., & Tyler, J. D. (1990). Mental health values and preferences for mental health resources of Japanese-American and Caucasian-American students. *Professional Psychology: Research and Practice, 21,* 291-296.

Sue, D. W. (1994). Asian-American mental health and help-seeking behavior: Comment on Solberg et al. (1994), Tata and Leong (1994), and Lin (1994). *Journal of Counseling Psychology, 41,* 292-295.

Sue, D. W. & Sue, D. (2003). *Counseling the Culturally Diverse: Theory and Practice, 4th ed.* John Wiley & Sons, Inc.

Taylor, R., Chatters, L., Jakody, R., & Levin, J. (1996). Black and White differences in religious participation: A multisample comparison. *Journal for the Scientific Study of Religion, 35,* 403-410.

Tobin, D. L., Holroyd, K. A., Reynolds, R. V., & Wigal, J. K. (1989). The hierarchical factor structure of the coping strategies inventory. *Cognitive Therapy and Research, 13,* 343-361.

Treharne, G. J., Lyons, A. C., & Tupling, R. E. (2001). The effects of optimism, pessimism,social support, and mood on the lagged relationship between daily stress and symptoms. *Current Research in Social Psychology, 7,* 60–81.

Triandis, H. C. (1989). The self and social behavior in differing cultural contexts. *Psychological Review, 96,* 506-520.

Triandis, H. C. (1995). *Individualism and collectivism.* Boulder, CO: Westview Press.

Triandis, H. C., Leung, K., Villareal, M. V., & Clark, F. L. (1985). Allocentric versus idiocentric tendencies: Convergent and discriminant validation. *Journal of Research in Personality, 19,* 395-415.

Trommsdorff, G., & Friedlmeier, W. (1993). Control and responsiveness in Japanese and German mother-child interactions. *Early Development and Parenting, 2,* 65-78.

United States Census Bureau (2000). *Highlights from the census 2000 demographic profiles.* Retrieved September 3, 2004 from http://factfinder.census.gov/servlet/SAFFFacts?_sse=on

United States Department of Health & Human Services (2001). Retrieved September 3, 2004 from http://www.hhs.gov/specificpopulations/index.shtml#ethnic

Wasti, S. A., & Cortina, L. M. (2002). Coping in context: Sociocultural determinants of responses to sexual harassment. *Journal of Personality and Social Psychology, 83,* 394-405.

Weisz, J. R., Rothbaum, F. M., & Blackburn, T. C. (1984). Standing out and standing in: The psychology of control in America and Japan. *American Psychologist, 39,* 955-969.

Wong, P. T. P. (1993). Effective management of life stress: The resource-congruence model. *Stress Medicine, 9,* 51-60.

Yang, K. S. (1986). Chinese personality and its change. In M. H. Bond (Ed.), *Psychology of the Chinese people* (pp.107-170). Hong Kong: Oxford University Press.

Yeh, C. J., & Wang, Y-W. (2000). Asian American coping attitudes, sources, and practices: Implications for indigenous counseling strategies. *Journal of College Student Development, 41,* 94-103.

Yeh, C. J., & Inose, M. (2002). Difficulties and coping strategies of Chinese, Japanese and Korean immigrant students. *Adolescence, 37,* 69-82.

Yeh, C. J., Inose, M., Kobori, & Chang, T. (2001). Self and coping among college student in Japan. *Journal of College Student Development, 42,* 242-256.

Yeh, C. J., Inman, A., Kim, A. B., & Okubo, Y. (2004a). Asian American families' collectivistic coping strategies in response to 9/11. Manuscript submitted for publication.

Yeh, C. J., Chang, T., Leong, F. T. L., Arora, A., & Kim, A. (2004b). Reliability, validity and factor analysis of the collectivistic coping scale. Manuscript submitted for publication.

Yue, X. (2001). Culturally constructed coping among university students in Beijing. *Journal of Psychology in Chinese Societies, 2,* 119-137.

Zaff, J. F., Blount, R. L., Phillips, L., & Cohen, L. (2002). The role of ethnic identity and self-construal in coping among African American and Caucasian American seventh graders: An exploratory analysis of within-group variance. *Adolescence, 37,* 751-773.

COPING WITH SUFFERING:
The Buddhist Perspective

Yu-Hsi Chen

1. INTRODUCTION

Buddhism, originated in India, has been an influential cultural force in Asia for more than 2500 years. In recent decades, it has gained increasing acceptance in the West, especially North America, largely through mindful meditation. As a religious philosophy, its distinctive feature consists in the attainment of spiritual liberation through awakening of the mind from the bondage of greed, hatred, and delusion. Unlike theistic religions, Buddhist faith is directed first towards Buddha's teachings and then towards the moral and spiritual qualities of the historical Buddha, the celestial Buddhas (regarded as awakened sentient beings) and other Buddhist saints. While the Pure Land School of Buddhism seeks salvation through faith in Amitabha Buddha and His Pure Land, ultimately that faith is tied to a mental capacity to surrender one's ego so that spiritual awakening and liberation can be achieved.

Considered as a major religion today, Buddhism was founded by Siddhartha Gautama, the prince of an ancient Indian state, initially as a system of mental cultivation aimed at achieving liberating insights and compassion. Following his death, he was revered as the Buddha (meaning the Awakened One in Sanskrit), and his followers held several councils over a period of some 600 years to verify and compile his teachings. As a result, two major streams have come into existence: the conservative Theravada (Southern Buddhism) and the more evolved and adaptive Mahayana Buddhism (great vehicle). The former, now prevalent in Thailand, Sri Lanka, Burma, and Laos, adheres to the early scriptures believed to embody the authentic teachings of the Buddha. Because its practice emphasizes the individual's liberation rather than the salvation of all sentient beings, it is also called Hinayana (lesser vehicle) by its detractors. By contrast, the latter, dominant in China, Taiwan, Japan, Korea, and Vietnam, stresses the ideal of Bodhisattvas – enlightened beings who vow to save all sentient beings from suffering. In addition to the early scriptures, the Mahayana is enriched by the profound commentarial literature of a number of prominent scholars, who respectively helped establish several Mahayana schools, including Madhyamika (Middle Way), Yogacara

Yu-Hsi Chen, Fo Guang College of Humanities and Social Sciences; Yu-Hsi Chen, Professor, Department of Religious Studies, Fo Guang College of Humanities and Social Sciences, 160, Linwei Road, Chiao-Hsi, Ilan County, Taiwan

(Mind-Only), Pure Land, Avatamsaka (Hua Yen) and the Esoteric (being practiced in Tibet). The Mahayana also owns a tremendous number of evolved scriptures, such as the Lotus Sutra, Surangama (Leng Yen) Sutra, Amitabha Sutra, Avatamsaka (Hua Yen) Sutra, etc., just to name a few. These texts, along with the commentarial literature, develop insights into the nature of the mind and the Ultimate Reality. For the first time in the history of spiritual philosophy, the transcendental non-dual Absolute known as *Sunyata* (Pure Emptiness) was revealed as the highest possible stage in the evolution of human consciousness. It is called Emptiness because in that supreme state of enlightened consciousness, the mind is pure and "empty" of all mental constructs and defilements and transcends the dualistic consciousness. Along with Pure Emptiness comes the realization of wisdom and intelligence of the highest order as well as unconditioned love and compassion.

A special feature of Mahayana Buddhism is the development of Zen (*Chan* in Chinese) Buddhism. Based on no particular scripture, Zen is a practice aimed at enlightenment through "direct seeing" of the true nature of the mind. It was introduced to China in the sixth century by an Indian monk named Bodhidharma and transmitted all the way to the Sixth Patriarch Hui Neng (638-713 A.D.), whose teachings embodied in the *Platform Sutra* stand out as a brilliant example of enlightenment through intuitive insights into the "self-nature" (true Self). Zen later found its way to Japan and has exerted a powerful influence on the Japanese culture and art. Japanese Zen master and scholar D. T. Suzuki introduced it to the West through his English writings in the early 20th century. Thanks to Suzuki's efforts, Westerners are familiar with the Japanese term "Zen" rather than its Chinese origin.

1.1. The Story of Siddhartha Gautama

Prince Siddhartha was endowed with an extraordinary sensitivity to feel human sufferings and the unfulfilling nature of human existence, even though he was born to a royal family with all its luxuries and material comforts. He decided to pursue the truth of life so that he might save fellow humans from sufferings. For this purpose he renounced his position as a successor to the throne, left his beloved wife, son and father behind and went in search of spiritual wisdom at the age of 29. After six years he became fully enlightened and spent the next 45 years teaching the principles and techniques of spiritual liberation until his death at the age of 80. Legends have it that he developed psychic powers to see his previous lives and sentient beings in all realms of the Cosmos. But from the perspective of spiritual knowledge, what is really significant and relevant is that he succeeded in purifying himself of the mental defilements of craving, aversion and ignorance, and transforming his human consciousness into a supreme state of enlightened consciousness, whereby he developed unconditional love and compassion, and also gained profound insights into the universal laws of causation and the nature of existence. Among other things, he discovered that all things and lives arose from complex causation and co-existed in cosmic networks of interdependence. According to his teachings, people who understand the Four Noble Truths and practice the Eightfold Path (see introduction below) in earnest will arrive at a deep realization of these universal truths, thereby realizing their oneness with all beings and freeing themselves from the fetters of the illusory ego to achieve the same enlightenment and liberation as the Buddha himself had experienced. However, he emphatically warned against taking his teachings as dogmas and stressed the importance of experimenting through practice.

1.2. The Buddhist Perspective on Stress and Coping

Buddhism provides a very unique perspective on stress, which differs, both in assumptions and emphasis, from the prevailing paradigm on stress and coping in American psychology. Buddhism offers a more general framework of suffering and stress, and this conceptual framework characterizes the Buddhist view of the human condition. In the West, stress is originally an engineering concept referring to the external pressure exerted on some structure or material. Therefore, psychological stressors typically refer to events external to the individual. In contrast, Buddhism locates the primary source of stress and suffering within individuals – it is the psychological mechanism of craving and aversion and the ignorance about its workings that are responsible for most of our troubles and difficulties in life.

Similarly, Buddhism also provides a much broader and proactive view of coping. Firstly, coping is more than a reaction to a specific stressful situation, but a pathway to be free from all of life's troubles and sorrows. Secondly, the goal of coping is not stress reduction but the transformation of whatever that is troubling us. Thirdly, effective coping depends on personal transformation, which can be achieved only through mental disciplines and enlightenment. Finally, successful personal transformation not only results in freedom from distress and suffering, but also in attainment of an inner state of serenity and compassion.

In order to practice the Buddhist way of coping, we need to understand the basic tenets known as the Four Noble Truths, which are the original teachings of the Buddha. (Rahula, 1972, chapters 2-5; Keown, 1996, chapter 4)

1. The Truth of Suffering (*Dukkha*): Life is full of suffering. In the Buddhist context, "suffering" not only refers to pain and distress caused by adverse circumstances, but more importantly, to spiritual vacuum and disillusionment resulting from the unfulfilling, illusory nature of desires, and to tension, stress and afflictions that stem from emotional attachments to worldly possessions. Thus the relevant implications of the Buddhist teachings on suffering should be found in the overall unhappiness as well as the widespread neuroses and mental troubles that plague modern society.
2. The Truth of Arising of Suffering (*Tanha*): Suffering comes from craving and aversion. Craving causes suffering in the way that fire consumes wood. In a vivid metaphor, "the Buddha spoke of all human experience as being 'ablaze' with desire. Fire is an appropriate metaphor for desire since it consumes what it feeds on without being satisfied. It spreads rapidly, become attached to new objects, and burns with the pain of unassuaged longing"(Keown, 1996, p. 49). It should be noted that craving always goes together with its antithesis – aversion – to form a psychological mechanism of defense. When we crave for something, such as pleasant sensations, we tend to reject its opposite, such as unpleasant sensations. This defense mechanism of craving and aversion, which is responsible for suffering, results from the primordial ignorance of the truth of human existence. Thus when Buddhism speaks of craving (or greed) and aversion (or hatred), it also speaks of ignorance (or delusion).
3. The Truth of Liberation from Suffering (*Nirvana*): We can be freed from suffering by transforming our craving and aversion, or equivalently, by dispelling the dark clouds

of ignorance and confusion with the light of liberating wisdom. The resulting mental state of perfect peace, serenity, and compassion is called *Nirvana*. One who attains *Nirvana* also attains freedom from rebirth after death. As Keown (1996, pp. 52-53) explains, "What is extinguished, in fact, is the triple fire of greed, hatred, and delusion which leads to rebirth. Indeed, the simplest definition of nirvana-in-this-life is as 'the end of greed, hatred, and delusion.'" Furthermore, the state of "final Nirvana" after death, namely, freedom from rebirth, is neither annihilation nor the eternal existence of a personal soul (Keown, 1996, p. 53). It transcends all dualities.

4. The Truth of the Eightfold Path (*Magga*): Liberation from suffering can be achieved through the cultivation and practice of eight disciplines, namely, right speech, right action, right living, right effort, right mindfulness, right meditation, right thought, and right understanding. These eight factors are divided into three categories: Morality, Meditation, and Wisdom. Right speech, right action, and right living are the basic moral disciplines required for spiritual transformation. In this regard, the most important thing to remember is not to speak, to act and to make a living in such a way as to harm others and oneself. The second category of Meditation requires assiduous efforts to practice mindfulness in everyday life as well as in formal meditation. This practice leads to increasingly high levels of mental concentration and awareness that give rise to Wisdom, the third category of disciplines. Liberating wisdom consists of unselfish, compassionate thoughts and intuitive insights into the truth of life (right understanding). Wisdom in this context implies a mental capacity to let go of the reactive mechanism of craving (greed) and aversion (hatred) as well as all mental defilements and negativities that stem from that mechanism. In other words, wisdom in the Buddhist sense is always the wisdom of spiritual liberation.

The following sections of this chapter will focus on Buddhist concepts, principles, and practices that are essential for our understanding of the Buddhist way of coping with suffering.

2. THE BUDDHIST CONCEPTION OF SUFFERING

The first sermon that the historical Buddha gave was on "suffering" and the way to cope with it. Throughout the Buddhist history, "suffering" is a recurring theme for practitioners, preachers, and scholars of Buddhism. Buddhists tend to associate life with a "boundless sea of suffering." And a major goal of the Buddhist spiritual practice, as interpreted by Chinese Buddhism, is "to end suffering and gain happiness." What do these statements actually mean? Since the Chinese term for suffering, *Ku*, also means "pain" and "hardship," these statements are often misinterpreted to mean that Buddhism has an aversion to the adverse circumstances and a preference for "happiness". Nothing can be further from the truth.

A deeper look into the Buddhist psychology shows that its approach to suffering is existentially based rather than metaphysical abstraction. The first thing we need to know is that although the Sanskrit word "*dukkha*" (literally translated as "suffering") refers to specific sufferings of life originating from external circumstances, such as wars, famines, and diseases, it also conveys more subtle meanings that are foreign to the Western mind.

As we have seen in the above section, Buddhism traces suffering to an internal causation, namely, the psychological mechanism of craving and aversion. Suffering in the

Buddhist sense also comes from the psychological experience of the law of "imperma-nence," i.e., the feelings of satisfaction and pleasure disappear quickly. As Keown aptly explains, "The problem.... is that good times do not last; sooner or later they fade away, or one becomes bored with what once seemed novel and full of promise. In this context the word *dukkha* has a more abstract and pervasive sense: it suggests that even when life is not painful it can be unsatisfactory and unfulfilling. In this and many other contexts 'unsatis-factoriness' captures the meaning of *dukkha* better than 'suffering.'" (Keown, 1996, p. 47)

2.1. Ignorance of Truth as the Root Cause of Suffering

The Buddha points to the cognitive ignorance of the truth of life as the root cause of all sufferings. That ignorance, or delusion, which is identified as a universal primordial trait of human existence, gives rise to the reactive mechanism of clinging and rejecting, or of craving and aversion. We hold on to whatever is seen as desirable, such as pleasure and success, while rejecting whatever is seen as undesirable, such as pain and failure. Our crav-ing for pleasure, good fortune and good health necessarily causes us to reject their antithe-ses, i.e., pain, misfortune, and illnesses. But the latter are unavoidable occurrences in our everyday lives, and when they come, they cause suffering precisely because we reject them, or relate to them with fear and aversion. Even pleasure cannot last, insofar as all pleasant sensations diminish in intensity from one moment to another, manifesting the universal law of "impermanence." Our emotional attachments to what is impermanent inevitably generate the feelings of emptiness, disappointment and disillusionment, which constitute part of *dukkha* by definition. Such feelings can accumulate and escalate into the distress-ing experience which we call "suffering."

2.2. Liberation from Suffering

Insofar as the Buddhist sees suffering as a symptom of man's primordial ignorance and delusion, it is a moral imperative – and not just a therapeutic need – to end suffering, and this is accomplished by learning – through insight and wisdom – to accept pain and adversities. The more a person can bear pain and adversities with equanimity, the less he or she will experience "suffering" and the greater is his or her mental capacity to achieve inner freedom, serenity, and happiness. In other words, Buddhism teaches that we can become liberated from suffering by learning to be liberated from the ego's desires, fears, and other mental defilements.

According to Buddhism, the reactive pattern of the mind implies one's refusal to accept both pain and pleasure as inevitable aspects of human existence. This failure to embrace life's experience in its entirety is at the root of suffering. Thus from the Buddhist perspective, to end suffering ultimately means to be liberated from the bondage of delu-sion and of its concomitant mechanism of clinging and rejecting. Rather than rejecting pain and holding on to pleasure, we learn to accept both, to eliminate our habitual pat-tern of the reactive mind and attain "equanimity" – a state of even-mindedness in which we see things as they are without reacting with negative emotions. As meditation teacher Goenka (1992) explains, "once one learns to observe objectively without identifying with the sensations, then the process of purification starts, and the old habit of blind reaction of multiplying one's misery is gradually weakened and broken" (p. 39).

3. THE HEALING FORCE OF BUDDHIST MEDITATION

As we have already explained in Section 1, in the time of the Buddha, the way to end suffering is known as the "Eightfold Path", which provides a set of principles and methods to achieve personal transformation. The Eightfold Path focuses on moral conduct and mental discipline. The moral aspect prescribes that one does no harm to oneself and others, and that mental defilements, such as greed, excessive desire, hatred, anger, animosity, selfishness, etc., be eradicated. This moral discipline is combined with the mental training of meditation and contemplation to achieve insights and wisdom that emancipate the mind from the primordial ignorance and the concomitant reactive mechanism of craving and aversion. In line with the teachings of the Eightfold Path, subsequent developments of Buddhism all emphasize mindful meditation as an effective method of purifying mental defilements and attaining the wisdom of liberation.

3.1. Meditation as a Way of Transformation and Coping

In talking about the Buddhist perspective on coping with stress and suffering, we should not neglect the healing and transformational forces of meditation. There are various schools of meditation in Buddhism. The meditation techniques of Southern Buddhism (the Theravada) emphasize the cultivation of mindfulness and awareness directed toward the body, feelings, sensations, and mental activities. Equally important is to develop equanimity, i.e., to learn to remain non-judgmental with regard to whatever happens internally and externally. Mindfulness coupled with equanimity is essential to purify the mind of the three basic defilements of craving, aversion and ignorance, thereby eradicating the roots of suffering (Goenka, 1992).

Apart from Southern Buddhism, the Zen School, the Tibetan Esoteric, the Tien Tai School, etc., have also developed different techniques of meditation, all aimed at spiritual liberation and enlightenment. The Esoteric meditation resorts to visualization and contemplation on a divine symbol or image, combined with a bodily gesture and recitation of a mantra. It is claimed to be an effective way to develop spiritual energy. However, it could produce harmful effects if done without a basic discipline in mental purification and proper guidance by a qualified teacher (Moacanin, 2003, chapter 6).

When practiced with proper guidance, Buddhist meditation of all styles can be remarkably efficacious in improving general health conditions, both physical and mental. Above all, it helps relieve stress and anxiety. In many cases it is reported to have positive effects on depression and other neurotic disorders. We need to note, however, that meditation in Buddhism is not intended to be an exercise or a therapy for health purpose. Rather, it is regarded as an integral part of the Buddhist practice aimed at achieving spiritual liberation and personal transformation. Its efficacy for the relief of stress and the cure of neuroses is considered as only a by-product of that practice. As liberation in the Buddhist sense means to free the mind from the primordial ignorance and delusion marked by the ego's habitual pattern of grasping and rejecting, any intent to change things as they are or to get rid of something undesirable falls into that pattern and therefore stands in the way of spiritual awakening and liberation. This does not mean that one should not take a meditation course unless he or she is prepared to follow the Buddhist path. This does mean that in taking the course, one should not be motivated by a utilitarian desire for gains, but should learn to develop a new outlook on life, a new mental attitude that emphasizes unconditional acceptance of one's own situation, no matter how difficult it may be. In fact, this new mentality is an integral part of the Buddhist meditation training. Once a practitioner learns to surrender his ego's desires and fears and to accept himself with equanimity, he is empowered with a liberating insight that will go a long way towards improving his health conditions. By the Buddhist standard, one is not considered a successful practitioner of meditation unless such an insight is attained.

3.2. The Practice of Mindfulness

This being said, we can now turn to the practice of mindfulness. Right mindfulness is the seventh component of the Eightfold Path. As Levine (2000) states, "Mindfulness is an essential process in attaining self-transformation and enlightenment. It is through mindfulness that we come to verify the teachings. It also contributes to other components of the path" (p. 73). For example, mindful meditation can be practiced to increase self-awareness of feelings, thoughts, and bodily functions. Right mindfulness detects mental defilements as soon as they arise and, as a result, helps eliminate the habitual pattern of emotional reactions. Furthermore, it sharpens the mental force of self-introspection so that the karmic complexes hidden deep in the unconscious can be brought to light and dissolved. Goenka (1992) explains how the process works as follows: "In such a moment (of mindful observation of breathing and sensations), the mind is free from the three basic defilements, that is, it is pure. This moment of purity at the conscious level has a strong impact on the old impurities accumulated in the unconscious. The contact of these positive and negative forces produces an explosion. Some of the impurities hidden in the unconscious rise to the conscious level, and manifest as various mental or physical discomforts." When one faces such a situation, he/she is advised not to react to the discomforts with fear and anxiety. Instead, "it would be wise to understand that what seems to be a problem is actually a sign of success in the meditation, an indication that in fact the technique has started to work" (p. 6).

A beginner is directed to develop mindfulness by paying full attention first to the breath. It involves learning to inhale and exhale slowly and observing the breathing with attentiveness but without making any judgment. After a period of training on breathing, the practice shifts to mindfulness of bodily sensations and whatever occurs within the body and the mind. Finally the practitioner can be trained to develop full awareness, which includes insights into one's own mind as well as the impermanent nature of all phenomena.

The practice of mindfulness puts a great emphasis on "bare" attention and "pure" awareness in the sense that the practitioner is not drawn into the mind's old habit of making discriminative judgments, which lead to the reactive pattern of craving for what is judged as pleasant and aversion to what is judged as unpleasant. This non-judgmental quality allows one to be freed from emotional reactivity and to observe the mental conditions with an unbiased open mind, thereby cultivating the mental capacity of unconditional self-acceptance. All of these combine to produce what is called *panna* (liberating insights or wisdom), along with a positive therapeutic effect on stress and suffering and overall mental health.

3.3. Health Benefits of Meditation

On the physiological and neurological levels, numerous medical studies have shown that meditation can boost the immune system and "rewire" the brain to reduce stress by increasing the theta brain waves and bringing about a more balanced secretion of neurotransmitters such as endorphins. These subtle physiological and neurological changes provide an effective antidote to stress, anxiety and depression. According to a recent cover story of *Time Magazine,*

> *Meditation is being recommended by more and more physicians as a way to prevent, slow or at least control the pain of chronic diseases like heart conditions, AIDS, cancer and infertility. It is also being used to restore balance in the face of such psychiatric disturbances as depression, hyperactivity and attention-deficit disorder (ADD). In a confluence of Eastern mysticism and Western science, doctors are embracing meditation not because they think it's hip or cool but because scientific studies are beginning to show that it works, particularly for stress-related conditions (Stein, 2003, p. 49).*

There are reports that chronic depression was cured or at least relieved by the practice of mindful meditation. One such case is cited in the *Time* story, which quotes Professor John Teasdale of Cambridge University as saying that mindful meditation helped chronically depressed patients, reducing their relapse rate by half. It also quotes Wendy Weisel, the daughter of two Holocaust survivors and author of *Daughters of Absence*, as saying that she took medication for most of her life until she started meditating two years ago. "There's an astounding difference," she reports. "You don't need medication for depression or for tension. I'm on nothing for the first time in my life"(Stein, 2003, p. 52). A question arises as to whether it is practical to recommend meditation as a therapy for depression and other neuroses. It is noted that many sufferers of depression lack a will and determination strong enough to sit through a meditation session, even if they care to try in the first place. Moreover, some Western psychotherapists appreciate meditation but are nevertheless concerned that cultural differences may prevent Western patients from developing a mental attitude commensurate with the practice of meditation. The classical psychologist Carl Jung, for all his enthusiasm for the Buddhist practice, hesitated to recommend meditation of the Tibetan style to his patients of neuroses because he thought that Westerners might not be able to comprehend the essence of Tibetan Buddhism properly due to cultural gaps, and that the Tibetan style of contemplative meditation without adequate spiritual preparation could evoke negative psychical forces from the unconscious that could aggravate rather than improve the mental health conditions of the patient (Moacanin, 2003, chapter 6). As a matter of fact, there have been cases where students suffered from a recurrence of their mental illness during the course of meditation.

However, psychologist and meditation teacher John Welwood (1983 and 2000) has stressed all the way that negative feelings and emotions do not have to be a problem if we know how to relate to them directly through insight meditation. When one judges his feelings of sadness negatively and gets entangled in the emotional story lines, Welwood explains, these feelings become "frozen" and – if in the absence of mindfulness these story lines are allowed to spin into a vicious circle – can lead to more intense emotions of depression. However, if we learn from Buddhist meditation how to open our hearts to feelings and emotions, befriending them, touching them with tenderness and accepting them as impermanent, ever-changing phenomena like floating clouds, then even the frozen emotions of depression can be "transmuted" into a spiritual treasure that enriches our lives (Welwood, 2000; 1985, pp. 79-90). Thus, the question of whether meditation is beneficial to neurosis patients really depends on individual cases and on what kinds of meditation techniques are employed. Generally speaking, when therapeutic work has succeeded in changing the life attitude of a patient, insight meditation that aims at self-acceptance can be safely recommended, if the therapist is an experienced meditation practitioner himself. A Buddhist meditation course directed by a qualified teacher appears to be safe and beneficial for the general public except those with a history of serious mental illness. In any case, the importance of learning through meditation to cultivate a new mental attitude of tolerance, forgiveness, and acceptance needs to be emphasized.

4. THE POSITIVE PSYCHOLOGY OF BUDDHIST COMPASSION

This article begins with a discussion of how suffering arises from delusion and the consequent reactive pattern of the mind, and how suffering can be overcome with insight, wisdom, and personal transformation. Now we are talking about love and compassion as an outcome of transformation and as an antidote to suffering. To be enlightened is to be filled with love and compassion for those who are still in the bondage of suffering. The Buddha is known both as The Enlightened One and The Compassionate One. The Buddha's mission is to share the wisdom of enlightenment in order to liberate everyone from suffering.

4.1. The Oneness of Love, Compassion, and Wisdom

Therefore, from the perspective of Buddhist psychology, wisdom and love are interrelated. As the Indian sage Nisargadatta Maharaj observes, "Wisdom tells me I am nothing. Love tells me I am everything. Between the two my life flows." In terms of Buddhism, this means that when a person develops the insight that the ego consciousness is a delusion – a false view of the self as a "real" entity separate from other beings, he or she is liberated from the straitjacket of the ego to embrace all beings – the larger Self – with universal love and compassion. However, this does not mean that love is uncovered only when wisdom presents itself, but rather that the two come in an interactive circle, that a measure of love and compassion is needed to open the heart shut off by ego-centeredness so that wisdom can flow. As love and compassion grows, so will the wisdom of liberation, and vice versa.

Thus the practice of loving-kindness as taught by Salzberg (1997) is consistent with the teaching of the Buddha, and should be taken as a useful practice that helps to open the heart with love to accept all situations and all people. With the sunshine of loving-kindness, the dark clouds of fear, aversion, and suffering are dispelled, giving way to joy and happiness. The attainment of love, compassion, joy, and equanimity in a transpersonal sense is identical to the attainment of insight and wisdom as conceived by Buddhism.

In this connection, a theoretical issue with regard to suffering needs to be mentioned in passing. According to *the Abhidharma*, an earliest Buddhist canon containing the Buddha's teachings on human psychology, insight and wisdom is the key determining factor of mental well-being. Where insight and wisdom is, delusion cannot be; and when insight and wisdom is present, the other healthy factors, such as love, joy and equanimity, also arise (Goleman, 1980, p. 133).

Consequently, when Buddhism talks about ending suffering with wisdom, the purpose is not merely to make people "feel better," or to bring about happiness as such, but more importantly, to achieve perfect mental well-being, and to allow for personal growth and development on a transpersonal level beyond the reach of mainstream psychology. To end suffering also implies the fulfillment of the Four Noble States of Mind – love, compassion, sympathetic joy, and equanimity – which mark a Bodhisattva, the ideal type of a fully awakened person who is committed to working for the salvation of all sentient beings.

4.2. The Practice of Loving-kindness

Not everybody can meet such an arduous challenge. But there are alternative methods with a similar transpersonal orientation that can be easily practiced in our everyday lives. Sharon Salzberg (1997), for example, recommends the practice of loving-kindness as a "revolutionary art of happiness." It includes contemplative reflections on one's own goodness and loving-kindness as a way of enhancing self-worth. As she explains,

> We begin to develop rapture by rejoicing in our own goodness. We reflect on the good things we have done, recollecting times when we have been generous, or times when we have been caring. Perhaps we can think of a time when it would have been easy to hurt somebody, or to tell a lie, or to be dismissive, yet we made the effort not to do that. Perhaps we can think of a time when we gave something up in a way that freed our mind and helped someone else. Or perhaps we can think of a time when we have overcome some fear and reached out to someone. These reflections open us to a wellspring of happiness that may have been hidden from us before (Salzberg, 1997, pp. 14-15).

The beneficial effect of meditation can be enhanced and reinforced by the practice of loving-kindness, which includes charitable actions and the practice of forgiveness as well as love-sharing through meditative contemplation. An overriding feature of this Buddhist approach is the emphasis placed on love as a unique power to overcome fear, hatred, and mental suffering. As Salzberg observes, "love can uproot fear or anger or guilt, because it is a greater power" than "the forces in the mind that bring suffering" (Salzberg, 1997, p. 23). And the practice of *metta* (loving-kindness) begins with befriending ourselves. She quotes the Buddha as saying, "You can search throughout the entire universe for someone who is more deserving of your love and affection than you are yourself, and that person is not to be found anywhere. You yourself, as much as anybody in the entire universe, deserve your love and affection" (Salzberg, 1997, p. 25). The psychological implications of self-love as a foundation for loving others become clear when we realize how people with low self-esteem are deprived of the capacity to love. Yet, self-love is not to be confused with narcissism and self-centeredness. It comes from a process of healthy personal growth in which the actualization of our personal potentials, especially in the service of others, brings us joy and happiness, and enhances our self-worth rather than self-conceit. To love ourselves is to be continuously in touch with this source of joy and happiness, and to learn to appreciate the goodness we have in us. Self-love in this sense is eroded by all egoistic and narcissistic tendencies, including self-aggran-dizement and self-abasement. Conversely it is enriched by our willingness to open our hearts and minds to accept all situations and all people, to touch our pain and sorrow with tender-ness and compassion, and to reach out to others in need of help (Chen, 2004).

According to Salzberg (1997), self-love can be cultivated through the contemplative process of directing *metta* (loving-kindness) to ourselves in meditation, and of reflecting on our own good deeds as discussed above. The process goes on to direct loving-kindness, peace ,and joy derived from meditation to those closest to us, and then to those whom we know and other sentient beings whom we do not know, and finally to our enemy – those with whom we have difficulty. The more we learn to love ourselves and others, the greater is our mental capacity to endure hardship and to overcome suffering.

5. THE NATURE OF BUDDHIST PSYCHOTHERAPY

A classical example of how the Buddha helped to end suffering is offered by the episode of a young woman who came to see the Buddha with her dead baby in her embrace. She wept tearfully and implored the Buddha to revive her baby's life with his magic power. The Buddha pondered that even if he could perform the miracle, it could not benefit the woman spiritually in the way of ending her suffering. He decided to help her see the light of the truth, and sent her to visit families in town to see if any of them was spared the woe of infant mortality. She came back with the report that there was none. At this point, the Buddha began to lecture her on the impermanence of worldly affairs, get-ting across the point that her emotional attachments to life and rejection of death were at the root of her suffering, and that it was up to her to eradicate that root. Upon hearing the lecture, her mind was awakened and she went on to become an "arhat" – a Buddhist saint who has achieved liberation from the primordial ignorance and delusion, and thus from the vicious circle of life and death.

5.1. A Behaviorist Approach with Love

This case and many others serve to remind us that a combination of the behaviorist and the cognitive approaches to psychotherapy was practiced by the Buddha some 2600 years ago. To help people overcome grief, fear, anger, and hatred, he had them go through the process of "relearning" from the environments and the actual experience of life. The point is to make them understand that these negative feelings and emotions are largely self-inflicted out of ignorance of the truth of existence, and therefore they must take the responsibility to resolve their own emotional difficulties. In this case the cognitive capac-ity for a "right understanding" of the truth through actual experience is emphasized. A Buddhist analogy is given of a person who mistakes a coil of rope for a snake at twilight and becomes terrified. The only way to assuage his fear is to make him see the rope for what it really is (Keown, 1996, p. 68).

As far as Buddhist psychotherapy is concerned, the behaviorist-cognitive approach would not be complete without a third ingredient – love and compassion. As we have already seen, Buddhism considers love and compassion as the most effective antidote to all negative emotions. The Buddha is often quoted as saying that "hatred can never be ceased by hatred; it is ceased by love alone." And this truth applies to fear and anger as well.

The legend has it that the Buddha once sent a group of monks to meditate in a forest at night. As these monks were terrified by the tree spirits that came out to disturb their meditation, they begged their teacher to send them to a safer place. But the Buddha insisted that they go back to the same forest and meditate with loving-kindness for the tree spirits. It turned out that by following their teacher's advice, they not only had their fear dispelled, but also so moved the tree spirits with their loving-kindness that the tree spirits vowed to serve the monks in all ways (Salzberg, 1997, p. 20). The implications of this story for psychotherapy is that the wise way to relate to fear is not to run away from it, but to face up to what is being feared with loving-kindness and to befriend it. Again, this Buddhist approach is similar to what behaviorist psychotherapy calls "systematic desensitization," except that it puts emphasis on love as an antidote to fear.

Mahatma Gandhi provides yet another example of how it works. An Indian father was excessively grieved by the murder of his son at the hand of a Muslim. To relieve his grief and hatred, mainstream psychotherapy would have resorted to ego-oriented approaches such as "getting even" with the murderer or some form of catharsis therapy that seeks vicarious outlets for the pent-up emotions. But Gandhi chose a transpersonal approach and advised the father to adopt a Muslim orphan and treat him as his own son. By so doing the Indian father learned to overcome his grief, hatred, and animosity with the power of love that transcends personal limits, and this was done through the seemingly impossible experience of caring for the enemy combined with the cognitive capacity that affirms the inner strength of love and compassion as a means of self-transcendence. Without the actual experience of caring for the orphan, there would be no existential base on which the potentials of love can be developed; and yet without a transpersonal perspective to affirm and recognize the positive power of love, mere experience may not go very far. Such a behaviorist approach of overcoming hatred by love through actual experience is exactly what the Buddha emphatically prescribed and practiced.

This implies that Buddhist psychotherapy expands the cognitive capacity far beyond the realm of ego-psychology. The need for self-esteem, which mainstream psychology sees as an important factor in mental health, can lead into the blind alley of narcissism if the self-esteem in question is too much ego-oriented. By contrast, Buddhist psychotherapy encourages the use of one's talents and skills in the service of others, thereby affirming a sense of self-worth and self-fulfillment which can have greater therapeutic effects than if the talents and skills are used to serve one's own interests. Moreover, Buddhist psychology recognizes that an important source of self-esteem rests with the affirmation of one's own transpersonal qualities such as loving-kindness, compassion, generosity, etc. Self-worth based on personal success and achievements can be a source of suffering, first because it is ego-oriented, and secondly because we so often meet with failures in our lives. On the other hand, self-worth based on love and other transpersonal qualities can bring greater happiness because it rises above the ego and is available to all of us at all times.

5.2. Buddhist Approach to Grief Counseling and Therapy

Like other religions, Buddhism offers effective grief therapy to people who suffer from the loss of loved ones, cancers and other kinds of personal misfortune. In these cases a strong faith in Amitabha Buddha (the Buddha of Infinite Light and Infinite Life), Bodhisattva Avalokitesvara (Goddess of Compassion, or Kuan Yin) or some other celestial Buddha/Bodhisattva (such as the Buddha of Medicine) is essential. Above all, the Pure Land School of Buddhism plays a vital role in helping devotees cope with grief and suffering. Through his compassionate vows and commitments to the salvation of sentient beings, Amitabha Buddha was experienced by ancient Buddhist sages as having created his Western Pure Land, where a devotee can have rebirth after death by virtue of pure faith, a strong will to be reborn there as well as persistent single-minded recitation of the sacred name of Amitabha Buddha.

Once spiritual communion with Lord Amitabha is established through faithful practice, the devotee feels secure about life and death. His fear of death and suffering of life are gone now that the promise of rebirth in the Pure Land is experienced and understood to be something real that will be honored by Lord Amitabha.

5.2.1. The Meaning of Infinite Life

While the Chinese Pure Land School emphasizes the ultimate goal of rebirth after death, Japanese Pure Land followers, many of them scholars with considerable intellectual breadth, appear more concerned about how the gospel of Pure Land can be brought to bear with the reality of this world. Faith in the Pure Land will be incomplete if the devotee is only concerned with what happens after death. After all, life and death cannot be seen as separate or antithetic to each other. So faith in the Pure Land should be able to help uncover the meaning of life and death, to see them as an integrated whole that signifies an infinite and eternal life that embraces all beings and is unaffected by the cycle of birth and death. The infinity of life also means that life and death are not simply a matter of the individuals seen as separate from one another, but a boundless cosmic network of interdependence that involves every one of us. If this new insight can be achieved, Pure Land is not just a vision for the future, but is with us here and now. The insight thus gained is not different from the insight gained through other Buddhist practices as we have discussed in the preceding sections of this chapter, except that it is the result of faith in Amitabha Buddha and His Pure Land – a devotional approach that distinguishes itself from other Buddhist schools.

Japanese scholar-monk Obata Bunsho points out that to appreciate the teachings of the Pure Land School, one needs to think about life in relation to death. In his view, those people who pursue the pleasure of life while pretending that death does not exist can never see the truth of life as expounded by the Pure Land School. The false perception of life as opposed to death is a source of suffering. Only when this opposition is transcended can one be reborn in the eternal bliss of the Pure Land. To develop such an insight, Obata has made many trips to India to experience the grim realities of life and death. The heart-rending scenes of corpses lying on Indian streets unattended by no one but flies, of dead bodies summarily cremated on the roadside, etc., serve as a vivid reminder of life's sufferings, and drive home a moral urgency to end the sufferings. He concludes that the only way out is to discover a "true new life" that is deeper and broader than the limited personal life, and the new life is possible only by "relying on the power of vows" of Amitabha Buddha. As he observes, "If we fail to be in touch with this power of vows, we are not really alive even if we have lived a hundred years. If we touch this power of vows, we obtain a true new life even though we have only ten or five more years to live"(Tashira, 1997, p. 126).

What distinguishes Buddhism from other religions is the Buddha's profound insight into the oneness of all beings living in an interrelated and interdependent universe. The Chinese Pure Land School seldom if ever expounds this cosmic truth, but Obata's discourse makes it clear that the understanding of Pure Land is not complete without taking the insight of a larger self into account. As he observes,

> *Life and death are not just the business of an individual. I need to explain this point again. People always say, "Death is my own business, and life is my own business." But the truth is that life and death go beyond our ego. We are in fact born and die in a much broader world. If we live and die all by ourselves, we fail to see how deep and broad life and death really are. As a result, we are unconcerned about others' lives, and we are unconcerned about their deaths also. We are not even concerned and critical about the death of modern society. If we cannot understand that our life and death are related to this broad world, and only live and die as an individual, then we plunge into the dark abyss of suffering, despair and loneliness, Therefore, it is imperative that we try to understand and show insight into the deep broad life that lies beyond our limited lives. I think this is the message I need to get across when I talk about rebirth in the Pure Land which is the teaching of Jodo Shinshu, True Pure Land School in Japan (Tashira, 1997, p. 128).*

5.2.2. How Pure Land Faith Helps Cancer Victims

There are many cases in which cancer victims face pain and death calmly without fear and distress because they have developed faith in the Pure Land. Another Japanese monk, Wada Kosho, tells a story of how Pure Land faith had supported his daughter, Keiko, a cancer victim, and helped her to live her final years with complete dignity. An enlightening lesson we learn from this case is that the hope of rebirth in the Pure Land is not accompanied by a desire to abandon the painful body and the hopeless life. On the contrary, Keiko repeatedly wrote in her diary about how she appreciated her "good life" in spite of her fatal disease, and she encouraged her children to follow her example of 'Buddha reciting"(repeated chanting of Amitabha Buddha's name) so that they could "meet again in the Pure Land." Religious faith is not just a spiritual opiate to soothe pain and distress; it is also a source of inner strength that enables the patient to face pain and distress with bravery and equanimity. Shortly before Keiko died, she wrote her father a New Year card, which read: "Peaceful time has gone by, so have sorrow and joy, and the good days that I so cherish. The coming New Year will be filled with the same joy, warmth and sorrow. How wonderful life is! With my heart filled with peace, I wish to extend to you, dear dad and mom, my heartfelt gratitude. I thank you for helping me to live out a beautiful and good life. Your dear daughter will be waiting for you in the Pure Land" (Tashira, 1997, pp. 28-29).

Venerable Wada concludes his discourse with the following message: "As Keiko's father, I can accept her death with calm and equanimity because my heart is full of fond hope that we will meet again soon in that world." And he adds that Keiko's wish to wait for dad and mom in the Pure Land was not empty words. "If someone says he will meet you at Nagoya Station, he must be there, otherwise it would be a lapse of courtesy. He who promises to meet you somewhere will certainly be there. My daughter promised to wait for us in the Pure Land, so she will be there. She is waiting in the Pure Land. This is a fact for sure." Buddhism believes that vows and will are self-fulfilling. And who is going to doubt that Venerable Wada and her daughter will meet again in the Pure Land?

6. THE POWER OF SURRENDER BY FAITH

There has been much debate as to whether Buddhist practice should rely on "self power" (i.e., the practitioner's own efforts) or "other power" (spiritual empowerment by the Buddhas). Zen Buddhism is clearly based on "self power" in the sense that Zen practitioners relies on their own mental discipline to develop the potentials for enlightenment rather than praying the Buddhas for spiritual empowerment. On the other hand, the Pure Land School considers liberation to be a grace from Amitabha Buddha and devout praying to Amitabha Buddha with faith and trust is essential for salvation. Pure Land masters criticize Zen practitioners for unrealistically over-estimating the human capacity to achieve the supra-human goal of spiritual liberation. Conversely, the Pure Land practice is criticized for neglecting the mundane world and for its attachments to rebirth after death. A middle-of-the-road position argues that "other power" and "self power" complement each other, and that the former has to work through the latter. A similar debate can also be found in Christian circles as to whether salvation depends on grace alone, good work alone or a combination of both.

From the perspective of religious psychology, a crucial point is often missing in these arguments: The essence of the "other power" approach consists in the total surrendering of the practitioner to that power. The emphasis on "other power" should not be taken to mean that "self-power" is not important. Rather, it should be understood as a convenient way to let go of the ego through faith in the divine power of Amitabha Buddha. When Pure Land masters warn against the use of "self power" to achieve enlightenment, they are in effect warning against the possibility that the self-righteous egoistic tendencies associated with "self power" can compromise the ability of the practitioner to surrender himself.

The reactive pattern of craving and aversion that we have discussed above is a primary hindrance to all spiritual progress. Even our inner striving for progress, for making a difference from what we are, is part of that mechanism, and is therefore, paradoxically, an obstacle to progress. The ability to surrender in spiritual practice means the ability to let go of that reactive pattern. In the Pure Land practice, as in other spiritual traditions, salvation through faith is achieved only when the faith and trust in the divine power inspire the practitioner to surrender himself or herself totally, to give up his or her craving for gains and fear of losses, and to be free from all egoistic tendencies. If one can surrender oneself this way, life poses no problems at all, and one is always grateful for whatever happens, be it bad health or bad fortune. In many cases, surrendering, coupled with faith and trust in the divine power, brings about a miraculous cure of illnesses.* The Pure Land practice of surrender by faith is similar to evangelical Christians' belief in salvation through total surrender to Christ. In both cases, spiritual transformation or regeneration is made possible by grace through faith and surrender.

---

* The Chinese Pure Land School does not seem to pay attention to the psychological principle of surrendering. William James, however, presents an insightful discussion of how Christianity and the mind-cure movement in the West attached importance to surrendering as a means to salvation. See Lectures IV and V on mind-cure movement in James' well-known work *Varieties of Religious Experience*. New York: Modern Library, 1994.

A Buddhist case of surrender by faith is offered by a Japanese college teacher named Kawamura Toshiko (Tashira, 1997, pp. 70-71). She testified how surrender through Pure Land faith helped her to overcome sufferings from stomach cancer and intestine cancer. She said, "I entrusted everything to Lord Amitabha Buddha as I was faced with the painful moment of truth for the first time in my life. When I genuinely surrendered my life and death to Lord Amitabha Buddha, I experienced tremendous joy and happiness."

According to Master Shinran (1173-1262), founder of the True Pure Land School in Japan, Amitabha Buddha promises by His vow that "salvation is bound to come; just keep faith with your whole heart and rejoice in it." Kawamura's response to this vow and promise is: "Thank you! I surrender myself to you with my whole heart." (Tashira, 1997, p. 67) It sounds so simple! The simplicity of practice seems to befit the illiterate simple-minded country folks, and yet beneath the apparent simplicity there must be faith, wisdom and love that make genuine surrendering of one's life and death possible.

7. CONCLUSION

Suffering in the Buddhist sense is rooted in man's primordial ignorance and delusion that gives rise to the reactive psychological mechanism of clinging and rejecting, craving and aversion. This mechanism covers a whole range of mental defilements and negativities, such as greed, craving, hatred, anger, animosity, fear, jealousy, etc., which Buddhism sees as depriving a human being of his inner freedom and mental well-being. Thus in dealing with suffering, Buddhism does not simply aim at relieving suffering to make people feel better, but more importantly, at freeing the mind from the bondage of delusion and the conditioning of blind impulses. To end suffering is equivalent to breaking through the bondage of delusion and the conditioning mechanism so that one can become the master of his own mind and affirm the meaning of his existence marked by mental serenity, joy, love and compassion. This ultimate concern of human existence is now recognized by transpersonal psychology and existential psychology in the West.

A convenient approach to ending suffering is through faith in the Pure Land. The goal of the Pure Land practice is not only rebirth in the paradise after death, but rather to create a "pure land" in the heart and mind, a "pure land" out of the impure mundane world just as a pure lotus rises out of the dirty mud. The Pure Land faith should help the practitioner to gain a new insight that his or her life runs deeper and broader than he or she has known – an infinite life that transcends our ego consciousness of life and death. Embracing this infinity enables the practitioner to take life's pain and suffering in stride.

Furthermore, the secret of the Pure Land faith, like other spiritual traditions, lies in the readiness to surrender oneself to the divine power of Amitabha Buddha. Surrendering implies first and foremost the letting go of the reactive pattern of craving for gains and fear of losses, along with all egoistic and narcissistic tendencies. The ability to surrender oneself in this way is the key to spiritual salvation, and the process of surrendering is facilitated by faith and trust in "other power" (the divine power of Amitabha Buddha). With surrendering, one is able to see that life poses no problems even in the face of extreme difficulties. In many cases, surrendering helps cure or alleviate pain, suffering and physical illnesses. But again, the Pure Land faith is ultimately concerned not with the temporary relief of pain and suffering, but with spiritual liberation and salvation as we have discussed above.

The Buddhist approach to coping can be regarded as transformational or transformative coping (Wong, Wong & Scott, Chapter 1), because the focus is on personal transformation through mental self-discipline and/or surrender to a higher power. The resulting transformation extends far beyond cognitive reframing or cognitive restructuring, because it permeates one's basic values, attitudes and worldviews. It can be a powerful approach to coping if one is prepared to undertake the necessary moral and mental disciplines, even if only in connection with a course on Buddhist meditation. Many stressors automatically disappear as one embarks on the process of mental purification. It needs to be re-emphasized, however, that while in this Buddhist approach coping with suffering is a legitimate goal for reasons we have elaborated in this chapter, coping with daily stress is not necessarily so, unless we are prepared to address the issue of stress on the same philosophical footing as Buddhism addresses *dukkha* (suffering). A Buddhist meditation teacher would decline to accept students who are solely motivated by a desire to reduce stress and enhance well-being, for the simple reason that the goal of liberation requires a strong commitment and determination to change one's basic values and attitudes, and that a desire for gains is regarded as a hindrance to progress on the path leading to spiritual liberation. Ideally, the Buddhist approach to coping with suffering is an end in itself rather than a means to curing and healing, which is considered only as a by-product. Although one can simply employ some aspects of the Buddhist approach, such as mindful meditation, as a way of coping with stress, it is essential to remember that effective coping in this context embraces the Buddhist values and attitudes. In the process, one's life can be transformed and enriched by exploring the integration between coping efforts and the spiritual insights of Buddhism.

REFERENCES

Chen, Y.-H. (2004). "The Buddha on Compassion: An Existential Approach," in *Positive Living E-Zine*, International Network on Personal Meaning, Posted March, at http://www.meaning.ca.

Goenka, S. N. (1992). *The Discourse Summaries for Vipassana Meditation*. India: Vipassana Vishodhan Vinyas

Goleman, D. (1980). "Mental Health in Classical Buddhist Psychology," in Roger Walsh and Frances Vaughan, ed., *Beyond Ego: Transpersonal Dimensions in Psychology*. Los Angeles: J. P. Tarcher, Inc.

Keown, D. (1996). *Buddhism: A Very Short Introduction*, Oxford University Press.

Levine, M. (2000). *The Positive Psychology of Buddhism and Yoga: Paths to a Mature Happiness*. Mahwah, NJ: Lawrence Erlbaum Associates.

Moacanin, R. (2003). *The Essence of Jung's Psychology and Tibetan Buddhism*, Boston: Wisdom Publications.

Salzberg, S. (1997). Loving Kindness: The Revolutionary Art of Happiness. Boston: Shambhala.

Stein, J. (2003)."The Science of Meditation," cover story, *Time Magazine*. August 4.

Sutra Translation Committee of the US and Canada (1998). *The Seeker's Glossary of Buddhism* (New York, San Francisco and Toronto).

Suzuki, D. T. (1988). *An Introduction to Zen Buddhism*, London: Rider and Co.

Tashira, S. (Ed.) (1997). *Hearts Feeling Life and Death and Buddhism* (Chinese version translated by Kuo Min-chun). Taipei: Tung-ta Books.

Thynn, T. (1997). *Living Meditation, Living Insight: The Path of Mindfulness in Daily Life*. Buddhist Association of the United States.

Rahula, Walpola Sri (1972). *What the Buddha Taught*, Grove/Atlantic, Inc.

Welwood, J. (2000). *Toward A Psychology of Awakening*. Boston: Shambhala Publications.

Welwood, J. (1983). *Awakening the Heart: East-West Approaches to Psychotherapy and the Healing Relationship*. Boston: Shambhala Publications.

THE WAY OF NATURE AS A HEALING POWER

Yu-Hsi Chen

1. INTRODUCTION

The philosophy of Taoism is well known to have espoused a natural way of life. The Way of nature is defined as one of simplicity, authenticity, and spontaneity. Throughout the Chinese history, "return to a genuine and simple way of life" has been held as an idealistic vision for those who are fed up with the vanity of worldly affairs and as a way of coping with the hardships in life. Taoism, along with Buddhism and Confucianism, has remained an influential philosophy that enables the Chinese to bear the unbearable and attain a sense of well-being in the midst of suffering. The strength of Taoism is that it not only teaches a philosophy of life on how to live a contented, serene life regardless of circumstances, but also prescribes physical and breathing exercises that reduce stress and enhance physical and mental well-being. Therefore, Taoism has much to offer to psychologists in the West regarding the oriental wisdom of coping with stress.

1.1. Basic Concepts of Taoism

In identifying Taoism with "the Way of nature," a word of clarification is needed. The Chinese word *Tao* literally means the "Way"—the ultimate creative principle that gives birth to the entire universe. According to Lao-tzu, the founding philosopher-sage of Taoism, *Tao* is beyond all thinking and description, without image or form, but he nevertheless identifies a number of the spiritual properties of *Tao* for the purpose of teaching. Among them are the qualities of being selfless, simple, authentic, and spontaneous. As far as function is concerned, *Tao* creates and nourishes everything in the Cosmos, and yet It appears to "do nothing" (*wu wei* in Chinese), which means that *Tao*, being spontaneous, has no intent or impulse to strive, to act, and to react as we humans do; It simply allows things to take their own courses. Paradoxically, because It takes no action, It is the source of all actions. And because It does nothing, there is nothing It cannot do. Rather than identifying *Tao* with God, Lao-tzu refers to It as "the Way of nature." But here the concept of "nature" not only means the great Cosmos, but also includes our true nature – the Origin

Yu-Hsi Chen, Fo Guang College of Humanities and Social Sciences of our life. By letting go of our ego in a mental state of "do nothing," Lao-tzu teaches, we can achieve perfect "tranquility" and access our Origin, thereby attaining serenity, wisdom, and enlightenment (Lao-tzu, trans., 2000, chapter 16).

Thus, the Way of nature as expounded by Taoism goes deeper and broader than a matter of life style. Among other things, it brings forth the insight that all things in the universe exist in polarity (or duality), with the two opposites in a polarity complementing each other and making the existence of each other possible. For example, goodness cannot exist without evil; and as Lao-tzu observes, "Fortune owes its existence to misfortune, and misfortune is hidden in fortune"(Lao-tzu, trans., 2000, chapter 58). With this insight one will not be overwhelmed by the vicissitudes of life, and the ups and downs of human affairs. As the psychologist Swami Ajaya (1997) says, "In Taoism it is believed that when one is unaware that the two sides of a polarity support one another to form a whole, he identifies with only one side of the polarity. This in turn leads to suffering and self-destruction. But understanding how the two poles support one another leads to a peaceful and integrated life" (Ajaya, 1997, p. 45).

In *Tao Te Ching,* the main text that embodies Lao-tzu's teachings, it is explained that "when the world knows beauty as beauty, without knowing that it depends upon its opposite, i.e., ugliness, then beauty turns out to be ugly. Similarly, when people know goodness as goodness, without knowing that it co-exists with evil, goodness tends to become evil" (Lao-tzu, trans., 2000, chapter 2). This teaching has profound implications for both mundane affairs and psychotherapy. When psychologists talk about "unconditional acceptance" as a crucial approach to emotional disorders, it is necessary to recognize that the failure to accept oneself and others is at least partly rooted in a judgmental, discriminative mentality in connection with polarity. Just consider how many people are emotionally troubled by a negative self-image that they do not look good or pretty. This problem is epitomized by a girl student in Asia who committed suicide years ago because she had reportedly failed in her attempts to lose weight and to beautify her face. Other suicide cases can be traced to a similar root cause that the victims cannot accept their failures one way or another. How often everyone of us feels frustrated or distressed simply because we cling to our preconceptions of success, good fortune, etc. while rejecting their opposites. If only we can accept the polarity of beauty and ugliness, success and failure, etc. as a unity, as Lao-tzu teaches, a lot of mental problems can be effectively avoided.

1.2. Following the Cosmic Pattern of Change

Taoism also explains this unified polarity as a dynamic of change. According to Lao-tzu, cosmic change takes place in a cyclical or circular pattern in which everything eventually reverts to its opposite. When misfortune reaches the limit, good fortune comes around, and the extreme of adversity ushers in prosperity in the same fashion as winter gives way to spring. So to live by the Way of nature means to understand and accept this pattern of circular change with equanimity in all circumstances. Thus, we choose not to be complacent over success, and not to lose heart over failure. As Alan Watts (1969) says of Taoism, "The sage no more seeks to obliterate the negative – darkness, death, etc. – than to get rid of autumn and winter from the cycle of the seasons. There emerges, then, a view of life which sees its worth and point not as a struggle for constant ascent but as a dance. Virtue and harmony consist, not in accentuating the positive, but in maintaining a dynamic balance" (p. 54). In contrast, Western thinking tends to favor a mechanical opposition of the positive against the negative. "By and large Western culture is the celebration of the illusion that good may exist without evil, light without darkness, and pleasure without pain, and this is true of both its Christian and secular, technological phases" (Ajaya, 1997, p. 48).

This Taoist concept of change is also seen as related to the post-modernist thinking in the West. Since cosmic things are constantly changing and related to one another, no truth can be considered as fixed or constant. What we see as true depends upon a particular frame of reference of time and space, and upon a specific perspective. When the frame of reference and the perspective shift, truth takes on a different face. This insight helps people readjust their rigid ways of thinking; the stereotypes that see things in a self-righteous, uncompromising way, as a result, bring on conflicts and suffering. How often we identify ourselves with a particular label or role, such as "I am a CEO", and take pride in it. Certainly it gives us self-esteem that we so desperately need. But consider how many people suffer from depression – and even end up in suicide – just because the vicissitudes of life suddenly deprive them of a label or role with which they have so dearly identified. An American author calls this "King Lear syndromes" – a mental health problem resulting from the sudden loss of power, privileges or positions, or a fall from grace. (Remember that King Lear became crazy after giving up power to his daughters). Keeping the insights of Taoism in perspective, we can allow for change in personal fortune, thereby learning to take things in stride when the change takes place.

2. CONTENTMENT AS A WAY OF NATURE

The perspective of Taoism not only enables people to cope with change and negative events with equanimity, but also shows them the path to happiness even when things go bad. Different from Western psychologists who focus on reactive coping and stress reduction, Taoism focuses on proactive coping, transcendence, and stress transformation. By adopting the Taoist way of thinking, we not only become free from worries and anxieties, but also achieve serenity and contentment.

Contentment in the Taoist sense means to be satisfied with what we have and to refrain from excessive desires for fame, wealth, pleasure, and other worldly possessions. From the psychological perspective, contentment refers to a state of mind in which the potential psychic energy known as libido in Western psychology is "transformed" to serve a higher purpose rather than actualized as a desire that needs to be "gratified" or repressed. In this way, contentment is accompanied by a sense of fulfillment and abundance. That is probably why Lao-tzu says that "those who know contentment are enriched." And he speaks of contentment on the same footing as self-knowledge and self-conquest: "Those who know themselves are enlightened" and "those who conquer themselves are strong" (Lao-tzu, trans., 2000, chapter 33). Furthermore, if contentment comes from the conquest of greed, craving and desire, it must also be present under adverse circumstances. Where contentment is, there cannot be hatred, anger, fear, aversion, and other negativities. In this sense, contentment is close to the Buddhist concepts of sympathetic joy and equanimity.

Taoist sages Lao-tzu and Chuang-tzu inculcate that craving for fame and wealth often results in moral depravity, and in many cases personal destruction. As Lao-tzu warns, "The greatest of woes comes from not knowing contentment; the greatest of faults comes from craving for gains"(Lao-tzu, trans., 2000, chapter 46). He argues that the nature of humanity, and for that matter, of all creatures, is to live in a simple and plain way, no more than what is needed to maintain the healthy growth of the organism. Beyond that limit one gets involved in "selfish craving" and "extravagance" that cause him to lose his genuine simplicity and spontaneity. Therefore, "A sage is free from excessive pursuit, extravagance and arrogance" (Lao-tzu, trans., 2000, chapters 19 and 29). From Lao-tzu's perspective, a sage is simply someone who lives according to his authentic nature – simplicity and spontaneity. This is an integral part of *Tao* – the great Way of nature. Alienation from *Tao* is seen as the root cause of all human problems.

Chuang-tzu picked up the same theme and uses a vivid analogy to get across the message that contentment is in the very nature of all living beings. "Amid the exuberance of woods, a bird needs only one branch to build its nest," he wrote. "And from the broad expanse of a deep river, a mouse drinks only enough to fill its stomach"(Wang, 1998, p. 145). Therefore, Chuang-tzu suggested that a human being could be happy with just a minimum of material means.

What are the implications of this Taoist thinking for modern people? First of all, one may raise the question that, unlike animals, human needs to extend far beyond the physiological realm to cover psychological, emotive, and spiritual needs. Even physical needs change as civilization progresses. For example, people in some Asian countries were content with riding on a bicycle several decades ago, but today driving a car has become a necessity. Does it make sense to compare human needs to the needs of a bird or a mouse? Do we have to give up the material amenities and comforts of modern civilization if we take the Taoist teaching seriously?

To be sure, ancient Taoists believed that simplicity of the mind could not be separated from simplicity of the life style. But the essence of the Taoist teaching is probably not that human needs are comparable to the needs of animals, but that we humans, like animals, can and should live a simple, spontaneous way of life by freeing ourselves from greed and craving for more than we need, regardless of how we define "need" in different social and cultural contexts. In their writings, the Taoist sages dwell upon the harmfulness of greed as it can impoverish people morally and spiritually. On the other hand, "those who know contentment are enriched," and "a contented person always lives in abundance" (Lao-tzu, trans., 2000, chapters 33 and 46).

While Buddhism also emphasizes contentment, it does not see material simplicity as a necessary condition. The Buddhist insight into simplicity and spontaneity centers around the transcendental quality of non-attachment and non-reactivity. Buddhist psychology has discovered a human potential for self-actualization neglected by Western psychology, that is, the potential to free the mind from its habitual pattern of grasping and rejecting, and of craving and aversion – a psychological mechanism seen as the root cause of mental suffering. A well-attained Buddhist can live in material abundance and yet keep his or her mind "detached," i.e., free from craving for material possession. This means that he or she will be just as contented and happy if he or she has to live in poverty. From the Buddhist perspective, this insight of non-attachment and non-reactivity is the source of blissful contentment. It also suggests that the Western concept of "gratification of desires" can cover up the subtle psychological mechanism of attachment to what is desired, and as the Buddhist sees it, it is precisely this emotive attachment that causes mental suffering. If so, gratification of desires does not ensure happiness, but on the contrary, it can lead to unhappiness and suffering if attachment to desires becomes very strong. In Buddhism as in Taoism, the energy of desires can be "transformed" into a higher spiritual quality so that neither "gratification" nor repression is necessary.

The traditional Freudian psychology is not concerned with greed or desire as a morbidity that can lead to emotive disorders and mental suffering. Instead, it hypothesizes that the gratification of desires is a necessary condition for mental health and happiness. Viktor Frankl's (2000) logotherapy has offered an insightful challenge to this Freudian view, arguing that the key to mental health and happiness lies in discovering the meaning of life, not in the pursuit of gratification of desires. According to Frankl, what people really need is "the will to meaning" rather than "the will to pleasure." Although logotherapy does not talk about contentment as Taoism does, it concurs with Taoism that the pursuit of pleasure or happiness can only result in unhappiness. This is so because the sensations of pleasure or happiness quickly diminish and revert to its opposites in accordance with the cosmic law of change, and also because such a pursuit inevitably gives rise to aversion and rejection to what is seen as unpleasant or unhappy. Logotherapy explains that happiness can only come as a by-product of working for a good cause that confers meaning. Taoism prescribes contentment as a reliable source of happiness.

3. "DO NOTHING" AS A WAY OF COPIING

3.1. Integrating the Opposites

The art of "do nothing" as a way of coping stems from Taoist basic understanding of duality of nature. Starting from simplicity, the Way of nature embraces the entire cosmic complexity in great harmony – in the integrated whole. The two opposites of a dualistic pair are seen as balancing and complementing each other. Thus to the Taoist, the cycle of life and death is as natural as the cycle of day and night, and fortune and misfortune embrace each other. With this insight in view, contentment is possible even under extreme adverse circumstances. When Chuang-tzu's wife died, for example, he grieved at first, but then beat a drum in joyous celebration. When his friend criticized him for this bizarre behavior, he explained that death was merely an extension of life, with each complementing the other; and if life was worth celebrating, so was death.

3.2. The Importance of "Do Nothing"

When the negative and the positive are seen as an integrated whole in harmony, life has no problems at all. All problems are created by humans out of ignorance of the Way of nature. So Taoism teaches that we need not worry about anything. "Has a bird ever worried about its food for tomorrow?" the Taoist asks. Just relax and let go, and things will take care of themselves. Lao-tzu's motto of "do nothing" (wu-wei in Chinese) means that a wise person knows how to let go of his or her personal will and desires, to surrender his or her impulse to strive for gains, be it good health or good fortune, and to allow nature to take its own course. In Tao Te Ching, "do nothing" is a recurring theme for self-cultivation. For example, in the chapter entitled "wu wei" (do nothing), Lao-tzu teaches, "Tao is always doing nothing, and yet there is nothing It cannot do. If government leaders know how to grasp this principle, all things will take care of themselves" (Lao-tzu, trans., chapter 37). In Lao-tzu's view, the virtue of "do nothing" is cultivated through learning the Tao, the Truth of life, thereby letting go of the ego's will and impulse. Here is how he explains,

In pursuing academic knowledge, we gain something each day. What we gain is knowledge, and with it our ego's desires. In pursuing the Tao, we lose something each day. What we lose is our ego's desires. We lose and lose, until finally we learn the virtue of wu wei (do nothing). Do nothing, and there is nothing you cannot do. If you aspire to govern the country, you must learn the art of "no business," namely, the principle of non-interference. If you interfere too much, there is no way you can govern (Lao-tzu, trans., 2000, chapter 48; True Tao, trans., 2004, chapter 48).

The importance of this teaching on "do nothing" for spiritual cultivation and personal development cannot be exaggerated. What can spiritual liberation mean if not the liberation from our psychological impulse to strive to be different from what we are, or liberation from the aforesaid mechanism of craving and rejecting? Furthermore, it also has invaluable implications for modern psychotherapy, first because we know that emotive disorders are often closely related to the impulse of striving, and secondly because the art of "do nothing" has proved efficacious for the treatments of not only emotive disorders, but also physical illnesses.

There is a striking parallelism between Taoist teaching of "do nothing" and William James' (1999) description of cases in which illnesses were miraculously cured by "passive relaxation," by letting go of "the tension of their personal will", and surrendering to a "greater Self".

As James (1999) explains,

Passivity, not activity; relaxation, not intentness, should be now the rule. Give up the feeling of responsibility, let go your hold, resign the care of your destiny to higher powers, be genuinely indifferent as to what becomes of it all, and you will find not only that you gain a perfect inward relief, but often also, in addition, the particular goods you sincerely thought you were renouncing. This is the salvation through self-despair, the dying to be truly born, of Lutheran theology, the passage into nothing of which Jacob Behman writes (p. 125).

Salvation is available to all who know how to surrender their personal will to a greater power, be it God or the *Tao*. It is in this connection that we discover that Taoism, for all its unique Oriental mysticism, shares a common basic belief with Western religion. "Salvation through faith" applies to Christianity as well as to Taoism, the crux being that faith in the Truth should inspire one to surrender himself or herself totally to the Truth. In Christianity, surrender to Christ by faith leads to rebirth by grace – a new life with new hope and meaning. In Taoism, surrender brings about serenity and contentment in accord with the cosmic Truth.

3.3. Taoism and Western Psychotherapy

Some Western psychologists and psychotherapists have drawn inspirations from the Taoist philosophy in innovating their therapeutic approaches. One example is the rational-emotive-behavioral therapy (REBT) developed by Albert Ellis (2004), which focuses on the irrational, inflexible, and self-defeating patterns of thinking as a major cause of emotional troubles. This approach to psychotherapy argues that it is not adverse circumstances, but rather people's attitudes and reactions to these circumstances, that cause distress and suffering. Very often one is emotionally upset by the irrational preconception that if he or she fails to do something well, he or she will be disgraced, will become worthless, etc. Partly based on ancient wisdom, including that of Taoism, REBT teaches clients how to develop flexibility in thinking, and to look at their problems from a broader new angle. In short, all is in flux, so our thinking should be allowed to flow rather than stagnate. This is the Way of nature – and the Taoist secret to overcoming suffering.

As far as psychotherapy is concerned, the art of "do nothing" can prove to be extremely effective in treating stress-related disorders and is worth further exploration by Western psychology. This art is similar to the approach of "unconditional acceptance" being used by several schools of Western psychotherapy, including humanist psychology, existential psychology, REBT and yoga psychology. The concept of unconditional acceptance is based on the assumption that neurotic problems are often related to the patient's refusal to accept certain aspects of himself or herself that he or she consciously or unconsciously regards as bad, unfortunate, ugly, inferior, etc. The therapist aims to help the patient understand that this negative self-image is not based on reality and that his or her problems will be relieved once he or she learns to accept the unwanted aspects of his or her experience. The point is to let go, to befriend oneself, and to surrender the impulse to strive to be different from what one is. As Swami Ajaya (1997) aptly observes:

> As with a Chinese finger lock, the more one struggles, the more he becomes entrapped. Paradoxically, when one accepts himself, he becomes more fluid, and begins to change. The way out of this client's conflict is not to struggle to become a success, but to accept all aspects of himself. The ultimate goal in this case is to transcend the polarized conception of success and failure...

> The client comes to therapy disowning the parts of himself that he considers unacceptable. He believes that those unacceptable aspects of himself create his suffering, but it is actually his non-acceptance and disowning of aspects of himself that create all the melodramas and unhappiness in his life. When one accepts the unwanted parts of himself, they cease to dominate him. The yoga therapy, therefore, encourages the client to acknowledge all aspects of himself (Ajaya, 1997, p. 230).

Ajaya (1997) is of the opinion that "all psychotherapeutic methods are insignificant in comparison with the expression of unconditional acceptance." If we can befriend and accept ourselves unconditionally, pain and suffering will serve a useful function and lead to significant growth (p. 230, & p. 233). Psychotherapeutic research has found that many mental and psychosomatic problems feed upon themselves through the patients' rejection of these problems, and as a result bring on increasing pain and suffering. If a patient learns to let go and accept his own problems with equanimity, he will be relieved of his suffering, and in many cases the problems can also be alleviated or cured. One highly intriguing discovery in this regard is that self-esteem or self-worth, which psychologists in general consider as crucial for healing purpose, can turn out to be an illusory preoccupation that stands in the way of healing rather than facilitating it. By surrendering the preoccupation with self-esteem, the patient can feel a blissful relief and have his emotional troubles resolved. Ajaya, for example, has dramatically demonstrated in his clinical work that a neurotic client could be counseled to accept that it is okay to be "unworthy," that one does not have to become "worthy." In the end, the client felt he could relax and no longer had to defend himself. As one client put it, "If I accept my unworthiness, there won't be anything to feel unworthy about, so I'll feel worthy" (Ajaya, 1997, pp. 231-232).

Ajaya is not alone in challenging the Western value of self-esteem. Renowned psychologist Albert Ellis (2005) also makes the point that self-esteem based on personal success and accomplishments is dangerous and counterproductive, and that USA (unconditional self-acceptance) is the right way to change the patient's problematic belief system that causes him emotional troubles. Ellis (2005) has even come up with the view that "self-esteem is a sickness" and that one can learn not to let self-esteem become a problem.* Of course, he does not mean that self-esteem is not important. He means that preoccupation with self-esteem causes trouble, and that one can get rid of the trouble by learning to accept oneself unconditionally. With unconditional self-acceptance, whether one is worthy or unworthy becomes an irrelevant question.

3.4. The Psychology of Self-Acceptance

The question is: how can unconditional self-acceptance be started when those who most need to practice it are people entrapped in low self-esteem that leaves no room for befriending and accepting themselves? Taoism has never answered this question, because it seems to assume that neuroses do not exist, and that human nature is in accord with the *Tao*, which embraces and accepts everything. Unfortunately, human situations are far more complex than meet the eye. The *Tao* is not readily accessible to common people. Modern psychotherapy, starting with Carl Rogers (1995a, b), places the responsibility on the therapist for showing unconditional acceptance to the client. If the client feels that he is being unconditionally accepted, he will learn to develop the capacity to accept himself too. As Ajaya observes, "To the extent that the therapist can express and the client can experience unconditional acceptance, growth and healing take place; to the extent that acceptance by the therapist is lacking, growth and healing are restricted" (Ajaya, 1997, p. 230). Some Western psychologists with a larger spiritual perspective have developed unique clinical techniques, along with a personal commitment to unconditional acceptance of clients, to help the clients learn to accept themselves. But the question remains as to how many therapists are prepared to accept unconditionally neurotic patients with a personality and character that are hardly acceptable to most people.

This was the dilemma that Buddhist psychologist John Welwood (2000) encountered when he was a graduate student in psychology. He says that he was intrigued and puzzled by Carl Rogers's term "unconditional positive regard." "Although it sounded appealing as an ideal therapeutic stance, I found it hard to put into practice. First of all, there was no specific training for it. And since Western psychology had not provided me any understanding of heart, or the intrinsic goodness underlying psychopathology, I was unclear just where unconditional positive regard should be directed." Welwood explains that it was only after turning to the Oriental meditative traditions that "I came to appreciate the unconditional goodness at the core of being human, and this in turn helped me understand the possibility of unconditional love and its role in the healing process" (Welwood, 2000, p. 165).

---

* Albert Ellis will discuss the idea that "self-esteem is a sickness" in a workshop scheduled for April, 2005. See the Workshops and Lectures section of the Albert Ellis Institute on website, www.rebt.org.

It is at this point that Welwood finds it vitally important to integrate the meditative traditions with Western psychology. Through his own experience as a Buddhist meditative practitioner, he discovers the "unconditional presence" of a true being at the core of the human unconscious. The presence of this "true self beyond ego" is unconditional in the sense that it is unaffected by all adverse circumstances and all neurotic conditions, in the same fashion as the sun and the blue sky are never disturbed by the turmoil of dark clouds and storms. According to Welwood (2000), the true self is the ultimate source of *maitri* (Sanskrit word for unconditional friendliness or loving-kindness) that makes it possible for us to be unconditional with ourselves, no matter what we are going through. Cultivating *maitri* through meditation and other Buddhist practice shows us the way to befriend our emotions and the unwanted aspects of ourselves, to let them be as they are.

Paradoxically, without an awareness of *maitri* to begin with, the power of *maitri* cannot grow. Meditation is not a mechanical process through which something called *maitri* is produced; it is a dialectical process in which the practice of *maitri* feeds upon itself to reproduce more *maitri*. This means that in meditation we make an effortless effort to surrender ourselves, to let things be and to be non-judgmental about whatever is being experienced, be it pleasant sensations or unpleasant ones. In terms of Taoism, the art of "do nothing" does not come out of nothing, but is cultivated through practicing it in meditation and in everyday life, with the *Tao,* the Way of nature that includes our true nature as our guide.

4. TAOIST MEDITATION AND HEALING

4.1. Mind-Body Integration

This leads us to examine the role that Taoist meditation plays in the healing process. Traditional Taoist masters have developed the techniques of meditation that are similar to the Buddhist meditation in style. In addition to sitting, Taoists also practice moving exercises such as *Tai Chi Chuan* and other kinds of vital energy exercises (*chi kung or Qigong*). Unlike Buddhism, which emphasizes cultivation of the mind to develop liberating insights, Taoism seeks to integrate the body and the mind in its spiritual practice, with the belief that the spiritual energy known as *chi* connects humans with the *Tao*, or the ultimate essence of the great Cosmos, and therefore the cultivation of *chi* through breathing exercise is the very first step on the path. Like some schools of Buddhist meditation, the Taoist approach emphasizes concentration of the mind, mostly on a spot about one or two inches below the navel. Known as *tan tien* (literally elixir field), this bodily spot is believed to be the energy center where the rudimentary energy of *ching* (literally sperm, which seems to refer to certain endocrinal secretions and other bio-chemicals that produce the sperm) can be "refined" into the vital energy called *chi*. The vital energy circulates through the "energy channels" (*ching mai*) of the body and can be further transmuted into the "divine energy" (*shen*) if meditation is practiced earnestly and properly. The "divine energy" brings the practitioner into spiritual union with the cosmic power and is therefore the source of psychic power, wisdom, and longevity. Continuing "refinery" of the divine energy gives rise to the elixir of life (*tan* or *yao*) that transforms a human into a celestial immortal, according to the traditional Taoist literature.

While celestial immortal has largely remained a legend, the Taoist meditative practice has significant empirical relevance. First of all, it shows that spiritual attainments need a solid physical and physiological foundation – a point which Buddhism does not bother to explore probably for fear of becoming attached to the ego. The Tantric yoga tradition in India has concurred with Taoism in developing a sophisticated system of practice integrating mind and body, which fully recognizes the importance of endocrinal secretions, neurotransmitters, and perhaps other types of bio-chemical energy for the purpose of spiritual transformation. Both the Taoist and the yoga traditions emphasize the fact that consuming the bio-chemical energy for sexual pleasure is devastating for spiritual practice, and that properly guided practice can channel internal secretions into spiritual energy for a higher purpose so that sexual impulse is automatically "transformed" without having to be gratified or suppressed. There is ample documented evidence that throughout the Chinese history, numerous Taoist and Buddhist masters had successfully "transformed" their sexual energy while demonstrating great physical vigor. It is not uncommon that successful Taoist practitioners have their sexual organs shrunk as a sure sign of energy transformation and transmutation.** The point here is that the Taoist practice, like its counterpart in the yoga tradition, seems to provide a scientific guidance that can assist practitioners in building physical health and mental serenity while avoiding sexual violations that are said to be widespread among religious celibates the world over.

According to the Taoist tradition, the first stage of successful practice is achieved when the vital energy of *chi* developed from the energy center begins to flow through the two major channels in the front and back of the body respectively. This flowing is not accomplished automatically, however. The practitioner needs to skillfully direct and guide the energy flow with his power of attention. This accomplishment, known as the "small heavenly cycle," is said to ensure an automatic cure of old ailments as well as a marked improvement of general health conditions, both physical and mental. A higher stage of successful practice is achieved when the vital energy continues to flow into various minor channels throughout the body. This is called the completion of the "big heavenly cycle," which reportedly makes the practitioner immune to all illnesses and capable of living a long and healthy life. Further advanced practice will lead to the formation of the radiant elixir of life, which is essential for the ultimate cosmic union and spiritual transformation.

4.2. Tranquility as a Healing Force

In *Tao Te Ching,* Lao-tzu reveals his spiritual realization that can be paraphrased as follows:

> *Attaining the ultimate Void and maintaining a state of the deepest tranquility, I observe the myriad things in the phenomenal world returning to their Origin. Complex and active as they are, eventually they all return to their Origin. Returning to the Origin brings about tranquility. In tranquility we access the Origin of our life, which is constant and immutable. Understanding this constant and immutable principle of the Cosmos, we attain serenity, illumination and enlightenment (Lao-tzu, trans., 2000, chapter 16; True Tao, trans., 2004, chapter 16).*

** In the 1960s Taoist practitioner Li Le-chiu published a book in Taiwan entitled Fang Tao Yu Lu (Dialogues of Taoist Practitioners), in which the author documented the experience of scores of Taoist meditators, including a Catholic father. In that book, the interviewed meditators spoke of the transformation of sexual energy and the shrinking of sexual organ as an actual experience.

Although Lao-tzu did not discuss meditative techniques, the above statement was taken by latter-day Taoists as the theoretical foundation of the Taoist meditation. Without visualization and contemplation, which are commonly found in yoga and Buddhist meditation, the Taoist practitioner aims to attain the utmost tranquility by training breathing and focusing attention on the body point below the navel. In order to attain this goal, it is essential for the practitioner to observe Lao-tzu's teachings on simplicity and abstention from excessive desires and wants, especially sexual desire. Following this moral precept helps the practitioner embark on the path. If the meditative practice goes well, it succeeds in transforming the body energy for a higher purpose, and thus facilitates the observation of the precept. Furthermore, in meditation as well as in everyday life, the practitioner is expected to cultivate the mental attitude of "do-nothing" (*wu wei*), i.e., to let go the instinctual impulse to strive and to react. This attitude is cultivated in an effortless and spontaneous manner, so that the practitioner can relax his mind and body and to let go of all thoughts during meditation. The mental tranquility thus obtained helps bring about a balance in the internal secretions, and increase the level of endorphins, which are said to produce the feelings of love, joy, and happiness. Consequently, the Taoist meditation is found to be efficacious for the treatments of neuroses and drug and alcohol addiction. It is particularly effective for the relief of stress and anxiety.

Because the Taoist meditation is relatively free of religious contents, it used to be practiced by religious and non-religious people in ethnic Chinese communities. In the early decades of the 20th century, meditation teachers in China and Japan had refined the Taoist techniques and come up with new meditative styles of their own to cater to the needs of the general public. Foremost among them were Yin Shih Tzu Meditative Method in China and Okata Meditative Method in Japan.

The fact that the refined Taoist meditative techniques are non-religious and are used primarily as a therapeutic exercise have made them popular for a while. But precisely because of this non-religious feature, their popularity has markedly declined in recent decades when different schools of Buddhist meditation find their way to the international and ethnic Chinese communities. The Taoist techniques as a therapeutic exercise have paled in significance when compared with the Buddhist practice that emphasizes spiritual awakening and liberation. Buddhist meditation has thrived as an integral part of the renaissance of contemporary Buddhism as a new religious movement. By contrast, Taoist meditation has become less attractive except among some New Age-styled religious-cultural groups in Taiwan, where meditative techniques are combined with *Tai Chi* exercise and/or some other forms of innovation to attract followers. However, *Tai Chi Chuan* has become increasingly popular in both China and Western countries as a way of improving health and reducing tension. This form of exercise is especially appealing to older people, because of its gentle movements and health benefits.

5. CONCLUSION

Taoism offers a unique perspective on stress and coping. In many ways, it is the forerunner of Western positive psychology, because its main message is that we can achieve contentment and health regardless of circumstances if we can understand and practice the Way of Nature and transcend the limiting factors in our daily lives. Instead of trying to confront problems and conquer nature, Taoism teaches that we need to transform our thinking and our way of life so that we can live in harmony with the Way of Nature. Taoism represents a philosophical and spiritual teaching with very practical implications for stress and coping. Different from the American psychology of coping, Taoism advocates a proactive and transformative approach to coping. By embracing the Taoist way of thinking and way of life, automatically we become free from all kinds of stressors and stress-related symptoms, such as anxieties and depression. By adopting the art of surrendering and "do nothing", we can overcome powerful negative forces without confronting them. Through the practice of *Tai Chi* and *Qigong,* we can maintain our physical and mental health even in very stressful and adverse environments.

Here is a summary of the main teachings of Taoism:

1. Taoism espouses a life style in accord with the *Tao*, the ultimate cosmic Truth, which is described as being selfless, simple, authentic, and spontaneous. Following a life style of luxury and extravagance not only wastes money, but also can be harmful to our health and mental well-being.

2. The Way of nature not only refers to the great Cosmos; it also includes our true nature – the Origin of our life. Lao-tzu teaches that by surrendering our ego, we can achieve perfect "tranquility" and access the Origin, thereby attaining serenity, wisdom, and enlightenment.

3. Craving for wealth and material possessions impoverishes us morally and spiritually, while freedom from such craving enriches us by enhancing our capacity for love, serenity, good health, and happiness.

4. All things in the universe exist in polarity (or duality), with the two opposites in a polarity complementing each other and making the existence of each other possible. Learning to develop a new insight that fortune and misfortune contain each other, can help us avoid mental frustration when misfortune strikes. The same insight applies to other dualities such as success and failure, health and illness, praise and blame, etc.

5. Taoism reveals that cosmic change takes place in a cyclical or circular pattern, in which everything reverts to its opposite when going to the extreme. With this insight, we learn to avoid excesses, and to remain equanimous in all circumstances. We do not become complacent over success or lose heart over failure.

6. The impulse of striving to be different from what we are causes tension and stress. Learning to master the art of "do nothing," i.e., surrendering our instinctive impulse to strive and to react, has enormous benefits for our mental and physical health. The Taoist principle of "do nothing" is consistent with the psychotherapeutic approach of "unconditional self-acceptance," which is considered by several schools of psychotherapy as crucial for the treatments of emotional disorders.

7. In the Taoist philosophy, "do nothing" also means that we take action in a spontaneous, effortless way, and avoid imposing our subjective thinking and beliefs on others, especially when we are in a leader's position. A successful leader is someone who can keep his or her mind open to all ideas and delegate authority and duty properly to those working under him or her. According to Taoism, dictatorship is doomed to failure because the dictators, by interfering too much, violates the principle of "do nothing" and causes disharmony (though often disguised as "harmony") within their society.

8. Taoist meditation in "passive relaxation" helps improve our physical and mental health. It is efficacious for the treatments of neuroses, especially stress and anxiety. Through Taoist meditation, one also learns to cultivate the art of "do nothing," which is a secret to good health, self-culture, and worldly success.

9. Taoism teaches that all is in flux, so our thinking should be allowed to flow rather than stagnate. We invite trouble if we act against this cosmic principle by sticking to a rigid, self-righteous way of thinking. Taoism and psychotherapy agree that flexibility in our way of thinking and outlook on life is important to avoid emotional troubles.

10. Taoism teaches that the *Tao*, the great Way of nature, has no selfish motives and that Mother Nature nurtures and nourishes without claiming anything in return. Learning from this cosmic virtue is the ultimate guarantee for a life of happiness and contentment. So, the Taoist message of contentment does not imply a passive resignation to fate, but rather a humble, selfless devotion to the well-being of humanity.

REFERENCES

Ajaya, S. (1997). *Psychotherapy East and West: A unifying paradigm.* Honesdale, Penn.: The Himalayan International Institute.

Ellis, A. E. (2004). *Rational emotive behavior therapy: It works for me – it can work for you.* Prometheus Books.

Ellis, A. E. (2005). *Workshop on self-esteem* (April). Workshops and Lectures section, the Albert Ellis Institute on website, www.rebt.org.

Frankl, V. E. (2000). *Man's search for ultimate meaning.* Cambridge, Mass.: Perseus Publishing.

James, W. (1999). *Varieties of Religious Experience.* New York: Modern Library.

Lao-tzu (2000). *Tao Te Ching* (translated into modern Chinese by Lin An-Wu). Ilan, Taiwan: Tu-Cheh Cultural Enterprise Co.

Rogers, C. (1995a). *A Way of Being.* Houghton Mifflin Co.

Rogers, C. (1995b). *On Being a Person: A Therapist's View of Psychotherapy.* Houghton Mifflin Co.

True Tao (2004). *Tao Te Ching.* www.truetao.org.

Wang, D. (1998). *Laozhuang Yijing yu Xiandai Rensheng* (in Chinese, Spiritual Realms of Lao-tzu and Chuang-tzu and Modern Life). Beijing: Chinese Broadcasting TV Press.

Watts, A. W. (1969). *The Two Hands of God: The Myths of Polarity.* Toronto:Macmillan.

Welwood, J. (2000). *Toward A Psychology of Awakening.* Boston: Shambhala Publications.

ADVANCE IN THE STUDY OF RELIGIOUS AND SPIRITUAL COPING

Derrick W. Klaassen, Marvin J. McDonald, and Susan James

1. INTRODUCTION

Over the past 15 years scholarly interest in the psychology of religion and spirituality has increased dramatically (Emmons & Paloutzian, 2003; Hill & Pargament, 2003). Particular attention has been paid to the relationship between religion and spirituality and mental and physical health. Notable recent contributions to this subdiscipline include: (1) a chapter in the Annual Review of Psychology (Emmons & Paloutzian), (2) special issues in the *American Psychologist* (2003) and *Psychological Inquiry* (2002), (3) the development and publication of new and innovative journals, such as the *International Journal of the Psychology of Religion* and *Mental Health, Religion and Culture*; (4) numerous comprehensive research reviews of the relationship between religion and physical and mental health (e.g., Harrison, Koenig, Hays, Eme-Akwari, & Pargament, 2001; Hackney & Sanders, 2003; Koenig, McCullough & Larson, 2001); and (5) a variety of recent meta-analytic studies of the relationship between religious practices and various psychological and physical health indicators (e.g., Baer, 2003; Smith, McCullough & Poll, 2003). Furthermore, scholars of spirituality are finding their work more frequently included in mainstream reviews of other subdisciplinary domains (e.g., Folkman & Moskowitz, 2004; Aldwin & Parke, 2004; Peterson & Seligman, 2004). And while it may be argued that the sheer volume of research in the psychology of religion has contributed to its recent renaissance, wider social and cultural factors, such as a renewed interest in the understanding of faith-based worldviews following the worldwide resurgence of international terrorism, should not be discounted (Bibby, 2002; Meisenhelder, 2002; Plante & Canchola, 2004).

One of the most vibrant domains of investigation into the relationships between religion/spirituality and health is the research on religious and spiritual coping (Folkman & Moskowitz, 2004; Pargament, 1997). This well established area emerged out of the research on the contextual model of coping, which has spawned a great deal of research in the social, behavioural, and medical sciences over the past thirty-five years. Much of the

Derrick W. Klaassen, M.A., The University of British Columbia; Marvin J. McDonald, Ph. D., Trinity Western University; Susan James, Ph. D., The University of British Columbia credit for this proliferation can be attributed to the work of Richard Lazarus and his colleagues (Lazarus & Folkman, 1984). The contextual model of coping outlined by Lazarus has been particularly attractive to researchers and clinicians because of its widespread empirical support and immediate relevance to psychotherapy. In addition to the more widely publicized methods (problem-focused, emotion-focused, social, and meaning-focused coping), religious and spiritual coping methods have gained increasing scholarly acceptance (Folkman & Moskowitz; Pargament, 1997, 2002a).

Numerous reviews of the psychology of religious and spiritual coping have summarized the recent advances in our collective understanding of this area. The foci of these analyses have included its epidemiology, (Harrison et al., 2001), the costs and benefits of religiousness, specifically positive and negative religious coping (Pargament, 2002a), health related stress (Siegel, Anderman, & Schrimshaw, 2001), marriage and parenting (Mahoney, Pargament, Tarakeshwar, & Swank, 2001), and its prevalence and expression in Sweden (Lewin, 2001). However, most of these studies have focused almost exclusively on research conducted in the United States with a largely Christian population (primarily Protestant). Few authors have included qualitative and cross-cultural studies in their reviews, in spite of the fact that these studies have much to offer to psychologists who often work with individuals and groups of various faith perspectives and cultures.

Thus, our aim in this chapter is to draw attention to neglected elements of the psychology of religious and spiritual coping. The first portion of the chapter presents a review of research and theoretical literature on religious/spiritual coping, focusing on studies which largely employ etic research methodologies (mostly cross-sectional, correlational and longitudinal designs). This section includes: (1) definitions of religion, spirituality, coping and religious/spiritual coping and their theoretical underpinnings; (2) expressions of religious/spiritual coping, such as its styles and methods; (3) recent developments in the assessment and measurement of religious/spiritual coping; (4) recent advances in the understanding of the outcomes of religious/spiritual coping, including psycho/social/spiritual well-being (e.g. depression, schizophrenia, life satisfaction, spiritual well-being, etc.), and physical health (e.g. cancer, HIV/AIDS, chronic illness, pain, etc.).

The second section of this chapter includes a review of some of the emic and cross-cultural approaches to understanding religious/spiritual coping. These studies have employed numerous qualitative methodologies (e.g., hermeneutic, grounded theory, phenomenological, etc.) and focused either on marginalized groups in the United States (e.g., Asian Americans, Native Americans) or on populations outside of the United States (e.g., Asian immigrants to the UK, Swedes etc.). Moreover, the complexity of the datasets is multiplied by the fact that many of these studies have employed non-Christian samples (e.g., Hindus, Bhuddists, Jews, Muslims, etc.). Thus, the obvious theological differences between these groups may and do in fact translate into substantive differences in terms of religious/spiritual coping. Interestingly, however, several studies also demonstrate substantial and functional commonalities in the coping practices of various faith traditions.

Finally, the chapter will conclude with a brief case study on religious and spiritual coping that one of the authors (Susan James) conducted in her work with Portuguese immigrants to the United States and Canada. Results from this study underscore the importance of employing culturally sensitive research strategies that are able to capture the complexity of religious/spiritual coping in diverse contexts.

2. REVIEW OF RELIGIOUS/ SPIRITUAL COPING

2.1. What is religious/spiritual coping?

Many of the recent advances in the understanding and measurement of religious/ spiritual coping can be traced to the persistent and thorough work of Kenneth Pargament and his associates. Thus, reviews of definition of religious/spiritual coping cannot be entirely separated from Pargament's definitions of coping, religion and spirituality, since these form the bedrock for his theory and his widely employed religious coping instruments. An observant reader may have noticed that we have chosen to add the word 'spiritual' to the common term 'religious coping'. The inclusion of the term 'spiritual' reflects not only our attempt to include a wide variety of religious/spiritual coping studies that may have been omitted in other reviews, but also our commitment to practice and encourage dialogue amongst multiple research traditions. Our hope is to build bridges between the various stakeholders who have a common interest in understanding how religion and spirituality contribute to the coping process.

Pargament (1997) defined religion as "a search for significance in ways related to the sacred" (p. 32). He highlights the point that this definition bridges functional and substantive traditions in the psychology of religion since it incorporates both the process or means of attaining personal value as well as a destination or direction for one's search. The sacred can relate to either facet of the journey, pathway or destination. Pargament notes that he is "defining religion in the classic tradition of our field. The search for significance in ways related to the sacred encompasses both individual and institutional; it includes both traditional and the novel; and it covers the good and the bad" (Pargament, 1999, p. 12). In contrast to other authors (e.g., Helminiak, 1996), Pargament's definition of spirituality is conceptually narrower than his definition of religion. Pargament (1999) defines spirituality as "a search for the sacred" (p. 12), which he views as the most central task of a religion, its heart and soul. Religion, in contrast to spirituality, is defined primarily by the search for objects of significance, some of which may be related to the sacred. Spirituality, on the other hand, is defined by its search for one specific object of significance, the sacred. It is notable that the primary motivation underlying Pargament's definition of religion and its distinction from spirituality, appear to be an attempt to undermine subtle and more obvious forms of psychological and biological reductionism (cf. Pargament, 2002b).

Pargament (1997) traces the historical origins of the construct of coping through its psychodynamic roots and arrives at a contextual and transactional definition of coping. After comparing numerous prominent definitions within the wider coping literature (e.g. Lazarus & Folkman, 1984), he defines coping as "a search for significance in times of stress" (p. 90). Pargament notes that his definition, which views coping as a response that emerges out the encounter between the person and the situation, adopts eight fundamental assumptions about the coping process: (1) people seek significance; (2) events are constructed in terms of the their significance to people; (3) people bring an orienting system to the coping process; (4) people translate the orientation system into specific methods of coping; (5) people seek significance in coping through the mechanisms of conservation and transformation; (6) people cope in ways that are compelling to them; (7) coping is embedded in culture; (8) the keys to good coping lie in the outcomes and the process (Pargament, 1997). It is important to note that when individuals are pushed beyond their limits by circumstances outside of their control, a coping process is evoked in which the individual chooses his or her coping strategies based upon a pre-existing orienting system, which for many people includes their religious faith (Harrison et al., 2001). Pargament's theory thus extends and elaborates the process model of Lazarus and Folkman (1984) and contends that one's spiritual/religious faith can permeate the entire coping process, including resources, strategies and appraisal.

In contrast to some of the prevailing stereotypes about the function of religion and spirituality in the larger coping literature (e.g., Rammohan, Rao & Subbakrishna, 2002), religious/spiritual coping can and should be viewed as a multidimensional process that cannot be reduced to simple behavioural indicators (e.g., prayer, going to a place of worship) or restricted to passive or defensive functions of the psyche (denial, rationalization, etc.). It incorporates active, passive, problem-focused, emotion-focused, intrapsychic (i.e. cognitive, behavioural) and interpersonal methods of managing stress (Folkman & Moskowitz, 2004; Harrison et al., 2001; Krause, Ellison, Shaw, Marcum & Boardman, 2001; Mahoney et al., 2001; Pargament, Koenig & Perez, 2000).

Religious/spiritual coping actually reflects a wide range of strategies spanning the entire range of coping options (Harris et al., 2001; Pargament, 1997). What seems to distinguish religious/spiritual coping is the incorporation of spiritual resources (either personal or social), appraisal processes that take sacred significance into account, or the selection of coping outcomes that acknowledge the search for the sacred. As in other domains, any specific strategy may function differently for different people facing different demands or deficits in resources. Prayer practices may, for instance, function as emotion-focused coping while living through grief in one instance, while in another they may serve as a problem-focused coping method of arousal reduction for a cardiac rehabilitation patient.

2.2. How is religious/spiritual coping conceptualized and measured?

Early conceptualizations (e.g., Pargament, Kennell, Hathaway, Grevengoed, Newman & Jones, 1988) of religious/spiritual coping focused largely on three distinct styles: self directing, deferring, and collaborative religious coping (Pargament, 1997; Pargament et al., 1988). Operationalized in the *Religious Problem Solving Scale,* self-directed coping was defined primarily as an approach in which individuals coped by relying on themselves rather than on God. Examples of items that such copers might endorse include "after I've gone through a rough time, I try to make sense of it without relying on God". Deferring approaches to religious coping, on the other hand, are characterized primarily by the refusal to take responsibility for the coping process. Instead, the coper chooses to rely exclusively on divine intervention in the process of their struggle. Deferring copers might endorse such items as "rather than trying to, with the right solution to problem myself, and that God decide how to deal with it". Collaborative religious coping is characterized by the attempt of the coper to involve God in his or her attempts to gain control. Someone coping in this manner might endorse items such as "when it comes to deciding how to solve a problem, God and I work together as partners" (Pargament, 1997, p. 181).

Research into the relationships between these various styles of coping has produced relatively stable results. Self-directed religious coping and collaborative religious coping have generally been linked to higher self-esteem and a greater sense of control or mastery (although, there have been some mixed results for self-directed religious coping – cf. Phillips,

Pargament, Lynn & Crossley, 2004; Fabricatore, Handal, Rubio & Gilner, 2004), while deferring religious coping has shown negative relationships with these outcome variables (Pargament, 2002a). While recent investigations have tended to focus on newer, more contextually sensitive religious/spiritual coping instruments (rather than the more static 'styles') some exceptions to this general trend are worth noting. For example, Wong-McDonald & Gorsuch (2000) recently proposed that, Surrender to God, might be considered a fourth coping style and developed a 12-tem Surrender Scale with adequate reliability and incremental validity above and beyond a pre-existing religious coping styles. Phillips et al. (2004) further investigated the relationship between self-directed religious coping and various measures of mental health. Reanalysis of the self directing religious coping scale given to 262 undergraduate students at a university in the Midwestern United States revealed the presence of two factors; a deistic, supportive and non-intervening God factor and an abandoning God factor. The first factor showed both positive and negative relationships with various mental health measures, while the latter revealed only negative relationships. Both of these studies are promising advances to Pargament's original style-oriented measurement of religious/spiritual coping and point to the complexity of the religious/spiritual coping process.

Moving beyond religious coping styles, recent efforts at conceptualizing and measuring religious/spiritual coping have focused on more situationally located strategies, as well as emphasizing both negative and positive coping methods (cf. Hill & Pargament, 2003; Moberg, 2002). These include the *Negative Religious Coping Scale*, the *RCOPE* and *Brief RCOPE*, the *Hindu Religious Coping Scale* and the *Process Evaluation Model* (Butter & Pargament, 2003; Egbert, Mickey & Coeling, 2004; Hill & Pargament, 2003; Pargament, Koenig & Perez; 2000; Pargament, Smith, Koenig & Perez, 1998; Pargament, Tarakeshwar, Ellison & Wulff, 2001; Pargament, Zinnbauer, Scott, Butter, Zerowin & Stanik, 1998; Tarakeshwar, Pargament, & Mahoney, 2003).

Shortly after the publication of his his landmark text in 1997, Pargament and his colleagues published the *Negative Religious Coping Scale*, which identifies religious/spiritual warning signs or 'red flags' (Pargament et al., 1998). The purpose of this scale was to identify and measure three dimensions of ineffective or maladaptive religious coping. The dimensions included the *Wrong Direction*, which "refers to religious involvement in goals or values that reflect an imbalance of self concerns or concerns that go beyond oneself" (p. 79). The second dimension was labelled as the *Wrong Road*, or the employment of religious coping strategies that demonstrate the lack of fit in relation to the stressor or the ends sought. The third dimension of the scale was labelled *Against the Wind*, and focused on religious conflict within the individual, in relation to his or her belief system and supporting religious community.

The *Negative Religious Coping Scale* was validated on two separate samples, including a largely Catholic church sample of 49 participants, and a sample of 196 students from one large Midwestern state university. As predicted, most of the subscales of the measure were related to negative mental health outcomes (e.g., low self-esteem, high anxiety). The strongest of these relationships included religious apathy, God's punishment, anger at God, religious doubts, interpersonal religious conflict, and conflict with church dogma (Pargament et al., 1998).

The development of the *Negative Religious Coping Scale* set the stage for the work on the most comprehensive measure of religious/spiritual coping to date, the *RCOPE*, and its shorter version, the *Brief RCOPE* (Pargament et al, 1998; Pargament et al, 2000; Pargament et al, 2001). In contrast to the unidimensional characterizations of religious/spiritual coping, the *RCOPE* represents a theoretically grounded and functionally oriented attempt at measuring religious/spiritual coping. Drawing upon the work of such notable scholars as Clifford Geertz, Erich Fromm and Emile Durkheim, Pargament et al. (2000) proposed that religion serves five main functions, which in turn constitute the five dimensions of the *RCOPE*. (1)The first dimension is identified as the process of *finding meaning* in the face of unexplainable and often horrific circumstances. (2) The second dimension and function of religion was defined as religious methods of coping to *gain control*. (3) The third dimension included religious methods of coping aimed at *gaining comfort from achieving closeness to God*. (4) The fourth dimension was defined as religious coping methods which lead to *intimacy with others and closeness with God*. (5) The final dimension of the scale focused on religious methods of coping in the service of *life transformation*.

Initial validation of this comprehensive measure of religious coping has proven to be encouraging. The *RCOPE* has been utilized with numerous and diverse populations, including 540 college students and 551 elderly hospital patients. Shortened versions of the 105 item measure have been employed with 296 members of two churches in Oklahoma City (following the Oklahoma City bombing in 1996), and a sample of 1260 clergy, 823 elders and 735 members of the Presbyterian Church of United States. Both the *RCOPE* and the *Brief RCOPE* have demonstrated satisfactory internal validity, predictable and consistent relationships with measures of religious orientation, and physical and mental adjustment (e.g., stress-related growth, emotional distress, symptoms of post traumatic stress disorder), evidence of incremental validity above and beyond global or distal religious measures and nonreligious coping. Thus, both instruments seem promising and will hopefully contribute to moving the religious/spiritual coping research beyond some of its methodological shortcomings.

A third and promising approach to measuring religious/spiritual coping places a greater emphasis on clinical applicability and contextual sensitively. While religious/spiritual coping has generally been construed as a dynamic process (Lazarus & Folkman, 1984; Folkman & Moskowitz, 2004), much of the research has focused on its outcomes and efficacy. In a recent publication, Butter & Pargament (2003) posited that effective or positive coping is conceptualized as integrated and balanced; conversely, ineffective or negative religious coping is viewed as unbalanced and uncoordinated in terms of its means and/or ends (i.e. 'goodness of fit', 'wrong road', 'wrong direction'). In order to assess this process evaluation model, the authors constructed six vignettes, two for each type of coping process. They conducted a reliability study with 42 graduate students in psychology and found that the vignettes were consistently rated as well integrated or poorly integrated, according to the way in which they were constructed and in which the authors intended for them to be understood. In the main study, the authors gathered data from mental health practitioners and clergy. One hundred and sixty six professionals completed the study, including eighty-three mental health practitioners and eighty-three clergy. The results of the study indicated that for all three vignettes the general and religious evaluation measures showed to be reliable measures of internal consistency, with Cronbach alphas ranging from .59 to .85. The results of the study provide some support for the validity of the process evaluation model of religious coping. While holding the outcomes of the particular of coping constant, the authors varied the methods of coping. And despite the fact that the outcomes were the same, mental health practitioners and clergy were able to distinguish poorly and better integrated ways of coping. The findings in this study are important because they expand the clinical usefulness of the religious/spiritual coping literature.

A fourth and notable contribution to the measurement of religious/spiritual coping was recently published by Pargament and two of his students (Tarakeshwar, Pargament & Mahoney, 2003), and represents a significant step towards understanding cross-cultural and interfaith approaches to religious/spiritual coping. In light of the significant theological differences between Hindus, the population under investigation, and Christians, specifically the doctrine of karma and reincarnation, the authors decided to begin the study inductively by consulting 15 Hindus from Northwest Ohio, about their practices of religious coping. Results of these interviews indicated that religious/spiritual coping for Hindus served the same five main functions that had emerged in the construction of the *RCOPE* and *Brief RCOPE*: (1) finding meaning, (2) gaining control, (3) gaining comfort and closeness to God, (4) gaining intimacy with others, and (5) achieving life transformation. In addition to this significant functional overlap, some distinctives emerged as well. Although participants in the interviews did not specifically mention the doctrine of karma, "many of the participant's comments, such as performing their duty, acknowledging limited control over one state, and not focusing on earthy desires, are tied to this notion. In addition, a few religious coping methods previously reported in person samples were not mentioned in the interviews with Hindus. These include demonic reappraisal, religious forgiving, and interpersonal religious discontent" (Tarakeshwar et al., 2003, p. 614).

In light of the results of the interviews and the recent developments in religious/spiritual coping measurement, the authors constructed a 23 item self-report measure. The *Hindu Religious Coping Scale* was administered to 164 Hindus across United States, along with some measures of mental health, acculturation, and religiosity. Participants in the study reported moderate levels of religiosity and spirituality, average levels of acculturation, relatively low levels of depressed mood, and relatively high levels of life satisfaction and marriage. Exploratory factor analysis yielded three factors, which were subsequently employed as the subscales of the scale: God focused coping, spirituality focused coping, and religious guilt, anger, and passivity coping.

2.3. How does religious/spiritual coping function?

The manner in which religious/spiritual coping aides the individual in his or her has been the topic of a great deal of investigation and theorizing. Two models are generally considered in the literature – the stress buffering model (or stress moderator) and the stress-deterrent model (or main effect and/or mediator). The former model hypothesizes that religious/spiritual coping functions best under high stress situations in which the coping response is elicited from a pre-existing religious/spiritual orienting system, while the latter postulates that it is effective regardless of the level of stress. The literature has demonstrated support for both models (Fabricatore, Handal, Rubio, & Gilner, 2004; Pargament, 1997, 2002a; Siegel, Anderman, & Schrimshaw, 2001). Before engaging this debate more substantially it is perhaps helpful to remain mindful of the theoretical and methodological context of the religious/spiritual coping process.

In contextual models of coping, the first step in research is to identify the appropriate level of analysis. The key focus for this task is to identify the location of religious/spiritual variables in the stress and coping process. Do the religious variables in a particular investigation reflect social or personal coping resources, appraisal activities, or selection of outcomes? The goodness of "fit" of these factors with the rest of adaptation processes defines the role of religious coping in each situation. In their review of daily process studies on coping strategies and alcohol consumption, Tennen, Affleck, Armeli, and Camey (2000), found that intra-individual analyses revealed significant relationships that were obscured in the nomothetic, cross-sectional statistics. This highlights the problems arising when "investigators continue in their attempts to answer inherently within-person questions regarding stress, coping, and adaptation with between-person research designs and analytic strategies" (p. 628).

Numerous reviews of religious/spiritual coping have pointed to its role as a mediator between personality and health variables (e.g., Fabricatore et al., 2004; Siegel et al., 2001). In one of the few studies which directly investigated a mediation hypothesis, Fabricatore et al. (2004) found that the collaborative religious coping style mediated the relationship between religiousness and (lower) distress and (higher) well-being in a sample of 175 undergraduate students. In short, religious variables can act as distal factors that strengthen the operation of other well-established psychological processes (such as health behaviours and social support) or they can directly strengthen physical resilience and strength through enhanced psychological states such as faith, hope, or inner peace (cf. Oman & Thoresen, 2002). Religious/spiritual coping can act directly on health through proximal pathways or through more distal, indirect paths to strengthen health. Religion, like culture, pervades the processes of stress and coping, and thus may emerge at multiple locations in the overall process.

Religious/spiritual coping can also operate as a moderating (deterring) factor shaping relationships between stressors and coping outcomes. In their review of this literature, Siegel et al. (2001) found that both private (e.g., prayer) and public (e.g., attending a church service) religions/spiritual practices buffered the relationship between various health measures and mental health. In the same study noted above, Fabricatore et al. (2004) noted that deferring religious coping moderated the relationship between stressors and several measures of psychological well being and distress. Contrary to expectations, however, collaborative religious coping did not moderate this same relationship.

Psychologists need to remember that the stress-buffering and stress-deterrent models are not antithetical or mutually exclusive. Not surprisingly from a contextual perspective, spiritual and religious coping strategies can be identified in virtually every facet of the human response to stress, and not one feature of the process is the sole, universal core of religious/spiritual coping. As investigators begin to systematically include religious/spiritual coping in their research, its contribution will continue to become clearer.

2.4. Who engages in religious/spiritual coping?

One of the frequent questions that emerges in the literature concerns the prevalence of religious/spiritual coping. The simple and short answer to this question is that we do not have any large-scale, sociological studies which investigate the prevalence of religious/ spiritual coping in a systematic and thorough manner in the general populace. Moreover, even if we did have the access to these statistics, we would expect that the prevalence would vary on the basis of the person and his/her context. Consistent with this assumption, it is thus not surprising to find that the limited numbers that have emerged from other research have varied widely. For example, Harrison et al (2001) note that the prevalence of religious coping in for recent studies with medical patients varied from 42.3% to 86%. While researchers have not yet been able to give specific, reliable statistics on the prevalence of religious/spiritual coping, the research does reveal several broader principles that bear notice: (1) The frequency of religious/spiritual coping varies between various countries and ethnic groups. For example, countries which report high rates of religiousness (specifically conservative Protestant religion), such as the United States, also report greater use of religious/spiritual coping (Ferraro & Kelley-Moore, 2001; Taylor 2001). In his review of the Swedish literature on religious coping, Lewin (2001) points to some of the sociological differences between Sweden and the United States, such as a widespread discomfort with organized, public religion in Sweden. Thus, one would expect overall to find fewer people employing spiritual/religious methods of coping in times of stress. It should be noted that scholars of religion in the United States and Canada have also recently pointed to the need to understand the religious and denominational diversity (Wuthnow, 2004; Bibby, 2002). Much basic research is still needed to gain an ecumenical understanding of the prevalence and nature of spiritual/religious coping in North America. (2) Similarly to religiousness in general, the use of religious/spiritual coping increases with age (Pargament, 1997). This finding is not surprising, considering the fact that the vast amount of studies point to the fact that religious/spiritual coping increases in the face of unchangeable and relatively stable stressors, such as the presence of a chronic illness (which, in turn, is positively correlated with age). (3) Religious/spiritual coping increases when people are presented with an extraordinary and overwhelming stressor, such as the diagnosis of a terminal illness or the presence of natural disaster (Pargament, 2002a). (4) There are some differences between religious groups (e.g. Hindus vs. Christians) and within Christian denominations. For example, Osborne & Vandenberg (2003) recently conducted a study of 153 Catholic and Protestant (Disciples of Christ) church members, which revealed that that Catholics engaged in significantly more negative religious/spiritual coping strategies, such as pleading with God and religious discontent, than their Protestant counterparts. In their investigation of Hispanic women with early-stage breast cancer, Alferi, Culver, Carver, Arena, and Antoni (1999), found that greater religiosity was linked to increased distress among Catholic participants, while the opposite was true for Evangelical women. These results are consistent with previous findings (e.g., Tix & Frazier, 1998) and bear further investigation in regards to the reasons for these differences.

2.5. What are the outcomes of religious/spiritual coping?

Over the past six years the vast amount of research on religious/spiritual coping has focused on its outcomes, and more precisely, its relationships with various forms of mental and physical health (Harrison, et al., 2001). Overall, these results tend to point to the fact that religious/spiritual coping strategies represent beneficial ways of encountering everyday and extraordinary stress. Relationships that run counter this trend should be subjected to closer theoretical and methodological scrutiny. Perhaps the results are spurious due to poor measurement (e.g., single behavioural item). It behoves psychologists of religion to remember, however, that all human behaviour, including religious/spiritual coping, runs the gamut between good and evil, functional and maladaptive, appropriate and inappropriate, "noble and nefarious" (Zinnbauer et al., 1999). Moreover, health researchers must take note of the fact that for many religious and spiritual individuals, the attainment of physical and psychological health is often considered of secondary importance relative to their religious and spiritual goals. Religious/spiritual coping must therefore be examined contextually.

2.5.1. Psychological & Social Outcomes

Much of the recent research has (not surprisingly) investigated the relationship between positive and negative religious/spiritual coping and various measures of mental health, including daily stress (Fabricatore et al., 2004; Plante, Saucedo & Rice, 2001; Smith, Pargament,

Brant & Olive, 2000), post-traumatic stress (Meisenhelder, 2002; Plante & Canchola, 2004; Witvliet, Phipps, Feldman & Beckham, 2004), depression and psychotic disorders (Bosworth, Park, McQuoid, Hays & Steffens, 2003; Reger & Rogers, 2002; Rogers, Poey, Reger, Tepper & Colemank, 2002; Smith, McCullough & Poll, 2003; Taylor, 2001; Wang & Patten, 2002), attachment (Belavich & Pargament, 2002); church based social support (Krause, Ellison, Shaw, Marcum & Boardman, 2001; Nooney & Woodrum, 2002), autism (Tarakeshwar & Pargament, 2001), and dementia (Kinney, Ishler, Pargament & Cavanaugh, 2003).

These studies add to the previously well-established research findings of others (e.g., Koenig, McCullough & Larson, 2001), which have consistently and robustly demonstrated the positive relationships between religion and religious/spiritual coping and mental health. A few key examples from this current review will serve to demonstrate the continuity of the research. Adding to the vast number of studies that have already demonstrated the significant relationship between religious/spiritual coping and stress, Smith et al. (2000) found that religious/spiritual coping, in addition to religious dispositions and attributions, predicted psychological and religious outcomes in church members following a large Midwest flood. In addition, path analyses also lent further support to Pargament's (1997) call for the use of proximal measures of religion, such as religious/spiritual coping, instead of more distal measurements, such as religious orientation, as the former and not the latter was significantly related to religious outcome. In a study with 209 (6 weeks post flood) and 139 (6 months post flood) respondents, Smith et al. found that positive religious coping mediated the relationship between religious dispositions and religious outcomes at six weeks and six months after the flood. A further study (Fabricatore et al., 2004) also found that collaborative religious coping mediated the relationship between religiousness and well-being and distress in the sample of 175 undergraduate students.

Religion in general and religious/spiritual coping methods in specific have been posited and demonstrated to be an important resource for those suffering from depression (Rogers et al., 2002). In general, the use of positive religious/spiritual coping strategies, such as seeking and giving spiritual support, benevolent reappraisal of a stressful situation, and a collaborative religious coping style, has been shown to be associated with better mental health, while negative religious/spiritual coping strategies, such as a deferring religious coping style, negative reappraisal of an event, and spiritual discontent, have been associated with the increased presence of depressive symptoms (Harrison et al., 2001). In a recent meta-analytic study of the relationship between religiousness and depression, Smith et al. (2003) examined 147 independent investigations ($N = 98,975$) and found a small but significant negative relationship between religiousness and depressive symptoms, that was independent of gender, age, or ethnicity. Interestingly, and in contrast to this general positive trend, negative religious coping was associated with higher levels of depressive symptoms. Consistent with Pargament's (1997) suggestion that religious/spiritual coping increases when individuals encounter a stressor that is above and beyond their normal coping resources, Rogers et al. (2002) found that individuals with more severe depressive symptomatology were more likely to engage in religious coping strategies. In a unique comparison between those suffering from schizophrenia, schizoaffective and bipolar disorder, Reger & Rogers (2002) found that after controlling for age and gender "those with diagnoses of schizophrenia and schizoaffective disorder... indicated that religion was more helpful when compared to those suffering with depressive disorders" (p. 345). Finally, Bosworth et al. (2003) were able to demonstrate in a longitudinal study with 114 elderly patients that positive religious/spiritual coping, was negatively related to depression above and beyond social support, demographic variables, and clinical measures.

Several studies have also investigated the role of religious/spiritual coping in the lives of those who support individuals living with serious, pervasive, and perennial mental illness. In their study with 63 families of children who are coping with autism, Tarakeshwar & Pargament (2001) found that positive religious/spiritual coping methods were associated with greater stress related growth, while negative religious/spiritual coping methods increase the likelihood of depression and, to a lesser extent, anxiety. Their faith served numerous functions for these families, including providing a sense of meaning in the face of incomprehensible situations and providing social support. Kinney et al. (2003) in turn found that in emotion focused coping and collaborative coping amongst 64 caregivers to spouses with dementia increased the likelihood of the presence of depressive symptoms.

Numerous studies have also investigated the role and importance of church based social support in the coping process. In a nationwide study of the Presbyterian church of the United States (N = 770), Krause, et al. (2001) found that increased spiritual support from church members and emotional support from the pastor was significantly and positively related to increased employment of religious coping methods. Moreover, Nooney & Woodrum (2002) demonstrated that church based social support and individual religious religious/spiritual styles mediate the effects of church attendance and prayer and contribute to decreases in depression.

2.5.2. Health Outcomes

In addition to the importance of religion and religious/spiritual coping in dealing with various mental illnesses, researchers have investigated its role in relation to many physical health concerns, including kidney transplant surgery (Tix & Frazier, 1998), living with HIV/AIDS (Simoni, Martone, & Kerwin, 2002; Somlai & Heckman, 2000), end stage renal disease (Snethen, Broome, Kelber & Warrady, 2004), chronic pain (Bush, Rye, Brant, Emery, Pargament & Riessinger, 1999), mortality (Krause, 1998), bereavement (Murphy, Johnson & Lohan, 2003), and cancer (Alferi et al., 1999; Gall, 2000; Laubmeier, Zakowski & Pair, 2004; McClain, Rosenfeld & Breitbart, 2003; Nairn & Merluzzi, 2003; Soothill, Morris, Harman, Thomas, Francis & McIllmurray, 2002; Stanton, Danoff-Burg & Huggins, 2002). While it would go beyond the scope of this chapter to review all of these studies in detail, the following examples should shed some light on common relationships.

Similar to the relationships between religion and religious/spiritual coping and mental health, the overall picture that one gains from reviewing the relationship between religious coping and self-reported physical symptoms is generally positive, although ambiguous or negative relationships continue to emerge. In a longitudinal study of 239 patients and 179 significant others, Tix & Frazier (1998) found that religious/spiritual coping was associated with improved psychological adjustment and decreased distress, even after controlling for nonreligious coping and social support. Simoni et al (2002) researched psychological adaptation among 230 predominantly African-American and Puerto Rican low income women living with HIV/AIDS in New York City, and found that spirituality was positively correlated with psychological adaptation (even after controlling for demographics, social support, and drug use). Krause (1998) reported that religious/spiritual coping was negatively correlated with mortality in a sample of 819 older adults who employed these methods in relation to a stressor that they faced in a highly valued role. In a five-year, longitudinal study with 138 parents who have lost a child by accident, suicide, or homicide, Murphy et al. (2003) found that parents who had found meaning in the death of their child were significantly more likely to report lower mental distress, higher marital satisfaction, and better physical health. Religious/spiritual coping was found to be a significant predictor of the ability to find meaning five years post-death. Nairn & Merluzzi (2003) reported that in their study of 292 people with cancer that deferring and collaborative religious coping styles were significantly correlated with self-efficacy, which in turn predicted better adjustment. On the other hand, religious/spiritual coping did not correlate significantly with a quality of life measure.

3. LIMITATIONS OF THE RELIGIOUS/SPIRITUAL COPING LITERATURE

Any recent analysis of the religious/spiritual coping literature is likely to mention several common shortcomings. Most of these critiques of the extant literature focus on the unsophisticated research methodologies, such as: (1) employing uni-dimentional, single item measures of religious/spiritual coping, (2) a high preponderance of cross-sectional, correlational studies, (3) the lack of diversity in samples (mostly Christian and mostly Protestant), (4) the lack of adolescent and clinical samples (mostly college students or elderly), and (5) the lack of longitudinal studies. These deficiencies are serious and must be rectified if we are to make progress in this domain. In our opinion, however, these methodological limitations pale in comparison to their theoretical counterparts, which remain largely unacknowledged.

3.1. Atheoretical Research

The most obvious theoretical limitation in the literature is that references to theory – whether contextual coping theory in general or more specifically religious/spiritual coping theory – are virtually absent. Most researchers, with a few exceptions (e.g., Butter & Pargament, 2003; Tarakeshwar, Pargament, & Mahoney, 2003), tend to ignore the theoretical import their studies and focus almost exclusively on its application or relationship to previous empirical work. Thus, for all intents and purposes much of the deliberation on religious/spiritual coping seems to be atheoretical in nature. In their review of the literature, Siegel et al (2001) note that "though many studies demonstrated significant associations between aspects of religiosity and mental health outcomes, few provide a theoretical framework for explaining these and other associations... Perhaps as a result of these limitations, the study of religiousness as a variable in the traditional stress and coping paradigm has not been well integrated into mainstream psychological and sociological research" (p. 646). We strongly concur with this conclusion and urge researchers of spiritual/religious coping to consider the theoretical import of their empirical work.

3.2. Key Theoretical Constructs

In light of the widespread theoretical confusion and/or omission, a brief reminder about the key theoretical constructs and definitions in the contextual model of coping is in order. In the contextual model, coping has been defined as the dynamic, effortful process, "the thoughts and behaviors used to manage the internal and external demands of situations that are appraised as stressful" (Folkman & Moskowitz, 2004, p. 745). These efforts are referred to as coping "strategies" that in which people seek to manage a dynamic "fit" among perceived: (a) demands of the situation (primary appraisal), (b) perceived levels of resources to meet those demands (secondary appraisal), (c) the function served be responding to those demands, and (d) the desired outcomes sought as a result of coping. It is important to note both the conceptual and empirical interdependence of key terms in process models. Not only can changing resources or appraisals redefine the coping process, but equally profound changes can emerge when one examines coping in from different faith traditions or cultural contexts. This complexity is both strength and weakness of the process theory of coping (Lazarus, 1999).

Different vocabulary is often used for different applications of coping theory. The term "coping methods" frequently refers to classes of coping strategies that share similar activities (e.g., behavioural or cognitive methods), similar approaches (e.g., benevolent religious reappraisals), or similar functions (e.g., problem-focused or emotion-focused). Terminology for different kinds of strategies is particularly chaotic in the literature, with many authors arbitrarily introducing synonyms or partially overlapping terms without definition or even acknowledgement of others' patterns of usage. Thus one finds the literature replete with coping "responses," "actions," "behaviours," "activities," and so on, often with little effort made to clearly articulate the levels of analysis appropriate to a particular study or application. Lazarus and Folkman, on the other hand, have consistently acknowledged such complexity and outlined the basic tools necessary for a scientifically and clinically useful theory of coping (e.g., Lazarus & Folkman, 1984; Lazarus, 1999). To adequately specify the process of coping in any particular investigation or application, coping strategies are defined in the context of identified stressors, coping resources, appraisal processes, coping constraints, and outcomes. And for each investigation or application, the level of analysis can vary from general to specific.

Lazarus' process theory also incorporates the dispositional models popular in some quarters. When a person consistently employs a pattern of coping strategies over time or across different stressors, that consistent coping pattern, called a "coping style," can be treated as a (somewhat) decontextualized personality characteristic or individual differences variable. Research and clinical approaches that emphasise traits often prefer to simplify the complexity of a transactional approach by reducing coping processes to relatively stable coping styles. Lazarus' approach supports investigation of coping styles while leaving open the possibilities that in some applications coping processes may not cohere into person-specific styles. In some research, for instance, flexibility of coping strategies (change over time) and complexity of coping strategies (use of many different strategies) can yield better outcomes (cf., Butter & Pargament, 2003; Tennen, et al., 2000).

3.3. Isolation from Literature

In addition to the lack of theory and its resultant confusions, few researchers make reference to the larger debates within the psychology of religion, such as the perennial disagreement over the functional and substantive definitions of "religion" and "spirituality". Also, the definitional differences between "religion" and "spirituality" are generally ignored or the author's preference is delineated by the use of one term in lieu of the other rather than through argument and in conversation with the larger scholarly community. Most studies give the informed reader some hints about the worldview or ideological surround of the authors (cf. Watson, Morris, Hood, Milliron, & Stutz, 1998) by their diction. Traditional psychologists of religion generally prefer to employ the theoretically laden term "religious coping", while most other psychologists seemed to prefer the more generic "spiritual coping"[1]. In spite of some efforts within the psychology of religion at coming to a consensus on its key terms (cf. Hill, Pargament, Hood, McCullough, Swyers, Larson, et al., 2000), it is obvious that many researchers have either ignored these efforts or have decided to disagree tacitly via their definitions of religion and spirituality.

The lack of theoretical reflection and sophistication leads directly to methodological difficulties and ambiguities, since many of the authors fail to engage alternative paradigms for understanding religious/spiritual coping, or even compare their theoretical predilections with those employed within the psychology of religion. For example, few authors have engaged Wong's (1993; Wong & McDonald, 2002) research on existential coping and have delineated this spiritual approach to coping from Pargament's contextual model. This sort of isolation in turn leads to one of the ironies in the psychology of religion. For years many psychologists of religion have bemoaned the fact that their work is continually ignored by the rest of the discipline. For example, Pargament (2002) recently noted rather humorously that "my colleagues and I have joked ruefully that the psychology of religion is an attractive field to those who are comfortable working in obscurity" (p. 239). And while there is certainly a case to be made that psychology as a whole needs to pay attention to the study of religion and spirituality, one could also certainly argue that psychologists of religion need to take note of other related areas of the discipline that might enhance and invigorate their research – cross cultural psychology (e.g. James, 2002), developmental psychology (Klaassen & McDonald, 2001) or existential psychology (Wong & Fry, 1998) readily come to mind.

3.4. Dichotomization of Religious/Spiritual Coping

A final theoretical concern relates to the dichotomization of religious/spirtual coping into positive vs. negative coping. In their initial conceptualizations of religious/spirtual coping, Pargament and his colleagues went to some trouble to emphasize the fact that the terms positive and negative religious coping were not intended to be value laden; i.e., positive was not necessarily related to effective and negative to ineffective methods of religious/spiritual coping. Pargament et al. (1998) note that "it is also possible that the religious pain and discontent embodied in the negative religious coping may be short-lived and relatively inconsequential... after all, struggle within the religious literature and within many models of religious and psychological development is a precursor to growth... negative religious coping may be relatively harmful to some people, inconsequential to others, and a source of growth to still others" (pp. 721-22). Unfortunately, this theoretical caveat has appears to have fallen by the wayside of research in the vast number of studies reviewed. Research in the past six years has demonstrated that in fact many authors do in fact tend to favour positive coping over negative coping because of its empirical links to mental and physical health measures. This dichotomization thus seems to oversimplify religious/ spiritual coping and run counter the stated intention for the RCOPE and its theoretical

---

[1] We found one exception to this general rule. In their study of childhood systic fibrosis, Cavalli, Pargament, and Nasr (2002) used the term "religious/spiritual coping". We felt that this term also fit our more inclusive purposes in this review chapter, and have thus employed it as well.

moorings in a process oriented theory of stress and coping. To the extent that researchers ignore the inherent complexity of the coping process in favour of trait oriented measurement strategies, we will continue to encounter confusing and conflicting results in the study of positive and negative religious/spiritual coping.

4. EMIC AND CROSS-CULTURAL RESEARCH ON RELIGIOUS/SPIRITUAL COPING

In order to understand and appreciate the complexity of the coping process in general and the religious/spiritual coping process specifically, it is vital that researchers begin to employ research methodologies that are able to capture the diversity of its incarnations. For example, a recent qualitative study of religious/spiritual coping strategies of children with cystic fibrosis pointed to a unique coping strategy that had not been previously identified – declarative religious coping (Pendleton, Cavalli, Pargament & Nasr, 2002). Many researchers have called for increased attention to the diversity of religious/spiritual coping, which includes investigations that employed multi-faith, cross-cultural and qualitative designs, yet few researchers have taken up this difficult task (Harrison et al., 2001; Pargament, 1997). It is interesting to note that nearly every major publication on religious/spiritual coping has emphasized the importance of, (a) treating religious/spiritual coping as a process that should be researched as such, (b) moving to cross-cultural, multi-faith samples, (c) employing research designs and methodologies that go beyond the typical cross-sectional, correlational design and are sensitive to the diversity of the phenomenon under investigation, and (d) contributing to the theoretical development of religious/spiritual coping, thus permitting the development and testing of further hypotheses. In spite of the rapid growth of ethnic and religious minorities in North America (Tarakeshwar et al., 2003, Wuthnow, 2004) and the increasing sophistication of qualitative research strategies, much publications on religious/spiritual coping continue to employ cross-sectional, correlational research designs with single faith samples.

To date the psychology of religion has made some progress towards internationalization. For example, the *International Journal for the Psychology of Religion* included an international and multi-faith report on the First International Congress on Religion and Mental Health which took place in April 2001 in Tehran, Iran (Khalili, Murken, Reich, Shah & Vahabzadeh, 2002). Due to its location, specific attention was paid to the relationship between western, Judeo-Christian based psychology and the development of an Islamic psychology. The authors favourably noted the good international attendance at this conference and pointed to the need to understand the diverse cultural and religious dimensions which undergird various incarnations of psychology.

Unlike natural sciences such as physics or chemistry, which are based on natural laws recognized worldwide, psychology of religion deals with people of rather different cultures, attitudes, and degrees of religiousness. Therefore, it is debatable to what extent, in psychology of religion, the recent findings from one particular culture can claim universal validity, even if they prove helpful in the original setting. If psychology of religion wants to become international discipline recognized by all researchers in the field, whatever their location and religion, and these issues need to be clarified and discussed. In other words, one has to avoid both simply assuming the universal validity of a given approach and refusing to enter the discussion because one does not see its necessity or potential fruitfulness (p. 218).

If psychology, and particularly the research concerning religious/spiritual coping, wants to rise to the challenge of recognizing the diverse and contextually embodied experiences of its research participants, it must employ strategies that lend themselves to such sensitive investigations. In tandem with the widespread and generally accepted methods of quantitative psychology, qualitative approaches will serve the development of religious/spiritual coping by highlighting new and unique findings and contributing to its theoretical development (cf., Mattis, 2002).

That said, it is encouraging to note that increasing attention has been paid to the role of religious/spiritual coping in various faiths and ethnic groups. These include numerous studies with African American men and women (Hines Smith, 2002; Mattis, 2002; Pointdexter, Linsk, & Warner, 1999; Spencer, Fegley & Harpalani, 2003; Wallace & Bergeman, 2002), Native Americans (Hazel & Mohatt, 2001), Asian women (Hussain & Cochrane, 2003), Asian immigrants to the United States (Bjorck, Cuthbertson, Thurman & Lee, 2001; Yeh & Inose, 2002; Wong & Reker, 1985; Wong & Ujimoto, 1998); Kosovar and Bosnian refugees to the United States (Ai, Peterson & Huang, 2003), Hindus living in the United States (Tarakeshwar, Pargament, & Mahoney, 2003), East Indian medical patients and their relatives (Pandey, Latha, Mathew, Ramdas, Chaturvedi, Iype et al., 2003; Rammohan, Rao & Subbakrishna, 2002); Orthodox Jews in Israel (Heilman & Witztum, 2000), and Christian, Hindu and Muslim depressed patients in the United Kingdom (Loewenthal, Cinniralla, Evdoka & Murphy, 2001). And while some of the above noted studies employed traditional, etic strategies of investigation (e.g. Ai et al., 2003; Bjorck et al., 2001), a wide variety of emic research methodologies were also employed, such as semi-structured interviews (Mattis), grounded theory research within a constructivist paradigm (Hussain & Cochrance; Pendleton et al., 2002), computerized text analysis (Gordon, Feldman, Crose, Schoen, Griffing & Shankar, 2002; Siegel & Schrimshaw, 2002), focus groups (Hazel & Mohatt), phenomenological analysis (Hines Smith, Pointdexter et al., Wallace & Bergeman), case study (Heilman & Witztum), hermeneutic analysis (Strang & Strang, 2001).

Various studies have demonstrated the importance of paying attention to the diverse cultural, ethnic and religious dimensions of religious/spiritual coping (Ai et al., 2003; Bjorck et al., 2001; Rammohan et al., 2002; Yeh & Inose, 2002). For example, Bjorck et al. conducted a study with 220 participants, 86 of which were Caucasian, 93 Korean, and 49 Filipino with near the equal participation of men and women in each subsample. Notable results included the finding that ethnicity demonstrated a significant effect on appraisal and on coping. Koreans appraised more events as losses relative to their Caucasian counterparts, and both Koreans and Filipinos appraised more events as greater challenges relative to the Caucasians. According to the researchers, the significant results may be due to worldview differences between Asians than Caucasians. They note that, "the eastern view, which values accepting fate and submitting to authority, has more made the Koreans more ready to appraise events as losses that they must accept. In contrast, the Western emphasis on individualism and self-assertion may have made the Caucasians more prone to protest or attempt to change a situation, effectively delaying, or even eliminating the need for loss appraisal" (Bjorck et al., 2001, p. 436). Bjorck et al. also reported a significant effect of ethnicity and appraisal on coping. As expected, Koreans and Filipinos scored higher than their Caucasian counterparts on accepting responsibility, religious coping, distancing, and escape avoidance scales. These results may also be explainable by the diverse worldviews and values associated with the various ethnic groups (cf. Yeh & Inose).

Pargament and his colleagues (Pargament et al., 2000) have posited that religion serves five broad functions, and that these functions, which form the theoretical groundwork for the *RCOPE* and the *Hindu Religious Coping Scale*, are embodied in the religious/spiritual coping strategies of North Americans. Overall, qualitative and cross-cultural studies have both confirmed and extended the findings in the previous literature. As elucidated below, the results of numerous studies confirm that religion/spirituality aides the coper through finding meaning, gaining control, gaining comfort from and closeness to God, finding intimacy and closeness with others, and achieving life transformation. In addition to these dimensions of religious/spiritual coping that have been demonstrated in the previous literature (Pargament et al., 2000; Tarakeshwar, Pargament, & Mahoney, 2003), qualitative and cross-cultural studies have also pointed to the importance of culture/ethnicity in facilitating development of a sense of self and identity. This presents a potentially novel contribution to the religious/spiritual coping literature that may have emerged due to the contextually-sensitive research methodologies employed.

4.1. Finding Meaning

Numerous studies have confirmed that religious/spiritual coping strategies facilitate the construction of finding meaning in adversity. In their interviews with 63 older, HIV-infected adults, Siegel and Schrimshaw (2002) noted that the religious and spiritual beliefs of the participants helped them find a sense of meaning and purpose in their illness, which in turn aided them in coming to terms and accepting their diagnosis. In their study of 10 African American elders, Wallace and Bergeman (2002) noted that "across interviews, respondents indicated that religion or spirituality served as mechanisms through which they were able to find meaning, or a sense of coherence, in their lives. In particular, oftentimes spiritual or religious beliefs were used to find meaning in change, or to help explain or understand life's circumstances" (p. 148). In their case study of an schizoaffective patient, Heilman & Witztum (2000) found that religion and specifically the religious terminology of Judaism allowed their schizoaffective client to accept the presence of his mental illness. Gall and Cornblat (2002) noted that in their interviews with 39 survivors of breast cancer, religious faith facilitated adjustment to and acceptance of their disease. Finally, in her study of 23 African American women, Mattis (2002) noted that religion and spirituality served as a vehicle of recognizing purpose and destiny for her research participants. She notes that "forty-eight percent of the women in the study insisted that there is a purpose (a plan) both to their existence and to the negative as well as positive events that they experience. This knowledge permitted them to put extraordinary as well as mundane happenings into perspective and shape the kinds of appraisals and attributions that they made" (p. 314).

The research of Paul Wong (Wong & Fry, 1998; Wong, Reker, & Peacock, Chapter 11; Wong & Ujimoto, 1998) and his students (Dumerton, 2004) with various ethnic minorities in Canada (e.g., First Nations, Asian Canadians) is also of importance in this regard. In contrast to Pargament and his colleagues, whose usage of 'meaning' focuses largely on the cognitive appraisal of the significance of an event, Wong emphasizes *existential coping*, which consists of finding positive meaning in negative situations. The latter dimension is considered the central tenet of Frankl's tragic optimism (Frankl, 1984), and has also provided the groundwork for Wong's research in this domain (Wong & McDonald, 2002).

4.2. Gaining Control

The ability to gain a sense of control, either directly or vicariously, was a second dimension that was echoed in the studies. Siegel & Schrimshaw (2002) noted that a common theme among their participants was that religion and spirituality offered strength, empowerment and control in the face of an uncontrollable illness – HIV/AIDS. Gall and Cornblat (2002) found the same theme emerged for breast cancer survivors. Mattis (2002) noted that spiritual surrender, the giving up of one's control to a higher power, was a key theme for her participants. She states that, "any and all aspects of an adverse situation may be surrendered. Women surrender their emotions, their confusions, as well as the lives of others... It appears that by 'turning things over' women gain the power to more clearly see and understand the side(s) of the circumstances in which they found themselves. Further, turning things over to a higher power invited individuals into relationship (with God, other divine entities, and/or other humans). Through these relationships and the resultant intimacy, individuals were able to gain the insight, protection, and guidance needed to envision and achieve outcomes that they would not have been able to see or achieve on their own" (p. 313). The contribution of religious faith in accepting one's condition was also echoed in a study of Muslim women suffering from depression (Hussain & Cochrance, 2003) and in a clinical case study of a young, Jewish man with schizophrenia. Heilman & Witztum (2000) point to the importance of religion practices in grounding a schizophrenic client into reality. "His religious concerns and the rituals associated with them served to thrust back into a reality and at least partially to put his disorder and anxieties aside. They offered him a kind of overarching orientation, however limited, that gave him some respite from his anxieties, torments and hallucinations. (p. 119).

4.3. Gaining Comfort and Closeness to God

This third dimension was widely confirmed in the cross-cultural and emic studies. Siegel & Schrimshaw (2002), for example, identified four themes in their study of religious/spiritual coping that could be grouped under this heading. These included (a) finding that religious coping eased the emotional burden of illness, (b) that it evoked comforting emotions, (c) that it relieved the fear and burden of one's impending death, and (d) that it offered spiritual support through a personal relationship with God. They note that for people coping with HIV/AIDS, "many who could not speak with others about their illness because they had not disclosed their HIV diagnosis found God to be a valuable confidant. Those who were physically unable to attend formal religious services, or those who felt rejected by and estranged from organized religion, often spoke of the sustenance they drew from their personal relationship with God" (p. 96).

In their study of 20 African American caregivers of persons with HIV, Pointdexter, Linsk & Warner (1999) echo these findings, noting that their participants gained a distinctive inner strength from their faith, in spite of the fact that they did not feel the sense of support from their fellow church members. They note that "while their congregations may have failed most of them as a source of direct social support, the answer is not for them to leave the church, for the church also provides the linguistic and cultural context which sustains the reality of the God on whom they rely" (p. 239). Again, the sense of inner comfort from their relationship with God was echoed by survivors of breast cancer (Gall & Cornblat, 2002).

4.4. Gaining Intimacy with Others

The importance of receiving social support and gaining a sense of intimacy with others has been consistently described as one of the most important functions of religious/spiritual coping (Pargament, 1997; Hazel & Mohatt, 2001; Krause et al., 2001). Siegel & Schrimshaw (2002) found that in spite of the stigma attached to HIV/AIDS, their participants repeatedly noted the importance of receiving social support from fellow church members and gaining a sense of belonging from their faith community. In their study of African American elders, Wallace & Bergeman (2002) found that the importance of social support is more complex than initially assumed. Social support meant not only receiving the care of fellow believers, but also extended to the reciprocal dimension of caring for others, as well as the importance of keeping active within one's community.

4.5. Achieving Life Transformation

Not only did religion served to protect and preserve some of the important dimensions of life, various studies also noted its potential for and contribution to life transformation and personal and spiritual growth. Gall & Cornblat (2002) noted that religion and spirituality facilitated adjustment in breast cancer survivors through enabling a positive attitude, receiving guidance from God, and inner strength to cope with the illness. Mattis (2002) noted that spirituality both highlighted and enabled her participants to transcend their personal boundaries and achieve growth and transformation. For example, one of her co-researchers, Grace, "asserted that even while she remained fully aware of the limitations basing her, she was able to transcend potentially desperate life circumstances by using her relationship with a Higher Power as a means of (re)envisioning and (re)creating her destiny (and the destinies of her sons)" (p. 314). These results strongly echo the work of Tedeschi & Calhoun (1995) on post-traumatic growth.

4.6. Contextual dimensions of religious/spiritual coping

Moving beyond the functions of religion/spirituality suggested by Pargament and his colleagues, a novel and more contextually sensitive theme emerged in the research, that does not seem to be subsumed in the previous five dimensions. Much of the religious/spiritual coping literature has been consumed with the identification, measurement, and validation of behaviours and cognitions which facilitate this process. However, it may be argued that the search for the constituent components of religious/spiritual coping may have omitted some of the larger, pervasive dimensions of faith (e.g., Ai et al., 2003; cf., Ganzevoort, 1998).

Several qualitative studies have pointed to the role that religion/spirituality play in the development of a sense of self and of one's identity. Wallace and Bergeman (2001), for example, note that in their study of African American elders, "religion and spirituality fostered self-concept for these individuals by providing a safe, supportive, and accepting environment" (p. 145). They also point to the importance of religion and spirituality throughout the life span. Particularly, participants in the study noted the importance of being brought up in the faith that contributed to their present sense of stability and of viewing the church as a second home. Spencer et al (2003) echo this sentiment in their study of African American youth, by noting that especially for males, "religion and spirituality and cultural pride as a form of coping are important in the development of a healthy sense of self and a healthy sense of self and relation to others (p. 187). Similarly, Pointdexter, Linsk & Warner (1999) point to this unique cultural and religious phenomenon for African-American Christians. They note that, "rather than being the product of an individualized search, their personal religiosity is culturally defined, anchored in the traditional, community-oriented, shared experience of the Protestant, and specifically African-American, Christian tradition" (p. 239).

In their study of sobriety amongst Native Americans in Alaska, Hazel & Mohatt (2001) similarly identified the importance of identity and its relationship to the land and the cultural and spiritual practices. They learned from their participants that their Native spirituality is an immensely embodied faith, which cannot be separated from their land-bound lifestyle (e.g., maintaining a connection to the land through hunting, fishing, agriculture, etc). Thus, a thorough understanding of their religion and culture were pre-requisite to the development of any program seeking to further sobriety amongst Native Americans. They note that

> *Issues of cultural identity and cultural-spiritual awareness have a particular relevance to prevention. Several authors have argued the importance of addressing what is perceived as problems related to cultural identity and esteem in substance abuse prevention programs for American Indian youth... the results of this research suggest that these and similar prevention programs and models that incorporate and enhance cultural and spiritual dimensions deserve more attention. It is clear from this research that issues of cultural identification, which is highly interrelated with spirituality, is important not only for American Indians and Alaska Natives who are recovering from alcohol addiction but also for the prevention of alcohol abuse within Native communities (p. 556).*

This emerging dimension of culture, which undergirds and conflates with personal religious ideology, is one that psychologists need to take serious in their study of religious/spiritual coping.

5. AGONIAS AND RELIGIOUS/SPIRITUAL COPING

Many researchers have consistently argued for the importance of investigating religious/spiritual coping in a contextually sensitive manner. Our work with Portuguese immigrants from the Azores Islands (James, 2002; James & Prilleltensky, 2002) certainly supports that theory. In our investigations into *agonias* (meaning 'the agonies'), a culture-specific somatic phenomenon of Portuguese immigrants, we have found a number of unique ways in which this group copes with various stressors. These include communal coping, visiting multiple healers, and culture-specific coping strategies. Each of these methods will be discussed below in more detail.

5.1. Communal suffering and coping

Suffering for community members is not seen as situated only within the individual but takes on a socio-religious meaning as well. One Portuguese clinician noted,

> *Suffering is a way to build relationships with other people.... When suffering is one's cross to bear and there is purpose in suffering, it takes on a totally different meaning and it is something that you are not ashamed to share with others. People look for empathy through suffering, empathy from friends and from the community.*

Thus, bodily suffering mediates relationships.

For many of the participants, suffering is imbued with power. One woman said, "God doesn't respond immediately all the time ... God wants to see that we really want our faith and our power." Another empowering notion is that the suffering, no matter how difficult presently, will not continue forever but merely exists in the present world. One mental health provider remarked, "I think that many women, especially in the reality of domestic problems, like domestic violence, marital issues, and problems with their children are saying, 'this is my cross to bear....' They see a purpose in their suffering, if not in this world, then in the other world." Empowerment is certainly a welcome concept to a group that has often been disempowered in North America and in their home country.

Similar to the other research in this volume (e.g., Wong, 2005; Yeh, 2005), which has pointed to use of collective coping strategies, our research with Portuguese immigrants has demonstrated that community members help each other when they are ill. This strategy moves beyond receiving social support in that the community itself takes on an individual's problem as their own; thus, it ceases to be the concern of simply one person and becomes the concern of the group. One community member said "As the Great Physician helps His people in a time of need; we in turn help our neighbours when they are suffering". The priest suggested that this is a way for them to serve the Divine as Christ indicated when he said, "Truly, I say to you, as you did it to one of the least of these my brethren, you did it to me." Matt. 25:40 (Revised Standard Version).

5.2. Commensurable multiple systems

The above quote also provides an example of how medicine and spirituality are inextricably linked. Rather than seeing divine healing as separate from medical healing the two are interwoven as is evident when the respondent referred to God as "The Great Physician". Consequently, some of the healers felt that they were expected to fulfil multiple roles. One physician has noticed that "or medical care has to be all-encompassing for this group. I find myself not only being a physician but a priest and a social worker as well". The priest agreed, "a lot of time people will come in with what I would consider psychological, emotional or deeper problems."

Not only did the Portuguese community seek allopathic and religious healers, they also sought traditional healers as well, such as herbalists, shamen (*curandeiros*) and mediums. The utilisation of these three healing systems is commensurable because allopathic and indigenous healers are just extensions of God's domain. A Portuguese physician commented,

> *There is a connection between the spiritual and scientific that goes beyond both realms. My approach is to tackle the problem in as many ways as possible and make all of the treatments available to the patient. I think that one of the advantages of being Portuguese and dealing with Portuguese patients is that they don't need to hide from me that they're seeking out other forms of healing.*

5.3. Coping strategies

Portuguese immigrants employ a wide range of strategies in coping with *agonias*. Many community members help each other and visit community healers when they are suffering. Second, the sharing of information plays a large role in their coping strategies. For instance, the waiting room of a Portuguese Health Clinic in the United States also served as a location for the continual exchange of information between patients. Patients who had seen their health care provides chatted with other patients for long periods of time. Many times they are sharing health information. One participant remarked,

> *In the Azores people talk about their health all of the time so that they can learn about the health secrets of others. They probably did this out of necessity because health care was so poor that it was helpful to disseminate health information aurally.*

This method of sharing health information is not lost in the new context. Whereas before they were trying to discover the secrets of health, now they discuss health issues because they are trying to discover the secrets of another mystery, negotiating the American health care system.

Another strategy that the community employs is prayer and church attendance. In their meta-analysis of the role of religion in coping with depression, Smith et al. (2003) found that church attendance and prayer can be linked with a decrease in depression. This was consistent with how many of the therapists talked about church attendance. The therapists suggested that they can tell the state of their clients' psychological condition by whether or not they went to church the previous weekend. At church they receive support from the priest or other congregants.

Many of the participants in the study talked of how they completely surrendered their problem to God and envisioned and active Deity acting on their behalf. One woman explained, "God is the one who knows. The Saint and God take care of me... The suffering will last until the day God wants. The day that He says close your eyes and come here with me."

Although many participants talked of completely surrendering to God, that did not mean that they did not comply with medical treatments as one might suspect. With this population, natural remedies are not to be dismissed. Rather, it is believed that God works through the mechanisms in the body and it is a person's duty to employ natural remedies from traditional healers or medication from physicians without relying on them exclusively (Thomas, 1997). One Physician explained,

> *They feel that we have the power to help them but the ultimate outcome is dictated by God's will. If it's meant to be, they will get better. On the other hand, they also feel that doctors should be consulted and that we are not trying to take God's place. God is working through us. If it's meant for them to get better, it's a way of getting better faster. In other words, going to a doctor is not against their religion.*

Portuguese community members engage in a number of active coping strategies by supporting each other, praying, consulting priests, health providers, and traditional healers, attending church, and gathering information. Even though they are engaged in these activities they are sometimes labeled as "passive" by psychotherapists serving this community because they are not behaving in the way that the therapists expect active copers to behave. For instance, they are not reading the literature the therapist provides because they are gathering their information aurally from each other and their reading levels (especially in English) are not very well-developed. The clients might not be completing homework assigned because they are working on the problem at other levels and the suggestion of the therapist to focus on psychological aspects could be seen as lower priority.

There are some future directions that emerge from the study of immigrant communities. Within the immigrant research literature different acculturation styles have been explored. The one that is given the most attention and is seen as the most favourable for mental health and adjustment is a bicultural acculturation style which means that the person adopts North American culture but at the same time maintains his or her home culture. This is seen as the most advantageous because the person can draw resources from two systems as opposed to one. Future research could investigate whether people who are bicultural have more access to religious and spiritual coping strategies than other groups. A second area of consideration involves the cultural relevance and validity of various measures of psychological well being and distress (such as the *Satisfaction with Life Scale*). Is this questionnaire appropriate for all cultural groups? For instance, for the Portuguese, a good person suffers and is not striving to be satisfied so the measure would need to be validated for the community with that in mind. Lastly, the research in the religion and spiritual coping domain often does not include investigate the practice of seeking traditional healers. This literature could be expanded by including traditional healing systems when investigating practices for a more complete look at the person and his or her lived experience (cf., Hazel & Mohatt, 2001).

6. CONCLUSION

As a discipline, psychology has made significant strides towards the inclusion of religion and spirituality in its theoretical and empirical investigations. The domain of religious/spiritual coping within the wider context of the contextual theory of coping, has established itself as a unique and valid process that concerns itself with the search for the sacred as a response to human suffering. We have attempted to give a broad overview of significant developments in religious/spiritual coping theory that have taken place since

1997. In addition to reviewing mainstream religious/spiritual typologies, methods, means of assessment and outcome studies, we have also included a significant review of cross-cultural and emic studies, which support and extend mainstream research findings. Moreover, our case study of religious/spiritual coping among Portuguese immigrants to Canada and the United States from the Azores has demonstrated the necessity of employing contextually sensitive research methodologies to capture unique cultural and spiritual coping dimensions of this ethnic and religious community.

Future investigations into spiritual/religious coping must take recent the developments documented in this review seriously. It is no longer sufficient to employ measures and methodologies that obscure the complexity of religious/spiritual coping for the sake of research expedience. Scholars of spirituality now have the opportunity take advantage of the significant advances over the past seven years and can engage in research that is contextually sensitive, methodologically rigorous and theoretically coherent. We hope that our review and critique of the domain of religious/spiritual coping will encourage and enable such exploration.

REFERENCES

Aldwin, C. M. & Park, C. L. (2004). Coping and physical health outcomes: An overview. *Psychology & Health, 19*, 277-281.

Alferi, S. M., Culver, J. L., Carver, C. S., Arena, P. L., & Antoni, M. H. (1999). Religiosity, religious coping, and distress: A prospective study of catholic and evangelical Hispanic women in treatment for early-stage breast cancer. *Journal of Health Psychology, 4,* 343-356.

Ai, A. L., Peterson, C. & Huang, B. (2003). The effect of religious-spiritual coping on positive attitudes of adult Muslim refugees from Kosovo and Bosnia. *The International Journal for the Psychology of Religion, 13*, 29-47.

Baer, R. A. (2003). Mindfulness training as a clinical intervention: A conceptual and empirical review. *Clinical Psychology: Science & Practice, 10*, 125-143.

Baumeister, R. F. (2002). Religion and psychology [Special issue]. *Psychological Inquiry, 13(3)*.

Belavich, T. G. & Pargament, K. I. (2002). The role of attachment in predicting spiritual coping with a loved one in surgery. *Journal of Adult Development, 9*, 13-29.

Bjorck, J. P., Cuthbertson, W., Thurman, J. W. & Lee, Y. S. (2001). Ethnicity, coping, and distress among Korean Americans, Filipino Americans, and Caucasian Americans. *The Journal of Social Psychology, 141*, 421-442.

Bibby, R. W. (2002). *Restless gods: The renaissance of religion in Canada*. Toronto: Stoddart.

Bosworth, H. B., Park, K. S., McQuoid, D. R., Hays, J. C. & Steffens, D. C. (2003). The impact of religious practice and religious coping on geriatric depression. *International Journal of Geriatric Psychiatry, 18*, 905-914.

Bush, E. G., Rye, M. S., Brant, C. R., Emery, E., Pargament, K. I. & Riessinger, C. A. (1999). Religious coping with chronic pain. *Applied Psychophysiology and Biofeedback, 24*, 249-260.

Butter, E. M. & Pargament, K. I. (2003). Development of a model for clinical assessment of religious coping: Initial validation of the process evaluation model. *Mental Health, Religion & Culture, 6*, 175-194.

Culver, J. L., Arena, P. L., Antoni, M. H. & Carver, C. S. (2002). Coping and distress among women under treatment for early stage breast cancer: Comparing African Americans, Hispanics, and Non-Hispanic Whites. *Psycho-Oncology, 11*, 495-504.

Dumerton, L. (2004). *Tragic optimism and choices: The Life Attitudes Scale with a First Nations sample.* Unpublished Masters Thesis, Trinity Western University, Langley, BC.

Egbert, N., Mickley, J., & Coeling, H. (2004). A review and application of social scientific measures of religiosity and spirituality: Assessing a missing component in health communication research. *Health Communications, 16*, 7-27.

Emmons, R. A. & Paloutzian, R. F. (2003). The psychology of religion. *Annual Review of Psychology, 54*, 377-402.

Fabricatore, A. N., Randal, P. J., Rubio, D. M., Gilner, F. H. (2004). Stress, religion, and mental health: Religious coping in mediating and moderating roles. *International Journal for the Psychology of Religion, 14,* 97-108.

Ferraro, K. F. & Kelley-Moore, J. A. (2001). Religious seeking among affiliates and non-affiliates: Do mental and physical health problems spur religious coping? *Review of Religious Research, 42,* 229-251.

Folkman, S. & Moskowitz, J. T. (2004). Coping: Pitfalls and promise. *Annual Review of Psychology, 55,* 745-774.

Fowler, R. D. (Ed.) (2003). *American Psychologist, 58*(1).

Gall, T. L. & Cornblat, M. W. (2002). Breast cancer survivors give voice: A qualitative analysis of spiritual factors in long-term adjustment. *Psycho-Oncology, 11,* 524-535.

Gall, T. L. (2000). Integrating religious resources within a general model of stress and coping: Long-term adjustment to breast cancer. *Journal of Religion and Health, 39,* 167-182.

Ganzevoort, R. R. (1998). Religious coping reconsidered, Part One: An integrated approach. *Journal of Psychology & Theology, 26,* pp. 260-275.

Gordon, P. A., Feldman, D., Crose, R., Schoen, E., Griffing, G., & Shankar, J. (2002). The role of religious beliefs in coping with chronic illness. *Counseling & Values, 46,* 162-174.

Hackney, C. H. & Sanders, G. S. (2003). Religiosity and mental health: A meta-analysis of recent studies. *Journal for the Scientific Study of Religion, 42,* 43-55.

Harrison, M. O., Koenig, H. G., Hays, J. C., Eme-Akwari, A. G. & Pargament, K. I. (2001). The epidemiology of religious coping: A review of recent literature. *International Review of Psychiatry, 13,* 86-93.

Hazel, K. L. & Mohatt, G. V. (2001). Cultural and spiritual coping in sobriety: Informing substance abuse prevention for Alaska native communities. *Journal of Community Psychology, 29,* 541-562.

Helminiak, D. A. (1996). A scientific spirituality: The interface of psychology and theology. *International Journal for the Psychology of Religion, 6,* 1-19.

Heilman, S. C. & Witztum, E. (2000). All in faith: Religion as the idiom and means of coping with stress. *Mental Health, Religion & Culture, 3,* 115-124.

Hill, P. C. & Pargament, K. I. (2003). Advances in the conceptualization and measurement of religion and spirituality. Implications for physical and mental health research. *American Psychologist, 58,* 64-74.

Hill, P. C., Pargament, K. I., Hood, Jr., R. W., McCullough, M. E., Swyers, J. P., Larson, D. B., et al. (2000). Conceptualizing religion and spirituality: Points of commonality, points of departure. *Journal for the Theory of Social Behaviour, 30,* 51-77.

Hines Smith, S. (2002). "Fret no more my child...for I'm all over heaven all day": Religious beliefs in the bereavement of African American, middle-aged daughters coping with the death of an elderly mother. *Death Studies, 26,* 309-323.

Hussain, F. A. & Cochrane, R. (2003). Living with depression: Coping strategies used by South Asian women, living in the UK, suffering from depression. *Mental Health, Religion & Culture, 6,* 21-44.

James, S. (2002). Agonias: The social and sacred suffering of Azorean Immigrants. *Culture, Medicine, and Psychiatry, 26,* 87-110.

James, S., & Prilleltensky, I. (2002). Cultural diversity and mental health: Towards integrative practice. *Clinical Psychology Review, 22,* 1133-1154.

Khalili, S., Murken, S., Reich, K. H., Shah, A. A., Vahabzadeh, A. (2002). Religion and mental health in cultural perspective: Observations and reflections after The First International Congress on Religion and Mental Health, Tehran, 16-19 April 2001. *The International Journal for the Psychology of Religion, 12,* 217-237.

Kinney, J. M., Ishler, K. J., Pargament, K. I., & Cavanaugh, J. C. (2003). Coping with the uncontrollable: The use of general and religious coping by caregivers to spouses with dementia. *Journal of Religious Gerontology, 14,* 171-188.

Klaassen, D. W. & McDonald, M. J. (2001). Quest and identity development: Re-examining pathways for existential search. *International Journal for the Psychology of Religion, 12,* 189-200.

Koenig, H. G., McCullough, M. E., & Larson, D. B. (2001). *Handbook of religion and health.* Oxford: Oxford University Press.

Krause, N. (1998). Stressors in highly valued roles, religious coping, and mortality. *Psychology and Aging, 13,* 242-255.

Krause, N., Ellison, C. G., Shaw, B. A., Marcum, J. P. & Boardman, J. D. (2001). Church-based social support and religious coping. *Journal for the Scientific Study of Religion, 40,* 637-656.

Laubmeier, K. K., Zakowski, S. G. & Bair, J. P. (2004). The role of spirituality in the psychological adjustment to cancer: A test of the transactional model of stress and coping. *International Journal of Behavioral Medicine, 11,* 48-55.

Lazarus, R. S. & Folkman, S. (1984). *Stress, appraisal, and coping.* New York: Springer.

Lazarus, R. S. (1999). *Stress and emotion: A new synthesis.* New York: Springer.

Lewin, F. A. (2001). Investigating religious and spiritually oriented coping strategies in the Swedish context: A review of the literature and directions for future research. *Illness, Crisis & Loss, 9,* 336-356.

Loewenthal, K. M., Cinnirella, M., Evodoka, G. & Murphy, P. (2001). Faith conquers all? Beliefs about the role of religious factors in coping with depression among different cultural-religious groups in the UK. *British Journal of Medical Psychology, 74,* 293-303.

McClain, C. S., Rosenfeld, B., Breitbart, W. (2003). Effect of spiritual well-being on end-of-life despair in terminally-ill cancer patients. *Lancet, 361,* 1603-1607.

Mahoney, A., Pargament, K. I., Tarakeshwar, N. & Swank, A. B. (2001). Religion in the home in the 1980s and 1990s: A meta-analytic review and conceptual analysis of links between religion, marriage, and parenting. *Journal of Family Psychology, 15,* 559-596.

Mattis, J. S. (2002). Religion and spirituality in the meaning-making and coping experiences of African American women: A qualitative analysis. *Psychology of Women Quarterly, 26,* 309-321.

McCullough, M. E., Hoyt, W. T., Larson, D. B., Koenig, H. G. & Thoresen, C. (2000). Religious involvement and mortality: A meta-analytic review. *Health Psychology, 19,* 211-222.

Meisenhelder, J. B. (2002). Terrorism, posttraumatic stress, and religious coping. *Issues in Mental Health Nursing, 23,* 771-782.

Miller, W. R. & Thoresen, C. E. (2003). Spirituality, religion, and health: An emerging research field. *American Psychologist, 58,* 24-35.

Moberg, D. O. (2002). Assessing and measuring spirituality: Confronting dilemmas of universal and particular evaluative criteria. *Journal of Adult Development, 9,* 47-60.

Murphy, S. A., Johnson, L. C., & Lohan, J. (2003). Finding meaning in a child's violent death: A five-year prospective analysis of parents' personal narratives and empirical data. *Death Studies, 27,* 381-404.

Nairn, R. C. & Merluzzi, T. V. (2003). The role of religious coping in adjustment to cancer. *Psycho-Oncology, 12,* 428-441.

Nooney, J. & Woodrum, E. (2002). Religious coping and church-based social support as predictors of mental health outcomes: Testing a conceptual model. *Journal for the Scientific Study of Religion, 41,* 359-368.

Oman, D. & Thoresen, C. E. (2002). Does religion cause health?": Differing interpretations and diverse meanings. *Journal of Health Psychology, 7,* 365-380.

Osborne, T. L. & Vandenberg, B. (2003). Situational and denominational differences in religious coping. *The International Journal for the Psychology of Religion, 13,* 111-122.

Pandey, M., Lantha, P. T., Mathew, A., Ramdas, K., Chaturvedi, S. K., Iype, E. M. & Nair, K. M. (2003). Concerns and coping strategies in patients with oral cancer: A pilot study. *Indian Journal of Surgery, 65,* 496-499.

Pargament, K. I. (1997). *The psychology of religion and coping.* New York: Guildford.

Pargament, K. I. (1999). The psychology of religion and spirituality? Yes and no. The *International Journal for the Psychology of Religion, 9,* 3-16.

Pargament, K. I. (2002a). The bitter and the sweet: An evaluation of the costs and benefits of religiousness. *Psychological Inquiry, 13,* 168-181.

Pargament, K. I. (2002b). Is religion nothing but...? Explaining religion versus explaining religion away. *Psychological Inquiry, 13,* 239-244.

Pargament, K. I., Kennell, J., Hathaway, W., Grevengoed, N., Newman, J., & Jones, W. (1988). Religion and the problem-solving process: Three styles of coping. *Journal for the Scientific Study of Religion, 27,* 90-104.

Pargament, K. I., Koenig, H. G., & Perez, L. M. (2000). The many methods of religious coping: Development and initial validation of the RCOPE. *Journal of Clinical Psychology, 56,* 519-543.

Pargament, K. I., Smith, B. W., Koenig, H. G. & Perez, L. (1998). Patterns of positive and negative coping with major life stressors. *Journal for the Scientific Study of Religion, 37,* 710-724.

Pargament, K. I., Sullivan, M. S., Balzer, W. K., Van Haitsma, K. S. & Raymark, P. H. (1995). The many meanings of religiousness: A policy-capturing approach. *Journal of Personality, 63,* 953-983.

Pargament, K. I., Zinnbauer, B. J., Scott, A. B., Butter, E. M., Zerowin, J. & Stanik, P. (1998). Red flags and religious coping: Identifying some religious warning signs among people in crisis. *Journal of Clinical Psychology, 54,* 77-89.

Pendleton, S. M., Cavalli, K. S., Pargament, K. I., & Nasr, C. Z. (2002). Religious/spiritual coping in childhood systic fibrosis: A qualitative study. *Pediatrics, 109,* 8-19.

Peterson, C. & Seligman, M. E. P. (Eds.) (2004). *Character strengths and virtues: A handbook and classification.* Washington: APA Press.

Phillips, R. E., Pargament, K. I., Lynn, Q. K., & Crossley, C. D. (2004). Self-directing religious coping: A deistic God, abandoning God, or no God at all? *Journal for the Scientific Study of Religion, 43*, 409-418.

Plante, T. G. & Canchola, E. L. (2004). The association between strength of religious faith and coping with American terrorism regarding the events of September 11, 2001. *Pastoral Psychology, 52*, 269-278.

Plante, T. G., Saucedo, B., & Rice, C. (2001). The association between strength of religious faith and coping with daily stress. *Pastoral Psychology, 49*, 291-300.

Poindexter, C. C., Linsk, N. L., & Warner, R. S. (1999). "He listens...and never gossips:" Spiritual coping without church support among older, predominantly African-American caregivers of persons with HIV. *Review of Religious Research, 40*, 230-243.

Rammohan, A., Rao, K. & Subbakrishna, D. K. (2002). Religious coping and psychological wellbeing in carers of relatives with schizophrenia. *Acta Psychiatrica Scandinavica, 105*, 356-362.

Reger, G. M. & Rogers, S. A. (2002). Diagnostic differences in religious coping among individuals with persistent mental illness. *Journal of Psychology and Christianity, 21*, 341-348.

Roesch, S. C. & Ano, G. (2003). Testing an attribution and coping model of stress: Religion as an orienting system. *Journal of Psychology and Christianity, 22*, 197-209.

Rogers, S. A., Poey, E. L., Reger, G. M., Tepper, L. & Coleman, E. M. (2002). Religious coping among those with persistent mental illness. *The International Journal for the Psychology of Religion, 12*, 161-175.

Siegel, K. & Schrimshaw, E. W. (2002). The perceived benefits of religious and spiritual coping among older adults living with HIV/AIDS. *Journal for the Scientific Study of Religion, 41*, 91-102.

Siegel, K., Anderman, S. J. & Schrimshaw, E. W. (2001). Religion and coping with health-related stress. *Psychology and Health, 16*, 631-653.

Simoni, J. M., Martone, M. G. & Kerwin, J. F. (2002). Spirituality and psychological adaptation among women with HIV/AIDS: Implications for counseling. *Journal of Counseling Psychology, 49*, 139-147.

Smith, B. W., Pargament, K. I., Brant, C. & Oliver, J. M. (2000). Noah revisited: Religious coping by church members and the impact of the 1993 Midwest flood. *Journal of Community Psychology, 28*, 169-186.

Smith, T. B., McCullough, M. E. & Poll, J. (2003). Religiousness and depression: Evidence for a main effect and the moderating influence of stressful life events. *Psychological Bulletin, 129*, 614-636.

Snethen, J. A., Broome, M. E., Kelber, S. & Warady, B. A. (2004). Coping strategies utilized by adolescents with end stage renal disease. *Nephrology Nursing Journal, 31*, 41-49.

Somlai, A. M. & Heckman, T. G. (2000). Correlates of spirituality and well-being in a community sample of people living with HIV disease. *Mental Health, Religion & Culture, 10*, 57-70.

Soothill, K., Morris, S. M., Harman, J. C., Thomas, C., Francis, B. & McIllmurray, M. B. (2002). Cancer and faith. Having faith -does it make a difference among patients and their informal carers? *Scandinavian Journal of the Caring Sciences, 16*, 256-263.

Spencer, M. B., Fegley, S. G. & Harpalani, V. (2003). A theoretical and empirical examination of identity as coping: Linking coping resources to the self processes of African American youth. *Applied Developmental Sciences, 7*, 181-188.

Stanton, A. L., Danoff-Burg, S. & Huggins, M. E. (2002). The first year after breast cancer diagnosis: Hope and coping strategies as predictors of adjustment. *Psycho-Oncology, 11*, 93-102.

Strang, S. & Strang, P. (2001). Spiritual thoughts, coping and 'sense of coherence' in brain tumour patients and their spouses. *Palliative Medicine, 15*, 127-134.

Tarakeshwar, N. & Pargament, K. I. (2001). Religious coping in families of children with autism. *Focus on Autism and Other Developmental Disabilities, 16*, 247-260.

Tarakeshwar, N., Pargament, K. I. & Mahoney, A. (2003). Initial development of a measure of religious copuing among Hindus. *Journal of Community Psychology, 31*, 607-628.

Tarakeshwar, N., Stanton, J. & Pargament, K. I. (2003). Religion: An overlooked dimension in cross-cultural psychology. *Journal of Cross-Cultural Psychology, 34*, 377-394.

Taylor, N. M. (2001). Utilizing religious schemas to cope with mental illness. *Journal of Religion and Health, 40*, 383-388.

Tedeschi, R.G. & Calhoun, L.G. (1995). *Trauma and transformation: Growing in the aftermath of suffering.* Thousand Oaks, CA: Sage.

Tennen, H., Affleck, G., Armeli, S., & Carney, M. A. (2000). A daily process approach to coping: Linking theory, research, and practice. *American Psychologist, 55*, 626-636.

Thomas, K. (1997). Health and morality in early modern England. In A. Brandt and P. Rozin (Eds.), *Morality and Health*. New York: Routledge.

Tix, A. P. & Frazier, P. A. (1998). The use of religious coping during stressful life events: Main effects, moderation, and mediation. *Journal of Consulting and Clinical Psychology, 66*, 411-422.

Wallace, K. A. & Bergeman, C. S. (2002). Spirituality and religiosity in a sample of African American elders: A life story approach. *Journal of Adult Development, 9*, 141-154.

Wang, J. & Patten, S. B. (2002). The moderating effects of coping strategies on major depression in the general population. *Canadian Journal of Psychiatry, 47*, 167-173.

Watson, P. J., Morris, R. J., Hood, Jr., R. W., Milliron, J. T., & Stutz, N. L. (1998). Religious orientation, identity, and the quest for meaning in ethics within an ideological surround. *International Journal for the Psychology of Religion, 8*, 149-164.

Witvliet, C. V. O., Phipps, K. A., Feldman, M. E., & Beckham, J. C. (2004). Posttraumatic mental and physical health correlates of forgiveness and religious coping in military veterans. *Journal of Traumatic Stress, 17*(3), 269-273.

Wong, P. T. P. (1993). Effective management of life stress: The resource-congruence model. *Stress Medicine, 9*, 51-60.

Wong, P. T. P. & Fry, P. S. (Eds.) (1998). *The human quest for meaning: A handbook of psychological research and clinical applications*. Mahwah, NJ: Lawrence Erlbaum.

Wong, P. T. P., & McDonald, M. (2002). Tragic optimism and personal meaning in counselling victims of abuse. *Pastoral Sciences, 20*, 231-249.

Wong, P. T. P. & Ujimoto, K. V. (1998). The elderly Asian Americans: Their stress, coping, and well-being. In L. C. Lee & N. W. S. Zane (Eds.), *Handbook of Asian American Psychology* (pp.165-209). Thousand Oaks, CA: Sage Publications.

Wong-McDonald, A. & Gorsuch, R. L. (2000). Surrender to God: An additional coping style? *Journal of Psychology and Theology, 28*, 149-161.

Wuthnow, R. (2004). Presidential address 2003: The challenge of diversity. *Journal for the Scientific Study of Religion, 43*, 159-170.

Yeh, C. & Inose, M. (2002). Difficulties and coping strategies of Chines, Japanese, and Korean immigrant students. *Adolescence, 37*, 69-82.

Zinnbauer, B. J., Pargament, K. I, & Scott, A. B. (1999). The emerging meanings of religiousness and spirituality: Problems and prospects. *Journal of Personality, 67*, 889-919.

Zinnbauer, B. J., Pargament, K. I., Cole, B., Rye, M. S., Butter, E. M., Belavich, T. G., et al. (1997). Religion and spirituality: Unfuzzying the fuzzy. *Journal for the Scientific Study of Religion, 36*, 549-564.

7

COPING STRATEGIES AND CULTURALLY INFLUENCED BELIEFS ABOUT THE WORLD

Roger G. Tweed and Lucian Gideon Conway, III

1. INTRODUCTION

Doing cultural psychology is like drawing caricature cartoons. Caricature cartoonists exaggerate bodily characteristics in ways that help people recognize features distinctive to particular individuals. Prior to seeing a caricature cartoon, casual observers may be able to recognize that a given individual's face is unique, but may not take the time to or may be unable to verbalize which features make it so. Caricatures help make the features explicit. Yet the very act of thus bringing these features into the public eye involves an exaggeration of their true nature.

Cultural psychologists, like their more visual cartoonist counterparts, also exaggerate particular features of the pictures they are (metaphorically) drawing. This has the same advantages, as well as the same dangers, as drawing caricatures. The act of distinguishing different features of a culture helps observers become aware of legitimate cultural differences. Humans are sometimes sensitive to even minute differences between cultural groups, but often may not take the time to understand or may actively misinterpret these differences. Like recognizing that a face is distinct but not knowing why, humans may recognize that other cultures "seem different," but lack ability to articulate the reasons. Cultural psychologists help to clarify these differences between cultural groups which are noticed by many, but clearly and accurately described by few.

For example, Markus and Kitayama (1991) in a frequently cited paper explained that some cultural groups (e.g., Japanese) conceive of the self as being interdependent with others, but that other cultural groups (e.g., North Americans) conceive of the self as being independent. Sophisticated observers, and Markus and Kitayama themselves, will recognize that this statement oversimplifies and exaggerates reality. Few if any Americans (perhaps only the autistic or true hermits) will believe the self is truly free of dependence on others. Likewise, few if any Japanese will claim that the self completely lacks some sense of independent existence from others. Furthermore, consideration of the nature of normal distributions suggests that there will probably be many Americans who are more interdependent than many Japanese; consider, for example, the interdependence expressed when Americans cheer on

Roger G. Tweed, Kwantlen University College; Lucian Gideon Conway, III, The University of Montana their favorite sporting team. Thus, such blanket generalizations about cultural differences may capture something accurate about reality, but if taken as literal monolithic statements, such statements tend to be crude at best.

Of course, the underlying goals of the cultural psychologist and cartoonist are generally quite different: Cultural psychologists seek not the humor and divisiveness that the political caricature cartoonist seeks, but rather understanding and conciliation. Cultural psychologists face the difficult task of trying to increase understanding of group differences and similarities while not increasing the human tendency to prejudge individuals from particular racial or cultural groups.

Cultural psychologists thus always face the risk that their findings will be abused. Does this mean cultural psychologists should cease their activity? We believe not. Increased understanding of culturally distant values may promote learning from ways unlike one's own and may highlight important but previously unrecognized differences within cultural groups (e.g., Tweed and Lehman, 2002). As children's activities may not make sense to an adult observer, but will make sense from the perspective of the child, likewise, activities of one cultural group may not initially make sense to individuals from a culturally distant group, but will often make sense if members of the second group attempt to understand the meaning system of the first group. Even though cultural psychological findings simplify and possibly exaggerate differences between groups, they often nevertheless reflect something accurate about average differences between cultural groups. Even though Markus and Kitayama's (1991) explanation simplifies reality, it has nevertheless helped to clarify a way in which cultural groups *do* tend to differ, and in that sense, has contributed to increased understanding.

We mention the caricature analogy (and the dangers therein) as a caveat to the work we plan to cover here. In the remaining pages, we intend to discuss cross-cultural differences in beliefs and coping, focusing in particular on how culturally influenced beliefs about the world shape the ways in which people respond to life's difficulties. We think this discussion has merit, but its merit does not lie in identifying differences in belief structures that apply to every member of the cultural groups under investigation, or even to every domain within those cultures. Rather, its merit lies in highlighting – like the caricature artist – those aspects of culturally-influenced beliefs that often shape coping styles and that reflect average differences between cultural groups. We hope this picture has usefulness for researchers, clinicians, and others in understanding cultures other than their own. But we realize that we exaggerate cultural differences here for the purpose of understanding. We hope that once that purpose has been achieved, the exaggerations will be recognized as such and not misappropriated.

2. WHY STUDY CULTURE AND COPING?

Coping with stressful life events is one of the fundamental aspects of human existence. Everyone has stress (see, e.g., Kohn, Lafreniere, and Gurevich, 1991). If such psychological strain is left unchecked, it becomes detrimental to humans' psychological and physical well-being. People simply cannot function well for very long at high levels of stress: Their minds and bodies eventually break down. Thus, all people everywhere are forced to find ways to cope with negative life events and subsequent negative emotions. People may cope in a number of ways such as avoiding the problem, distracting themselves, confronting others, forming a plan, reinterpreting the situation, or any of a number of different strategies (Folkman and Lazarus, 1985), and the choice of coping strategies is no small decision: How people cope with life events may have implications for mental and physical health (e.g., Burns, 2000; McKenna et al., 1999; Mulder et al., 1999; Park and Adler, 2003; Terry and Hynes, 1998).

Habits of coping, though, may differ around the world. Consider the contrasting views taught by the world's great religions. The Four Noble Truths of Buddhism teach one to cope by cultivating detachment. These Truths suggest that suffering results from desire, so according to this teaching, one will escape suffering by becoming detached from worldly objects and activities. In contrast, the Taoist tradition teaches a method of coping by means of adapting oneself to the environment. Water has great power, according to this tradition, but water travels mainly by flowing over or around barriers rather than by fighting against the barriers. Likewise, humans can cope by adapting to the environment. In further contrast, the Confucian tradition teaches that if one diligently strives to learn and to acquire righteousness, then one will cope well with unforeseen future circumstances. Thus, the Confucian tradition teaches the value of acquiring personal resources prior to encountering difficulty. These brief summaries are very selective and thus in some ways misrepresent each of these traditions, but nonetheless highlight the fact that differing traditions teach different coping strategies. The differences between these traditions further suggest that coping habits in regions influenced by these traditions may tend to differ from those of other regions because of the influence of these traditions.

So there is good reason to suspect that people from cultures with often vastly different approaches to suffering, adaptation, and the environment would in fact cope differently. Indeed, anecdotal reports further suggest that coping differences across cultures exist. Lebra (1984), for example, argued that many cultures will allow for direct confrontation when coping with interpersonal conflict, but that Japanese culture cultivates habits of indirect confrontation. Japanese, Lebra suggests, will use subtle cues, which other Japanese will understand, to communicate their feelings. Japanese will also recruit neutral third parties for assistance or will express anger at a third party in the presence of the offending party in order to communicate their feelings to the offending party. Lebra's insightful discussion highlights the role culture can play in coping. Empirical research (e.g., Tweed, White, and Lehman, 2004; Yeh and Inose, 2002) also provides further evidence of cross-cultural differences in coping habits. A number of studies of culturally influenced coping tendencies will be described later in this chapter. For many people, the mere existence of coping differences across cultures may be sufficient to justify research on coping and culture.

The reasons to study coping and culture, however, reach beyond curiosity alone. For example, understanding the Taoist perspective on coping may facilitate skills in adapting to a demanding situation. Understanding the detachment orientation may facilitate a healthy and appropriate ability to remove oneself from the sources of stress. Thus, for clinicians and mentors, the study of coping and culture can potentially benefit those they lead because the clinician's or mentor's toolkit of coping resources may potentially be expanded by understanding coping strategies common in a culture not one's own (Chiu and Hong, in press). Further, it is vital for clinicians to understand the most typical coping strategies – and their outcomes – that persons seeking help might use. In an increasingly multi-cultural world, it thus becomes paramount that clinicians have at least a rudimentary grasp of how coping strategies might differ across cultures. Otherwise, they may begin counseling from false assumptions about their clients' psychological functioning, and may make unnecessary missteps in the counseling process.

Thus, given how pervasive and significant coping is, and given that coping likely differs across cultures and contexts, it is important to explore the ways that culture might influence coping. That is the goal of this chapter.

3. CULTURALLY-INFLUENCED BELIEFS ABOUT THE WORLD AND THEIR ORIGINS

Often, cultural researchers focus on behaviors as touchstones for understanding cultural differences (e.g., Conway, Tweed, Ryder, and Sokol, 2001; Pekerti and Thomas, 2003; Schnieder et al., 2000). This approach has yielded useful theoretical and empirical fruit relevant to coping (e.g., Essau and Trommsdorff, 1996; Tweed, White, Lehman, 2004). For example, some East Asian groups are more likely to using coping styles that focus on adapting themselves to the situation than are Euro-Canadian groups (Tweed et al, 2004). While we fully endorse this focus and acknowledge its usefulness (indeed, we discuss behavior differences between cultures herein), focusing exclusively on coping behaviors also limits our understanding of the factors influencing those behaviors. In particular, knowing that cultural differences in coping behaviors exist only begs the question: What sorts of cultural processes contributed to the rise of those behaviors? Why, for example, do some East Asian groups tend to cope by adapting themselves to their environment more than do North Americans groups? Many potential angles exist for understanding the nature of coping differences between cultures. But we focus here only on one: The link between culturally influenced beliefs about the world and coping strategies.

Focusing on beliefs in order to study culture has been called the "theory" approach to cultural psychology (Peng et al., 2001). In particular, this approach seeks to understand cultural differences in people's folk theories (or implicit theories) about the world and the ways these differences are manifested. It is worth noting that some of the most interesting cultural beliefs may seldom be vocalized by respondents because they seem so obvious and indisputable or because they are below consciousness. Shweder, (1993) borrowed the term "experience-near beliefs" (Geertz, 1973) to describe these types of implicit theories that are expressed in behavior though not frequently spoken. Implicit theories provide an opportunity to examine underlying factors that may in some ways explain the more obvious behavioral differences across cultures.

A number of prior researchers have examined cultural differences in implicit theories. Chiu et al. (2000), for example, argued that Chinese culture cultivates an implicit theory that groups initiate behavior, but that North American culture cultivates a belief that individuals initiate behavior. For example, when told that a pharmacy distributed improperly prepared medication, Chinese participants tended to blame the clinic, but North Americans blamed the individual pharmacist. When told a story about a bull escaping from an enclosure, North Americans under time pressure attributed agency to that particular bull, but Chinese under time pressure tended to blame the herd as a whole. Thus even when participants were discussing animals, the implicit theories seemed to influence responses.

The implicit theories approach has also been applied to research within particular cultures. Dweck's (2000) program of research has examined the implicit theory that intelligence is malleable and has found that this belief seems to facilitate academic success. Wong (1998) examined individual's implicit theories about the nature of a meaningful life. He distinguished factors that people perceived to be associated with the meaningful life (e.g., community relations and fair treatment) and also examined which components were actually most strongly associated with the experience of meaningfulness (e.g., transcendence via serving a purpose beyond oneself and achievement striving).

Prior to our discussion of the nature of cultural beliefs, the source of cultural differences in beliefs deserves some comment. The source of cultural beliefs is a much larger question than can be addressed adequately in this chapter, but in brief, at least a few sources of cultural differences are especially worthy of consideration. Human epistemic needs, belongingness motives, terror management, communication processes, and rational responses to social and geographic environments may be some of the factors contributing to cultural differences in belief systems and ultimately in coping habits (see Conway and Schaller, in press; Lehman et al., 2004).

People have an innate desire to accurately understand their world. This human epistemic need, may in part account for the origins of cultural belief systems (see Richter and Kruglanski, 2003). Other people provide salient sources of information, and our deeply rooted need to have an understanding of our world often causes us to accept their explanations as fact. (We would often rather believe uncertain knowledge as fact than live with uncertainty). As a result, people tend to influence and be influenced by the people directly around them (see Conway and Schaller, in press), and thus belief systems emerge that are more stable and enduring if they are shared with geographically near others. This tendency for epistemic needs to contribute to the emergence of culture is perhaps strongest in times of widespread uncertainty, doubt, or difficulties (Richter and Kruglanski, 2003). It is in these sorts of culturally-shared trials (e.g., famines, wars) that great upheavals in cultural belief systems often occur, and new cultures are formed in the aftermath. Thus, the epistemic approach to culture not only provides a general explanation for why cultural beliefs emerge and differ, but also suggests when culture is especially likely to begin and change.

Of course, people are motivated by more than a need for knowledge, and these other motives also impact the formation of cultural beliefs. Two related motives in particular seem directly tied to the origins of culture. First, people are fundamentally motivated to belong (Baumeister and Leary, 1995). This desire directly explains why culture exists at all: It exists in part to help people feel like they "fit it." If I can share the beliefs of those directly around me, this helps me feel like I have found a place in the world that I belong.

We are also motivated by a desire to avoid death. Terror management theory (e.g., Greenberg et al., 1997) suggests that cultural belief systems emerge in part to buffer people against the inevitable psychological consequences of the consciousness of one's own impending death. Membership in a group of culturally likeminded individuals creates a sense that one is serving values and purposes beyond oneself. This serves purposes that extend beyond one's own mortal existence, thereby alleviating the threat that one's impending death will bring an end to all that one creates. Much empirical evidence supports the relationship – deduced from the principles of terror management theory – between the awareness of one's death and upholding or defending the cultural worldview. (Greenberg et al., 1997).

All of these approaches implicitly suggest that we are more influenced by people geographically close to us in space. Indeed, research on the emergence of culture from communication – much of it collected under the rubric of Dynamic Social Impact Theory (Latane, 1996; Lehman et al., 2004) – highlights the role of physical proximity in shaping culture. This work suggests that all that is necessary for cultural "pockets" to emerge is (1) an arrangement in physical space so that persons cannot communicate with equal frequency with everyone else in that space, (2) initial variability in beliefs, and (3) individual differences in the persuasion "power" of the individuals comprising the initial focal population. Because persuasion tends to be directed at others who live geographically nearby, belief systems will tend to cluster in particular geographic regions. Thus, cultural differences emerge as a result of this tendency for communication and persuasion to be directed at geographically near others. In other words, cultural differences emerge because people over time persuade geographically near others of the value of particular beliefs.

So epistemic needs, belongingness motives, terror management, and communication processes all conspire together to produce local pockets of shared beliefs that we call culture. However, all of these approaches are devoid of *content*. They suggest the motives and processes underlying culture, but say little about why *specific* beliefs come to comprise *specific* cultures. From our discussion so far, it may seem as if "any old belief will do" – that all beliefs are equally likely to become the objects of cultural belief systems, and that the processes that determine the actual, real-world contents of culture are random.

But it is not so (see Conway and Schaller, 2004). Many factors influence the specific contents of culturally-shared beliefs, ranging from how memorable they are (Norenzayan and Atran, 2003) to how much they match the surrounding cultural milieu (see Conway and Schaller, in press). We focus here on one factor that seems most likely to have influenced the development of specific cultural beliefs relevant to coping: The particular environmental and socio-historical context within which those beliefs emerged.

In particular, rational responses to the social and/or geographic context in which a particular group lives may help explain the contents of some belief systems (see, e.g., Berry, 1994; Conway, Ryder, Tweed, and Sokol, 2001; Lehman, Chiu and Schaller, 2004; Vandello and Cohen, 1999). For example, Chinese beliefs that one best copes by adapting oneself to the situation may result from the history of experience that has shaped Chinese beliefs. Thus, people within China have not merely developed different beliefs about the same world and reality than some other cultural groups, but rather they have developed beliefs about a different world and reality. One could argue that they have experienced problems and difficulties that tend to be external, chronic, pervasive, unyielding and unforgiving – natural disasters, foreign invasions, civil wars, tyrannies, widespread poverty – all of which are beyond one's control, and one rational way to maintain sanity was to transform their worldviews to accept the bleak reality and still live with contentment. Similarly, one can also imagine oneself in an African country ravaged by AIDS, genocide, and natural disasters. How would one cope in that kind of a situation? In order to contextualize coping, we need to recognize that different cultural groups really have lived in very different historical, socio-economic-political contexts which shape their beliefs.

For our purposes, we will discuss beliefs that are *already* shared – or viewed as culturally representative – by some substantial percentage of a cultural population (see Conway and Schaller, in press; Schaller, Conway, and Crandall, 2003; Tweed, Conway, and Ryder, 1999). Thus, we will not primarily be attempting to explain where these beliefs came from, but – given that they exist – what consequences they have on coping. Below, we examine belief in an entity view of the world, in a benevolent purpose for events, in the ubiquity of change, in traditional Chinese values, in the utility of personal preparation, in the value of standing out, in the utility of effort, in a variety of religious doctrines, and in particular categories of illness. This review will of necessity provide a limited exploration of culturally-influenced beliefs that might be relevant to coping. A broad set of beliefs fit within the wide latitude of this definition, so this chapter can at most provide examples of the utility of this approach and provide suggestions for further research, but cannot provide a thorough catalogue of beliefs influencing coping. Also, the empirical research on cultural beliefs and coping is still too limited to provide a thorough picture. Indeed, herein we often follow a rough formula for highlighting how culture and coping overlap: We illustrate (1) that cultures tend to differ on X belief and (2) that X belief tends to have consequences for coping. This approach leaves many gaps, but some of these gaps reflect the actual state of the literature, and we hope that they will soon be filled. One aim of this chapter, then, is to provide an impetus for future research on this important topic. After we consider these different types of beliefs, we then turn our attention to the impacts that such beliefs have on health outcomes and to potential implications for cultural and clinical psychologists.

3.1. Belief in the Utility of Effort

People who believe in the utility of effort (Heine et al., 2001) assume that many outcomes in life are controlled by one's own exertion of energy. Recent research by Bond (2004) has affirmed that this construct has importance in cross-cultural research. In particular, Bond conducted an ecological factor analysis of belief statements in order to identify some of the most important belief constructs that differ across cultures. (In an ecological factor analysis, average scores for cultural subgroups are used as cases in the factor analysis, thus producing results that highlight dimensions on which the cultures tend to differ.) His questionnaire listing sixty social axioms had been distributed to 7,672 students from 41 cultural groups. The social axioms were general statements about the world and the self that were likely to vary across individuals. The statements were designed to be descriptive and factual rather than normative or moral. Thus, "we should be devoted to our family" would not be included because it makes a normative rather than factual claim. Two examples of the social axioms used are "Good deeds will be rewarded" and "It is rare to see a happy ending in real life." The participants rated their agreement with each statement. Average scores were calculated for each item within each cultural group. The cultural group average scores were then subjected to a factor analysis in a method similar to that used by Hofstede (1980) in his classic work. Belief that effort makes a difference emerged as a major factor differentiating cultural groups (sample item: "Adversity can be overcome by effort," Bond, 2004, p. 557).

The Confucian tradition teaches the value of perseverance in response to difficulty, so one could expect that belief in the utility of effort would be affirmed especially often in China and possibly in other East Asian countries influenced by the Confucian tradition.

Stevenson and others (Stevenson and Stigler, 1992; Stevenson et al., 1993) highlighted the importance of this belief in cross-cultural research comparing East Asian and North American samples. They presented evidence that Japanese students are more likely to believe that effort determines success than are American students. Heine et al. (2001) also examined a similar construct: The "utility of effort." They developed a questionnaire assessing belief in the utility of effort and found evidence that Japanese participants affirmed this belief more than did North American participants.

These same researchers (Heine et al., 2004; Stevenson and Stigler, 1992; Stevenson et al., 1993) also presented evidence that this belief seems to be associated with particular types of coping in response to demanding situations. Stevenson presented evidence that Japanese students, because they tend to believe that effort determines success, see more hope for creating and controlling their personal success, so as a result put forth more effort when facing demanding academic tasks. They further argued that this belief accounts in part for the academic success of Japanese students relative to American students.

Strong evidence that this belief influences behavior can only be provided, however, by true experimental studies in which this belief is manipulated and the effects are measured. Heine et al. (2001) did in fact manipulate participants' belief in the utility of effort and thereby presented experimental evidence that this belief induced greater persistence following failure on a task. Heine et al. thus supported the contention by Stevenson and others (Stevenson and Stigler, 1992; Stevenson et al., 1993) that belief in the utility of effort contributes to perseverant effort in response to demanding situations.

The role of this belief may be much broader, however, than the work by Stevenson (Stevenson and Stigler, 1992; Stevenson et al., 1993) and Heine et al. (2004) might initially seem to suggest. Belief that effort is efficacious may contribute to persistent coping not only for academic tasks and tasks assigned during psychology studies. Persistent coping in response to failure in other domains such as sports, relationships, and work potentially could be induced by this belief. Indeed, in keeping with this expectation, one would expect that East Asian samples may be especially likely to report coping by persevering. Yeh and Inose (2002; see also Wong and Ujimoto, 1998) did in fact find that East Asian immigrant youth reported using the strategy of enduring in the face of difficulty. This tendency to endure is congruent with an underlying belief that effort is efficacious. Thus, belief in the utility of effort seems to be relevant to cross-cultural examinations of coping. The evidence suggests that this belief in the utility of effort is influenced by one's cultural context and that this belief induces persistence in response to failure.

3.2. Religious Beliefs

Even a cursory glance at the major religious systems across different parts of the world's geography suggests that religion varies across cultures. Also, the importance attributed to religious beliefs seems to differ across cultures. In Bond's (2004) ecological factor analysis of belief statements, the second factor, "dynamic externality" affirms that religious beliefs play an important role in life (sample item: "Belief in a religion helps one understand the meaning of life," p. 557; Bond, 2004). The emergence of this factor in a cross-cultural ecological factor analysis suggests that cultural groups differ in the extent to which they tend to affirm these items. The exact implication of a culture being high or low on dynamic externality (affirming a central role for religion) is difficult to discern unless the exact nature of the religion is specified (e.g., beliefs in benevolent deity or vengeful deity, active deity or deistic deity). However, it is clear that cultures *do* differ, and differ substantially, in both the importance they attach to religion as well as the specific religious viewpoints themselves. Many people may not adhere strictly to the tenets of their religion, but even if relatively few people in a culture were to consistently attempt to live according to the society's traditional religious beliefs, the associated implicit beliefs about the world may live on in the cultural meaning system of much of the population.

Religious beliefs can profoundly influence how people cope. Although a relatively small proportion of empirical coping studies directly examine religious beliefs, some studies *do* suggest that religiosity plays an important role in coping (e.g., McIntosh, Silver, Wortman, 1993; Pargament, 1997). For example, research suggests that African-Americans often successfully use a belief in God's love to overcome the negative effects of prejudice (Blaine and Crocker, 1995). Pargament has developed a program of research examining religious coping (e.g., Pargament, 1997; Pargament, Koenig, and Perez, 2000). Some types of religious coping such as having a sense that one is collaborating with God in solving a problem are associated with positive psychological outcomes (Pargament et al., 1990), but others such as interpreting trauma as divine punishment are associated with negative outcomes (Pargament, 1997). Cultural differences in religious belief create some obvious effects on coping particularly when the religious beliefs require particular rituals at times of stress. Parkes, Laungani, and Young (1997) edited a fascinating volume highlighting the diverse ways in which cultures deal with death, and many of the practices discussed were dictated by religious beliefs about death.

Indeed, clinicians may want to consider these issues of religiosity and coping further because of the potential to produce better outcomes through being responsive to their clients' religious belief systems. For example, Razali et al. (2002) conducted a four-cell study providing standard treatment for generalized anxiety disorder with either an added religious component or not to Muslim patients who were either religious or not. For the non-religious Muslims, the added religious component produced no positive or negative effect, but for the religious Muslims, those assigned to the psychotherapy plus a religious component experienced greater symptom reduction than did those experiencing standard psychotherapy alone. Similar results have been found with largely Christian populations of cancer patients: When doctors were encouraged to talk about spiritual issues, patients showed reduced depression, greater satisfaction with their care, greater well-being, and an improved sense of interpersonal caring when compared to control patients (Rhodes and Kristeller, 2001).

It is worth noting that religiosity includes multiple constructs including personal ideology, ritualistic behavior, internal emotional experience, intellectual knowledge, and social experience (Tarakeshwar et al., 2004). Thus, researchers cannot examine religiosity merely by assessing attendance at religious events or perceived importance of religion. Some recent publications provide useful guidance for those wanting to measure major dimensions related to religiosity (e.g., Hill and Pargament, 2003; Hill and Wood, 1999). Researchers interested in religion's influence on coping would do well to consider that these different dimensions of religiosity may have widely discrepant impacts on how people cope and on coping success. The relation between religious belief and coping has not, however, received extensive attention in the cross-cultural psychology literature. This absence might not be too surprising given the general neglect of religious themes by cross-cultural psychologists (see Tarakeshwar, Stanton, and Pargament, 2004) Thus, religious influences on coping probably deserve significantly more attention than they currently receive. Indeed, throughout this chapter we will return to the potential religious underpinnings of particular culturally-shared beliefs: The Buddhist belief that detachment eradicates suffering, the Christian belief that all events can be reappraised as working for the good of the righteous, and the Taoist belief in the ubiquity of change all have pervasive influences in their respective cultures.

3.3. Belief in an Entity View of World

Another set of beliefs, entity versus incremental beliefs about the self have been examined in a well developed program of research (Chiu et al., 1997b; Dweck, 2000; Levy et al., 1999). Incremental theorists, according to this framework, assume that the self is malleable; one can change oneself. Entity theorists, in contrast, believe that efforts to change the self are futile.

Studies of incremental versus entity orientation have focused mainly on lay theories about the self and have provided evidence that these implicit self-theories influence coping behavior (Dweck, 2000). In the cultural domain, however, lay theories about the self may be less important than lay beliefs about the world. In particular, findings by Chiu et al. (1997a) suggest that individuals from some East Asian cultures are more likely than Euro-Americans to perceive the world as difficult to change. When asked about the nature of the outside social world, the East Asian participants were less likely than the Euro-Americans to say that they could alter the nature of the outside world.

Traditional landscape art also seems to illustrate in a symbolic sense these underlying beliefs about the environment in relation to the self. Many traditional Chinese and also some traditional Japanese paintings include large mountains or rivers with one or a few human figures who appear small in comparison to the geographic features. These portraits illustrate in a very realistic sense the scale differences between relatively small humans and large geographic objects. The paintings also make humans appear relatively weak and impotent in relation to the fixed nature of the physical surroundings. Western art by English speakers or Europeans, in contrast, often excludes people from paintings of land-scapes. Clearly, links between art and psychology are difficult to draw, but the parallels are instructive. The culture that in art portrays humans as small figures within a large domi-nating uncontrollable environment seems to perceive the world as difficult to change.

We know of no direct tests of whether manipulating entity beliefs about the world influences coping behavior (though there is evidence that manipulating entity beliefs about the self influences coping; Dweck, 2000). Nonetheless, one could expect that an entity view of the world could motivate efforts to adapt the self to the environment rather than vice verse because efforts to change an unchangeable world will be less efficacious than efforts to change the self.

Thus, one would expect cultures high an entity view of the world (e.g., East Asian cul-tures) to focus on efforts to change the self in response to stressful circumstances. Indeed, that is exactly the effect that has been observed, though admittedly the available data is still somewhat limited. In particular, Tweed, White, and Lehman (2004) asked respondents to describe their biggest problem of the last 6 months. The respondents then completed the Ways of Coping Checklist (WOCC; Folkman and Lazarus, 1985) and some other cop-ing questions. The WOCC lists a number of coping responses (e.g., "I stood my ground and fought for what I wanted"), and respondents rated the extent to which they engaged in each strategy. As hypothesized, the participants influenced by East Asian cultures were more likely than the Euro-North Americans to assert that they coped by attempting to control themselves. In particular, East Asian cultural influence was associated with strate-gies of accepting the problem, distancing oneself from the problem, and waiting. Each of these strategies includes efforts to control the self rather than directly controlling the exter-nal world.

3.4. Belief in a Benevolent Purpose for Events

The theory that events have a benevolent purpose may also be relevant to coping. Traditional religious instruction in Western English speaking areas and in Europe suggests that events, even events causing suffering, work for the good of righteous people (Erickson, 1983; Simundson, 1985; Thiessen and Doerksen, 1979). This belief that events have a benevolent purpose differs somewhat from the related Chinese traditional belief that persistence in the face of hardship brings benefits. In the former, it is the events them-selves that induce the benefit, but in the latter, it is the individual's response that brings the benefit either because of the personal growth resulting from perseverance or because the situation may become more favorable and the perseverance may thus produce benefits. The Buddhist tradition, in contrast to both of these perspectives, teaches that attachment to the physical world brings suffering. From the Buddhist perspective, suffering is not conceived of as serving a positive purpose; a major goal is to escape this suffering by minimizing ego and personal desire.

One could wonder whether the traditional Western belief in a benevolent purpose for events still has relevance for people in modern Western cultures, but Janoff-Bulman (1992) found in congruence with this teaching that among North American samples the assumption of a benevolent world was central to the human response to trauma. In particular, she found that trauma causes people to question this assumption and that coping requires rebuilding this and other assumptions shattered by the trauma. Likewise, many anecdotal reports suggest that construing benefits from tragedy is a common response to suffering in North America (e.g., Affleck and Tennen, 1996; Lehman et al, 1993; McFarland and Alvaro, 2000; Sittser, 1996).

In a direct cross-cultural comparison, Tweed, White, and Lehman (2004) found evidence that Euro-North American respondents coped in this way more often than did Japanese respondents. In particular, they examined the positive reappraisal scale of the Ways of Coping Checklist which operationalizes benefit finding (Folkman and Lazarus, 1985). The scale's items ask whether the respondent personally grew, rediscovered the important things in life, found faith, or became a better person as a result of the tragedy. The results thus support the hypothesis that Western English speakers will believe there to be, and thus will cope by seeking benefits in the midst of trauma.

Though religious traditions may be largely inactive, seldom accessed, or even barely understood for many people, the religiously influenced assumption that events do or do not have benevolent purpose still can serve as an implicit belief that influences coping responses. (It is worth keeping in mind that the vast majority of the people on earth still claim a religious affiliation, so we do not wish to underemphasize the *explicit* role religion plays).

3.5. Values (Individualism/Collectivism; Traditional Chinese Values; Standing Out)

Values, one could argue, are particular types of beliefs. To be more specific, values can be defined as principles regarding the importance of certain life outcomes (e.g., Schwartz et al., 2001). For example, some cultures may tend to value confrontation in business meetings while other cultures may value harmony. Some cultures may value hedonic behavior more than do other cultures.

Individualism/Collectivism: Hofstede (1980; for other traditions of values research see Chinese Culture Connection, 1987; Schwartz et al., 2001; Smith and Schwartz, 1997) conducted a massive study to determine the nature of culturally-influenced values. Some have criticized the methodology by which he factor analyzed country scores on a 32-item work values survey (Heine et al., 2002), but his first dimension, individualism-collectivism, has become central to much cross-cultural psychology. He concluded that cultures valuing individualism "assume individuals look primarily after their own interests and the interests of their immediate family" (Hofstede, 1984, p. 390). Collectivistic societies, in contrast, assume precedence will be given to group goals. Although the exact nature of cultural differences on individualism/collectivism is the source of much debate (Oyserman et al., 2002), it is clear that these differences exist in some capacity, and that they have consequences on behavior and psychological functioning (e.g., Conway et al., 2001; Smith et al., 1996; Triandis, 1996).

These values may influence coping. For example, collectivistic values may induce additional effort to preserve in-group harmony. Individuals from collectivistic cultures have been shown to select coping strategies such as compromise and self-adjustment that are less likely to disrupt social connections, (Coates, 1968; Kirkbride et al., 1991; Trubisky et al., 1991; Tweed, White, Lehman, 2004; Willmann et al., 1997). Lebra (1984) provided a richly detailed discussion of Japanese nonconfrontational conflict strategies which preserve in-group harmony. One such strategy, which Lebra argued is especially common in Japan, is to accept a situation rather than to openly express anger. A mode of Japanese therapy titled Morita therapy has been built up from this practice of accepting difficult situations. Clients in Morita therapy learn to accept their world and learn that they can adapt to their world by accepting difficulty rather than by trying to change the world. Traditional Morita therapy (see Ishiyama, 2003) includes, of course, much more than a simple exhortation to accept difficulty, but acceptance is nonetheless central. Morita therapy begins with an inpatient treatment in which patients are inactive for a time, but then slowly return to more strenuous work. During the treatment, the patients learn to accept their situation and their symptoms and even to transform the energy from their symptoms in a positive direction. The method is rooted in Buddhist assumptions about the value of detachment from worldly concerns. This focus on acceptance of difficulties also is evident in a proverb some mothers in Japan quote to children when they fight: "To lose is to win" (Kojima, 1984). The message of the proverb is that the one who becomes aggressive and possibly angry and dominates in conflict actually loses. The winner of the conflict is the one who controls emotion and aggression and accepts the difficult situation with maturity. Unrestrained display of anger and aggression indicates personal failure. Lebra (1984) also reports that third party intervention is common in Japan, and this strategy likewise may serve to preserve harmony. Person A, who is in conflict with person B approaches a higher status person X who can act as a mediator for the conflicting parties. The third party may take responsibility for the conflict and apologize on behalf of person A. Alternatively, if the reconciliation is slow in coming, the intermediary may call on persons A and B to "save my face" by becoming reconciled and saving the intermediary from the embarrassment of failing in the reconciliation effort. Lebra also claims that self-blame is often used to avoid interpersonal conflict. A Japanese therapy labeled Naikan therapy builds upon this tendency to blame the self. The client meditates on how much others have done for him or her and how little has been given in return. This practice is intended to produce new joy and purpose by motivating the client to strive to pay back some of these debts. Thus, the client can regain joy in living and manage perceived conflict with others without engaging in open confrontation with other people but instead by blaming the self.

Traditional Chinese Values: Other research also suggests that values may influence coping responses. For example, adherence to traditional Chinese values (civic harmony, industry, and prudence) is associated with coping via defensive pessimism in response to SARS-related fears (Chang and Sievam, 2004; see also Bond et al., 2004). This means that traditional Chinese values are associated with strategically being somewhat pessimistic about one's future in order to avoid disappointment. The exact nature of the relation (i.e., causal, mediated, direct) between these values and defensive pessimistic coping is not, however, yet known.

According to Wong and Ujimoto (1998), East Asian cultures tend to be influenced by Taoist thinking which values passive acceptance of difficulties. Tweed, White, and Lehman (2004) included an acceptance scale in their coping study, and as was suggested by Wong and Ujimoto, they found Japanese scored higher on acceptance than did North Americans. Tendency to cope by accepting difficulty could also be measured by the existential scale on Wong's Inventory of Coping Schemas (Peacock and Wong, 1996).

Traditional Chinese teachings (see Wong and Ujimoto, 1998) also value preservation of particular relationships. Confucius, for example, assumed that proper societal functioning depended on individuals maintaining appropriate relations with others. Appropriate relational behavior according to traditional Chinese values includes honor to those of higher status and care for those of lower status. Aggressive confrontation would be seen as unacceptable in most circumstances because of the potential cost to others' dignity. Devotion to family is also valued. Wong and Ujimoto (1998) argue that for many East Asians, preserving harmony is more important than solving many problems. Thus, Asian values could cultivate a tendency to follow the Confucian tradition of courageously persevering in the face of difficulty rather than potentially disrupting stable relations with others.

Value of Standing Out or Standing In: Weisz, Rothbaum, and Blackburn (1984) argued compellingly that Americans value standing out from others, but Japanese value standing in. Thus, Americans are more likely to seek attention, but Japanese are more likely to seek to match the surrounding crowd. This distinction obviously oversimplifies the cultural difference, as we warned in the introduction to this chapter, but nonetheless the distinction draws our attention to important cultural realities. Two proverbs cited by Weisz, Rothbaum, and Blackburn illustrate their point. According to a common American proverb, the squeaky wheel gets the grease. The American proverb teaches that drawing attention to oneself brings benefits. In contrast, according to a Japanese proverb, the nail that sticks out gets pounded down. The Japanese proverb teaches that setting oneself apart from one's peers, even if one is reaching higher than one's peers, leads to pain from being banged back into one's place. Japanese students have reported to us that performing far above average in school compared to their peers would bring them great discomfort. North American students in contrast reported to us that they had a hard time understanding the Japanese perspective. Bellah et al. (1985) discussed this cultural distinction in their classic book entitled "Habits of the Heart." In that work, they discussed the expressive individualism tradition in North America which purports that "each person has a unique core of feeling and intuition that should unfold and be expressed..." (p. 334).

Western English speaking cultural beliefs in the value of standing out (or standing in) are congruent with, and possibly account for, important coping differences across cultures. People seeking to stand out would be expected draw attention to their unique problems for the sake of having the attention of others. In keeping with this expectation, preliminary data suggests that North Americans more frequently cope by telling others about their feelings than do Japanese (Tweed and Lehman, unpublished data). This tendency fits with a belief in the value of standing out, of drawing attention to one's uniqueness, and in this case, particularly to one's emotional experience.

Those seeking to stand in would seek to avoid drawing attention to their problems and uniqueness unless there is good reason to do otherwise. Yeh and Inose (2002; see also Wong and Ujimoto, 1998) found evidence that East Asian participants frequently cope with silent perseverance. For the East Asian students, keeping to oneself and enduring were not uncommon coping strategies. Also, there is preliminary evidence that when East Asian participants do seek social support, they seek, not attention, but instead concrete assistance (Tweed and Lehman, unpublished data). Wong (1993) called this "collective coping": In collective coping, social support is activated, not merely by providing emotional support or attention to an individual's problem, but instead by having the group focus on providing practical help to solve the problem of an individual member.

3.6. Belief in the Ubiquity of Change

Another fundamental theory about the world, belief in the ubiquity of change, was explored by Li-Jun Ji (2001). She found that her Chinese participants were more likely to affirm that change is ubiquitous in the world than were her Euro-American participants. Thus, Chinese shown graphs of trends in cancer rates, economic growth, and other trends were more likely than Americans to predict a reversal in the direction of change. Even when predicting their own happiness in the future as compared to the change in their happiness over time in the past, Chinese participants (though not any more or less optimistic than Americans) were more likely to predict a change in the direction of the trend. She also provided some evidence that those who expect reversals of fortune are perceived as wise by others of Chinese cultural background.

This high expectation of change and of change in the direction of change (reversal of trends) coheres with the Taoist tradition of China. The Tao Te Ching (Lao Tzu, 1989) thought to have been written in approximately 400 BCE by Lao Tzu, a central figure in Taoism, includes numerous texts about the ubiquity of change. For example, chapter 77 of the Te asserts that the Way is like a flexing bow that springs back to where it started. The Way gives to those who do not have enough, but takes away from those who have excess; it elevates the lowly and brings down those who are high (Lao Tzu, 1989). Thus, reversal of fortune is to be expected. The Christian Bible also asserts that reversals of fortune should be expected (e.g., Jesus said "many who are first will be last and many who are last will be first" Matthew 19:30; New International Version), but those reversals are often expected to occur in the afterlife. In contrast, Lao Tzu taught his readers to expect many reversals of fortune in this life.

Ji (2001) suggested that Chinese anticipation of reversals may promote persistence in the face of temporary hardship. She suggests that those who anticipate reversals of fortune (e.g., lost games for athletes or failed tests for students) will not be as surprised by the setbacks and will be more likely to expect that persistence may bring a further reversal back to good fortune. The belief in the ubiquity of change, and in particular, the belief that trends will reverse, would thus be interesting to further explore in relation to coping. Further research could explore whether it is true, as Ji (2001) suggests, that people from cultures endorsing this belief will be less distressed by setbacks when trying to achieve their goals. Lin Yutang (1939) provided an anecdotal account of the prototypical older Chinese person who will neither be surprised by setbacks, nor overly excited by successes. He called this type of person the "old rogue" (p. 52) and argued that the old rogue character is central to Chinese culture. As is often the case in cultural psychology, a rich anecdotal account written by a non-scientist foreshadowed the findings derived from good empirical research.

3.7. Beliefs about Illness

Cultural beliefs about health and illness will also influence coping. For example, the Kmer culture passes on beliefs in kyol goeu, a fainting syndrome said to be a response to rushes of air inside the body (Hinton, 2001). This specific belief about illness produces catastrophizing in response to certain autonomic sensations, and thus influences how individuals cope with these sensations. This belief will thus influence behavior. Likewise, many Japanese are familiar with the concept of taijin kyofusho (Ono et al., 2001), a particular syndrome including fear of social relations. People familiar with the construct may assume that if they experience some of the symptoms, then the others will be forthcoming. The beliefs about which symptoms co-occur may thus influence future coping such as by avoiding anxiety provoking social situations. These and many other culture-specific constructs of illness could be explored further.

3.8. Belief in the Utility of Personal Preparation

The belief in the utility of personal preparation could also be examined further. Confucius taught his disciples that if they prepared well by mastering the basics of his teaching (which included being transformed into morally upstanding individuals), then they could be assured of exemplary performance in future demanding situations. We expect that this belief may have ongoing influence in Chinese-influenced cultures. In particular, we expect that Chinese culture cultivates belief in the utility of personal preparation to assure that future events turn out well. As a result, we expect that Chinese-influenced individuals will more frequently engage in conscious preventive coping (Wong, 1993) in which they gather personal resources to assure positive outcomes in the future. As of yet, though, this hypothesis is somewhat speculative and in need of quantitative examination.

4. THE BENEFITS OF MULTI-CULTURAL EXPERIENCE: THE COPING TOOLKIT

We have so far documented various dimensions of culturally-influenced beliefs, how cultures differ on those beliefs, and what consequences these differences might have on coping styles. We have thus behaved like a caricature artist by focusing on distinctives rather than similarities. There is, of course, much variability within cultural groups and there are many people who will not fit these cultural patterns (see, e.g., Conway et al., 2001; Tweed et al., 1999).

Also, individuals will likely vary over time in the extent to which they express particular implicit beliefs. Hong et al. (2000) presented compelling evidence that cognitive priming can influence whether cultural belief systems influence behavior. They exposed Hong Kong students to primes associated with Western nations (e.g., Eiffel Tower, Superman, White House) or to primes associated with Chinese culture (Chinese opera singer, Confucius) and asked participants to complete a questionnaire for which Chinese and American participants are known to differ. Participants were not aware of the purpose of the study, but nonetheless, those primed with Western images were more likely to respond as if they were from America than were those primed with Chinese images. Thus, situational primes may influence whether cultural belief systems are expressed in coping.

To this point, we have discussed primarily the impact of cultural beliefs on coping strategies, without considering explicitly the impact of different cultural beliefs on coping *outcomes*. Some of the consequences of coping strategies are perhaps obvious. Sometimes, particular culturally-influenced beliefs may encourage coping strategies that are maladaptive. For example, the implicit belief in "catharsis" held by many Americans leads them to adopt a "venting" strategy to cope with their anger – they lash out, not at the object of their anger, but at some other animate or inanimate object. However, research suggests that this strategy of dealing with anger is counterproductive by almost any standard (Bushman, 2002; Bushman et al., 2001).

Of course, the picture for most coping strategies is rarely that simple. One may be tempted to ask whether coping strategies more prototypical of certain cultural groups (e.g., Chinese) are more or less adaptive than coping strategies more prototypical of a second cultural group (e.g., North American). Such a question would pose some interesting research possibilities, but we expect that in most cases, such a question would be overly simplistic. The adaptiveness of a coping strategy may depend on the nature of the cultural environment. For example, departure from coping norms for a particular cultural context (whether those norms be for seeking social support, or for persevering, or for externally-targeted control) could create social disharmony with one's valued peers. Thus, there may be value in examining which strategies are most adaptive, but these effects may be moderated not only by the problem-type, but also by the cultural context.

The very idea of what makes a good "outcome" is itself subject to cultural variability, and researchers should be wary of over-applying particular measures of psychological coping success (e.g., increases in self-esteem) in cultures where these measures have less meaning for that purpose. Also, the success of a particular coping strategy is almost certainly contingent on multiple factors.

At this point, we are not far enough along in coping research to make many specific recommendations about which culturally-influenced coping strategies are most effective in various cultural contexts. However, instead we would like to make a more general point about the potential usefulness of cultural contact.

Culture has been viewed by some researchers as providing a toolkit (Chiu and Hong, in press). Cultural socialization provides beliefs and repertoires of behavioral responses available to individuals. The greater the diversity of persons we encounter, the more likely we are to increase the range of potential responses we may have because exposure to multiple cultures seems to induce a greater repertoire of value systems and cognitive processes (Ervin, 1964; Hong et al., 2000). Consistent with this, group essays often have higher levels of complexity than individual essays (Gruenfeld and Hollingshead, 1993); the process of group involvement almost by default necessitates increasing one's complexity to deal with diversity. This is especially true when those other persons have an entirely different cultural background.

Likewise, in the coping domain, exposure to multiple cultures may provide a greater repertoire of responses to activate when coping with stress, thus providing a bigger toolkit of possible coping responses. One lesson from previous work related to coping is that an ability and willingness to employ multiple strategies for coping may lead to more satisfactory outcomes than a singular focus on one strategy. Cheng (2003) conducted an interesting study suggesting that flexibility in coping may promote better personal adjustment.

Tendency to use different coping responses in different situations was associated with better adjustment.

This suggests that there may, as a general rule, be coping advantages to multi-culturalism. Although no work to date that we are aware of directly addresses this hypothesis, Essau and Trommsdorff (1996) presented some interesting data that point in that direction. They compared the coping strategies of Malaysian respondents to the coping strategies of Americans and Germans. The Malaysians were more likely to use emotion-focused coping than Americans and Germans. However, more interesting was their finding that Americans and Germans who coped more like the Malaysians reported fewer physical symptoms than other Americans and Germans. Malaysians who coped more like Americans and Germans reported fewer physical symptoms than other Malaysians. The data are limited, but provide preliminary support that those who learn the coping strategies of other cultures (whether this be through cross-cultural contact or not) may gain benefits by so doing.

5. CONCLUSION

The primary purpose of this chapter was to suggest the potential of culturally influenced beliefs as resources for developing hypotheses about culture and coping. In thus painting this caricature of different cultures, we hoped to highlight the ways in which beliefs across cultures sometimes differ, and to illustrate how these different beliefs can have consequences for coping. An examination of individualism and collectivism, belief in an entity view of the world, in a benevolent purpose for events, in the ubiquity of change, in traditional Chinese values, in the utility of personal preparation, in the value of standing out, in the utility of effort, in a variety of religious doctrines, and in particular categories of illness suggests hypotheses about coping, a number of which have received some empirical support. Further examination could explore the cultural differences in coping responses suggested by these and other culturally-influenced beliefs about the world. For example, future researchers could examine the extent to which Confucian beliefs in the value of preventive coping persist as implicit beliefs in East Asian cultures and the extent to which these beliefs influence behavior. Researchers could also further examine entity views of the world. So far, there is some evidence that an entity view of the world is associated with internally-targeted control in responses to stress, but an experimental study manipulating this belief (see Chiu, Hong, and Dweck, 1997b; Levy, Stroessner, and Dweck, 1999) could assess the contexts within which this belief influences coping behavior. An additional series of studies could examine what happens when apparently contradictory cultural beliefs are made simultaneously salient. For example, Chinese cultures apparently cultivate beliefs in the utility of effort and ubiquity of change while simultaneously cultivating an entity view of the world. Of course similar apparent contradictions could be found in the beliefs taught in any culture, but the interesting question would be how individuals cope when these apparent contradictions are made salient.

Furthermore many relevant beliefs have not been discussed here (e.g., Wong and Ujimoto, 1993), so exploratory research could seek to identify the implicit beliefs on which people from various cultures rely when making coping decisions. Perhaps because the relations between cultural beliefs and coping are still relatively unexplored, open-ended exploratory research on implicit beliefs (e.g., Wong, 1998) may be especially valuable.

REFERENCES

Affleck, G., and Tennen, H. (1996). Construing benefits from adversity: Adaptational significance and dispositional underpinnings. *Journal of Personality 64*: 899-922.

Baumeister, R. F., and Leary, M. R. (1995). The need to belong: Desire for interpersonal attachments as a fundamental human motivation. *Psychological Bulletin 117*: 497-529.

Bellah, R. N., Madsen, R., Sullivan, W. M., Swidler, A., and Tipton, S. M. (1985). *Habits of the heart: Individualism and commitment in American life*. Harper and Row Publishers, New York, NY.

Berry, J. W. (1994). Ecology of individualism and collectivism. In U. Kim, H. C. Triandis, C. Kagitcibasi, S-C. Choi, and G. Yoon (eds.), *Individualism and collectivism: Theory, method, and applications* (pp. 77-84). Sage, Thousand Oaks, CA.

Blaine, B., and Crocker, J. (1995). Religiousness, race, and psychological well-being: Exploring social psychological mediators. *Personality and Social Psychology Bulletin 21*: 1031-1041.

Bond, M. H. (2004). Culture-level dimensions of social axioms and their correlates across 41 cultures. *Journal of Cross-Cultural Psychology 35*: 548-570.

Bond, M. H., Leung, K., Au, A., Tong, K. K., and Chemonges-Nielson, Z. (2004). Combining social axioms with values predicting social behaviours. *European Journal of Personality 18*: 177-191

Burns, J. W. (2000). Repression predicts outcome following multidisciplinary treatment of chronic pain. *Health Psychology 19*: 75-84.

Bushman, B. J. (2002). Does venting anger feed or extinguish the flame? Catharsis, rumination, distraction, and aggressive responding. *Personality and Social Psychology Bulletin 28*: 724-731.

Bushman, B. J., Baumeister, R. F., and Phillips, C. M. (2001). Do people aggress to improve their mood? Catharsis beliefs, affect regulation opportunity, and aggressive responding. *Journal of Personality and Social Psychology 81*: 17-32.

Chang, W., and Sivam, R. W. (2004). Constant vigilance: Heritage values and defensive pessimism in coping with severe acute respiratory syndrome in Singapore. *Asian Journal of Social Psychology 7*: 35-53.

Cheng, C. (2003). Cognitive and motivational processes underlying coping flexibility: A dual-process model. *Journal of Personality and Social Psychology 84*: 425-438.

Chinese Culture Connection (1987). Chinese values and the search for culture-free dimensions of culture. *Journal of Cross-Cultural Psychology 18*: 143-164.

Chiu, C. Y., and Hong, Y. Y. (in press). Cultural competence and dynamic processes. In: Elliot, A., and Dweck, C. S. (eds.), *Handbook of competence and motivation*. Guilford, New York.

Chiu, C. Y., Dweck, C. S., Tong, J. Y. Y., and Fu, J. H. Y. (1997a). Implicit theories and conceptions of morality. *Journal of Personality and Social Psychology 73*: 923-940.

Chiu, C. Y., Hong, Y. Y., and Dweck, C. S. (1997b). Lay dispositionism and implicit theories of personality. *Journal of Personality and Social Psychology 73*: 19-30.

Chiu, C. Y., Morris, M. W., Hong, Y. Y., and Menon, T. (2000). Motivated cultural cognition: The impact of implicit cultural theories on dispositional attribution varies as a function of need for closure. *Journal of Personality and Social Psychology 78*: 247-259.

Coates, A. (1968). *Myself a mandarin*. Muller, London.

Conway, L. G., III, Ryder, A. G., Tweed, R. G., and Sokol, B. W. (2001). Intra-national cultural variation: Exploring further implications of collectivism within the United States. *Journal of Cross-Cultural Psychology 32*: 681-697.

Conway, L. G., III, and Schaller, M. (in press). The emergence of cultural norms through communication. In: Fiedler, K. (ed.), *Frontiers of Social Psychology: Social communication*. Psychology Press, New York.

Dweck, C. S. (2000). *Self-theories: Their role in motivation, personality, and development*. Psychology Press, Philadelphia, PA.

Erickson, M. J. (1983). *Christian theology*. Baker Book House, Grand Rapids, MI.

Ervin, S. M. (1964). Language and TAT content in bilinguals. *Journal of Abnormal and Social Psychology 68*: 500-507.

Essau, C. A., and Trommsdorff, G. (1996). Coping with university-related problems: A cross-cultural comparison. *Journal of Cross-Cultural Psychology 27*: 315-328.

Folkman, S., and Lazarus, R. S. (1985). If it changes it must be a process: A study of emotion and coping during three stages of a college examination. *Journal of Personality and Social Psychology 48*: 150-170.

Folkman, S., Lazarus, R. S., Dunkel-Schetter, C., DeLongis, A., and Gruen, R. J. (1986). Dynamics of a stressful encounter: Cognitive appraisal, coping, and encounter outcomes. *Journal of Personality and Social Psychology 50*: 992-1003.

Geertz, C. (1973). *The interpretation of cultures*. Basic Books, New York.

Greenberg, J., Solomon, S, Pyszczynski, T. (1997). Terror management theory of self-esteem and cultural worldviews: Empirical assessments and conceptual refinements. *Advances in Experimental Social Psychology 29*: 61-139.

Gruenfeld, D. H., and Hollingshead, A. B. (1993). Sociocognition in work groups: The evolution of group integrative complexity and its relation to task performance. *Small Group Research 24*: 383-405.

Heine, S. J., Kitayama, S., Lehman, D. R., Takata, T., Ide E., Leung, C., and Matsumoto, M. (2001). Divergent consequences of success and failure in Japan and North America: An investigation of self-improving motivations and malleable selves. *Journal of Personality and Social Psychology 81*: 599-615.

Heine, S. J., Lehman, D. R., Peng, K. P., and Grennholtz, J. (2002). What's wrong with cross-cultural comparisons of subjective Likert scales? The reference-group effect. *Journal of Personality and Social Psychology 82*: 903-918.

Hill, P. C., and Pargament, K. I. (2003). Advances in the conceptualization and measurement of religion and spirituality: Implications for physical and mental health research. American Psychologist *58*: 64-74.

Hill, P. C., and Wood, R. W. Jr. (1999). *Measures of religiosity*. Religious Education Press, Birmingham, AL.

Hinton, D., Um, K., and Ba, P. (2001). Kyol goeu ('wind overload') Part I: A cultural syndrome of orthostatic panic among Khmer refugees. *Transcultural Psychiatry 38:* 403-432.

Hofstede, G. H. (1980). *Culture's consequences: International differences in work-related values*. Sage Publications, Beverly Hills, CA.

Hofstede, G. (1984). The cultural relativity of the quality of life concept. *Academy of Management Review 9*: 389-398.

Hong, Y. Y., Morris, M. W., Chiu, C. Y., and Benet-Martinez, V. (2000). Multicultural minds: A dynamic constructivist approach to culture and cognition. *American Psychologist 55*: 709-720.

Ishiyama, F. I. (2003). A bending willow tree: A Japanese (Morita therapy) model of human nature and client change. *Canadian Journal of Counselling 37*: 216-231.

Janoff-Bulman, R. (1992). *Shattered assumptions: Towards a new psychology of trauma*. The Free Press, New York.

Ji, L. J. (2001). Culture, change, and prediction. *Psychological Science 12*: 450-456.

Kirkbride, P. S., Tang, S. F. Y., and Westwood, R. I. (1991). Chinese conflict preferences and negotiating behavior: Cultural and psychological influences. *Organization Studies 12*: 365-386.

Kojima, H. (1984). A significant stride toward the comparative study of control. *American Psychologist 39*: 972-973.

Kohn, P.M., Lafreniere, K., and Gurevich, M. (1991). Hassles, health, and personality. *Journal of Personality and Social Psychology 61*: 478-482.

Lao-Tzu (1989). *Te-Tao Ching* (R. G. Henricks, trans.). Ballantine Books, New York (Original work published c.a. 400 BCE).

Latane, B. (1996). Dynamic social impact: The creation of culture by communication. *Journal of Communication 6*: 13-25.

Lebra, T. S. (1984). *Nonconfrontational strategies for management of interpersonal conflicts*. In: Kraus, E. S., Rohlen, T. P., and Steinhoff, P. G. (eds), Conflict in Japan (pp. 41-60). University of Hawaii Press, Honolulu HI.

Lehman, D. R., Chiu, C. Y., and Schaller, M. (2004) Psychology and culture. Annual Review of Psychology *55*: 689-714.

Lehman, D. R., Davis, C. G., DeLongis, A., Wortman, C. B., Bluck, S., Mandel, D. R., and Ellard, J. H. (1993). Positive and negative life changes following bereavement and their relations to adjustment. *Journal of Social and Clinical Psychology 12*: 90-112.

Levy, S. R., Stroessner, S. J., and Dweck, C. S. (1999). Stereotype formation and endorsement: The role of implicit theories. *Journal of Personality and Social Psychology 74*: 1421-1436.

Lin, Y. (1939). *My country and my people*. The John Day Company, New York.

Markus, H. R., and Kitayama, S. (1991). Culture and the self: Implications for cognition, emotion, and motivation. *Psychological Review 98*: 224-253.

McFarland, C., and Alvaro, C. (2000). Impact of motivation on temporal comparisons: Coping with traumatic events by perceiving personal growth. *Journal of Personality and Social Psychology 79*: 327-343.

McIntosh, D., Silver, R. C., and Wortman, C. B. (1993). Religion's role in adjustment to a negative life event. *Journal of Personality and Social Psychology 65*: 812-821.

McKenna, M. C., Zevon, M. A., Corn, B., and Rounds, J. (1999). Psychosocial factors and the development of breast cancer: A meta-analysis. *Health Psychology 18*: 520-531.

Mulder, C. L., Griensven, G. J. P., Vroome, E. M. M., Antoni, M. H., and Sandfort, T. G. M. (1999). Avoidance as a predictor of biological course of HIV infection over a 7-year period in gay men. *Health Psychology* 18: 107-113.

Norenzayan, A., and Atran, S. (2003). *Cognitive and emotional processes in the cultural transmission of natural and nonnatural beliefs*. In M. Schaller and C. S. Crandall (eds.) *The psychological foundations of culture* (pp. 149-170).Lawrence Erlbaum Associates, Mahwah, NJ.

Ono, Y., Yoshimura, K., and Yamauchi, K. (2001). Taijin kyofusho in a Japanese community population. *Transcultural Psychiatry 38:* 506-514.

Oyserman, D., Coon, H. M., and Kemmelmeier, M. (2002). Rethinking individualism and collectivism: Evaluation of theoretical assumptions and meta-analyses. *Psychological Bulletin 128*: 3-72.

Pargament, K. I. (1997). The psychology of religion and coping: Theory, research, and practice. Guildford, New York, NY.

Pargament, K. I., Koenig, H. G., Perez, L. M (2000). The many methods of religious coping: Development and initial validation of the RCOPE. *Journal of Clinical Psychology 56*: 519-543.

Park, C. L., and Adler, N. E. (2003). Coping style as a predictor of health and well-being across the first year of medical school. *Health Psychology 22*: 627-631.

Parkes, C. M., Laungani, P., and Young, B. (1997). *Death and bereavement across cultures*. Routledge, London, UK.

Peacock, E. J., and Wong, P. T. P. (1996). Anticipatory stress: The relation of locus of control, optimism, and control appraisals to coping. *Journal of Research in Personality 30*: 204-222.

Pekerti, A. A., and Thomas, D. C. (2003). Communication in intercultural interaction: An empirical investigation of idiocentric and sociocentric communication styles. Journal *of* Cross-Cultural Psychology *34*: 139-154

Peng, K., Ames, D., and Knowles, E. (2001). Culture and human inference: Perspectives from three traditions. In: Matsumoto, D. R. (ed.), *Handbook of cross-cultural psychology*. Oxford University Press, Oxford, UK, pp. 245-264.

Peng, K., and Nisbett, R. E. (1999). Culture, dialectics, and reasoning about contradiction. *American Psychologist 54*: 741-754.

Razali, S. M., Aminah, K., and Khan, U. A. (2002). Religious-cultural psychotherapy in the management of anxiety patients. *Transcultural Psychiatry 39*: 130-136.

Richter, L., and Kruglanski, A. W. (2003). Motivated closed mindedness and the emergence of culture. In M. Schaller and C. S. Crandall (eds.) *The psychological foundations of culture* (pp. 101-122).Lawrence Erlbaum Associates, Mahwah, NJ.

Rhodes, M., and Kristeller, J. L. (2001). *The OASIS Project: Oncologist-Assisted Spirituality Intervention Study*. Unpublished data, Indiana State University, Terre Haute, IN.

Schaller, M., Conway, L. G., III and Crandall, C. S. (2003). The psychological foundations of culture: An Introduction. In: Schaller, M. and Crandall, C. S. (eds.) *The psychological foundations of culture* (pp. 3-12). Lawrence Erlbaum Associates, Mahwah, NJ.

Scheider, B. H., Fonzi, A., Tomada, G., and Tani, F. (2000). A cross-national comparison of children's behaviour with their friends in situations of potential conflict. *Journal* of *Cross-Cultural Psychology 31:* 259-266.

Schwartz, S. H., Melech, G., Lehmann, A., Burgess, S., Harris, M., and Owens, V. (2001). Extending the cross-cultural validity of the theory of basic human values with a different method of measurement. *Journal of Cross-Cultural Psychology 32*: 519-542.

Shweder, R. A. (1993). Cultural psychology: Who needs it? *Annual Review of Psychology* 44: 497-424.

Simundson, D. J.. (1985). Suffering. In: Achtemeier, P. J. (ed.), *Harper's Bible dictionary* (pp. 997-999). Harper and Row Publishers, San Francisco, CA.

Sittser, G. L. (1996). *A grace disguised: How the soul grows through loss*. Zondervan Publishing House, Grand Rapids, MI.

Smith, P. B., Dugan, S., and Trompenaars, F. (1996). National culture and the values of organizational employees: A dimensional analysis across 43 nations. *Journal of Cross-Cultural Psychology 27*: 231-264.

Smith, P. B., and Schwartz, S. (1997). Values. In: Berry, J. W., Segall, M. H., and Kagitcibasi, C. (eds.), *Handbook of cross-cultural psychology, Volume 3: Social behavior and applications* (2nd ed., pp. 77-118). Allyn and Bacon, Boston, MA.

Stevenson, H. W., Chen, C., and Lee, S. -Y. (1993). Mathematics achievement of Chinese, Japanese, and American children: Ten years later. *Science 259*: 53-58.

Stevenson, H. W., and Stigler, J. W. (1992). *The learning gap: Why our schools are failing and what we can learn from Japanese and Chinese education.* Simon and Schuster, New York.

Tarakeshwar, N., Stanton, J., and Pargament, K. I. (2003). Religion: An overlooked dimension in cross-cultural psychology. *Journal of Cross-Cultural Psychology 34*: 377-394.

Terry, D. J., and Hynes, G. J. (1998). Adjustment to a low-control situation: Reexamining the role of coping responses. *Journal of Personality and Social Psychology 74*: 1078-1092.

Thiessen, H. C., and Doerksen, V. D. (1979). *Lectures in systematic theology,* rev. ed. William B. Eerdmans Publishing Company, Grand Rapids, MI.

Triandis, H. C. (1996). The psychological measurement of cultural syndromes. *American Psychologist 51*: 407-415.

Trubisky, P., Ting-Toomey, S., and Lin. S. L. (1991). The influence of individualism-collectivism and self-monitoring on conflict styles. *International Journal of Intercultural Relations, 15,* 65-84.

Tweed, R. G., Conway, L. G. III, Ryder, A. G. (1999). The target is straw or the arrow is crooked. *American Psychologist 54*: 837-838.

Tweed, R. G., and Lehman, D. R. (2002). Learning considered within a cultural context: Confucian and Socratic approaches. *American Psychologist 57*: 88-99.

Tweed, R. G., White, K., and Lehman, D. R. (2004). Culture, stress, and coping: internally- and externally-targeted control strategies of European-Canadians, East Asian-Canadians, and Japanese. *Journal of Cross-Cultural Psychology 35*: 652-658.

Vandello, J. A., and Cohen, D. (1999). Patterns of individualism and collectivism across the United States. *Journal of Personality and Social Psychology 77*: 279-292.

Weisz, J R., Rothbaum, F., and Blackburn, T. C. (1984). Standing out and standing in: The psychology of control in America and Japan. *American Psychologist, 39,* 955-969.

Welch, J. (2001). *Jack: Straight from the gut.* Warner Business Books: New York.

Willmann, E., Feldt, K., and Amelang, M. (1997). Prototypical behaviour patterns of social intelligence: An intercultural comparison between Chinese and German subjects. *International Journal of Psychology 32*: 329-346.

Wong, P. T. P. (1993). Effective management of life stress: The Resource-Congruence Model. *Stress Medicine 9*: 51-60.

Wong, P. T. P. (1998). Implicit theories of meaningful life and the development of the Personal Meaning Profile. In: Wong, P. T. P. and Fry, P. (eds), *The human quest for meaning.* Lawrence Erlbaum Associates Publishers, Mahwah, NJ, (pp. 111-140).

Wong, P. T. P., and Ujimoto, K V. (1998). The elderly: Their stress, coping, and mental health. In: Lee, L. E, and Zane, N. W. S. (eds.), *Handbook of Asian American psychology.* Sage Publications, Thousand Oaks, CA.

Yeh, C. and Inose, M. (2002). Difficulties and coping strategies of Chinese, Japanese, and Korean immigrant students. *Adolescence 37*: 69-82.

8

PERSONALITY SYSTEMS AND A BIOSOCIOEXISTENTIAL MODEL OF POSTTRAUMATIC RESPONSES BASED ON A KOREAN SAMPLE

Hong Seock Lee

1. INTRODUCTION

"Nature does not know complex principles. Its method of working can be only elementarily simple. Since psychological reactions are natural processes, their underlying principles or causal laws must also be elementarily simple." (D. G. Garan, 1968)

The phenomenon of personality transformation as a response to suffering has been recognized for centuries. Religion and literature have comforted people in suffering by providing a vision that they will be close to wisdom, truth, and God through the experiences (Tedeschi & Calhoun, 1995) Existential philosophers and psychologists also have long recognized opportunities for growth in trauma and suffering (Kierkeggard, 1983; Nietzsche 1955; Tillich, 1952; Fromm, 1976, Ebersole, 1970).

Systematic research about positive reorganization of personality system due to traumatic experiences such as life crisis (Schaefer and Moos, 1992), death of a loved one (Nerken, 1993), a period of psychological disequilibrium (Mahoney, 1982), etc has provided some evidence that personality systems may be transformed in face of life adversity.

These researchers have variously termed the metamorphosis of personality system "Thriving" (O'Leary & Ickovics, 1995), "Transformational coping" (Aldwin, 1994), "Quantum change" (Miller & C'deBaca, 1994), and "Posttraumatic growth" (Tedeschi & Calhoun, 1995). Finkel (1974, 1975) proposed the concept of trauma-to-stren transformation; according to him "stren" are "health-promoting" or "growth-potentiating" experiences. He seemed to arrive at the conclusion that certain persons had the ability to convert trauma into growth through some "cognitive restructuring mechanism"

Hong Seock Lee, The Catholic University

1.1. THREE BASIC QUESTIONS IN PERSONALITY RESEARCH

In this chapter, I will raise some fundamental and yet unanswered (questions) in the field of personality studies. And then I will propose a theory that may shed some light on these questions.

My first question is: Is there continuity in the reorganized or or transformed personality systems? There is some empirical support of the continuity of the reorganized personality structure (Costa and McCrae, 1989; Park, Cohen, & Murch, 1996), but the issue is not completely resolved.

My second question is the process of the changes in personality system gradual or abrupt? There are longstanding contradictions in personality research. Majority of the theoretical literature on positive reorganization of personality system reflects the gradual change: "working through" and moderated "dosing" of traumatic material into awareness (Greenberg, 1995; Horowitz, 1986), gradual changes in one's view of oneself and the world through repeated comparisons of an experienced trauma with existing schemas (Janoff-Bulman, 1992), graduate growth following loss through incremental change (Nerken, 1993), and the incremental transformational process as the result of coping with some unexpected and uncontrollable trauma (Tedeschi and Calhoun, 1995).

However, the literature also reports dramatic transformations that occur abruptly through mechanisms that are not yet fully appreciated (Tennen and Affleck, 1998). For example, the theory of Quantum Change proposed by Miller and C'deBaca (1994) describes sudden, unexpected deviations in the lives of people that result in permanent and ubiquitous change. Also, Finkel's (1974, 1975) concept of trauma-to-stren transformation supports the abrupt, sudden changes of personality.

The implication of this contradiction is not that one is right and the other is wrong. Tennen and Affleck (1998) posited that the abrupt, unintentional type of change must be considered as distinct from the gradual, intentional type of change. Their position implies that the two types of change may occur through different mechanisms.

My last question is: Is there any particular structure of personality system, which is conducive to transformation as a result of suffering?

1.2. POSTULATES OF THE BIOSOCIOEXISTENTIAL MODEL

In order to answer the above questions, I propose a Biosocioexistential (BSE) model of personality. This model provides a simple causal principle that can explain chaotic behavior of personality systems. The major postulates are: (1) the minimal unit of systems, the union of opposites, creates transcendence between the opposites. (2) repeated transcendence brings transformation of structures (i.e., monistic, bipartite, or triadic structures) out of personality system depending on the nature of input from environment and individual's willingness to accept the input. (3) when individuals personality systems acquire triadic structure, three subsystems produce their unique psychological experiences at different levels, biologically by polarity system, existentially by duality system, and socially by dialectical system.

Regarding to my first question, according to the BSE model, the union of opposites is the fundamental, general, and minimal set of personality systems. These unchanging two-opposite templates of personality systems give rise to consistency of individual personality systems, when the personality system was observed through the method of factor analysis. Meanwhile, the works of the union of opposites are complex and make the personality system "transcend-able" and "transformable". These mechanisms of personality against the oppositeness create the inconsistency of personality. Regarding to my second question, BSE model explains the transcend-ability of personality system as the abrupt changes of personality system and the transformability as the incremental changes of personality system.

Regarding my last question, BSE model hypothesizes the three different personality structure's hierarchical degree of the transformability. In other words, BSE model of personality proposes that the union of opposites gives birth to the phenomena of transcendence and transformation, which eventually create evolutionary systems to the psyche.

2. THEORETICAL CONSTRUCTS

Whatever personality may be, it has the properties of an *open system* (Allport, 1961, p. 109), which is a dynamic order of parts and processes standing in mutual interaction (Bertalanffy, 1952). In order to understand the complexity of personality systems, we need to return to the place where the complexity was born-that is, the union of opposites, which gives birth to a system.

Although frequently regarded as pathological, tension itself actually plays a key role in evolutionary changes (Jung, 1953; Levy, 1992; Festinger, 1957). There can be no development or change without tension, which is created from the union of opposites. The union of opposites is the basic causation of mental phenomena.

This union of opposites is literally synonymous with a paradoxical system having opposite elements in the same entity: in the "oneness" (i.e., the union of opposites), there exist "two-ness" (i.e., two opposites). Paradoxical systems display three interlocking essential features: (a) the interpenetrating back and forth interplay, (b) the opposite effect of the same entity, and (c) the oscillative or cyclical dynamics. Undergoing interpenetrating back and forth interplay between the opposite, the opposites in the union each display their own unique effect alternatively so that oscillative or cyclical dynamics emerge. The newly emerged cyclical dynamic is a cycle, a pattern, a dimensional organization, or a structure created at higher hierarchical level. In this sense, paradoxical system is creative. However, the creativeness of the paradoxical system is not possible without its opposite elements or subsystems, maintaining their qualitative oppositeness consistently. From a relative point of view, the subsystems of the paradoxical system are non-paradoxical.

This theory will explain that the union (oneness) of differentiated opposites (two-ness) gives transcend-ability and transformability to the personality system: Transcendence occurs between the differentiated opposites. And transformation of personality structure varies from a monistic structure to a triadic structure (three-ness), which is a minimal structure of a whole system that enable the repeated creation of self-similar fractal structures at each level of organization.

In this sense, triadic structure is infinite. Now, we will return to the departure point of systems – union of opposites.

2.1.   Minimal set of system's unit: union of form and force

From the standpoint of physics, the most fundamental union of opposites is that of matter (form) and anti-matter (force). When matter is not united with anti-matter or vice-versa, their further transformation is impossible. Therefore, all the systems reorganizing by themselves arise from the union of matter and anti-matter.

On the other hand, according to theories of evolution, every entity changes itself in a best way for surviving in the world where it belongs (Darwin, 1969). Similarly, a personality system, in which only psychological phenomena can be found, will take a best structure for the world in which it lives (Buss, 1978). Therefore, we can assume that the union of physical opposites, like form and force, must be found in personality systems. Psychological definition of the form is the state of "no difference" between mental cognitions. In the state of no difference, mental representations cannot gain their identity through their contrast with one another. But the state of differences brings different kinds of cognitions. Psychological equivalents of form and force can be found in the distinction between implicit knowledge and explicit knowledge, which is believed as essential cognitive agents from the perspective of cognitive psychology.

From this background, it is hypothesized that in personality systems the pair of two opposite elements, form (matter) and force (antimatter), is a minimal unit of transformable systems. In other words, union of form and force is the fundamental, general, and minimal set of personality system. In fact, prevailing definitions of "system" have ignored this principle of union between force and form, the unit of variants in form, or the unit of variants in force. However, in any open system, when a force is united to a force with no existence of a form as medium for the union, the system cannot produce anything meaningful to the system; the only system in which allows the union of a force and a force, and a form and a form, is a closed system.

2.2. Extension of the proposition

2.2.1. Transcendence between form and force and transformation into the third entity

Let me apply the proposition aforementioned into the developmental aspect of human psyche. At the developing stage that amorphous characteristics of form (i.e., body) and force (i.e., mind) of prototype are salient because form and force are not individualized yet as the opposites, they cannot interact with each other, just like in the symbiotic phase of the object relations theory.

But through the interaction with environment, form and force come to be individualized so that they can start to interact: the more the oppositeness of the opposites is individualized, the more the interaction is strengthened. As these individualized prototypic elements of system come to influence each other, form is transcended into a different kind of form by force. Simultaneously, by the transcendental process of the form a different kind of force is created which brings out change in character of the original force. The whole process including the interaction between form and force is defined as "*Transcendental Interpenetrating Interaction*" or "*Transcendence*," by which movement breaks out. The movement, generated by the interaction of force and mass, is the third entity, which has a totally different quality from the original force and form. The process of giving birth to the third entity, which is a large-scale change of structure, is called "*Transformation*" by Ashby (1956).

In other words, repeated transcendences between the prototypic form and force are a pre-condition of transformation: the more there are of abrupt changes in one's worldview such as insight and revelation, the more the gradual transformational changes of personality. This notion of the BSE model provides a mechanistic explanation toward Reker's (2000) conceptualization of transformation and transcendence. According to him, as a new possibility becomes actualized through transformation, the stage is set for other potentialities through transcendence. Transcendence is also the product itself (phenomenon) through transformational process.

2.2.2. Paradox of paradoxical system: Creation of non-paradoxical systems-Polarity system and Duality system

The first union of opposites, form and force, can be termed "paradoxical system" because it is created by the union of opposites. As the oneness of sperm and ovary eventually gives a birth to the two-ness, a unilateral sex of male or female, this prototype of paradoxical system eventually gives birth to variants of its opposite elements, non-paradoxical systems.

To explain, by the interaction between the prototypic form and force, form is bifurcated into two opposite extreme poles of a linear continuum: homogeneous form vs. heterogeneous form. By the process of form's bifurcation, force evolves into opposite poles such as entropy vs. free energy. Applying the proposition of this theory that an open system can only be produced by the interaction between form and force, the bifurcated variant (i.e., homogeneous form) of form cannot make a pair of unit with the other variant of form (i.e., heterogeneous form) in an open system, but only with one of the two variants of force (i.e., entropy or free energy). Accordingly, only four kinds of union of pairs can be made: a pair (1) between homogeneous form and entropy force, (2) between homogeneous and free energy, (3) between heterogeneous and entropy, and (4) between heterogeneous and free energy.

Four Pairs

1. *Homogeneous (form) + Entropy (force)*
2. *Homogeneous (form) + Free Energy (force)*
3. *Heterogeneous (form) + Entropy (force)*
4. *Heterogeneous (form) + Free Energy (force)*

Among the four pairs, the pair of (2) and (3) have relatively paradoxical, contradictory elements within one system and therefore, they are still remained as a paradoxical system, so that they keep changing themselves through transcendental interpenetrating interaction until they are transformed into a relatively stable non-paradoxical system.

On the contrary, the systems created by the pair of (1) and the pair of (4) are non-paradoxical systems because they are composed of non-paradoxical or parallel elements: homogenous form and force of entropy have the common goal pursuing the state of near equilibrium (Priogogine, 1980); heterogeneous form and force of free energy have the common goal pursuing the state of the far-from equilibrium (Priogogine, 1980). Therefore, purpose of the non-paradoxical systems is to be linear, consistent, intrinsic, internal and endogenous due to the aforementioned non-paradoxical, parallel nature of the pairs of unit creating the system. Also, because the purpose is always consistent, the system moves in an autonomous and predictable way. Here, the former non-paradoxical system will be called "*a Polarity System*," while the latter non-paradoxical system will be coined as "*a Duality System*."

Figure 1. Schematic functional definition of the polarity system and the duality system

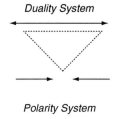

Meanwhile, the directions of works of the non-paradoxical systems are opposite to each other. To explain, polarity system brings polarity, which means the state of indifference between opposites (i.e., homogeneous mental representations), through the process of integration, identification, or dedifferentiation. Thereby, the polarity states acquired by the polarity system reduce tension between opposites and eventually bring the near equilibrium state to an entity. On the other hands, a duality system induces duality, which is a state of difference between elements (heterogeneous representations), through the process of disintegration, dis-identification, or differentiation. And by the differential impulse, it eventually increases tension between opposites, pursuing far-from equilibrium. In addition, while the polarity system usually directs the determined action to the external environment (because states of indifference cause no conflict), the actions of a duality system are directed to symbolic psychological world because the states of difference only induce comparison, conflicts, complaints, symbolization, verbalization, and meaning-creation, but not particular action to be acted.

Because of the ontological difference between the polarity system and the duality system and their tendency to be stabilized, the functional qualities gradually become bifurcated between them as they develop. In other words, the more the entity develops, the more the non-paradoxical systems are individuated, bifurcated, differentiated from each other. This process is "Individuation of the non-paradoxical systems."

The individuation of non-paradoxical systems directly indicates that non-paradoxical systems are created from the paradoxical system due to its unstable, paradoxical nature. This process is called "*Paradox of Paradoxical System.*"

Figure 2. Possible end-products of the polarity system and the duality system

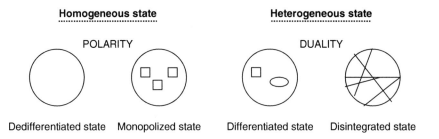

Figure 3. Individuation of non-paradoxical systems

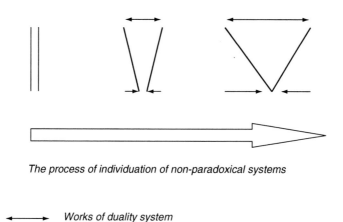

The process of individuation of non-paradoxical systems

Works of duality system

Works of polarity system

2.2.3. Paradox of non-paradoxical systems: Creation of paradoxical system (Dialectical system) from non-paradoxical systems

When the opposite non-paradoxical systems are individuated, paradoxically the very union of opposites reemerges. That is, the polarity system takes a form of matter compared to the duality system and at the same time the duality system takes a form of antimatter compared to the polarity system. Again, the more the oppositeness between the non-paradoxical systems is solidified through the individuation of non-paradoxical systems, the more the transcendental interpenetrating interaction between the non-paradoxical systems is strengthened. In turn, the more the transcendental interaction is heightened, the more the opposite non-paradoxical systems are unified into a newly created system at different hierarchical level.

Figure 4. Schematic functional definition of dialectical systems

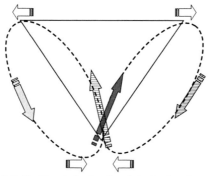

* Dotted line indicates the dialectical system

The newly created system from the non-paradoxical systems is also a paradoxical system because it is composed of paradoxical or opposite elements, the polarity and the duality systems. The only difference between the prototypic paradoxical system and the newly created paradoxical system is hierarchical level: Sabelli's (1989) priority of the simple belongs to the former, but the latter has the supremacy of the complex. This paradoxical system will be called *"Dialectical system."* And this process of creation of another paradoxical system from the individuated non-paradoxical systems will be called *"paradox of non-paradoxical systems.*

The reason for naming this paradoxical system as dialectical is that dialectic's concept of the alternative convergence (association) and divergence (dissociation) between opposites provides the excellent theoretical underpinnings for explaining the work of the dialectical system: (1) *dialectical system makes the linear movement of non-paradoxical system change into the alternating, cyclical, oscillative, and interpenetrating pattern; (2) according to the level of the dialectical system's efficiency and the maturity of the individuation of its subsystems, the degree of interaction between subsystems (convergence vs. divergence) is determined.* This notion in this theory is partially connected to the synergistic model of cognitive psychology integrating the bottom-up model and the top-down model, the Frank's (2002) enactment concept, P.L. Wachtel's (1982) cyclical psychodynamics conception, Kiesler's (2002) maladaptive transaction cycle, Carson's (1982) self-fulfilling expectancy model, Safran's (Safran & Segal, 1990) cognitive-interpersonal model, Andrew's (1989) self-confirmation model, and Strupp and Binder's (1984) cyclical maladaptive pattern.

For dialectical system, transformation resulted from the interrelatedness between the parts of a whole is emphasized over separateness. In this sense, transformability acquired from transcendental interpenetration of the non-paradoxical subsystems is a fundamental characteristic of this system.

2.2.4. Circle of Information

A dialectical system is constrained by external environment so that it permissively accepts input from external environment and assigns the accepted input to its subsystems (i.e., information flows from the environment into the dialectical system, and from the dialectical system to the non-paradoxical systems), while non-dialectical systems are encapsulated and constrained by the dialectical system, respond to the signals that are produced by the dialectical system, and finally send out their predetermined action toward environment (i.e., information flows from the non-paradoxical systems toward the environment). As a reaction to the action of the non-paradoxical systems, environment constrains the dialectical system. Thereby, "a circle of information" is formed at this point.

Important implications of this circle of information flow are that causal mechanism of the dialectical system is absolutely dependent on rewards from social, interpersonal, environmental, and cultural context. Meanwhile, the linear, consistent working mechanisms of the non-paradoxical systems are dependent on their predetermined nature and the signals from the dialectical system.

3. PSYCHOLOGICAL EQUIVALENTS OF THE THREE SUBSYSTEMS

Applied in the personality realm, the three systems play a unique role and each produces an unique psychological experience at three different levels, biologically by the polarity system, existentially by the duality system, and socially by the dialectical system; these will be called "the Biological system", "the Existential system", and "the Social system" of personality, respectively.

3.1. Biological system of personality: Polarity system

The homeostasis principle, which seeks to maintain equilibrium or a state without tensions, plays a crucial role in solidifying the polarity system of personality. That is, the main consequence of the polarity system's activity is tension reduction by acquiring the state of indifference and by canceling the effects of opposites. An instinctive property of the polarity system is that under the polarity system an entity tends to search for an immediate way (*causal searching*) in order to release tension (*pleasure principle*).

Polarity can be achieved through two largely opposite mechanisms: mature vs. immature. The former includes forms of psychic activity including integration, identification, causal appraisal, associative causal problem solving, the pleasure principle-driven behavior, and so forth. When all these mechanisms fail to establish an unified monopoly state, the polarity system finds its way to complete the task by means of immature, prior, and simple mechanisms: denial, dissociation, fugue, amnesias, and dedifferentiation.

We can find these characteristics from instincts, automatic skills, temperaments, and biological dimensions. Cognitive, emotional, and behavioral polarities achieved by the biological system are stored in "*implicit memory systems.*" Eventually, the saved polarities are genetically inherited by the next generation as a surviving strategy of individuals within society.

In these senses, the biological system of personality is simple, stable, prior, potential, autonomic, and implicit compared to its higher systems, the existential system and the social system.

3.2. Existential system of personality

The existential system (duality system), separating indifference into difference, is directed to something other than itself. Preserving the "otherness" means the meaning principle that is the motivation to reach to other states. Therefore, one person cannot be satisfied with the present and "what I am." So the monopolized identity or cognition acquired by polarity system, "what I am," is going to be dis-identified or fragmented.

Thereby, the differentiated mental representations, identities, goals, or emotions can be compared, explicitly. But, inescapably, unpleasant tension states such as conflicts, confusion, identity-diffusion, chaos, and complaints are caused by comparison with the opposite-value (Festinger, 1950). At this time, a main consequence of the duality system's activity increases tension. But, paradoxically, these amplified tensions become actually play a key role in evolutionary changes (Levy 1992): the comparison between the opposites gives rise to information, symbols, language, meanings and goals of life. The dualities, produced by the existential system (duality system), are to be saved in an explicit memory system. In the explicit memory system, the duality is presented as languages, symbols or meaning constructs according to the degree of information processing. The transformed qualities transcend to the next generation as a survival strategy of the species but not of individuals.

3.2.1. Existential attribution and existential coping

In order to achieve its goal, the duality system uses the following mechanisms: (1) existential attribution and (2) meaning principles. To explain, the cognitive properties of the duality system try to find the more fundamental reasons for the reality by using the mechanisms of existential attribution (Wong & Weiner, 1981; Wong, 1991). Existential attribution is mainly a quest for explanation based on one's subjective reflections and values; it represents a deeper level of processing than causal attribution. According to Wong (1991), it entails continued and repetitive quest for satisfactory reasons and purpose for a negative event or an unsatisfactory state of affairs. Tension may be increased in the course of searching for existential attributions.

Existential coping (Wong, 1993, Chapter 11) represents the result of a successful existential attributional search; it is consisted of accepting what cannot be changed and finding some positive meaning in a negative situation. Once one is able to employ existential coping, the tension of the existential quest is reduced.

Existential search is a process of "*auto-amplification of tension*," which plays a crucial role in completing duality system's task. This process is not different from the Kraft's (1974) experience of "nothingness"; which includes such negative emotions as anger, loneliness, depression, anxiety, guilt, frustration, anger, and boredom. People may actually increase their tension to heighten their pleasure when tension is subsequently decreased (Maddi, 1996). By amplifying tension, repetitive existential questions without immediate reinforcement play a role in the initiation of various symptoms of "existential sickness (Maddi, 1967)" and "nothingness (Kraft, 1974)." In spite of these negative by-products of existential attribution, amplification of inner tension is prerequisite for the attainment of new understandings of people's suffering from the inner world (i.e., tension attenuation by existential attribution) and external world (i.e., negative events). Murray and Kluckhohn (1956) contends that the absence of tension is less rewarding than the process of getting from higher to lower states of tension. In this sense, the sufferings, actually indicating autonomous amplification of the tension, are only the by-product of the works of the duality system, which is needed to accomplish its goal.

How can we endure these enormous sufferings and how can we postpone immediate satisfaction? The only way to transform the amplified tension into stren is to replace the pleasure principle into the meaning principle: According to the reinforcement principle, lack of reinforcement eventually leads to extinction of a certain coping strategy, unless an alternative strategy can be adopted (Wong, 1995). In terms of tension, meaning principle aims to find meaning and value in sufferings but not to gain pleasure or power (Wong, 1998). Individuals are willing to endure pain and hardship to the extent that suffering is transformed to a meaning. These statements do not insist that the meaning principle is a primary method of working on the mental apparatus, "dominance of the meaning principle," but convey that under the difficulties of the external world, the pleasure principle is replaced by the meaning principle. Another fundamental conflict in the meaning principle is the duality of positive existential givens and negative existential givens (Wong, 2005). Negative existential givens include ultimate loneliness, death anxiety, despair and the resulting feeling of meaninglessness of life (Yalom, 1980). However, Frankl (1963) and Wong (2005) have also identified positive existential givens that are potentially present in everyone to combat the negative existential givens; these positive existential givens include the affirmation of meaning, will to meaning, and faith in a

Higher Power. Existential coping consists of both acceptance of what cannot be changed and the affirmation of positive existential givens in the presence of negative reality (Wong & Reker, in press).

Therefore, it can be said that the system of the unpleasant tensions (duality system) is a higher system than biological system (polarity system), being characterized as more complex, unstable, dynamic, supreme, experiential and more intentional system than the biological system.

3.2.2. Roots of Non-paradoxical Systems in Psychology

We can find psychology's union of polarity system and duality system everywhere. The union of opposites such as matter vs. antimatter, entropy vs. free energy, closed system vs. open system, implicit memory system vs. explicit memory system, and temperament dimension vs. character dimension are the examples. Cognitive psychologists have tried hard to deal with issues raised by differences between the symbolic approach and the connectionist approach (Carver and Scheier, 1998, p. 331). This general idea recurs in several other theories (see Holyoak & Spellman, 1993; Buck, 1985;): the dichotomy of symbolic versus subsymbolic processing (Rumelhart et al., 1986), the dichotomy of conceptual (conscious processor) versus subconceptual processing (intuitive processor) (Smolensky 1988), the dichotomy of rule-based and associative (Sloman, 1996), the dichotomy of reflective and reflexive (Shastri and Ajjanadde, 1993), and the dichotomy of the conscious versus the unconscious (Jacoby et al. 1994).

Although theories differ, they all can be characterized as two-mode models of processing: conscious explicit experiences are concept-based and represented as words, images, or symbols about facts and events that have explicit meanings and functional relations with one another that we can retrieve consciously, declare verbally, and act on intentionally. In contrast, unconscious, implicit, or procedural memories involve presemantic percep-deriven processing that encodes concrete visuospatial structural information and affective valence; such perceptual processing can operate independent of abstract conceptual, intentional, or declarative processes (Cloninger, 1993; Squire et al., 1993).

The general idea of two modes of functioning has been around for a long time throughout various fields including personality psychology in particular. Indeed, Cloninger's psychobiological model of personality (1993), which is constructed based on two basic templates of personality including temperament and character dimensions, is another revival of cognitive psychology's two-mode models. In his psychobiological model, temperament involves automatic, preconceptual responses to preconceptual stimuli, presumably reflecting heritable biases in information processing by the preconceptual memory system. In contrast, character dimensions were related to conceptual memory system (Cloninger, 1993). He acknowledged that prior models of personality, such as Five Factor Model (FFM) or Big Five, failed to distinguish between distinct aspects of memory because they were derived by factor analysis of behavior, not by consideration of its underlying biological and social determinants. To him, thereby, personality is paradox of biological (i.e., temperament) and social determinants (i.e., character).

The aforementioned idea that people experience the world through two different modes of processing also appears in the literature of personality such as Epstein's cognitive-experiential self-theory (1994), which assumes the existence of two systems (i.e., the rational system and the experiential system) for processing information; Jung's rational and irrational functions of the mind (1953), which influences behavior in varying degrees; Kohut's the grandiose-exhibitionistic self and the child's idealized parental imago (1977); Heckhausen and Gollwitzer's deliberative and the implemental mindsets (Gollwitzer, Heckhausen, & Steller, 1990; Gollwitzer & Bayer, 1999); and Bowin's two basic templates of psychological defense mechanisms-dissociation and cognitive distortions (2004).

The template such as body (preconcept-based biological dimension), nature (inborn), implicit knowledge (automata), and temperamental dimension of Cloninger's biosocial model is parallel to the definition for the biological system (polarity system) of BSE model. On the other hand, the opposite template such as mind (concept-based cognitive dimension), nurture (education), and explicit knowledge (intention), and character dimension is to the definition for the existential system (duality system).

In sum, we live in the world of opposites. This is a truth. Here, the field of tension is established between subject and object, between the "I am" and the "I ought", between reality and ideal, between being and meaning, between homogeneity and heterogeneity, between monopoly and pluralism, between dedifferentiation and differentiation, between identification and dis-identification, between the implicit and the explicit, between the physical system and the symbolic system, between polarity and duality. Among these opposite bipolarities, a most representative bi-polarity seems to reside between the polarity and the duality.

3.3. Social System of Personality: Dialectical Systems

In order to maintain homeostasis and a state of "what I am," we construct, integrate, or dedifferentiate our mental representation. Whereas, in order to go beyond the limitations, we destruct, disintegrate, or differentiate the previous mental representation, "what I was." These mental processes are not different from the nature's evolutionary repetition of construction and destruction.

However, the two opposite systems are only a part of the whole. Thereby, they are incomplete, not self-sufficient, just like a catcher and a pitcher without a ball. These opposite mechanisms of the polarity system and the duality system are controlled by dialectical system, which is can be defined as "Social system (Dialectical system)."

3.3.1. The dialectical system

The social system (dialectical system), formed by the union of the biological system and the existential system, causally interconnects the polarity states with the duality states by transcending the former into the latter and vice versa.

The dialectical system has been regarded as nothingness to psyche because its existence is observed us as a non-linear pattern that is ruled by the reinforcement from the environment. Because of the external location of its mobilizing resources of this system, we cannot describe its nature on the dimension of matter or antimatter but on another dimension.

This third dimension is built for the continuous autonomic production of change by enhancing the interpenetrating oscillation between subsystems and by inducing transformation of structure of the whole system.

Generally, a part of our psyche is in the monopolized state and the other part is in the fragmented state, and these opposed states compete against one another. These competition eventually cause "essential tension," which is neither pleasant nor discomfort, and which prevents the whole system from reaching to the irreversible point of Bertalanffy's closed system. An absolute monopolized or absolute fragmented state is an irreversible state, which is the world of "non-living things." In this sense, the essential tension is the medium that enables to our psychic world oscillates between the state of unified cognition and the state of the fragmented state. Thus, the psyche can generate psychic energy at any time, at any situation. Then, how this is possible?

3.3.2. Mechanism of the dialectical system

The causal mechanism of the dialectical system (the social system) controlling its non-paradoxical subsystems can be explained by the synthetic view integrating Thorndike's law of effect (1910) and Allport's idea of conative perseverance (1937). The law of effect and idea of conative perseverance exactly opposes to each other: while the law of effect is that the greater the satisfaction or discomfort, the greater the strengthening or weakening of the S-R bond, the principle of the conative perseverance is that the uncompleted tasks set up tension that tends to keep the individual at work until they are resolved (Allport, 1937). However, the completion of the task itself has become a quasi-need with dynamic force of its own. Therefore, the conative perseverance can be revised as having this principle: the greater the satisfaction or discomfort, the greater the weakening or strengthening of the bond.

In order to control transcendental interpretation of its subsystem mentioned above as the law of effect and the conative perseverance, the dialectical system responds to rewards from the external environment and uses the two opposite reinforcement mechanisms in a synergistic way.

The incompatibility of their statements does not mean that one is correct and the other is wrong, rather their opposed notions wonderfully explain human phenomenon when diachronically considered, Thorndike's law of effect is truth in short-time observation (T1), while conative perseverance is also truth in long-term observation (T2). Therefore, reinforcement principles need to be revised: Positive reward strengthens the bond of stimuli and response temporarily, but eventually it weakens the bond; negative rewards weaken the bond temporarily, but eventually it strengthens the bond. That is, positive reward eventually terminates a certain behavior and negative reward eventually initiate a different kind of behavior.

This synthesis of these two opposite laws explains clearly how the dialectical system controls oscillating cyclical dynamics of its two opposite subsystems. At T1, the aforementioned existential principles of the existential system (the duality system) result in prolonged no reinforcement, while the biological principles of the biological system (the polarity system) attain immediate resolution of discomfort or offer positive rewards. Therefore, in the beginning even though movement of polarity system is strengthened, as time passes, the duality system, to which reward is not offered, becomes strengthened. At the same time, movement of the polarity system is weakened. Over time, the contrasting phenomena appear and eventually the two opposite non-paradoxical systems start to act alternatively.

Figure 5. Evolutionary progression of the union of opposites

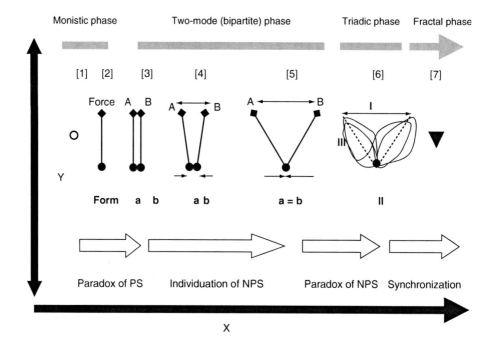

4. CREATIVE EVOLUTION OF THE UNION OF OPPOSITES

The figure 5 is a summary for the evolution of the system's minimal union.

X = TRANSFORMATION PROCESS
Y = TRANSCENDENCE PROCESS

1. *Amorphous form and force*
2. *Prototypic paradoxical system (Union of form and force)*
3. *Undifferentiated non-paradoxical systems*
4. *Moderately differentiated non-paradoxical systems*
5. *Optimally differentiated non-paradoxical systems*
6. *Newly created paradoxical system and its non-paradoxical subsystems*
7. *Synchronized system as oneness*
A: *Heterogeneous form   B: Force of free energy a: Homogeneous form   b: Force of entropy*
I: *Duality system = A^*B II: Polarity system = a^*b III: Dialectical system = I^*II*

4.1. Paradox of systems

4.1.1. Creation of circle of paradoxical system and non-paradoxical systems

In the figure, a prototypic paradoxical system [1-2] (i.e., a system consisting of form and force), by its paradoxical nature, creates relatively non-paradoxical systems [AB & ab, 3]. The emerged non-paradoxical systems are individualized [3-5] due to their own non-paradoxical nature. By the time they are optimally individuated, their union creates another paradoxical system (dialectical system) [6]. Dialectical system displays a new cyclical dynamics creating cycle, pattern, and dimensional organization.

In this evolutionary process, we can observe the phenomena of *"the Paradox of systems"* indicating the alternative emergence of the paradoxical systems [1, 2, 6] and non-paradoxical systems [3-5]. The "paradox of systems" induced by the aforementioned mechanisms such as "paradox of paradoxical systems," the "individuation of non-paradoxical systems," "paradox of non-paradoxical system," and "synchronization of triadic systems".

5. PERSONALITY STRUCTURES

Through the course of creative evolution of "the paradox of systems," the whole system of an individual personality system can be transformed dynamically into a structure among *"the Synchronized monistic structure," "the Bipartite (two-mode) structure," or "the Triadic structure,"* which is partially equivalent with Heraclitus's three different worldviews, respectively.

In Heraclitus's three principles, *"Dynamic Monism"* indicating that psyche and body are made of the same stuff, *"Union of Opposites,"* which was later supplanted by the separation of opposites, or their mutual neutralization, or by unilateral formulations of universal harmony (theology), or of a struggle of opposites (Marxist dialectics and Darwinian evolutionism), and *"Becoming,"* which was the belief in the creation and destruction of structures in opposing processes of evolution and involution (enantiodromia) (Sabelli, 1989) are interlocked. But their explicit meaning is not fully understood. BSE model provides a systematic understanding for these three interlocking principles.

From the aspect of BSE model, however, the systemic structure of personality is very transformable according to environmental conditions so that the structure cannot be understood along one or two selected structures. Rather, they must be considered in their transformability, which transforms flexibly into the synchronized monistic structure, the bipartite structure, or triadic structure. Seemingly contradicting each other, both are preconditions for the other. The true nature of a personality system can be appreciated only when we can understand the functional qualities of each structure and their interactions as a whole.

The monistic structure of a system [1-2, 7] is transformed into the bipartite structure [3-5] through the process of "the paradox of paradoxical system," and the bipartite structure is transformed into the triadic structure [6] through the process of "the paradox of non-paradoxical systems." If the dialectical interaction (transcendence) of the triadic structured system reaches to the optimal level, the triadic structure is synchronized as another monistic structure. In this case, the creative evolution (transformation) of a system's structure can be continued at different dimension (fractional dimensionality). However, in ordinary a system's whole structure, there is back and forth interplay between the triadic structure and the bipartite structure because of the difficulty to reach to the optimal level of dialectical interaction. In this case, there is no evolution in the whole system.

An excellent analogy of this transformational course can be found in the dimensional evolution of quantum physics: When the concept of the wave behavior of time-varying fields is considered, the single electromagnetic field derives the one-dimensional scalar, such as voltage and current (i.e., the monistic structure), the motion of vector fields in the form of the two-dimensional plane (rectangular) wave (i.e., bipartite structure), and finally the three-dimensional spherical waves found in the electromagnetic radiation emitted by antennas (i.e., triadic structure). It is important to note that all of its seemingly unrelated dimensional structures are derivable from a single electromagnetic field, which is cause by the gap between electric poles (i.e., the union of opposites). As far as the field is concerned, each of the different responses is due solely to a different frequency of excitation (i.e., transcendence caused by tension).

5.1. Monistic Structure

5.1.1. Mechanism

Synchronized monistic structure is a newly transformed organization, which can be acquired only when the frequency of the oscillating cycle (transcendental interaction) between the polarity system and the duality system is maximized by the dialectical system so that the three subsystems are synchronized into a new form. Therefore, monistic structure is a maximized dynamics and a new form at the same time.

5.1.2. Symptom formation and energy level

When personality system takes the monistic structure, subjectively there is no complexity, confusion, and conflict. But objectively dynamics of the psyche are maximized. That is, in this structured system a high level of energy is generated but the system stays in calm. Thereby, the monistic structure gives rise to "vitality," "creativity," "openness to other experiences," "a sense of otherness," "enchanted agnosia," or "peak experience."

5.1.3. Transformability

As soon as it is formed, another structure immediately follows. Because the personality system in monistic structure begins to be aware of, incorporate, and accept information, which is totally different or opposite from the previously synchronized cognitions, the structure is transformed itself.

5.1.4. Equivalents

Equivalents of this condition can be found in physics as synchronization or resonance, in chemistry as Prigogine's far-from equilibrium state (Prigogine, 1980), and in psychology as Maslow's "Being-Cognition" (Maslow, 1999). Two oppositely charged particles, which had no previous weight, created mass through synchronization. The far-from-chemical-equilibrium condition serves to bring out or activate the nonlinear factors in the chemical reaction, thereby, enabling bifurcation and self-organization phenomena to take place (Goldstein, 1962). "Being-Cognition" makes a psychic system complete, self-sufficient, unitary, independent in its own right, self-forgettable, conflict transcending, uncontaminated, self-organized, outside of time and space, eternal, universal, and general, self-justifying, absolute, resolution of dichotomies, ineffable, mutually interpenetrating, and dialectical.

5.2. Bipartite Structure

5.2.1. Mechanism

For the absence of dialectical system in an entity indicates that the polarity system and the duality system of the entity are scattered without active transcendental interaction. Thus they remain at an intermingled state in which the polarity system and duality system are not yet individualized. At this time, the whole system is observed as a "bipartite structured system" (dichotomous two-mode systems), which is the homeostatic-oriented structure. In this structure, the correlations of the subsystems are weak.

5.2.2. Transformability and energy level

Due to the qualities of this structure (i.e., premature individuation and weak interaction of the subsystems), the whole system of bipartite structure is resistant to both structural transformation (i.e., from bipartite to triadic) and functional transformation (i.e., from input to output). The level of creative tension is low to moderate. Therefore, in general, bipartite system is the one in which conflict (energy) is not generated by encountering two opposite elements. According to the principle of economy, developing a dominant, linear, and unilateral personality trait becomes a system's goal. Eventually, however, the system would be extinguished if it does not change itself anymore. The only way for an entity in this system to revive is to transform the system into the triadic systemic structure by achieving individualization of the polarity system and the duality system.

5.2.3. Phenotypes

Four phenotypes of personality can be created by the bipartite structured system. (1) When personality structure stays in the bipartite system, it is normal that unilateral behavior, emotion, self, or cognition appears consistently. That is, in a normal state of the bipartite system, stability, continuity, identity and organization come to entity's phenotype, and thus an *organized type* is commonly created. (2) However, in a case where interactions between the polarity system and the duality system is too weak owing to disordered individuation of non-paradoxical systems, there would be rather an obstacle in creating psyche energy and the obstacle can trigger a melancholic downcast type. (3-4) When balance between two subsystems is broken, two kinds of phenotypes are triggered: the dependent type (duality system >> polarity system) or the autocratic type (duality system << polarity system). All of the four types' energy level is much lower than those of the triadic structured system so then entity cannot transform the input (stimulus) to output (transcendence and transformation).

5.2.4. Symptom formation

On the other hands, when a systemic entity is captured in the bipartite structure, pathological conditions such as personality disorders, stagnation, allostatic load, developmental arrest or fixation may appear.

5.2.5. Equivalents in worldview

We can find numerous equivalents in dualism of matter vs. antimatter in physics, the mutual neutralization in mechanics, the struggle of opposites in Marxist dialectics and Darwinian evolutionism (1969), Bertalanffy's closed system and open system (1952), Ebstein's cognitive-experiential self-theory (1990, 1994) assuming the existence of two systems (the rational system vs. the experiential system) for processing information, Jung's rational and irrational functions of the mind (1971/1931), Kohut's bipolar concept of self (1977), Heckhausen and Gollwitzer's the declarative and the implemental mindsets (1987), the two-mode model (implicit memory system vs. explicit memory system) of cognitive psychology (Squire LR and Zola-Morgan S, 1991), and Cloninger's (1993) biopsychological model of personality (temperament vs. character).

5.3. Triadic Structure

5.3.1. Mechanism

When the opposite non-paradoxical systems are converged by the increase of transcendental interaction, the dialectical system is created and the whole system takes on a triadic structure. Meanwhile, the dialectical system cannot be created when the non-paradoxical systems are diverged so that the whole system will take on a bipartite structure but not triadic structure.

5.3.2. Transformability

As noticed above, the fact that the whole system has taken on a triadic system directly indicates that the dialectical system has been evolved from the two opposite non-paradoxical subsystems. Thereby, the triadic structure is a change (transcendence and transformation)-oriented structure of the whole system: (1) dialectical system's transcendental interaction brings changes to world view and offers brand new insight, and (2) as long as the interference does not occur in the process of synchronization and in the interaction with environment, it is transformed into the monistic structure, bipartite structure, and triadic structure at different hierarchical dimensions. Once the triadic structure is constructed, it repeatedly creates complex fractal structures in an evolutionary way. Therefore, when a system is transformed into the triadic system, it means that the system has been changed in a way that brings maximum internal change. In this sense, the triadic structure of systems is a minimal set on the hierarchy. This is a favorable structure for generating energy.

5.3.3. Symptom formation

When observed from the macroscopic level of the phenomenal world, the whole system can be characterized as a series of an entity's behaviors, consisting of transformation, growth, vitality, changeability, dynamic, creativity, and evolution. At the microscopic level, because triadic structured system indicates repeated alternate changes from the polarity system to duality system and vise versa, alternative appearance of the contradicting behaviors, emotions, and cognitions could be noticed.

5.3.4. Compositions

Triadic structure is formulated by three systems at different hierarchical levels: two opposite non-paradoxical systems (polarity system and duality system) and a paradoxical system (dialectical system). The prototypic paradoxical system mentioned above also can be called as "the dialectical system." Although their developmental roots are not different, hierarchical order is. In this line, even though the polarity system and the duality system can be categorized together as a non-paradoxical system, hierarchical order of the two systems differs. The prototypic paradoxical system is the lowest, or primary ordered systemic entity, in which its nature can be described as a physical dimension. The polarity system is located in the next upper hierarchical level and its nature clearly corresponds to biological dimension. The duality system resides at the next upper level of the polarity system to which symbolic or existential dimension corresponds. Finally, the dialectical system created by the union of the polarity and the duality systems is located in higher level of hierarchy, which corresponds to the social dimension than another subsystems are located.

Figure 6. Fractal self-organization of the triadic structure

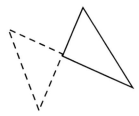

* ⌐/⌐ : Triadic physical system consisted of form, force, and movement

△ : Triadic personality system consisted of polarity (biological), duality (existential), and dialectical (social) subsystem

The above figure presents that the basic triadic structure revives repeatedly. The process of reviving for the triadic structure is defined as Transformation in this theory and can be explained as a causation of self-organization

5.3.5. Equivalents

This explanation is consistent with the triadic system, Salthe suggests. According to Salthe (1985), the smallest cluster of levels required to represent fundamental interactive relationship between entities at different levels is a triad of contiguous level. Thus, three adjacent levels should provide for a minimal description of any complex diachronic system.

5.3.6. Phenotypes

Also four phenotypes of personality can be created by the triadic structured system. (1) When amplitude, frequency, and balance of the dialectical system's transcendental dialectics are optimal, a *creative type* appears. While the creative type seems to be unstable externally, internally it is very vital and transformable.

However, in a situation where a dialectical system is over-hypertrophied before the subsystems are fully individualized, a negative result might be brought about. In this case, (2) the whole system can be disorganized (schizotypal type), or (3) the frequency of the cyclical oscillation might be too fast (cyclothymic or moody type), or (4) reward from the external environment cannot be provided (fanatical or paranoid). All of the four types generate high level of energy in the psyche because a triadic structure of the whole system can only be maintained in a far-from equilibrium state (steady state).

5.4. Complementarity of the systems three structures

Importantly, the classification of systems structures does not mean that one is superior to another, or inferior to the other. Rather, the three systems are complementary to each other. The monistic structure of the system becomes a core for individuation of non-paradoxical systems, which give rise to the bipartite structure. In turn, the individuation of non-paradoxical systems in the bipartite state also becomes precondition for the formation of the triadic system. Paradoxically triadic system can be transformed into another monistic structure at higher dimension when the synchronization occurs successfully.

In other words, in order to transform a personality system into triadic structure in the face of adversity that can destruct the whole system, in an ordinary situation an entity paradoxically delays its dialectical interaction as possible as it can, and maintains its bipartite structure on the purpose of individualizing non-paradoxical systems at optimal level. Also, after adjusting itself to change, during a period of dormancy (or as a resting stage), an entity exists as the two-mode system.

6. TRANSCENDENCE AND TRANSFORMATION

Transformation and transcendence of personality systems are not separated phenomenon, but deeply interconnected. Then, how do they co-work? The processes of their co-works are summarized by the figure as below.

The oscillating cyclical wave in dotted gray line is "the Transcendental Movement." The above figure indicates three movements. The first movement is "the Expansive Transcendence (1)," which means the process of transcendence from the polarity state to the duality state done by the duality system. The second is "the Contractive Transcendence (2)" that is the

Figure 7. Cyclical oscillation of transformation and transcendence

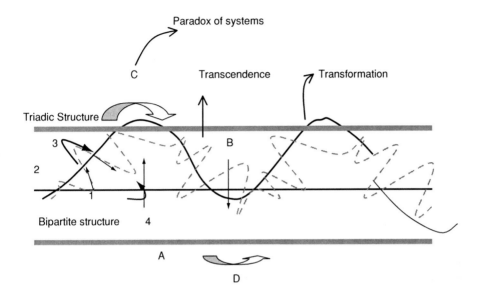

process of transcendence from the duality state to the polarity state done by the polarity system. On the other hands, there is "Paradoxical Transcendence (3, 4)," facilitated by dialectical system. The paradoxical transcendence creates an oscillating, rotary, and cyclical wave of transcendental movements. In this process, the transcendence from the polarity to the duality should be equal to the transcendental movement from the duality to the polarity.

Through the dialectical works of the dialectical system, convergence and divergence between non-paradoxical systems, the structure of the whole system is transformed: when the subsystems are converged, the bipartite structured system is transformed into the triadic structured system. This process will be referred as "the Expansive Transformation (A)." On the contrary, when the subsystems are diverged or scattered (i.e., when the transcendental interaction between them was decreased), the established triadic structure of the system is destructed into the bipartite structure through "Contractive Transformation (B)." "Paradoxical Transformation (C)" is a process of synchronization changing the triadic structure into the monistic structure so that it gives rise to the initial conditions for the creation of the fractal structures. When further paradoxical transformation is hampered, the whole system cannot maintain its triadic structure anymore and cannot create further fractals but returns to the bipartite structure.

6.1. Summary

The triadic structure of the whole system has a higher transformability as compared to the bipartite structure. Of an important part is, however, that the most efficient reorganization of a system in response to the world's chaos would be possible only by the complementary co-works of the monistic structure, the bipartite structure, and the triadic systemic structure. And if an entity system can be actively transformed, the characteristics of the eight phenotypes can appear variously. The varieties are not pathologic, but rather the varieties as diverse experiences of behaviors, emotions, self, cognition would help an entity understand and empathize its external world.

7. AN EMPIRICAL STUDY

The present study was designed to test the BSE model. It is a case-control study, which compared Traumatized Group with the Normal Control Group. , It was hypothesized that the bipartite structure will be the most prevalent system's structure in normal populations who are in low to moderate range of needs for transformation. Conversely, triadic structure will be the most prevalent structures in victimized individuals who are in a situation where the need for transformation is extremely high. That is, in ordinary peaceful life, we finger the piano, but in adversities we stand up with fist.

To test the hypothesis, we need a personality inventory that includes the equivalents of these subsystems of personality. Indeed, Cloninger's TCI (1994) make it possible to test this thesis because while its seven-factor structure rests on the bipartite view of the psychobiological model (Cloninger et al., 1993), all the three subsystems of BSE model are present in the TCI as its subscales.

To explain, its seven-factor structure, which is based on two basic templates of personality including the temperament and character dimensions, is actually lower-order primary scales of the three subsystem of the BSE model. In his psychobiological model, the temperament involves automatic, preconceptual responses to preconceptual stimuli, presumably reflecting heritable biases in information processing by the preconceptual memory system. In contrast, character dimensions were related to conceptual memory system (Cloninger, 1993). Moreover, personality factors associated with the existential system of this theory have usually been neglected from personality inventories, yet TCI adopts Self-transcendence, which represents the existential system (duality system), as one of the character dimensions.

7.1. Method

7.1.1. Subjects

Traumatized group was consisted of 71 victims of the Incheon Fire Disaster in 10/30/1999. Mean age was 16.23 years, and they experienced the extreme terror through the disaster. Eighty were injured and 54 died from the disaster. These victims experienced hearing the screaming of their friends, fear of death, near suffocation, loss of consciousness, etc. Subjects who reported any history of trauma as defined by the criteria of DSM-IV were excluded in control group. One hundred and ninety-eight high school boys (N = 98) and girls (N = 100) at Chuncheon city of Korea were recruited as a control group. Age of the samples was 17.23.

7.1.2. Procedure

TCI consists of temperament and character dimensions having 7 higher-order secondary scales. Again, these scales are composed of 25 primary subscales. Temperament dimensions of the TCI are defined as individual differences in associative learning in response to novelty, punishment, and reward, respectively, and persistence subscale was differentiated from reward dependence as an independent temperament dimension. Thereby, the temperament dimensions consist of four higher-orders including novelty seeking (NS), harm avoidance (HA), reward dependence (RD), and persistence (P). Character dimensions are defined as the three aspects of self-concept including conceptualization of the self as an autonomous individual, as an integral part of human society, and as an integral part of the universe. Thereby, three higher-order character dimensions include cooperativeness (CO), self-directedness (SD), and self-transcendence (ST). In order to create factorial summaries of the 25 subscales, we conducted the exploratory factor analysis by means of principal-components analysis and Promax rotation.

7.2. Results

The traumatized group indicated three-factor structure representing a Biological Factor, a Social Factor, and an Existential Factor, with 67.8% of the total variance. All of the RD, CO, and SD subscales, except for SD4 (self-acceptance), had the highest loadings on the Social Factor. And all NS and HA subscales, except for NS1 (exploratory excitability), had the highest loadings on the temperament Factor. All subscales of ST, P, NS1, RD1 (sentimentality), and SD4 loaded on the Existential Factor.

To explain, the subscales constituting the Existential Factor in the traumatized group, indeed, have been consistently suggested as prerequisites for self-transcendence and posttraumatic growth under the traumatic stress from the fields of meaning psychology and existential psychology: in order to transcend beyond our limitations as a human being (self-transcendence), such as suffering and mortality, at first we need to mourn over it (sentimentality), and we must accept the uncontrollable problems as the reality of life (self-acceptance), then, we should explore a new positive meanings in the negative experiences (exploratory excitability) and should put the new possibilities into action despite failures (persistence). Before we face life adversities, rarely we cast "why questions."

On the other hand, the Temperament Factor of this study clearly agrees with the two-factor theory of temperament (Gray, 1972), which posited that general motivational systems are consisted of BAS/BIS underlying behavior and affect. Andrew and Todd (2002) noted that Approach and Avoidance Temperament Factor represent fundamental structure of temperament. In fact, Cloninger's NS and HA dimensions exactly correspond with these two fundamental templates of temperament. However, RD and P dimensions, proposed as temperament dimensions by Cloninger, do not correspond to any dimension of BAS/BIS and approach/ avoidance. This conceptual ambiguity of RD and P dimensions may be related with the consistent evidences for the instability and the weak internal consistency of these scales (Giancola et al., 1994; Otter et al., 1995; Waller et al., 1991; Gutie'rrez et al., 2001).

Rather, actually the RD dimensions are more closely related with CO and SD dimensions functionally in that they are ruled by reinforcement principle. For instance, these dimensions are concerned with gaining and maintaining positive reward from society by depending on others (RD), identifying others (CO), and identifying one's goal (SD). In other words, these dimensions are concerned with same goal, which can be achieved through social relationship, but motivated by different objects. As predicted, RD dimension was collapsed with CO, and SD dimensions into a single factor, termed as Social

Factor. Moreover, the collapse of the three scales has been consistently reported from previous studies (Gutie'rrez et al., 2001; Sato et al., 2001).

In the control group, on the contrary, a scree test indicated five-factor solution, accounting for 59.7% of the total variance. The five-factor structure of the TCI is caused by the known instability of the RD and P temperament scales, which were scattered into CO and SD character scales. But the rest of the factors corresponded to Cloninger's original seven-factor model. Five-factor solution also emerged in the previous Korean normative samples. The internal consistency for the three factors solution in the victim group was higher than that of the original seven dimensions and that of the five factors in the present control group.

7.3. Interpretation of the present results

The results of this study directly support three major notions of the BSE model. Firstly, the existential system (duality system), which has been scattered throughout the personality system, has been individuated as a subsystem, in response of traumatic experiences.

Secondly, by applying the notion for the increased transcendental interaction between systems in triadic structured system, inter-correlations among the personality factors will be increased in the three-factor structure. As predicted, especially in the traumatized group, all of the seven scales were highly and positively inter-correlated with each other compared to the control group in this study. This strengthening of the correlations in the traumatized group may indicate the triadic system's enhanced synergistic interaction between the personality factors.

Thirdly, as predicted by the BSE model, the personality systems of the victim group were reorganized themselves into triadic (tripartite) structure from the bipartite structure, when need for transformation is heightened due to the traumatic experiences. Also, the three factor-solution of the victim group clearly corresponded to the three subsystems of the BSE model.

Although the discrepancy between the intuitive assumption of personality's consistency and the data from research indicating the lack of consistency has been regarded as "the personality paradox (Bem and Allen, 1974)," the variability of personality structure across different situations seen in this study is not simply random fluctuations. Rather, it is a key to understand the underlying causal mechanism that produces the plasticity of personality. Because the present findings have been acquired from Korean sample, however, the applicability and generality of this finding need to be examined in different cultures.

8. CONCLUSION

"How to float like a butterfly." R. B. Srygley and Adrian L. R. Thomas (2002) determined that butterflies use a number of "unconventional aerodynamic mechanisms to generate force. Accompanying commentary writes, "What is more astounding is that butterflies appear to switch effortlessly among these mechanisms from stroke to stroke." It is continued, if engineers ever succeed in understanding just how insects exercise control over such a wide range of abilities, "there will be a revolution in aeronautics (Graham, 2002)." In Greeks, butterfly is "psyche." The essence of the BSE model may not be different than the floating of butterflies: the psyche appears to switch effortlessly among the mechanisms of polarity (biological system), of duality (existential system) by means of dialectics (social system), and transforms with effort into the monistic, bipartite, or triadic structures, from stroke to stroke against life's adversities.

The BSE model of personality integrates dynamic mechanisms (functionalism) and structural descriptions (structuralism) about personality system by providing a principle that the union of opposites creates transcendence between the opposites, and that the repeated transcendence brings transformation of structures, which varies from monistic structure to triadic structure, out of personality system depending on the nature of input from environment and individual's willingness to accept the input. The principle is simple but implication is significant across the fields of psychology and psychiatry.

1. Defining taxonomy for the basic dimensions of personality has been a major task of personality researchers across the various fields of school. According to their positions, personality systems have been explained as one-dimensional structure based on monism, two-dimensional structure based on body-mind dichotomy, three-dimensional structure based on existential, philosophical, and religious schools, four-dimensional structure based on ancient Greek's philosophy, five-dimensional structure based on the lexical studies, or seven-dimensional structure based on the predictable pattern of behavior in response to specific classes of environmental stimuli. These apparently incontrovertible premises on personality structure do not give unacceptable or contradictory conclusions but describe partial pictures of the whole. According to the BSE model, the personality system appears as two-dimensional structure on certain points and as one- or three-dimensional structure on others, depending on the developmental stages and environmental needs.

2. Current cognitive psychology views cognitive architecture as dichotomous structure of the implicit and the explicit memory systems, or as the interaction between the two sides of the dichotomy including top-down (explicit learning first and implicit later), bottom-up (implicit learning first and explicit later), and parallel learning (simultaneous implicit and explicit learning), or at most as the synergy between the implicit and the explicit cognition. In the current understandings of cognitive psychology, there is no third system regulating the interaction between the two opposites, whether it will be top-down, bottom-up, parallel, or synergistic. Synergy is not a system but an effect. In this line, dichotomous views including Cloninger's (1997) biosocial model of personality (temperament vs. character), Kohut's (1997) bipolar self, Bowin's (2004) two basic templates of defense mechanism (cognitive distortion vs. dissociation), von Bertalanffy's (1952) general systems theory (closed system vs. open system), and etc., explain the interaction as transactional, non-linear, or at most synergistic. The BSE model gives room these dichotomous views to think about the third entity making the two opposites work together synergistically.

3. The BSE model provides systematic theoretical framework to the existential psychology's phenomenological description about transcendence and transformation and the ambiguous explanations about the relationship between transcendence

and transformation: the more the oppositeness is amplified (the more the tension is increased between the opposites), the more the transcendental interaction between the opposites is maximized. In turn, the more the transcendence is maximized, the more the structural transformation of the whole system is activated. Therefore, transcendence and transformation must not be treated as separated phenomena because each of them is prerequisite for another.

4. This theory provides an answer to the longstanding conflict: the transformation of personality occurs abruptly or gradually. According to this theory, abrupt, unintentional changes in attitude, insight, or world-view are works of transcendence, but gradual or incremental changes that occur intentionally probably involve the process of transformation. And, to the disputes regarding the trait vs. state notions of personality, the BSE model provides a third view that in the whole personality system, there are non-paradoxical subsystems making the personality system trait-like as well as paradoxical subsystem making personality system state-like.

5. The BSE model provides theoretical rationale to distinguish three levels of coping: *existential (tension amplifying) coping, causal (tension reducing) coping, and transformational (dialectical) coping*. Existential coping of the duality system (existential dimension), which consists of both acceptance of what cannot be changed and the affirmation of positive existential givens in the presence of negative reality (Wong, 2005), inevitably amplifies tension to individuals because plural state of mental representations caused by the duality system does not permit us to choose one simple truth. Instead, causal coping of the polarity system (biological dimension), which consists of denial of potential truth and the cognitive distortion of truth in order to affirm the feasible answer to the situations, effectively reduces individual's tension level. The directions of the both copings are consistently opposite each other. Transformational coping, however, is only possible by the complementary co-works of the existential and causal coping, just like light behaving as particle on certain weekdays and as wave on others. To explain the transformational coping from the position of the BSE model, transformation coping demands us to put the existential coping and the causal coping together in order to make paradoxical condition in our psyche. This process is carried by the dialectical system. By the repeated transcendental interpenetrating interaction between the opposite coping strategies, a building up and breaking down of the cognitions, emotions, behavioral patterns, self-images, and world-views occur in a state of a real-far-from equilibrium, which maximizes transformational process of the personality system. In other words, the paradoxical conditions, created by the transformational coping, brings out of transformation naturally as time passes, just like Winter is transformed into Spring through the repetition of day and night.

6. The BSE model provides a concept about the transformation-prone (or resistant) structure, transcendence-prone (or resistant) condition, and the minimal unit of personality structure (two non-paradoxical systems and a paradoxical system) to the development of personality measurements in particular. This indicates the necessity of the development of psychometry, which can provide us the comprehensive picture of individual's psychic world-in-the-life adversities.

The rest part of the BSE model, which is not shown in this chapter, contains the application of the model into hierarchical symptom formation process, hierarchical reorganization of psychiatric diagnostic system, and development of phase-specific treatment module.

There exist differences in coping strategies between Eastern culture and Western culture. Applying the BSE model to the dichotomy, it may seem that Western culture focuses on causal attribution, which facilitates prediction and control. While Eastern culture may favor existential attribution, which help deepens understanding. Western society's linear cause-and-effect instrumental approach has created a strong scientific base and a prosperous economy. In contrast, Eastern society is more interested in non-linear and paradoxical relationships and favors a more philosophical approach to life. From the perspective of the BSE model, duality system maybe dominant in Eastern cultures, whereas polarity system maybe dominant in Western cultures. However, under the influence of increasing interactions between East and West, the two opposite cultures may create a self-evolving triadic structure as a result of learning from each other's coping strategies

REFERENCES

Aldwin, C. M. (1994). Transformational coping. In C. M. Aldwin (Ed.), *Stress, coping, and development* (pp. 240-269). New York: Guilford.

Allport, G. W. (1937). *A psychological interpretation.* New York: Holt.

Allport, G. W. (1961). *Pattern and growth in personality.* New York: Holt, Rinehart & Winston.

Andrew J. D. (1989). Psychotherapy of depression: a self-confirmation model. *Psychological Review, 96*(4), 576-607.

Andrew J. E., & Todd, M. T. (2002). Approach-Avoidance Motivation in Personality: Approach and Avoidance Temperaments and Goals. *Journal of Personality & Social Psychology, 82*(5), 804-818.

Antonovsky, A. (1987). *Unraveling the mystery of health: How people manage stress and stay well.* San Francisco: Jossey-Bass.

Ashby, W. R. (1956). *An introduction to cybernetics.* London: Chapman and Hall.

Bertalanffy, L. von (1952). *Problems of Life* (p. 11). New York: Wiley.

Bowins, B. (2004). Psychological defense mechanisms: a new perspective. *The American Journal of Psychoanalysis, 64*(1), 1-26.

Buck, R. (1985). Prime theory: An integrated view of motivation and emotion. *Psychological Review, 92,* 389-413.

Buss, A. R. (1978). The structure of psychological revolutions. *Journal of the History of the Behavioral Sciences, 14,* 57-64.

Carver, C. S., & Scheier, M. F. (1998). *On the Self-Regulation of Behavior (pp. 331).* New York: Cambridge University Press.

Cloninger C. R., Przybeck T. R., & Svrakic D. M. (1991). The tridimensional personality questionnaire: U.S. normative data. *Psychological Reports, 69,* 1047-1057.

Cloninger C. R., Svrakic D. M., & Przybeck T. R. (1993). A psychobiological model of temperament and character. *Archive of General Psychiatry, 50,* 977-991.

Cloninger C. R., Przybeck T. R., & Svrakic D. M. (1994). *The temperament and character inventory (TCI): A guide to its development and use.* St. Louis Missouri: Center for Psychobiology of Personality.

Costa, P. T., Jr., & McCrae, R. R. (1989). Personality continuity and the changes of adult life. In M. Storandt & G. R. VandenBos (Eds.), *The adult years: continuity and change* (pp. 45-47). Washington, DC: American Psychological Association.

Darwin, C. (1969). The autobiography of Charles Darwin, N. Barlow (Ed.), New York: Norton.

Ebersole, P (1970). Effects of nadir experiences. *Psychological Reports, 27,* 207-209.

Epstein, S. (1990). Cognitive-experiential self-theory. In L. Pervin (Ed.), *Handbook of personality: Theory and research* (pp. 165-192). New York: Guilford.

Epstein, S. (1994). Implications of cognitive-experiential self-theory for new directions in personality and developmental psychology. In R. Parke, G. Tomlinson-Keasey, K. Widemen, & D. C. Funder (Eds.), *Studying lives through time: Approaches to personality and development.* Washington, DC: American Psychological Association.

Festinger, L. (1950). Informal social communication. *Psychological Review, 57,* 271-282.

Finkel, N. J. (1974). Strens and traumas: An attempt at categorization. *American Journal of Community Psychology, 2,* 265-273.

Finkel, N. J. (1975). Strens, traumas, and trauma resolution. *American Journal of Community Psychology, 3,* 173-178.

Frankl, V. E. (1963). *Man's search for meaning: An introduction to logotherapy.* (Original title: From Death Camp to Existentialism). New York, NY: Pocket Books.

Fromm, E. (1976). *To have or to be?* New York: Harper & Row.

Garan, D. G. (1968). *Relativity for psychology: A causal law for the modern alchemy.* New York, NY: Philosophical Library.

Giancola P.R., Zeichner A., Newbolt W. H., & Stennett R.B. (1994). Construct validity of the dimensions of Cloninger's tridimensional personality questionnaire. *Personality and Individual Differences, 17,* 627-636.

Goldstein, Jacobi ,& Yovits,. (1962) Self-Organizing Systems (Eds.). Spartan

Gollwitzer, P. M., Heckhausen, H., & Steller, B. (1990). Deliberative vs. implemental mind-sets: Cognitive tuning toward congruous thoughts and information. *Journal of Personality and Social Psychology, 59,* 1119-1127.

Gollwitzer, P. M., & Bayer, U. (1999). Deliberative versus implemental mindsets in the control of action. In S. Chaiken & Y. Trope (Eds.), *Dual-process theories in social psychology* (pp. 403-422). New York: Guilford.

Graham, S. (2002). How to float like a butterfly. *Scientific American, 12.*

Gray, J. A. (1972). The psychophysiological basis of introversion-extraversion: A modification of Eysenck's theory. In V. D. Nebylitsyn & J. A. Gray (Eds.), *The biological bases of individual behavior* (pp.182-205). San Diego, CA: Academic Press

Greenberg, M. A. (1995). Cognitive processing of traumas: The role of intrusive thoughts and reappraisals. *Journal of Applied Social Psychology, 25,* 1262-1296.

Gutie'rrez F., Torrens, N., Boget, T., Martin-Santos, R., Sangorrin, J., Pe'rez, G., & Salamero M. (2001). Psychometric properties of the Temperament and Character Inventory (TCI) questionnaire in a Spanish psychiatric population. *Acta Psychiatry Scandinavia, 103*(2), 143-147.

Harvey, M. R. (1996). An ecological view of psychological trauma and trauma recovery. *Journal of Traumatic Stress, 9,* 3-23.

Heckhausen, H., & Gollwitzer, P. M. (1987). Thought contents and cognitive functioning in motivational versus volitional states of mind. *Motivation and Emotion, 11,* 101-120.

Holyoak, K. J., Spellman, B. A. (1993). Thinking. *Annual Review of Psychology, 44,* 265-315.

Horowitz, M. J. (1986). *Stress response syndromes* (2nd ed.). Northvale, NJ: Aronson.

Jacoby, L., Toth, J., Yonelinas, A., & Debner, J. (1994). The relation between conscious and unconscious influence: Independence or redundancy? *Journal of Experimental Psychology: General, 123*(2), 216-219.

Janoff-Bulman, R. (1992). *Shattered assumptions: Toward a new psychology of trauma.* New York: The Free Press.

Jung, C. G. (1953). The relations between the ego and the unconscious. In H. Read, M. Fordham, & G. Adler (Eds.), *Collected works.* Princeton, NJ: Princeton University Press.

Kierkeggard, S (1983). *Fear and trembling.* (H. V. Long & E. H. Long, Trans.). Princeton, NJ: Princeton University Press.

Kobasa, S. C. (1979). Stressful life events, personality, and health: An inquiry into hardiness. *Journal of Personality and Social Psychology, 37,* 1-11.

Kohut, H. (1977). *The restoration of the self.* New York: International Universities Press.

Kraft, W. F. (1974). *A psychology of nothingness.* Philadelphia: Westminster Press.

Levy, S. (1992). *Artificial Life -The Quest for a New Creation.* Jonathan Cape.

McAdams, D. P. (1993). *The stories we live by: Personal myths and the making of the self.* New York: William Morrow.

Maddi, S. R. (1967). The existential neurosis. *Journal of Abnormal Psychology, 72,* 311-325.

Maddi, S. R. (1996). *Personality Theories: a comparative analysis.* Illinois: Waveland Press.

Mahoney, M. J. (1982). Psychotherapy and human change processes. In J.H. Harvey & M.M. Parks (Eds.), *Psychotherapy research and behavior change* (pp. 77-122). Washington, DC: American Psychological Association.

Mandelbrot, B. B. (1977). *The fractal geometry of nature.* San Francisco, CA: Freeman.

Maslow, A. H. (1999). *Toward a Psychology of Being* (3rd ed). New York: Wiley.

Miller, W. R., & C'deBaca, J. (1994). Quantum change: Toward a psychology of transformation. In T. F. Heatherton & J. L. Weinberger (Eds.), *Can personality change?* (pp. 253-281). Washington, DC: APA.

Mischel, W. (1973). Toward a cognitive social learning reconceptualization of personality. *Psychological Review, 80,* 252-283.

Mischel, W., & Shoda, Y. (1995). A cognitive-affective system theory of personality: Reconceptualizing situations, dispositions, dynamics, and invariance in personality structure. *Psychological Review, 102,* 246-268.

Murray, H. A., & Kluckhohn, C. (1956). Outline of a conception of personality. In C. Kluckhohn, H. A. Murray, & D. M. Schneider (Eds.), *Personality in nature, society, and culture* (2nd ed.) New York: Knopf.

Nietzsche, F. (1955). *Beyond good and evil.* (M. Cowan, Trans.). Chicago, IL: Henry Regnery.

Nerken, I. R. (1993). Grief and the reflective self: Toward a clearer model of loss and growth. *Death Studies, 17,* 1-26.

O'Connor, D., & Wolfe, D.M. (1991). From crisis to growth at midlife: Changes in personal paradigm. *Journal of Organizational Behavior, 12,* 323-340.

O'Leary, V. E., & Ickovics, J. R. (1995). Resilience and thriving in response to challenge: An opportunity for a paradigm shift in women's health. *Women's health: Research on gender, behavior, and policy, 1,* 121-142.

Otter C., Huber J., & Bonner A. (1995). Cloninger's tridimensional personality questionnaire: Reliability in an English sample. *Personality and Individual Differences, 18,* 471-480.

Park, C., Cohen, L., & Murch, R. (1996). Assessment and prediction of stress-related growth. *Journal of Personality, 64,* 71-105.

Pervin, L. A. (1994). Personality stability, personality change, and the question of precess. In T. F. Heatherton & J. L. Weinberger (Eds.), *Can personality change?* (pp. 315-330). Washington, DC: American Psychological Association.

Priogoine, I. (1980). *From being to becoming. Time and complexity in the physical sciences.* San Francisco, CA: Freeman.

Reker, G.T.(2000). Theoretical perspectives, dimensions, and measurement of existential meaning. In G.T. Reker, & K. Chamberlain (Eds.), Exploring existential meaning: optimizing human development across the life span (pp. 107-122). Thousand Oaks, CA: Sage Publications.

Rumelhart, D. E., McClelland, J. L., & PDP Research Group (Eds.) (1986). *Parallel distributed processing: Explorations in the microstructure of cognition: Vol. 1. Foundations.* Cambridge, MA: MIT Press.

Rutter, M. (1987). Psychological resilience and protective mechanisms. *American Journal of Orthopsychiatry, 57,* 316-331.

Sabelli, H. C. (1989). *Union of Opposites: A Comprehensive Theory of Natural and Human Processes.* Lawrenceville, VA: Brunswick.

Sabelli, H. C., & Carlson-Sabelli, L. (1989). Biological priority and psychological supremacy, a new integrative paradigm derived from process theory. *American Journal of Psychiatry, 146*(12), 1541-1551.

Salthe, S. N. (1985). *Evolving Hierarchical Systems.* New York: Columbia University Press.

Sato, T., Narita, T., Hirano, S., Kusunoki, K., Goto, M., Sakado, K., & Uehara, T. (2001). Factor validity of the temperament and character inventory in patients with major depression. *Contemporary Psychiatry, 42*(4), 337-41.

Schaefer, J. A., & Moos, R. H. (1992). Making the case for coping. In B. N. Carpenter (Ed.), *Personal coping: Theory, research, and application* (pp. 149-170). Westport, CT: Praeger.

Shannon, C. E., & Weaver, W. (1964). *The mathematical theory of communication.* Urbana, IL: University of Illinois. (Original work published 1949)

Shastri, L., & Ajjanagadde, V. (1993). From simple associations to systematic reasoning: A connectionist representation of rules, variables, and dynamic bindings using temporal synchrony. *Behavioral and Brain Sciences, 16,* 417-494.

Sloman, S. A. (1996). The empirical case for two forms of reasoning. *Psychological Bulletin, 119,* 3-22.

Smolensky, P. (1988). On the proper treatment of connectionism. *Behavioral and Brain Sciences, 11,* 1-23.

Squire, L., Knowlton, B., & Musen, G. (1993). The structure and organizatin of memory. *Annual Review of Psychology, 44,* 453-495.

Srygley, R. B., & Thomas A. L. (2002). Unconventional lift-generating mechanisms in free-flying butterflies. *Nature, 12, 420*(6916), 660-664.

Strupp, H. H., & Binder, J. L. (1984). *Psychotherapy in a new key: A guide to time-limited psychotherapy.* New York: Basic Books.

Tedeschi, R. G., & Calhoun, L. G. (1995). *Trauma and transformation: Growing in the aftermath of suffering.* Thousand Oaks, CA: Sage.

Tedeschi, R. G., Park C. L., & Calhoun, L. G. (1998). Posttraumatic Growth. In I. B. Weiner (Eds.), *Posttraumatic growth: Conceptual issues* (pp.1-22). Mahwah, New Jersey: Lawrence Erlbaum Associates.

Tennen, H., & Affleck G. (1998). Posttraumatic Growth. In I. B. Weiner (Eds.), *Personality and Transformation in the Face of Adversity* (pp.65-98). Mahwah, New Jersey: Lawrence Erlbaum Associates.

Thorne, A. (1989). Conditional patterns, transference, and the coherence of personality across time. In D. M. Buss & N. Cantor (Eds.), *Personality psychology: Recent trends and emerging directions* (pp. 149-159). New York: Springer-Verlag.

Thorndike, E. L. (Ed.) (1949). *Selected writings from a connectionist's psychology*. New York: Greenwood Press.

Tillich, P. (1952). *The courage to be*. New Haven: Yale University Press.

Van Denburg, T. F., & Kiesler, D. J. (2002). An interpersonal communication perspective on resistance in psychotherapy. *Journal of Clinical Psychology, 58*(2), 195-205.

Wachtel, P. L. (Ed.) (1982). *Resistance: Psychodynamic and behavioral approaches*. New York: Plenum.

Waller, N. G., Lilienfeld, S. O., Tellegen, A., & Lykken, D. T. (1991). The Tridimensional Personality Questionnaire: Structural validity and comparisons with the Multidimensional Personality Questionnaire. *Multivariate Behavioral Research, 26,* 1-23.

Werner, E. E. (1989). High-risk children in young adulthood: A longitudinal study from birth to 32 years. *American Journal of Orthopsychiatry, 59,* 72-81.

Wong, P. T. P. (1989). Personal meaning and successful aging. *Canadian Psychology, 30*(3), 516-525.

Wong, P. T. P. (1991). Existential versus causal attributions: The social perceiver as philosopher. In S. L. Zelen (Ed.), *New models, new extensions of attribution theory*. New York: Springer-Verlag.

Wong, P. T. P. (1993). *Personal meaning and spiritual coping in the elderly*. An invited lecture given at the Summer Institute on Gerontology at McMaster University, Hamilton, ON.

Wong, P. T. P. (1995). A stage model of coping with frustrative stress. In R. Wong (Ed.), *Biological perspectives on motivated activities* (pp. 339-378). Norwood, NJ: Ablex.

Wong, P. T. P. (2005). Victor Frankl: Prophet of hope for the 21st century. In A. Batthyany, & J. Levinson (Eds.), Anthology of Viktor Frankl's logotherapy. Tulsa, AZ: Zeig, Theisen & Tucker Publishing.

Wong, P. T. P., & Reker, G. T. (1984 August). *The coping behaviors of successful agers*. Paper presented at the Annual Meeting of Western Gerontological Association, Anaheim, CA.

Wong, P. T. P., Reker, G. T., & Peacock, E. (in press). Development of the Coping Schemas Inventory: Reliability and Validity. In P. T. P. Wong & L. C. J. Wong (Eds.) *Handbook of multicultural perspectives on stress and coping*. New York: Springer

Wong, P. T. P., & Weiner, B (1981). When people ask why questions and the heuristics of attributional search. *Journal of Personality and Social Psychology, 40,* 650-663.

Section 2

Methodological Issues

FREQUENTLY IGNORED METHODOLOGICAL ISSUES IN CROSS-CULTURAL STRESS RESEARCH

Juan I. Sanchez, Paul E. Spector, and Cary L. Cooper

1. INTRODUCTION

Globalization and free trade have underscored the need to ascertain whether psycho-logical theories developed primarily in English-speaking countries can be transferred to other cultural settings (Boyacigiller & Adler, 1991; Church & Lonner, 1998; Maruyama, 1984; Triandis, 1994a). At the core of this aspiration seems to be the identification of aspects of stress that are culture-general and those that are culture specific (often referred to as the etic-emic distinction, which is borrowed from the linguistic differentiation between phonetics and phonemics, Berry, 1969). However, in addition to sharing the same limitations and problems of studies done within countries or cultures, conducting stress research across countries and cultures presents unique methodological challenges.

This chapter focuses on issues of establishing equivalent samples and on methods that permit reasonable inferences about culture effects, hence minimizing sampling and measurement artifacts potentially confounded with culture. In our view, cross-cultural/cross-national (CC/CN) stress researchers should pay close attention to two major aspects of equivalence, namely measurement and sampling equivalence. First, CC/CN comparisons require the administration of the same measures across countries/cultures and, therefore, they often require foreign-language translations of measures that were originally developed and tested in a single language, most often English. Unfortunately, carefully done translations, albeit linguistically correct, may not necessarily produce equivalent instruments, even when back-translation procedures are employed (Brislin, 1986). Second, valid conclusions about culture differences necessitate samples that differ only on culture. In CC/CN research, there are numerous factors poten-tially confounded with culture or country. For instance, a nation's tax structure affects the personal finances (and therefore the individuals' ability to cope with stressors) of two peo-ple earning equivalent salaries in terms of currency exchange but living in two countries

Juan I. Sanchez, Florida International University; Paul E. Spector, University of South Florida; Cary L. Cooper, Lancaster University, UK with marked differences in tax structure (e.g., Canada vs. the U.S.). A myriad of factors confounded with culture represent potential rival explanations of culture effects.

2. MEASUREMENT EQUIVALENCE BETWEEN TRANSLATED INSTRUMENTS

The Sapir-Whorf or Whorfian hypothesis (Werner & Campbell, 1970) maintains that language acts as a filter between individuals and the objective reality that surrounds them. According to this hypothesis, language is thought to filter the evaluative, connotative, and affective meaning of scale items, thereby preventing comparisons between linguistically different groups. This notion of language as an insurmountable obstacle in the way of CC/CN comparisons, however, has not been shared by a majority of researchers, who have developed various approaches to study cultural differences in spite of linguistic differences.

A potential source of measurement non-equivalence stems from the use of closed-ended scales, which are widely employed to gauge work stressors and strains. Using such scales, research participants respond to items varying along the continuum of interest. However, some items are typically more extreme than others, and such differences affect participant responses (Spector, Van Katwyk, Brannick, & Chen, 1997). For example, an individual who agrees with an item, "I am sometimes tense at work", will not necessarily endorse a more extremely worded item like "I sometimes find myself in a panic at work." That is, even though both items reflect anxiety, they represent different degrees of the anxiety construct. Individuals or groups of individuals who complete the same sets of items can be compared to determine their relative standing on the underlying construct. However, if different samples of individuals interpret the items differently, or if translations modify the extremity to which the item expresses the construct, sample comparisons cannot be made without error. Such extremity differences can occur even when back-translation suggests equivalent meanings.

The translation of measures creates a potential confound of language and culture effects (e.g., responses from a Japanese and a U.S. sample may differ because of not only cultural but also linguistic biases in the Japanese version of the measure). Thus, before any observed differences are attributed to culture as opposed to language, researchers need to rule out linguistic biases in their measures (Berry, 1969; Brislin, 1986; Geisinger, 1994; Lytle, Brett, Barsness, Tinsley, & Janssens, 1995; Riordan & Vanderberg, 1994; Spirrison & Choi, 1998). The need to sort out linguistic from cultural effects arises from the fact that culture and language are normally confounded, because individuals from different cultures often speak different languages.

Most of our stress research instruments were originally developed using the English language, and almost all were developed in countries that are culturally similar (e.g., the United Kingdom and the United States). Using these instruments in a set of relatively homogeneous countries may not pose serious problems of measurement equivalence. Participants will tend to interpret the words and phrases in each item similarly across countries for the most part. The more different the culture, even within the English speaking world, the less likely it is that interpretations will remain exact (Liu, Borg, & Spector, 2004). A participant from India, for example, might not see an item as representing the exact same degree of the construct than an Australian counterpart. Thus, comparing sample means becomes problematic, because we cannot be certain that the degree of the construct represented by the scale values associated with each item is equivalently calibrated across countries.

If we cross languages, the problem becomes even worse. English is a language that admits flexible uses of words and phrases. Nouns can be transformed into verbs, adverbs, or even adjectives by simply adding a suffix to them. With less flexible languages, expressing the same idea may require a lengthier stream of words that, in the English language, can be condensed into a single term. Indeed, an exact match that reflects the same scale value might not exist. Even a very good translation will not necessarily produce close matches in terms of extremity, even though the basic idea underlying each item is clearly conveyed. Thus a back translation might be technically correct, but it does not guarantee that items are sufficiently equivalent for mean comparisons. Even if the same construct is assessed, the different language versions may not be equivalently calibrated. To illustrate this point, consider an item that reads "I love my job." A linguistically correct Spanish translation of this item will be "Yo amo mi trabajo." However, the verb "amar" (to love) in Spanish is usually confined to people, and it is seldom or never used to refer to things or social constructs like a job. Thus, this Spanish translation of the item may reflect a much more extreme degree of job satisfaction than its English counterpart.

Still another example of potential non-equivalence between translated instruments is found in the Likert scale-type anchors employed in many job stress instruments. Translators will admit that finding equivalent anchors for the extreme points of the scale is relatively easy, but finding equivalent anchors for the mid-points can be challenging. For instance, a suitable Spanish translation of "very much agree" would be "muy de acuerdo," but translating the anchor "agree slightly" is not that straightforward because the exact degree conveyed by the word "slightly" does not have an immediate synonym in Spanish.

In the stress domain, where theorists have argued that subjective interpretations of the environment are sometimes more important than the environment itself (Lazarus, 1966), non-equivalent items representing distinct degrees of the focal construct may trigger different interpretations. Such item non-equivalence may result in flawed attributions of observed differences to culture rather than faulty instruments. Thus, it can be concluded that the equivalence of translated instruments should not be taken for granted, even if the instruments successfully passed the back-translation test.

Contrary to what is sometimes argued, measurement properties, for instance, a high level of scale reliability does not guarantee the equivalence of the translated and the original instrument. Let us illustrate this point with an example. In one of our recent data-collection efforts undertaken in three countries (U.K., U.S.A., and Spain), the mean alpha reliability coefficient across 26 scales related to work stress was: .70, .75, and .69 for the U.K., the U.S., and Spain, respectively. Thus, the back-translated scales employed in Spain seemed to have at least the same level of reliability than the original English scales employed in the U.K. and the U.S. However, a LISREL 7 comparison of the covariance structures of one of these measures, namely Spector's (1988) Work Locus of Control Scale, between the U.K. and Spanish samples suggested that inter-item relationships differed between the two countries, Chi-Square(136) = 197.76, p < .0001, GFI = .82, RMSR = .10. An inspection of the correlation matrix of the Spanish sample revealed that the item "if you know what you want out of a job, you can find a job that gives it to you" had practically null correlations with most of the other scale items (median r = .10), whereas in the U.K. this item had generally larger and statistically significant correlations with other items in the scale (median r = .23). This differential item functioning should not be surprising to anyone familiar with the relatively high levels of what some have termed "chronic unemployment" in Spain. Thus, it makes sense that "internals" (individuals who believe they can generally control things at work) in Spain are less confident about their ability to find a fulfilling job than are internals in the U.K., where unemployment has been typically lower. This example illustrates that even if a construct exists across cultures, its behavioral manifestations would vary considerably (Lonner, 1990). Thus, an apparently adequate level of reliability does not necessarily constitute a sign of the equivalence between the original and the translated instrument.

To rule out linguistic biases such as those inherent in poorly translated instruments, back-translation procedures have become a widely accepted standard in cross-cultural research (Brislin, 1986). Back-translation involves translating the measure to the target language first, and then independently translating it back to the source language and comparing the two versions to ascertain linguistic problems in the translation. Nevertheless, back-translations do not necessarily guarantee measurement equivalence. For instance, back-translators share knowledge that may lead them to consider terms as if they were synonyms whereas respondents do not see them that way (e.g., "simpático" in Spanish and "friendly" in English may not always mean the same thing, but translators may see them that way due to their learned semantic connection between the two languages).

Still another potential problem of back-translations is that they may retain the grammar and idiomatic expressions of the source language, which may be easy to back-translate but may not have the same meaning to monolinguals in the target language. For example, an item developed for a Chinese scale (i.e., "one should not be afraid of the change of heavens"), which measured beliefs of control in China was successfully back-translated from English to Chinese, but it obviously lacks unambiguous meaning for English-speaking monolinguals (Siu & Cooper, 1998).

Because back-translation does not guarantee the absence of language effects on cross-cultural comparisons, research designs that either analyze or control language effects have been employed. Such designs include some or all of the following features: (1) between-participant comparisons across languages that hold culture constant, such as for example comparing the English and French versions of a measure using samples from the same nation (e.g., Canadians) (Candell & Hulin, 1987), (2) between-participant comparisons across cultures holding language constant, such as, for instance, comparing U.S. versus Australian samples or Spaniards versus Mexicans (Ryan, Chan, Ployhart, & Slade, 1999), and (3) within-participant comparisons of responses in different languages provided by bilinguals, such as having bilingual respondents complete an English and a Spanish version of the same measure (Hulin, Drasgow, & Komocar, 1982; Katerberg, Hoy, & Smith, 1977; Rybowiak, Garst, Frese, & Batinic, 1999).

Not surprisingly, each one of these approaches has limitations. First, between-participant comparisons across languages that attempt to hold culture constant may not succeed due to self-selection. Take for instance the case of a sample of 1,931 Canadians enlisted in the Canadian Armed Forces used by Candell and Hulin (1987). Among 596 participants who identified French as their primary language, 235 chose to complete the English version of a survey. It is likely that the 235 French-Canadians who responded in English were more acculturated to the patterns of English-speaking Canada than those who chose the French version and, therefore, culture was in part confounded with language in comparing these two groups of French Canadians.

Second, between-participant comparisons across cultures that hold language constant (e.g., Australia vs. U.S.; Brazil vs. Portugal) are still influenced by sample differences in third variables that are often confounded with nation. For instance, a public notary typically enjoys a much higher social status in Europe than in the U.S., and therefore comparing public notaries across countries may yield differences associated with third variable effects rather than with culture. We further elaborate on this issue on the section entitled "Sample Equivalence Between Cultures" included later in this chapter.

Finally, within-participant comparisons suffer from the before-mentioned issues that multilinguals may differ from monolinguals both culturally and linguistically. Individuals who study foreign languages will be exposed to the cultures of countries in which those languages are spoken, and they may interpret the translated version differently than a monolingual.

2.1. Construct Equivalence In Stress Research

So far we have discussed how translation can distort the meaning and scale value of items and response choices in scales. However, there is a more fundamental problem that can arise in that the underlying construct of interest may not be equivalent across countries and/or cultures. It is possible that a translation could perfectly capture the same linguistic meaning and scale value, but a scale reflects different constructs. Furthermore, a given construct might manifest itself differently across countries/cultures, so that different items would be needed in both places (Lonner, 1990).

Wong (1993) noted that culture can affect what people appraise as stressful, so a condition that might be a stressor for people in one country might not be for people in another. For example, direct disagreements among employees might be more likely to be perceived as interpersonal conflict among Chinese for whom group harmony is an important value than among Americans who are less sensitive to direct confrontation. Liu (2003) in an analysis of stressful work incidents found that Americans were more likely to report having direct conflicts with others, whereas Chinese were more likely to report having indirect. In another study when asked to describe a stressful incident at work, Americans but not Indians reported instances of lack of control and work overload, whereas Indians but not Americans reported instances of lack of structure and equipment/situational constraints (Narayanan, Menon & Spector, 1999). Of particular concern is that the most often noted stressor for Americans and Indians was opposite—too little control for one and too little direction for the other. This raises questions about the interpretation of responses on an autonomy or structure scale between samples from the two countries and whether the same score means the same thing.

Construct nonequivalence has received far less attention than measurement nonequivalence. Some of the same approaches can be used to deal with both, but establishing the construct validity of a scale among countries/cultures is a far more difficult process than establishing equivalent psychometric properties or calibration of scores. Ultimately, it would require an accumulation of evidence to support viability of the construct interpretation of a measure. For scale development in a single country/culture, this means among other things compiling data to explore the nomological network of relationships of a given scale with other variables. In CC/CN research this can be more complex as it is not a foregone conclusion that nomological networks are unaffected by cultural or national differences, and therefore theories of a construct might differ across locations. This suggests that CC/CN research has additional challenges of jointly having to explore equivalence of constructs, measures, and theories.

2.2. Response Biases

A final difficulty with CC/CN research is the existence of culture/national differences in response biases or tendencies (Triandis, 1994b; van de Vijver & Leung, 1997). It has been suggested that culture influences how individuals use rating scales, with people from some countries preferring extreme responses and others avoiding them. These tendencies may be complex, however, as Iwata, Umesue, Egashira, Hiro, Mizoue, Mishima, and Nagata (1998) found that Japanese were less likely than Americans to use extreme responses for positively worded depression items, but there were no differences for negatively worded items. Thus compared to Americans Japanese avoided reporting extreme positive feelings, but not extreme negative.

Cultural and national response biases might not just affect how people use response choices in rating scales. Ross (2004) discusses how people in some countries might be more apt to respond in accordance to what they believe the researcher wants, thus being more subject to experimenter effects. This suggests that care must be taken, not only in the translation of scales, but in how instructions are phrased and the mode of presentation. It might not be enough to just standardize procedures, as what might serve as response cues to one group might not to another.

Response biases and tendencies can make it difficult to compare means across groups. Thus a given score might not reflect the same level of a construct across people in different groups. Of course, it is not clear than the same score means the same thing between two people within the same group, but the problem arises when group (e.g., country) is confounded with response tendency. Furthermore, it is not necessarily the case that response tendency differences within a group are equivalent across all scales or even all items within a scale, as shown by Iwata et al. (1998). Finally, we cannot be certain that a given difference can be attributable to response tendencies just because one group usually scores higher or lower than others. In other words, do the Japanese in the Iwata et al. (1998) study avoid extreme positive reports because of cultural modesty tendencies, or do Japanese accurately report that they experience less positive affect than Americans? The possibility that observed differences might or might not be attributable to response biases makes it difficult to find simple solutions to this problem.

2.3. Research Strategies to Rule Out Rival Explanations When Using Translated Measures

Let us now turn to possible strategies that can help in ruling out rival hypotheses arising from the non-equivalence of translated instruments. Note that this potential problem is aggravated by the inattention to measurement criteria that pervades back-translation procedures. That is, no clear guidelines exist for deciding when a back-translated scale is sufficiently close to the original version, as this decision is usually left to the translators' professional judgment.

3. BILINGUALISM VS. BICULTURALISM OF TRANSLATORS

Although translators may be linguistically competent, their ability to ascertain cultural nuances in the manifestation of stress across cultures may be limited. We believe that translators should be carefully selected according to not only their linguistic competence, but also the extent to which they are truly "bicultural" individuals who are familiar with the subtleties inherent in the ways in which individuals in the two cultures express their attitudes and emotions. In some cases, a linguistically imperfect translation may provide better psychological equivalence than a linguistically perfect one. Let us offer an example of what we mean here. The Spanish term "de pronto," whose linguistically correct English translation could be "all of a sudden," is often used in some Latin American countries located in the Andean cordillera to mean "perhaps" or "maybe." A linguistically competent Spanish-English translator may fail to realize this colloquial usage of the term, hence rendering a technically correct but non-equivalent translation of an item including this term. Biculturalism, more than even the most impressive academic credentials of bilingual competence, may be a required skill for translators in charge of producing equivalently calibrated instruments.

3.1. Studies Involving Monolinguals

Perhaps the easiest way to explore measurement equivalence is to administer a given scale to monolinguals in two or more countries. Likely the scale was developed in one country in a single language, and translation (and back-translation) will be needed for at least some countries. The psychometric properties of the scale across countries can be compared to test for equivalence, and a number of alternatives exist for this purpose. Perhaps the simplest test would be to compare the internal consistencies of the scale across samples. Although this is not a very conclusive test, failure to maintain internal consistency reliability is a sign that the scale is not functioning well.

More complex approaches are often preferred, including structural equation modeling (SEM) and approaches based on item response theory (IRT). SEM can be used to compare the item variances and covariances across samples to see if the underlying factor structure of a scale is equivalent (Bollen, 1989; Byrne, 1994; Byrne, Shavelson, & Muthén, 1989; Ghorpade, Hattrup, & Lackritz, 1999; Schaffer & Riordan, 2003; Vandenberg & Lance, 2000; Van de Vijver & Leung, 1997). IRT methods can be used to compare item responses for each item across samples from different countries (Raju, Laffitte, & Byrne, 2002). Although both approaches provide a great deal more information than internal consistency, these analyses alone cannot guarantee that scales have equivalent meaning.

3.2. Studies Involving Bilinguals

One approach that can be helpful would be to test for equivalence of two versions by administering them to the same sample of bilingual respondents. Studies of bilinguals are scarce, probably because large samples of bilinguals are not readily available. However, the participation of bilinguals permits a within-participant design that employs a different language in each administration, thereby holding constant the aforementioned extraneous variables plaguing between-participant designs. This kind of check on the equivalence of back-translations through a within-participant design provides the most robust control of the extraneous variables inherent to between-participant designs.

The employment of bilinguals, nevertheless, is not a panacea in the study of cross-cultural differences. Two sets of issues have been raised in relation to the study of bilinguals: (1) issues related to research design and (2) issues related to the manner in which bilinguals process information. The first design-related issue involves the need to address practice effects. Practice effects refer to the change in scores obtained in the second administration brought about by taking the test more than once. In studies employing bilinguals who take the same measure in two languages, one can gauge practice effects by adding a control group where the focal measure is also administered twice, but in the same language. Differences across the two administrations index the practice effect.

One also needs to consider order effects in the presentation of the two versions of the same measure. For instance, let us assume that individuals are asked to complete the original English version first, and then they are asked to complete the Spanish version on a second administration. Even if the Spanish translation is not accurate, respondents may still recall the English version and answer accordingly. Counterbalancing the order of language presentation can remedy this problem.

Still another variable that has remained uncontrolled in research designs involving bilinguals is language proficiency. Differences in the extent to which respondents master either the source or the target language may account for the observed differences between the two linguistic measures of a survey. In the absence of information regarding language mastery, such differences may be erroneously attributed to linguistic biases.

The manner in which bilinguals process information has also been debated. There seem to be two schools of thought arguing in opposite directions. Some argue that even though responses by bilinguals are comparable across the two languages, such a pattern misleadingly underestimates the number of biased items encountered when comparing monolingual samples. For instance, Hulin, Drasgow, and Komocar (1982) found that virtually no Job Descriptive Index (Smith, Kendall, & Hulin, 1969) items were biased when comparing responses by the same sample of bilinguals in English and Spanish. However, when the same versions were administered to monolinguals in Mexico and in the U.S., about 30% of the items were biased. Candell and Hulin (1987) explained this kind of result by arguing that bilinguals may use their knowledge of both the source and the target language when responding to a translated survey, and hence attenuate any linguistic biases owing to poor translation. For instance, a Spanish version of an organizational measure may show signs of poor translation in the form of items that have a "Spanglish" flavor ("Spanglish" is a colloquial term used to refer to the English-influenced Spanish that is sometimes spoken in Latin "barrios" throughout the U.S.). When answering the poorly translated "Spanglish" version of the survey, respondents will use their knowledge of the source language (i.e., English) and respond as if they were answering to the English version. As Hulin (1987) pointed out, *amigo, friend*, and *tovarish* are not always synonyms, but bilinguals sharing a number of rules-of-thumb may interpret them similarly whereas monolinguals see unique meaning in each one of them. Of course, this explanation assumes that the increased number of biased items found when comparing monolinguals in Mexico and the U.S. was due to linguistic rather than cultural effects.

The second argument regarding how bilinguals process information claims that they adapt to the culture associated with the language employed in the measure, so that the same bilingual respondent would give different answers to the two versions of the same measure. This effect has been labeled cultural accommodation (Bond & Yang, 1982). Cultural accommodation implies "Whorfian" thinking about language, which is seen as an evolved cultural pattern intrinsically linked to socialization (Bandura, 1986). Under this approach, the use of a specific language will inevitably lead to culturally-biased responses. For example, Ralston, Cunniff, and Gustafson (1995) found differences between bilingual (i.e., Chinese and English) managers in Hong-Kong. Specifically, managers using the English version of an attitudinal survey scored higher on important Western values than those answering the Chinese version. The latter in turn scored higher on important Eastern values than those using the English version. However, as mentioned earlier, this kind of between-groups design opens the doors to a selection bias. Given the high respect for and loyalty to one's superiors (i.e., power distance) in the Chinese culture, it is not unreasonable to think that the employed students who "snowballed" these surveys to their superiors tried to accommodate those superiors who, upon finding that the survey was in English, might have requested a Chinese version. Thus, those managers who had the best command of the English language (and therefore were more Western-oriented) might have ended up filling out the English version. Regardless of possible problems in the assignment of participants to languages, between-group designs do not lend themselves to a true test of the cultural accommodation hypothesis, whose prediction that the *same* individual would change his/her responses to accommodate the survey's language calls for a within-group design. An example of a study that did indeed use a within-participant design was carried out by Rybowiak, Garst, Frese and Batinic (1999). They found generally higher mean scores in the Dutch than in the English version of their Error Orientation Questionnaire. Rybowiak et al.'s results, however, might have been explained by differences in language proficiency between the two languages, because their Dutch respondents might have been more proficient in their native tongue than in English. It is also possible that the order of scale presentation and the practice effects inherent in any re-test might have been confounded with the language effects in their study.

Hulin and Mayer (1986) argued that the Whorfian thinking implied in the cultural accommodation hypothesis seems unlikely, at least when drawing comparisons across similar languages. That is, although it can be argued that languages like Cantonese and English may create somewhat discrepant mental worlds that interfere with cross-language comparisons, English has its roots in the larger group of Indo-European languages that also involves the majority of the Western languages. Therefore, English shares at least basic semantic structures with many other languages such as French, German, or Spanish.

A noteworthy design feature that has been overlooked in prior research involving bilinguals is the use of relatively long time frames of at least two or three months, so that participants are unlikely to recall their responses to the first administration. In addition, control for the effects of language proficiency through the employment of bilinguals with similar levels of reading comprehension in both the source and the target language is recommended. For instance, studies of bilinguals whose command of the second language is limited may suggest language effects, but we would counter that such effects are more parsimoniously explained by the participants' limited language proficiency.

Counterbalancing and/or analyzing order of language administration, so that half of the participants receive the English version first while the other half receive the foreign language version first, also helps establish the absence of significant language effects. That is, the manipulation of language order helps rule out that bilinguals' recall of the source (e.g., English) version affects their responses to the target (e.g., Spanish) version.

The cultural accommodation hypothesis predicts that when bilinguals respond to a measurement instrument, the language in which the instrument is taken influences their responses. However, languages such as English and Spanish are not as distinct as the languages (i.e., English and Chinese) in which accommodation effects have been reported (Ralston, Cunniff, & Gustafson, 1995). But when comparing two versions of their Error Orientation Questionnaire in more similar languages such as Dutch and English, Rybowiak, Garst, Frese and Batinic (1999) did not find as much similarity in results in their sample of Dutch bilinguals. In their study the Dutch version tended to yield somewhat higher mean scores but patterns of correlations with other variables were similar. They argued that the mean differences might have been attributed to subtle translation differences (both language versions were translated from the original German questionnaire). Smaller differences between languages might be obtained among samples that are bicultural in addition to being bilingual; that is, when participants are used to employing both languages on a daily basis more so than the Dutch participants were in the Rybowiak et al's sample.

Notwithstanding the strengths of any research design, not every threat to its internal and external validity can be always controlled for or ruled out. For example, as mentioned, some authors maintain that the semantic structures of bilingual participants are unique because they allow them to switch languages without problems of meaning congruity (Hulin, 1987). Although such pervasive semantic connections between languages may exist in professional translators, they seem unlikely in to exist across individuals with different levels of reading comprehension in any two languages (e.g., Spanish and in English).

Some might argue that comparing bilinguals' responses to those from monolinguals sheds light on whether bilinguals process semantic information differently. However, we would counter that virtually any sample of monolinguals is likely to differ from a sample of bilinguals in not only linguistic but also cultural factors. That is, monolinguals would not share the dual familiarity with either culture that bilingual participants typically enjoy. If such cultural differences affect bilinguals' answers, it would be impossible to isolate language from culture effects because there would be a confound between the two factors.

Note that studies involving bilinguals can rule out solely linguistic biases. Cultural biases can hardly be studied through bilingual samples. However, research designs involving bilinguals can minimize or hold constant the cultural differences that characterize between-participant comparisons. Thus, even when translated scales are subject to this type of study by employing a bilingual sample, the results do not guarantee measurement equivalence. When drawing cross-cultural comparisons, stress measures may very well vary as a function of cultural or economic factors such as unemployment rates and the ease with which one could find a good job. For instance, a comparison between American monolinguals and Spanish monolinguals in, say, Guatemala City may reveal unique cultural biases that compromise the measurement equivalence of the generic Spanish translations in the context of such a cultural setting. However, researchers who detect measurement non-equivalence of translated scales of proven measurement equivalence in bilingual samples could reasonably rule out linguistic problems in the translations as the cause of the measurement non-equivalence.

Measurement equivalence is not a panacea in cross-cultural research. The source scales are often developed in English according to theories developed in English-speaking countries and, therefore, they may fail to capture the nuances of how the focal constructs are manifested in cultures elsewhere (Maruyama, 1984; Weisz, Rothbaum, & Blackburn, 1984). That is, even if a construct exists across cultures, its behavioral manifestations could vary considerably (Lonner, 1990). As a result of not being fully aware of the manner in which constructs are manifested across cultures, researchers may build their cultural biases into the definition and operationalization of constructs (Boyacigiller & Adler, 1991). The answer to whether stress constructs have different cultural manifestations awaits much needed research regarding how measures of such constructs developed in other languages fare when they are translated into English.

Language and culture are so intrinsically tied that disentangling the effects of linguistic and cultural biases is not easy. To do so requires a design that does not confound language with culture and other sample characteristics. Carefully back-translated measures seem necessary but not sufficient to disentangle potential confounds. We believe that research designs incorporating the recommendations provided here would begin to test cultural differences under minimal contamination by linguistic biases, but additional approaches are necessary.

4. MULTI-CULTURAL SCALE DEVELOPMENT PROCEDURES

A potentially serious limitation to much CC/CN research is the reliance on measures that are developed in a single country and exported for use elsewhere. Even if the items are successfully translated linguistically, there exists the possibility that the individual items don't do a good job of reflecting the construct universally. In other words the scale suffers from ethnocentricity in its development. A procedure to help eliminate that problem is to enlist researchers in multiple countries to have input into scale development from the beginning.

This procedure begins by assembling a diverse team of research partners from culturally distinct countries. Each member should be fluent in a common language, most likely English given its widespread use. The team then goes through a multi-stage procedure for scale development that is more complex than the typical process. First, a clear definition of the construct of interest is discussed and written so everyone has a similar understanding of what the items should reflect. Second, each team member independently writes a set of scale items. Third, the items are mixed up and compiled into a questionnaire that is administered to a sample of subjects. This can be done initially in a single country, or it can be done in parallel in multiple countries. Item analysis or more complex analyses such as factor analysis can be applied to help select items for the final scale. Fourth, the final scale should be administered to samples in at least the countries of the research partners to verify internal consistency reliability and possibly factor structure. The scale will have to be translated and back-translated for use in countries with different languages. Fifth, validation studies should be conducted in multiple countries, although it should be kept in mind that relationships between the construct of interest and other constructs might vary across culturally dissimilar countries.

Spector, Sanchez, Siu, Salgado, and Ma (2004) used this approach in developing new control belief scales that could be used cross-nationally. Partners from three countries (China, Spain, and the U.S.) each wrote items that were combined into an initial large item pool. The items were administered to a sample of Americans, and item analysis was used to create internally consistent scales that contained items written by all coauthors. The final scales were translated into Chinese, back-translated, and then administered to samples in Hong Kong, People's Republic of China, and the U.S.. They maintained internal consistency reliability across samples, in contrast to some other American scales that lost internal consistency when administered to Chinese samples.

This procedure can be used as a first step in CC/CN research to create scales with the potential to maintain equivalence across translation and national borders. It should be used with other procedures, such as within-subject bilingual studies to explore how equivalent a scale might be. A series of studies might be necessary to give complete confidence that a scale can be used successfully internationally and that differences in results can be attributed to cultural/national differences as opposed to measurement problems. This can be particularly important in the measurement of constructs that have been difficult cross-culturally, such as culture values.

4.1. Sample Equivalence Between Cultures

The second issue of concern is the selection of equivalent groups across countries. Our interest in cross-cultural research is the impact of culture, not the impact of confounding variables. One problem in much cross-cultural stress research is the availability of equivalent participant samples. Thus we sometimes compare individuals who vary, not only in country, but in demographics such as occupation, income (relative to society) and status. Even within the same occupation, differences in work conditions can masquerade as cultural differences. Suppose we compare physicians in the U.S. who are highly paid and work 80-hour weeks with physicians in a country with socialized medicine whose incomes are modest and who work regular 40-hour weeks. If we find the Americans are more highly stressed, should we conclude that the U.S. is a more stress-producing culture? Clearly, with so many potential third-variable effects, we need to be extremely careful to match subjects on relevant variables so we can draw appropriate conclusions about the effects of culture itself.

However, matching participants in all potential third-variables so that one ends up with comparable samples across countries may be far-fetched because of wide variation across cultures. For researchers who study employed populations, economic and social factors can make it difficult to identify equivalent samples. In contrast to North America, there are countries where large private corporations are rare. In other countries, state-managed enterprises dominate the economic landscape and, therefore, even matching for industry sector will not rid comparisons of selection bias, because organizations in the same sector (e.g., oil production and distribution) will still differ in meaningful ways like whether they are private or state-run enterprises. Even those who study college students might find differences across countries. In the U.S. a far greater proportion of the general population attends college than in countries where college attendance tends to be limited to the upper echelons of society. Thus, statistically controlling for factors representing rival explanations seems necessary even in the best of matched samples.

One partial solution to this problem is to gather as much information as possible about the samples, which goes beyond what we usually do. One should try to match on variables likely to cause confounded results. We should look carefully at economic (e.g., relative standard of living, economic system, and tax structure), political, and social factors. For research conducted in organizations, data on industry sector, organizational structure, and power structure should be collected. To the greatest extent possible, samples should be matched, and comparisons of multiple samples per country would be helpful. With the physician example, one could have samples of American physicians from different settings, such as private practice versus public health facilities. If the Americans regardless of setting score higher on the stressor measures, one gains confidence that results might be due to culture. As one compares more and more occupations and continues to find the same results, one begins to establish a pattern of cultural differences.

In choosing control variables, researchers should be careful about operationalizing such measures in terms of subjective appraisals rather than reports of objective factors. Consider for example the case of social support, whose effects on the stressor-strain relationship have been widely studied (Viswesvaran, Sanchez, & Fisher, 1999). A majority of measures of social support rely on subjective appraisals of received support. Reports of social support are influenced by the extent to which societies are collectivistic vs. individualistic and, therefore, interpretations of what constitutes a high, average, or low level of support may vary considerably across countries (Triandis, 1994a). Thus, matching samples on the extent to which individuals feel that they had support from supervisors, co-workers, or even family members may be misleading, given the variations on what various cultures would consider an adequate level of support. Similarly, appraisals of potentially stressful working conditions are likely to differ as a function of what constitute normal working conditions in the country. For example, the nasty working conditions of a sweatshop may not look so bad to workers without job mobility who do not count on better ways to make a living.

5. CONCLUSION

In summary, several research design features are advocated here as potentially instrumental in establishing the absence of the kind of language and selection biases that are often confounded with culture effects. First, the use of bilinguals with similar levels of acculturation and reading comprehension in both the source and the target language reduces the likelihood of selection bias introduced by differences in language proficiency. Second, the use of a within-participant design eliminates the threat of selection bias that plagues non-equivalent groups in cross-cultural research. Third, the manipulation of language order can help rule out order effects such as recall of the source (e.g., English) version when responding to the target (e.g., Spanish) version. The kind of research design advocated here can test the cultural accommodation hypothesis, which predicts that when bilinguals respond to a measurement instrument, the language in which the instrument is taken influences the responses.

Problems of measurement calibration and sample equivalence are but two of the major issues involved in CC/CN. They provide challenges to researchers interested in comparing people across countries. With the globalization of the economy, cross-cultural comparisons are becoming more important than ever. Research procedures and measurement tools that minimize measurement and sampling error in cross-cultural comparisons are needed if we are to draw valid inferences about culture and nationality effects.

REFERENCES

Bandura, A. (1986). *Social foundations of thought and action: A social cognitive theory*. Englewood Cliffs, NJ: Prentice-Hall.

Berry, J. (1969). On cross-cultural comparability. *International Journal of Psychology*, 4:119-128.

Bollen, K.A. (1989). *Structural equations with latent variables*. New York: Wiley.

Bond, M.. H. & Yang, R. (1982). Ethnic affirmation versus cross-cultural accommodation. *Journal of Cross-Cultural Psychology*, 13: 169-185.

Boyacigiller, N. A., & Adler, N. J. (1991). The parochial dinosaur: Organizational science in a global context. *Academy of Management Journal*, 16, 262-290.

Brislin, R. W. (1986). The wording and translation of research instruments. In W. J. Lonner & J. W. Berry (Eds.), *Field Methods in Cross-Cultural Research*. Newbury Park, CA: Sage.

Byrne, B. M. (1994). *Structural equation modeling with EQS and EQS Windows*. Thousand Oaks, CA: Sage.

Byrne, B. M., Shavelson, R. J., & Muthén, B. (1989). Testing for the equivalence of factor covariance and mean structures: the issue of partial measurement invariance. *Psychological Bulletin*, 105, 456-466.

Candell, G. L., & Hulin, C. L. (1987). Cross-language and cross-cultural comparisons in scale translations. *Journal of Cross-Cultural Psychology*, 17: 417-440.

Church, A. T. & Lonner, W. J. (1998). The cross-cultural perspective in the study of personality: Rationale and current research. *Journal of Cross-Cultural Psychology*, 29, 32-62.

Geisinger, K. F. (1994). Cross-cultural normative assessment: Translation and adaptation issues influencing the normative interpretation of assessment instruments. *Psychological Assessment*, 6(4): 304-312.

Ghorpade, J., Hattrup, K., & Lackritz, J. R. (1999). The use of personality measures in cross-cultural research: A test of three personality scales across two countries. *Journal of Applied Psychology*, 84, 670-679.

Hulin, C. L. (1987). A psychometric theory of evaluations of item and scale translations. *Journal of Cross-Cultural Psychology*, 18: 115-142.

Hulin, C. L., & Mayer, L. J. (1986). Psychometric equivalence of a translation of the Job Descriptive Index into Hebrew. *Journal of Applied Psychology*, 71: 83-94.

Hulin, C. L., Drasgow, F., & Komocar, J. (1982). Application of item response theory to analysis of attitude scale translations. *Journal of Applied Psychology*, 67: 818-825.

Iwata, N., Umesue, M., Egashira, K., Hiro, H., Mizoue, T., Mishima, N., & Nagata, S. (1998). Can positive affect items be used to assess depressive disorder in the Japanese populations? *Psychological Medicine*, 28, 153-158.

Katerberg, R., Smith, F. J., & Hoy, S. (1977). Language, time, and person effects on attitude scale translations. *Journal of Applied Psychology*, 62: 385-391.

Lazarus, R. S. (1966). *Psychological Stress and the Coping Process*. New York: McGraw-Hill

Liu, C. (2003). A comparison of job stressors and job strains among employees holding comparable jobs in Western and Eastern societies. Unpublished Doctoral Dissertation, University of South Florida, Tampa.

Liu, C., Borg, I., & Spector, P. E. (2004). Measurement equivalence of a German job satisfaction survey used in a multinational organization: Implications of Schwartz's culture model. *Journal of Applied Psychology*, 89, 1070-1082.

Lonner, W. J. (1990). An overview of cross-cultural testing and assessment. In R. W. Brislin (Ed.), *Applied Cross-Cultural Psychology*, Vol 14. Newbury Park, CA: Sage.

Lytle, A. L., Brett, J. M., Barsness, Z. I., Tinsley, C. H., & Janssens, M. (1995). A paradigm for confirmatory cross-cultural research in organizational behavior. *Research in Organizational Behavior*, 17:167-214.

Maruyama, M. (1984). Alternative concepts of management: Insights from Asia and Africa. *Asia Pacific Journal of Management*, 1(1): 100-111.

Narayanan, L., Menon, S., & Spector, P. E. (1999). A cross-cultural comparison of job stressors and reactions among employees holding comparable jobs in two countries. *International Journal of Stress Management*, 6, 197-212.

Ralston, D. A., Cunnif, M. K., Gustafson, D. J. (1995). *Journal of Cross Cultural Psychology*, 26: 714-727.

Raju, N. S., Laffitte, L. J., & Byrne, B. M. (2002). Measurement equivalence: A comparison of methods based on confirmatory factor analysis and item response theory. *Journal of Applied Psychology*, 87, 517-529.

Riordan, C. M., & Vandenberg, R. J. (1994). A central question in cross-cultural research: Do employees of different cultures interpret work-related measures in an equivalent manner? *Journal of Management*, 20(3): 643-671.

Ross, N. (2004). *Culture & cognition: Implications for theory and method*. Thousand Oaks, CA: Sage.

Ryan, A. M., Chan, D., Ployhart, R. E., & Slade, L. A. (1999). Employee attitude surveys in a multinational organization: Considering language and culture in assessing measurement equivalence. *Personnel Psychology*, 52: 37-58.

Rybowiak, V., Garst, H., Frese, M., & Batinic, B. (1999). Error orientation questionnaire (EOQ): Reliability, validity, and different language equivalence. *Journal of Organizational Behavior*, 20: 527-547.

Schaffer, B. S., & Riordan, C. M. (2003). A review of cross-cultural methodologies for organizational research: A best-practices approach. *Organizational Research Methods*, 6, 169-215.

Siu, O. L., & Cooper, C. L. (1998). A study of occupational stress, job satisfaction and quitting intention in Hong Kong firms: The role of locus of control and organizational commitment. *Stress Medicine*, 14: 55-66.

Smith, P. C., Kendall, L. M., & Hulin, C. L. (1969). *Measurement satisfaction in work and retirement*. Chicago: Rand McNally.

Spector, P. E. (1997). *Job satisfaction*. Application, assessment, causes, and consequences. Thousand Oaks, CA: Sage.

Spector, P. E (1988). Development of the Work locus of Control Scale. *Journal of Occupational Psychology*, 61: 335-340.

Spector, P. E., Sanchez, J. I., Siu, O. L., Salgado, J., & Ma, J. (2004). Secondary control, socioinstrumental control, and work locus of control in China and the U.S. *Applied Psychology: An International Review*, 53, 38-60.

Spector, P. E., Van Katwyk, P. T., Brannick, M. T., & Chen, P. Y. (1997). When two factors don't reflect two constructs: How item characteristics can produce artifactual factors. *Journal of Management*, 23, 659-677.

Spirrison, C. L., & Choi, S. (1998). Psychometric properties of a Korean version of the revised NEO-personality inventory. *Psychological Reports*, 83: 263-274.

Triandis, H. C. (1994a). Cross-cultural industrial and organizational psychology. In H. C. Triandis, M. D. Dunnette, and Leatta M. Hough (Eds.), *Handbook of industrial and organizational psychology* (pp. 103-172). Palo Alto, CA: Consulting Psychologists Press.

Triandis, H. C. (1994b). *Culture and social behavior*. New York: McGraw-Hill.

Vandenberg, R. J., & Lance, C. E. (2000). A review and synthesis of the measurement invariance literature: Suggestions, practices, and recommendations for organizational research. *Organizational Research Methods*, 3, 4-69.

Van de Vijver, F., & Leung, K. (1997). *Methods and data analysis for cross-cultural research*. Thousand Oaks, CA: Sage.

Viswesvaran, C., Sanchez, J. I., & Fisher, J. (1999). The role of social support in the process of work stress: A meta-analysis. *Journal of Vocational Behavior*, 54, 314-334.

Weisz, J. R., Rothbaum, F. M., & Blackburn, T. C. (1984). Standing out and standing in: The psychology of control in America and Japan. *American Psychologist*, 39: 955-969.

Werner, O., & Campbell, D. (1970). Translating, working through interpreters, and the problem of decentering. In R. Carroll and R. Cohen (Eds.), *A handbook of method in cultural anthropology*, New York: Natural History Press, 398-420.

West, S. G., Finch, J. F., & Curran, P. J. (1995). Structural equation models with nonnormal variables: Problems and remedies. In R. H. Hoyle (Ed.), *Structural equation modeling: Concepts, issues, and applications* (pp. 56-75). Thousand Oaks, CA: Sage.

Wong, P. T. P. (1993). Effective management of life stress: The resource-congruence model. *Stress Medicine*, 9, 51-60.

10

PROBLEMS AND STRATEGIES WHEN USING RATING SCALES IN CROSS-CULTURAL COPING RESEARCH

Roger G. Tweed and Anita DeLongis

1. INTRODUCTION

Culture may significantly influence people's coping strategies. The possibility of cultural differences in coping strategies is suggested in part by the differences between the coping prescriptions of traditional belief systems. For example, the Taoist tradition prescribes adapting oneself to the environment. In this tradition, water provides a model of successful coping because water adapts to the contours of its environment (Lao-Tzu, 1989, chapter 77 Te). Alternatively, the Hebrew and Christian traditions prescribe ruling over the environment, at least as embodied in the cultural mandate in which humans are directed to subdue and have dominion over the Earth; furthermore, in the Hebrew and Christian traditions, when personal efforts fail, humans are encouraged to enlist the assistance of an all-powerful deity to change the environment.

Many additional examples of differing advice can be found when comparing traditional belief systems. Confucius provides a further point of comparison because he, in contrast to the Hebrew and Christian cultivation of dependence on a deity, told his followers to avoid becoming overly interested in questions about spirits. Confucius recommended efforts directed toward self-improvement. In the Buddhist tradition, elimination of personal desire is prescribed as a means of coping with the demands of life. Personal desire is a source of suffering, according to the Four Noble Truths of Buddhism, so elimination of desire brings freedom from suffering.

Thus, depending on which tradition one follows, the appropriate prescription for coping may be to adapt to the environment, bring the environment into submission, rely on a deity, eliminate personal desire, or seek self-improvement. These strategies are not all mutually exclusive, yet these differing ideals suggest possible continuing cultural differences in regions influenced by one or more of these or other traditions. Empirical research has the potential to clarify the extent of variation and consistency in coping around the world.

Roger G. Tweed, Kwantlen University College; Anita DeLongis, University of British Columbia

Studying coping, however, is challenging. Qualitative methods such as ethnographies, grounded theory, or discourse analysis rely on the researcher to select and interpret representative segments from respondents' reports. These methods can be very enlightening, but many psychologists would be unwilling to rely on qualitative methods of study alone because of the possibility that the prior beliefs, assumptions, and the cultural background of the researcher will color the selection and interpretation of the respondents' words. These dangers were illustrated in Freeman's (1999) allegations regarding Margaret Mead's classic book, Coming of Age in Samoa (1928). Her book reported how Samoan adolescents coped with the transition from childhood to adulthood. According to Freedman and at least one of Mead's informants, Mead's book expressed Mead's theories about sexuality more accurately than it portrayed Samoan adolescent strategies for coping with this developmental transition. The accuracy of Mead's work can still be debated as can the selection and interpretation by Freeman, but the incident nonetheless illustrates the danger of relying on selection and interpretation from extended interviews with a small number of informants.

2. CONTEMPORARY COPING RATING SCALES

Quantitative methods such as the use of Likert-type rating scales reduce the role of interpretation (or of hermeneutics to be more precise) in the research process. The rating scales are used as follows: Participants are instructed to recall a particular stressful circumstance. Sometimes the event is specified by the researcher as in Halamandaris and Powers' (1999) study of student responses to exam stress. Other times, the respondent is asked to think of the most stressful event within a particular time period (e.g., in the last 6 months or the last 24 hours). Some of the coping scales are designed to be applicable to a wide range of problems (e.g., Ways of Coping Scale, WOC, Folkman et al., 1986a), but others apply only to specific contexts (e.g., Coping with Health Injuries and Problems scale, CHIP; Endler and Parker, 2000; Chronic Pain Coping Inventory, Jensen et al., 1995; Romano et al., 2003). After reading the instructions, the participants may be asked to write a description of the stressful circumstance under consideration.

Next, the participants read each item on the scale and rate the extent to which they used each strategy listed to cope with the specific stressor described. For example, the first item may say "I stood my ground and fought for what I wanted" (WOC; Folkman et al., 1986a) and beside that item will be the numbers from 0 to 5. One participant may decide that he didn't use that strategy at all, so he will circle a zero for that item. Another participant may decide that she used that strategy somewhat and circle a 3 for that item. A third participant may decide that she used that strategy extensively, so will circle a 5 for that item.

The COPE (Carver et al., 1989) differs from these others in initially being used to assess coping dispositions or habits; in the initial study, participants were not asked to recall a specific event, but instead were asked to report how they generally respond under conditions of stress. In a separate study (also reported in Carver et al., 1989), the COPE was also used more like the other scales to assess coping with a specific stressful situation. Thus, the authors of the COPE suggested that the instrument could be used effectively either to assess coping dispositions by asking participants how they usually cope or to assess situational coping by asking participants to recall a particular incident and report how they coped with that situation.

Factor analyses and theoretical considerations have provided guidance for grouping items on coping scales into clusters measuring particular latent constructs. The Ways of Coping Scale (WOC), for example, a widely used measure, assesses confrontive coping (e.g., "expressed anger to the person who had caused the problem"), distancing (e.g., "went on as if nothing had happened"), self-control (e.g., "tried to keep my feelings to myself"), seeking social support (e.g., "talked with someone to find out more about the situation"), accepting responsibility (e.g., "criticized or lectured myself"), escape/avoidance (e.g., "wished the situation would go away or somehow be over with"), planful problem solving ("made a plan of action and followed it"), and positive reappraisal (e.g., "changed or grew as a person in a good way"; Folkman et al., 1986a). The Coping Inventory for Stressful Situations (CISS; Endler and Parker, 1999) assesses task-oriented, emotion-oriented, and avoidance-oriented coping. The COPE (Carver et al., 1989) assesses a number of constructs including active coping, planning, suppression of competing activities, restraint, seeking instrumental social support, seeking emotional social support, alcohol-drug disengagement, and turning to religion. Recently, attention has been directed toward developing rating scales of coping to assess interpersonal modes of coping, such as empathic responding (O'Brien and DeLongis, 1996) and protective buffering (Lyons et al., 1998). These latter dimensions have been referred to as relationship-focused coping; they tap communal or interconnected ways of coping. Given differences across cultures in interpersonal roles and responsibilities (e.g., Markus and Kitayama, 1991; Miller, 1994), such dimensions of coping may be particularly important for the study of cultural differences. The Coping Schemas Inventory (Peacock and Wong, 1996) is an interesting scale that includes some subscales such as self-restructuring and acceptance that may be especially relevant in culturally Chinese contexts. The inventory is based on the Resource Congruence model (Wong, 1993) which assumes stress involves not only processes of conflict between the self and the environment, but also intrapsychic conflict. The Resource Congruence model also includes a role for proactive coping strategies that build personal resources so that one can cope better with unforeseen future events.

The use of rating scales such as these reduces the need for experimenters to select from and interpret respondents' open-ended responses. The scales, because they rely on self-reports, also allow assessment differentiating not only coping behavior, but also differentiating the cognitions and motivations behind the coping. For example, self-reports can begin to distinguish respondents who are stunned into inaction from respondents who are strategically waiting for an appropriate time to act. Likewise, via self-reports researchers can begin to distinguish cognitive reappraisal from passivity. In most circumstances, coping research will include self-report data, but in spite of the benefits offered by these quantitative self-reports of coping, as with all self-report data, some difficulties arise. This chapter will discuss some of the challenges faced by researchers relying on self-reports, and in particular, those challenges faced by researchers relying on rating scales in cross-cultural coping research.

3. CONCERNS WITH CROSS-CULTURAL USE OF RATING SCALES

Cross-cultural psychologists have highlighted a number of challenges faced by researchers attempting to use rating scales across cultures. Most of these problems are not unique to coping research and do not necessarily invalidate rating scales, but nonetheless are cause for concern.

3.1. Nay-Saying

First, cultures differ in their tendency to nay-say (Hofstede, 1980). In our experience and according to Hofstede's data, North American participants tend to less strongly endorse items on rating scales than do Chinese respondents. These findings suggest that culturally North American participants tend toward nay-saying more than do culturally Chinese participants (or one could interpret this as a Chinese tendency toward yea-saying). Of course, there are exceptions for particular scales, but across a number of questionnaire studies we have observed a general trend consistent with Hofstede's data when comparing Euro-North American respondents to Chinese respondents. This tendency suggests, and our experience supports this hypothesis, that when researchers calculate an average score across all scales in a coping inventory, the North American participants will tend to have lower averages than the Chinese participants. Japanese participants in our data, however, produced overall averages similar to those of the North Americans. The reasons for the response bias are not completely understood, but the bias creates problems in data analysis because the true differences in coping strategies can be difficult to distinguish from apparent differences due to nay-saying bias.

3.2. Extremism

Second, cultural differences in extremism on rating scales may sometimes create problems. Chen et al. (1995) found that Americans were more likely than Japanese to use extreme ends of rating scales. They conducted studies to examine whether this response bias creates problems in group comparison. According to their results, this response bias will not usually influence substantive findings, but the bias is nonetheless concerning simply because of the potential to obscure substantive findings.

3.3. Reference Effect

Third, a reference effect exists such that responses to rating scales can be influenced by participants' implicit choice of a comparison group to which they compare themselves (Heine et al., 2002). For example, if the data are being collected at a university in Turkey, the participant may implicitly be comparing him or herself to other students at that same university. When asked whether he or she strongly agrees with the value of freedom, he or she may strongly agree, but the researcher may not be aware that the strongly agree is relative to the level of endorsement he or she perceives in his or her peer group. This reference effect seems to be less of a problem when the questionnaire asks objective questions about behaviors than when the questionnaire asks about values (Peng et al., 1997), so this effect may be less concerning when using coping rating scales than when using values questionnaires. Also, the effect may be lessened when the respondents are currently residing in the same environment, such as when data is collected in one university with a multicultural student body.

3.4. Translation Problems

Fourth, translation of standard coping questionnaires may alter the meaning of the items in ways that the researchers do not anticipate. These translation problems can result from low quality translations or from more complex problems. Some questionnaire items may include idioms that translate poorly. The Ways of Coping Scale (Folkman and Lazarus, 1985), for example, asks the respondents to rate their agreement with the following: "stood my ground and fought for what I wanted." The figurative use of "stood my ground" may not translate well into all languages.

3.5. Imposed-Etic Research

Fifth, imposed etic research (Berry, 1989) can create problems. Imposed etic research uses unaltered instruments from one culture for research in a second culture and assumes that the constructs relevant to one culture will also be relevant to the other culture. An imposed-etic approach can create problems because constructs meaningful in one culture may not be meaningful in another (e.g., "Confucian work dynamism" Chinese Culture Connection, 1987). Also constructs central to one of the cultures being examined may not be well represented on common coping scales. This tendency for imposed-etic research to exclude culturally relevant constructs is well illustrated by research with the Chinese Personality Assessment Inventory 2 (CPAI 2, see Cheung et al., 2003 for a review of Asian personality inventories) which includes a personality factor of "interpersonal relatedness." This factor of interpersonal relatedness includes the following facets: harmony, face, and an orientation to reciprocity in relationships (*renqing*). This factor separated from the Big 5 in a joint factor analysis of the CPAI-2 and the NEO-FFI (Costa and McCrae, 1992; Cheung et al., 2001) and offered incremental validity beyond the Big 5 in predicting social psychological variables (Zhang and Bond, 1998), but only became widely known by using an emic approach. Emic methodology, unlike imposed-etic methodology, uses measures derived within and for the culture being examined. Purely emic methodology would produce completely distinct measures for each cultural context, and thus would preclude quantitative comparisons of cultures. A combination of etic and emic methods, however, can increase cultural sensitivity while also allowing quantitative comparison of similarities and differences across cultural groups.

Tweed, White, and Lehman (2004), for example, used the Ways of Coping Scale (WOC; Folkman and Lazarus, 1985) for research in Japan and Canada, but conducted factor analyses in each cultural group to assure that the items showing internal consistency in the West also showed internal consistency in Japan. Also, they noted that two central constructs for the Japanese seemed to be missing from the Ways of Coping. In particular, they spoke to natives of Japan and an expert on Japanese culture and also reviewed a stress and coping questionnaire constructed by Japanese researchers (Ozeki et al.,1994) and noted that the constructs of "waiting" and "accepting the problem" seemed to be relevant to the Japanese, but were not well represented in the WOC items. Thus, items related to waiting (e.g., "waited until I was able to do something about the matter," "I leave things to the passing of time") and accepting the problem (e.g., "tried to think of it as not being all that important") were modified or created in the WOC format. In stress and coping theory, these have been considered largely under cognitive appraisals of stress (Folkman et al., 1986b), rather than as coping strategies *per se*. Given the importance of these concepts for examining cultural differences in stress and coping processes, it would seem important for future research to assess not only differences in coping with stress, but also, and perhaps more importantly, differences in cognitive appraisals of stress.

Similarly, Cameron et al. (2004) noted, that indirect coping is not well represented on common coping scales though this strategy may be especially common in interdependent cultures (Lebra, 1984). Indirect coping includes keeping a low profile, seeking assistance of a third party, saving face, and drawing on group traditions or resources. They did find evidence that, within a multicultural North American sample, interdependent self-construal was associated with indirect coping, supporting their contention that this coping strategy may be particularly relevant for particular cultural groups.

These types of creative approaches to cross-cultural research are needed because mainstream instruments developed in North America tend to neglect some important coping constructs. As a further example, the Confucian tradition of silent endurance in response to trials is evident in modern research with students from East Asia (Yeh and Inose, 2002), yet this construct is not well represented in mainstream North American coping instruments. Also, there is reason to believe that East Asian participants will often seek social support not primarily as a source of emotional comfort as might be the case for Euro-North American participants, but primarily as a source of advice and concrete assistance (Tweed and Lehman, unpublished data). Wong (1993) used the term "collective coping" to refer to this type of collective effort to solve the problems of a single group member. The Coping Schemas Inventory (Peacock and Wong, 1996) which was built on Wong's (1993; see also Wong and Ujimoto, 1998) Resource Congruence model includes some coping strategies (e.g., accepting the problem and self-restructuring) that might be particularly important in cross-cultural research, but that are not well represented on mainstream North American scales.

Thus, cross-cultural research with coping rating scales raises a number of difficulties. In particular, nay-saying, extremity, reference group differences, or translation problems across cultures can obscure true cross-cultural differences and/or similarities. Also, imposed-etic research can result in miscommunication and/or the neglect of important constructs. Strategies for coping with each of these problems will be discussed, but these are not the only problems facing coping researchers.

4. CONCERNS WITH COPING RATING SCALES IN GENERAL

Even in monocultural environments, if one could find such a research context, coping research would be difficult. Coping researchers in recent years have become more aware of some of the difficulties with studying coping in any context. A number of writers have bemoaned the lack of progress in coping research (e.g., Coyne and Gottlieb, 1996; Somerfield and McCrae, 2000), citing, in particular, the disjunction between the many coping studies that have been conducted and the limited number of theoretically important or clinically useful findings. Some have attributed the lack of progress in part to the way in which coping rating scales have been used (Coyne and Gottlieb, 1996). A second, related reason cited for the lack of progress has been a lack of fit between coping theory and the methodologies that have been employed (Tennen and Affleck, 2000; DeLongis and Holtzman, in press).

4.1. Memory Problems

One of the major difficulties is that most coping research has relied on participants accurately recalling their coping responses. Memory errors, if they are unsystematic, will decrease measurement reliability, and thereby decrease statistical power of all analyses, but will not introduce systematic bias. There is reason to expect, however, that memory errors will sometimes be systematic and biased. Individuals differ in their biases in recollection of past events, and one could even argue that biased recall is itself a coping strategy (Wong and Watt, 1991). Furthermore, in other research domains, both respondents' current state and respondents' theories about the world seem to influence recall of past situations (McFarland and Buehler, 1997; McFarland et al., 1992). There is no reason to believe that recall of coping is immune to these effects, and in fact Ptacek et al. (1994) report surprisingly low correspondence between concurrent and retrospective reports of coping.

Further evidence suggests that retrospective recall of coping will produce over-reporting of some types of coping and underreporting of others. For example, Stone et al. (1998) asked participants to carry handheld computers in order to record coping within one hour after occurrence. The participants were randomly prompted by an audible beep on average every 40 minutes over a two day period and asked whether they had been thinking about, discussing, or doing something about a conflict or issue related to work, marriage, or something else. If so, they were asked to identify the issue and report their coping on a 33-item scale. After the two day study, participants were interviewed and asked retrospectively about their coping at those prior time points. The retrospective reports produced higher endorsement of behavioral coping and lower endorsement of cognitive coping than did the momentary reports. Stone et al. argued that retrospective reporting is not necessarily invalidated by these findings. They argued that retrospective coping may accurately capture some broader coping strategies not reported in momentary assessment, but that nonetheless retrospective coping is subject to memory reconstruction heuristics.

If memory reconstruction is influenced by personal theories of the respondents (McFarland and Ross, 1987), then one could expect that in cross-cultural research, individual reports of coping will drift toward the respondents' culturally-influenced theories of how coping proceeds. The drift within various cultures could involve psychological defense mechanisms in which one recalls one's own coping as favorably in line with the culturally prescribed norm. Also, the drift could take place even without defense mechanisms, simply as a result of respondents filling in missing memories with a narrative that make sense to the respondent. Thus, for example, North Americans may drift toward agentic accounts of their coping. In other words, as time passes, North American recollections of coping may drift toward the Judeo-Christian ideal of actively seeking to control the environment. This, admittedly speculative, hypothesis that North American recollections tend to drift toward agentic coping accounts would in part explain Stone et al.'s (1998) finding of increased reports of behavioral coping in retrospective as opposed to momentary reports. In contrast, Taoism, as described above, prescribes adaptation to the environment as the normative coping response, so in Taoist-influenced cultures retrospective memory reconstruction may tend to drift toward the theory that coping takes place as one adapts to the environment. Because memory is somewhat reconstructive, respondents will report more than they can know without even realizing they are doing so.

If retrospective coping reports drift toward cultural narratives, then this tendency creates both potential and problems for cross-cultural research with retrospective coping reports. If this drift occurs, then comparisons of retrospective coping reports across cultures may uncover both cultural differences in actual behavioral and in cultural theories of coping.

Thus, retrospective coping studies have value as first steps in examining cultural similarities and differences. A problem with retrospective coping studies is their inability to distinguish these sources of variance: culturally influenced memory reconstruction versus culturally influenced behavior differences. Only a combination of momentary and retrospective reporting will be able to distinguish which source is causing cross-cultural differences in coping reports. If, for example, Taoist-influenced cultural groups report greater acceptance of the problem both on momentary and retrospective reports, then this would suggest actual differences in coping strategies. If, however, the cultures differ only on retrospective reports and not on momentary reports, then this would suggest that the cultural groups are showing similar coping responses, but that their reconstructions are being influenced by cultural norms.

4.2. Automatic and Habitual Coping

Coyne and Gottlieb (1996) have criticized coping researchers for neglecting to examine habitual, automatic or anticipatory coping responses. For example, defense mechanisms in which the respondent distorts reality (e.g., denial) will likely be unavailable in the respondent's consciousness, so will be largely unavailable on self-reports (Somerfield and McCrae, 2000). One cannot expect respondents to consistently and reliably report whether they distorted reality (e.g., denying the severity of the event or denying their role in causing the event) in response to the stressor. This problem is not limited to rating scales; unconscious processes will be difficult to measure with any form of self-report and even be difficult to assess reliably with more formal diagnostic interviews. The outlook is not totally bleak; some unconscious responses have been operationalized successfully as, for example, with Paulhus' (1984) measurement of self-deception with the Balanced Inventory of Desirable Responding, but nonetheless, unconscious processes will in general remain difficult to measure.

This insensitivity to unconscious coping processes may be particularly concerning for cultural research. Culture has many times been compared to the water in which a fish swims (original source unknown). Fish live within the water, but do not question the nature of the water. Likewise, people live within culture, but until they cross into another culture, they may never question or even recognize the beliefs and assumptions that make their culture unique. For example, according to Markus and Kitayama (1991), people within interdependent cultures will assume that self is defined by its relationships, but people in independent cultures will assume that the self is defined by its traits. These assumptions may not be questioned or even recognized by most people within the culture. Likewise habitual culturally cultivated coping beliefs and responses may be below the awareness of most respondents. For example, North Americans may more frequently than Japanese respond to stressors by taking actions to protect their own self-esteem by distorting reality (Heine et al., 1999), but the North Americans may be unaware of the purpose of their responses, and the responses may be so automatic that they occur without conscious deliberation or realization.

These unconscious processes are an interesting topic of cultural psychology. Shweder (1993), in particular, argued for the importance of unconscious interpretations and representations for cultural psychologists. Shweder has used the term "experience-near concepts" (see also Geertz, 1973) which he described as implicit concepts that influence behavior, that are activated spontaneously, and that are often unconscious. He argued that these concepts reside in a realm for which respondents know more than they can tell. He argued that these experience-near concepts are the appropriate object of study for cultural psychologists. Measurement, however, is exceedingly difficult in regards to implicit beliefs. In-depth interviews or clinical work may begin to uncover these concepts, but raise other equally serious methodological concerns.

4.3. Brevity and Vagueness of Coping Items

Items on coping scales are necessarily written briefly and in relatively simple language, which can lead to problems of multiple interpretations (Coyne and Gottlieb, 1996). For example, Tweed, White, and Lehman (2004) compared Japanese to Canadian respondents on the WOC and found some evidence that Japanese participants engaged in more internally targeted control. They noted, however, that the planful problem solving (e.g., "I made a plan of action and followed it") items on the scale were disappointingly vague. The cultural groups did not differ on the planful problem solving items even though the Japanese reported a greater tendency to "leave things to the passing of time" and "try to think of it as not being that important" (items adapted from Ozeki et al., 1994). This similarity of endorsement for planful problem solving may have hidden very different plans selected by the different cultural groups. Possibly, follow-up interviews (Coyne and Gottlieb, 1996) or think aloud procedures during the completion of the questionnaires would help clarify the meaning of these items to each cultural group.

One of the reasons items on coping scales have historically been worded briefly and, perhaps more importantly, vaguely, has been to allow the items to apply to coping with a wide range of stressful situations. Although such wide applicability obviously has the potential to allow for greater generalizability of findings across situations and populations, there are clear shortcomings to this approach. It may be that, at least in some cases, the meaning of the items varies depending upon the situation in which they are used. The assessment of problem-focused coping efforts seems particularly vulnerable to this problem. For example, Newth and DeLongis (2004) examined coping with pain among patients with rheumatoid arthritis, and found that problem-focused coping was associated with increases in pain. They argued that, in the context of chronic pain, problem-focused coping as assessed by items such as "I doubled my efforts to make things work", might have served as a marker for over-exertion. It may not be problem-solving *per se* that is associated with increases in pain, but rather the over-exertion that might be reflected in such a "doubling" of effort – particularly if that effort is directed towards physical activity. If, on the other hand, one's problem-solving efforts involved seeking appropriate medical care and following a recommended regimen of exercise, diet, and medication, then it appears unlikely that such "problem-solving" efforts would be associated with negative health outcomes. This result provides further evidence that vague items can cause problems.

4.4. One Shot Administrations

Lazarus and DeLongis (1983), Coyne and Gottlieb (1996), Tennen and Affleck (2000) and others have criticized coping researchers for relying on single administrations of a coping checklist. In particular, they argued that this method is inconsistent with the transactional model of coping assumed by many of the researchers. To be consistent with the transactional perspective, the researchers must assume stress is a dynamic and bi-directional relationship between the person and the situation. Coyne and Gottlieb cite the example of coping with an exam. On a single administration of a coping scale, students may endorse an item stating that in response to exam stress, they "avoided being with people in general." Prior to the exam, this type of behavior may indicate problem-focused coping, in particular, focusing one's time on studying. After the exam, this item could indicate social withdrawal due to poor performance. Thus, to be true to the model, coping research should examine not only the type of coping, but also the timing of the coping. One-shot administrations of coping scales will have value as preliminary examinations of cultural similarities and differences, but in order to assess how the timing of coping influences outcomes in various cultures, multiple administrations will be required.

4.5. Non-Representative Samples

One difficulty in psychological research is finding representative samples. Coping research, more than research in many other areas of psychology has drawn on diverse populations including persons with a variety of illnesses, of all ages, from a variety of occupations, and with a variety of stressful life situations. Unfortunately, the few studies examining coping cross-culturally have tended to rely on university students. These studies have value, but a complete portrait of coping requires examination of a wider range of individuals within a culture. An over-reliance on student samples likely minimizes differences in stressors and masks critical differences in coping that might emerge in dealing with more diverse sets of stressors than are typically experienced by students.

4.6. Misguided Reliance on Statistical Controls

Coyne and Gottlieb (1996) criticized researchers who statistically control for important variables such as event type, event stressfulness, participant gender or even participant ethnicity in the hope that this process will make the participants comparable. They argue that this decontextualization of coping will lead to nonsense because coping is always tied to a particular situation and person as indicated by the transactional perspective. Certainly, this concern must be applied to the role of culture in coping as well. Efforts to describe the antecedents and consequences of coping within a cultural vacuum by statistically controlling for ethnicity or culture are problematic. Thus, coping researchers who use multicultural samples and try to use statistical controls to justify ignoring the diversity, risk obscuring the truth.

5. STRATEGIC RESPONSES TO THESE CHALLENGES

Some of these problems are difficult to overcome when using rating scales to study coping. Nonetheless, some suggestions will be made for best practices in studying coping.

5.1. Nay-Saying

A variety of data transformations have been suggested for dealing with nay-saying bias (Fischer, 2004). One strategy is to use a modified ipsatization procedure, variants of which have received extensive use in cross-cultural research using self-report data (Fischer, 2004). This modified ipsatization procedure converts the scores to relative scores, so that each item score indicates whether the respondent used that coping strategy more or less than he or she tended to use other strategies. The procedure is conducted as follows: One calculates separately for each respondent the mean of all coping items, and then subtracts this value from each of the respondent's scores. Tweed, White, and Lehman (2004) found that ipsatization of their WOC data, when comparing Japanese and Canadian partici-pants, left the substantive findings unchanged, but tended to increase effect sizes. Vitaliano et al. (1990) suggested a similar procedure in which coping scores are trans-formed into proportional scores. Variants of ipsatization, but not variants of proportional scoring have been used often in cross-cultural research.

A complete discussion of the advantages and disadvantages of ipsatization and of the various techniques of ipsatization would go beyond the scope of this chapter (Tweed, Conway, Ryder, and Lehman, 2004), but the basic procedure is less complicated than it might initially seem. If one is using SPSS syntax, for example, one writes a statement com-puting the mean across all items for each individual (e.g., meancope=mean(qn1 to qn45)). Then, for each item, one writes a statement calculating a corrected variable (e.g., ips_qn1=qn1-meancope). This procedure centers all scores around zero. In other words, each respondent will have an average score of zero on the coping items. A positive score for a particular item will indicate that the individual endorsed that item more than they tended to endorse the other items. A negative score will indicate that the individual endorsed that item less than they tended to endorse other items. Because negative scores make tables dif-ficult to read, one can add a constant to all scores to raise the scores above zero.

5.2. Extreme Responding

The ipsatization techniques discussed above can also be modified to correct for extrem-ity, but we recommend that in most cases simple ipsatization as described above is a better choice. Simple ipsatization may be a better choice because according to the studies by Chen et al. (1995), extremity differences usually do not affect substantive findings and also because the correction procedure can introduce unwanted biases (Tweed, Conway, Ryder, and Lehman, 2004). The transformation to correct for extremity differences is often labeled sim-ply "standardization," but is not the same as more typical standardization of data, so we pre-fer the term "within-person standardization." In within-person standardization, both the mean and the standard deviation of each participant are transformed. The commands are only slightly modified from those for ipsatization (In SPSS: A. meancope=mean(qn1 to qn45), B. sdcope=sd(qn1 to qn45), C. std_qn1=(qn1-meancope)/sdcope).

Alternatively, by examining relations within persons across time, researchers can reduce many of the problems inherent in self-report methodologies (DeLongis and Holtzman, in press). For example, differences in response styles, such as nay-saying, are controlled because these are presumably constant within a person across time, allowing an examination of the relationship between, for example, coping and pain without contamination by differences in response sets. More will be said about within-person studies in our discussion of memory problems and our discussion of statistical control.

5.3. Reference Effect

The reference effect discussed above is clearly problematic in research on values. The effect may not be as significant in coping research because people are reporting responses rather than explicitly comparing their responses to those of others (Heine et al., 2002). Nonetheless, there is value is conducting research not only across cultural settings (e.g., comparing Japanese in Japan to North Americans in North America), but also conducting research within multicultural settings in order to reduce the likelihood that results are obscured due to a reference effect. Within a multicultural setting, the likelihood is increased that participants, if they are using a reference group, are comparing themselves to others in the same setting, thereby reducing problems due to different cultural groups using completely distinct reference groups.

5.4. Translation Problems

Translations will never be perfect, but Brislin (1970) recommended back translation to improve translation quality. In this procedure, questionnaires are translated by one person, and then back-translated into the original language by another person. The quality of the original translation can then be assessed by comparing the original questionnaire with the back-translation. His advice is as relevant now as it was over thirty years ago.

5.5. Imposed-Etic Research

As discussed above, combining emic and etic research procedures will allow comparison across cultures. In particular, researching indigenous coping constructs prior to finalizing the research design reduces the likelihood of ignoring important constructs. Researchers can consult with indigenous individuals when planning studies, ask indigenous individuals to review all research materials, and run small pilot studies possibly with a think aloud format. All of these procedures will help uncover poorly worded items, absent constructs, and other problems associated with imposed-etic research. Coyne and Gottlieb (1996) have suggested the use of in-depth interviews with all participants following completion of the coping checklists in order to assess how the participants interpreted the items. Resource limitations, however, may make their suggestion unrealistic for many researchers except during pilot studies or with a small subsample of respondents.

Factor analysis can also help provide a partial assessment of whether constructs translate well across cultures. In particular, the coping inventories can be factor analyzed separately in each cultural group to assess whether items loading on each construct in one culture also load on the same construct in the second culture. Tweed, White, and Lehman (2004) conducted factor analyses of a brief form of the Ways of Coping Checklist in North America and Japan and found that most of the constructs showed coherence in both cultural contexts. Future research papers could go even further and make the replicability of coping factors across cultures a major topic of examination. In particular, confirmatory factor analyses could be used to explore the replicability of these factors. Also, convergent validity could be examined; in particular, a researcher could examine whether the coping scales show anticipated correlations with other variables (e.g., the Big Five personality factors) in all cultures being examined. It would also be of great value to include measures of continuous cultural variables (e.g., Triandis, 1996) with any coping questionnaire because many research consumers will want to know not only whether two cultures differ, but also which continuous variables (Tweed, Conway, and Ryder, 1999) account for the coping differences.

Collaborations between researchers from different cultural groups will help avoid the problems of imposed-etic research. The collaborations may be difficult to build, but offer many potential benefits.

5.6. Memory Problems

In order to reduce the role of reconstructive memory, coping self-reports can be gathered near in time to the actual coping response. Newth and DeLongis (2004), for example, asked people with rheumatoid arthritis to keep daily diaries of their coping, mood, and pain. Daily diary studies not only overcome some of the restrospective memory problems, but also allow within-person analyses over time, thus providing better evidence of causality than do between person comparisons. Newth and DeLongis found that for people with rheumatoid arthritis, cognitive reframing predicted reduced pain. This within-person finding that cognitive reframing predicts reduced pain provides more compelling evidence that coping influences pain than would a between-person finding. In contrast, a between person finding showing a relation between reframing and pain reduction would raise questions about the direction of causality; in particular, reduced pain could be allowing sufficient relaxation to enable cognitive reframing or instead the reframing could be causing the pain reduction. The within-person effect, however, provides stronger evidence that reframing causes pain reduction. Sometimes, the within-person analyses produce different results than the between-person analyses. For example, in a study of alcohol use, Shroder and Perrine (2004) reported, based on a two-year daily diary study that across persons, women with higher stress levels tended to drink more than other women. The opposite was true for men. Within-persons, however, both men and women tended to drink less during periods of increased stress. The within-person findings address different questions than the between-person findings, and one could argue that the within-person analyses are more relevant to the transactional perspective (i.e., an assumption that stress involves an ongoing negotiation between the individual and their environment) than are the cross-sectional between-person analyses.

Newth and DeLongis (2004) used traditional paper and pencil questionnaires for their daily diaries. Likewise, Valiente et al. (2004) asked parents to complete a pencil and paper daily diary for 14 days. For each day, parents were asked to describe the most stress-ful experience their child had encountered in the prior 24 hours, rate the stressfulness of the event, and check off the item best describing how their child coped. Compliance can be problematic especially in diary studies. To encourage compliance, research assistants can call participants weekly or on some other regular basis to remind them that their information is required and is valued (e.g., Todd et al., 2004).

One concern could be that participants might neglect to complete the daily diary for a number of days, and then use retrospective recall to fill in information for those inter-vening days. Todd et al. (2004) sought to overcome this problem by asking participants to complete the measures each evening and then post the envelope the next day. The post-mark date could then be checked to assure that the daily diary had been completed on time. In a study we are currently conducting (Holtzman and DeLongis, 2004), we are col-lecting thrice daily brief telephone interviews to track stress, coping, and social support across time. Still others (Perrine et al., 1995) have used automated telephone answering systems to collect and time-stamp data. And of course, there is always the collection of data via the internet to allow time-stamping (e.g., Lee-Baggley, DeLongis, Voorhoeve, and Greenglass, 2004).

Stone and Shiffman (1994) have helped pioneer the use of ecological momentary assessment (EMA) in order to reduce the role of reconstructive memory in self-reports. In EMA, participants are prompted by a beeper at various times through the day and imme-diately complete a self-report using either a palm-type device or pencil and paper. Stone et al. (1998; see also Litt et al., 2004) used handheld computers which offer the advantage of recording the time of all entries, thereby making it impossible for participants to pro-crastinate until the end of the study and then retrospectively fill in the supposedly momen-tary reports of coping.

Momentary coping assessments are not, however, a panacea. Coyne and Gottlieb (1996) suggest that asking participants to consider a very recent event may cause some participants to choose relatively nonstressful events, thus making the findings potentially less useful. Allowing participants a longer retrospective period may allow them all to draw on a truly stressful event and may improve cooperativeness. Also, Holtzman, Newth, and DeLongis (2004) discuss the onerous requirements of momentary analysis and suggest that these requirements, especially when coupled with the often necessarily high pay for compliance may lead to poorer data because the financially motivated respondents may not respond conscientiously. We expect that continued use of retro-spective coping assessments will be necessary for a complete picture of similarities and differences across cultures.

5.7. Automatic or Habitual Coping

Automatic coping is inherently difficult to assess because the responses often occur without the respondent's awareness. Respondents may be unaware, for example, that they are engaging in repression. Some measures of automatic responses have been developed and some interesting findings have emerged. Repression, for example, seems to have mal-adaptive effects (e.g., Burns, 2000; McKenna et al., 1999). Also, Edith Chen's work exam-ining children coping with asthma from a variety of socioeconomic backgrounds is one useful approach that could be applied meaningfully to the cross-cultural domain (e.g.,

Chen et al., 2003). Chen uses an experimental paradigm in which she provides vignettes to children and asks them about their cognitive appraisals of these situations. Thus, some guidance based on past research is available. Nonetheless measuring automatic responses will continue to be challenging and will require creativity on the part of researchers.

5.8. Brevity and Vagueness of Coping Items

Brevity of coping items can lead to misunderstanding, but coping items are brief for good reason. Long items will try the patience and reading comprehension of respondents. As suggested above, the use of pilot studies with debriefing afterward will help clarify which items are misunderstood or interpreted in a variety of ways by respondents, and these items can be revised. Further, if scales are adapted specifically to be used within a given population coping with a specific stressor, then such problems can be minimized. For example, measures have been developed to tap the use of problem-focused coping (e.g., medication usage; activity limitation) with chronic pain (e.g., Jensen et al., 1995). Even relatively brief items can have a specific meaning if they are written with a particular context and group of people in mind. Coyne and Gottlieb (1996) argue that participants will choose to respond to different types of stressful events, and thus the coping strategies they endorse will have very different meanings within those contexts. Given this, it may be particularly important in cross-cultural work to identify samples coping with similar life stressors. For example, one could limit participants within a particular study to rheumatoid arthritis (RA) patients, and ask them to endorse strategies used within a given (brief) time-frame to cope with the pain caused by their disease. In doing so, one has the ability to compare persons coping with very similar stressors (pain due to RA) on a number of dimensions (c.f., Holtzman, Newth, and DeLongis, 2004).

5.9. One Shot-Administrations

One-shot administrations of coping scales are not without value in cross-cultural research, but the daily diaries and momentary assessment techniques described above provide an opportunity to go beyond one-shot administrations to conduct longitudinal within-person analyses. These longitudinal methods in some ways are more relevant to the transactional model of stress and coping (Coyne and Gottlieb, 1996), can provide more compelling evidence that coping influences outcome, and may provide better answers of which coping strategies at which point in the coping process predict positive life outcomes.

5.10. Nonrepresentative Samples

Research samples are rarely perfectly representative of the population of interest, but creative data collection techniques can improve representativeness. An increasing proportion of studies are being conducted online. In the not too distant past, online data collection required significant technical acumen, but more recently, web hosting agencies such as Surveymonkey and others allow even near technical illiterates to conduct online research. The use of online data collection can enable more work to be conducted with individuals who are not near a university or who are even in a different country. Further, they can allow quick and timely assessment of geographically distributed crises such as 9/11 (Silver, 2004) and the SARS epidemic (Lee-Baggley et al., 2004).

5.11. Misguided Reliance on Statistical Controls

If we are to further our understanding of the role of culture in coping, it is going to have to be by examining coping across and within diverse cultural groups and making explicit comparisons, rather than by trying to eliminate the differences with statistical controls.

One naturalistic approach, is to use multilevel modeling (Raudenbush et al., 2001; Snijders and Bosker, 1999) to nest participants within their cultural group. In this way, one can examine the effect of culture on stress and coping processes, and can also use the person as his or her own control to examine within person changes in stress, coping and outcomes across time. There are a number of distinct advantages to the use of multilevel models to analyze this type of data (DeLongis and Preece, in press). First, simpler methods, such as ordinary least squares regression analysis, do not take into account the grouping of participants within cultural groups, and therefore the models are misspecified and the results unreliable. A second advantage of multilevel models is that the observed variance is decomposed into variance due to differences between persons and variance due to differences between families so that explanatory variables can be modeled separately. A third advantage is that this method of analysis considers variance in the slopes separately from variance at either level.

This type of analysis is also useful for the examination of daily diary data (DeLongis, Hemphill, and Lehman, 1992). Our approach is to consider days as nested within individuals (e.g., DeLongis, Capreol, Holtzman, O'Brien, and Campbell, 2004; Preece and DeLongis, in press). In turn, these individuals can be nested within the larger cultural groups. When complex data are aggregated, relations between macro-levels cannot be used to make assertions about micro-level relations. However, multilevel analyses allow examination of micro-level relations, as well as how these micro-level relations varied depending upon macro-level variables. That is, we can examine not only how changes in coping across time are associated with changes in mood, health or other outcomes of interest, but also how such relationships vary across cultural groups.

6. CONCLUSION

These strategies suggested above cannot solve all the problems associated with the use of rating scales in cross-cultural research on coping, but can help to increase the validity of these methods. No method of research is perfect. Rating scale data will continue to be sometimes difficult to interpret, but nonetheless, by employing some of these strategies, rating scale data can begin to improve the available portrait of ways in which coping is similar and different across cultures.

Some of the most challenging, but important strategies relate to building scales sensitive to coping strategies particularly common outside of North America. Some researchers have sought to diversify the nature of coping strategies receiving attention (e.g., Wong and Ujimoto, 1998) and these efforts are to be applauded. Future research collaborations across cultural groups may be especially helpful in highlighting previously ignored coping constructs. These collaborations can draw from the knowledge of multiple cultural groups to increase the likelihood that coping models specify culturally appropriate constructs.

REFERENCES

Berry, J. W. (1989). Imposed etics-emics-derived etics: The operationalization of a compelling idea. *International Journal of Psychology* 24: 721-735

Brislin, R. W. (1970). Back-translation for cross-cultural research. *Journal of Cross-Cultural Psychology* 1: 185-216.

Burns, J. W. (2000). Repression predicts outcome following multidisciplinary treatment of chronic pain. *Health Psychology* 19: 75-84.

Cameron, R. P., Tabak, M., Fuentes, A. J., Lynch, A., Abrishami, G., Meyers, L. S., and Wagner, L. S. (2004). *Toward a measure of indirect coping strategies.* Paper presented at the 112th Annual Convention of the American Psychological Association, Honolulu, Hawaii, July 29-August 1, 2004.

Carver, C. S., Scheier, M. F., and Weintraub, J. K. (1989). Assessing coping strategies: A theoretically based approach. *Journal of Personality and Social Psychology* 56: 267-283.

Chen, C., Lee, S. -Y. and Stevenson, H. W. (1995). Response style and cross-cultural comparisons of rating scales among East Asian and North American students. *Psychological Science* 6: 170-175.

Chen, E., Fisher, E. B., and Bacharier, L. B. (2003). Socioeconomic status, stress, and immune markers in adolescents with asthma. *Psychosomatic Medicine* 65: 984-992.

Cheung, F. M., Leung, K., Zhang, J. X., Sun, H. F., Gan, Y. Q., Song, W. Z. and Xie, D. (2001). Indigenous Chinese personality constructs: Is the Five Factor Model complete? *Journal of Cross-Cultural Psychology* 32: 407-433.

Cheung, F. M., Cheung, S. F., Wada, S., and Zhang, J. X. (2003). Indigenous measures of personality in Asian countries: A review. *Psychological Assessment* 15: 280-289.

Chinese Culture Connection (1987). Chinese values and the search for culture-free dimensions of culture. *Journal of Cross-Cultural Psychology* 18: 143-164.

Costa, P. T. and McCrae, R. R. (1992). *Revised NEO Personality Inventory (NEO-PI-R) and NEO Five-Factor Inventory (NEO-FFI) professional manual.* Psychological Assessment Resources, Odessa, FL.

Coyne, J. C., and Gottlieb, B. H. (1996). The mismeasure of coping by checklist. *Journal of Personality* 64: 959-991.

DeLongis, A., Capreol, M., Holtzman, S., O'Brien, T. B., and Campbell, J. (2004). Social support and social strain among husbands and wives: A multilevel analysis, *Journal of Family Psychology* 18: 470-479.

DeLongis, A., and Holtzman, S. (in press, to appear in Dec 2005). Coping in Context: The role of personality and social relationships. *Journal of Personality. Special issue on daily process methodology.*

DeLongis, A., Hemphill, K. J., and Lehman, D. R. (1992). *A structured diary method for the study of daily events.* In: Bryant, F. B. and Edwards, J. (eds.), Methodological issues in applied social psychology (pp. 83-109). Plenum Press, New York.

Endler, M. B., and Parker, J. D. A. (2000). Coping with Health Injuries and Problems (CHIP) manual. Multi-Health Systems, Toronto, Canada.

Fisher, R. (2004). Standardization to account for cross-cultural response bias. *Journal of Cross-Cultural Psychology* 35: 263-282.

Folkman, S., Lazarus, R. S., Dunkel-Schetter, C., DeLongis, A., and Gruen, R. J. (1986a). Dynamics of a stressful encounter: Cognitive appraisal, coping, and encounter outcomes. *Journal of Personality and Social Psychology* 50: 992-1003.

Folkman, S., Lazarus, R. S., Gruen, R., and DeLongis, A. (1986b). Appraisal, coping, health status, and psychological symptoms. *Journal of Personality and Social Psychology* 50: 571-579.

Freeman, D. (1999). *The fateful hoaxing of Margaret Mead: A historical analysis of her Samoan research.* Westview, Boulder, CO.

Geertz, C. (1973). *The interpretation of cultures.* Basic Books, New York.

Halamandaris, K. F., and Power, K. G. (1999). Individual differences, social support and coping with the examination stress: A study of the psychosocial and academic adjustment of first year home students. *Personality and Individual Differences* 26: 665-685.

Heine, S. H., Lehman, D. R., and Markus, H. R. (1999). Is there a universal need for positive self-regard? *Psychological Review* 106: 766-794.

Heine, S. J., Lehman, D. R., Peng, K. P., and Grennholtz, J. (2002). What's wrong with cross-cultural comparisons of subjective Likert scales? The reference-group effect. *Journal of Personality and Social Psychology* 82: 903-918 .

Hofstede, G. H. (1980). *Culture's consequences: International differences in work-related values.* Sage Publications, Beverly Hills, CA.

Holtzman, S., Newth, S., and DeLongis, A. (2004). The role of social support in coping with daily pain among patients with Rheumatoid Arthritis. *Journal of Health Psychology* 9: 677-695.

Jensen, M. P., Turner, J. A., Romano, J. M. (1995). The Chronic Pain Coping Inventory: Development and preliminary validation. *Pain* 60: 203-216.

Lao-Tzu (1989). *Te-Tao Ching* (R. G. Henricks, trans.). Ballantine Books, New York (Original work published c.a. 400 BCE).

Lazarus, R. S., and DeLongis, A. (1983). Psychological stress and coping in aging. *American Psychologist* 38: 245-254.

Lee-Baggley, D., DeLongis, A., Voorhoeve, P. and Greenglass, E. (2004). Coping with the threat of Severe Acute Respiratory Syndrome: Role of threat appraisals and coping responses in health behaviors . *Asian Journal of Social Psychology: Special issue on Severe Acute Respiratory Syndrome* 7: 9-23.

Lebra, T. S. (1984). *Nonconfrontational strategies for management of interpersonal conflicts.* In: Kraus, E. S., Rohlen, T. P., and Steinhoff, P. G. (eds), Conflict in Japan (pp. 41-60). University of Hawaii Press, Honolulu HI.

Litt, M. D., Shafer, D., and Napolitano, C. (2004). Momentary mood and *coping* processes in TMD pain. *Health Psychology* 23: 354-362.

Lyons, R. F., Mickelson, K., Sullivan, M. J. L., and Coyne, J. C. (1998). Coping as a communal process. *Journal of Social and Personal Relationships* 15: 579-605.

McFarland, C., and Buehler, R. (1997). Negative affective states and the motivated retrieval of positive life events: The role of affect acknowledgement. *Journal of Personality and Social Psychology* 73: 200-214.

McFarland, C., and Ross, M. (1987). The relation between current impressions and memories of self and dating partners. *Personality and Social Psychology Bulletin* 13: 228-238.

McFarland, C., Ross, M., and Giltrow, M. (1992). Biased recollections in older adults: The role of implicit theories of aging. *Journal of Personality and Social Psychology* 62: 837-850.

McKenna, M. C., Zevon, M. A., Corn, B., and Rounds, J. (1999). Psychosocial factors and the development of breast cancer: A meta-analysis. *Health Psychology* 18: 520-531.

Markus, H. R., and Kitayama, S. (1991). Culture and the self: Implications for cognition, emotion, and motivation. *Psychological Review* 98: 224-253.

Mead, M. (1928). *Coming of age in Samoa: A psychological study of primitive youth for Western civilization.* Blue Ribbon Books, New York.

Miller, J. G. (1994). Cultural diversity in the morality of caring: Individually oriented versus duty-based interpersonal moral codes. *Cross-Cultural Research: The Journal of Comparative Social Science* 28: 3-39.

Newth, S., and DeLongis, A. (2004). Individual differences, mood and coping with chronic pain in rheumatoid arthritis: A daily process analysis. *Psychology and Health* 19: 283-305.

O'Brien, T. B., and DeLongis, A. (1996). The interactional context of problem-, emotion-, and relationship-focused coping: The role of the big five personality factors. *Journal of Personality* 64: 775-813.

Ozeki, Y., Haraguchi, M., and Tsuda, A (1994). A covariance structural analysis of psychological processes in university students. *Japanese Journal of Health Psychology* 8: 20-36.

Paulhus, D. L. (1984). Two-component models of socially desirable responding. *Journal of Personality and Social Psychology* 46: 598-609.

Peacock, E. J., and Wong, P. T. P. (1996). Anticipatory stress: The relation of locus of control, optimism, and control appraisals to coping. *Journal of Research in Personality* 30: 204-222.

Peng, K., Nisbett, R. E. and Wong, N. Y. C. (1997). Validity problems comparing values across cultures and possible solutions. *Psychological Methods* 2: 329-344.

Perrine, M. W., Mundt, J. C., Searles, J. S., and Lester, L. S. (1995). Validation of daily self-reported alcohol consumption using interactive voice response (IVR) technology. *Journal of Studies on Alcohol* 56: 487-490.

Preece, M., and DeLongis, A. (in press). *A contextual examination of stress and coping processes in stepfamilies.* In: Revensen, T. A. R., and Kayser, K. (eds.), Coping among couples. American Psychological Association Press, Washington, DC.

Ptacek, J. T., Smith, R. E., Espe, K., and Raffety, B. (1994). Limited correspondence between daily coping reports and retrospective coping recall. Psychological Assessment 6: 41-49.

Raudenbush, S.W., Bryk, A.S., Cheong, Y.F., and Congdon, R.T. (2001). *HLM5 Hierarchical linear and non-linear modeling*. Scientific Software International, Chicago, IL.

Romano, J. M., Jensen, M. P., Turner, J. A., (2003). The Chronic Pain Coping Inventory-42: Reliability and validity. *Pain* 104: 65-73.

Schroder, K. E. E., and Perrine, M. W. B. (2004). *Patterns of mood and alcohol consumption in two-year daily self-reports*. Paper presented at the 112th Annual Convention of the American Psychological Association, Honolulu, Hawaii, July 29-August 1, 2004.

Shweder, R. A. (1993). Cultural psychology: Who needs it? *Annual Review of Psychology* 44: 497-424.

Silver, R. C. (2004). Conducting research after the 9/11 terrorist attacks: Challenges and results. *Families, Systems, and Health* 22: 47-51.

Snijders, T. A. B., and Bosker, R. J. (1999). *Multilevel analysis: An introduction to basic and advanced multilevel modeling*. Sage Publishers, London.

Somerfield, M. R., and McCrae, R. R. (2000). Stress and coping research: Methodological challenges, theoretical advances, and clinical applications. *American Psychologist* 55: 620-625.

Stone, A. A., Schwartz, J. E., Neale, J. M., Shiffman, S., Marco, C. A., Hickcox, M., Paty, J., Porter, L. S., and Cruise, L. J. (1998). A comparison of coping assessed by ecological momentary assessment and retrospective recall. *Journal of Personality and Social Psychology* 74: 1670-1680.

Stone, A. and Shiffman, S. (1994). Ecological momentary assessment (EMA) in behavioral medicine. *Annals of Behavioral Medicine* 16: 199-202.

Tennen, H., Affleck, G., and Armeli, S. (2000). A daily process approach to coping: Linking theory, research, and practice. *American Psychologist* 55: 626-636.

Todd, M., Tennen, H., Carney, M. A., Armeli, S., and Affleck, G. (2004). Do we know how we cope? Relating daily coping reports to global and time-limited retrospective assessments. *Health Psychology* 86: 310-319.

Triandis, H. C. (1996). The psychological measurement of cultural syndromes. *American Psychologist* 51: 407-415.

Tweed, R. G., Conway, L. G. III, Ryder, A. G. (1999). The target is straw or the arrow is crooked. *American Psychologist* 54: 837-838.

Tweed, R. G., White, K., and Lehman, D. R. (2004). Culture, stress, and coping: internally- and externally-targeted control strategies of European-Canadians, East Asian-Canadians, and Japanese. *Journal of Cross-Cultural Psychology 35*: 652-658.

Tweed, R. G., Conway, L. G., Ryder, A. G., and Lehman, D. R. (2004). *Ipsatization: Reducing measurement error in cross-cultural research*. Unpublished manuscript.

Valiente, C., Fabes, R. A., Eisenberg, N., and Spinrad, T. L. (2004). The relations of parental expressivity and support to children's coping with daily stress. *Journal of Family Psychology* 18: 97-106.

Vitaliano, P. P., DeWolfe, D. J., Maiuro, R. D., Russo, J., and Katon, W. (1990). Appraised changeability of a stressor as a modifier of the relationship between coping and depression: A test of the hypothesis of fit. *Journal of Personality and Social Psychology* 59: 582-592.

Wong, P. T. P. (1993). Effective management of life stress: The resource-congruence model. *Stress Medicine* 9: 51-60.

Wong, P. T. P., and Ujimoto, K V. (1998). The elderly: Their stress, coping, and mental health. In: Lee, L. E, and Zane, N. W. S. (eds.), *Handbook of Asian American psychology*. Sage Publications, Thousand Oaks, CA.

Wong, P. T. P., and Watt, L. M. (1991). What types of reminiscence are associated with successful aging? *Psychology and Aging* 6: 151-158.

Yeh, C. and Inose, M. (2002). Difficulties and coping strategies of Chinese, Japanese, and Korean immigrant students. *Adolescence* 37: 69-82.

Zhang, J. X. and Bond, M. H. (1998). Personality and filial piety among college students in two Chinese societies: The added value of indigenous constructs. *Journal of Cross-Cultural Psychology* 29: 402-417.

11

A RESOURCE-CONGRUENCE MODEL OF COPING AND THE DEVELOPMENT OF THE COPING SCHEMAS INVENTORY

Paul T. P. Wong, Gary T. Reker, and Edward J. Peacock

1. INTRODUCTION

For most people, living is a fulltime occupation, which exacts a great deal of effort and energy. At times, life can also be a risky business, with hidden traps and lightning strikes. Considering the manifold sources of stress in modern life that cover the whole gamut from traumatic events, interpersonal conflicts, situational obstacles, existential crises to everyday hassles, one wonders why more people have not succumbed to stress-related disorders, and why so many people are still able to transcend their difficulties and lead a healthy, fulfilling life.

The key to answering these questions is *coping*. The ability to cope is essential to surviving and thriving in a rapidly changing and highly competitive global village. That is one of the reasons why coping has become a key concept in psychology and health disciplines. This chapter is all about the art and science of coping as a major part of the larger story of human adaptation and survival (Wong, Wong, & Scott, Chapter 1). The art aspect draws from human experiences and theoretical speculations, while the science part draws from empirical studies.

Even to a casual observer of people, there are vast individual differences in how we react to life stress. While some are vulnerable and become easily overwhelmed by stress, others are very resilient and made even stronger by their stress-encounters. Why do similar misfortunes lead one person to distress and another person to success? What accounts for these differential effects of stress? What are the mediating variables? What are the most effective ways to cope with life's demand? Should we **approach** it as a problem to be solved **or avoid** it as an unsolvable problem? Alternatively, should we simply **embrace** life in its totality as a mystery to be appreciated?

After more than 10,000 research articles, we still do not have a clear roadmap to help us journey through life's obstacle course. In this chapter, we review what has been accomplished in coping research, present our own thinking and research findings, and then

Paul T. P. Wong, Trinity Western University; Gary T. Reker, Trent University; Edward J. Peacock, Correctional Service of Canada propose future research directions in a world that is increasingly multicultural. Coping after all is a universal human drama. How can we gain a deeper understanding without a broader lens?

1.1. A historical overview

Just as we need to know what the stressors are, so we need to know what kinds of coping strategies are at our disposal. This chapter is primarily concerned with psychological rather than physiological and genetic coping mechanisms.

Sir Walter Cannon's (1936) landmark research on emotional stress led to his discovery not only of physiological arousal reactions to signals of danger, but also the instinctive fight-and-flight coping patterns. Cannon considered stress and its "emergency response" as vitally important to survival and adaptation. However, it was not until Selye (1976) that research on stress and coping was introduced to the larger scientific community as well as the public arena.

The psychoanalytical literature is another rich source on coping responses, which are largely unconscious. S. Freud's (1894/1962) psychoanalytical formulations of defence mechanisms were primarily concerned with unconscious mechanisms to protect the ego against neurotic anxiety. Haan (1977) and Vaillant (1977) have continued this analytical tradition in their research on coping and defence.

The next major development focuses on traits/styles of coping. Various scales have been developed to measure individual differences such as repressors vs. sensitizers (Byrne, 1971), screeners vs. nonscreeners (Baum, Calesnick, Davis, & Gatchel, 1982), monitors vs. blunters (Miller, 1979), and Type A vs. Type B individuals (Glass, 1977). More recent research favoring the trait approach includes McCrae's (1982) personality-based coping, Epstein and Meier's (1989) constructive thinking, and Carver, Scheier & Weintraub's (1989) dispositional coping styles.

However, both the psychoanalytic and trait approaches have been criticised for failing to capture the complexity of coping and for their inability to predict coping behaviors, in specific situations. Lazarus and Folkman's (1984) seminal publication continues to dominate the field because of its emphasis on identification of functional categories of specific coping behaviors to deal with specific situations. Folkman (1984) provides a comprehensive definition of stress and coping:

> "The cognitive theory of stress and coping on which this discussion is based is relational and process oriented. The relational characteristic is evident in the definition of stress as a relationship between the person and the environment that is appraised by the person as taxing or exceeding his or her resources and as endangering his or her well-being. Coping refers to cognitive and behavioral efforts to master, reduce, or tolerate the internal and/or external demands that are created by the stressful transaction" (p. 840).

The impact of the cognitive-relational approach was greatly enhanced by the development of The Ways of Coping Questionnaire (Folkman & Lazarus, 1980), which was designed to measure two functionally different broad coping categories. Problem-focused coping consists of various learned instrumental strategies while emotion-focused coping includes some of Freud's (1936) defence mechanisms and other types of cognitive strategies.

Wong (1993) in his discussion of the evolution of coping has emphasized the following coping strategies as being important for future research: creative, proactive, collective, existential, and spiritual coping. Various chapters in this volume attest to the gradual inclusion of these additional coping categories in the literature.

1.2. Lack of progress in stress and coping research

Several contributors in this volume have bemoaned the lack of progress in stress and coping research (Chapters 1, 2, 3, 4, 7, and 8). One frequent complaint is the ethnocentric bias in stress and coping research. Related to this bias is the undisputed hegemony of the cognitive-relational approach; somehow researchers, including the present authors have difficulty going beyond this conceptual framework.

Recent reviews of the coping literature indicate very little cross-cultural research on stress and coping (Folkman & Moscowitz, 2000; Snyder, 1999a; Chapters 1 and 2). Given the importance of the sociocultural context in shaping every aspect of the stress and coping process, the next major step in the psychology of effective coping needs to seriously consider culture-related variables.

1.3. The need for a comprehensive measure of coping

Several researchers have suggested that research in this area has been hindered by the lack of valid and comprehensive coping measures (Parker & Endler, 1992, 1996; Fleming, Baum, & Singer, 1984). For example, Amirkhan (1990) has criticised that most studies focus on specific coping strategies related to specific life situations rather than "more universal modes of response" (p. 1066). We wonder whether the "more universal modes of response" can be discovered without cross-cultural studies.

Folkman and Lazarus (1981) have long pointed out the need for developing a comprehensive and general taxonomy of coping without sacificing the richness of specific cognitive and behavioral coping strategies. However, without some consensus regarding a comprehensive taxonomy, progress in both research and applicatioins will remain difficult.

1.4. The need for a comprehensive theory of coping

The lack of an integrative and comprehensive coping theory has also been cited as a hindrance to progress. Parker and Endler (1992) point out the need for "the development of a systematic understanding of the empirical and theoretical relationships among coping behaviors and both mental and physical health" (p. 339). Similarly, Carver, Scheier, and Weintraub (1989) argue for a more theoretical approach to scale development in order to achieve a more systematic understanding of the stress-coping process. Litt (1988) emphasizes the need to more clearly differentiate the various components in the stress process.

Ideally, a comprehensive theory needs to accomplish at least three goals: (a) Take into account the major stressors in life and most commonly employed coping strategies,

(b) Specify the stress process and the relationships between different variables, and
(c) Illuminate both the conditions and mechanisms of effective coping.

1.5. The need for innovative approaches

Clearly, innovative approaches are needed. First of all, we need to learn a great deal more about coping from various countries. The fact that China has survived more than 5000 thousand years of tumultuous times means that the Chinese must have learned a great deal about coping. The top-down arm-chaired approach to developing theories and measures of coping, a preferred way of many researchers in North America, will not capture the real coping strategies people use in surviving wide-spread famines, chronic poverty, prolonged civil wars, catastrophic natural disasters or genocides like the Holocaust and the Nanjing massacre.

The implicit theories approach (Wong, 1998a) provides a bottom-up view and seems particularly suitable for cross-cultural research. Similarly, field research by indigenous psychologists in different countries can also expand our knowledge of coping. There is so much we can learn from those who have survived adversities that is unthinkable to psychologists in ivory towers.

Historical and archival records can be a goldmine to study how people coped with and survived major events, such as natural disasters, plagues, national tragedies, and personal traumas, in past centuries and foreign cultures. These studies can shed some light on the timeless and universal nature of the fundamental principles of coping.

Another innovative approach is to conceptualize the coping process in terms of complex patterns of reactions, which may include seemingly contradictory coping responses. For example, to ensure success in applying for a job, one may choose to depend on one's own track record and interview skills, but at the same time pray to God for help as well as ask some influential persons to pull some strings.

Wong and Sproule (1983) have argued that internal and external control can co-exist. Similarly, Wong and McDonald (2002) have pointed out that many lives hang in the balance between despair and hope; they provide a strong case for the co-existence between realistic pessimism and idealistic optimism as a necessary condition for individuals to survive trauma. Carver and Scheier (1999) report that optimists tended to accept the reality of negative events, but also tried to see something positive in a bad situation. Folkman (1997) in a longitudinal study of the care-giving partners of men with AIDS found the co-occurrence of both positive and negative psychological states during the difficult circumstances of caring and grieving. These ideas have important implications for understanding the complex internal dynamics in the coping process.

2. COPING MEASURES BASED ON DEDUCTIVE TAXONOMIES

Existing measures are either based on an empirical (deductive) or rational (inductive) approach. Sometimes, test development employs both deductive and inductive methodologies. We will evaluate the strengths and weaknesses of each approach before reviewing major coping measures.

2.1. Advantages of the deductive approach

The deductive approach is very appealing, not only because the broad theoretical categories are conceptually clear, but also because they are derived from a theory or conceptual framework. Another advantage is that deductive taxonomies have achieved some level of generality, and can be applied to many stressful situations. As a result, they are more likely to be employed in research, either to test the theory or validate the coping measure.

The best known deductive taxonomy is problem-focused vs. emotion-focused coping (Folkman & Lazarus, 1980), which makes intuitive sense, and has been incorporated into most coping measures. Another widely accepted deductive taxonomy is approach vs. avoidance (Roth & Cohen, 1986), which parallels the natural instinctive fight-flight tendencies; this too has been incorporated into many coping measures (e.g., Billings & Moos, 1984; Endler & Parker, 1990a,b; Moos & Billlings, 1982).

2.2. Limitations of the deductive approach

The most common problem is that theoretically generated items do not always belong to a priori conceptual categories. For example, the distinction between problem-focused coping and emotion-focused coping is not as simple as it seems. Wong and Reker (1983) found that judges often failed to agree whether a particular item was problem- or emotion-focused. Furthermore, there were differences between age-groups – the older one gets, the more likely one considers emotion-focused items as problem-focused, perhaps, to increase one's sense of control. Thus, deductive categories often fail to survive the empirical validation process (Amirkhan, 1990).

A related problem is that coping categories may lack conceptual clarity, because they may include items that logically do not belong together. For example, in one study (Folkman, Lazarus, Gruen, & DeLongis, 1986), an item relating to prayer was loaded on a factor labeled positive reappraisal along with items dealing with personal change and doing something creative. Another major problem is that a priori categories are often too broad or too vague to be relevant to specific stressful situations, let alone to predict coping behaviors. Finally, the coping categories measured are limited by both the theory and the coping items generated by the theory. As a result, coping strategies essential for survival are often omitted in deductive measures.

3. COPING MEASURES BASED ON INDUCTIVE TAXONOMIES

Inductive taxonomies can be based on factor analysis of actual coping behaviors reported or observed in specific situations. As such, they seem to provide a more accurate picture of how individuals actually cope with specific situations.

However, in some cases, inductive taxonomies are based on factor analyses of items pooled from several existing coping scales (Amirkhan, 1990; Endler & Parker, 1990a,b). The resulting taxonomies tend to have more adequate psychometric properties than the original measures. For example, Endler & Parker's (1990a,b) multidimensional model has been cross-validated on different populations.

3.1. Advantages of the inductive approach

Inductive taxonomies tend to contain more coping categories and are more predictive of coping in specific situations. "Inductive taxonomies have usually proven more exhaustive than deductive ones, containing a greater number and variety of categories" (Amirkhan, 1990, p. 1066).

When the coping measure is based on factor analysis of items from several measures, the resulting factors tend to be more stable and internally reliable. Therefore, it tends to show greater factorial invariance across samples (Endler & Parker, 1990a,b).

3.2. Limitations of the inductive approach

There are also limitations inherent in inductive taxonomies. When the measure is based on factorial analysis of actually coping behaviors, the resulting coping categories tend to lack generality. In other words, coping measures derived from factor analysis of a specific sample in a specific stressor may not be generalized to other samples and different stressors. Factor analysis of the same coping measure used in different stressful situations tends to to yield different results (Amirkhan, 1990).

When inductive taxonomies are based on factor analysis of items from existing scales, naturally they tend to report similar factors (e.g., Amirkhan, 1990; Endler & Parker, 1990a,b). Consequently, coping research tends to focus on the same old coping categories, and continues to ignore other coping strategies, such as relaxation or existential coping.

The most common criticism of factor analysis is that the number of factors identified is dependent on the number and nature of the items. With few exceptions, the initial item pool usually failed to include a broad range of different types of coping, thus, resulting in only a few coping categories. However, if large number of items is used, it tends to require a much larger sample size and yield a large number of factors. For example, McCrae (1984) factor analysed 118 items and obtained 28 coping factors; some of the factors were not very meaningful or reliable, because they only contained one or two items.

There is also a measurement problem with the inductive approach based on factor analytical procedures. "Because these procedures generate scales based on statistical rather than conceptual criteria, they are unlikely to yield adequate measures of the intended theoretical constructs" (Edwards & Baglioni, 1993, p. 28).

Finally, empirically derived scales tend to be linked to "theoretical principles only somewhat loosely and post hoc" (Carver, Scheier & Weintraub, 1989, p. 268). Therefore, it is difficult to use empirically derived measures to determine how coping is related to other constructs, such as appraisal and outcome variables as specified by any general theories of coping.

4. A CRITICAL REVIEW OF EXISTING COPING SCALES

Recently, a number of papers have criticised existing coping scales (e.g., Carver, Scheier & Weintraub, 1989; Coyne & Gottlieb, 1996; Endler & Parker, 1990a,b; Parker & Endler, 1992; Stone & Neale, 1984).

The common critiques include weak psychometric properties, lack of empirical validation, unstable factorial structures, unrepresentative samples, inadequate links to theories, and the difficulty of generalizing from one stressful situation to another. We now review some of the more specific critiques directed to a few widely used coping scales.

4.1. Folkman and Lazarus' Ways of Coping Questionnaire (WCQ)

The WCQ (Folkman & Lazarus, 1980, 1985, 1988) is by far the most widely used coping measure. The current version consists of 66 items. Because of its popularity, the WCQ has also been subjected to the most scrutiny. Parker and Endler (1992) comment: "The continued use of scales, such as the WCQ, appears to be more a matter of convenience than anything else" (p. 336).

Parker and Endler (1992) have identified a number of psychometric weaknesses of the WCQ. First of all, the WCQ often yields different number of factors, depending on the sample. Factor analyses of the WCQ have resulted in anywhere between five to eight categories rather than two broad categories (Aldwin & Revenson, 1987; Folkman & Lazarus, 1985; Folkman, et al., 1986; Vitaliano, Russo, & Maiuro, 1985).

Secondly, the absence of test-retest reliability in the WCQ manual remains problematic, notwithstanding Folkman and Lazarus' (1985) claim that temporal stability is irrelevant because coping is a process which changes over time. Parker and Endler also question the practice by researchers of frequently adding or dropping coping items from the WCQ, and even thought such practice was actually encouraged by Folkman and Lazarus (1988). This lack of standardization makes it difficult to compare results from different studies employing different versions of the WCQ. Their overall assessment is as follows:

"Ways of Coping measures are of considerable theoretical interest, and the authors have made important theoretical and empirical contributions to the coping area. However, their coping measures have probably been used more often than is justified by the psychometric properties of these scales" (p. 334).

Carver, Scheier and Weintraub (1989) also criticise that some of the coping items are conceptually ambiguous. For example, the item "Took a big chance or did something risky" might mean different things, such as reckless driving, or gambling. Furthermore, they point out that the broad categories of problem and emotion-focused coping may obscure coping responses which may be distinct from each other, and may have different implication for coping effectiveness. For example, denial and positive reinterpretation both are considered as emotion-focused coping, but they may have very different psychological functions. Similarly, taking direct action and seeking assistance are very different problem-solving activities; the former is likely to be used in situations perceived as manageable by oneself, while the latter is more likely to be needed when the situation is perceived as beyond one's control.

Another criticism, which is common to many existing scales, is the limited range of coping responses measured by the WCQ. Although these may reflect the coping experiences of the professors and graduate students who generated the initial pool of items (Folkman and Lazarus, 1980), they certainly do not reflect the life experiences of people living in a very different kind of world.

From our perspective, we think that the WCQ should be used to validate any new measure of coping, since a great deal of information is already available about its psychometric properties. However, researchers need to move beyond the WCQ to explore new ways of measuring new dimensions of coping. If we continue to stay within the comfort zone provided by Folkman and Lazarus, the field of stress and coping research will not move forward in any significant way.

4.2. Moos' Coping Response Inventory (CRI)

The CRI developed by Moos (1988, 1993) measures eight types of coping responses, each of which is measured by six items. These respondents select a recent (focal) stressor and rate their reliance on each of the 48 coping items on 4-point scales from *not at all* (0) to *fairly often* (3). The eight types of coping are: 1. Logical Analysis (LA), 2. Positive Reappraisal (PR), 3. Seeking Guidance and Support (SG), 4. Problem Solving (PS), 5. Cognitive Avoidance (CA), 6. Acceptance or Resignation (AR), 7. Seeking Alternative Rewards (SR), and 8. Emotional Discharge (ED).

These eight dimensions can be classified according to **approach vs. avoidance** orientations and **cognitive vs. behavioral** coping strategies. Approach coping is measured by the first four subscales; avoidance coping is measured by the second four subscales. Subscales 1, 2, 5, and 6 reflect cognitive coping strategies, while subscales 3, 4, 7, and 8 reflect behavioral coping strategies.

It has three parallel versions: Adult, Youth and Ideal. In the Ideal version of the CRI-Adult, the respondents are asked to indicate what they believe would be the best way to cope with the stressor. The Ideal version seems a good instrument to study individuals' implicit theories about what coping responses work best for what stressor.

According to Moos, the approach-avoidance classification has to do with the **orientation** or focus of coping, whereas cognitive or behavioral coping has to do with the **methods** or ways of coping. Approach coping is similar to problem-focused coping, while avoidance coping is similar to emotion-focused coping. Almost all the available coping measures focus on cognitive and behavioral coping strategies (Billings & Moos, 1984; Folkman & Lazarus, 1985; Roth & Cohen, 1986).

By combining approach vs. avoidance with cognitive vs. behavioral methods, Moos not only generates and expands the taxonomy of coping, but also brings greater conceptual clarity to the different coping responses. The CRI has been employed with a variety of populations, such as alcoholic patients, depressed and medical patients, work stress, aging, etc. Reliablility and validity for most of the subscales are good (Moos, 1988; 1993).

Our main criticism is that by forcing various coping responses within the confines of a classification system based on approach vs. avoiadance and cognitive vs. behavioral coping, Moos also has to restrict the interpretation and meaning of various coping responses. For example, "seeking alternative rewards" cannot be simply limited to "behavioral attempts to get involved in subsitute activites"; this coping strategy could also mean changing one's beliefs and values, which are more cognitive and spiritual than behavioral.

Similarly, "acceptance or resignation" cannot be limited to "cognitive attempts to react to the problem by accepting it", because it can also mean behavioral surrender to situational demands without giving up hope. Acceptance can also mean to operate within one's financial or situational constraints.

Many psychologists can not resist the seductive appeal of a 2 x 2 contingency table: it is simple and elegant, and the factorial combination can yield very interesting categories. However, they often have to arbitrarily restrict the rich meanings of the constructs in order to neatly fit them into the tiny 2 x 2 table.

4.3. Stone and Neal's Measure of Daily Coping

Initially, Stone & Neal (1984) intended to develop a checklist of coping responses for use in longitudinal studies with repeated assessments. Eventually they gave up attempts to develop a coping checklist based on rationally derived categories, because they were unable to obtain satisfactory internal consistency and inter-rater reliability. For example, in one of the studies reported, they asked participants to sort the checklist items into different categories, representing different types of coping. They discovered that often only a few items for a category were checked. Furthermore, subjects perceived the coping items differently; for example, there were several coping items that could be classified as belonging to either the relaxation or distraction category. Consequently, they chose to develop an open-ended questionnaire listing eight coping categories.

The open-ended assessment presents one-sentence descriptions of the eight different modes of coping strategies and asks them to check whether they "Did not use" or "Used" any of these coping responses in handling the problem or situation they have just described. Any "yes" response is followed by an open-ended question asking them to describe action(s) or thought(s). The eight coping strategies are described as follows:

Category	Description printed on the form
1. Distraction	Diverted attention away from the problem by thinking about other things or engaging in some activity.
2. Situation redefinition	Tried to see the problem in a different light that made it seem more bearable.
3. Direct Action	Thought about solutions to the problem, gathered information about it, or actually did something to try to solve it.
4. Catharsis	Expressed emotions in response to the problem to reduce tension, anxiety, or frustration.
5. Acceptance	Accepted that the problem had occurred, but that nothing could be done about it.
6. Seeking Social Support	Sought or found emotional support from loved ones, friends, or professionals.
7. Relaxation	Did something with the implicit intention of relaxing.
8. Religion	Sought or found spiritual comfort and support.

This brief questionnaire was administered to 120 married individuals for 21 consecutive days. Sex of respondents was associated with the type of coping. For example, females were more likely to use distraction, relaxation, catharsis, seeking social support and religion, while males were more likely to use direct action. The type of coping was also associated with the level of appraisal. For example, acceptance was more associated with "no control" appraisal than with "Quite a lot/complete control". Similarly, catharsis, seeking social support, relaxation, and religion tended to be associated with "severe" appraisals (i.e., extremely undesirable, extremely changing). A moderate amount of within-subject consistency in coping with the same problem over time was also observed.

This type of questionnaire seems useful not only in determining which coping categories are used most frequently, but also providing information about the specific actions and thoughts associated with the coping strategy employed. However, the lack of evidence of validity and reliability, and the difficulty of quantifying the open-ended responses may discourage researchers from using it for quantitative studies.

Overall, we find this measure of the coping process promising. A combination of quantitative and qualitative measures can provide a more complete picture of the dynamic process of coping in different individuals. Another good thing is that this approach has also renewed a debate regarding the merits of measuring situation-specific coping (Folkman, 1992; Tennen, Affleck, Armeli, & Carney, 2000).

4.4. Carver, Scheier and Weintraub' (1989) COPE

The COPE is based on a deductive rather than an inductive approach to test-construction. This coping measure was guided by Lazarus and Folkman's cognitive-relational model as well as their own model of behavioral self-regulation (Carver & Scheier, 1981, 1983, 1985; Scheier & Carver, 1988). Their self-regulatory process of coping (Carver & Scheier, 1999) came from a control-process perspective (Carver, Lawrence, & Scheier, 1996).

The instrument consisted of 13 conceptually distinct scales. Five scales were based on functionally distinct aspects of problem-focused coping (active coping, planning, suppression of competing activities, restraint coping, seeking of instrumental social support). Another five scales measured different aspects of what might be viewed as emotional-focused coping (seeking of emotional social support, positive reinterpretation, acceptance, denial, turning to religion). The remaining three scales measured coping responses that as they believed, are arguably less useful (focus on and venting of emotions, behavioral disengagement, mental disengagement).

The COPE is made up of the following scales:

1. *Active coping:* Taking action, exerting efforts, to remove or circumvent the stressor.
2. *Planning:* Thinking about how to confront the stressor, planning one's active coping efforts.
3. *Seeking Instrumental Social Support:* Seeking assistance, information, or advice about what to do.
4. *Seeking Emotional Social Support:* Getting sympathy or emotional support from someone.
5. *Suppression of Competing Activities:* Suppressing one's attention to other activities in which one might engage in order to concentrate more completely on dealing with the stressor.
6. *Religion:* Increased engagement in religious activities.
7. *Positive Reinterpretation and Growth:* Making the best of the situation by growing from it, or viewing it in a more favorable light.

8. *Restraint Coping:* Coping passively by holding back one's coping attempts until they can be of use.
9. *Acceptance:* Accepting the fact that the stressful event has occurred and is real.
10. *Focus on and Venting of Emotions:* An increased awareness of one's emotional distress, and a concomitant tendency to ventilate or discharge those feelings.
11. *Denial:* An attempt to reject the reality of the stressful event.
12. *Mental Disengagement:* Psychological disengagement *from the goal with which the stressor is interfering*, through daydreaming, sleep, or self-distraction.
13. *Behavioral Disengagement:* Giving up, or withdrawing effort from, the attempt to attain *the goal with which the stressor is interfering*.
14. [*Alcohol/Drug Use:* Turning to the use of alcohol or other drugs as a way of disengaging from the stressor.]
15. [*Humor:* Making jokes about the stressor.]

Although all social support items loaded on a single factor, they still believe that the theoretical distinction between instrumental social support and emotional support needs to be maintained. Similarly, Planning and Active Coping loaded on a single factor, but they saw some merit in treating them as separate scales because these two types of coping occupy different points in the temporal continuum of problem-focused coping. Two Scales, Alcohol/Drug Use and Humor were developed later and were not reported in the 1989 article.

Following the implicit logic of congruence, they predict that Scales 1, 2, 5, 7, and 8 would probably be adaptive in situations where active coping efforts yield good outcomes, while Scales 10, 11, and 12 would be maladaptive in such circumstances. However, they are less sure as to what coping responses would be adaptive in situations that are uncontrollable.

The scale items have been developed in three different formats: (a) a "trait" version in which respondents indicate the degree to which they typically do each of the things listed when under stress, (b) a time-limited version in which respondents indicate the degree to which they actually did use each of the coping strategies during a period in the past, and (c) a time-limited version in which respondents indicate the degree to which they have been using each of the strategies during a period up to the present.

The COPE has clearly expanded the coping taxonomy as compared to the WCQ. We find the categories indeed representative of functional coping strategies. We also agree that it is beneficial to take a more theoretical approach to scale construction. Our only reservation is that Carver and Scheier's (1999) model of self-regulation may restrict their view of the coping process. After all, life cannot be viewed simply as a series of behavioral regulations to attain various goals. For example, for those who are confined in the hospice or palliative care unit, living out their last few days of earthly life, perhaps the best they can do is to cope by living one day at a time. We need to go beyond analyzing individual behavior to move into the realm of the philosophy of life and collaborative efforts in community building. These are challenges for all coping researchers.

4.5. Ender and Parker's MCI and CISS

In view of the psychometric weaknesses of existing coping measures (Parker & Endler, 1992), Endler and Parker (1990a) developed the Multidimensional Coping

Inventory (MCI), which had 44 items, based on a 5-point frequency Likert-type of scale. Factor analysis yielded three basic coping styles: task-oriented, emotion-oriented, and avoidance-oriented coping. Construct validity was established by correlating the scale with depression, anxiety, and personality measures.

The MCI was later revised and renamed as Coping Inventory for Stressful Situations (CISS) (Endler & Parker, 1990b, 1999). New items were added to strengthen the avoidance dimension and create equal number of items for the three dimensions, resulting in 48 items. Separate factor analyses of the avoidance items yielded two factors: an 8-item distraction subscale and a 5-item social diversion subscale. Distraction is a task-oriented avoidance strategy, because it involves switching to a substitute task. Social diversion is a person-oriented avoidance strategy, because it involves seeking out other people. These two sub-scales help expand our understanding of the avoidance coping.

Endler and Parker (1990b) reported a stable factor structure and good test-retest reliability over a 6-week interval. Considerable research has been done employing the CISS (e.g., Endler & Parker, 1994; McWilliams, Cox, & Enns, 2003). There is good evidence of validity and reliability with different populations. For those interested in the functional properties of the three basic coping styles, CISS is clearly a better instrument than other existing coping measures. However, if one intends to investigate a broader range of coping behaviors, the CISS would not be the instrument of choice.

5. A RESOURCE-CONGRUENCE MODEL OF EFFECTIVE COPING

5.1. What constitutes effective coping

One of the persisting questions in stress and coping research is to determine what constitutes effective coping, and what constitutes maladaptive coping. Various attempts have been made to differentiate adaptive defence mechanisms from non-adaptive and pathological defence mechanisms (Haan, 1977; Vaillant, 1977). However, the long entrenched idea that some coping responses are inherently adaptive, and mature, whereas some are inherently maladaptive and primitive, has been challenged.

Epstein and Meier (1989) have identified the problem that "a particular mode of coping that is effective for a particular person in a particular setting may be ineffective when used by the same person in another situation or by a different person in the same situation" (p. 348). Litt (1988) concludes: "Interestingly, the nature of the coping strategy per se does not appear to account for the generally beneficial effects of cognitive coping. That is, no single strategy appears to be superior for coping with stressful stimuli." (p. 242). Folkman (1984) clearly states that according to cognitive-relational theory, coping simply refers to efforts to transact with situational demands, regardless of the outcome of those efforts. In other words, coping effectiveness is not inherent in any given coping strategy (Folkman and Lazarus, 1985).

Wong, Wong, and Scott (Chapter 1 of this volume) have pointed out that a great deal depends on cultural values. For example, if collectivistic values are cherished, then active coping to achieve personal success at the expense of group harmony would not be regarded as effective coping. We have also made the case that coping efficacy depends on whether the coping response is congruent with the nature of the stress and the cultural context in which the stress takes place (Wong, 1993; Peacock, Wong, & Reker, 1993).

5.2 A resource-congruence model of effective coping

The model posits that sufficient resources and appropriate utilization of these resources are essential to effective coping. Conversely, deficient resources and/or gross deviations from congruence would lead to ineffectual coping and make the individual vulnerable to stress-related disorders. Figure 1 is a schematic presentation of the resources-congruence model of effective coping.

An important feature of this model is the emphasis on creative coping. If an individual constantly develops a variety of resources, he or she will reduce the likelihood of stress encounters. By the same token, an individual can reduce or remove a stressful situation by transforming and developing existing resources. For example, the person can seek a religious conversion and transform his or her barren and broken spiritual resources. Interestingly, none of the existing coping scales explicitly measure creative coping.

Reactive coping begins as soon as a problematic condition is declared by primary appraisal. At this stage, two types of congruence are important for effective coping. First, appraisal should accurately reflect reality and be based on an objective, rational assessment of the demands and available resources. Secondly, the strategies selected need to be congruent with the nature of the stressor and the cultural context. Most of the coping measures are concerned with reactive coping without paying too much attention to issues of cultural congruence.

Adequate resources and congruent coping would eventually lead to a reduction of stress and enhancement of one's well-being. At the same time, one needs to employ protective coping to conserve personal resources, until one is able to invest further energy into

Figure 1. A schematic presentation of the resource-congruence model of effective coping.

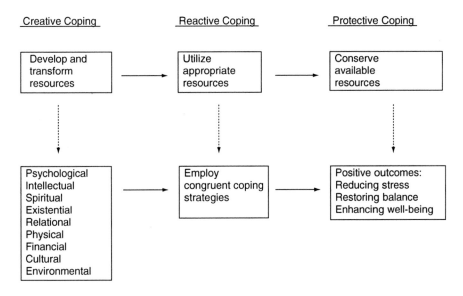

creative coping. Thus, this cycle of positive coping may be repeated many times each day. When reactive coping is not successful because of lack of resources or congruence, then one will not have the luxury of enjoying a period of relaxation and recovery in order to conserve energy.

5.3. The importance of congruence

Most of the time, people cope with daily routines in a habitual, mindless manner. The well-established patterns are carried out efficiently without conscious efforts of planning and decision-making. However, when the daily routines are disrupted or when people are confronted with an unexpected difficulty or emergency, the attribution process (Wong & Weiner, 1981) as well as the coping process are activated.

According to Carver et al. (1989), coping often proceeds in a trial-and-error manner. However, we reason that it would be too time-consuming if this trial-and-error process was random. We propose that people do possess coping schemas about what works in what types of situations, based on past experience. Therefore, the trial-and-error search would be focused on certain types of coping responses. For example, if the situation is appraised as controllable, the search will be focused on active, instrumental coping responses.

It is difficult to achieve congruence by reacting to stress emotionally, impulsively, instinctively or habitually. The best way to achieve appropriate matching is through intel-lectualization: What would be the most logical solution to this problem? What kind of appropriate response would achieve the desired result? Rational analysis is most likely to yield the best results, because it would optimize the selection of coping schemas.

Recent research has provided some evidence suggesting that to be effective, a person's coping efforts should be congruent with the controllability of the event. Thus, active, problem-focused coping strategies are favored in situations appraised to be controllable, while emotion-focused coping strategies are more likely to be used in conditions appraised as of low controllability (Aldwin, 1991; Carver et al., 1989; Folkman & Lazarus, 1980; Terry, 1994).

We propose that the mechanism underlying congruence involves the activation of coping schemas by secondary appraisal. According to Lazarus and Folkman (1984), pri-mary appraisal of the presence of a threat or challenge would lead to secondary appraisal of coping resources and options. Secondary appraisal would process such relevant infor-mation as: What is troubling me? What kind of problem is it? What can be done about it? Is it within my control?

When the problem is brought on by oneself such as poor time management, or bad habits, then the obvious solution is to make certain changes in one's behaviors. Similarly, when a problematic situation cannot be changed, such as being trapped in an oppressive work situation, then one has to change one's attitude to regain a sense of control; this may include secondary control (Rothbaum, Weisz, & Snyder, 1982). Self-restructuring includes both behavioral and cognitive restructuring and personal transformation. Some evidence already exists regarding the hypothesized linkages between these three aspects of the per-son and appropriate coping strategies (Peacock, 1992; Peacock & Wong, 1996). More specifically, Wong and Reker (1983) have demonstrated that people are able to choose appropriate coping strategies in terms of appraised controllability as follows:

- Controllable situational stress —— Task-oriented (instrumental) coping
- Situational stress beyond one's resources but controllable with help from others ——
  Seeking practical social support
- Situational stress uncontrollable by any human beings —— Religious and existential coping.

The present schema-based model of congruent coping also has implications for multicultural psychology. When an individual is transplanted to a different culture, some coping schemas acquired in the home culture may no longer be adaptive. The same coping response that used to work well in a particular situation back home may no longer work in the new culture, because each culture has its own shared implicit rules of coping with difficulties.

5.4. The duality of psychological resources

Cultivating coping resources is perhaps the most neglected but most potent contributor to effective coping. Figure 1 indicates the various kinds of resources, which may be conceptualized as capital. Thus, spiritual resources can be considered as spiritual capital. As such, capital can be depleted, when one keeps on drawing without replenishing. Capital can also be built up continually.

Psychological resources are important for coping (Lazarus & Folkman, 1984; Scheier and Carver, 1996; Wong, 1993). It is instructive to keep in mind that psychological resources often co-exist with psychological deficiencies. For example, hope and despair may co-exist (Wong & McDonald, 2002). Courage and fear may be both evoked by a dangerous situation. The deficiencies tend to sap our energies, make us feel bad about ourselves and reduce our effectiveness in coping. Deficiencies represent a parallel cognitive-emotional system that counteracts psychological resources. Thus, optimism and self-doubt may be waging a constant tug-of-war, while one's sense of mastery is trying desperately to ward off feelings of powerlessness. The net psychological resources available to the person depend not on the amount of resources one possesses, but on the balance between resources and deficiencies.

In view of the above analysis, to enhance stress-resistance and improve mental health requires that we cultivate psychological resources and reduce deficiencies at the same time. To increase resources, we need to foster a sense of mastery while recognizing external constraints and internal limitations; we need to explore sources of personal meaning; we can also cultivate our capacity for dreaming and hoping. In dealing with the deficiencies, we need to work on personal life history and replace irrational beliefs with more coping schemas; we need to identify the character flaw that frequently defeats the individual's best intentions and efforts.

5.5. Clarifying the relationship between appraisal and coping

The present model extends cognitive relational theory not only by specifying the mechanisms for effective coping, but also by clarifying the relationship between appraisal and coping.

There is some empirical support of a positive association between appraisal and coping (Bjorck, Cuthbertson, Thurman & Yung, 2001; Folkman & Lazarus, 1980; Folkman, Lazarus, Dunkel-Schetter, Delongis & Gruen, 1986; Mikulincer & Victor, 1995). Chung, Langebucher, Labouvie, Pandina, & Moos (2001) study even suggested that cognitive appraisal of threat could predict avoidance coping at 6- and 12-month follow-ups. However, Forsythe and Compas (1987) found that perceived control of an event was associated with problem-focused coping for major life events but not for daily problems. In short, the linkage between control appraisals and coping strategies is neither clearly established nor well understood. Overall, there is only weak empirical support of the two fundamental propositions of cognitive-relational theory: the first is that appraisal influences coping and the second is that appraisal and coping mediate stress outcomes (Peacock & Wong, 1996).

There is also the problem of confound. For example, Lazarus and Folkman (1984) consider reappraisal as both a revised appraisal and a type of cognitive coping, which is variously called coping centered appraisal, defensive reappraisal, and cognitive reappraisal. They claim that the problem stems from the fact that these concepts '. . . are inherently fused' (p. 167). This argument is difficult to understand, because if appraisal and coping are indeed separate constructs, as Lazarus and Folkman have maintained, then it must be possible to make clear conceptual distinctions between them and provide independent measures of these constructs. Close correspondence between appraisal and coping items in some of the coping scales (e.g., the WCQ) increases the probability that both sets of items are tapping the same underlying construct. A further problem is that subjective measures of appraisal and coping may simply reflect personality variables or prior mental health status (Watson, 1988).

To minimize the confound between appraisal and coping, we need to ensure that items used to measure these two constructs do not overlap in wording or conceptualization. The present resource-congruence model clarifies the conceptual relationship between appraisal and coping: appraisal provides the mechanism for activating the appropriate coping schemas, and is measured by items that are distinctly different from coping measures (Peacock & Wong, 1990). The congruence model also generates several specific predictions concerning appraisal-coping relations.

5.6. Advantages of the present model

The resource-congruence model provides a novel and comprehensive approach to stress management. It goes beyond traditional concerns with reactive coping and emphasizes the genius of proactive measures. Effective stress management has to be better than merely putting out fires; it requires a new vision and a new approach to resource development that would minimize the need to put out fires.

Another contribution of the model is that it recognizes the vital role of cultural knowledge and rational analysis in achieving congruence. The ethnic background of the client and the cultural context of stress need to be taken into account in interventions. Further, the cognitive skills of realistic appraisal and selecting appropriate strategies can be acquired.

Finally, the heuristic values of the model need to be mentioned. It has greatly expanded our vista of resilience research. Hardiness is no longer a limited set of personality traits but a long list of personal resources that can be cultivated and acquired. We can now systematically investigate how these resources operate singly and in different combinations to enhance resistance to various types of stressors. We can also study what kinds of resources are most importantly involved in resistance to reactive depression. The concept of parallel cognitive-emotive systems is also a fertile ground for research on the interactions of psychological resources and deficits and their effects on memory, affect, and behavior.

The model also allows for continued expansion of both new kinds of stressors and appropriate types of coping. In other words, whenever we are confronted with a stressful situation, which has not been researched, we can decide what kind of coping should be more appropriate on the basis of personal experience, rational analysis, and cultural knowledge. This kind of expansion of the taxonomy of coping seems both natural and consistent with the resource-congruence model.

In sum, the resource-congruence model has made the following contributions to stress and coping research:

1. A broader spectrum of stressors
2. A broader spectrum of general life problems
3. Based on the coping schemas acquired by various peoples
4. Recognizing the importance of cultivating and conserving resources
5. Taking into account the importance of cultural context
6. Providing a comprehensive theoretical framework for predicting what works in what situation
7. Clarifying the general mechanisms for effective coping and resilience

From the perspective of the present model, effective coping is flexible, creative, and resourceful not only in the development and management of resources, but also in the wise use of appropriate coping strategies. The following are some indices of effective coping: efficiency in terms of expenditure of energy and resources; efficacy in achieving the desired goal of removing stress and restoring balance; personal growth in terms of enhanced competence, self-esteem, and well-being, and contributions to the group and humanity. Thus, successful coping yields both short-term and long-term benefits for both the self and others.

6. MAJOR SOURCES OF STRESS

The most common source of stress is situational; it originates from the environment and is external to the person. It encompasses a wide array of stressors, from loud noise, high temperature to too much work. Given that the concept of stress originates from engineering, traditional research has focused on situational or enviromental stressors (Wong, 1990, 1993). However, there are also internally generated stressors. There are at least three common types of stress, which originate from within the person – emotional distress, existential concerns, and personality difficulties. Furthermore, we cannot conceptualize external stress merely in terms of discrete situational encounters. External stress can also be a pervasive, chronic oppressive or threatening environment that totally envelops individuals residing in a particular region from which there is little chance of escape. The reinforcement-congruence model sheds some light on these under-researched stressors.

6.1. Emotional distress

Emotional stress refers to an emotional tension or tumult triggered by catastrophising a rather harmless event. Emotional distress can also be initiated by a past trauma. Often, the emotional residue of a past trauma takes on a life of its own and becomes an internal source of stress in its own right (Wong, 1993). For example, in the case of post-traumatic stress disorders, one has to cope with the recurrent fear and tensions. Victims of childhood abuse may endure deep-seated emotional scars of humiliation, guilt, and anger. In the case of pathological grief, one has to struggle with feelings of pain and sorrow even after many years of bereavement.

What would be the appropriate coping responses to emotional distress? From the perspective of the resource-congruence model, emotion-focused coping alone would not be adequate. Some meaning reconstruction is needed to transform the nature of past traumatic events so that they would no longer trigger emotional distress.

6.2. Existential crisis

Existential crisis can be triggered by a personal tragedy or normal life transition (Frankl, 1988, 1992; Yalom, 1981). It refers to one's inner struggle with such existential issues as the meaning of human existence and suffering and the reconstruction of one's presumptive world (Janoff-Bulman, 1992). The present model predicts that an existential crisis calls for existential and religious ways of coping (Wong, 1993).

These two types of coping are similar in that they deal with ultimate concerns, but they involve different worldviews and belief systems. The philosophical or existential way of coping typically includes acceptance of what cannot be changed and constructing positive meanings from negative, unchangeable situations. Religious coping, on the other hand, involves additional concepts and beliefs such as God and afterlife.

Frankl (1988) affirms "meaning can be found in life literally up to the last moment, up to the last breath, in the face of death" (p. 76). Such affirmation of meaning can transform despair into hope and triumph (Frankl 1988, 1992, Wong, 2005). Based on Frankl's logotherapy, Breitbart and colleagues are able to apply meaning-centered psychotherapy to address existential and spiritual suffering in terminally ill patients (Breitbart, 2002; Breitbart & Heller, 2003; Breitbart, Gibson, Poppito, & Berg, 2004). Breitbart et al. (2004) point out the vital role of meaning as a resource in coping with emotional and existential suffering as one nears death.

The present model also emphasizes the need to build up one's existential and spiritual resources to help overcome existential crises. Similarly, Lazarus and DeLongis (1983) also recognize the importance of the person's central storyline or sources of personal meaning. Others (Coward, 2000; Reed, 1991) emphasize the human capacity for expanding self-transcendence to cope with end-of-life existential issues.

6.3. Personal disabilities and weaknesses

Personal handicaps encompass all sorts of difficulties such as physical disabilities, maladaptive habits, and character defects. It is obvious that any kind of physical disability can create frustration and stress, because it hinders one's ability to live independently and productively. What kinds of coping responses are most appropriate for physical disabilities? Seeking professional help and instrumental social support would be the most appropriate coping responses. In addition, existential and religious copings are also appropriate in such situations because of the need for meaning-reconstruction and spiritual healing.

However, psychological disabilities, such as self-handicapping strategies or personality defects, are less visible, and often can go on undetected for a long time. For example, rigidity in personality can make adjusting to new situations very difficult and stressful. It has often been said that we are our worst enemies, but the coping literature seldom addresses stresses that are generated by one's personal issues. In such situations, neither problem-focused coping nor emotion-focused coping will be of much help. When the self is the problem, the only appropriate mode of coping is to engage in some kind of self-restructuring, such as attitude change.

6.4. Societal stress or national disasters

Societal stress refers to the stressful living condition that affects large segments of the population in a city, nation, or region. Such stress may be caused by natural disasters, terrorism, wars, pandemic, famine, or a brutal and oppressive government. What immediately comes to mind are images of survivors of the recent Asian tsunami, victims of AIDS in Africa, the mayhem caused by bombings in the Middle East, and starving children in various third world countries. Naji's chapter (Chapter 20) provides a glimpse of the suffering and agony of the people in the Middle East.

For those living in such hellish conditions, which adversely affect every aspect of one's life, how should one cope? The resource-congruence model predicts that given the multifaceted nature of the stress, one needs to muster all the coping skills. When one's instrumental efforts are not able to have any impact on harsh realities, existential and religious coping (Klaassen, McDonald & James, Chapter 6) would be appropriate in dealing with unavoidable and uncontrollable problems. For example, Buddhist and Taoist ways of coping (Chen, Chapters 4 and 5) could help restore one's inner serenity and contentment in the midst of sufferings and frustrations.

However, both the resource-congruence model and common sense dictate that collective coping would be of primary importance in dealing with large-scale disasters. Community services offered by non-governmental organizations, such as the Red Cross and the Salvation Army, Government emergency relief efforts, and international aids are needed to ensure personal safety and meet basic survival needs of the victims. Individual efforts alone are simply not sufficient to meet the demands of extraordinary catastrophes.

7. MAJOR TYPES OF COPING

Effective coping with a variety of stressors requires a large repertoire of coping strategies. The following major types of coping have been well-established by research:

- Problem-focused vs. emotion-focused coping (Lazarus & Folkman, 1984)
- Approach vs. avoidance (Roth & Cohen, 1986; Suls & Fletcher, 1985).
- Primary control vs. secondary control (Rothbaum, Weisz, & Snyder, 1982).

- Mastery vs. meaning coping (Taylor, 1983).
- Emotional vs. tangible social support (Schaefer, Coyne & Lazarus, 1981)

The present paper will focus on two major types of coping, which are considered important according to the resource-congruence model Creative (proactive) coping and existential coping. These two coping strategies have not received sufficient attention in both the theoretical and empirical literatures.

7.1. Creative coping

Traditional research has almost exclusively focused on what we call reactive coping, because the coping process is triggered by a stressful encounter. In this chapter, we emphasize the importance of creative coping, which often takes place in the absence of any specific stressful encounter. The differences between reactive and creative coping are schematized in Figure 2.

The upper panel shows the typical process of reactive coping. An externally or internally generated stressor is appraised as demanding coping efforts. In the case of a

Figure 2. A schematic presentation of reactive and creative coping strategies and their effects.

Reactive Coping

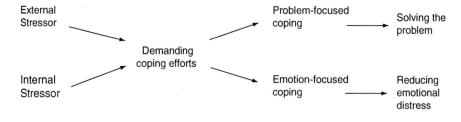

Creative Coping

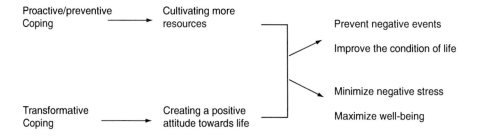

controllable stressor, problem-focused coping may resolve the problem and reduce the stress. In the case of an uncontrollable stress, emotion-focused coping may achieve some success in reducing emotional distress.

The lower panel shows two different pathways of creative coping. Proactive or preventive coping means efforts devoted to developing resources in order to reduce the likelihood of stress and improve the general condition of life. For example, if you succeed in building up a sizable bank account, you will be less likely to encounter problems of not being able to pay your bills. The transformative pathway involves some kind of meaning reconstruction and attitude change. For example, you may attain the level of enlightenment of a Zen Buddhist to the point of becoming impervious to both negative and positive life events, regarding them as mere passing illusions (Chen, Chapter 4). In fact, even the mindful meditation can reduce stress and improve well-being outcomes (Brown & Ryan, 2003; Burrows, 2004; Kabat-Zinn, 2003).

7.1.1. Creative coping as positive coping

Creative coping can also be conceptualised as positive coping. Schwarzer and Knoll (2003) consider proactive coping as the prototype of positive coping because the focus is on creating positive opportunities.

"Proactive coping reflects efforts to build up general resources that facilitate promotion toward challenging goals and personal growth. In proactive coping, people hold a vision. They see risks, demands, and opportunities in the distant future, but they do not appraise them as potential threat, harm, or loss. Rather, they perceive demanding situations as personal challenges. Coping becomes goal management instead of risk management. Individuals are not reactive, but proactive in the sense that they initiate a constructive path of action and create opportunities for growth. The proactive individual strives for life improvement and builds up resources that ensure progress and quality of functioning. Proactively creating better living conditions and higher performance levels is experienced as an opportunity to render life meaningful or to find purpose in life. Stress is interpreted as "eustress," that is, productive arousal and vital energy.

Preventive and proactive coping are partly manifested in the same kinds of overt behaviors, such as skill development, resource accumulation, and long-term planning. It makes a difference, however, if the motivation emanates from threat or challenge appraisals because worry levels are higher in the former and lower in the latter. Proactive individuals are motivated to meet challenges, and they commit themselves to their own personal high-quality standards" (Schwarzer & Knoll, 2003).

Consistent with our analysis, Schwarzer (2003) also recognizes that another form of proactive coping is to build up personal resources, such as competencies, skills, self-efficacy and optimistic beliefs. These inner resources will reduce the likelihood of stress appraisals. However, Schwarzer has not considered the transformative pathway through meaning-reconstruction or mindful meditation as a form of proactive coping.

7.2. Meaning-focused coping and existential coping

A number of coping researchers have recognized the important role of meaning in the stress process (Janoff-Bulman, 1992; Lazarus,1991; Lazarus & Folkman, 1984; Folkman & Moskowitz, 2000; Park & Folkman, 1997; Taylor, 1983). The quest for meaning is particularly relevant in effective coping with aging (Wong, 1989), chronic or life-threatening illnesses (Carlisle, 2000; Greenstein & Breitbart, 2000; Wong & Stiller, 1999). However, there are different conceptualizations of meaning, and not all of them can be classified as existential coping. For example, according to Taylor's (1983) theory of cognitive adaptation to threatening events, the three main dimensions of adaptation are: search for meaning, sense of mastery, and self-enhancement. Taylor suggests that meaning "invokes a need to understand why a crisis occurred and what its impact has been" (1983, p. 112). Causal understanding of an event will increase one's sense of mastery in dealing with it. Here, the emphasis is on causal attribution as a form of cognitive meaning.

Park and Folkman (1997) review meaning in relation to coping with stress and traumatic events. They describe meaning as a general life orientation, as appraisal of personal significance, as attribution of causality, as a coping mechanism, and as a coping outcome. They differentiate between situational and global meaning. The former is equated with stress appraisal, which precedes coping. The latter is concerned with more generalized meaning about one's life and existential assumptions. Global meaning can be conceptualized as the meaning of life. Searching for life meaning in the midst of adversities is important in reconstructing one assumptive world (Janoff-Bulman, 1992; Wortman, Silver, & Kessler, 1993). In a similar vein, Folkman and Moskowitz (2000) recognize three meaning-related coping strategies in the context of prolonged stress: positive reappraisal, problem-focused coping, and imbuing life events with positive meaning.

Meaning-seeking is particularly important in chronic or life-threatening situations. In studying 29 persons with spinal cord injuries, Bulman and Wortman (1977) found that their need to ascribe meaning to the event was an important part of coping. Dunbar, Mueller, Medina, & Wolf (1998) conducted a qualitative study to better understand women living with HIV. Thirty-four women living with various stages of HIV were interviewed. Five of them were identified to be important in their psychological and spiritual well-being: reckoning with death, life affirmation, creation of meaning, self-affirmation, and redefining relationships.

Acceptance is also adaptive for terminal patients. Mok (2001) conducted a qualitative study to understand Chinese cancer patients' conceptualization of empowerment. In-depth interviews of 12 Chinese patients with cancer revealed that empowerment is a process whereby patients develop a sense of inner strength through connection with families, friends, and health care professionals. Meaning-reconstruction also played an adaptive role – they were able to transform their conditions through an active process of developing new perspectives and reinterpreting their illness. The acceptance of illness was facilitated by their beliefs in Confucianism and Taoism.

Still another angle to meaning is conceptualized in terms of benefit-finding (Affleck & Tennen, 1996; Tennen & Affleck, 1999, 2003). They are primarily concerned with the issue of finding positive meaning in adversities. They further distinguish between benefit-finding and benefit reminding (Tennen & Affleck, 2003). The former refers to the adaptive benefit-related cognitions and beliefs **following a crisis**. We would consider such beliefs as affirmations in the potential for good outcomes or the goodness of life. The latter refers to active coping efforts in the form of recalling benefits **during difficult times** in order to ease the negative impact of the stressful encounter.

Davis, Nolen-Hoeksema, & Larson (1998) find evidence of a two-dimensional construal of meaning as "sense-making" and "benefit-finding". Sense-making relates to finding an explanation for what happened in an attempt to integrate the negative event with an existing schema or belief/meaning system. Therefore, it is similar to Wong's existential attribution (Wong 1991; Wong & Weiner, 1981). Benefit-finding, on the other hand, is related to finding positive meaning and positive implications in an adverse situation.

Space will not allow a thorough review of the different conceptions of meaning in the psychological literature. Here we will summarize the various adaptive functions of meaning-related coping.

1. **Cognitive function** – Causal attribution and stress appraisal increase one's understanding of the nature and significance of negative events and enable one to cope with these events effectively.
2. **Instrumental function** – Cognitive understanding guides one's instrumental actions and increases one's sense of mastery and efficacy.
3. **Communicative function** – Expressing one's needs, intentions, and affective states to other people.
4. **Affective function** – Meaning-affirmation and benefit-finding generate positive affects, such as feelings of happiness; experiences of happiness, hope, and personal significance also feed into one's overall assessment that life is meaningful.
5. **Motivational function** – Affirmation of positive meaning and the attribution of positive purpose provide the motivation to persist in pursuing certain life goals.
6. **Spiritual function** – The quest for ultimate meaning invariably triggers a spiritual quest in the service of both survival and personal growth.
7. **Existential function** – Acceptance of unchangeable harsh realities coupled with the affirmation of meaning and purpose will enable one to transcend existential givens and retain meaning and hope in the midst of difficult conditions.

The first two functions are more related to the traditional cognitive/behavioral coping efforts. The last four functions are all related to the broader category of existential coping, because they increase one's capacity to cope with chronic or uncontrollable stressful situations through meaning-related functions. We differentiate between meaning-based cognitive/behavioral coping and existential coping, because the latter involves a holistic view of human beings and recognizes the importance of resolving existential issues in addition to the need for task-oriented and problem-focused coping strategies.

8. RATIONALE FOR THE PRESENT COPING MEASURES

The above review of the stress and coping literature from the perspective of the resource-congruence model has recognized the following:

- A wider spectrum of stressors calls for additional categories of coping.
- The conceptual framework of resource-congruence provides a rational basis for predicting what works in what situation.
- Predictions based on the matching model call for finer functional differentiation of broad coping categories, such as problem-focused and emotion-focused coping.

- Comprehensive coping measures require both deductive and inductive approaches. It needs theory-guided research on major coping responses. But it can also need inductive methods to provide validation of coping components.

Edwards and Baglioni (1993) recommend: "Future efforts to develop coping measures will be greatly facilitated by clearly defining the relevant coping dimensions, generating multiple items that convincingly represent these dimensions, and evaluating the resulting measures using confirmatory procedures such as those illustrated here" (p. 28).

In view of the above considerations, we embarked on a systematic research program to develop a comprehensive coping measure in 1982. We adopted a four-pronged research strategy. Firstly, we interviewed people and learned from them how they coped with various life problems. This is the bottom-up approach. Secondly, we developed a resource-congruence model as a conceptual framework to systematically relate coping strategies to various stressors. Thirdly, we rationally deduced from this theory prototypical coping responses to various kinds of stressors and collect some pilot data to determine if people indeed possess the coping schema regarding what coping works with what kinds of problems. Finally, we revised and validated the coping measures through factor analysis and correlational studies. The present chapter only presents the main findings of this research program.

8.1. Coping schemas

Two constructs play a vital role in our efforts to develop a comprehensive coping measure: coping schema and prototypical coping. The concept of cognitive schema has gained wide acceptance in social cognition (Fiske & Taylor, 1984). To put it simply, schemas are cognitive structures based on abstraction and generalization of accumulated life experiences. Coping schemas are goal schemas in the sense that the objective of coping is to attain the goal of resolving problems and overcoming obstacles. It seems reasonable to assume that in their daily struggles for survival and pursuing life goals, individuals have acquired generalized knowledge of what coping strategies are effective in dealing with a given common life problem. In other words, survival and adjustments demand the acquisition of knowledge of what coping behaviors work in what situation.

In any given culture, most individuals have acquired certain skills in coping with the common, predictable life stresses. When faced with a stressful situation, individuals know how to utilize coping schemas to select appropriate coping strategies (Beck & Emery, 1985). Without such knowledge, individuals would have to cope with every demand on a trial-and-error basis, as if it we encounter it for the first time. This would lead to adjustment difficulties. Acculturation stress occurs to the extent that coping knowledge acquired in one's home land no longer applies to the host country.

8.2. Prototypical coping responses

A prototype generally refers to members of a conceptual class that possess certain representative or defining characteristics. Prototypes are typical examples of a conceptual category. For example, "chairness" may be defined by a prototypical chair.

Prototypes provide a conceptual framework to generate and classify coping responses suitable to different types of stressors. For each coping response, we ask two questions:

What is the unique function of this response in the stress process? In what kind of stressful situation will this coping response be most effective or appropriate? The first question allows us to group coping responses into various units of special functions. For example, the unit of behavior control consists of coping strategies that share the special function to changing a problematic situation through one's own actions. The unit of practical social support consists of utilizing existential resources to change a stressful situation.

The second question allows us to determine the prototypical coping response in different stressful situations. Each special category of coping is, on the basis of rational analysis, conceptualized as a typical effective way of coping with a particular stressor. Thus, the unit of behavior control is considered a typical appropriate strategy to coping with stressful situations that are appraised as within one's competence and control. The prototype concept makes it easier to generate representative items for different types of stressful situations.

The mechanism of coping schema is conceptualized as consisting of an adaptive prototypical (typical) coping response activated by cognitive appraisal of a particular stress encounter. Therefore, the construct of prototype is integral to the mechanism of coping schema.

9. RESEARCH STRATEGY AND METHODS

Based on our critical review of the research strategies of existing measures of coping, we have developed a research strategy that incorporates the advantages, while avoids the disadvantages of previous approaches. We have developed and employed a consistent research strategy to guide the different stages of our research project. The most unique feature of our research strategy is that it is open-ended, as it allows for inclusion of additional coping categories, when theoretical development and field research so demand. At different stages of development of the present coping project, different methods were used.

9.1. Research strategy

Our research strategy may be characterized by the following:
- It is **deductive**, because the generation of coping categories and responses is guided by the resource-congruence model, particularly its concepts of coping schemas and prototypes.
- It is also **inductive**, because the generation of coping categories and responses is also dictated by field research and existing coping measures.
- It is both **qualitative** and **quantitative**. Item-generation relies heavily on people's narrative on how they cope, but item-selection and scale-validation depend on quantitative analyses.
- It employs both **subjective** sorting and **objective** factor analysis.
- It is open-ended and **comprehensive**, because the measure can be expanded to accommodate new coping categories and responses.
- It has a **multicultural** orientation, because from item-generation to scale-validation, our samples included subjects from different ethnic backgrounds.

Throughout the entire research process, we attempted to identify major life stressors (Wong, 1993). We then tried to deduce the appropriate coping schemas and prototypical

(typical) responses within each schema. This deductive process involved a rational analysis of the existing literature on stress and coping as well as personal coping experiences of the research team (the three authors of this chapter).

The inductive method involved extensive field research to discover how people coped with various kinds of stressors. It also involved reviewing all the major existing coping measures to identify the various coping responses that have been reported.

Three criteria were used to develop a comprehensive coping taxonomy: (1) It has to incorporate all the major findings on stress and coping in the literature. (2) It has to incorporate all the coping responses discovered in our own field research. (3) It has to pass a validation process.

The search for common life problems was systematic: We began with the external situational problems that are controllable and emotional problems that are uncontrollable, because these two were the most studied area. Then, we focused on future problems that could be avoided or prevented; existential crises that are inherent in the human conditon; and finally, spiritual needs and struggles that are also common.

9.2. Research method

Over a ten-year period, more than 600 subjects were recruited for generating coping categories and responses and for subjective validation purposes. In addition, more than 10 studies were completed, including theses and student research projects. Serious attempts were made to include a range of age groups and ethnic minorities. For example, more than 100 Chinese participants were involved in various stages of the study.

Three methods were used to generate coping items: (1) We specified a certain type of stressor (e.g., a situational problem that is considered controllable by oneself, controllable by others, etc.) and asked participants what would be the typical or appropriate coping responses based on their experiences. (2) We specified a certain type of stressor and asked the participant to describe a specific event that fits that description, and then recall how he or she coped with that event. (3) We asked subjects to focus on certain major life domains, such as family, finance, and health, and indicate how they coped with problems in any one of these domains. We employed either the face-to-face interview format or a paper-and-pencil questionnaire format; the interview format was mainly used with seniors (age 65 years and above), because they might have difficulty understanding the written instructions without any explanations. During the interview, the verbal responses were taped and then transcribed for content-analysis.

Two methods were used for subjective validation by sorting: (1) We asked subjects to sort a group of coping items into the appropriate coping categories as described by the researchers. Each coping item was written on a 3×5 index card. Each coping category or prototype was described on a larger index card. Typically, we asked them to sort the cards into different piles according to broad categories, and then within each category, asked them to sort the cards according to prototypes. (2) We asked subjects to match individual coping responses with specific stressors on the basis of appropriateness or suitability. For both sorting tasks, we recruited subjects spanning different age groups. Coping items, which met the criterion of 70% correct classification, were retained. Sometimes, the sorting task was repeated until all resulting items met the 70% criterion.

A three-step procedure was used in content-analysing open-ended narrative data. The first step was to group coping behaviors on the basis of *semantic* similarities. The second step was to reduce the number of coping behaviors according to their *conceptual* similarities. Finally, the resulting strategies were further classified on the basis of distinctive *psychological functions* in the coping process, such as instrumental coping, practical social support, etc.

9.3. Summary of the stages of research

The present coping research project went through three stages of development as summarized below:

In **Stage 1**, the main objective was to generate items, develop the **57-item Coping Inventory** and test its validity. The Coping Inventory consisted of five coping categories: Problem-focused coping, Emotion-focused coping, Preventive/Proactive coping, Religious coping, and Existential coping. There were nine prototypes. Problem focused coping was further classified into Internal control, External control, and Secondary control. Emotion focused coping was subdivided into Denial/escape, Wishful thinking, Expressiveness, and Self-blame. Existential coping was further divided into Acceptance and Positive meaning.

In **Stage 2,** we revised and expanded The Coping Inventory into the **81-item Coping Orientation and Prototype** (The COAP). It consisted of six coping categories. Self-restructuring was added as a new coping category. Each of the six coping categories was further subdivided, resulting in a total 16 prototypes. The following seven new prototypes were added: Tension reduction, Self-improvement, External improvement, Religious beliefs, Religious practices, Cognitive restructuring, and Behavioral restructuring. Quantitative analyses were conducted to validate the COAP. The merit of this deductively based coping measure is that it measures coping at two levels: broad coping categories and specific coping prototypes. The variety of 16 prototypes makes the scale relevant for a broad range of stressors. Furthermore, additional categories and prototypes can be added without revamping the entire questionnaire.

In **Stage 3**, factor analyses were used to create the **65-item Coping Schema Inventory**. This reductive method resulted in nine coping schemas: Situational, Self-restructuring, Practical social support, Active emotion, Passive emotion, Relaxation, Acceptance, Positive Meaning and Religious coping. Several prototypes of the COAP did not survive the inductive validation process. Several items were added to Acceptance, Relaxation and Active Emotion sub-scales because of unsatisfactory reliability; this led to the creation of the **72-item Coping Schema Inventory Revised**. Numerous studies were conducted to validate the CSI.

10. THE FIRST STAGE: THE COPING INVENTORY

Initially, we generated 132 items based on Wong and Reker (1982, 1985c), Folkman and Lazarus (1980), and our own explorative qualitative field research. Note that Wong and Reker (1985c) was a cross-cultural study comparing the coping behaviors of Chinese and Caucasian elderly. Thus, from the very outset, both item generation and coping classification included contributions from Chinese samples as well as P. T. P. Wong.

We resorted to the subjective sorting task to select coping items that belong to various coping categories. At the first level, items were classified into **Problem-focused coping, Emotion-focused coping, Preventive coping, Religious coping,** and **Existential coping**. At the second level, problem-focused coping items were further classified into three prototypes: Internal control, External control, and Secondary control. Emotion-focused items were subdivided into six prototypes: Acceptance, Denial/Escape, Optimism, Wishful thinking, Self blame, and Expressiveness. These finer differentiations are important as they represent functionally different coping strategies suitable for different stressors. Furthermore, the prototypes provide a more complete and more realistic picture of the coping strategies that are actually employed by people. Only 57 items survived two rounds of subjective sorting task. Face validity was demonstrated in successful sorting of these items into appropriate categories and prototypes (Wong & Reker, 1983).

10.1. Age differences

Construct validity was also provided by age differences. Wong and Reker (1983) provided 94 items pooled from Folkman and Lazarus' (1988) Ways of Coping Scale and their own Coping Inventory. They then asked 40 young adults (ages 18-29), 40 middle-aged and 40 elderly to classify these items as either problem-focused or emotion-focused. There was a significant interaction. Young and middle-aged subjects were more likely to classify coping items as emotion-focused, whereas older subjects tended to classify coping items as problem-focused. For example, "Maintain my pride and keep a stiff upper lip" was treated by 62.5% of the elderly as problem-focused, whereas less than 30% of the middle-aged and young samples classified it as instrumental. One reason might be that the elderly have fewer coping resources (Koenig, Kvale & Ferrel, 1988). Consequently, they may want to regain a sense of control by viewing emotion-focused coping as problem-focused coping. One important implication of this finding is the need to include older adults in the process of test-development.

10.2. Construct validity

Wong and Reker (1983, 1985b) also presented some initial findings on construct validity. For example, when subjects were directed to think of either controllable or uncontrollable stress events, their problem-focused coping was more frequently employed for controllable than uncontrollable stress, but emotion-focused coping was more frequently used for uncontrollable stress than for controllable stress. Similarly, participants used internal control more than external control for problems perceived as controllable by themselves, but the reverse was true for problems perceived as controllable by others.

A number of studies on Type A behavior have provided support for the validity of the Coping Inventory. For example, Type A individuals scored higher in problem-focused coping than Type B counterparts (Greenglass, 1988; Wong & Reker, 1985a). Furthermore, preventive and existential coping are negatively associated with burnout socres, but positively related to quality of life measures (Greenglass, Burke & Ondrack, 1990). This finding clearly demonstrates the adaptive value of preventive and existential coping.

10.3. Coping behavior of successful agers

The construct validity of the Coping Inventory was further strengthened by Wong and Reker (1984) in a study of the coping behaviors of older adults (ages 65+). On the basis of a structured intensive interview, elderly subjects (ages 65+) were rated on three scales: mental health, physical health, and adjustment. A wellness score was derived from the summation of the three scales. Subjects were then divided into successful and unsuccessful groups according to a median split of wellness scores. The main purpose of the study was to determine the difference between the successful and unsuccessful agers in their ways of coping.

We also did some validity check on our Coping Inventory. The purpose was to determine whether the coping strategies extracted from the subjects' narratives matched the coping categories and protoypes of the Coping Inventory. The fact that most of their reported ways of coping can all be classified according to our Coping Inventory provides some support of the validity of our taxonomy. Two trained judges were able to classify all coping strategies an inter-judge agreement that ranges between of 72% to 95%.

Construct validity was provided by the finding that successful agers tended to use preventive strategies significantly more frequently than unsuccessful agers. It is also noteworthy that successful agers had a stronger tendency to use existential strategies than their unsuccessful counterparts. These two types of coping are of obvious importance in promoting wellness; unfortunately, they have not received much attention in coping research.

Preventive and existential strategies may be labeled *creative coping* in that these strategies help create an external/internal environment, that spawns positive events and at the same time reduces the likelihood of negative events. The positive external environment includes good interpersonal relationships, financial security, and pleasant living conditions. The positive internal environment includes a sound body and a sound mind, coupled with a positive attitude towards life. A schematic presentation of creative coping and reactive coping is shown in Figure 2. Preventive and existential strategies are treated as coping strategies, because apart from their ability to reshape the environment, they are effective in dealing with potential as well as philosophical problems, respectfully. Both types of problems, if unresolved, can become a significant source of stress.

Successful agers used more internal but fewer external strategies than the unsuccessful group, even though the two groups did not differ in overall problem-focused coping strategies. Similarly, the two groups did not differ in overall emotion-focused coping, but the successful agers employed denial, expressiveness, and wishful thinking less than unsuccessful ones. These findings further support the value of finer differentiation of problem- and emotion-focused coping categories. To ensure that differences in strategies were not due to the possibility that the two groups experienced different kinds of problems, we compared their coping responses to three specific problems: health, finance, and family. It is interesting to note that the two groups still differed.

The main contributions of the first stage of research were: demonstrating the initial validity of the Coping Inventory and providing the empirical foundation for our resource-congruence model. Therefore, we were encouraged to further refine the coping inventory theoretically and empirically.

11. THE SECOND STAGE OF DEVELOPMENT: THE COAP

During the second stage, we decided to expand the coping categories as well as the prototypes under each category. The broad categories were now renamed Orientations to indicate the initial cognitive search for appropriate coping schemas. We theorized that the coping schema actually involves two cognitive steps: Individuals initially focus or orient towards a certain broad conceptual categories before selecting prototypical responses appropriate for the situation. For example, when the problem is appraised as potentially solvable, the coping efforts will be at once oriented towards problem-focused coping strategies. A final appraisal of the nature of the stressor – whether it is controllable by self or by other people will activate the appropriate coping schema, which will select the appropriate coping prototype. Thus, externally controllable situations will elicit external control strategies, while internally controllable situation will elicit internal control strategies (Wong & Reker, 1983).

Recall that a coping prototype refers to a group of coping behaviors that share a common psychological function. Prototypes of coping are conceptualized as what a rational person would typically do in a particular stressful situation. Thus, prototypes are assumed to be appropriate or effective coping behaviors. In other words, coping efficacy of individuals can be assessed by the extent they employ prototypical coping responses. A major assumption of the resource-congruence model was that generally, people attempt to match their coping behavior to perceived situational demands. Consequently, a broader range of coping prototypes was identified. In order to emphasize the importance of prototypes, the revised and enlarged Coping Inventory was renamed Coping Orientations and Prototypes (COAP) (Wong, Reker, & Peacock, 1987).

The coping prototypes were grouped into broad coping orientations on the basis of their common conceptual focus. For example, two prototypes were grouped together to form the Situational Orientation because both of these involve attempts to change an existing situation or problem; one of these prototypes involves one's own efforts to change the situation and the other involves relying on other individuals to change the situation. Specific items are intended to represent typical strategies used for a given prototype rather than an exhaustive list of all strategies representing that coping strategy.

11.1. A description of the COAP

The 81-item COAP has six orientations or foci. Each orientation subsumes two or more prototypes (see Appendix A for a complete outline of each orientation and prototype).

The **Situational Orientation** involves strategies that focus on solving an existing problem by changing the situation, either by one's own efforts or by relying on the help of others. It includes the prototypes of instrumental behavior and practical social support.

The focus in the **Emotional Orientation** is on managing one's emotional reaction without changing the situation or solving the problem. This orientation encompasses six prototypes: distancing, wishful thinking, expressiveness, self-blame, emotional social support, and tension reduction.

The **Preventive Orientation** focuses on reducing the likelihood of anticipated problems. It includes the prototypes of self-improvement and external improvement.

The **Existential Orientation** involves strategies that are aimed at maintaining a sense of meaning or an attitude of acceptance. Acceptance and existential meaning are the two prototypes included in this orientation.

The **Religious Orientation** takes into account God or religion in dealing with anticipated or existing situations. The two prototypes within this orientation are religious beliefs and religious practices.

The focus in the **Self-Restructuring Orientation** is on changing one's own cognitions, behaviors, and attitudes. It encompasses cognitive restructuring and behavioral restructuring prototypes.

Scale scores are obtained for each respondent by calculating the average score across the items comprising each scale; thus, scale scores can vary from 1 to 5. Scale means and standard deviations obtained in several studies of undergraduates' coping with anticipatory stress are shown in Table 1.

11.2. Internal consistency

Internal consistency estimates for the six orientations are good. Across three studies in which undergraduate students reported their coping behaviors associated with three different anticipatory stressors, the following median coefficient alphas were obtained:

Table 1. Means obtained for each COAP scale

| | Type of Anticipatory Stress | | | |
COAP	AIDS VIRUS (N = 80)	Unemployment (N = 75)	Examination (N = 153)	Employment Decisions (N = 118)
Orientations				
Situational	2.8	3.1	3.1	3.4
Emotional	2.3	2.6	2.5	2.4
Preventive	2.9	3.3	3.3	3.5
Religious	2.2	2.1	2.5	2.5
Existential	2.8	3.1	3.3	3.2
Self-Restructuring	2.7	3.0	3.2	3.3
Prototypes				
Instrumental	2.9	3.5	3.5	3.7
Practical Social Support	2.7	2.8	2.5	2.9
Distancing	1.8	2.0	2.0	2.0
Wishful Thinking	2.6	2.7	2.6	2.4
Expressiveness	2.7	3.1	3.0	3.1
Self-Blame	2.0	2.3	2.4	2.1
Emotional Social Support	2.9	3.5	3.3	3.4
Tension Reduction	1.9	1.8	2.0	1.9
Self-Improvement	2.9	3.3	3.3	3.4
External-Improvement	2.9	3.4	3.2	3.6
Religious Beliefs	2.3	2.2	2.7	2.6
Religious Practices	2.1	2.1	2.4	2.4
Acceptance	2.8	3.0	3.3	3.1
Existential Meaning	2.9	3.2	3.3	3.3
Cognitive Restructuring	2.6	3.0	3.0	3.1
Behavioral Restructuring	2.8	3.1	3.4	3.4

.83 (situational), .86 (emotional), .79 (preventive), .79 (existential), .97 (religious), and .85 (self-restructuring). Similarly, the alphas for the 16 prototypes were also satisfactory. See Table 2 for individual values obtained in each study.

In two subsequent studies, internal consistency estimates were of a similar, if not greater, magnitude. Median alphas ranged from . 80 to . 97 for the orientations and .68 to .96 for the prototypes (see Table 3).

11.3. Evidence of validity

Previous coping measures have been criticised because of a lack of evidence of validity (Cohen, 1987). However, demonstrating the validity of a coping instrument is a diffi-

Table 2. Internal consistencies of COAP scales in three studies

| | Stressor | | |
COAP	Psychology Examination (N = 100)	AIDS VIRUS (N = 73)	Unemployment (N = 67)
Orientations			
Situational	.83	.94	.82
Emotional	.82	.91	.86
Preventive	.79	.91	.72
Religious	.96	.97	.98
Existential	.79	.86	.64
Self-Restructuring	.85	.90	.70
Prototypes			
Instrumental	.85	.92	.88
Practical Social Support	.75	.86	.66
Distancing	.74	.79	.73
Wishful Thinking	.71	.83	.72
Expressiveness	.71	.73	.57
Self-Blame	.78	.91	.87
Emotional Social Support	.91	.92	.93
Tension Reduction	.79	.85	.78
Self-Improvement	.76	.88	.62
External-Improvement	.59	.75	.55
Religious Beliefs	.92	.95	.96
Religious Practices	.94	.94	.94
Acceptance	.66	.77	.73
Existential Meaning	.83	.82	.66
Cognitive Restructuring	.73	.72	.49
Behavioral Restructuring	.84	.88	.70

Table 3. Internal consistencies for COAP scales in two other studies

COAP	Study 1	Study 2		
	Academic Examination (N = 153)	Employment Decisions (N = 118)	Natural Disaster (N = 119)	Teacher Bias (N = 120)
Orientations				
Situational	.78	.80	.88	.86
Emotional	.85	.88	.82	.86
Preventive	.73	.79	.81	.83
Religious	.97	.97	.97	.98
Existential	.78	.84	.83	.78
Self-Restructuring	.82	.85	.83	.85
Prototypes				
Instrumental	.82	.87	.89	.88
Practical Social Support	.81	.76	.85	.80
Distancing	.77	.82	.72	.80
Wishful Thinking	.73	.76	.76	.80
Expressiveness	.66	.74	.67	.69
Self-Blame	.80	.87	.86	.89
Emotional Social Support	.88	.91	.91	.89
Tension Reduction	.71	.82	.75	.79
Self-Improvement	.63	.69	.72	.74
External-Improvement	.57	.72	.69	.70
Religious Beliefs	.96	.96	.96	.97
Religious Practices	.95	.95	.95	.96
Acceptance	.64	.75	.77	.65
Existential Meaning	.76	.80	.78	.79
Cognitive Restructuring	.67	.68	.52	.69
Behavioral Restructuring	.80	.83	.88	.85

cult and on-going task. Because the COAP is a new instrument, validity data is still limited. Nevertheless, the process used to develop the COAP ensures a high degree of content validity; items were based on actual responses reported in the literature and by our respondents. These items are representative of a broad range of coping strategies that people actually use. In developing the initial Coping Inventory, judges sorted items into orientations and only those items for which there was a 70% or greater agreement rate were retained (Wong & Reker, 1983).

Data from three pilot studies with the COAP also support its validity. In one prospective study that investigated how undergraduates cope with a forthcoming examination, the nature of the relationships between coping orientations and residualized psychological symptoms and dysphoric mood (controlling for initial levels of symptoms and mood reported three weeks prior to the examination) were consistent with predictions. For example, greater use of emotional coping reported one week before the examination was associated with higher levels of residualized psychological symptoms and dysphoric mood, reported immediately before the examination. In another study, the COAP was able to distinguish differences in the coping used by undergraduates for two anticipatory stressors (unemployment and exposure to AIDS virus) that consensually were judged as requiring different coping strategies. Similarly, in another study, the COAP identified three different patterns of coping used to deal with three different anticipatory stressors (natural disaster, employment decisions, teacher bias). Thus, the initial evidence supports the validity of the COAP.

Concurrent construct evidence was further provided by two other studies which correlated the COAP with other psychological measures. Table 4 presents the correlations of the six orientations with the WCQ Scales. What was noteworthy was the relatively high correlations between WCQ's Positive Reappraisal with our Existential Coping and Religious coping, suggesting that Positive Reappraisal may be existentially and spiritually based rather than just cognitively based. Table 5 shows that Existential coping is positively correlated with Sense of Coherence (Antonovsky, 1979, 1987, 1992), the Life Orientation Test (Lot; Scheier & Carver, 1985, 1987), and Perceived Physical Well-being (Reker & Wong, 1984). These findings further suggest the adaptive value of existential coping.

The COAP has also been employed to study coping in old age. Van Ranst and Marcoen (2000) found that the participants made maximum use of existential orientation

Table 4. Construct Validity Correlations between the COAP and WCQ

N = 79	The COAP					
	SIT	PRV	RST	EMO	EXI	REL
Confrontive	.32**	.31**	.22	.20	.10	.04
Distancing	−.18	−.08	.10	.04	.26*	.11
Self-control	.13	.29**	.10	.19	.23*	.22*
Social support	.52***	.34**	.23*	.27*	.19	.09
Accept respon	.03	.12	−.02	.11	−.05	−.03
Escape-avoid	−.09	.04	−.21	.48***	−.16	.20
Planful prob	.39***	.34**	.38***	−.12	.30**	.15
Positive reap	.31**	.43***	.43***	.17	.50***	.49***

Note: SIT = Situational
PRV = Preventive
RST = Self-Restructuring
EMO = Emotional
EXI = Existential
REL = Religious
*** p < .001
** p < .001
* p < .05

Table 5. Concurrent Validity Correlations of the COAP

	The COAP					
	SIT	PRV	RST	EMO	EXI	REL
SOC (N=84)	.27**	.24*	.30**	−.37**	.28**	.17
LOT (N=119)	.18	.20*	.23*	−.31**	.20*	.03
LOC (N=119)	−.12	−.15	−.22*	.29**	−.08	.10
(N=142)	−.16	−.14	−.19*	−.18*	−.01	.02
BSI (N=142)	.15	.19*	.11	.49***	−.06	.05
Phy. Well-being (N=84)	.21	.17	.17	−.23*	.28**	.10
Psy. Well-being (N=84)	.01	.10	.10	−.31**	.18	−.06

Note: SIT = Situational
PRV = Preventive
RST = Self-Restructuring
EMO = Emotional
EXI = Existential
REL = Religious
SOC = Sense of Coherence Scale
LOT = Life of Orientation Test
LOC = Rotter Locus of control (Scored in direction of externality)
BSI = Brief Symptom Inventory
Phy. Well-being = Perceived Physical Well-Being
Psy. Well-being = Perceived Psychological Well-Being
*** $p < .001$
** $p < .001$
* $p < .05$

in trying to accept what had already happened to them and could not be undone. In addition to active, instrumental coping, they also depended on religious beliefs and practices for comforts and support, thus confirming the important adaptive role of religious coping in old age (Koenig, 1994)

11.4. Potential usefulness of the COAP

The COAP is a promising instrument for measuring coping efforts. The classification of coping is based on a rational-empirical approach that combines the strengths of logical classification of coping with empirical support. The COAP also has the advantage of allowing coping to be investigated at two levels of analysis. Broad coping categories are obtained by examining coping at the level of the six coping orientations. These broad categories encompass a wider range of coping strategies than available in a number of previous coping measures. Preventive, Existential and Religious Orientations represent important coping categories frequently ignored or given inadequate representation in other coping instruments. Initial findings with the COAP provide evidence that these are important coping strategies. Further, strategies that involve restructuring of one's cognitions and behaviors are also included; such coping efforts have been emphasized by cognitive-behavioral psychologists as important for effective stress management (e.g. Meichenbaum, 1977).

Depending on the nature of the application, coping can be investigated at either the orientation level or the prototype level. For many applications, the orientation scores will provide the most appropriate summary information. However, for other applications, there will be a need to make finer differentiations than allowed by the orientations; in such instances, it will be necessary to examine coping in terms of the specific prototypes.

Another advantage of the COAP is that additional orientations and prototypes can be added as new stressful situations in other cultures demand research attention. These additions can be validated independently of existing orientations and prototypes. Furthermore, specific orientations and prototypes can be selected to study various types of stressors. Thus, the COAP approach provides a great deal of flexibility and expandability in coping research and promises a comprehensive coping measure.

12. THE THIRD STAGE OF DEVELOPMENT: THE CSI

In the third and final stage of development, we attempted to develop a version of the new coping measure that passed the validating process of factor analyses. We wanted to find out to what extent the empirically determined factors corresponded to theoretically determined prototypes. This new version was called the Coping Schema Inventory (CSI) in order to differentiate it from the theoretically deduced COAP. We adopted the term schema to emphasize the role of coping schema in triggering various types of coping strategies.

Based on structural modeling (Peacock, 1992), the original 16 coping prototypes of the COAP were regrouped into eight coping schemas: **instrumental (situational), self-restructuring, preventive, active emotional, passive-emotional (avoidance/escape/denial, wishful thinking, self-blame), practical social support, existential (acceptance and meaning), and religious/spiritua**l. Validity data supporting these coping schemas comes from moderate to high correlations of the schemas to various personality variables, outcome measures and other coping scales (Peacock, 1992; Wong, Reker, & Peacock, 1993). Cronbach's Alphas for the eight coping schemas were: .88 (instrumental), .81 (preventive), .81 (passive-emotional), .80 (social support), .80 (active-emotional), .82 (existential), .84 (self-restructuring), and .97 (religious/spiritual) (Peacock & Wong, 1996). Existential coping and religious coping were significantly predicted by appraised uncontrollability, while emotion-focused coping was significantly predicted by appraised threat (Peacock, Wong, & Reker, 1993).

12.1. Study 1A: Factorial Structure of the CSI

The purpose of the present study was to determine the factorial structure of the CSI. To overcome some of the methodological weaknesses mentioned earlier, the CSI was used to measure coping responses with a variety of life stressors in different samples; thus, the emerging factorial structure is not specific to a particular situation or sample. If our present conceptual analysis is correct, then the underlying dimensions of coping should match the eight coping schemas.

A large sample (N = 967) of university students from two Ontario universities took part in the study. To establish factorial invariance, the sample was evenly divided into two samples. The result of the factor analysis is shown in Table 6.

Table 6. Study 1A: Varimax rotated principal components factor loadings for CSI across two independent samples

Scale name and items	Sample 1 (N=484)	Sample 2 (N=483)
	Loading	
Situational		
Be determined and persistent in attacking the problem.	.76	.73
Confront the problem by taking appropriate action.	.68	.70
Make a plan of action and follow it.	.67	.66
Double my efforts to change the situation.	.66	.67
Do something about the situation.	.64	.57
Actively seek out information on my own.	.63	.61
Break down the problem into smaller steps and work on it one at a time.	.55	.57
Take the problem into my own hands by fighting back.	.52	.56
Self-restructuring		
Change my pace to suit the situation.	.68	.63
Restructure my own actions in light of the problem.	.64	.62
Do what is necessary to fulfil the requirements of the situation.	.63	.65
Rearrange my activities to accommodate the situation.	.59	.60
Develop better time management skills so that I will be more efficient in the future.	.53	.55
Change my attitude in view of this problem.	.49	.47
Change my negative attitude toward this problem into a more positive one.	.47	.51
Try to look at the problem from a new perspective.	.46	.37
Active Emotional		
Seek emotional support from others.	.77	.69
Depend on friends for emotional/moral support.	.74	.69
Look to others for moral support.	.71	.67
Share my feelings with a confidant.	.67	.74
Express my feelings and thoughts.	.65	.69
Air my complaints and frustrations.	.59	.65
Release my pent-up emotions.	.50	.53
Passive Emotional		
Blame myself for what has happened.	.78	.73
Feel guilty for what has happened.	.76	.76
Feel sorry for what I have done.	.75	.73
Feel ashamed for my inadequacies.	.73	.68
Wish that I were a different person.	.71	.58
Wish that I could undo the past.	.67	.63
Wish that a miracle or something fantastic would happen.	.57	.46

Continued

Table 6. Study 1A: Varimax rotated principal components factor loadings for CSI across two independent samples—cont'd

Scale name and items	Sample 1 (N=484)	Sample 2 (N=483)
	Loading	
Put off doing something about the problem.	.55	.63
Wish that the situation were different.	.53	.46
Run away from the problem or situation.	.50	.53
Suppress or avoid facing my own emotions.	.47	.45
Ignore the problem and pretend it doesn't exist.	.45	.54
Meaning		
Believe that valuable lessons can be learned from undesirable experiences.	.67	.55
Believe that there must be a purpose in the suffering I experience.	.60	.48
Derive meaning from my past.	.58	.59
Believe that there is meaning and purpose to the things that happen to me.	.53	.56
Acceptance		
Accept/tolerate life as it is and make the best of it.	.72	.64
Accept what has happened because eventually things will work out as well as can be expected.	.60	.66
Accept the present situation because no matter how bad things are they could always be worse.	.60	.67
Don't worry about the past or the future, accept each day as it comes.	.49	.52
Look at the humorous side of this problem.	.48	.40
Avoid thinking about the problem or things that are upsetting.	.47	.16
Religious		
Believe that God will answer prayers.	.93	.91
Believe that God watches over me.	.92	.92
Pray to God.	.92	.91
Seek help and direction from God.	.92	.91
Believe in an almighty God.	.91	.90
Believe that I can communicate with God.	.90	.90
Do what is necessary to maintain a personal relationship with God.	.90	.90
Follow religious principles.	.87	.87
Believe that God will execute final justice.	.84	.89

Table 6. Study 1A: Varimax rotated principal components factor loadings for CSI across two independent samples—cont'd

Scale name and items	Sample 1 (N=484)	Sample 2 (N=483)
	Loading	
Social Support		
Rely on people who have successfully coped with the problem.	.66	.70
Depend on opinions of people who have experienced similar problems.	.64	.71
Depend on the experts and follow their advice.	.63	.68
Rely on available connections to solve the problem.	.58	.64
Rely on others to do what I cannot do myself.	.54	.51
Receive practical help from friends.	.47	.54
Tension Reduction		
Practise muscle relaxation techniques.	.82	.78
Practise meditation techniques to reduce tension.	.82	.77
Practise controlled breathing techniques.	.76	.77
Engage in mental exercise (such as imagery) to reduce tension.	.61	.62

Note. Items are ranked in order of strength of loadings for Sample 1.

After deleting items that loaded on two or three factors as well as items with a loading lower than .40, only 65 items remained. The Preventive factor did not emerge, because some of the items related to improving external environment loaded on situational coping, while items related to internal improvement either went to Self-Restructuring or Relaxation. The two prototypes of Existential coping: Acceptance and Meaning appeared as two separate factors. Except for the dissolving of Preventive coping into other factors and the emerging of the Relaxation factor, the result of the factor analysis was very similar to the result from Peacock's (1992) results based on structural modeling. It was also significant that except for the Relaxation factor, all factors were the same as those in the COAP. In other words, there is a convergence of support from both deductive and inductive methods of test-construction.

Alpha coefficients, means, and standard deviations are shown in Table 7. Internal consistency as reflected by Cronbach's alpha coefficient was good. Except for the Acceptance factor with an alpha of .65, all other factors have satisfactory alphas, ranging from .78 to .97. In terms of means, the most frequently used coping schemas are situational (instrumental) and active emotional expression. Tying for third place are Meaning and Self-restructuring. Therefore, the existential coping of meaning making can no longer be ignored as a commonly used coping strategy.

Gender differences as shown in Table 8 show that females consistently score higher almost on all coping schemas than males. This may reflect a gender bias in response style rather than an actual tendency to use these schemas to cope more frequently. The problem of response style remains a challenge in test construction.

Table 7. Study 1A: Alpha coefficients, means, and standard deviations among a large sample (N=967) of university students for the CSI scales

CSI Scales	Alpha	Mean	SD
Situational	.84	3.35	.76
Self-restructuring	.82	3.18	.72
Active Emotional	.86	3.36	.86
Passive Emotional	.87	2.30	.80
Meaning	.78	3.18	.90
Acceptance	.65	2.95	.71
Religious	.97	2.40	1.39
Social Support	.81	2.71	.84
Tension Reduction	.78	1.75	.87

Correlations among CSI scales are shown in Table 9. The highest correlation is between Situational coping and Self-restructuring (.79). This is expected because Self-restructuring contained many items, which used to belong to Secondary control, and Situational coping was previously labelled Internal Control; these two types of control are called Problem-focused Coping. It is also worth noting that Meaning Making and Religious coping are correlated at .51 level, higher than most other correlations, thus providing some empirical support that existential meaning and religious/spiritual coping are closely related.

Table 8. Study 1A: Gender differences in frequency of use, rank, and pattern of coping on the CSI

CSI Scales	Female (N=506)			Male (N=162)			T
	Mean	SD	Rank	Mean	SD	Rank	
Situational	3.37	.77	2	3.21	.83	1	2.29*
Self-restructuring	3.20	.72	4	2.91	.83	2	4.25***
Active Emotional	3.54	.79	1	2.77	.89	5	0.48***
Passive Emotional	2.33	.83	8	2.01	.80	7	4.26***
Meaning	3.21	.91	3	2.83	.93	3	4.65***
Acceptance	2.92	.72	5	2.83	.81	4	1.33
Religious	2.48	1.43	7	1.80	1.24	8	5.47***
Social Support	2.87	.86	6	2.47	.93	6	5.02***
Tension Reduction	1.71	.85	9	1.54	.91	9	2.11*

* $p < .05$, ** $p < .01$, *** $p < .001$.

Table 9. Study 1A: Correlations among CSI scales (N = 967)

CSI Scales	1	2	3	4	5	6	7	8	9
1. Situational	–	.76	.42	–.10	.32	.23	.18	.35	.30
2. Self-restructuring		–	.44	.07	.46	.40	.29	.47	.39
3. Active Emotional			–	.20	.36	.18	.25	.59	.24
4. Passive Emotional				–	.27	.26	.23	.32	.18
5. Meaning					–	.40	.51	.34	.26
6. Acceptance						–	.25	.23	.23
7. Religious							–	.33	.18
8. Social Support								–	.28
9. Tension Reduction									–

Note. All correlations are significant at the .01 level.

12.2. Study 1B: Correlates of CSI with Stress Appraisal and Ways of Coping

This study provides further evidence of the construct validity of the CSI. The correlations between the CSI and Stress Appraisal Measure (Peacock & Wong, 1990) are presented in Table 10. The results replicate our earlier findings (Peacock & Wong, 1996; Peacock, Wong, & Reker, 1993). As predicted, Challenge and Controllability are positively correlated with Situational coping and Self-restructuring. Stress appraised as controllable by others leads to seeking Social Support as well as Active Emotional coping of complaining about the problem to others.

The correlations between the CSI and WCQ are shown in Table 11, and they replicate our earlier findings on the COAP and WCQ. Again, it is worth pointing out that positive-reappraisal is correlated with Meaning making, Religious coping and Self-restructuring, suggesting that positive-reappraisal is more than cognitive reframing.

13. RELIABILITY AND VALIDITY OF THE REVISED CSI (R-CSI)

Because we wanted to enhance the reliability for Active Emotional, Acceptance and Tension Reduction, we added three items to Acceptance, three items to Tension Reduction, and one item to Active Emotional, to create a **72-item CSI** and it is now called the **Revised CSI** (R-CSI).

13.1. Study 1: Evidence of reliability

The internal reliability of the R-CSI is shown in Table 12. The alpha coefficients are now much improved over the previous CSI. The test-retest reliability over a 6-week period was also satisfactory. Thus the R-CSI has acceptable levels of reliability.

Table 10. Study 1B: CSI and Stress Appraisal

	Stress Appraisal Measure (SAM)			
CSI scales	Threat (n=97)	Challenge (n=98)	Centrality (n=98)	Stressfulness (n=98)
Situational	−.10	.26**	.09	.05
Self-restructuring	−.17	.35***	.08	−.10
Active Emotional	.01	.19	.19	.18
Passive Emotional	.36***	.00	.20	.36***
Meaning	−.05	.28**	.14	.17
Acceptance	−.27**	.00	−.28**	−.19
Religious	.01	.00	.08	.01
Social Support	.15	.02	.17	.16
Tension Reduction	−.16	.18	−.03	−.18

	Stress Appraisal Measure (SAM)		
CIS scales	Controllable by self (n=96)	Controllable by others (n=97)	Uncontrollable by anyone (n=98)
Situational	.33***	.10	−.19
Self-restructuring	.32**	.10	−.15
Active Emotional	.18	.44***	.00
Passive Emotional	−.44***	−.12	.17
Meaning	.05	.11	.01
Acceptance	.26**	−.01	.01
Religious	−.04	.14	.10
Social Support	.00	.36***	.09
Tension Reduction	.11	.17	.05

$^*p < .05,\ ^{**}p < .01,\ ^{***}p < .001.$

13.2. Study 2A Revised CSI with CISS and COPE

A sample of 35 students completed a battery of questionnaires including R-CSI, Endler and Parker's (1990b) CISS, and Carver, Scheier and Weintraub' (1989) COPE as part of a larger study on coping. They were asked to think of a critical incident of stressful encounter in recent months. A stressful event was critical if it was appraised as having a significant impact on their lives. The event could have taken place at the university or at home. The stressful event could also be primarily an inner crisis triggered by some experience. Participants were asked to describe this critical incident in as many details as possible and then indicate how they coped with it by completing three coping questionnaires.

Table 11. Study 1B: CSI and Ways of Coping (WCQ)

	Ways of Coping (WCQ)			
CSI scales	Confrontive Coping (n=93)	Planful Problem Solving (n=92)	Positive Reappraisal (n=92)	Seeking Social Support (n=95)
Situational	.29**	.53***	.23*	.22
Self-restructuring	.17	.42***	.41***	.16
Active Emotional	.24*	.28**	.22*	.65***
Passive Emotional	.00	−.40***	−.14	−.15
Meaning	.18	.28**	.41***	.23*
Acceptance	.00	.06	.17	−.05
Religious	.06	.16	.47***	.09
Social Support	.15	.05	.30**	.64***
Tension Reduction	.03	.27**	.43***	.15

	Ways of Coping (WCQ)			
CSI scales	Distancing (n=93)	Accepting Responsibility (n=95)	Escape-Avoidance (n=95)	Self-Controlling (n=95)
Situational	−.18	.06	−.29**	.12
Self-restructuring	−.05	.04	−.22*	.02
Active Emotional	−.22*	−.04	.03	.02
Passive Emotional	.16	.22*	.54***	.14
Meaning	.08	.01	.10	.28**
Acceptance	.51***	−.09	−.18	.11
Religious	.20*	−.03	.20*	.27**
Social Support	−.08	−.03	.16	.08
Tension Reduction	−.01	−.13	−.04	.01

$^*p < .05,\ ^{**}p < .01,\ ^{***}p < .001.$

The correlations between R-CSI and CISS are shown in Table 13. The positive correlations between Situational coping, Self-restructuring, and Active Emotional coping simply confirm that all these coping strategies belong to the category of problem-focused coping. Active emotional coping is similar to other problem-focused strategies in that it is direct and confrontational and may have the effect of resolving a problem, so says the proverbial statement that the squeaky wheel gets the grease. Passive emotional coping is positively correlated with Emotional Orientation, because both are emotion-focused coping. Meaning was negatively correlated with Task Orientation, suggesting that when problems are controllable and solvable by direct actions, people are less likely to resort to Meaning-making. The positive correlation between Seeking Social Support and Social

Table 12. Study 1: Alpha coefficients and 5-week stability coefficients for the R-CSI

R-CSI Scales	Alpha (N = 63)	Test-rest (N = 60)
Situational	.88	.74
Self-restructuring	.85	.69
Active Emotional	.92	.67
Passive Emotional	.87	.68
Meaning	.77	.81
Acceptance	.85	.70
Religious	.98	.94
Social Support	.72	.74
Tension Reduction	.87	.78

Diversion are predicted because both involve reaching out to other people; but functionally, we do not see Social Diversion as helpful as Seeking Practical Social Support, because Social Diversion is an avoidance strategy. The overlapping construct between seeking Practical Social Support and seeking avoidance through Social Diversion needs to be clarified through further research. The positive correlation between Tension Reduction and Task Oriented Coping can only be understood in terms of the preventive and adaptive nature of relaxation. When one is gaining more self-composure and confidence through meditation and other relaxation practices, one is better able to take on the problems.

Table 13. Study 2A: Revised CSI and the CISS

	Coping Inventory for Stressful Situations			
			Avoidance	
R-CSI scales	Task Oriented	Emotion Oriented	Distraction	Social Diversion
Situational	.84***	−.10	−.01	−.03
Self-restructuring	.66***	−.22	.01	−.10
Active Emotional	.42*	.22	.26	.41*
Passive Emotional	−.38*	.78***	.24	.15
Meaning	−.45*	−.22	−.10	−.12
Acceptance	.15	−.01	.14	−.06
Religious	.04	.05	−.18	−.15
Social Support	.27	.06	.06	.47**
Tension Reduction	.50**	−.40*	−.24	−.43**

N=35.
* $p < .05$, ** $p < .01$, *** $p < .001$.

The correlations between the R-CSI and the COPE are shown in Table 14. The positive correlations between Situational, Self-restructuring and Active Emotional coping strategies are predicted, because functionally they all have the capacity to solve problems. Self-restructuring is positively correlated with Active Coping, Positive Planning and Reinterpretation further clarifying the functional properties of the strategy of changing oneself. This is important, because in many difficult situations there is little we can do except changing ourselves – our behaviors, attitudes, and philosophies, etc. It is also important because of its anticipatory and preventive nature. For example, we can avoid many problems and improve our life conditions by adopting better attitudes towards people and life. Meaning is primarily associated with Reinterpretation, Behavioral disengagement, and Humor, but negatively correlated with Active Coping; these findings clarify the functions of Meaning-making and shed some light on Behavioral disengagement. From the perspective of control theory, Carver et al. (1989) feel that Behavioral disengagement may not be a very positive coping response, because it reduces the likelihood of goal-attainment. However, from the perspective of Taoism, or wu-wei, disengagement can be very adaptive, because it conserves energy and replaces the futile behavioral striving with an attitude of acceptance and going with the flow; such behavioral disengagement will allow time for meaning-exploration. The positive relationships betweenTension Reduction with Positive Planning and Reinterpretation further highlight the preventive function of Tension Reduction.

13.3. Study 2B: Revised CSI and the CRI

Similar to Study 2A, 55 subjects were asked to describe a recent stressful encounter and then indicate how they have coped with this event by completing the Revised CSI and the CRI.

It is interesting that Situational Coping, Self-restructuring and Tension Reduction appear to have similar adaptive functions by virtue of their positive associations with Logical Analysis, Positive Reappraisal, Seeking Guidance, and Problem-solving; all four are considered by Moos (1988, 1993) as representing approach strategies. Both Meaning and Religious Coping are positively correlated with Logical Analysis, Positive Reappraisal, and Seeking Guidance, implicating cognitive strategies in these two types of coping. As expected, Social Support was positively related with Seeking Guidance/Support, but different from prediction, Acceptance and Resignation/Acceptance were not correlated. Perhaps, according to our thinking, Acceptance simply means accepting the situation as unchangeable, but it does not imply resignation, because one can still engage in Meaning-making, Self-restructuring and Tension-reduction rather than giving up.

14. GENERAL DISCUSSION AND CONCLUSIONS

To live is to suffer. To survive is to cope. To succeed is to adapt effectively and creatively. For most people, the journey of life is continued education on coping and survival in the school of hard knocks. Through eons of time and the cumulative wisdoms of human adaptation, a vast repertoire of coping strategies is now available to people. We no longer depend on the primitive brain and instinctive responses to cope with complex

Table 14. Study 2A: Revised CSI and the COPE scale

R-CSI scales	COPE Scale			
	Active Coping	Positive Planning	Reinterpretation	Social Support-Emotional
Situational	.75***	.79***	.43**	.04
Self-restructuring	.51**	.64***	.77***	.00
Active Emotional	.28	.25	−.04	.71***
Passive Emotional	−.33*	−.21	−.41*	.08
Meaning	.30	.40*	.63***	−.04
Acceptance	−.13	−.03	.25	−.07
Religious	−.01	−.02	.22	.12
Social Support	.31	.13	.06	.54***
Tension Reduction	.39*	.51**	.68***	-.22

R-CSI scales	COPE Scale			
	Social Support Instrumental	Suppressing Competing Activities	Religion	Denial
Situational	.18	.49**	−.11	−.10
Self-restructuring	.12	.21	.18	.04
Active Emotional	.70***	.17	−.06	.00
Passive Emotional	−.08	−.12	−.04	.35*
Meaning	.04	.08	.40*	.24
Acceptance	.12	−.12	.20	−.07
Religious	−.02	−.24	.93***	.19
Social Support	.51**	.02	.18	.01
Tension Reduction	−.18	.15	.04	.10

R-CSI scales	COPE Scale			
	Acceptance	Mental Disengagement	Behavioral Disengagement	Venting Emotion
Situational	−.05	−.36*	−.21	.17
Self-restructuring	.23	−.14	.09	−.13
Active Emotional	.07	−.03	.07	.63***
Passive Emotional	− .03	.44**	.16	.37*
Meaning	.20	−.18	.38*	−.32
Acceptance	.59***	.18	.11	−.16
Religious	.19	.05	.23	−.07
Social Support	.27	.00	.24	.30
Tension Reduction	.09	−.14	.00	−.35*

Table 14. Study 2A: Revised CSI and the COPE scale—cont'd

R-CSI scales	COPE Scale		
	Restraint Coping	Alcohol/Drug Use	Humour
Situational	−.05	−.12	.12
Self-restructuring	.14	−.24	.31
Active Emotional	−.23	.04	.11
Passive Emotional	−.20	.15	.08
Meaning	.10	−.04	.43[*]
Acceptance	.18	−.14	.15
Religious	.01	−.10	−.02
Social Support	−.18	−.09	−.08
Tension Reduction	.30	.08	−.03

N=35.
$^* p < .05, ^{**} p < .01, ^{***} p < .001.$

problems. In most situations, we also do not depend on the process of trial and error. More likely we can take advantage of the coping knowledge and wisdoms already stored in our memories in the form of coping schemas of what works in what situations. None of the existing coping measures even come close to capturing the variety of coping strategies available to people in their coping with the harsh realities of living. In this chapter, we have at least described the process to develop a comprehensive schema-based measure of coping.

Our biggest contribution is to follow the resource-congruence model by asking people what would be the appropriate, prototypical ways of coping with various types of stressors. We can then employ the subjective sorting task (Carver, Scheier, & Weintraub, 1989) to validate the prototypes. With each type of stressor, we can deduce and verify the prototypical coping responses. Therefore, this open-ended deductive approach allows researchers to add new modules to the COAP without having to start over again the elaborate validating process as required by the inductive approach. In Section 6, we have identified several major sources of stress, which have not received research attention. There are bound to be additional sources of stress and suffering for those living in others parts of the world, but unknown to denizens of North America. Eventually, the COAP can be extended to the point of encompassing the majority of coping strategies employed by people in different situations and cultures. Another advantage of the COAP is that researchers can choose the specific Orientations or Prototypes to study coping reactions to a specific stressor. Stone, Greenberg, Kennedy-Moore, & Newman (1991) have raised the provocative question: What are self-report, situation-specific coping questionnaires measuring? The COAP provides a partial answer to this question – it measures the typical responses people adopt in a specific situation. Finally, the COAP provides a powerful research strategy to study the cross-cultural psychology of coping. For example, one can hold the stressor constant across cultures and ask equivalent samples what the most typical and

Table 15. Study 2B: Revised CSI and the CRI

R-CSI scales	Coping Responses Inventory (CRI)			
	Logical Analysis	Positive Reappraisal	Seeking Guidance/ Support	Problem Solving
Situational	.57***	.54***	.40**	.73***
Self-restructuring	.49***	.49***	.41**	.67***
Active Emotional	.24	.25	.48***	.32*
Passive Emotional	−.17	−.12	−.04	−.41**
Meaning	.42***	.51***	.39**	.18
Acceptance	.11	.22	.17	.03
Religious	.37**	.48***	.51***	.09
Social Support	.10	.21	.50***	−.13
Tension Reduction	.37**	.48***	.50***	.28*

R-CSI scales	Coping Responses Inventory (CRI)			
	Cognitive Avoidance	Acceptance/ Resignation	Alternate Rewards	Seeking Emotional Discharge
Situational	−.33*	−.32*	.18	.03
Self-restructuring	−.21	−.17	.11	−.04
Active Emotional	−.10	−.06	.21	.21
Passive Emotional	.63***	.55***	.05	.40**
Meaning	.11	.16	.17	.24
Acceptance	.15	.20	.09	−.01
Religious	.05	.07	.17	.12
Social Support	.21	.28*	.30*	.19
Tension Reduction	−.05	.03	.22	.16

N=55.
$^{*}p < .05,\ ^{**}p < .01,\ ^{***}p < .001.$

appropriate way of coping with this kind of stressor would be. This would allow researchers to identify both universal and cultural-specific aspects of coping prototypes.

Our inductively developed R-CSI also has some advantages over most existing coping measures for three reasons. First, it is both theory-based (Carver et al., 1989; Lazarus, 1990) and empirically-based; it has survived both deductive and inductive validation processes. Second, it has very good psychometric properties in terms of reliability and validity and has overcome some of the weaknesses in other coping scales. Thirdly, it includes major coping strategies, such as Existential Meaning Coping, Self-restructuring and Tension Reduction, which have not been included in other coping measures. The adaptive functions of Existential coping remain largely unexplored, although it has been discovered that such strategies are used in coping with a wide range of stressful situations, such as cancer (Breitbart, 2002); AIDS (Carlisle, 2000), chronic illnesses (Mok, Lai, & Zhang, 2004; Taylor & Aspinwall, 1992), incest (Silver, Boon, & Stones, 1983), chronic disabilities (Stephenson & Murphy, 1986), combat deaths (Florian, 1989), and aging (Wong, 1998b). There are promising new theoretical and empirical developments in meaning research (Reker & Chamberlain, 2000; Thompson & Janigian, 1988; Wong & Fry, 1998); such research will further clarify the various functions of meaning in Existential coping.

Self-restructuring is another major coping strategy with important adaptive functions. When the source of stress is one's own bad habits, negative attitudes, or some other personal handicaps, clearly the most appropriate coping response is Self-restructuring. But when one lives in situations with chronic and pervasive problems, Self-restructuring can also be very effective. For example, both Buddhist coping (Chapter 4) and Taoist way of nature (Chapter 5) entail fundamental self-restructuring, which may be considered a kind of transformational coping. Tension Reduction also holds a great deal of promise as both a reactive and proactive coping strategy. Apart from reducing immediate stress, regular practices of tension reduction exercises, such as mindful meditation and Qigong can even prevent the development of tension. At present, there are already several mindfulness-based stress reduction programs (Chang et al, 2004) and psychological interventions (Kabat-Zinn, 1998, 2003).

14.1. Contributions to research on effective coping

Fleming, Baum, & Singer (1984) point out the difficulties of discovering methods of effective coping. They point out that while intellectualization may work for one person for a problem, another person may use denial and come to the same satisfactory solution. Similarly, a strategy may work for an individual in a specific situation at time I, but may not work that well in the same situation for time II. Of course, it will be extremely difficult to predict precisely which strategy works in what situation for which person. However, our theory and research provide several principles to serve as guidelines on effective coping and resourcefulness (Rosenbaum, 1990).

Congruence is one key factor. Congruence not only means that the coping response matches the nature of the stressor, but it also means that the coping response is congruent with implicit cultural values and practices. Various chapters in this book (Chapters 1, 2, 3 and 7) have emphasized the importance of cultural values and beliefs in determining what constitute socially desirable coping responses and outcomes. Thus, congruence requires both coping knowledge and cultural knowledge. Lacking either knowledge, one has to rely on trial and error to discover congruence.

Another key factor is resource availability. The general principle is that the more external and internal resources one possesses, the more likely one is able to cope with the demands of life. The emphasis on coping resources thus shifts the focus from reacting to stressful encounters to preventive and transformative coping. When one is armed with adequate resources, one is less likely to appraise situations as threatening or harmful.

The third key factor is self-restructuring. The success or failure of coping depends not so much on skills as on the person. The same strategy works for one person but not for another in an identical situation, because of individual differences in terms of attitudes and personalities. A resilient person is not necessarily someone with a lot of coping skills, but must be someone with the right stuff, such as endurance, determination, optimism, flexibility, creativity, wisdom, humility, faith, integrity, and equanimity. The mediating roles of these positive attributes represent another new frontier for coping research.

14.2. Concluding remarks

Since Lazarus' (1966) landmark publication, stress and coping has become a major research area for several sub-disciplines of psychology, such as social and personality, clinical and consulting, health psychology, organizational psychology, sports psychology, life-span development, and cross-cultural psychology. Such positive developments are not unexpected, because effective coping is so essential not only for individuals' mental and physical health, but also for the well-being of community and society.

In musing over the future of coping research, Snyder (1999b) asks whether coping constructs are by-products of Western society and emphasizes the need of keeping an eye on the societal and cultural context in which our coping models are developed. Thus, he implicitly acknowledges the need for cross-cultural research if the psychology of coping is going to move forward. We need to move the frame of reference from individualistic achievements to broader considerations of how people in other cultures cope, and why community harmony and collective coping are just as important as personal success. Snyder's concluding statement in his book is prophetic: "Wherever coping goes, so too will our civilization...and vice versa" (p.333). We will even go further by stating that the survival of humanity depends on how we cope with such global problems as poverty, AIDS, inequality, discrimination, corruption, abuse of power, and clash of cultural values. As we look into the future, we need to venture out of our confines of neat coping models and paradigms and learn from history, the wisdom literature and the heroic stories of survival and resilience in different cultures. We believe that in the post 9/11 world, coping research will gain even more importance, if we are willing to get out of our comfort-zone and get into the uncharted areas alluded to throughout this chapter.

APPENDIX A

Coping Orientations and Prototypes (COAP)

Definitions and Classifications of Coping Strategies

1. *Situational Orientation* (Focus is on efforts to change an existing situation.)
    (a) *Instrumental* (Depends on one's direct actions to change the situation or solve the problem.)
        *2. Do something about the situation.
        5. Confront the problem by taking appropriate actions.
        15. Break down the problem into smaller steps and work on one at a time.

---

* The number for each item represent the number on the COAP Questionnaire, on which all the different items of coping were randomized.

26. Take the problem into my own hands by fighting back.
30. Actively seek out information on my own.
40. Make a plan of action and follow it.
56. Be determined and persistent in attacking the problem.
68. Double my effort to change the situation.

(b) *Practical Social Support* (Depends on others to change the situation or solve the problem. It involves receiving practical social support.)
1. Rely on others to do what I cannot do myself.
25. Rely on people who have successfully coped with the problem.
49. Rely on available connections to solve the problem.
58. Receive practical help from friends.
61. Depend on the experts and follow their advice.
80. Depend on opinions of people who have experienced similar problems.

2. *Emotional Orientation* (Focus is on regulation of one's emotional reactions without changing the situation or solving the problem.)

(a) *Distancing* (Distancing oneself from an existing problem by denial, avoidance, escape or procrastination.)
8. Run away from the problem or situation.
17. Suppress or avoid facing my own emotions.
34. Put off doing something about the problem.
42. Ignore the problem and pretend that it doesn't exist.
43. Avoid thinking about the problem or things that are upsetting.

(b) *Wishful thinking* (Entertains unrealistic wishes or fantasies.)
3. Wish that I could undo the past.
31. Wish that I were a different person.
36. Wish that a miracle or something fantastic would happen.
45. Wish that the situation were different.

(c) *Expressiveness* (Expresses one's feelings to release tension.)
4. Express my feelings and thoughts.
18. Air my complaints and frustrations.
44. Do something physical to let off my anger.
67. Release my pent-up emotions.

(d) *Self-blame* (Blames one's own behavior or character from the problem.)
21. Feel guilty for what has happened.
32. Feel ashamed for my inadequacies.
55. Feel sorry for what I have done.
72. Blame myself for what has happened.

(e) *Emotional social support* (Seeks emotional/verbal support from others.)
28. Share my feelings with a confidant.
41. Look to others for moral support.

57. Seek emotional support from others.
75. Depend on friends for emotional/moral support.

(f) *Tension reduction* (Engages in some activity/exercise to achieve immediate reduction of tension.)
12. Talk to myself to reduce tension.
22. Practise controlled breathing techniques.
27. Engage in mental exercise (such as imagery, etc.) to reduce tension.
52. Practise muscle relaxation techniques.
79. Practise meditation techniques to reduce tension.

3. *Preventive Orientation* (The focus is on anticipated or potential problems.)
   (a) *Self-improvement* (Attempts to improve self to be better prepared for the future)
   10. Pursue a health promoting lifestyle (exercise, diet, mental stimulation or activities, etc.) to prepare myself for the future.
   20. Develop mental toughness so that I will be better prepared for future difficulties.
   33. Rehearse the anticipated situation in my mind.
   38. Try to develop a positive self concept or self image so that I can better face future uncertainties.
   65. Know my limits so that I will not get into difficulties later on.
   70. Develop better time management skills so that I will be more efficient in the future.
   78. Rehearse the planned action in my mind.

   (b) *External improvement* (Attempts to improve one's conditions or network to be better prepared for the future.)
   14. Try to improve my situation in anticipation of future needs.
   19. Develop/maintain good interpersonal relationships with family/others to prevent conflicts.
   46. Develop connections/contacts that one day may be useful.
   71. Develop/maintain relationships with people who are likely to contribute to my personal goals.

4. *Religious Orientation* (Focus is on God or religion in dealing with both existing and anticipated problems.)
   (a) *Religious beliefs* (Relies on religious beliefs and convictions.)
   7. Believe that I can communicate with God.
   37. Believe that God will answer prayers.
   47. Believe that God watches over me.
   73. Believe in an almighty God.
   76. Believe that God will execute final justice.

   (b) *Religious practices* (Relies on religious practices.)
   6. Do what is necessary to maintain a personal relationship with God.
   29. Seek help and direction from God.
   51. Follow religious principles.
   60. Pray to God.

5. *Existential Orientation* (Focus is on philosophical issues of human existence, such as suffering, meaning, etc.)
   (a) *Acceptance* (Accepts the inevitable or givens in life in a rational and philosophical manner.)
      11. Accept what has happened because eventually things will work out as well as can be expected.
      16. Accept/tolerate life as it is and make the best of it.
      35. Accept the present situation because no matter how bad things are they could always be worse.
      69. Don't worry about the past or the future, accept each day as it comes.

   (b) *Existential meaning* (Discovers or creates a sense of meaning or purpose.)
      39. Believe that there must be a purpose in the suffering I experience.
      53. Maintain a sense of purpose, optimism and zest for life.
      62. Try to maintain a sense of contentment or fulfillment in life.
      66. Believe that there is meaning and purpose to the things that happen to me.
      74. Believe that valuable lessons can be learned from undesirable experiences.
      77. Derive meaning from my past.

6. *Self-Restructuring Orientation* (Focus is on changing one's own cognitions and behaviors.)
   (a) *Cognitive Restructuring* (Changes in one's attention, and attitudes in response to a present problem/situation that cannot be changed or that mainly exists in one's mind.)
      23. Change my negative attitude toward this problem into a positive one.
      48. Mentally transform the situation into something less threatening.
      54. Change my attitude in view of this problem.
      63. Try to look at the problem from a new perspective.
      81. Look at the humorous side of this problem.

   (b) *Behavioral Restructuring* (Changes in one's behavior in response to a present problem or situation which cannot be changed or is brought on by one's own behaviors.)
      9. Do what is necessary to fulfill the requirements of the situation.
      13. Change my habit(s) in view of the problem.
      24. Change my pace to suit the situation.
      50. Change my behavior to better fit the situation.
      59. Restructure my actions in light of the problem.
      64. Rearrange my activities to accommodate the situation.

APPENDIX B

Coping Schemas Inventory-Revised

To what extent do you usually use each of the following strategies to cope with_____?
In making your rating, use the following scale:

1	2	3	4	5
Not At All (Never)	A Little Bit (Rarely)	A Moderate Amount (Occasionally)	A Considerable Amount (Often)	A Great Deal (Always)

Please circle the appropriate number for each coping strategy.

1. Rely on others to do what I cannot do myself 1 2 3 4 5
2. Do something about the situation 1 2 3 4 5
3. Wish that I could undo the past 1 2 3 4 5
4. Express my feelings and thoughts 1 2 3 4 5
5. Confront the problem by taking appropriate actions 1 2 3 4 5
6. Do what is necessary to maintain a personal relationship with God .1 2 3 4 5
7. Believe that I can communicate with God 1 2 3 4 5
8. Run away from the problem or situation 1 2 3 4 5
9. Do what is necessary to fulfill the requirements of the situation 1 2 3 4 5
10. Accept what has happened because eventually things will work
    out as well as can be expected 1 2 3 4 5
11. Break down the problem into smaller steps and work on one
    at a time 1 2 3 4 5
12. Learn to live with the problem, because nothing much can be
    done about it 1 2 3 4 5
13. Confront and understand my own feelings .1 2 3 4 5
14. Accept/tolerate life as it is and make the best of it 1 2 3 4 5
15. Learn to accept the negative realities of life 1 2 3 4 5
16. Suppress or avoid facing my own emotions 1 2 3 4 5
17. Air my complaints and frustrations 1 2 3 4 5
18. Feel guilty for what has happened 1 2 3 4 5
19. Practice controlled breathing techniques 1 2 3 4 5
20. Change my negative attitude toward this problem into a
    positive one 1 2 3 4 5
21. Change my pace to suit the situation 1 2 3 4 5
22. Rely on people who have successfully coped with the problem 1 2 3 4 5
23. Take the problem into my own hands by fighting back 1 2 3 4 5
24. Look at unavoidable life events as part of my lot in life 1 2 3 4 5
25. Engage in mental exercise (such as imagery) to reduce tension 1 2 3 4 5
26. Share my feelings with a confidant 1 2 3 4 5
27. Try to reduce my anxious thoughts 1 2 3 4 5
28. Seek help and direction from God 1 2 3 4 5
29. Actively seek out information on my own 1 2 3 4 5
30. Wish that I were a different person 1 2 3 4 5

31. Feel ashamed for my inadequacies 1 2 3 4 5
32. Put off doing something about the problem 1 2 3 4 5
33. Accept the present situation because no matter how bad
    things are they could always be worse 1 2 3 4 5
34. Wish that a miracle or something fantastic would happen 1 2 3 4 5
35. Believe that God will answer prayers 1 2 3 4 5
36. Believe that there must be a purpose in the suffering
    I experience 1 2 3 4 5
37. Make a plan of action and follow it 1 2 3 4 5
38. Look to others for moral support 1 2 3 4 5
39. Ignore the problem and pretend that it doesn't exist 1 2 3 4 5
40. Avoid thinking about the problem or things that are upsetting 1 2 3 4 5
41. Wish that the situation were different 1 2 3 4 5
42. Believe that God watches over me 1 2 3 4 5
43. Mentally transform the situation into something less threatening . . .1 2 3 4 5
44. Rely on available connections to solve the problem 1 2 3 4 5
45. Follow religious principles 1 2 3 4 5
46. Try *not* to focus on likely negative outcomes 1 2 3 4 5
47. Practice muscle relaxation techniques 1 2 3 4 5
48. Change my attitude in view of this problem 1 2 3 4 5
49. Feel sorry for what I have done 1 2 3 4 5
50. Be determined and persistent in attacking the problem 1 2 3 4 5
51. Seek emotional support from others 1 2 3 4 5
52. Receive practical help from friends 1 2 3 4 5
53. Restructure my actions in light of the problem 1 2 3 4 5
54. Pray to God 1 2 3 4 5
55. Depend on the experts and follow their advice 1 2 3 4 5
56. Look at the humorous side of this problem .1 2 3 4 5
57. Try to look at the problem from a new perspective 1 2 3 4 5
58. Rearrange my activities to accommodate the situation 1 2 3 4 5
59. Believe that there is meaning and purpose to the things that
    happen to me 1 2 3 4 5
60. Release my pent-up emotions 1 2 3 4 5
61. Double my effort to change the situation 1 2 3 4 5
62. Don't worry about the past or the future, accept each day
    as it comes 1 2 3 4 5
63. Develop better time management skills so that I will be more
    efficient in the future 1 2 3 4 5
64. Blame myself for what has happened 1 2 3 4 5
65. Believe in an almighty God 1 2 3 4 5
66. Believe that valuable lessons can be learned from undesirable
    experiences 1 2 3 4 5
67. Depend on friends for emotional/moral support 1 2 3 4 5
68. Believe that God will execute final justice .1 2 3 4 5
69. Derive meaning from my past 1 2 3 4 5
70. Remind myself that worrying will not accomplish anything 1 2 3 4 5
71. Practice meditation techniques to reduce tension 1 2 3 4 5

72. Depend on opinions of people who have experienced
    similar problems 1 2 3 4 5

Items of the Coping Schemas Inventory-Revised

Situational (8 items):   Items 2, 5, 11, 23, 29, 37, 50, and 61
Self-Restructuring (8 items):   Items 9, 20, 21, 48, 53, 57, 58, and 63
Active Emotional (8 items):   Items 4, 13, 17, 26, 38, 51, 60, and 67
Passive Emotional (12 items):   Items 3, 8, 16, 18, 30, 31, 32, 34, 39, 41, 49, and 64
Meaning (4 items):   Items 36, 59, 66, and 69
Acceptance (9 items):   Items 10, 12, 14, 15, 24, 33, 40, 56, and 62
Religious (9 items):   Items 6, 7, 28, 35, 42, 45, 54, 65, and 68
Social Support (6 items):   Items 1, 22, 44, 52, 55, and 72
Tension Reduction (8 items):   Items 19, 25, 27, 43, 46, 47, 70, and 71

REFERENCES

Affleck, G., & Tennen, H. (1996). Construing benefits from adversity: Adaptational significance and dispositional underpinnings. *Journal of Personality, 64*, 899-922.

Aldwin, C. M. (1991). Does age affect the stress and coping process? Implication of age differences in perceived control. *Journal of Gerontology, 46*, 174-180.

Aldwin, C. M., & Revenson, T. A. (1987). Does coping help? A reexamination of the relation between coping and mental health. *Journal of Personality and Social Psychology, 53*, 337-348.

Amirkhan, J. H. (1990) A factor analytically derived measure of coping: the coping strategy indicator. *Journal of Personality and Social Psychology, 59*, 1066-1074.

Antonovsky, A. (1979). *Health, stress and coping*. San Francisco, CA: Jossey-Bass.

Antonovsky, A. (1987) *Unraveling the mystery of health: How people manage stress and stay well*. San Francisco: Jossey-bass.

Antonovsky, A. (1992). Can attitudes contribute to health? *Advances, 8*(4), 33-49.

Baum, A., Calesnick, L. E., Davis, G., & Gatchel, R. J. (1982). Individual differences in coping with crowding: Stimulus screening and social overload. *Journal of Personality and Social Psychology, 43*, 821-830.

Beck, A. T., & Emery, G. (1985). *Anxiety disorders and phobias*. New York: Basic Books.

Billings, A. G. & Moos, R. H. (1984) Coping, stress and social resources among adults with unipolar depression. *Journal of Personality and Social Psychology, 46*, 877-891.

Bjorck, J. P., Cuthbertson, W., Thurman, J. W., & Yung, S. L. (2001). Ethnicity, coping, and distress among Korean American, Filipino American, and Caucasian Americans. *Journal of Social Psychology, 141*(4), 421-443.

Breitbart, W. (2002). Spirituality and meaning in supportive care: Spiritual-and-meaning-centered group psychotherapy interventions in advanced cancer. *Support Care Cancer, 10*, 272-280.

Breitbart, W., & Heller, K. S. (2003). Reframing hope: Meaning-centered care for patients near the end of life. *Journal of Palliative Medicine, 6*, 979-988.

Breitbart, W., Gibson, C., Poppito, S. R., & Berg, A. (2004). Psychotherapeutic interventions at the end of life: A focus on meaning and spirituality. *Canadian Journal of Psychiatry, 49*(6), 366-372.

Brown, K. W., & Ryan, R. M. (2003). The benefits of being present: Mindfulness and its role in psychological well-being. *Journal of Personality and Social Psychology, 84*(4), 822-848.

Bulman, R. J. & Wortman, C. (1977) Attributions of blame and coping in the "real world": Severe accident victims react to their lot. *Journal of Personality and Social Psychology, 35*, 351-363.

Burrows, G. D. (2004). *Stress and health: Journal of the International Society for the Investigation of Stress*. West Sussex, UK: John Wiley & Sons, Ltd.

Byrne, D. (1971). *The attraction paradigm*. New York: Academic Press.

Cannon, W. B. (1936). *Bodily changes in pain, hunger, fear, and rage* (2nd ed.) New York: Appleton-Century.

Carlisle, C. (2000). The search for meaning in HIV and AIDS: The carers' experience. *Qualitative Health Research, 10*(6), 750-765.

Carver, C. S., & Scheier, M. F. (1981). *Attention and self-regulation: A control-theory approach to human behavior*. New York: Springer-Verlag.

Carver, C. S., & Scheier, M. F. (1983). A control-theory model of normal behavior, and implications for problems in self-management. In P.C. Kendal (Ed.), *Advances in cognitive-behavioral research and therapy* (Vol. 2, pp. 127-194). New York: Academic Press.

Carver, C. S., & Scheier, M. F. (1985). Self-consciouslness, expectancies, and the coping process. In T. Field, P. M. McCabe, & N. Schneiderman (Eds.), *Stress and coping* (pp. 305-330). Hillsdale, NJ: Erlbaum.

Carver, C. S., & Scheier, M. F. (1999). Optimism. In C. R. Snyder (Ed.), *Coping: The psychology of what works* (pp. 182-200). New York: Oxford University Press.

Carver, C. S., & Scheier, M. F. (1999). Stress, coping, and self-regulatory processes. In L. A. Pervin and O. P. John (Eds.), *Handbook of Personality* (2nd ed.) (pp. 553-575). New York: Guilford Press.

Carver, C., Scheier, M., & Weintraub, J. (1989). Assessing coping strategies: A theoretically based approach. *Journal of Personality and Social Psychology, 56*, 267-283.

Carver, C. S., Lawrence, J. W., & Scheier, M. F. (1996). A control-process perspective on the origins of affect. In L. L. Martin & A. Tesser (Eds.), *Striving and feeling: Interactions between goals and affect* (pp. 11-52). Hillsdale, NJ: Erlbaum.

Chang, V. Y., Palesh, O., Caldwell, R., Glasgow, N., Abramson, M., Luskin, F., Gill, M., Burke, A., & Koopman, C. (2004). The effects of a mindfulness-based stress reduction program on sress, mindfulness self-efficacy, and positive states of mind. In G.D. Burrows (Ed.), *Stress and Health: Journal of the International Society for the Investigation of Stress*, (pp.141-147). West Sussex, UK: John Wiley & Sons, Ltd.

Chung, T., Langebucher, J., Labouvie, E. Pandina, R. J., & Moos, R. H. (2001). Changes in alcoholic patients' coping responses predict 12-month treatment outcomes. *Journal of Consulting and Clinical Psychology, 69*(1), 92-100.

Cohen, F. (1987). Measurement of coping. In S. V. Kasl and C. L. Cooper (Eds.), *Stress and health: Issues in research methodology* (pp. 283-305). New York: Wiley.

Coward, D. D. (2000). Making meaning within the experience of life-threatening illness. In In G. T. Reker & K. Chamberlain (Eds.), *Exploring Existential Meaning: Optimizing human development across the life span*. Thousand Oaks, CA: Sage Publications, Inc.

Coyne, J. C., & Gottlieb, B. H. (1996). The mismeasure of coping by checklist. *Journal of Personality, 64*, 959-992.l

Davis, C., Nolen-Hoeksema, S., & Larson, J. (1998). Making sense of loss and benefiting from the experience: Two construals of meaning. *Journal of Personality and Social Psychology, 75*, 561-574.

Dunbar, H. T., Mueller, C. W., Medina, C., & Wolf, T. (1998). Psychological and spiritual growth in women living with HIV. *Social Work, 43*(2), 144-154.

Edwards, J. R. & Baglioni, Jr., A. J. (1993). The measurement of coping with stress: construct validity of the Ways of Coping Checklist and the Cybernetic Coping Scale. *Work & Stress, 7*, 17-31.

Endler, N. S., & Parker, J. D. (1990a). Multidimensional assessment of coping: a critical evaluation. *Journal of Personality & Social Psychology, 58*(5), 844-854.

Endler, N. S., & Parker, J. D. A. (1990b). *Coping Inventory for Stressful Situations (CISS): Manual*. Toronto: Multi-Health Systems, Inc.

Endler, N. S., & Parker, J. D. A. (1994). Assessment of multidimensional coping: Task, emotion, and avoidance strategies. *Psychological Assessment, 6*, 50-60.

Endler, N. S., & Parker, J. D. A. (1999). *Coping Inventory for Stressful Situations (CISS): Manual* (Revised Edition). Toronto: Multi-Health Systems.

Epstein, S. & Meier, P. (1989) Constructive thinking: A broad coping variable with specific components. *Journal of Personality and Social Psychology, 57*, 332-350.

Fiske, S. T., & Taylor, S. E. (1984). *Social cognition*. Reading, MA: Addison-Wesley.

Fleming, R., Baum, A., & Singer, J. E. (1984). Toward an integrative approach to the study of stress. *Journal of Personality and Social Psychology, 46*(4), 939-949.

Florian, V. (1989) Meaning and purpose in life of bereaved parents whose son fell during active military service. *Omega, 20*, 91-102.

Folkman, S. (1984). Personal control and stress and coping processes: A theoretical analysis. *Journal of Personality and Social Psychology, 46*(4), 839-852.

Folkman, S. (1992). Improving coping assessment: Reply to Stone and Kennedy-Moore. In H.S. Friedman (Ed.), *Hostility, coping, and health* (pp. 215-223). Washington, DC: American Psychological Association.

Folkman, S. (1997). Positive psychological states and coping with severe stress. *Social Science & Medicine, 45*(8) 1207-1221.

Folkman, S. & Lazarus, R. S. (1980) An analysis of coping in a middle-aged community sample. *Journal of Health and Social Behavior, 21*, 219-239.

Folkman, S. & Lazarus, R. S. (1981) Reply to Shinn and Krantz. *Journal of Health and Social Behavior, 22*, 457-459.

Folkman, S. & Lazarus, R. S. (1985) If it changes it must be a process: A study of emotion and coping during three stages of a college examination. *Journal of Personality and Social Psychology, 48*, 150-170.

Folkman, S., & Lazarus, R. S. (1988). *The ways of coping questionnaire.* Palo Alto: Consulting Psychologists Press.

Folkman, S., & Moskowitz, J. (2000). Positive affect and the positive side of coping. *American Psychology, 2*, 300-319.

Folkman, S., Lazarus, R. S., Dunkel-Schetter, C., DeLongis, A. & Gruen, R. J. (1986) Dynamics of a stressful encounter: Cognitive appraisal, coping and encounter outcomes. *Journal of Personality and Social Psychology, 50*, 992-1003.

Folkman, S., Lazarus, R. S., Gruen, R. J., & DeLongis, A. (1986) Appraisal, coping, health status, and psychological symptoms. *Journal of Personality and Social Psychology, 50*, 571-579.

Forsythe, C. J., & Compas, B. E (1987). Interaction of cognitive appraisals of stressful events and coping: Testing the goodness of fit hypothesis. *Cognitive Therapy and Research, 11*, 473-485.

Frankl, V. E. (1988). *The will to meaning: Foundations and applications of logotherapy, expanded edition.* New York: Penguin.

Frankl, V. E. (1992). *Man's search for meaning* (4th ed.). Boston, MA: Beacon Press.

Freud, A. (1936). *The ego and the mechanisms of defense.* New York: International Universities Press.

Freud, S. (1962). The neoro-psychoses of defense. In J. Strachey (Ed. And Trans.) *The standard edition of the complete psychological works of Sigmund Freud* (Vol. 3, pp. 45-61). London: Hogarth Press. (Original work published 1894).

Glass, D. C. (1977). *Behavior patterns, stress, and coronary disease.* Hiillsdale, NJ: Erlbaum.

Greenglass, E. (1988). Type A behavior and coping strategies in female and male supervisors. *Applied Psychology: An international review, 37*, 271-288.

Greenglass, E., Burke, R. J., & Ondrack, M. (1990). A gender-role perspective of coping and burnout. *Applied Psychology: An international review*, 39, 5-27.

Greenstein, M., & Breitbart, W. (2000). Cancer and the experience of meaning: A group psychotherapy program for people with cancer. *American Journal of Psychotherapy, 54*, 486-500.

Haan, N. (1977). *Coping and defending.* New York: Academic Press.

Janoff-Bulman, R. (1992). *Shattered assumptions: Toward a new psychology of trauma.* New York: Free Press.

Kabat-Zinn, J. (1998). Meditation. In J.C. Holland (Ed.), *Psycho-oncology* (pp. 767-779). New York: Oxford University Press.

Kabat-Zinn, J. (2003). Mindfulness-based interventions in context: past, present, and future. *American Psychologist, 10*(2), 144-156.

Koenig, H. G. (1994). *Aging and God: Spiritual pathways to mental health in middle and later years.* New York: Haworth Pastoral Press.

Koenig, H. G., Kvale, J. N., & Ferrel, C. (1988) Religion and well being in later life. *The Gerontologist, 28*, 18-28.

Lazarus, R. S. (1966). *Psychological stress and the coping process.* New York: McGraw-Hill.

Lazarus, R. S. (1990). Theory-based stress measurement. *Psychological Inquiry, 1*, 3-13.

Lazarus, R. S. (1991). *Emotion and adaptation.* New York: Oxford University Press.

Lazarus, R. S. & DeLongis, A. (1983). Psychological stress and coping in aging. *American Psychologist, 38*, 245-254.

Lazarus, R. S. & Folkman, S. (1984). *Stress, appraisal and coping.* New York: Springer.

Litt, M. D. (1988) Cognitive mediators of stressful experience: Self-efficacy and perceived control. *Cognitive Therapy and Research, 12*, 241-260.

McCrae, R. R. (1982). Age differences in the use of coping mechanisms. *Journal of Personality and Social Psychology, 44*, 1144-1156.

McCrae, R. R. (1984). Situational determinants of coping responses: Loss, threat, and challenge. *Journal of Personality and Social Psychology, 46*(4), 919-928.

McWilliams, L. A., Cox, B. J., & Enns, M. W. (2003). Use of the Coping inventory for stressful situations in a clinically depressed sample: Factor structure, personality correlates, and prediction of distress. *Journal of Clinical Psychology, 59*(4), 423-437.

Meichenbaum, D. (1977). *Cognitive-behavior modification*. New York: Plenum Press.

Mikulincher, M. & Victor, F. (1995). Appraisal of and coping with real-life stressful situation: The contribution of attachment styles. *Personality and Social Psychology Bulletin, 21*(4), 406-415.

Miller, S. M. (1979). Coping with impending stress: Psychophysiological and cognitive correlates of choice. *Psychophysiology, 16*(6), 572-581.

Mok, E. (2001). Empowerment of cancer patients: From a Chinese perspective. *Nursing Ethics, 8*(1), 69-76.

Mok, E., Lai, C., & Zhang, ZX (2004). Coping with chronic renal failure in Hong Kong. *International Journal of Nursing Studies, 41*(2), 205-213.

Moos, R. H. (1988). *The Coping Responses Inventory Manual*. Palo Alto, CA: Social Ecology Laboratory, Stanford University and Department of Veterans Affairs Medical Center.

Moos, R.H. (1993). *Coping responses inventory: Adult form* (Professional Manual). Odessa, FL.: Psychological Assessment Resources, Inc.

Moos, R. H. & Billings, A. G. (1982) Conceptualizing and measuring coping resources and processes. In L. Goldberger & S. Breznitz (Eds.) *Handbook of stress: Theoretical and clinical aspects* (pp. 212-230). New York: Free Press.

Park, C., & Folkman, S. (1997). Meaning in the context of stress and coping. *Review of General Psychology, 1*, 115-144.

Parker, J. D. A. & Endler, N. S. (1992) Coping with coping assessment: A critical review. *European Journal of Personality, 6*, 321-344.

Parker, J. D. A., & Endler, N. S. (1996). Coping and defense: An historical overview. In M. Zeidner, and N. S. Endler (Eds.), *Handbook of coping: Theory, research, application* (pp. 3-23). New York: Wiley.

Peacock, E. J. (1992). *Coping with anticipatory stress: A study of appraisal, personality, and situational variables*. Doctoral Dissertation, University of Toronto.

Peacock, E. J., & Wong, P. T. P. (1990). The stress appraisal measure (SAM): A multidimensional approach to cognitive appraisal. *Stress Medicine, 6*, 227-236.

Peacock, E. J., & Wong, P. T. P. (1996). Anticipatory stress: The relation of locus of control, optimism, and control appraisals to coping. *Journal of Research in Personality, 30*, 204-222.

Peacock, E. J., Wong, P. T. P., & Reker, G. T. (1993) Relations between appraisals and coping schemas: Support for the congruence model. *Canadian Journal of Behavioral Science, 25*, 64-80.

Reed, P. (1991). Toward a theory of self-transcendence: Deductive reformulation using behavior. In M. Rosenbaum (Ed.), *Learned resourcefulness: On coping skills, self-control, and adaptive behavior* (pp. 3-30). New York: Springer.

Reker, G. T., & Chamberlain, K. (Eds.) (2000). *Exploring existential meaning: Optimizing human development across the life span*. Thousand Oaks, CA: Sage Publications.

Reker, G. T., & Wong, P. T. P. (1984). Psychological and physical well-being in the elderly: The Perceived Well-Being Scale (PWB). *Canadian Journal on Aging, 3*, 23-32.

Rothbaum, F., Weisz, J. R., & Snyder, S. (1982). Changing the world and changing the self: A two-process model of perceived control. *Journal of Personality and Social Psychology, 42*, 5-37.

Rosenbaum, M. (Ed.) (1990). *Learned resourcefulness: On coping skills, self-control, and adaptive behavior* (pp. 3-30). New York: Springer.

Roth, S., & Cohen, L. J. (1986). Approach, avoidance, and coping with stress. *The American Psychologist, 41*(7), 813-819.

Schaefer, C., Coyne, J. C., & Lazarus, R. S. (1981). The health-related functions of social support. *Journal of Behavioral Medicine, 4*, 381-406.

Scheier, M. F. & Carver, C. S. (1985). Optimism, coping, and health: Assessment and implications of generalized outcome expectancies. *Health Psychology, 4*, 219-247.

Scheier, M. F., & Carver, C. S. (1987). Dispositional optimism and physical well-being: The influence of generalized outcome expectancies on health. *Journal of Personality, 55*, 169-210.

Scheier, M. F., & Carver, C. S. (1988). A model of behavioral self-regulation: Translating intention into action. In L. Berkowitz (Ed.), *Advances in experimental social psychology* (Vol. 21, pp. 303-346). New York: Academic Press.

Scheier, M. F., & Carver, C. S. (1996). Psychological resources matter, no matter how you say it or frame it. *The Counseling Psychologist, 24*, 736-742.

Schwarzer, R. (2003). Manage stress at work through preventive and proactive coping. To appear in E. A. Locke (Ed.), *Basic principles of organizational behavior: A handbook*. Oxford, UK: Blackwell.

Schwarzer, R., & Knoll, N. (2003). Positive coping: Mastering demands and searching for meaning. In S. J. Lopez & C. R. Snyder (Eds.), *Positive Psychological Assessment: A handbook of models and measures*. Washington, DC: American Psychological Association.

Selye, H. (1976). *The stress of life*. New York: McGraw-Hill.

Silver, R. L., Boon, C., & Stones, M. H. (1983). Searching for meaning in misfortune: Making sense of incest. *Journal of Social Issues, 39*, 81-102.

Snyder, C. R. (Ed.) (1999a). *Coping: The psychology of what works*. New York: Oxford University Press.

Snyder, C. R. (1999b). Coping: Where are you going? In C. R. Snyder (Ed.), *The psychology of what works* (pp.324-333). New York: Oxford University Press.

Stephenson, J. S., & Murphy, D. (1986). Existential grief: The special case of the chronically ill and disabled. *Death Studies, 10*, 109-119.

Stone, A. A., & Neale, J. M. (1984). New measure of daily coping: Development and preliminary results. *Journal of Personality and Social Psychology, 46*(4), 892-906.

Stone, A. A., Greenberg, M. A., Kennedy-Moore, E., & Newman, M. G. (1991) Self-report, situation-specific coping questionnaires: what are they measuring? *Journal of Personality and Social Psychology, 61*, 648-658.

Suls, J., & Fletcher, B. (1985). Self-attention, life stress, and illness: A prospective study. *Psychosomatic Medicine, 47*(5), 469-481.

Taylor, S. (1983). Adjustments to life-threatening events: A theory of cognitive adaptation. *American Psychologist, 38*, 1161-1173.

Taylor, S. E., & Aspinwall, L. G. (1992). Coping with chronic illness. In L. Goldberger and S. Breznitz (Eds.), *Handbook of stress: theoretical and clinical aspects* (2nd ed.; pp. 511-531). Toronto: The Fress Press.

Tennen, H., & Affleck, G. (1999). Finding benefits in adversity. In C. R. Snyder (Ed.), *Coping: The psychology of what works* (pp. 279-298). New York: Oxford University Press.

Tennen, H., & Affleck, G. (2003). Benefit-finding and benefit-reminding. In C. R. Snyder & S. J. Lopez (Eds.), *The handbook of positive psychology*. New York: Oxford University Press.

Tennen, H., Affleck, G., Armeli, S., & Carney, M. A. (2000). A daily process approach to coping. *American Psychologist, 55*, 626-636.

Terry, D. J. (1994). Determinants of coping: The role of stable and situational factors. *Journal of Personality and Social Psychology, 66*(5), 895-910.

Thompson, S., & Janigian, A. (1988). Life schemes: A framework for understanding the search for meaning. *Journal of Social and Clinical Psychology, 7*(2/3), 260-280.

Vaillant, G. E. (1977). *Adaptation to life*. Boston: Little, Brown.

Van Ranst, N., & Marcoen, A. (2000). Structural components of personal meaning in life and their relationship with death attitudes and coping mechanisms inlate adulthood. In G. T. Reker & K. Chamberlain (Eds.), *Exploring Existential Meaning: Optimizing human development across the life span* (pp.59-74). Thousand Oaks, CA: Sage Publications, Inc.

Vitaliano, P. P., Russo, J., & Maiuro, R. D. (1985). Locus of control, type of stressor, and appraisal within a cognitive-phenomenological model of stress. *Journal of Research in Personality, 21*, 224-237.

Watson, D. (1988). Intraindividual and interindividual analyses of positive and negative effect: Their relation to health complaints, perceived stress, and daily activities. *Journal of Personality and Social Psychology, 54*, 1020-1030.

Wong, P. T. P. (1989). Successful aging and personal meaning. *Canadian Psychology, 30*, 516-525.

Wong, P. T. P. (1990). Measuring life stress. *Stress Medicine, 6*, 69-70.

Wong, P. T. P. (1991). Existential vs. causal attributions. In S. Zelen (Ed.) *Extensions and new models of attribution theory* (pp. 84-125). New York: Springer-Verlag Publishers.

Wong, P. T. P. (1992). Control is a double-edged sword. *Canadian Journal of Behavioral Science, 24*, 143-146.

Wong, P. T. P. (1993). Effective management of life stress: The resource-congruence model, *Stress Medicine, 9*, 51-60.

Wong, P. T. P. (1998a). Implicit theories of meaningful life and the development of the Personal Meaning Profile (PMP). In P. T. P. Wong & P. Fry (Eds.) *The human quest for meaning: A handbook of psychological research and clinical applications* (pp. 111-140). Mahwah, NJ: Lawrence Erlbaum Associates, Inc., Publishers.

Wong, P. T. P. (1998b). Spirituality, meaning, and successful aging. In P. T. P. Wong & P. Fry (Eds.), *The human quest for meaning: A handbook of psychological research and clinical applications* (pp. 359-394). Mahwah, NJ: Lawrence Erlbaum Associates, Inc., Publishers.

Wong, P. T. P. (2005). Viktor Frankl: Prophet of hope for the 21st century. In A. Batthyany & J. Levinson (Eds.), *Anthology of Viktor Frankl's Logotherapy*. Tulsa, AZ: Zeig, Theisen & Tucker Publishers.

Wong, P. T. P., & Fry, P. (Eds.) (1998). *The human quest for meaning: A handbook of psychological research and clinical applications*. Mahwah, NJ: Lawrence Erlbaum Associates.

Wong, P. T. P., & McDonald, M. (2002). Tragic optimism and personal meaning in counseling victims of abuse. *Pastoral Sciences, 20*(2), 231-249.

Wong, P. T. P., & Reker, G. T. (1982). *The coping strategies of Caucasian and Chinese elderly*. Paper presented at the Annual Meeting of the Canadian Association on Gerontology, Winnipeg.

Wong, P. T. P. & Reker, G. T. (1983) *Face validity of the Coping Inventory*. Paper presented at the annual meeting of the Canadian Association on Gerontology, Moncton, Canada.

Wong, P. T. P., & Reker, G. T. (1984). *Coping behaviors of successful agers*. Paper presented at the 30th Western Gerontological Society Annual Meeting in Anaheim, California.

Wong, P. T. P., & Reker, G. T. (1985a, June). *Coping behavior of Type A individuals*. Paper presented at the Annual Meeting of the Canadian Psychological Association, Halifax.

Wong, P. T. P. & Reker, G. T. (1985b, November). *Effective coping and health: A matching model*. A workshop given at the Canadian Gerontological Association Meeting, Vancouver.

Wong, P. T. P., & Reker, G. T. (1985c). Stress, coping, and well-being in Anglo and Chinese elderly. *Canadian Journal on Aging, 4*(1), 29-37.

Wong, P. T. P., Reker, G. T., & Peacock, E. J. (1987). *Coping Orientations and Prototypes (COAP)*. Unpublished manuscript, Trent University, Peterborough,ON.

Wong, P. T. P., Reker, G. T., & Peacock, E. J. (1993). *The Coping Schema Inventory*. Unpublished manuscript. Trent University.

Wong, P. T. P., & Sproule, C. F. (1983). An attribution analysis of the locus of control construct and the Trent Attribution Profile. In H. M. Lefcourt (Ed.), *Research with the locus of control construct* (Vol. 3, pp. 309-360). New York, NY: Academic Press.

Wong, P. T. P., & Stiller, C. (1999). Living with dignity and palliative care. In B. de Vries (Ed.), *End of life issues: Interdisciplinary and multidimensional perspectives* (pp. 77-94). New York: Springer.

Wong, P. T. P., & Ujimoto, K. V. (1998). The Asian American elderly: Their stress, coping, and well-being. In L.D. Lee & N. Zane (Eds.) *Handbook of Asian American psychology* (pp. 165-209). Newbury Park, CA: Sage.

Wong, P. T. P., & Weiner, B. (1981). When people ask "Why" questions and the heuristic of attributional search. *Journal of Personality and Social Psychology, 40*, 650-663.

Wortman, C. B., Silver, R. C., & Kessler, R. C. (1993). The meaning of loss and adjustment bereavement. In M. S. Stroebe, W. Stroebe, & R. O. Hansson (Eds.), *Bereavement: A source book of research and intervention* (pp. 349-366). London: Cambridge University Press.

Yalom, I. (1981). *Existential psychotherapy*. New York: Basic Books.

Section 3

Acculturative Stress

12

ACCULTURATIVE STRESS

John W. Berry

1. INTRODUCTION

The concept of "*acculturative stress*" was introduced (Berry, 1970) as an alternative to the term *culture shock* (Oberg, 1960). The reasons for coining this new term will be outlined below, following a discussion of the concept of *acculturation* itself, and how it has come to be employed in cross-cultural psychology. The chapter then presents a framework for understanding how groups and individuals experience and manage the process of acculturation, focusing on the concept of "acculturation strategies" as a way of coping with acculturative change. Then, attention turns to the core notion of "acculturative stress" itself. Finally, we consider the concept of "adaptation", as an long term outcome of the process of acculturation.

2. ACCULTURATION CONCEPT

The initial interest in acculturation grew out of a concern for the effects of European domination of colonial and indigenous peoples (Thurnwald, 1927). Later, it focused on how immigrants (both voluntary and involuntary) changed following their entry and settlement into receiving societies. More recently, much of the work has been involved with how ethnocultural groups[1] relate to each other, and change, as a result of their attempts to live together in culturally plural societies. Nowadays, all three foci are important, as globalization results in ever-larger trading and political relations: indigenous national populations experience neo-colonization, new waves of immigrants, sojourners and refugees flow from these economic and political changes, and large ethnocultural populations become established in most countries (see Chun, Balls-Organista & Marin, 2003; Sam & Berry, 2005 for overviews).

John W. Berry, Queen's University

[1] I employ the term *ethnocultural* group (rather than *minority* or *ethnic* group) in order to signal my contention that many groups trace their ancestry to a particular heritage culture, and are composed of individuals who identify with that heritage culture and group: such groups and individuals have a *culture*! Of course, some groups are dominant, and others are non-dominant; this power differential is important, but should not overshadow the cultural reality. Moreover, I prefer to mention specific ethnocultural groups (rather than "official" categories, such as Asian or Hispanic) since their cultural realities are unique, and the object of identification by their individual members.

Early views about the nature of acculturation are a useful foundation for contemporary discussion. Two formulations in particular, have been widely quoted. The first is:

Acculturation comprehends those phenomena which result when groups of individuals having different cultures come into continuous first-hand contact, with subsequent changes in the original culture patterns of either or both groups... under this definition, acculturation is to be distinguished from culture change, of which it is but one aspect, and assimilation, which is at times a phase of acculturation... (Redfield, Linton, & Herskovits, 1936, pp. 149-152).

In another formulation, acculturation was defined as:

Culture change that is initiated by the conjunction of two or more autonomous cultural systems. Acculturative change may be the consequence of direct cultural transmission; it may be derived from non-cultural causes, such as ecological or demographic modification induced by an impinging culture; it may be delayed, as with internal adjustments following upon the acceptance of alien traits or patterns; or it may be a reactive adaptation of traditional modes of life (Social Science Research Council, 1954, p. 974).

In the first formulation, acculturation is seen as one aspect of the broader concept of culture change (that which results from intercultural contact), is considered to generate change in "either or both groups", and is distinguished from assimilation (which may be "at times a phase"). These are important distinctions for psychological work, and will be pursued later. In the second definition, a few extra features are added, including change that is indirect (not cultural but "ecological"), delayed (internal adjustments, presumably of both a cultural and psychological character take time), and can be "reactive" (that is, rejecting the cultural influence and changing towards a more "traditional" way of life, rather than inevitably towards greater similarity with the dominant culture).

As for all cross-cultural psychology (Berry, Poortinga, Segall & Dasen, 2002), it is imperative that we base our work on acculturation by examining its cultural contexts. We need to understand, in ethnographic terms, both cultures that are in contact if we are to understand the individuals that are in contact. Thus a linkage is sought between the acculturation of an individual's group and the *psychological acculturation* of that individual. For Graves (1967), psychological acculturatioin refers to changes in an individual who is a participant in a culture contact situation, being influenced both directly by the external culture, and by the changing culture of which the individual is a member. There are two reasons for keeping these two levels distinct. The first is that our field insists that we view individual human behavior as interacting with the cultural context within which it occurs; hence separate conceptions and measurements are required at the two levels. The second is that not every individual enters into, and participates in, or changes in the same way; there are vast individual differences in psychological acculturation, even among individuals who live in the same acculturative arena.

3. ACCULTURATION FRAMEWORK

A framework that outlines and links cultural and psychological acculturation, and identifies the two (or more) groups in contact is presented in Figure 1. This Framework serves as a

Figure 1. A General Framework for Understanding Acculturation

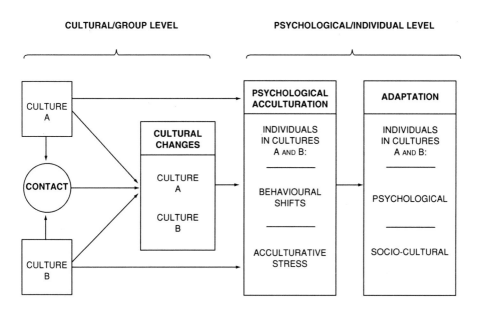

map of those phenomena which I believe need to be conceptualized and measured during acculturation research. At the cultural level (on the left) we need to understand key features of the two original cultural groups (A & B) prior to their major contact, the nature of their contact relationships, and the resulting cultural changes in both groups and in the emergent ethnocultural groups, during the process of acculturation. The gathering of this information requires extensive ethnographic, community-level work. These changes can be minor or substantial, and range from being easily accomplished through to being a source of major cultural disruption. At the individual level (on the right) we need to consider the psychological changes that individuals in all groups undergo, and their eventual adaptation to their new situations. Identifying these changes requires sampling a population and studying individuals who are variably involved in the process of acculturation. These changes can be a set of rather easily accomplished behavioral shifts (e.g., in ways of speaking, dressing, eating and in one's cultural identity) or they can be more problematic, producing acculturative stress as manifested by uncertainty, anxiety, and depression (Berry, 1976). Adaptations can be primarily internal or psychological (e.g., sense of well-being, of self-esteem) or socio-cultural, linking the individual to others in the new society as manifested for example in competence in the activities of daily intercultural living (Searle & Ward, 1990). General overviews of this process and these specific features can be found in the literature (e.g., Berry, 1980, 1990, 1997; Berry & Sam, 1997; Birman, 1994; Ward, 1996).

4. ACCULTURATION STRATEGIES

Not all groups and individuals undergo acculturation in the same way; there are large variations in how people seek to engage the process. In much of the earlier research, it was assumed that individuals changed from being "traditional" in their attitudes and behaviours, to become more like the dominant society that was influencing them. This 'assimilationist' view of how people changed served the purposes of those who considered that the goal of acculturation was to achieve a 'melting pot ,in which all peoples would come to share one language, one identity and one set of values. However, beginning in the 1980's (see Berry, 1980), this unidimensional conception of acculturation began to change, and yield to a more complex, and multidimensional views (Ryder, Alden & Paulhus, 2000). These various orientations are termed *acculturation_attitudes* (see Berry et al, 1989), or *acculturation strategies*. Which strategies are used depends on a variety of antecedent factors (both cultural and psychological); and there are variable consequences (again both cultural and psychological) of these different strategies. These strategies consist of two (usually related) components: *attitudes* and *behaviors* (that is, the preferences and actual outcomes) that are exhibited in day-to-day intercultural encounters.

The centrality of the concept of acculturation strategies can be illustrated by reference to each of the components included in Figure 1. At the cultural level, the two groups in contact (whether dominant or non-dominant) usually have some notion about what they are attempting to do (e.g., colonial policies, or motivations for migration), or what is being done to them, during the contact. Similarly, the kinds of changes that are likely to occur will be influenced by their strategies. At the individual level, both the behavioral changes and acculturative stress phenomena are now known to be a function, at least to some extent, of what people try to do during their acculturation; and the longer term outcomes (both psychological and socio-cultural adaptations) often correspond to the strategic goals set by the groups of which they are members.

Four acculturation strategies have been derived from two basic issues facing all acculturating peoples. These issues are based on the distinction between orientations towards one's own group, and those towards other groups (Berry, 1970, 1974, 1980). This distinction is rendered as a relative preference for maintaining one's heritage culture and identity and a relative preference for having contact with and participating in the larger society along with other ethnocultural groups.[2] This formulation is presented in Figure 2.

These two issues can be responded to attitudinal dimensions, represented by bipolar arrows. For purposes of presentation, generally positive or negative ("yes" or "no" responses) to these issues intersect to define four acculturation strategies. These strategies carry different names, depending on which ethnocultural group (the dominant or non-dominant) is being considered. From the point of view of non-dominant groups (on the left of Figure 2), when individuals do not wish to maintain their cultural identity and seek daily interaction with other cultures, the Assimilation strategy is defined. In contrast, when individuals place a value on holding on to their original culture, and at the same time wish to avoid interaction with others, then the Separation alternative is defined.

When there is an interest in both maintaining one's original culture, while in daily interactions with other groups, Integration is the option. In this case, there is some degree

---

[2] Variations in the attitude objects presented in Issue 2 have been varied in recent research (see section on Focus, below).

Figure 2. Four Acculturation Strategies Based Upon Two Issues, in Ethnocultural Groups, and the Larger Society

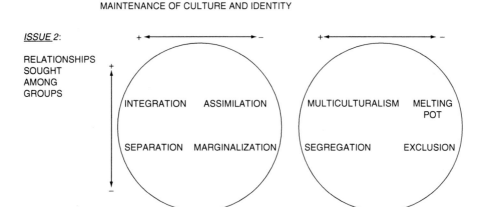

ISSUE 1:

MAINTENANCE OF CULTURE AND IDENTITY

of cultural integrity maintained, while at the same time seeking, as a member of an ethno-cultural group, to participate as an integral part of the larger social network. Integration can take a number of forms. One are similar to how a bilingual person switches between languages, depending on the linguistic context, speaking either language in the appropriate setting. Another is when there is a blending, in which features of both cultures are merged into a new behavioural repertoire that is distinct from both original cultures. This may be compared to a 'joint venture' in which practices of one corporation are adapted to better fit the requirements of working with another corporation in their home setting.

Finally, when there is little possibility or interest in cultural maintenance (often for reasons of enforced cultural loss), and little interest in having relations with others (often for reasons of having experienced exclusion or discrimination) then Marginalization is defined. In this situation, there is confusion, uncertainty, and frequently signs of social and psychological problems (such as substance of family abuse, school failure or inability to keep a job).

This presentation was based on the assumption that non-dominant groups and their individual members have the freedom to choose how they want to acculturate. This, of course, is not always the case (Berry, 1974). When the dominant group enforces certain forms of acculturation, or constrains the choices of non-dominant groups or individuals, then other terms need to be used (see below).

Integration can only be "freely" chosen and successfully pursued by non-dominant groups when the dominant society is open and inclusive in its orientation towards cultural diversity (Berry, 1991). Thus a mutual accommodation is required for Integration to be attained, involving the acceptance by both groups of the right of all groups to live as culturally different peoples. This strategy requires non-dominant groups to adopt the basic values of the larger society, while at the same time the dominant group must be prepared to adapt national institutions (e.g., education, health, labor) to better meet the needs of all groups now living together in the plural society.

These two basic issues were initially approached from the point of view of the non-dominant ethnocultural groups. However, the original anthropological definition clearly established that *both* groups in contact would become acculturated. Hence in 1974, a third dimension was added: that of the powerful role played by the dominant group in influencing the way in which mutual acculturation would take place (Berry, 1974; 1980). The addition of this third dimension produces the right side of Figure 2. Assimilation when sought by the non-dominant acculturating group was termed the "Melting Pot," but when demanded by the dominant group, it was called the "Pressure cooker." When Separation was desired by the acculturating group it was termed "Withdrawal," but when forced by the dominant group it was "Segregation." Marginalization, when sought by members of a group, is termed "Marginality" but when imposed by the dominant group it is "Ethnocide." Finally, Integration, when diversity is a feature of the society as a whole, is termed "Pluralism" and when this diversity is desired by the various ethnocultural groups, it is called "Multiculturalism" (Berry, 1980).

With the use of this framework, comparisons can be made between individuals and their groups, and between non-dominant peoples and the larger society within which they are acculturating. The ideologies and policies of the dominant group constitute an important element of ethnic relations research (see Berry, et al, 1977; Bourhis, et al 1997), while preferences of non-dominant peoples are a core feature in understanding the process of acculturation in non-dominant groups (Berry et al., 1989). Inconsistencies and conflicts between these various acculturation preferences are sources of difficulty for acculturating individuals. Generally, when acculturation experiences cause problems for acculturating individuals, we observe the phenomenon of *acculturative_stress* (see below).

5. ACCULTURATIVE STRESS

Three ways to conceptualize outcomes of acculturation have been proposed in the literature (see Figure 3). In the first (*behavioural shifts*) we observe those changes in an individual's behavioural repertoire that take place rather easily, and are usually non-problematic. This process encompasses three sub-processes: culture shedding; culture learning; and culture conflict (Berry, 1992). The first two involve the selective, accidental or deliberate loss of behaviors, and their replacement by behaviors that allow the individual a better "fit" in with the larger society. Most often this process has been termed "adjustment" (Ward & Kennedy, 1993a), since virtually all the adaptive changes take place in the acculturating individual, with few changes occurring among members of the larger society. These adjustments are typically made with minimal difficulty, in keeping with the appraisal of the acculturation experiences as non-problematic. However, some degree of conflict may occur, which is usually resolved by the acculturating person yielding to the behavioral norms of the dominant group. In this latter case, Assimilation is the most likely outcome.

When greater levels of conflict are experienced, and the experiences are judged to be problematic but controllable and surmountable, then the second approach (*acculturative*

Figure 3. Three Approaches to Conceptualizing Psychological Difficulties During Acculturation

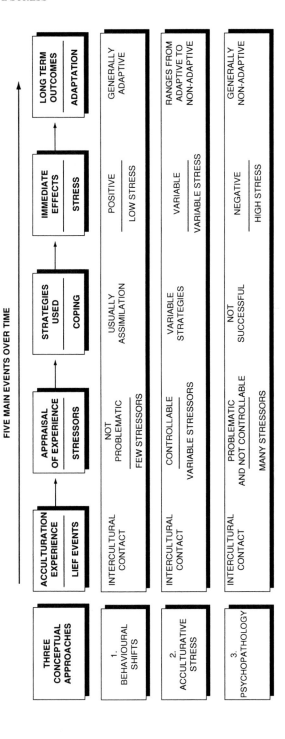

stress) is the appropriate conceptualization (Berry, 1970; Berry, Kim, Minde & Mok, 1987). In this case, individuals experience change events in their lives that challenge their cultural understandings about how to live. These change events reside in their accultura- tion experiences, hence the term "acculturative" stress. In these situations, they come to understand that they are facing problems resulting from intercultural contact that cannot be dealt with easily or quickly by simply adjusting or assimilating to them. Drawing on the broader stress and adaptation paradigms (e.g., Lazarus & Folkman, 1984), this approach advocates the study of the process of how individuals deal with acculturative problems on first encountering them, and over time. In this sense, acculturative stress is a stress reac- tion in response to life events that are rooted in the experience of acculturation.

A third approach *(psychopathology)* has had long use in clinical psychology and psy- chiatry. In this view, acculturation is almost always seen as problematic; individuals usu- ally require assistance to deal with virtually insurmountable stressors in their lives. However, contemporary evidence (eg., Berry & Kim, 1988; Beiser, 2000) shows that most people deal with stressors and re-establish their lives rather well, with health, psychologi- cal and social outcomes that approximate those of individuals in the larger society.

Instead of using the term *culture shock* (see Ward, Bochner & Furnham, 2001) to encompass these three approaches, we prefer to use the term *acculturative stress* for two reasons.

First, the notion of *shock* carries only negative connotations, while *stress* can vary from positive (*eustress*) to negative (*dis-stress*) in valence. Since acculturation has both pos- itive (eg., new opportunities) and negative (eg., discrimination) aspects, the stress concep- tualization better matches the range of affect experienced during acculturation. Moreover, *shock* has no cultural or psychological theory, or research context associated with it, while *stress* (as noted above) has a place in a well-developed theoretical matrix (ie., stress-coping- adaptation). Second, the phenomena of interest have their life in the intersection of *two* cul- tures; they are intercultural, rather than cultural in their origin. The term *culture* implies that only one culture is involved, while the term *acculturation* draws our attention to the fact that two cultures are interacting, and producing the phenomena. Hence, for both rea- sons, we prefer the notion of *acculturative stress* to that of *culture shock*.

Relating these three approaches to acculturation strategies, some consistent empirical findings allow the following generalizations (Berry, 1997; Berry & Sam, 1997). For behav- ioral shifts, fewest behavioral changes result from the Separation strategy, while most result from the Assimilation strategy; Integration involves the selective adoption of new behaviors from the larger society, and retention of valued features of one's heritage cul- ture; and Marginalization is often associated with major heritage culture loss, and the appearance of a number of dysfunctional and deviant behaviors (such as delinquency, and substance and familial abuse). For acculturative stress, there is a clear picture that the pur- suit of Integration is least stressful (at least where it is accommodated by the larger soci- ety) while Marginalization is the most stressful; in between are the Assimilation and Separation strategies, sometimes one, sometimes the other being the less stressful. This pattern of findings holds for various indicators of mental health (Berry & Kim, 1988; Schmitz, 1992), and for self-esteem (Phinney, Chavira & Williamson, 1992).

Individuals engage in the appraisal of these experiences and behavioral changes. When they are appraised as challenging, some basic coping mechanisms are activated. Lazarus and Folkman (1984) have identified two major coping functions: problem- focused coping (attempting to change or solve the problem) and emotion-focused coping (attempting to regulate the emotions associated with the problem). More recently, Endler and Parker (1990) have identified a third: avoidance-oriented coping. It is not yet clear how the first two coping strategies relate to acculturation strategies since both forms of coping are likely to be involved in Assimilation and Integration. However, the third (avoidance) closely resembles the Separation and possibly the Marginalization strategies.

6. ADAPTATION

As a result of attempts to cope with these acculturation changes, some long-term adaptations may be achieved. As mentioned earlier, adaptation refers to the relatively stable changes that take place in an individual or group in response to external demands. Moreover, adaptation may or may not improve the "fit" between individuals and their environments. It is thus not a term that necessarily implies that individuals or groups change to become more like their environments (i.e., adjustment by way of Assimilation), but may involve resistance and attempts to change their environments, or to move away from them altogether (i.e., by Separation). In this usage, adaptation is an outcome that may or may not be positive in valence (i.e., meaning only well-adapted). This bi-polar sense of the concept of adaptation is used in the framework in Figure 1 where long term adaptation to acculturation is highly variable ranging from well- to poorly-adapted, varying from a situation where individuals can manage their new lives very well, to one where they are unable to carry on in the new society.

Adaptation is also multifaceted. The initial distinction between psychological and sociocultural adaptation was proposed and validated by Ward and colleagues (Searle & Ward, 1990; Ward, 1996; Ward & Kennedy, 1993a). Psychological adaptation largely involves one's psychological and physical well-being (Schmitz, 1992), while socio-cultural adaptation refers to how well an acculturating individual is able to manage daily life in the new cultural context. While conceptually distinct, they are empirically related to some extent (correlations between the two measures are in the +.4 to +.5 range). However, they are also empirically distinct in the sense that they usually have different time courses and different experiential predictors. Psychological problems often increase soon after contact, followed by a general (but variable) decrease over time; sociocultural adaptation, however, typically has a linear improvement with time. Analyses of the factors affecting adaptation reveal a generally consistent pattern. Good psychological adaptation is predicted by personality variables, life change events, and social support while good sociocultural adaptation is predicted by cultural knowledge, degree of contact, and positive intergroup attitudes. Both aspects of adaptation are usually predicted by the successful pursuit of the Integration acculturation strategy and by minimal cultural distance (Ward & Kennedy, 1993b; Ward, 1996).

Other forms of adaptation have been proposed, including "economic adaptation" (Aycan & Berry, 1996), and "marital adaptation" (Ataca & Berry, 2002). Both of these forms of adaptation tend to blend psychological and sociocultural features. In the case of economic adaptation, immigrants often experience an initial loss of economic status on arrival in the country of settlement, followed by a period of slow recovery until they regain, or even surpass, the economic level with which the left their country of origin. Since work life is an integral part of how people deal with their new social context, it is a core component of their sociocultural adaptation. However, there are psychological components involved as well: loss of economic status is often accompanied by feelings of depression and lowered self-worth. These psychological aspects interact with the social ones, interfering with ones ability to look for or hold a job, leading to a spiral of declining adaptation. In the case of marital adaptation, spouses often experience acculturation differentially. Sometimes the husband is more engaged with the larger society, while the wife remains in the home or involved with the ethnocultural community. These differing patterns of contact are associated with differing kinds of life changes, strategies and stressors. Occasionally, the pattern is reversed, where the husband works outside the home, but entirely within an ethnospecific work setting having little contact with the larger society, whereas the wife may engage the community at large when dealing with schooling and health care needs of the children. Whichever the pattern of acculturation experience, it is the "differential" experience that places stressors on the marital relationship, leading to both psychological and sociocultural difficulties.

Research relating adaptation to acculturation strategies allows for some generalizations (Berry, 1997; Ward, 1996). For all forms of adaptation, those who pursue and accomplish Integration appear to be better adapted, while those who are Marginalized are least well-adapted. And again, the Assimilation and Separation strategies are associated with intermediate adaptation outcomes. While there are occasional variations on this pattern, it is remarkably consistent, and parallels the generalization regarding acculturative stress.

7. CONCLUSION

There is now widespread evidence that most people who have experienced acculturation actually do survive! They are not destroyed or substantially diminished by it; rather they find opportunities, and achieve their goals sometimes beyond their initial imaginings. The tendency to "pathologize" the acculturation process and outcomes may be partly due to the history of its study in psychiatry and in clinical psychology. Second, researchers often presume to know what acculturating individuals want, and impose their own ideologies or their personal views, rather than informing themselves about culturally-rooted individual preferences and differences. One key concept (but certainly not the only one) to understand this variability was emphasized in this chapter (acculturation strategies).

The generalizations that have been made in this chapter on the basis of a wide range of empirical findings allow us to propose that public policies and programs that seek to reduce acculturative stress and to improve intercultural relationships should emphasize the Integration approach to acculturation. This is equally true for national policies, institutional arrangements, and the goals of ethnocultural groups; and it is also true for individuals in the larger society as well as members of non-dominant acculturating groups.

In some countries, the integrationist perspective has become legislated in as policies of Multiculturalism, which encourage and support the maintenance of valued features of all cultures, and at the same time support full participation of all ethnocultural groups in the evolving institutions of the larger society. What seems certain is that cultural diversity and the resultant acculturation are here to stay in all countries. Finding a way to accommodate each other poses a challenge and an opportunity to social and cross-cultural psychologists everywhere. Diversity is a fact of contemporary life; whether it is the "spice of life", or the main "irritant", is probably the central question that confronts us all, citizens and social scientists alike.

REFERENCES

Ataca, B. & Berry, J.W. (2002). Sociocultural, psychological and marital adaptation of Turkish immigrant couples in Canada. *International Journal of Psychology*, 37, 13-26.

Aycan, Z. & Berry, J.W. (1996). Impact of employment-related experiences on immigrants' psychological well-being and adaptation to Canada. *Canadian Journal of Behavioural Science*, 28, 240-251.

Berry, J. W. (1970). Marginality, stress and ethnic identification in an acculturated Aboriginal community. *Journal of Cross-Cultural Psychology*, 1, 239-252.

Berry, J. W. (1974). Psychological aspects of cultural pluralism: Unity and identity reconsidered. *Topics in Culture Learning*, 2, 17-22.

Berry, J. W. (1976). *Human ecology and cognitive style: Comparative studies in cultural and psychological adaptation*. New York: Sage/Halsted.

Berry, J. W. (1980). Acculturation as varieties of adaptation. In A. Padilla (Ed.), *Acculturation: Theory, models and findings* (pp. 9-25). Boulder: Westview.

Berry, J. W. (1984). Multicultural policy in Canada: A social psychological analysis. *Canadian Journal of Behavioural Science*, 16, 353-370.

Berry, J. W. (1990). Psychology of acculturation. In J. Berman (Ed.), *Cross-cultural perspectives: Nebraska symposium on motivation* (pp. 201-234). Lincoln: University of Nebraska Press.

Berry, J. W. (1991). Understanding and managing multiculturalism. *Journal of Psychology and Developing Societies*, 3, 17-49.

Berry, J. W. (1992). Acculturation and adaptation in a new society. *International Migration*, 30, 69-85.

Berry, J. W. (1997). Immigration, acculturation and adaptation. *Applied Psychology*, 46, 5-68.

Berry, J. W. Kalin, R., & Taylor, D. (1977). *Multiculturalism and ethnic attitudes in Canada*. Ottawa: Supply & Services.

Berry, J. W., & Kim, U. (1988). Acculturation and mental health. In P. Dasen, J. W. Berry, & N. Sartorius (Eds.), *Health and cross-cultural psychology* (pp. 207-236). Newbury Park: Sage.

Berry, J. W., Kim, U., Minde, T., & Mok. D. (1987). Comparative studies of acculturative stress. *International Migration Review*, 21, 491-511.

Berry, J. W., Kim, U., Power, S., Young, M., & Bujaki, M. (1989). Acculturation attitudes in plural societies. *Applied Psychology*, 38, 185-206.

Berry, J.W., Poortinga, Y.H., Segall, M.H. & Dasen, P.R. (2002). *Cross-cultural psychology: Research and applications (2nd ed.)*. New York: Cambridge University Press.

Berry, J. W., & Sam, D. (1997). Acculturation and adaptation. In J. W. Berry, M. H. Segall. & Kagitcibasi (Eds.), *Handbook of cross-cultural psychology. Vol. 3, Social behavior and applications* (pp. 291-326). Boston: Allyn & Bacon.

Birman, D. (1994). Acculturation and human diversity in a multicultural society. In E. Trickett, R. Watts, & D. Birman (Eds.), *Human diversity* (pp. 261-284). San Francisco: Jossey-Bass.

Bourhis, R. (et al) (1997). Towards an interactive acculturation model: A social psychological approach. *International Journal of Psychology*, 32, 369-386.

Chun, K., Balls-Organista, P.,& Marin, G. (Eds.) (2003). *Acculturation: Advances in theory, measurement and applied research*. Washington: APA Books.

Endler, N., & Parker, J. (1990). Multidimensional assessment of coping. *Journal of Personality and Social Psychology*, 58, 844-854.

Graves, T. (1967). Psychological acculturation in a tri-ethnic community. *South-Western Journal of Anthropology*, 23, 337-350.

Ho, E. (1995). Chinese or New Zealander? Differential paths of adaptation of Chinese Adolescent immigrants in New Zealand. *New Zealand Population Review*, 21, 27-49. *Studies*, 27, 1-15.

Lazarus, R. S., & Folkman, S. (1984). *Stress, appraisal and coping*. New York: Springer.

Oberg, K. (1960). Cultural shock: Adjustment to new cultural environments. *Practical Anthropology*, 7, 177-182

Phinney, J., Chavira, V., & Williamson, L. (1992). Acculturation attitudes and self-esteem among school and college students. *Youth and Society*, 23, 299-312.

Redfield, R., Linton, R. & Herskovits, M. (1936). Memorandum on the study of acculturation. *American Anthropologist*, 38, 149-152.

Ryder, A., Alden, L., & Paulus, D. (2000). *Is acculturation unidimensional or* bidimensional? *Journal of Personality and Social Psychology*, 79, 49-65

Sam, D. & Berry, J. W. (Eds.) (2005). *Cambridge handbook of acculturation psychology*. Cambridge: Cambridge University Press.

Schmitz, P. (1992). Acculturation styles and health. In S. Iwawaki, Y. Kashima, & K. Leung (Eds.), *Innovations in cross-cultural psychology* (pp. 360-370). Amsterdam: Swets and Zeitlinger.

Searle, W., & Ward, C. (1990). The prediction of psychological and sociocultural adjustment during cross-cultural transitions. *International Journal of Intercultural Relations*, 14, 449-464.

Social Science Research Council. (1954). Acculturation: An exploratory formulation. *American Anthropologist*, 56, 973-1002.

Thurnwald, R. C. (1927). The psychology of acculturation. *American Anthropologist*, 34, 557-569.

Ward, C. (1996). Acculturation. In D. Landis & R. Bhagat (Eds.), *Handbook of intercultural training* (2nd ed., pp. 124-147). Newbury Park: Sage.

Ward, C., Bochner, S. & Furnham, A. (2001). *The psychology of culture shock*. London: Routledge.

Ward, C., & Kennedy, A. (1993a). Psychological and sociocultural adjustment during cross-cultural transitions: A comparison of secondary students overseas and at home. *International Journal of Psychology*, 28, 129-147.

Ward, C., & Kennedy, A. (1993b). Where's the "culture" in cross-cultural transition? Comparative studies of sojourner adjustment. *Journal of Cross-Cultural Psychology*, 24, 221-249.

13

THE EFFECTS OF ACCULTURATIVE STRESS ON THE HISPANIC FAMILY

Amado M. Padilla and Noah E. Borrero

1. INTRODUCTION

Much has been written about the increasing rates of divorce in the United States over the past 40 years. However, most research has focused on the effects of divorce on middle-class White American families. While there has been an increase in research on marital instability among Black American families (McLoyd, Cauce, Takeuchi & Wilson, 2000), there is much less information about evolving family structures among Hispanics (Vega, 1990; Oropesa & Landale, 2004). Further, there is a dearth of information on the divorce rates among Hispanics and what effect they might be having on children. Because the Mexican American subgroup is the largest of the various ethnic groups categorized as Hispanic and about which there is the most written, this chapter will focus primarily on Mexican Americans, but where appropriate information will be extended to other Hispanic groups.

An important consideration in this chapter will be such issues as familism, gender roles, immigration and acculturation, religion, socioeconomic status and the role that each of these plays in the Hispanic family. Further, we will utilize a theoretical framework that capitalizes on acculturative stress and coping in our analysis of the marital bond in Hispanic families. Oropesa and Landale (2004) in their assessment of the future of marriage among Hispanics note that migration is stressful and risky, and requires flexibility in responsibilities and roles for immigrants to experience success in their new environment. This coupled with the greater freedom enjoyed by women in the United States may result in changes in the role that marriage has traditionally played in Hispanic culture.

Hispanic men and women experience many of the same general stressors as anyone else regardless of ethnicity or race; however, there is a class of stressors associated with immigration and acculturation that needs to be taken into consideration when discussing the Hispanic family (Cervantes, Padilla, & Salgado de Snyder, 1991; Flores, Tschann, Marin, & Panotja, 2004). Finally, this chapter will deviate from other works on the Hispanic family in a very significant way. Most of the literature on the Hispanic family has focused on the theme that the family or "*la familia*" is sacred in the Hispanic culture.

Amado M. Padilla and Noah E. Borrero, Stanford University

This literature capitalizes on the strong familial bonds between family members extending over multiple generations and the sacrifices that family members make for each other (Contreras, Hendrick, & Hendrick, 1996; Zambrana, 1995). The literature on "la familia" is replete with positive stereotypes of the Hispanic family and often these positive images are contrasted with family patterns found among other ethnic groups (Falicov, 1982; Williams, 1990). In this chapter we take the position that the Hispanic family is not monolithic and that these families, like all families, encounter daily stressors that often culminate in broken relationships and divorce. More importantly, we agree with Oropesa and Landale (2004) that acculturative stress and exposure to American culture will erode the traditional values associated with marriage among Hispanics and their descendents.

2. ACCULTURATION STRESS AND COPING

Stress is a normal occurrence in a person's life. In fact, there are many reasons why stress can be a good thing. Stress can function as a motivator to change our behavior if something is not going as well as we would hope. For example, if an individual finds his job to be unsatisfying or if he has a strong difference of opinion from that of his supervisor, he might find going to work stressful and consequently seek a new position or even consider a change in occupation. If the person feels that he is making a good decision about a career shift or a job change, then this would be a good example of stress serving as a positive influence in a person's life. However, when we speak of stress in our life we typically think about stress as something negative that causes us undue anxiety. This type of stress can occur from many sources. A sampling of typical stressors that we encounter in the stress literature are: interpersonal difficulties with family members such as parents, siblings, spouses, children; problems with peers, co-workers, or even strangers; financial obligations and/or inability to meet basic necessities such as food, shelter, and clothing; environmental conditions such as pollutants, excessive noise, over crowded living conditions; and stress associated with personal poor health or of people we are close to. No one is immune from these types of stressors. Fortunately some individuals have more social support systems in place (e.g., family and friends, religion, access to public social services) or personal resources (e.g., self-esteem) to enable them to more effectively cope with these stressors.

Another major class of stressors that researchers and mental health clinicians have begun to study has to do with acculturation and the adaptation process that immigrants and their offspring experience following migration to a new country and culture (e.g., Berry, 1994; Cervantes et al., 1991; Flores et al., 2004). In the general stress and coping literature (e.g., Lazarus & Folkman, 1984) there is seldom mention of how acculturation related stressors that are common with immigrants add a layer of stress that is not experienced by the general population. For example, in a scale developed for assessing acculturative stress among immigrants from Latin America, Cervantes et al. (1991) found that immigrants reported the following items as particularly stressful:

- Due to poor English, people treated me badly.
- I felt guilty leaving behind family/friends in my home country.
- I felt like I would never regain the status/respect I had in my home country.
- I have felt unaccepted by Americans due to my [Latino] culture.
- I am discriminated against because of my race or background.

In addition to these items, another cluster of items emerged through factor analysis that reflected cultural and family conflict that occurs following immigration. These stressors are related to differential rates of acculturation between males and females because of greater autonomy enjoyed by woman in this country compared to women in more traditional cultures. Among the stress items identified by Cervantes et al. are:

- My personal goals conflicted with my family's goals.
- Some family members have become too individualistic.
- I noticed that religion is less important to me than before.
- Due to my acculturation, I've had arguments with my family.
- Family members have considered divorce for marital problems.

A final class of stressors that were identified through factor analysis and that relate directly to the topic of this chapter – marriage and divorce – are items specific to marital conflict among Hispanic immigrants and their descendents who may still be experiencing acculturative stress. Before turning to these items, it is important to emphasize that married Hispanic couples experience the full range of psychosocial stressors that all married couples irrespective of ethnicity or culture experience (e.g., conflicts in relationship dynamics, financial difficulties, etc.). However, acculturative stressors may impact Hispanic married couples in unique ways that make coping more difficult because the usual cultural and social supports (e.g., extended family, Catholic Church) that are available to couples in the home country may not be readily available in the adopted country. Thus, the added emotional burden of acculturative stress on less acculturated Hispanics may significantly disrupt their family life and further fracture their connection with the home culture.

Hispanic married couples that differ in their rate of acculturation may find that their changing values and lifestyles are at odds with each other. Some of the pressures that Hispanic couples encounter as they make the transition to life in the United States are reflected in the following stress items reported by Cervantes et al.:

- My spouse and I disagree on which language to speak at home.
- My spouse expected me to be more traditional in our relationship.
- My spouse hasn't been adapting to the American way of life.
- It's hard to see why my spouse wants to be more Americanized.
- My spouse and I find it hard to combine Hispanic and American culture.
- My spouse and I disagree on the importance of religion in the family.

Little research exists on how exactly acculturative stress impacts the life of Hispanics as they become assimilated into the American mainstream. In a study of 140 newly married Mexican women who immigrated to the United States after the age of 14, Salgado de Snyder (1987) found a significant correlation between acculturative stress and depressive symptomatology (as measured by the Center for Epidemiologic Studies Depression Scale (CES-D)). Additionally, acculturative stress by itself significantly predicted 16% of the variance in depressive symptomatology. However, the ways in which Hispanics can be resilient to the negative consequences of stress in their lives generally, and more specifically in their marital relationships is in need of investigation. What is apparent is that acculturative stress may influence how Hispanics view divorce and single parenthood as a viable option in the United States. In Latin America the view that marriage "is forever" is changing and divorce is becoming more acceptable; nonetheless, divorce is still generally frowned upon and not always readily granted by the state. Further, the concept of "no fault" divorce, while not uniquely American, is much less common in more traditional countries. In other words, divorce has not entered into the cultural fabric of the Latin American family structure in the same way that it has in this country. With approximately 50% of all marriages ending in divorce in this country, divorce is not a surprise nor is it viewed as a tragedy for the family when it happens. In Latin America though, divorce is still viewed by most people as a negative stigma for the extended family and it creates additional stress for both sides of the family. As immigration from Latin America continues and as Hispanics acculturate to American culture, it appears that divorce is another behavioral (i.e., coping) outcome that emerges with acculturation to the values and norms of American culture (Oropesa & Lansdale, 2004).

3. CULTURAL AND HISTORICAL CONTEXT OF RELATIONSHIP STRESS

3.1. Demographic Information on Hispanics

In the 1990 census, Hispanics[1] numbered 22.4 million (Stroup and Pollock, 1999). In the 2000 census, the number of Hispanics grew to 35.3 million, or 12.5 percent of the population (U. S. Bureau of the Census, March 2001). Mexican Americans numbered 21 million, or 7.3 percent of the American population. The Mexican origin population is by far the largest of the Hispanic groups with approximately 21 million, followed by 3.41 million Puerto Ricans, and 1.24 Cuban Americans. In recent years, there have also been sizable increases of Hispanic immigrants from Central and South America. In proportion to their number, it is the new Latinos for whom the figures are most changed. These new Hispanics have increased in number by 2.4 million between 1990 and 2000. Conservatively, 335,000 additional Dominicans and Salvadorans have settled in the United States between 1990 and 2000 bringing the total up to 1.42 million. Add to this another 91,000 Columbians who have entered after 1990 and this group's population is approximately 471,000. Other large groups include approximately 372,000 Guatemalans and 218,000 Hondurans who call the United States home. Three groups are quickly approaching the three quarters of a million mark – these groups are Ecuadorians, Peruvians, and Hondurans. Finally, the 2000 census counted another 670,000 new Latinos from a total of 9 other Latin American countries (U.S. Bureau of the Census, March, 2001).

These groups all share a common language – Spanish, and a value system that encompasses specific gender roles and interpersonal relationships. Nonetheless, there are important differences between Hispanic subgroups which one might expect considering that each group has a distinct colonial history to Spain. Part of the uniqueness across groups also stems from the fact that the countries differ in their geography, political and

---

[1] Since most national statistics are given in terms of the percentage of Hispanics in the total American population, we will use the term Hispanic rather than Latino. Also, if particular authors use specific subgroup designations such as Mexican American, that is the term we use in the chapter.

social institutions, their own respective immigration histories to the U.S., and in their relationship with their European and indigenous roots. Despite their differences, there are enough similarities to engage in a discussion of the role of the family in the context of Hispanic culture, the pressures of minority status and acculturative stress, and family disruption and the effects of this on children.

Forty three percent of Hispanics reside in the West and 33% in the Southern part of the U.S. The total U.S population is concentrated in the West (36%), but is more evenly distributed across the other regions than is the Hispanic population. In the West, Hispanics represent as much as 18% of the total population while in the South they represent about 12% of the population. The ten states with the largest Hispanic populations include: California [11 million], Texas [6.7 million], New York, Florida, New Jersey, Arizona, New Mexico, Colorado, Washington, and Illinois. These data show that about 50% of all Hispanics are concentrated in two states – California and Texas. However, the average growth in the top ten states (33%) was outpaced by the growth of Hispanics in states that were not traditionally populated by Hispanics. Census data show that growth rates quadrupled in the last decade in North Carolina, Arkansas, Georgia, and Tennessee, while this rate tripled in states such as South Carolina, Alabama, and Kentucky. Other states that evidenced a large growth of Hispanics include Nevada, Nebraska, and Minnesota. Collectively, these population statistics indicate that Hispanics are increasingly found in areas that differ from their previous geographic preferences, and consequently are transforming geographic areas that had not previously had large Hispanic presences. Moreover, Hispanics represent the largest minority group in all but New York, New Jersey, and Illinois.

The regional preferences of Hispanic groups in 2000 indicate that most Cubans live in the South (74%), the majority of Puerto Ricans live in the Northeast (61%), and most Mexicans live in the West (55%). Contrary to some stereotypes, the overwhelming majority (91%) of Hispanics live in urban areas and the proportion of urban dwellers has remained unchanged since 1990.

Current rates of divorce for Hispanics have remained similar to rates between 1960 and 1980. In the 2000 census, 7.4% of Hispanics age fifteen years and older were divorced. This compares to a national average of 9.7%, and the "non-Hispanic White" rate of 10.1%. Conversely, the marital separation only rate for this group of Hispanics was 3.6% compared to the national separation rate of 2.2%, and the "non-Hispanic White" rate of 1.4% (Kreider and Simmons, 2003). Thus, Hispanics are below the national norm for divorce, but above it for separation. Bean and Tienda (1987) corroborated this finding when they reported that when separation statistics are included in marital disruption, differences between non-Hispanic whites and Hispanics disappear. Teachman, Tedrow, & Crowder (2000) reported that Hispanics are following national trends in both marriage and divorce rates. For Hispanic women aged 40-44, divorce rates rose from 20% to 27% between 1980 and 1990, and as of the 2000 census the overall rate for Hispanic females who were once married and are divorced or separated is 21.5%. Thus, Hispanic females have caught up with White non-Hispanic counterparts and the national average of 21.1% for all divorced or separated families (Teachman et al., 2000). These percentages do not take remarriages into account, so the total percentage of people who have ever been divorced or separated is higher than the stated rates.

Based on these statistical data, we can assert safely that, for a large portion of the Hispanic population, the stereotype of having stronger familial ties than the rest of the

American population is not well founded. The rates for separation and divorce among Hispanics indicate that many couples are under undue psychological stress and that one negative consequence is separation and/or divorce. Another less positive view is that Hispanics are acculturating to the dominant family norms of American culture, since their divorce and separation rates straddle the national averages. Other forces at work that are known to be correlated to marital stress and family instability are low socioeconomic status, lower levels of educational attainment, and earlier entrance into marriage (Wang & Amato, 2000).

3.2. Historic Perspective of Hispanics' Rates of Divorce

Although Hispanic families, and in particular Mexican American families, have historically had lower rates of divorce than other groups, divorce is not uncommon in the Mexican American family. An early call for the need for research on divorce among Hispanics was put forth by Wagner (1993) who argued that research on Hispanics was fixated on the notion of *la familia* as a stable and enduring institution that was the cornerstone of Hispanic life. Accordingly, research efforts were dedicated to the intact nuclear and extended family, rather than on factors that might disrupt family structure and functioning despite a caring and supportive extended family. Further, Wagner believed that the effects of marital discord and divorce needed to address all family members: father, mother, children, and extended family. How the family as a collective and how individual family members cope with stress and family discord may be different for Hispanics than it is for families of other ethnic groups. In addition, the rapid increase of the Hispanic population in the last three decades and the fact that this group is now the largest ethnic group in the United States makes the study of this population all the more important.

A common stereotype of Hispanic culture is that it has clearly defined gender roles for different members of the family (Ginorio, Guiterrez, Cauce, & Acosta, 1995). The father has a dominant, bread-winner role, and the mother has a subordinate, child-bearer role. This stereotype is another reason that Mexican Americans are seen as having stable families. Since married couples are expected to have little tension in the marriage caused by gender role conflict, these families are not expected to have high divorce rates. For instance, Neff, Gilbert, & Hoppe (1991) in their work with Mexican American families in the Southwest state,

> ...while marital instability (defined as the sum of remarried, divorced, and separated) among ever married women in the Southwest increased between 1960-80 from 23% to 31% for Anglos and from 38% to 43% for Blacks, marital instability among Mexican Americans during that period increased only from 19% to 21%. (p. 76)

However, as noted above, more recent census information (see Oropesa & Landale, 2004) contradicts the Neff et al. (1991) conclusion. Thus, the stereotypes of having stronger familial ties than other American groups and clearly defined gender roles, if in fact true, do not serve as protective factors shielding Hispanics from marital distress and divorce. In fact, it is likely that Hispanics, as they acculturate to the dominant norms and values of American society, also adjust their stance on divorce and avail themselves of the legal protection through no fault divorce law offered anyone else about the freedom to choose to remain married or not.

3.3. Hispanics and Catholicism

Catholicism plays a significant role in the lives of people throughout Latin America, and by extension among Hispanics in the United States. There is evidence that religion and spirituality play a protective role in moderating the effects of stress in people's lives. Studies have also shown the importance that religiosity plays in the life of Hispanics, especially for women. Thus, it makes sense to examine the role of the Catholic Church and its relevance to divorce among Hispanics. Since a large portion of the Hispanic population is at least nominally Roman Catholic, it is important to examine the influence that religion has on the family life of Hispanics. In Catholicism, marriage is a sacrament, thus divorce is not accepted in the Catholic faith (Jenks and Woolever, 1999, p. 46). In fact, Catholics who marry in the Church, but who later want to divorce must undergo the long process of seeking an annulment of the marriage. The process involved in obtaining an annulment is complicated and is not "fault-free" as we see today in family law. Jenks and Woolever (1999) describe the process for seeking an annulment as follows:

> *Typically, the divorced person who is seeking an annulment makes some contact with his/her parish priest. Usually after some discussion, the person is directed to the marriage tribunal of his or her archdiocese. The tribunal then gathers information about the people involved in the marriage and the marriage itself... As part of this process, the petitioner is asked to provide the names of witnesses who can provide information about the partners and their marriage as requested by the tribunal. If it is determined that the petition for an annulment has merit, a "judge" is assigned the case... the judge may also ask that psychological evaluations be conducted... a "defender of the bond" is also presented with the arguments... Once this is complete, the judge renders his verdict... If an annulment is granted, it is automatically appealed and reviewed. When the original decision is upheld by the appeal board... the process is complete. (p. 48)*

The annulment is a declaration that the marriage was never valid. Further, if the annulment is granted, both former spouses are considered to be in good standing in the Church and they are free to remarry, even in the Church if they so choose. The annulment process is a long, involved one. It seems that both the attitude of the Church and the difficulty of the annulment process would dissuade many couples from seeking an official annulment from the Church. This, of course, would only be applicable to the segment of the population that believed an official annulment was necessary. Since a large percentage of the Hispanic population is only nominally Catholic, this may not apply to all. Also, the process intimidates many people because it entails contact with clergy about personal matters that they may feel uncomfortable disclosing to a priest. The process, while not costly in the monetary sense, does involve a psychological cost (e.g., stress and anxiety) because of the layers of religious bureaucracy involved and a long period of uncertainty of whether the annulment will be granted whereas in no fault divorce the outcome is certain.

The literature on Catholicism and Hispanics is minimal, especially on the question of divorce. Thus, we do not expect to see useful information on the role of the Church until a major study is conducted. As a measure of the scarcity of literature, the Jenks and Woolever (1999) study is the first ever written on Catholic annulments and the study had only a small sample of Hispanic respondents. In the study, 213 Catholics throughout the country were surveyed. The sample consisted of mostly White middle-class respondents, and the number of annulled, divorced Catholics was about the same as the number of non-annulled, divorced Catholics. The small number of Hispanic Americans in the study represented 5.6 % of the annulled Catholics, and 2.5 % of the non-annulled, divorced Catholics. The larger percentage of Hispanics in the annulled group may reflect their stronger desire to seek official annulment from the Church, but a small sample and sampling concerns limit any firm conclusions that can be drawn from this study. An interesting finding from the study was that current monthly attendance at worship services and the average number of hours spent each month with church groups were the only two variables that were significantly correlated with higher rates of annulment for the total sample.

It seems that the requirement for Catholics to seek annulment may deter Catholics from divorce, since these people would likely desire to fulfill the Catholic requirement that their marriage be annulled. In addition, they may delay longer in seeking an annulment than they would a "no fault" divorce, because the Church first fosters the idea of reconciliation. In fact, "Whereas nationally the average length of the divorced person's first marriage is approximately 11 years, the average duration here is between fifteen and sixteen years" (Jenks and Woolever, 1999, p.54). No information is provided about the duration of marriage among Hispanics prior to divorce and seeking an annulment.

It is also important to note the rapid increase in the number of annulments granted by the American Roman Catholic Church since the Second Vatican Counsel. Prior to the Second Vatican Counsel the regulations guiding policy on annulments were stricter than they are now following the changes made by the bishops at the conclusion of the Second Vatican Counsel. The Church now recognizes many psychological reasons that justify an annulment, whereas, before Vatican II, only insanity, fraud, and impotence were recognized as legitimate bases for annulment. Jenks and Woolever (1999) note that "Within a twenty-year period, from 1968 to 1988, grants for annulments rose from 368 to approximately 50,000 nationwide... also... a majority (80%) of these annulment petitions are granted" (p.46). The current number of American annulments is 60,000, which accounts for 77% of annulments given worldwide.

In sum, it seems that the Church's influence on the matter of divorce is waning, at least in the United States. Hispanic divorce rates are increasing beyond the rates of non-Hispanic whites, and policy shifts within the Catholic Church have resulted in extremely high numbers of annulments relative to the numbers allowed prior to the Second Vatican Council. In seeking annulments, Hispanic Americans may also be approaching rates similar to the general American Catholic population.

In addition to religiosity when we discuss divorce among Hispanics we also have to consider generational differences, poverty, low average level of education, and age of first marriage. There are now a large number of studies that have examined the relationship between generational level (i.e., immigrant generation versus later American born) and acculturation among Hispanics (Keefe & Padilla, 1987; Portes & Rumbaut, 2001). Let's turn now to an examination of generation of respondents in the context of marital stability.

3.4. Acculturation and Relationship Distress

A major confounding variable in research comparing diverse ethnic groups is *acculturation*. Although we discussed acculturative stress in an earlier section of this chapter more discussion is in order. Acculturation *refers to* the degree to which an individual has adopted the beliefs, values, and norms of behavior of the dominant culture. For example, an early study (Tharp, Meadow, Lennhoff, & Satterfield, 1968) found that Mexican American wives relatively high in acculturation (as measured by language preference) subscribed to marital roles that were more egalitarian in nature than those of relatively less acculturated Mexican American wives who held on to the belief that the male was the decision maker in the relationship. In a later study, Vega, Kolody, and Valle (1988) hypothesized that marginal acculturation may function as an independent stressor because it causes the less acculturated spouse to feel less capable of managing her new cultural environment and forces her to be dependent on her more acculturated spouse. Feelings of personal isolation and alienation may ensue which create marital conflict. In their study, Vega et al. found support for their hypothesis with a sample of 550 Mexican American immigrant women. Less acculturated women reported increased marital stress, self-denigration, and the loss of the ability to negotiate as a response to marital conflict.

In contrast, other studies have suggested that marital distress is linked to higher, rather than lower, levels of acculturation. In a study comparing Mexican American couples born in Mexico with Mexican heritage persons born in the United States, Casas and Ortiz (1985) identified higher marital satisfaction in the former group and concluded that "the more acculturated U.S.-born couples may be more exposed to the stressors inherent in the redefining of traditional husband/wife roles" (p. 1027). For example, Mexican American couples relatively high in acculturation have been shown to make significantly more joint decisions for purchases than less acculturated couples (O'Guinn, Imperia, & MacAdams, 1987; Webster, 1994), but in so doing they also experience more distress possibly because of differences in acculturation levels. In a study of 151 Mexican American husbands and wives, Flores et al. (2004) found that more acculturated couples reported significantly more marital conflict than those couples who identified strongly as Mexican and who were more likely to be immigrants. The study probed specific levels of both acculturation and inter-spousal conflict. Flores et al. concluded that higher levels of acculturation reflected more direct expressions of power issues between husbands and wives resulting in greater conflict and potential marital dissolution.

In a study that compared Mexican American and non-Hispanic White couples on marital satisfaction, Negy and Snyder (1997) found no differences on marital satisfaction between non-Hispanic White males and Mexican American males regardless of level of acculturation. There were no significant differences between non-Hispanic husbands and wives on marital satisfaction. However, the more acculturated Mexican American wives expressed greater marital distress on two dimensions: time together and sexual dissatisfaction. Here time together is an expression of time shared in leisure activity and sexual dissatisfaction reflects displeasure with the frequency and quality of intercourse. A conclusion that can be drawn from these findings is that acculturation and any accompanying distress due to acculturation has a greater impact on the woman and her role as wife.

A different approach to the question of marital cohesion and distress focuses on changes in economic dependency between the husband and wife (e.g., Teachman, Tedrow, and Crowder, 2000; Oropesa & Landale, 2004). The median income for Hispanic men declined from $18,800 in 1980 to $16,200 in 1997, and as more Hispanic women enter the labor force, economic independence may be propelling divorce rates (Teachman et al., 2000). It may be that the higher distress among highly acculturated Mexican American couples in the Casas and Ortiz (1985) study reflects increased stress associated with pressures to redefine their marital roles, expectations, and adjustment while also trying to remain loyal to their traditional family background.

As Mexican Americans acculturate they come into direct contact with an American individualist ethos that some researchers hypothesize is the factor behind the American "culture of divorce" (Oropesa & Landale, 2004). This American ethos conflicts with Mexican traditional values of family unity, but it is likely that more acculturated Mexican Americans, especially woman, are pulled more in the direction of the values of their adopted country and come to see divorce as a viable option to marital discord. Clearly, much more research on the relationship of acculturation and acculturative stress to marital satisfaction, and the differential impact on Hispanic men and women, is needed. Acculturation does alter a person's relationship to members of her/his family; however, little is known about how respective family members cope with these changes when they impact interpersonal dynamics between husbands and wives and their children.

3.5. Generational Differences and Marital Stability

Because the Hispanic population consists of immigrants and their descendents, it is important to disaggregate data by generational levels to understand the effects of acculturation. The significance of this is that with other populations such as non-Hispanic whites and African Americans, generational differences are often of little relevance when considering an issue like divorce. However, when intergroup comparisons are made about marriage and divorce rates across non-Hispanic whites, African Americans, and Hispanics it is very important to be able to specify whether the Hispanics are first generation immigrants or later generation Hispanics and whether or not they resemble non-Hispanic whites in terms of family-related values.

In a study of single mothers in San Jose, California generational differences were found to influence social support networks among Mexican Americans. According to Schaffer and Wagner (1996), "It was striking that the generational differences were statistically significant in both the proportion of kin and the number of friends, which were precisely the two variables for which ethnicity was not a significant predictor" (p. 84). First-generation Mexican American women had fewer relatives living close to them and the greatest number of non-relatives in their support group. The second-generation Mexican American women had high family involvement, as expected. Interestingly, the results for third-generation Mexican American women showed "... a bicultural adaptation pattern in which kin are not eliminated from the network, but rather friends are added" (Schaffer & Wagner, 1996, p.84).

Schaffer and Wagner (1996) show that generational differences can be important when considering women's social support networks, and if we believe that such support is important in how women cope with divorce, then it is evident that later generation Hispanic women would fare better than their first generation immigrant counterparts. More research is needed to determine whether this hypothesis is supported by the data.

At a more macro-level Oropesa and Landale (2004), in their analysis of census data, see a bleaker picture for Hispanics in terms of SES variables that have ramifications for understanding marital stability among this population. These authors hold that

If past is prologue, the future of marriage among Hispanics is likely to be shaped by the social and economic trajectories of the second and third generations. If the education and skill levels of these generations are similar to those of their parents, they will not be well positioned to support marriages and families in the future, especially because later generations will not have the countries of origin of their parents and grandparents as a frame of reference. Although the parents of second- and third-generation Hispanics typically have a strong prenuptial orientation, and although U.S. immigration policy favors the admission of immigrants who are married, there is little reason to expect that marriage will strengthen as an institution under the weight of Hispanicization and the larger economic and cultural processes currently underway in U.S. society. (p. 917)

4. EFFECTS OF DIVORCE AMONG HISPANICS

4.1. Effects of Divorce on Hispanic Men

Findings regarding the effects of gender on divorce distress and adjustment are inconsistent (Wang & Amato, 2000). The effects of divorce on Hispanic males are important since men cope differently with the stressors associated with marital instability and divorce (Flores et al., 2004). Latin culture is male oriented and machismo still reigns supreme in Latin America. What this means is that males hold power in the family and their pronouncements with respect to such things as the woman's role in the marriage, children, and household responsibility are generally followed. However, this view of the "macho" husband and father is breaking down and studies report that with acculturation there is more joint decision making in Hispanic families (e.g., Ginorio, et al, 1995). What is not well understood though is how Hispanic males are coping with these changing family patterns and whether they are threatened by their spouses' new found "sexual and marital" liberation. It might be that Hispanic males who traditionally are socialized to be "machos" in their relationships with women might have major difficulties in coping with marital separation and divorce when the wife indicates that she wants to terminate the relationship and is supported in this decision by her family and by "no fault" divorce laws in this country.

There are important questions as well having to do with differences in income and the amount of time spent with non-custodial children after divorce by fathers. Because a greater number of Hispanic families fall below the federal poverty guidelines, when a couple does separate and divorce, there are many Hispanic children growing up without their non-custodial fathers (Battle, 2002). Further, although the figures are difficult to gather, it appears that many divorced fathers, because of their already low wages, are unable to make regular and appropriate child care payments to the mother. As a consequence, Hispanic fathers may be considerably negligent in both the financial and emotional care of their children.

In a study of 556 Hispanics from a base of General Social Survey respondents, males suffered less economically than females (Stroup and Pollock, 1999). According to Stroup and Pollock, Hispanic women suffered a loss of 24% in their income level compared with no significant loss in income for males following divorce. Clearly, the economic consequences of divorce are worse for Hispanic females than for males. Importantly, this effect was shown to be significant across different socioeconomic strata. In the highest level,

Professional/Technical, no significant difference was shown for income differentials between men and women. However, in the lower four categories: Executive/Administrative/Sales, Crafts, Operatives, and Unskilled Labor, a significant income difference was found between men and women in each category. "In the lower four SES categories, the ratio of mean income of divorced to mean income of married is .81 or lower, indicating a loss of 19% or greater" (Stroup and Pollock, 1999 p.156). Even when controlling for socioeconomic status, females suffer a large economic loss, unless they have high levels of education and opportunity for income to overcome the effects. In the lowest category, Unskilled Labor, where a significant loss is most difficult to endure due to income levels that are already low, a loss of 25% was found in the data.

In the case of Hispanic men, Stroup and Pollock (1999) reported that for the 371 Hispanic males in their sample no difference was found between married men's income and divorced men's mean income. In fact, the data showed that there was not a gap between the two mean incomes. That is, the ratio was essentially equal to one. More importantly, Hispanic males with greater educational attainment showed an increase in their income ratio following divorce in comparison to comparable married Hispanic males (Stroup and Pollock, 1999). No information is available unfortunately that informs us if these divorced middle class Hispanic males paid child support. More research is needed to understand the emotional and financial burdens carried by divorced Hispanic fathers, because we know that a single mother with financial hardship suffers undue stress and humiliation because of poverty.

Importantly, this study does not control for the length of time since the divorce. For the non-Hispanic white population, income levels usually begin to show an increase for women beginning after about two years post-divorce (Hetherington & Kelly, 2002). Thus, more research is needed about post-divorce income for both Hispanic men and women to determine whether the same pattern of income recovery for Hispanic women holds as it does for non-Hispanic white women.

Another post-divorce consideration has to do with Hispanic fathers' contact with children following divorce. Gray (1989) found no significant difference between fathers' involvement with children in two types of post-divorce families: those who have two Hispanic natural parents, and those who have two non-Hispanic natural parents. Fathers' involvement was measured in the study by father-child contact in the number of hours spent with children, legal representation, and custody requests. One significant difference between Hispanic and non-Hispanic males is that in Hispanic families mothers were more likely to have sole custody of their children, whereas in the case of non-Hispanic families' joint custody of children was the norm. However, fathers in both ethnic groups did not differ in their involvement with children.

Interestingly, in the case of intermarried families (where only the father is Hispanic), the father's level of participation was higher than for fathers in non-Hispanic families (Gray, 1989). Intermarried families with a Hispanic father were found to score higher on "measures of father-child contact, custody requests (reflecting higher father involvement), legal representation of the father, divorce filings by the father, and the father's preference for custody" (Gray, 1989 p. 117). In sum, Hispanic fathers manifest a higher interest in their children after the divorce if they are of a different ethnicity than their wife. This may, however, be due to a self-selection bias, since fathers may be more likely to submit questionnaires if they are more involved with their children. Another important consideration that requires research has to do with Hispanic males involved in interethnic marriages.

One presumption is that intermarried Hispanic men are more acculturated and of a higher socioeconomic status and this may explain why they are more willing to exert time, money, and effort in maintaining contact with their children than are lower SES Hispanic males married to Hispanic women, or to non-Hispanic males of similar SES standing. A related question for which there is little research has to do with whether intermarried couples experience particular kinds of cultural conflicts that contribute to marital discord and divorce.

4.2. Effects of Divorce on Hispanic Women

As indicated above, Hispanic women suffer greater economic loss following divorce than do their former male partners. This is similar to trends in the general population that show greater economic loss for females after divorce (Amato, 2000). However, a study of 232 single mothers from inner city San Jose, California found that Hispanic mothers experienced a less dramatic loss in income than did non-Hispanic white mothers (Wagner, 1993).

Although these findings conflict with those reported earlier by the GSS study (Stroup and Pollock, 1999), there are various factors that are different in the two studies. The Stroup and Pollock study had a larger (150 divorced and 406 married) sample of Hispanic women. Further, the sample was more representative of the U. S. population because it was based on a stratified, national probability sample of women. On the other hand, Wagner's study focused on 135 Mexican American single mothers and 97 non-Hispanic single mothers living in San Jose. The GSS study spanned the years 1972-1994, whereas Wagner's study was a one-time view of the economic status of two groups of single mothers. In addition to the stratified national sample, the GSS study only assessed women who had been married, but were at the time of data collection divorced. On the other hand, Wagner's study included single women with children regardless of whether the women had never married, were divorced, separated, or widowed. Furthermore, the study offers a unique perspective into the factors confronting single mothers after divorce.

Wagner found that, in the population he studied, Mexican American single mothers had multiple disadvantages that should have predicted lower income after divorce. The multiple disadvantages included single mothers who were younger, who had more children, and who had completed fewer years of school. Despite these disadvantages, Hispanic women were able to restore their income to what it had been before becoming single parents. In comparison, this was not the case with the non-Hispanic white women. Wagner (1993) concludes "In spite of having higher average education and job skills, Anglo women were unable to achieve higher income levels than the Mexican Americans" (p. 121).

The demographics of the Mexican American and Anglo women in the Wagner study are important in interpreting the results. Mexican American women in the study had more children than their White women counterparts. Over 40% of the Mexican American women were pregnant at the time of the interview compared with less than one-third of the Anglo women (Wagner, 1993). The majority of women were unemployed at the time of the divorce, with (surprisingly) Anglo women having a statistically significant higher rate of unemployment. However, 57% of the Mexican Americans reported having no job skills, while only 27% of Anglos reported having none. Almost half of the women in both ethnic groups received Aid to Families with Dependent Children during their first year after becoming single mothers. Also, 43% of the Mexican Americans in the study relied primarily on earned income, compared with only 29% of Anglos. The Mexican Americans also relied more on family members, especially their own parents for economic and other resource support. On the other hand, Anglo women were more likely to rely on the father of their children for support.

Surprisingly, divorce or separation caused a "leveling effect" between the two groups. The non-Hispanic women experienced a large drop in income while the Mexican American women did not have a significant change in income. In other words, any differences that might have existed in income prior to divorce were eliminated with the divorce regardless of differences in educational level between the women (Wagner, 1993). Thus, despite greater employability because of their higher level of education the non-Hispanic women did not achieve a higher level of post-divorce earnings than did the less skilled women. Divorced women with children seem to fall victim to their circumstances as single mothers even if they do not struggle with discrimination and possess high levels of education and more job related skills. In fact, non-Hispanic women suffered the greatest losses, with over half of them losing $10,000 or more in annual income, compared with only 17% of the Mexican American women. However, in the first year, some women actually gained income. This was particularly true of Mexican American women with more education, of whom 16% gained income, in comparison with only 2.5% of the Anglo women with comparable levels of education.

The results of Wagner's study show us that despite cultural and SES differences, Mexican American single mothers cope better with their status as single mothers. This finding is surprising, but more research with larger samples is needed to test the robustness of Wagner's findings. We can speculate that women who endure poverty, minority status and discrimination, and possibly even the cycle of coming from a single parent home themselves have a more intact social support system as well as internal resources (e.g., persistence and hope) to cope positively with their own status as single mothers. Studies that focus on the resilience of Hispanic single mothers and their support systems and strategies for coping with the stress and economic hardship of caring for their dependent children are in order.

Although Mexican Americans as a group by necessity have more experience with economic hardship (Battle, 2002), this does not mean the transition into single parenthood is easy. As Wagner (1993) reveals, it is important to study the stresses unique to Mexican American women. Mexican Americans reported fewer than average stressors in their lives as well as differences in the kinds of stress that were more prevalent. For non-Hispanic women, feeling inadequate and overwhelmed, as well as feeling economically burdened was more prevalent than for Mexican Americans. Only two types of stressors were reported by more than half of the Mexican American women, these were "Having to share a residence" and "Feeling overwhelmed by daily responsibilities," respectively. The non-Hispanic women, on the other hand, ranked "Having to share a residence" as the tenth most prevalent type of stress.

The different types of stressors experienced by women in the two groups and how they ranked them is important for social workers, psychologists, teachers, and other social service personnel serving low income single women and their children. Social service agencies assisting single women and children need to adjust their services to meet their clients varying needs depending on culture and ethnicity, pre and post-divorce income levels, and availability of support from family and friends. More community surveys of the type carried out by Wagner in San Jose, California are needed with Hispanic single mothers.

4.3. Effects of Divorce on Hispanic Children and Adolescents

Reviews of the effects of divorce on non-Hispanic white children and adolescents are available (e.g., Amato, 2000; Hetherington & Kelly, 2001; Kelly, 2000). These syntheses of the research literature conclude that the psychological effects seen in children are generally present before the divorce, and thus not caused by the divorce. Further, syntheses of the research literature indicate that whatever effects there may be on non-Hispanic white children due to divorce, the symptoms are not long lasting and generally dissipate within the first two years following parental divorce. However, research with Hispanic children and the effects of divorce is not as abundant. One way to investigate the impact of divorce on adolescents is to consider performance and engagement in contexts outside of the home, especially in school. For example, how much does family instability contribute to academic achievement and/or school dropout rates for Hispanic students?

In a study of 8,483 students at eight San Francisco area high schools, Fraleigh (1990) found that Hispanic parents' educational attainment was much lower than that of parents in other ethnic groups. Also Hispanic students' combined GPA was lower than any other group except Blacks. However, whether Hispanic families consisted of one or both parents had no effect on student GPAs. Regardless of family stability, Hispanic students overall did poorly in school. According to Fraleigh (1990),

> *compared to Asians and Whites, the Black and Hispanic groups show substantially less variation in grades across family types. While family processes may indeed be operative in explaining the depressed levels of achievement among Black and Hispanic adolescents, the salient factor appears not to be family structure per se. (p. 286)*

It seems that other forces, such as perceived discrimination or low socioeconomic status make such a drastic difference in the lives of Hispanic American adolescents that marital conflict and divorce of parents does not make enough of a difference to contribute to the already low academic attainment of these students.

The patterns of parental education are different, amongst the types of families, for non-Hispanic whites and Hispanics. Parental education was positively correlated with familial stability for non-Hispanic white parents. That is, the more education those non-Hispanic white parents reported the more likely they were to be living in an intact relationship with a spouse (Fraleigh, 1990). However, a very different picture emerged with the Hispanic sample. According to Fraleigh (1990)

> *The Hispanic subsample is characterized not only by substantially lower levels of parental education overall, but also by a relative lack of differentiation amongst all but the mother-stepfather category. Indeed, except for the higher level of education among mother-stepfather families, the differences amongst the various Hispanic configurations are too small to be statistically significant. (p. 157)*

This means that Hispanic children do not have an advantage in terms of educational capital if they live in an intact family that is also poor. Importantly, the GPAs of Hispanic students reflect the lower levels of parental education and socioeconomic conditions and not the status of the family as intact and stable or unstable and guided by a single parent. Fraleigh concludes that the lower academic attainment of African American and Hispanic students, "... would [make it] appear that other structural constraints, such as institutionalized racism or varying subcultural values, may be operating independently of family structure to limit the achievement of Blacks and Hispanics" (p. 162). Although the sample in Fraleigh's study is large it is limited in scope to the San Francisco area, so additional studies that represent the larger Hispanic population are needed.

Beyond academic performance, there is some evidence suggesting that Hispanic youth are less vulnerable to the adverse psychological effects of family discord, separation, and divorce than are non-Hispanic White children (Amato & Keith, 1991). Little empirical data are available, but a theory of "embeddedness" has emerged. Essentially, some family researchers believe that, even within the American context, children who are embedded in extended family networks are less affected by the stresses of divorce and separation. The extended family provides protection from the negative psychosocial effects of parental conflict (McLoyd, Cauce, Takeuchi, & Wilson, 2000). Furthermore, research shows that Hispanic immigrants are the most likely of all ethnic groups to reside in extended family households (Glick, Bean, & Van Hook 1997). Thus, if embeddedness is a protective factor, Hispanic youth should fare better than children from other ethic groups who for various reasons demonstrate lower familial embeddedness.

Additionally, in keeping with other research that focuses on parsing the effects of familial discord (both prior to and following divorce) on the psychosocial adjustment of children and adolescents (e.g., Heatherington & Kelly 2002), similar longitudinal research is necessary with Hispanic families. Currently, there is no reason to believe that the coping responses of Hispanic youth due directly to the divorce of their parents (and not to confounding socioeconomic factors) will be different qualitatively or of longer duration than their non-Hispanic White counterparts.

Also important is the question of how effectively the extended family operates for later generation Hispanic parents and their offspring before and after marital dissolution. While notions of familial "embeddedness" may be plausible in the first and even second generation Hispanic family, the impact of acculturation on family lifestyle by the third generation as noted by Oropesa and Landale (2004) may mean that reliance on an extended family for support is not possible.

5. CONCLUSION

The effects of divorce on Hispanic families differ in important ways from those of non-Hispanic white families. As the Hispanic population continues to grow, so too does the need to study how marriage as an institution is faring among Hispanic immigrants and their later generation descendents. We have shown that Hispanics are not immune from divorce and that literature that focuses on *la familia* as an enduring cultural mainstay is not totally accurate. Because Hispanics on average have less education, fewer job skills, and consequently higher rates of poverty, it is not unreasonable to assume that they may be less successful in the long term in coping positively with multiple stressors.

For Hispanics, the pressures to acculturate may set into motion a variety of stressors associated with changes in language, gender roles, and traditional family values that may result in increased levels of marital conflict and subsequent divorce. The differential effects of acculturation and acculturative stress on Hispanic men and women indicate that women are more dissatisfied with marriage than Hispanic married males (Negy & Snyder, 1997). Although speculative at this time, it may be that Hispanic women have come to recognize divorce as a coping response that is available to them. Further, without the negative stigma that was once attached to divorce, Hispanics, and in particular Hispanic women, may see divorce as a viable coping response to marital conflict. Thus, while acculturative stress may augment marital discord, acculturation itself may provide the impetus for a Hispanic person to see divorce as a way to end an unhappy situation.

The evolving system of no fault divorce, coupled with the waning influence of the Catholic Church and the extended family among those of Hispanic descent presents an interesting paradox for Hispanics. On the one hand, acculturative stress places immigrants and less acculturated later generation Hispanics at greater risk for yet more psychological hardships as they assimilate into the American culture. Thus, rather than gaining protective factors to cope successfully with life's difficulties, Hispanics may in fact be shedding valuable protective resources. On the other hand, acculturation into a society where divorce is available may also have a liberating effect for a person(s) trapped in an unhappy marriage. This paradoxical outcome on marriage due to acculturation is fertile ground for research.

This chapter presents a fresh and perhaps more realistic view of the Hispanic family. Research is beginning to show that the assumed pillars of the Hispanic family (namely, defined gender roles, intergenerational interdependence, and traditional values of the "sacred" family) do not occlude the negative forces of acculturative stress, family conflict, and a culture of divorce that supports marital dissolution through its no fault laws. The harsh realities of poverty, low parental education, and perceived discrimination make research on acculturation and its effects on the Hispanic family challenging; however, the demystification of the stalwart family unit is a necessary step towards a more accurate picture of Hispanic families in America.

The research, practice, and policy implications of changing family structure among Hispanic Americans are immense. Hispanics are now the largest ethnic group in America and their numbers are expected to continue to grow for at least the next 30 to 50 years. The Hispanic population is marked by extreme heterogeneity in terms of country of origin, generational differences, geographic residence, assimilation patterns, etc. Accordingly, it is important for researchers, mental health professionals, and policy makers to be knowledgeable of the types of stressors that Hispanic men and women face during their assimilation into American society. Important too is how these stressors can alter family structure resulting in single parenthood and the re-deployment of traditional resources in support of non-traditional coping responses (Wagner, 1993). If stressors that are highly correlated with marital conflict can be prevented through education and intervention type services (e.g., family and marriage counseling) then this should be of high priority. If prevention is not possible or not available then it is essential that intervention programs be available in our schools, places of work, and communities that offer services in culturally appropriate ways to the needs of Hispanics of all ages that are experiencing family-related stress.

REFERENCES

Amato, P.R. (2000). The consequences of divorce for adults and children. *Journal of Marriage and the Family*. 62: 1269-1287.

Amato, P.R., & Keith, B. (1991). Parental divorce and adult well-being: A meta-analysis. *Journal of Marriage and the Family*. 53: 43-58

Battle, J. (2002). Longitudinal Analysis of Academic Achievement Among a Nationwide Sample of Hispanic Students in One-Versus Dual-Parent Households. *Hispanic Journal of Behavioral Sciences. 24(4)*: 430-447.

Bean, F. D.,& Tienda, M. (1987). *The Hispanic population of the United States*. (New York: Russell Sage Foundation.)

Berry, J. (1994). Acculturative stress. In W. J. Lonner & R. Malpass (Eds.), *Psychology and culture (p. 211-215)*. Needham Heights, MA: Allyn and Bacon.

Casas, J. M.,& Ortiz, S.(1985). Exploring the applicability of the Dyadic Adjustment Scale for assessing level of marital adjustment with Mexican-Americans. *Journal of Marriage and the Family*. 47: *1023*-1027.

Cervantes, R. C., Padilla, A. M., & Salgado de Snyder, N. (1991). The Hispanic Stress Inventory: A culturally relevant approach toward psychosocial assessment. *Psychological Assessment*. 3: 438–447.

Contreras, R., Hendrick, S.S., & Hendrick, C. (1996). Perspectives on marital love and satisfaction in Mexican American and Anglo-American couples. *Journal of Counseling and Development*. 74: 408-415.

Falicov, C. J.(1982). Mexican families. (In M. McGoldrick, J. K. Pearce, & J. Giordano (Eds.), *Ethnicity and family therapy* (pp. 134–163). New York: Guilford Press.)

Flores, E., Tschann, J., Marin, B., Pantoja, P. (2004) marital conflict and acculturation among Mexican American husbands and wives. *Cultural Diversity and Ethnic Minority Psychology*. 10, 1: 39-52.

Fraleigh, M. J. (1990). *The Relationship between Family Structure and Academic Achievement among Adolescents*. Stanford, CA: Unpublished Doctoral Dissertation.

Glick, J., Bean, F., & Van Hook, V.W. (1997). Immigration and changing patterns of the extended family household structure in the United States: 197-1990. *Journal of Marriage and the Family*. 59: 177-191.

Ginorio, A., Gutierrez, L., Cauce, A. M. & Acosta, M. (1995). The psychology of Latinas. In C. Travis (Ed.), *Feminist perspectives on the psychology of women* (pp. 331-342). Washington, DC: American Psychological Association.

Gray, K. D. (1989). *The Influence of Ethnicity on Fathers' Participation in Child Custody Arrangements: A Study of Divorcing Hispanic, Non-Hispanic and Intermarried Families*. Stanford, CA: Dissertation.

Hampson, R. B., Beavers, W. R.,& Hulgus, Y. (1990). Cross-ethnic family differences: Interactional assessment of White, Black, and Mexican-American families. *Journal of Marital and Family Therapy*. 16: 307-319.

Hetherington, E. M., & Kelly, J. (2001). *For Better or for Worse: Divorce Reconsidered*. W. W. Norton & Co.

Jaramillo, P. T.,& Zapata, J. T. (1987). Roles and alliances within Mexican-American and Anglo families. *Journal of Marriage and the Family. 49*: 727-735.

Jenks, R. J., & Woolever, C. A. (1999). Divorce and Annulment among American Catholics. *Journal of Divorce & Remarriage. 30(3/4)*: 45-54.

Keefe, S., & Padilla, A.M. (1987). *Chicano Ethnicity*. Albuquerque: University of New Mexico Press.

Kelly, J. B. (2000). Children's adjustment in conflicted marriage and divorce: A decade review of research. *Journal of the American Academy of child & Adolescent Psychiatry, 39*: 963-973.

Kreider, R., & Simmons, T. (2003). *Special Report on Marital Status: 2000, C2KBR-30*. Washington, D.C.: U.S. Bureau of the Census.

Lazarus, R. S., & Folkman, S. (1984). *Stress, Appraisal and Coping*. Springer, New York.

McLoyd, V., Cauce, A.M., Takeuchi, D., & Wilson, L. (2000). Marital processes and parental socialization in families of color: a decade review of research. *Journal* of Marriage and the Family. 62: 1070-1093.

Negy, C., & Snyder, D. K. (1997). Ethnicity and acculturation assessing Mexican American couples' relationships using the Marital Satisfaction Inventory – Revised. *Psychological Assessment, 9*, 414-421.

Neff, J., Gilbert, K., & Hoppe, S. (1991). Divorce likelihood among Anglos and Mexican Americans. *Journal of Divorce & Remarriage*. 15: 75-98.

O'Guinn, T. C., Imperia, G.,& MacAdams, E. A.(1987). Acculturation and perceived family decision-making input among Mexican-American wives. *Journal of Cross-Cultural Psychology. 18:* 78-92.

Oropesa, R. S., & Landale, N. S. (2004). The future of marriage and Hispanics. *Journal of Marriage and Family*. 66: 901-920.

Portes, A., & Rumbaut, R.G. (2001). *Legacies: The story of the immigrant second generation*. Berkeley, CA: University of California Press.

Salgado de Snyder, V.N. (1987). Factors associated with acculturative stress and depressive symptomatology among married Mexican immigrant women. *Psychology of Women Quarterly*. 11: 475-488.

Schaffer, D. M. & Wagner, R. M. (1996). Mexican American and Anglo Single Mothers: The Influence of Ethnicity, Generation, and Socioeconomic Status on Social Support Networks. *Hispanic Journal of Behavioral Sciences. 18(1)*: 74-86.

Stroup, A. L. & Pollock, G. E. (1999). Economic Consequences of Marital Dissolution for Hispanics. *Journal of Divorce & Remarriage. 30(1/2)*: 149-164.

Teachman, J., Tedrow, L., Crowder, K. (2000). The changing demography of America's families. *Journal of Marriage and the Family*. 62: 1234-1246.

Tharp, R. G., Meadow, A., Lennhoff, S. G.,& Satterfield, D.(1968). Changes in marriage roles accompanying the acculturation of the Mexican-American wife. *Journal of Marriage and the Family. 30:* 404-412.

U.S. Bureau of Census, March 2001, Overview of Race and Hispanic Origin. (www.census.gov/population/www/ socdemo/race.html).

Vega, W. A.(1990). Hispanic families in the 1980s: A decade of research. *Journal of Marriage and the Family. 52:* 1015-1024.

Vega, W. A., Kolody, B.,& Valle, R.(1988). Marital strain, coping, and depression among Mexican-American women. *Journal of Marriage and the Family. 50:* 391-403.

Vega, W. A., Patterson, T., Sallis, J., Nader, P., Atkins, C.,& Abramson, I.(1986). Cohesion and adaptability in Mexican-American and Anglo families. *Journal of Marriage and the Family. 48:* 857-867.

Wang, H., Amato, P.R. (2000). Predictors of divorce adjustment: stressors, resources, and definitions. *Journal and Marriage and the Family*. 62: 655-668.

Webster, C.(1994). Effects of Hispanic ethnic identification on marital roles in the purchase decision process. *Journal of Consumer Research. 21:* 319-331.

Wagner, R. M. (1993). Psychosocial Adjustments During the First Year of Single Parenthood: A Comparison of Mexican-American and Anglo Women. *Journal of Divorce & Remarriage. 19(1/2)*: 121-142.

Williams, N. (1990). *The Mexican American Family: Tradition and Change*. Dix Hills, NY: General Hall.

Wolchick, S. A., Ramirez, R., Sandler, I. N., Fisher, J. L., Organista, P. B. & Brown, C. (1993). Inner-City, Poor Children of Divorce: Negative Divorce-Related Events, Problematic Beliefs and Adjustment Problems. *Journal of Divorce & Remarriage. 19(1/2)*: 1-20.

Zambrana, R. E. (1995) (Ed.), *Understanding Latino families: Scholarship, policy, and practice*. Thousand Oaks, CA: Sage Publication.

COPING WITH DOMESTIC VIOLENCE BY JAPANESE CANADIAN WOMEN

Yoshiyuki Takano

1. INTRODUCTION

Domestic violence is a worldwide phenomenon and a serious issue regardless of cultural backgrounds, types of societies, and levels of living conditions. It creates a very stressful situation for the victims and often results in psychological or physical injuries. In the case of spousal abuse, the issue is even more complicated because the effects often extend multi-generationally.

Family violence is one of the most stressful issues for immigrant families because they have to deal with family problems in a completely foreign environment without their familiar social supports. In addition, language and cultural barriers may also prevent them from seeking appropriate help. In some cases, the existing social services may be inappropriate for immigrant families (Family Violence Situation Paper, 1993). The purpose of this present research is, first, to investigate the experience of violence and abuse against Japanese immigrant women in Canada; and secondly, to examine the women's coping strategies. It is my hope that findings from the research may be helpful for preventing domestic violence in immigrant families and developing cross-culturally sensitive counseling models.

1.1. Definition of Terms

In research on family violence, part of the challenge is the lack of consistency in defining relevant terms (Frankel-Howard, 1989; Gelles, 1990; Hotaling, Straus, & Lincoln, 1989). The clarity of the terms is particularly important. Upon careful review of the existing literature, definitions of the key terms are provided in the following section.

1.1.1. Conflict

Researchers agree that families are conflict prone by nature because a family is a gathering of members who have different opinions, roles, and values. It is normal to have

Yoshiyuki Takano, Douglas College

a clash of interests, desires, or values among family members (Giles-Sims, 1983; O'Brien, 1974). Violent behavior may or may not emerge from marital conflict and may or may not be used as a way to resolve the conflict (O'Brien, 1974). Marital conflict involves, therefore, mutual antagonism that issues from discrepancies between idealized expectations and the reality of insufficient resources, differences in personal goals and values and defensive reactions by partners to each other (Giles-Sims, 1983; Reber, 1985).

1.1.2. Violence

Frankel-Howard (1989) defined violence as the use of any physical force against another person. Straus and Gelles (1986) also defined violence as "an act carried out with the intention, or perceived intention, of causing physical pain or injury to another person" (p. 467). Violence can occur mutually among the members of a family with approximately the same size and physical strength, but is more likely to entail a stronger individual using force against a weaker individual. Violence may emerge as a result of a severe argument or can be used as a way to assert power and control. Violence may also occur as the means to release one's frustration at the nearest target with or without apparent reason.

1.1.3. Abuse

Wiebe (1985) defined abuse as any abusive act which intends to control one's partner through isolation, pain, and fear. Finkelhor (1984) stated that it is a situation where a more powerful individual takes control and advantage of a less powerful individual. In other words, there is a clear distinction between perpetrators and victims, and the intent of perpetrators is to harm their victims with or without controlling them. Therefore, the abusive act includes not only physical aggression, but also verbal, sexual, emotional, spiritual, and material/financial aspects.

The Department of Justice Canada (2005) defined "spousal abuse" as "the violence or mistreatment that a woman or a man may experience at the hands of a marital, common-law or same-sex partner" (p. 1). The spousal abuse can take many different forms, such as physical abuse, sexual abuse and exploitation, emotional abuse, economic or financial abuse, and spiritual abuse (The Department of Justice Canada, 2005).

Physical abuse involves any physical force, such as beating, hitting, shaking, pushing, choking, biting, burning, kicking, rough handling, confinement, restraint, and/or assaulting with a weapon to injure or put the partner at risk of being injured (The Department of Justice Canada, 2005). Pence and Paymar (1993) added that the physical assault can range from threats, to beating, to homicide. In addition, the physical assault is often accompanied or preceded by various degrees of psychological abuse. The other form of abuse is sexual abuse and exploitation. The Department of Justice Canada (2005) stated that sexual abuse and exploitation is any form of sexual assault, sexual harassment, or sexual exploitation which forces the partner to participate in undesired, unsafe and/or degrading sexual activity. It may attempt to degrade and control the partner's sexuality or reproductive choices. Psychological and emotional abuse can be defined as any attempt or act of making one's partner feel bad about him/herself and/or degrading his/her self-esteem (Pence & Paymar, 1993). The Department of Justice Canada (2005) defined psychological and emotional abuse as any form of verbal attack which includes yelling, screaming and name-calling. Criticism, verbal threats, social isolation, intimidation and/or exploitation are used to control the partner. It also includes criminal harassment, such as stalking, threatening the partner and/or his/her loved ones, damaging the partner's possessions, and/or harming the partner's pets. Discerning emotional abuse can be subtle because it does not tend to leave any trace of a visible wound (Gelles & Straus, 1988; Kelly, 1997). One distinct characteristic may be, as various research has indicated, that verbal and emotional abuse and violence are almost always accompanied by physical violence and abuse (Arias & Pape, 1999; Gelles & Straus, 1988). Gelles and Straus discovered that there are as many victims of emotional abuse as there are victims of physical abuse. Economic or financial abuse is another form of abuse. This type of abuse uses financial resources as a mean to control the partner. It involves stealing money from the partner, deceiving a partner, withholding the money for meeting the partner's basic living needs, such as buying food and/or medical treatment, manipulating a partner to gain money, refusing and/or restricting access to financial resources, and preventing the partner from working and/or making his/her own choice of occupation. Spiritual abuse involves manipulating, dominating and/or controlling the partner by using the partner's religious or spiritual beliefs, such as preventing the partner from engaging in religious practices, and/or degrading their beliefs.

2. REVIEW OF THE LITERATURE

2.1. Factors and Issues: Spousal Abuse Among Immigrant Families

Current research about spousal abuse in North America utilizes various theories that include feminist theory (Adams, 1988; Dobash & Dobash, 1979; Pressman, 1989), sociological perspective (Geller, 1992; Gelles & Cornell, 1990), family of origin, social learning theory (Ganley, 1989; Gelles, 1987; O'Leary, 1988), attachment theory (Bartholomew & Horowitz, 1991; Dutton, 1995, 1998; Dutton, Saunders, Starzomski, & Bartholomew, 1994; Roberts & Noller, 1998), and abusive personality theory (Dutton, 1995, 1998; Dutton et al. 1994; Hofeller, 1982; Mahler, 1971; Star, 1980). Bronfenbrenner (1979) introduced the ecological model where he discussed microsystems such as family, classroom, religious setting, and peer groups as intimate systems. Important aspects of the issue of abuse are attributed not only to the direct relationship between the spouses, but also to the involvement of their entire ecology which includes their immediate family setting and the social community to which they belong (Perilla, Bakeman, & Norris, 1994). These theories may be only partially applicable to spousal abuse of immigrant families, which may be vulnerable to spousal abuse because of acculturation stress, isolation, unemployment frustration, intergenerational conflict, communication difficulties, and possibility of racial discrimination.

2.1.1. Acculturation Stress

One of the vulnerability factors under consideration is acculturation stress. Various researchers agreed with the notion that acculturation is a stressful adjustment for immigrants (Atkinson, Morten, & Sue, 1989; Berry & Annis, 1974; Church, 1982; Cleary, 1987; Furnham & Bochner, 1986; Ishiyama, 1989; Oberg, 1960; Padilla, Wagatsuma, & Lindholm, 1985; Pedersen, 1991; Taft, 1977; Thomas, 1995). It is common for the recent immigrant to experience various intensive emotions, such as homesickness, insecurity, depression, loss and grief, cultural and personal uprootedness, loneliness, anger, frustration, self-doubt, and confusion (Ishiyama, 1989). They are also prone to a variety of psychiatric disorders and social maladjustment, such as depression, anxiety, psychosomatic symptomatology, cardio-vascular disease, adjustment disorder, deviant behaviors, and substance abuse because of this extensive acculturation stress (Berry, 1986; Cleary, 1987; Faris & Dunham, 1960). Acculturation stress can contribute significantly to the occurrence of abuse (Perilla, Bakeman, & Norris, 1994; Rhee, 1997; Wiebe, 1985).

2.1.2. Ethnic Identity Crisis

Issues of ethnic identity are also significant for immigrant people and families (Ishiyama, 1989, 1995; Sue & Sue, 1990). Ethnic identity does not simply mean where the individual lives and how long he/she has lived in one particular country. Ishiyama (1989) stated that identity is multi-lateral; it may involve many levels, such as physical, familial, and socio-cultural. Thus, developing one's ethnic identity may require a protracted process. This process may create stress on the immigrant family system. For instance, through the process of developing ones' ethnic identity, the transformation from one's traditional family role to a new family role may also take place and a role reversal from the traditional family role may occur. Contrary to the traditional family role, the wife may have to become bread-winner of the family and the husband may have to stay at home to care for the family. This adjustment process may cause stress and conflict in the family.

2.1.3. Isolation

The other vulnerability factor for immigrant families is isolation. Isolation is a serious issue for immigrant women who are in abusive and violent relationships (Abraham, 2000; Chin, 1994; Family Violence Situation Paper, 1993; Pilowsky, 1993; Wiebe, 1985). As the immigrant family relocates to the host culture, members may experience loss of social support, lack of trust in the host society, and inability to access to the mainstream facilities for necessary help. Such experiences create a sense of isolation and vulnerability. For minority women being abused, seeking help from their parents and extended families may be the only culturally acceptable way to deal with the abusive situations, but family support may not be available to immigrants.

Wiebe (1985) stated that there are three ways for immigrant women to experience isolation. First, battering husbands tend to isolate their wives by removing their social contact and restricting their rights. Abusive husbands may attempt to increase their wives' dependency on them by undermining their self-confidence and lack of confidence. Second, if the wife attempts to leave, the abusive husband may overpower her by threatening that he may no longer sponsor her, which may result in the possibility of her being deported (Chin, 1994). Third, the wife may have to depend on her husband financially and thus be terrified by the idea of her leaving the family and thereby, facing poverty and loneliness (Chin, 1994). If these women leave the relationship, they may have to face unemployment, poor job opportunities, low wages, lack of adequate accommodation, and fear of subjecting their own children to the experience of poverty. This may result in her remaining in the abusive relationship. These isolating factors may be important reasons why immigrant women stay in an abusive relationship.

Abraham (2000) stated that isolation is not simply feeling lonely, it is also an experience of being emotionally, socially, economically, and culturally disconnected. It is a state where individuals cannot have a meaningful relationship and connections with their society. Isolation may also negatively affect abusive men as well. Those men who are aware of their own issues, may have lost friends, family members, and their mentors with whom to openly discuss their issues. Abusive men may, therefore, lose the opportunity to seek help and have others intervene.

2.1.4. Sense of Shame and Embarrassment

Their sense of shame and embarrassment is one of the significant obstacles for Japanese immigrant women who are the victims of spousal abuse. Wiebe (1985) stated that in some cultures, women are taught to be self-sacrificial and dutiful in their maternal and spousal roles and such people seem to believe that the success or failure of their marriage is tantamount to their success or failure as women. Tamura and Lau (1992) added that in Japanese culture, psychological and behavioral issues are perceived as a lack of will-power, self-control, or self-discipline and discussing personal issues with someone else from outside of their kin creates a sense of shame. In Asian families, "loss of face" means losing the respect and status of the entire family in their community when one family member is shamed (Hsu, 1970). Therefore, to save face and to avoid further condemnation, these women tend to stay in the relationship, even if they are facing abuse. Many researchers have identified underreporting of issues for spousal abuse because of this sense of shame and responsibility in Asian immigrant families (Ho, 1990; Huisman, 1996).

In Japanese culture, Doi (1973) described how the sense of shame and sense of guilt are in close relationship and these two feelings are not separable. Doi stated that what is characteristic about the Japanese sense of guilt is that it most strongly emerges when loyalty to the group is betrayed by a member of the group. As Doi summarized, the sense of guilt will be generated within the self and its direction is outward in the form of apology; whereas, the sense of shame is caused by the awareness of the eyes of others and is directed toward the self.

According to Doi (1973), the source of shame, just as in the case of guilt, is in the relation to the group to which one belongs, and being excluded by the group is the greatest shame and dishonor that one may experience, just as betrayal of the group creates guilt. However, simultaneously, having a sense of shame is extremely important for the individuals who belong to a group because the sense of shame encourages individuals to conform to the group. As a result, it generally becomes very difficult for Japanese to transcend the group and make individual choices.

One's desperate attempt to avoid a sense of shame may make one feel responsible for the group's unity and well-being. Doi (1973) stated that in some cases, people's sense of solidarity with the group takes over true responsibility. For example, it is still a practice to take full responsibility for group disharmony by resigning from one's post, even when the disunity is caused by other people. The sense of shame can also emerge when individuals compare their thoughts, actions, and feelings with their internalized criteria or frame of reference (Sakuta, 1964).

The strong stigma about shame can be clearly perceived in the Japanese language. Tatara (1998) stated that the concept of *sekentei* which is one's perception of how the society or others view him/herself is very significant in Japanese society. *Sekentei* can be translated as face, reputation, appearance, and what people would say about who one is, and how one behaves, feels, and thinks. This can become a strong frame of reference and stigma in terms of judging one's social admirability. For example, in Japan, people often say, "stop acting like that or people will laugh at you." In this sense, the speaker was using "people" as an imaginative frame of reference. *Shigarami* is usually used in the negative connotation, as it refers to the restriction of individuals' choices because of the "chains" or "fetters" of traditions, customs, and long established social convention. People follow these conventions in order to maintain harmony. The words *sekentei* and *shigarami* both imply how one is perceived in comparison to the majority of others in society. Therefore, people in Japan are extremely careful not to bring any disgrace or shame on their family name. People prefer dealing with their issues as a family and acquiring some help from extended family members, rather than having their issues known outside of the family. As a result, women are prevented from seeking professional help in the community.

2.1.5. Unemployment and Underemployment

Economic hardship, unemployment, and underemployment are not only stressful to the primary workers, but they also affect the family as a whole (Conger, et al., 1990; Liem & Liem, 1988). Liem and Liem (1988) studied the emotional impacts of job dislocation on husbands and their wives, and reported that unemployment was associated significantly with higher psychological symptoms such as anxiety, depression, somatization, hostility, and paranoia, and greater conflict and less supportive attitude between spouses.

Underemployment can also be a unique experience to immigrant families. Chin (1994) discussed underemployment among those people who are professional in their home countries are no longer being able to get the employment in their professional fields in the new country because of their language issues and legal restrictions, and Such people are forced either to "down grade" or to change their career in order to work.

Unemployment and underemployment may also affect one's self-identity, self-worth, personal meaning, and self-esteem (Westwood & Ishiyama, 1991). Straus, Gelles, and Steinmetz (1980) and various others researchers (Chin, 1994; Dooley, & Catalano, 1984; Krishnan, Hilbert, Vanleeuwen, & Kolia, 1997) stated that low socio-economic status, financial pressure, unemployment, and underemployment are significant factors which create ecological instability and increase the risk of marital violence.

2.1.6. Intergenerational Conflict

Intergenerational conflict may severely affect the families which are suffering from spousal abuse. Wiebe (1985) stated that the abused immigrant women are often isolated and constrained about from accessing services in their own community and learning about available information. As a result, the gap between themselves and acculturated family members increases. Those women may also have to depend on their children for translation which may cause a role reversal whereby children lose respect for their mothers and the women themselves may lose self-esteem.

Padilla et al. (1985) examined the relationship between acculturation stress and its effect on Japanese immigrants in the United States throughout across generations. They cited Caudill and DeVos (1956) stating that interpersonal conflict between the first generation and second generation can occur because of value conflict between the first generation's traditional Japanese culture and the second generation's American culture. Padilla and colleagues stated that both second generation and third generation also experience readjustment of their culture because there is a value discrepancy between their home and their dominant culture. This also leads to intrafamilial role conflict.

2.1.7. Communication Difficulty

Research has revealed that violent husbands tend to lack the ability to communicate their feelings effectively (Hofeller, 1982; MacLeod, 1980; Roberts & Noller, 1998). Hofeller reported that the majority of women in her study indicated that there were verbal arguments in which they found they were not communicating effectively, often prior to battering. Hofeller stated that lack of effective verbal communication skills may be a precipitating factor in a violent episode. Communication difficulty can be serious, when couples are married inter-culturally. Ibrahim (1985) cited Maruyama's (1978) comment, which stated communication breakdowns can be attributed to both languages barriers and differences in philosophy of life, world views, and epistemology.

Communication difficulties also become an obstacle when immigrant women require help in the community. Wiebe (1985) found that in case of crisis, those immigrant women may not know where to go to get help or may not even know that assistance is available to them. In addition, immigrant women may not have the language skills to communicate their problems and needs fluently. Thus, they may feel reluctant to seek help from outside their family or from outside their cultural group. Wiebe also stated that the lack of fluency in language causes abused women to feel more powerless and isolated.

2.1.8. Racial Discrimination

Racial discrimination can be another vulnerability factor for immigrant families. Dummett and Dummett (1982) defined racism as an attitude or behavior of discrimination and prejudice which is based on a belief that human beings can be or should be differentiated from one another mainly or entirely on the basis of their ancestral background, some physical characteristics, and sometimes by behavioral characteristics. Racists believe that the "inferior" groups of people need to be categorized and to be treated differently in terms of their rights, capabilities, and basic needs. Racist attitudes not only affect relationships between people, but also social structures, laws, and educational systems.

Various research has reported that racism can be extremely damaging to one's psychological well-being (Fernando, 1984; Franklin & Boyd-Franklin, 2000; Harrell, 2000; Outlaw, 1993; Pedersen, 1997; Pence & Paymar, 1993; Sue & Sue, 1990; Utsy, Ponterotto, Reynolds, & Cancelli, 2000). Pence and Paymar stated that racism is consistent with a belief that one's own group is superior to another's and thus, it promotes rationalization for domination. Fernando (1984) explained that one of the reasons that racism is psychologically damaging to people is because it is subtle and can be hidden unless we dig it out. Fernando discovered that racism can cause depression for the victims by affecting them in three negative ways: damaging their self-esteem, causing a sense of loss and rejection from society, and causing learned helplessness.

2.2. Spousal Abuse in Japan

Recently there has been increased awareness of family violence and abuse in Japan. According to Yoshihama and Sorenson (1994), there were over 11,000 wives who filed for divorce mediation due to their husbands' physical abuse in 1991. In 1998, the very first survey about violence against women was conducted by the city of Tokyo. According to Hada (1998), results showed that among the 1553 women who responded, 750 reported that they experienced or were experiencing physical, emotional, or sexual abuse or violence. Among these 750 women, there were only 117 women who reported that they sought help. Among those who sought help, most sought help through their friends, acquaintances, and relatives. There were very few women who sought help through doctors/counsellors (4.3%), regional help line/crisis line (2.6%), or lawyers/police (1.7%). More interestingly, among those who had not sought help (339 women), the reason cited by the majority of women (65.5%), was that they thought it was not that necessary to seek help. Some (35.1%) reported that they thought it was their fault. Others (14.5%) reported that they thought they could sustain their marriage by simply enduring it. Still others (7.1%) reported that they could not speak up because they felt embarrassed. Finally, others (6.8%) reported that they did not want to get other people involved in their family matters.

According to Nazuna (2000), results from the Tokyo survey also showed the negative emotional impact on children who witnessed their mothers being abused. Reactions included anger and physical aggression toward their fathers and others, emotional and personality disturbances, dropping out from the school, apathy, lost contact with society, nervous breakdown and suicide attempt, and psychosomatic symptoms.

Until recently, there was no specific legislation in Japan which defined spousal abuse as a crime nor provided protection for the victims of spousal abuse (Yoshihama & Sorenson, 1994). Effective from 2001, a Law for the Prevention of Spousal Violence and the Protection of Victims in Japan has finally been established to define spousal abuse as a crime and legislate particular support systems such as the involvement of law enforcement for mediating of family disputes, in addition to providing restraining orders and public social support.

This Law for the Prevention of Spousal Violence and the Protection of Victims was further revised on December 2001. Its protection order can now be applied to partners who are divorced. It also now prohibits the perpetrators to not only their partners, but also to their partners' children for six months. It can also order the perpetrators to vacate the shared-premise for two months.

3. EXISTENTIAL-PHENOMENOLOGICAL APPROACH

An existential-phenomenological research method was utilized in the present study. The goal of existential-phenomenological psychology is to reveal or disclose the naïve experience as pure and real phenomena (Valle & King, 1978). Giorgi (1971b) stated a verbal description can reveal the meaning of the phenomenon for the participants. Therefore, the aim for using existential-phenomenology in human science is to reveal the content and meaning of the experience unique to individuals rather than measuring and quantifying their experiences. To ask for the qualities of specific experience is ultimately to ask individuals what that specific experience is like for them, and through this description of the experiences, the participants disclose also elements of the *meaning* of the phenomenon for them. Therefore, those who participate in the research are identified as "participants" or "co-researchers" because they are not the "subjects" of the study, but rather they are the ones who can provide their personal experiences and meanings of specific phenomena (Osborne, 1990).

4. RESEARCH DESIGN AND PROCEDURE

4.1. The Interview Structure

For the data collection, in-depth interviews were used. The interview questions and the interview procedures were formulated in a way to help participants "produce clear and accurate descriptions of a particular aspect of human experience" (Polkinghorne, 1989, p. 44). Polkinghorne also recommended that the interviews open-ended, unstructured, and provide enough time to explore the topic in depth. "The subject [sic] is required to concentrate on the experience of the phenomenon exactly as it is given to him [sic], and not to pre-judge it nor to see it through any specific perspective simply because of previous knowledge about the phenomenon" (Giorgi, 1971a, p. 9). Kvale (1983) also emphasized that the interview is not person-oriented, but theme-oriented and the use of basic counseling skills, such as empathy and probing are person-required to draw out accurate and clear descriptions and meanings of interviewees' life world.

The researcher had an initial contact either in person or over the telephone in order to inform the participants about the purpose of the research and to establish rapport. After receiving a signed consent form, and agreement to audio record the interview, the principal researcher moved onto the second phase where the actual interview took place and data was gathered. In order to enhance more immediate and authentic experiences, the participants' own mother tongue, Japanese, was used in the interview. The complete interview took approximately one to two hours in a location of the participants' choosing. There were six open-ended questions:

1. Would you please share with me as fully as you can your experience of your abusive relationship? (Additional question: What is your experience of living with someone who abuses you?)
2. What was it like for you to be in an abusive relationship as an immigrant wife? (Additional question: In what ways does being in an abusive relationship as an immigrant woman makes life more difficult for you?)
3. What does it mean to you to be in an abusive relationship? (Additional question: How does it affect life with your partner?)
4. What did you do to help yourself in your abusive situation?
5. What is your experience of getting help from _____ service?
6. In what ways can the service be more helpful to you and other immigrant women with similar problems?

These interview questions were, first, formulated in English, and then, translated into Japanese by the researcher. The accuracy of the Japanese translation of the questions was confirmed by asking another Japxanese-English, bilingual person, to translate the Japanese translated interview questions back into English.

These interviews were conducted in Japanese and transcribed word for word from the audiotape, and then all the transcriptions were translated into English. To ensure the accuracy of the researchers's translations, two of the interviews translated by the researcher were independently translated by another bilingual volunteer and compared with the researcher's translations. Then, a brief back-translation was performed. Back-translation is a translation process where a bilingual translator translates from the original language to the designated language, and then blindly translates it back to the original language (Brislin, 1986).

4.2. Selection of Co-Researchers

The first phase was to select appropriate participants who were able to share their experiences freely and accurately. Polkinghorne (1989) listed the requirements for selection of co-researchers as: first, co-researchers have had experiences of the phenomenon under investigation; and second, the co-researcher has "the capacity to provide full and sensitive descriptions of the experience under examination" (p. 47). Within the above mentioned requirements, nine Japanese immigrant women agreed to participate in this research. Participants were recruited through local churches, a Japanese community women's group, and Japanese community newspapers. All participants signed a consent form. To ensure that participants had experienced the phenomenon under investigation, Walker's (1984) definition of abuse was used to screen participants. All the participants had to be immigrants to Canada or be naturalized Candians. Also, all participants were current residents of Canada and had experience of abuse and violence in Canada. Participants could be still in the relationship with their partners or divorced or separated. The nationality of the partners was not specified for participation in this research.

5. DATA ANALYSIS

Data analysis followed the procedure outlined by Giorgi (1975), Colaizzi (1978), and Osborne (1990). It involved the following steps:

Step1. Read the protocol description in order to understand and to get the co-researchers' feelings from it. This process was to seek pure description of the participants' account through the meanings the researcher apprehended through written language.

Step 2. Review the protocol and extract phrases and sentences which are related to the investigating phenomenon. The first step was to find the transition in meaning which was perceived as significant meaning in spousal abuse experiences as immigrant women, reading the transcript slowly and analytically. After working through this procedure, the researcher was able to acquire a series of meaning units or constituents.

Step 3. Phrases in the protocol, that is the meaning units, were transformed into the researcher's words and meanings, and then themes were elicited out of these significant statements, phrases, or meaning units. Colaizzi (1978) stated that researcher's "formulations must discover and illuminate those meanings hidden in the various contexts and horizons of the investigated phenomenon which are announced in the original protocols" (p. 59).

Step 4. Organize these meanings into a cluster of themes in each protocol. Then, compare the clustered themes of all the protocols, and cluster them further into the categories based on the themes common to all the protocols.

Step 5. Organize and gather all results into an exhaustive description. This was to discover the structure of the experience of spousal abuse as reported by Japanese immigrant women. Colaizzi (1978) stated that the aim for this phase was to "formulate the exhaustive description of the investigated phenomenon in as unequivocal a statement of identification of its fundamental structure as possible" (p. 61).

Step 6. Examine the validity of the interpretations. Polkinghorne (1989) explained that "the researcher returns to each subject and asks, 'How do my descriptive results compare with your experience?' and 'Have any aspects of your experience been omitted?'" (p. 53). This procedure may discover new data which may revise the final description.

6. ESTABLISHING TRUSTWORTHINESS

In phenomenological perspective, the meaning of truth, validity, and reliability, are used differently from the conventional terms as they are applied in quantitative research. Verification and content of the data requires a new approach.

6.1. Validity Procedures

Kvale (1994) indicated that validity does not mean final product control or verification. Rather, "verification is built into the research process with continual checks of the credibility, plausibility, and trustworthiness of the findings" (p. 168). Producing verification is a process and, therefore, it is important for the researcher to implement verification processes throughout the research.

Osborne (1990) introduced four ways to assess the validity of the data. The first way is to use bracketing. Bracketing is a process of detailed self-reflection, and by presenting the researcher's self-reflection it helps readers understand the reports while taking the researcher's perspective into account (Osborne, 1990). The process of bracketing helps to suspend the researcher's biases and hunches while accessing the co-researchers' world view. The second way is to examine the researchers' interpretation of the data with the co-researchers through dialogue. The third way is to check the interpretation of the phenomenological data with the members of the research community to examine the coherence of the process. The fourth way is to examine the validity of the interpretations with the people who have experienced the phenomenon under examination.

For the verification of validity, several steps were taken in this research. First, bracketing was used to ensure the validity of the data. Secondly, throughout the data analysis, emergent themes were always verified by the research supervisor and colleagues who were familiar with Asian culture and existential-phenomenological research. According to Kvale (1989), it is "to test statements about the truth and falsity of propositions on the basis of argued points of view, and the best argument wins. The discourse is a form of argumentation where no social exertion of power takes place, the only form of power being the force of the better argument" (p. 84).

Thirdly, after completion of the data analysis, the principal researcher had a second telephone interview with participants to verify the validity of the extracted themes. Five out of nine participants were available to verify the themes. Only five participants were available to verify the results because of their safety concerns and because of having had to move to some other location. There was a high agreement between co-researchers and the principal researcher's extracted themes.

Finally, to verify the themes, the principal researcher conducted an extensive interview with a Japanese immigrant woman who was not in this study, but who had experienced spousal abuse and family violence in her marriage. All the themes were verified by this individual.

6.2. Reliability

According to Wertz (1986), the issue of reliability is that it is an estimate of the consistency of measuring the phenomenon. Wertz stated that reliability is context bound and implies the meaning of the measure for the observer. Meaning is intrinsically context bound and is relational. Therefore, it is inevitable to have multiple complex meanings and interpretations.

Miles and Huberman (1994) explained the focus of reliability is to ensure the process of the study is consistent, reasonably stable across researchers and methods. Reliability is thus concerned with examining the quality of the data and data analysis. Regarding reliability, Osborne (1990) also stated that "the nature of the construct being measured will have an effect upon how it is to be measured" (p. 87). Osborne also stated that "although there may be several interpretive perspectives on the same phenomenon, sameness (reliability) can arise out of the inconsistency, variability and relativity of human perception" (p. 87). One of the ways to examine reliability is to ask another phenomenological researcher to categorize the meanings into themes to determine if there may be any consistency of the clustering. To ensure reliability of the research the principal researcher first took 10 percent of the meaning units from the entire 783 meaning units and asked an Asian female Master's level counseling psychology student to categorize the meaning units into the given categories. Results were compared with the principal researcher's result and produced high (84%) intersubjective agreement (P. T. P. Wong, personal communication, 2001).

7. RESULTS

7.1. Meaning Units and Categories

Through explication of the themes from each of the nine interviews, 16 distinct meaning categories of experience of abuse and nine categories of coping strategies emerged. The 16 categories of experience of spousal abuse are listed in Table 1 together with the percentages of participants reporting such experiences. Table 2 provides a

Table 1. Participation Rate and Frequency of Meaning Units for Categories of Abuse

Categories	Co-Researchers									Participants' Rates	Frequency of Meaning Units
	1	2	3	4	5	6	7	8	9		
1. Experiences of acculturation	Y	Y	Y	Y	Y	Y	Y	Y	Y	100%	63
2. Sense of helplessness and powerlessness	Y	Y	Y	Y	Y	Y	Y	Y	Y	100%	54
3. Feeling remorse and regret for getting into a relationship with someone without knowing him well	Y	Y	Y	Y	Y	Y	Y	Y	Y	100%	32
4. Experience of violence and abuse	N	Y	Y	Y	Y	Y	Y	Y	Y	89%	104
5. Feeling and/or being responsible	Y	Y	Y	Y	Y	Y	Y	Y	N	89%	60
6. Significant family of origin experiences	Y	Y	Y	Y	Y	Y	Y	Y	N	89%	56
7. Domineering and controlling personality	N	Y	Y	Y	Y	Y	Y	Y	Y	89%	50
8. Experience of financial exploitation	N	Y	Y	Y	N	Y	Y	Y	Y	78%	38
9. Partner's alcohol and drug abuse	Y	Y	Y	N	Y	Y	Y	N	Y	78%	30
10. Marital conflicts	N	Y	Y	Y	Y	N	N	Y	Y	67%	43
11. Experience of communication difficulties	N	Y	Y	Y	Y	N	N	Y	Y	67%	10
12. Emotional difficulties in children	N	N	Y	N	Y	N	Y	Y	Y	56%	41
13. Partners' insecurity and low self-esteem	N	Y	Y	N	N	N	N	Y	Y	56%	16
14. Partners' infidelity	Y	Y	N	N	N	Y	Y	N	N	44%	12
15. Sense of shame	N	Y	Y	N	N	N	N	N	N	33%	13
16. Experience of racial discrimination and prejudice	Y	N	Y	Y	N	N	N	N	N	33%	10

Table 2. Categories of Abuse Experiences

Categories	Definition	Examples
1. Experiences of acculturation	It refers to the issues and experiences related to ethnic identity and acculturation such as development of a sense of belonging in the new culture, homesickness, isolation, and alienation.	"I do think of myself Japanese. But, sometimes I do think like a Canadian, depends on each situation... but both sides are all mingled up together right now. But I find myself being more Japanese." "I became homesick at the beginning for a while after I moved to Canada.... I became very lonely and became homesick."
2. Sense of helplessness and powerlessness	It refers to the participants' feelings of helplessness, powerlessness, depression, and inability to improve the situation.	"I felt that he was watching every single action that I took.... I felt almost like being in a bird cage. I felt like being put into the cage." "At that time, it was such a mess and I was at the bottom... It was almost like there was no more, no any worse life to live than that was. I was pushed into the corner...."
3. Feeling remorse and regret for getting into a relationship with someone without knowing him well	It refers to the participants' feeling remorse and regret for getting married or getting into the relationship without knowing their partners well.	"I got married to him without knowing his personality and other things.... I personally did not know anything about his personality." "I tell myself, why didn't we stay as friends longer before we dated. I think now, that our length of time of being just friends, no, what I mean is our length of time before dating was too short."
4. Experience of violence and abuse	It refers to any abusive acts, which included physical, sexual, emotional/mental, and verbal abuse.	"I was beaten, got angry at, and yelled at all night.... And I got bruises all over my body." "I was kicked around and beaten up so badly, and bleeding all over the place."

Continued

5. Feeling and/or being responsible	It refers to the participants' experiences of feeling responsible for their partners' and children's well being, maintenance of the family unity, and improvement of the relationship; they also felt guilty for failing to carry out the above responsibilities.	"I would not tell any negative things or bad news to people in Japan. It is just fine to share the positive things happening, but not bad news. They would worry a lot, if we live at a distance because they do not know exactly what is going on.... So, I think that I would never tell them anything bad that happened to me.... Not to parents and siblings...."
6. Significant family of origin experiences	It refers to the significant family of origin experiences and/or unfinished business which may be affecting their values and relational patterns in their marriage. These significant life experiences included witnessing and/or experiencing abuse as a child, traumatic experiences, neglect, alcohol problems at home, and parents' marital difficulties.	"I persevered through his insults for my child.", "It was very difficult. Here was the person who was born after the war and the person who experienced the war, I mean, he went through the chaos of the post war period as a child. We had a big difference in our experiences.... So, I did not experience these hardships and so, he pressured me to experience them.... That was very difficult." "My husband does not respect his father. He grew up without his father around, so, when his father came back from the war, he just treated his father as a stranger in the house.... So, the respecting father was not nurtured inside of my husband."
7. Domineering and controlling personality	It refers to the domineering and aggressive personality as their partners' prevailing characteristic. It means that partners were demanding, controlling and had explosive tempers.	"As a human being, he did not accept me. He never did accept me." "When he has some conversation, he still tries to show that he is always the superior to me, with his words."

Table 2. Categories of Abuse Experiences—cont'd

Categories	Definition	Examples
8. Experience of financial exploitation	It refers to the participants' experiences of financial exploitation by their partners with an intention of harming and/or controlling. This also included their partners using family finances without consideration of others.	"He really liked changing cars. In the matter of 16 years, he changed 29 times... After 16 years, I stopped counting because that makes me angry... It was just like that, he was always buying things for himself." "Sometimes, my husband treated me like he was giving money to a prostitute like this. (sobbing) Giving me only a minimum amount of money... and he did not give it to me by asking only one time..."
9. Partner's alcohol and drug abuse	It refers to the subjects' experiences of their partners misusing alcohol and/or drugs. The subjects stated that their partners were severely involved and frequently intoxicated.	"When I said things that do not mean anything, he took it very personally and became angry, especially when he was drunk, I did not mean anything, he became very angry and raised his voice and started arguing with me." "The major issue was his alcoholism... Alcoholism was the one. He was alcoholic and lost consciousness. And then he started yelling at me or physically attacking at me. At the end, he did something like choking me..."
10. Marital conflicts	It refers to Japanese immigrant women's experiences of non-abusive marital conflicts. These conflicts were the disagreements about children's education, issues of parenting, and their husbands' refusal to improve the relationships.	"I thought about getting divorced so many times, more than 100 times." "We just couldn't get along well.... I just could never understand him.... all my life."

11. Experience of communication difficulties	It refers to the communication difficulties as a result of language barriers, cultural differences, and the lack of communication among the couples.	"Because of my poor English skills, I could not communicate well.... I think I could discuss most things, but I could not explain deeper and more complicated things. So, if I could explain those kind of things, then.... I think we could have understood each other much better." "My husband doesn't know anything about Japan.... he does not at all."
12. Emotional difficulties in children	It refers to the participants' experiences of their children having emotional difficulties, such as an explosive temper, lacking remorse, emotional cut off between parents and children, depression, low self-esteem, irresponsibility with money, and difficulties at school.	"Sometimes, when she [my daughter] did not like something, then she just hit me. So, I think that kind of behavior comes from her growing up with watching what her father did. So, when she grew up, she has been hearing the message that 'mother is stupid, she cannot get it unless she is beaten.' So, she hit me too, she used to beat me." "Later, it became an issue that how much his father negatively affected my son.... I thought he is doing just fine. But it turned out that.... he has low self-esteem."
13. Partners' insecurity and low self-esteem	It refers to the Japanese immigrant women's perception of their partners' insecurity and low self-esteem, such as being emotionally dependent, and lacking leadership.	"Because he is very timid kind of guy.... And he wants to be domineering and proud and wants to show off." "I guess he is expecting that [being mother] kind of role of his wife, but a wife is not a mother...."
14. Partners' infidelity	It refers to the subjects' feelings regarding their partners' unfaithfulness and infidelity in general.	"From what I understand, his image of marriage is... having a wife he loves at home, and she will raise their children. But he will also have a sex life outside of marriage." "This is not the first time, but he got involved with many other women so many times.... I believe that he had more relationships behind my back."

Continued

Table 2. Categories of Abuse Experiences—cont'd

Categories	Definition	Examples
15. Sense of shame	It refers to the Japanese immigrant women's experiences of feelings of shame or losing face. They experienced feeling shame as a result of being abused and having family problems.	"I have pride as a Japanese.... It was very shameful..... it was very disgraceful, wasn't it?" "When I think about those *shigarami* (face, reputations), even though it is my own home town and it is just fine for me to go and visit for fun, I do not think that I can move back and start living there."
16. Experience of racial discrimination and prejudice	This refers to the participants' experiences of discrimination and prejudice. This also includes partners' attempts to prevent Japanese immigrant women from sharing their culture with their children.	"He says the most beautiful women in the world are Caucasian white with blond hair and big bust.... and he says look at the Japanese woman, the height of your cheek bone, or hair is black." "[getting racially discriminative remarks] is a different type of pain from being physically hurt by someone. You cannot quite remember the pain from being hurt physically, can you? But, the scar that being verbally hurt will stay very long. You can't forget about it.... I can still remember each word he said."

Table 3. Categories of Coping

Categories	Definition	Examples of Meaning Units
1. Seeking help from friends	The participants sought physical and emotional support from their friends.	"I wanted to get away from that house. But I did not have a car, so a friend helped me to move out." "They [friends] brought me some dinner, or things like that.... They did grocery shopping for me."
2. Seeking help from family members	The participants coped with the domestic violence and abuse by seeking help and support from their own family members.	"The last time that I went back to Japan was when my sister worried about me and told me to come back immediately. She said, if I did not have any money, then she would send some for me. Whenever I went back, my sister always had daily necessities, cosmetics, underwear, clothes, and everything for me. She prepared everything for me to live comfortably." "Once you are an immigrant, compared to the old time, you can always go back whenever you feel fed up with it. We can make a choice.... It is not like it is impossible for refugees to go back to their own country."
3. Seeking help from church members or pastor	The participants coped with the domestic violence and abuse by receiving help and mediation from their church members and/or pastors.	"Until that time, my pastor worried about us and visited us several times." "My friends, there is one of the church members, a lady, and she, too, came to see me.... came to me even in the middle of the night.... She came to mediate our fight.... Even at past midnight, she came to my house."
4. Getting out of the situation through separation or divorce	The participants coped with the domestic violence and abuse by physically removing themselves from the relationship.	"I am so glad that I was able to get out from the situation." "I got divorced three years ago,... And right now, I feel rather fulfilled right now, than I used to be."

Continued

Table 3. Categories of Coping—cont'd

Categories	Definition	Examples of Meaning Units
5. Finding strength and guidance through faith in God	The participants sought help by having faith in an omnipotent, omnipresent, and omniscient God to cope with their crisis.	"I overcome difficulties with faith, and there is a joy in that" "It was faith. In the night, after all the things I went through, I read the Bible and prayed, that was when I experienced a tremendous peace just like climbing up to the heaven. Without faith, I do not think I could have managed this far."
6. Finding and affirming meaning and purpose	The participants sought their personal meaning and purpose for their life in their crisis.	"The reasons why they are troubled and anguished is, through this anguish.... because this distress makes them search for the reasons why they are suffering like that right now." "After I got married and had children, my life became more joyful, I think I found happiness in my life. So, even though there were many things that happened through my marriage, I still feel content, so I do not regret that."
7. Experiencing personal growth	The participants sought personal growth in their difficulties.	"I would suggest to examine and learn about oneself. That was what happened to me so... I did not know about myself." "For me, it seems to me that these things are the footsteps for me to grow."
8. Remaining optimistic	The participants used optimism to cope with their crisis.	"I feel like I did not suffer at that time. I am rather an optimistic person." "I am optimistic and so, I do not take things so seriously."
9. Relying on own strong personality	The participants relied on their own strength and perseverance to cope with crisis.	"I persevered and brought myself up to this point by myself.... I came this far with my own willpower." "I think I'm aggressive... I think of myself as quite strong... I am not the type to cry. I think that's why I am able to survive on my own here."

definition of each of the categories with exemplars. Table 3 indicates the categories of coping strategies.

These results are the subjective description of the experience of domestic violence and abuse for Japanese immigrant women. Overview of the interview data for experience of abuse is described in Table 1. This table also shows participants' rating with respect to how many participants shared the category in their descriptions. Rates are arranged in descending order of agreement from the most to least. Thus, Category 1: Experiences of acculturation had a greater agreement rate (100%) among the participants compared to Category 16: Experience of racial discrimination and prejudice.

8. DISCUSSION OF ABUSE EXPERIENCE

In order to facilitate discussion first experiences of abuse will be grouped into the following four areas: (1) Discussion of abuse experience; (2) Characteristics of the abusive and violent husbands; (3) Marital and family problems; (4) Issues related to acculturation and racial discrimination. After the experience of abuse is discussed in these four groups, coping strategies reported by the participants and will be discussed as well as their implications.

8.1. Experiences of Abuse

Several types of abuse emerged from the interview that are consistent with previous research. Physical, sexual, and emotional abuse were present and clearly identified. As the initial emotional impact of the violence and abuse, these Japanese immigrant women experienced fear, shock, feeling threatened for their lives, and feeling isolation. I Ms. K. stated that "I was scared of being physically attacked again. Once I have experienced that, it really scares me a lot." Ms. S. shared her fear as, "I seriously thought that if I stay longer, I might get killed...." She also said, "that [being abused] was very shocking for me.... So, for me, it was very traumatic and... I thought that I cannot take it any more." They reacted with emotional shock, which is an emotional, cognitive, and behavioral state whereby the women cannot process what is happening to them (Pilowsky, 1993; Wiebe, 1985).

One of the challenges is to distinguish between the severe conflict in marriage and emotional abuse. Emotional abuse is subtle, but distinctly different from the state of severe marital conflict. Emotional abuse causes severe negative damage on individuals (Gelles & Straus, 1988; Pence & Paymar, 1993) and some research even suggests that emotional abuse is a significant predictor of posttraumatic stress disorders (Arias & Pape, 1999).

In this study, one way to identify emotional abuse is to identify any actions, whether verbal or non-verbal, visible or invisible, that are clearly oppressive, controlling, and/or hurtful to the partner. An example of this would be when the women were prevented from reaching out to the social realm by the participants' husbands. This enforced isolation expressed both verbally and by overt attempts at controlling them by moving to a rural area, preventing them from attending school, or not letting them answer phone calls.

One of the damaging long-term effects of emotional abuse is that the Japanese immigrant women experience isolation. Participants are forced to disconnect from their social support and have their self-reliance and self-esteem shattered by their abusive husbands.

This is consistent with Wiebe's (1985) research where she found one of the damaging effects of emotional abuse for immigrant women is isolation by their husbands who deprive them of social contacts and restrict their rights. Abraham (2000) agrees with this conclusion and explains that there are three levels of social isolation: the quality of a women's relationship with her husband; the quality and frequency of social networks, such as friends, relatives, and co-workers; and the accessibility of participating in community, such as community organizations, economic, legal, and political institutions.

Exploitation and control in financial matters can also be a form of emotional abuse. There are Two types of financial exploitation emerge in this study. The first type is the controlling type of financial exploitation in which the husbands are the primary wage earner and have control over their wives by not giving them enough money to buy daily necessities and food which creates real hardship and emotional stress. The second type is an irresponsible type of financial exploitation in which the wives are the primary wage earner or controller of the family finances. However, the husbands may squander the family resources and accumulate irresponsible debts without the consideration of family members. Both types of financial exploitation are a significant emotional burden for the immigrant women and result in feeling powerless, disregarded, humiliated, and non-existent. Abraham (2000) indicates that financial deprivation is a major source of isolation and powerlessness for immigrant women, as abusive husbands can use finances to restrict their wives' freedom and thereby isolate them from the outside world.

The results are also the consistent with Walker's (1984) theory of the cycle of abuse which describes the recurring phases of violence: tension building, the acute battering incident, and the loving contrition phase. Participants often recount that after the loving contrition phase, and in spite of their husbands' promises, they never stopped the violence. Walker (1984) also reports that this third phase positively reinforces the woman to stay in the relationship.

8.2. Sense of Helplessness and Powerlessness

The common experience of feelings of helplessness, powerlessness, depression, and feeling an inability to improve the situation is consistent with various research on victims of abuse (Cook & Frantz-Cook, 1984; Dutton, 1995; Gelles & Straus, 1988; Margolin & Burman, 1993; Seligman, 1992). Walker (1986) agrees with the existence of learned helplessness in victims of abuse and explains that battered women often become unable to predict and be hopeful that their efforts will have an effect on what can happen to them. Stith and Rosen (1990) state that victims of family violence quite often have low self-esteem and high external locus of control in which the individuals perceive powerlessness over events in their lives. Frieze (1979) discovers that the more severe the assault, the greater the tendency for assaulted women to attribute causality to the self. When the victim's internalized blame for abuse is severe, the depression and helplessness will be greater and the self-esteem will be decreased.

More interestingly, various studies show that the result of violence and abuse can lead to posttraumatic stress disorder (Davidson, 1994; Street & Arias, 2001). Results of the research reported here also support this view. The participants' description indicates symptoms of posttraumatic stress disorder in the victims of abuse, such as recurrent distressing recollections of the events, feeling of intense fear and helplessness as if the traumatic events were recurring, symptoms of depression, and some physiological reaction to the exposure of the symbolized events of the their abuse and violence (American Psychiatric Association [APA], 1994).

8.3. Feeling Remorse for Getting into a Relationship with Someone without Knowing Him Well

The Japanese immigrant women describe their feelings of regret that they did not spend enough time getting to know their partners before deciding to get married or starting the relationship. Most of the participants found that their husbands were rather pleasant in the early stages of the relationship, and they could not see their hidden personality traits such as having a domineering, aggressive, extremely jealous personality, and/or having alcohol problems. Consequently, as the relationship progressed, the women felt shocked when they gradually discovered their husbands' predominant personality and felt regret about getting married before they knew their husbands very well.

One contributing factor seems to have been that the abusive men tended to show two opposite sides of their personality and disguise their feelings with a "mask." Clow, Hutchins, and Vogler (1990) state that although abusive men can experience a variety of feelings and emotions, with limited self-awareness, they tend to suppress and mask their feelings. Dutton (1998) attributes this evidence to abusive personality theory and states that the Dr. Jekyll and Mr. Hyde descriptions given by the wives of abusive men can come from the wives' experience of borderline personality traits of their husbands who have a distinct split self-perception which cannot be well integrated.

The other contributing factor is that, in some cases with the inter-cultural relationships, the courtship was carried out only through the mail or via occasional visits. The long distance courtship was very difficult because years ago the cultural distance between Canada and Japan was much greater than it is today when we have more developed telecommunications. In addition, the gap between Japanese and Canadian currencies used to make travel from Japan to Canada more difficult for Japanese women so it was harder to get to know their prospective partners in person. The cultural distance has also diminished in recent times due to greater multiculturalisam in Japan and Canada.

8.4. Feeling Responsible

The important aspect of this category is that contrary to previous research (Frieze, 1979; Gelles & Straus, 1988; Star, 1980), none of the participants expressed that they felt responsible for provoking the abuse and violence. In this study, participants did experience feeling responsible, but they did not feel responsible for the cause of the abuse; rather, they felt responsible for maintaining the family harmony, protecting family members' well-being, improving the relationship, and protecting their children.

The participants also felt guilty as a result of failing to carry out the above responsibilities. This feeling seems to have emerged from more of a sacrificial attitude and loyalty toward their family members and children rather than being driven by feelings of guilt from the possibility that they provoked the abuse and violence. One of the participants shared her thoughts in the follow-up interview. She stated that Japanese women are committed to the family and it is not acceptable for them to simply give up and leave the family or seek divorce when the relationship becomes difficult. They are committed to protecting their children at any cost. Pedersen (1997) recognizes the strong devotion of mothers to their children in Japanese culture.

8.5. Sense of Shame

The sense of shame in the Japanese immigrant women has a close relationship with social stigma in Japanese culture. The concept of *Sekentei* and *Shigarami* became apparent throughout the interviews and was often mentioned. As indicated earlier, in Japanese culture, shame and embarrassment become evident in terms of the relationship with others and society rather than as an identity. The participants expressed embarrassment coming from the comparisons of themselves to others and to "the social standard." More interestingly, this is their own frame of reference and perception, and may not represent accepted social standards. Because this sense of shame and embarrassment relates closely to social stigma, avoiding shame/embarrassment and protecting their face prevents abused victims from reaching out for social support and it can produce social isolation from the community. One of the participants shared that she could not ask for help from the local Japanese community because the community is very small and she was afraid that rumors may be spread. For Japanese immigrant women, the sense of shame and embarrassment is a significant concern and it could facilitate social isolation.

9. CHARACTERISTICS OF ABUSIVE HUSBANDS

Several significant themes were extracted regarding the characteristics of the husbands. The personality components show domineering and controlling personalities, feelings of insecurity, and low self-esteem. The behavioral components of the husbands indicate issues of alcohol and drug abuse and infidelity.

9.1. Personality Components

Participants described their husbands as demanding, controlling, constantly irritable, having an explosive tempers, being malicious, jealous, unforgiving, and manipulative. The personality types of these abusive and violent husbands are consistent with current research which suggests distinct characteristics of abusive men including: being demanding, controlling, and possessive; pathological jealousy; lack of empathy; external blame and avoiding responsibility; poor impulse control; insecurity; and low self-esteem (Dutton, 1995, 1998; Hofeller, 1982; Pence & Paymar, 1993; Star, 1980; Stark & Flitcraft, 1988; Stith & Rosen, 1990). Clow, Hutchins, and Vogler (1990) also state that abusive and violent husbands tend to have erroneous and distorted cognitions, rationalizations, and justifications about their violence and abuse which may prevent them from taking responsibility for their actions.

Violence in the context of an intimate relationship can be different from violence in the social context. Dutton (1995) states that emotional abuse can be produced through attachment rage. Bowlby (1973) states that intimate anger has two major functions. First, anger may assist in overcoming any obstacles for the reunion of attachment figures.

Second, anger may discourage the loved one from leaving again. Therefore, this functional form of anger also has a purpose of reproach and punishment of the behavior which encourages reunion and discourages further separation of their loved ones. As is consistent with past research (Coleman, 1980), the result also showed that none of the partners had been violent outside of their marital relationships. They were rather described as a "nice person." Dutton (1995) also revealed in his studies that adult males who were both dominant and emotionally abusive also showed significant occurrence of fearful and preoccupied attachment. This indicates that those men who are violent may require the development of proper skills for managing their anger and effective communication of their thoughts and feelings to their partners.

In addition to the attachment patterns and anger management skills, the abusive and violent men's psychological status can be an important element. Some research has been indicating abusive and violent men's serious personality disorders, borderline personality disorder (Dutton, 1995, 1998) and family of origin issues, such as having observed and/or experienced violence as children (Coleman, 1980). Dutton (1995, 1998) states that borderline personality men attempt to split women into two conflicting images: ideal and devalued object. These men project their volatile impulses onto the devalued women-object and this results in the possibility of increasing intimate conflict and violence. Also, according to Beck (1999), cognitively, the abusive men tend to have egocentric and inflexible concepts about the marital relationship and about their wives. Abusive men tend to have skewed beliefs that they perceive themselves as vulnerable to their wives' words and actions.

9.2. Partner's Alcohol/Drug Abuse and Infidelity

The other characteristic of these husbands that the participants share is the propensity for alcohol and drug abuse. Partners are described as frequently intoxicated to the point where they fail to fulfill significant roles and obligations at work and/or home. Although the relationship between alcohol or drug use and marital abuse or violence is controversial, a considerable body of research reveals that abused women describe their husbands as having problems with alcohol (Hofeller, 1982; Leonard & Jacob, 1988; MacLeod, 1980; Ministry of Attorney General Police Services Division, 1999). Results of the present research show that the majority of participants (seven out of nine) said their partners' had a substance abuse problem.

Struggling with the problem of the husband's infidelity also emerges from the Japanese immigrant women's experiences. The participants described their husbands as having less commitment to their marriage, and they did not take responsibility for their relationship with their partner. Hofeller (1982) also discovered similar results in her qualitative research with 50 victims of wife abuse, where 32 percent of the women found that their husbands had confirmed sexual liaisons with others throughout their marriage.

10. MARITAL AND FAMILY PROBLEMS

10.1. Experience of Marital Conflict and Communication Problems

Apart from the experience of violence and abuse, the experience of marital conflict emerged independently. This category indicated that the relationship itself was not stable and conflicts were not resolved effectively. These conflicts involved disagreements about children's education, issues of parenting, and husbands' refusals to improve the relationship.

O'Leary (1988) states that marital satisfaction is one of the most significant distinctions between violent families and non-violent families. Her results indicate that couples who are satisfied with their marriage have few disagreements on many significant issues, such as finances, sex, and philosophy of life. A frequent finding of this research was that even though the Japanese immigrant women attempted tenaciously to resolve family conflicts or improve their relationships, the husbands were not cooperative and did not feel responsible for their relationships and families.

Another frequently cited difficulty in the marriages in this research was in the area of communication. Various studies reveal that violent couples often lack effective communication skills (Margolin, 1988; Margolin, Burman, & John, 1989; Roberts & Noller, 1998). Roberts and Noller state that couples in violent relationships tend to suffer from communication problems and they either withdraw or suppress, but tend to express their heightened emotions and anger during their conflict. In addition to these problems, intercultural married participants in this research reported that they experienced language barriers and cultural differences which compounded their communication difficulties.

10.2. Effects on Children's Emotional Growth

One of the significant categories related to the marital and family problems that emerged through the interviews was emotional difficulties in children. This result was consistent with previous research which revealed the negative effect that witnessing spousal abuse and violence has on children (Coleman, 1980; Dutton, 1995; Geffner, Rosenbaum, & Hughes, 1988; O'Leary, 1988; Stith & Rosen, 1990; Walker, 1986). These Japanese immigrant women recognized that their children had emotional difficulties such as explosive tempers, lack of remorse, being emotionally cut off from their parents, depression, low self-esteem, irresponsibility with money, and difficulties at school.

Although children in the dysfunctional family may not directly experience abuse or violence by their father, these children may experience violence as a part of family themes (Satir, Banmen, Gerber, & Gomori, 1991). In abusive and violent families, the lack of emotional separation between the parents and their children is prominent and this lack of emotional separation is much more emotionally damaging to the children. In the enmeshed relationship, the children may be forced to be a part of their parents' issues by being triangulated into the conflict by their parents. Triangular of children into parental conflict occurs when parents attempt to reduce emotional stress and anxiety in the emotionally charged relationship between the parents by creating a three-way interconnected relationship which displaces parental anxiety onto children (Kerr & Bowen, 1988). As a result, it creates emotional fusion and prevents differentiation of self from occurring.

10.3. Significant Family of Origin Issues

One of the significant themes that was extracted from the interviews was family of origin issues. This category refers to the significant family of origin experiences and/or unfinished business which may be affecting marital values and relational patterns. These significant life experiences include witnessing and/or experiencing abuse as a child, traumatic experiences, neglect, alcohol problems at home, and parents' marital difficulties.

According to O'Leary (1988), a social learning account of intergenerational transmission of spousal aggression explains the effect of family of origin in two ways: by observation and by actually experiencing violence as a child. Observing parents using physical aggression serves as models for generalized aggressive behavior as well as spouse specific aggression. If children observe their parents using physical aggression in a functional manner, these children will be more likely to use physical aggression as an acceptable method to relate and cope with stress, anger, and frustration in their own relationships (Stith & Rosen, 1990). Also, by actually experiencing abuse as a child, children will learn and use their parents' behavior as a model to cope with stress. Thus, the experience of violence will serve as an immature model of coping behavior with others outside the home.

The Empirical research reveals that children who witness family violence throughout their growth tend to become involved in violence and abuse in their adult relationships (Avakame, 1998; Dutton, 1995; Gelles, 1987; Halford, Sanders, & Behrens, 2000; Hutchison & Hirschel, 2001; Kalmuss, 1984; O'Leary, 1988; Stith & Rosen, 1990)

As a recurring theme of the relational patterns, both husbands' and wives' past experiences in family relationships and unresolved issues can emerge in present relationships. This result shows the multigenerational transmission of family themes. Kerr and Bowen (1988) explain that the cycles of distance and closeness of family members are not created by an individual. Rather the cycles are formulated through the relationships with each family member.

According to Papp and Imber-Black (1996), a framework of meaning and central themes in the family dictates that each individual and family system will perceive, interpret, and respond to life experiences in a specific way. They state that "these responses repeat themselves in different situations over time, forming overarching themes that run throughout people's lives. They shape events and relationships and, in turn, are reshaped by them" (p. 5). Themes and beliefs exist on the ideological level of functioning and this family ideology "regulates the internal processes of the family, determining its traditions, rules, and values, and shaping the quality of interpersonal relationships" (p. 5). The category of family of origin is a significant category because partners are re-visiting their past, examining their relational patterns with significant others, and attempting to make sense of their relationships and present relational patterns.

11. ISSUES RELATED TO ACCULTURATION AND RACIAL DISCRIMINATION

11.1. Experience Related to Acculturation

The category of issues and experiences related to acculturation is a unique experience of the Japanese immigrant women. This category refers to the issues related to ethnic identity and experiences of acculturation, such as development of a sense of belonging in the new culture, homesickness, isolation, and alienation.

The results clearly indicate that the experience of cultural disintegration and personal crisis resulting from immigration can be extremely stressful for immigrants (Berry, Trimble, & Olmedo, 1986; Pedersen, 1997). Ishiyama (1995) explained that "individuals learn that how they are treated, evaluated, and validated by others in the host culture follows different cultural rules, and realize that they can no longer have the kind of social validation that they used to enjoy back home" (p. 266). Relocation and acculturation contribute to the Japanese immigrant women's sense of isolation. Participants describe their experiences of isolation through homesickness and loss of support from their kinships and friends. On the other hand, once cultural adjustment progresses and for those people who have adjusted well to Canada, going back to Japan could be stressful as they may encounter a reverse culture shock. As a result, those who have acculturated may not be able to use Japan as their secure base in case of crisis.

11.2. Racial Discrimination and Prejudice

Racial discrimination and prejudice is another type of difficulty that the Japanese immigrant women have experienced. This is especially apparent in the relationship with their non-Japanese partners. This theme refers to any remarks, discrimination, and prejudice based on the participants being Japanese or partners' attempt to prevent Japanese immigrant women from sharing their culture with their own children.

Pedersen (1995) defines racism as "a pattern of systematic behaviors resulting in the denial of opportunities or privileges to one social group by another. These behaviors are observable, measurable, verifiable, and predictable" (p. 197). Pedersen (1995) also describes two types of racism. Overt racism is intentional racism whereby a specific group is judged inferior and/or undeserved. Covert racism is unintentionally having inaccurate assessments or giving inappropriate treatment to a particular group of people based on misinformation or wrong assumptions without being aware of it. Pence and Paymar (1993) provide a brief explanation and note that the effect of racial discrimination in the context of intimate relationships is based on "the belief that one's own group is superior to another's. This belief provides a rationalization for domination" (p. 81).

Various research indicates that racial discrimination can create detrimental stress to the individual (Choney, Berryhill-Paapke, & Robbins, 1995; Franklin & Boyd-Franklin, 2000; Harrell, 2000; Ivey, Ivey, & Simek-Morgan, 1997; Outlaw, 1993; Sue & Sue, 1990). Racial discrimination brutalizes and dehumanizes individuals, will severely damage their self-esteem (Pedersen, 1995; Sue & Sue, 1990), and can create learned helplessness. Racial discrimination is a significant form of emotional violence and abuse in inter-cultural marriages.

12. DISCUSSION OF COPING RESPONSES

How do Japanese immigrant women cope with the wide array of external and internal stressors related to spousal abuse? The results indicate they employ five major coping strategies: (1) Social support and collective coping; (2) Escape and avoidance; (3) Spiritual coping; (4) Existential coping; and (5) Perseverance and endurance. The use of these coping strategies seems to depend on their personal resources (Fernández-Esquer & McCloskey, 1999; Gelles & Straus, 1988), types of relationships, severity of the abuse and violence (Gelles & Straus, 1988), and the stages of crisis and abuse (Gelles & Straus, 1988; Follingstad, Brennan, Hause, Polek, & Rutledge, 1991). As Folkman and colleagues

(1986) state, "A range of personality characteristics including values, commitments, goals, and beliefs about oneself and world helps to define the stakes that the person identifies as having relevance to well-being in specific stressful transactions" (p. 572). The participants utilize various coping strategies to produce maximum benefits and reduce harm.

12.1. Social Support and Collective Coping

The first coping strategy extracted from this research is the securing of basic human needs from social supports. The significance of social support in coping is consistent with previous research (Brownridge & Halli, 2001; Fernández-Esquer & McCloskey, 1999; Finn, 1985). First and foremost, in the case of abuse in the family, Japanese immigrant women need to ensure their safety. The social support they received includes both tangible support (such as provisions of possible shelter, food, physical safety, and language needs) and emotional support (such as comfort, encouragement, empowerment, and validation).

The Japanese immigrant women in the present study also used a collective coping strategy. Wong (1993) explained that collective coping is different from social support being. Coping is a collaborative coping strategy with all the members of a group working together to deal with an issue which one of the group is facing. For example, pastors and their church members work together with the abuse victim to resolve the issue.

One noteworthy point in the results of this study is that there was only one participant who sought support from official social services, such as transition homes and women's abuse centers. This reduced frequency of immigrant women seeking public support is consistent with existing research (Abraham, 2000; Finn, 1985). Their reluctance to seek public support may be related to their sense of shame, mistrust of social agencies, and/or fear of negative consequences.

Doi (1973) commented that Japanese culture has clear distinctions and boundaries relating to a sense of inside as opposed to outside of the support network. When people regard individuals as an outsider they call these particular individuals *tanin*. *Tanin* means "persons with no blood relationship to oneself," or "persons unconnected with oneself" (Doi, 1973, p. 36). Doi stated that unless people know each other deeply and closely and the relationship becomes as close as one's family, the relationship cannot be considered as a real relationship and those people are called as *tanin*. If the one defines others as *tannin*, then *enryo* will play into the relationship. *Enryo* is a barrier or distance between the individuals. It is a line one preserves so that the individual will not impose or be imposed on by another.

Doi (1973) also introduced the concept of *amae*. *Amae* means to expect and depend upon each other's benevolence and nurturance in the relationship. The term is often used to describe the quality of the relationship within the family, such as parents and children, and wife and husband relationships (Pedersen, 1997). Doi described *amae* as a desire and urge for people to draw closer to each other, and at the same time, the individual who uses *amae* in the relationship, holds back with the idea that one must not take for granted too much of the other's good will. There is a slight *enryo* which exists in the relationship as a sign of respect. In other words, insiders, such as family members, would use *amae* as a part of their relationship where the members of the family presume and encourage dependency on the group, but it discourages one to be independent from the group in the true sense (Doi, 1973).

12.2. Escape and Avoidance

Another type of coping strategy was escape and avoidance. Research suggests that women who are the victims of abuse tend to use passive coping strategies rather than active, problem-solving behaviors (Fernández-Esquer & McCloskey, 1999; Finn, 1985). Coping by escape means that in order to cope with abuse, the participants choose to separate and divorce from their abusive husbands. In most cases, it is not an easy task simply because their husbands were persistent and attempted to take their wives back against their will. However, eventually, some participants managed to get away from their relationships.

One of the unique coping strategies that the Japanese immigrant women used is going back to Japan until things settled down. Traveling to Japan has become more accessible due in part to affordable airfare. Additionally, telecommunications, such as the internet, electronic mail, and the accessibility of long distance calling further facilitate communication. As a result, the Japanese immigrant women may escape from their social isolation by returning to their country of origin, thus giving them more options and the feeling of psychological security.

The avoidance coping strategy is an attempt by the immigrant women to avoid further escalation of anger by distancing or trying not to collide with their husbands. Gelles and Straus (1988) found that avoidance is one of the effective coping strategies for women who are suffering from "minor violence." In addition, from attribution theory's perspective, if women attribute the cause of the husbands' violence to themselves and blame themselves for the violence, the women would be more likely to stay in the relationship because they think that the cause of the family disturbances is attributed to themselves. Therefore, leaving the relationship would not improve the situation. If the women, on the other hand, perceive the cause of their husbands' violence as a stable attribution of the husbands, then the women would be more likely to leave than women who blame themselves for the violence and abuse (Frieze, 1979).

The avoidance coping strategy may also include denial and minimizing of the abuse and violence. Fernández-Esquer and McCloskey (1999) defined avoidance as distancing oneself psychologically or emotionally from a painful event by means of denial, minimizing, or trivializing the abuse and violence. Consequently, the women can freeze their emotional and psychological reaction to the attack and the infliction of pain. Avoidance can be very effective in preventing women from exhausting themselves from the abuse and violence.

12.3. Spiritual/Religious Coping

Resorting to religious faith is one of the effective coping strategies that the Japanese immigrant women used to deal with abuse. Faith was a source of refuge. Ms. S. explained her experience: "I overcome difficulties with faith, and there is a joy in... it was good that I have faith. That was where I could escape to." Ms. M. also found that faith helped her to deal with the crisis: "It was faith. In the night, after all the things I went through, I read the Bible and prayed, that was when I experienced a tremendous peace just like climbing up to the heaven. Without faith, I do not think I could have managed this far."

Through faith in an omnipotent, omniscience, and omnipresent God, these women experienced peace and joy. They trust and expect God to guide, provide, and bring justice.

The effectiveness of using faith as a coping strategy is consistent with previous research (Frankl, 2000; Koenig, George, & Siegler, 1988; Lazarus & Folkman, 1984; Pargament, Smith, Koenig, & Perez, 1998; Wong, 1993, 1998a).

Frankl (2000) stated that there is a spiritual noölogical dimension, which is distinct from a psychological dimension, but at the same time intermediate between the psychological and spiritual dimension of human beings. Frankl (1988) did not believe human beings can comprehend the ultimate meaning of human suffering. He stated that "the supra-meaning" is not to understand and comprehend, but is a matter of believing and having a faith.

Pargament et al. (1998) examined patterns of positive and negative religious coping with life stressors and the implications for health and adjustment. The positive coping methods were: seeking spiritual support, seeking forgiveness, coping with a collaboration, spiritual connection, religious purification, caring and compassionate religious reappraisal, and religious focus. The negative religious coping methods were: spiritual discontent, reappraisals of a punishing God, interpersonal religious discontent, demonic reappraisal, and reappraisal of God's powers.

McGrath (1991) described two important elements of faith in God. One element of faith is hope. Faith is maintained by hope. Faith is having expectations with the confidence that the contradictions, disappointment, and suffering will be resolved regardless of the current situation and reality. It is a perspective of seeing things from the resurrection instead of the crucifix. The other component of faith in God is trust. It is not simply a matter of believing that something is true, but it is a matter of acting according to one's own belief. In other words, coping by faith is a proactive strategy because having faith means having a vibrant relationship with God. People who have faith make decisions and act based on trust and expectation that the almighty God will guide, protect, and provide all of their resources. Therefore, utilizing faith as a coping strategy is not a passive attitude toward abuse.

12.4. Existential Coping

Existential coping means that the participants sought meaning in their crisis to cope with the difficulties. This does not mean that they found the answer for the reasons "why" it occurs, but rather, they derived meaning out of their crisis. Wong (1998b) stated that existential coping operates in two ways. One way is to accept uncontrollable and unavoidable problems as a part of reality of human lives. The second is to perceive and generate positive meanings out of negative life experiences. Wong stated that existential coping involves integrating both acceptance of the unavoidable nothingness, such as loneliness, depression, anxiety, guilt, frustration, anger, and boredom, and constructive transformation of such unavoidable suffering into cognitive coping processes. Reker (2000) also defined existential meaning as "the cognizance of order, coherence, and purpose in one's existence, the pursuit and attainment of worthwhile goals, and an accompanying sense of fulfillment" (p. 41). The significant point is that this coping strategy also leads to the sense of personal growth for the participants. For instance, the Japanese immigrant women who found meaning in faith also experienced a sense of spiritual growth. Ms. I. found the crisis in her life as a God given opportunity for her to grow spiritually: "I almost felt that I was given these many hardships for me to grow... it seems to me that these things are the footsteps for me to grow." If the individual finds meaning from a crisis experience and uses it as a stepping stone, it can lead to personal growth as well. After going through an extremely difficult period in her life, Ms. T. found meaning in her crisis and experienced a sense of personal growth: "I think, I have learned to become considerate of others, to be considerate toward other people's hearts.... I can empathize with others. Even any small things, even things that I have never experienced before.... I can relate to them."

Frankl (1959/1984) stated that one of the ways to discover the meaning of life is by creating a work, achieving, and accomplishing. This creative value that Frankl has mentioned is one of the effective ways that Japanese immigrant women used to cope with the abuse. One of the participants said that she was devoted to work, exercise, and music and she found them encouraging and empowering. Similarly, other participants mentioned that they discovered meaning in life by nurturing and seeing their children growing up in an abuse free environment in spite of the women's suffering. Other participants also mention that they found meaning in their lives by actively participating and leading the club to work together with other members.

Wong (1998a) introduced six avenues to enhance the meaning of life: creative work, relationship, self-transcendence, simple pleasures of life, hope for the future, and life review. With respect to life review, Wong suggested that this is not just bringing a sense of order and coherence to one's life, but resolves emotional issues, such as guilt and resentment which can promote meaning of life. Ms. E. experiences resolving resentment and said "From my husband's family, his siblings completely apologized to me and they said, 'I really apologize' to me... Just the one word like that will, my heart.... will be relieved." Ms. E. also added, "I felt that I brought some closure in all this."

12.5. Perseverance and Endurance

Coping by perseverance means that the participants utilized their own personal strength and resources such as optimism and commitment to overcome difficulties. They may commit to the relationship and believe that things will work out eventually and may use optimism to reframe the situation to overcome difficulties.

Coping by using optimism is one of the effective coping strategies that the Japanese immigrant women utilized consistently throughout their experience. Ms. K. said, "I feel like I did not suffer at that time. I am rather an optimistic person." Ms. W. also said, "I am optimistic and so, I do not take things so seriously." Mrs. E. found herself using optimistic personality and said, "I have a very laid-back personality, and I do not mind many things. My personality is almost like if I hear any bad news, it gets into the right ear and it comes right out from the left ear. So, I think that that is the reason why I was able to manage through this far." Extensive research has substantiated that using optimism is an effective way of dealing with stress and crisis (Frankl, 1959/1984; Fry, 1994; Lazarus & Folkman, 1984; Martin & Lefcourt, 1983; Nezu, Nezu, & Blissett, 1988; Scheier, Weintraub, & Carver, 1986; Seligman, 1998; Waldrop, Lightsey, Ethington, Woemmel, & Coke, 2001; Wong, 1998b).

Coping by commitment is another method that the Japanese immigrant women used to cope with the abuse. Lazarus and Folkman (1984) stated that commitment implies a strong emotional attachment to a specific interaction between the person and his/her objectives, in relation to relationships, objects, persons, ideals, values, and beliefs. Lazarus,

Coyne, and Folkman (1982) stated that commitment refers to cognitive components, such as choices, values, and/or goals, and it is also motivational which implies forward movement, intensity, persistence, affective salience, and direction. This coping strategy is closely tied to the sense of responsibility and the sense of shame.

The Japanese immigrant women used commitment to deal with their abusive relationships. Their commitment was to their family, especially to their children. This is an attitude of fighting back against the oppressors and negative situations by persevering through and protecting what they care for. Mrs. E. shared her thoughts: "After all, the reason why I am bearing with all this here is because I cannot abandon my son." Ms. E. also describes her experience of coping with abuse by commitment to her relationship: "The only reason that we decided to move (to Canada) was just because I care for the relationship between us."

From a Japanese cultural perspective, commitment tends to be considered as a virtue. In Japanese culture, commitment and perseverance compete with a sense of shame and embarrassment. Tatara (1998) stated *iji* is the mechanism for restoring lost face and honor. It is a type of defense mechanism to compensate, protect, and restore. *Iji* can be translated as commitment to working one's own way out, perseverance, will power, pride, honor, and determination to struggle against challenging situations and circumstances. Ms. J. described how she managed her difficult times by using *iji*: "I think of myself as quite strong.... I am not the type to cry. I think that's why I am able to survive on my own here." Ms. M. also persevered and said, "I was desperate, but I managed by myself." This can be a distinct experience of *iji*. The participant experienced racial discrimination, felt humiliation, resentment, and damage to her self-esteem. Instead of choosing a direct retaliation against her partner, "*iji*" emerged to attempt to sustain her and made her emotionally stronger throughout the difficult moment.

13. RESEARCH AND PRACTICAL IMPLICATIONS

This section will, first, address the cross-cultural comparison of abuse experiences and coping strategies between the Japanese immigrant women and non-immigrant women. Secondly, counseling implications will be discussed.

13.1. Cross-Cultural Comparisons

Although the actual experiences of abuse and violence between the Japanese immigrant women and non-immigrant women may be similar in many ways, the impact of abuse and violence may be more severe for Japanese immigrant women than it is for women who are born and raised in Canada. One of the significant differences in their experiences is the degree of isolation such that immigrant women experience. They seem to be much more isolated due to the lack of social supports and the existence of language and cultural barriers.

Japanese immigrants also seem to differ from the people who are born and raised in North America in two ways. Firstly, their self-blame is directed toward "failing" to preserve the family integrity and "failing" to provide a respectful life and well-being for their children. As a result, participants seem to choose the well-being of their family over their own interests and they attempt to endure abuse in order to maintain family harmony and protect the children. Secondly, for the Japanese immigrant women, the family is an extension of who they are. When family harmony is disrupted, the Japanese immigrant women experience guilt and shame. For women who are from a North American cultural background, their sense of shame stems from injury to their own identity and self-esteem (Dutton, 1995; Hofeller, 1982).

In terms of types of abuse and violence, one of the unique differences between interracial couples and same race couples seem to be the experience of racial discrimination. The abusive non-Japanese husbands may emotionally attack the women with racial slurs or may simply mistreat the women based on their prejudices. This is detrimental to the immigrant women's self-concept and sense of safety. In some cases, the women have to encounter racial discrimination both in society and at home.

Another unique difference is the issue of communication difficulties. For the interracial couples, it is not uncommon for the Japanese immigrant women to feel that their voices are not heard because their husbands' first language is English and the women have difficulties expressing their own thoughts and feelings. They may not be able to express themselves during marital conflict. Additionally, another unique experience of abuse and violence is the experience of financial exploitation. Although both immigrant and non-immigrant women may experience financial exploitation in an abusive relationship, the immigrant women experience the impact of financial exploitation more severely. They may have more difficulty finding a job because they may lack language skill and the social network needed to find a job. Their skills may not be transferable to Canadian society, or more likely, immigrant women may lack any relatives to ask casually for financial assistance.

In terms of coping strategies, one of the unique types of coping strategies for the participants was the use of Japan as a safe refuge. If the abuse and violence becomes too severe, the immigrant women can leave the country and seek help in Japan. Leaving abusive husbands and going back to Japan will, firstly, provide them a safe environment. Secondly, going back to Japan will provide the immigrant women with critical social support by their families, relatives, and friends. In other words, returning to Japan can provide the most secure safe house for the Japanese immigrant women.

Another interesting finding is that the Japanese immigrant women in this study used more reflective and internally focused coping strategies and used less problem focused and confrontational strategies. This is evidenced by the fact that only one out of the nine participants reported violent incidences to the police and furthermore, only one participant sought help from social services. These coping strategies seem unique to the Japanese immigrant women when compared to the types of coping strategies utilized by women from a North American cultural background where it was found that 9,681 spousal assault incidents in British Columbia were reported to the police in 1996 (Ministry of Attorney General Police Services Division, 1999). Another interesting finding with respect to the Japanese immigrant women in this study is the goal of the coping strategies. The aim of the coping for the Japanese immigrant women in this study was to restore their families, instead of seeking divorce, separation, and personal rights.

One explanation for the above tendencies is that the Japanese immigrant women are taught to have a significant role in preserving the integrity of the family and to sacrifice themselves to protect their children. This is also consistent with a collectivistic sense of self-concept in which Japanese people find *Kazoku* (family) and *Katei* (home, household) to be an extension of their identity. Further research is required to investigate the differences between immigrant women and women who are from a North American cultural background in coping with spousal abuse.

13.2. Intervention Implications

This research has provided several helpful insights with respect to culture-sensitive interventions. First of all, most of the participants sought the restoration of the family, rather than separation from their partners. One of the reasons why Japanese immigrant women were reluctant to seek social services seems to be that the Japanese immigrant women felt that social services might be able to save the victims of abuse but not restore the family.

To save a family, there seems to be several requirements. The first requirement is that any type of abuse and violence must be stopped and the women's physical and emotional safety must be assured. In case of emergency, immigrant women require a safe place to escape. To reduce stress for immigrant women, it would be effective to establish a culturally sensitive transition home. This means that rather than having women from different cultural backgrounds in the same transition home, each transition home would provide specific services for women depending on their cultural backgrounds. Thus, the facilities would provide culturally sensitive services, such as language, food, information and counseling, in their own language. This may reduce stress and anxiety for the women and help them come into the house. It would also provide a greater level of support for these women because they would be with others of the same cultural background.

Securing their safety also involves having meaningful social support, knowing the resources in the community, and language and cultural supports. It is very important to provide social services in Japanese and essential that helping professionals have a deep understanding of the Japanese culture. Meaningful social support also means having someone, such as friends and the clergy, whom they can trust, depend on, be validated by, and be supported by. This meaningful social support enhances empowerment and the meaning of life for the immigrant women. This culturally sensitive support is also necessary for the husbands who are violent and abusive. It is essential for abusive husbands to be able to receive treatment and it also has to be culturally sensitive.

The second requirement is that both parties have to be willing to work together for the improvement of their relationship. Abusive husbands must take responsibility for their own actions and commit themselves to improve their relationships. How do we promote that? This leads to a third requirement that indispensable. It is necessary to have a third person mediate such as a pastor or mentor who has authority and objectivity. Such a person can provide empathy and mediation at the same time, and would be less threatening and less likely to impose public shame on the couple.

The fourth requirement is that a thorough and accurate assessment of the family relationship should take place. Prior to the beginning of mediation, it is important to determine whether the particular case entails abuse, family violence, marital conflict, or any combination of these. Also, both husbands and wives have to separately assess and review aspects of their relationship, such as their level of violence, personality types, levels of anger management, stress coping strategies, family of origin issues, attachment types, and family themes. Methods of assessment might include, in-depth interviews, Family maps (Satir et al., 1991), and psychological assessments, such as Conflict Tactics Scale (Straus, 1979), The Self-Report Instrument for Borderline Personality Organization (Oldham et al., 1985),

Psychological Maltreatment of Women Inventory (Tolman, 1989), Trauma Symptom Checklist (Briere & Runtz, 1989).

Secondly, in terms of intervention strategies, education for both husbands and wives regarding abuse and violence seems to be an effective method. It is essential for immigrant women to have accurate information about abuse, such as the effect of abuse on themselves and their children in order for them to make appropriate decisions. For instance, it was commonly stated in the interview that participants stayed in the marriage because they thought it would be healthier for their children to have a father in the home rather than growing up in a single parent home. However, various research has contradicted this reasoning and revealed the negative effect on children who witness marital violence and abuse (Dutton, 1995; Geffner, Rosenbaum, & Hughes, 1988; O'Leary, 1988; Stith & Rosen, 1990; Walker, 1986). Thus, to avoid any misjudgement, it is essential to provide accurate information about family violence and abuse. A psychoeducational approach can also be an effective tool to help women develop efficient problem solving skills. It involves the exploring and expanding of resources they use to cope, such as developing skills to search for information and resources, analyzing situations to identify the issues, and generating alternative courses of action.

The psychoeducational intervention can also include the women's self-identified community or their support network. The result of this study indicated that the Japanese immigrant women sought friends and pastors for help and shelter more than they sought these from social services. The psychoeducational program can be beneficial not only to the couples who are having problems, but also to the community. The local agency can implement proactive strategies by providing information and training about abuse and violence in immigrant families to the community. Agencies can equip lay counselors, pastors, and local community groups, so that when the immigrant women seek help from the church and friends, the immigrant women and families can be helped more effectively.

Thirdly, when supporting the women who are victims of abuse, empowerment is essential. There are several ways to promote empowerment. First, having meaning in their lives is effective. The results indicated that various participants used existential coping whereby participants searched for intangible meaning for their lives. It is effective to help the victims of abuse and violence develop positive and constructive meanings as the foundation and fulfillment of their productive life. In other words, as Wong (1998b) stated, it is a process of clarification of one's values, purpose, and beliefs in life.

Validation is also important to enhance the meaning of life. By moving into a new culture, the immigrant's frame of reference is challenged, and mistrust of family members and the meaning of life can increase through the experience of voilence and abuse. The validation of the self would restore and reinforce the sense of self-worth, meaning in life, personal identity and competence. (Ishiyama, 1989) This validation would not only increase awareness of the struggles and issues in their lives, but would also help them to explore their inner struggles and determine effective ways of accessing and expanding their internal and external validation resources. (Ishiyama, 1989).

Finally, helping couples to establish better boundaries would be very effective. Through reviewing the existing research, it became apparent that one of the distinct features of the abusive relationship is that couples tend to become co-dependent. Co-dependency means that an individual's self-esteem and self-worth becomes dependent on another person's evaluation and appraisal. He/she becomes preoccupied with the other person's behaviors and needs, and then the individual loses the ability to generate their own sense of self-worth, and they neglect their true self (Whitfield, 1991). However, helping the Japanese immigrant families to establish boundaries is a challenging task to accomplish because the boundaries in the relationship may have a different meaning and distance in Japanese culture, and a simple application of a concept of boundary and co-dependency in western culture to the Japanese immigrant families may not be appropriate.

In Japan, the relationship norm among family members may be more interdependent than it is in the western culture. Pedersen (1997) pointed out that in Japan, boundaries between mothers and children are more blurred than in western cultures, as Japanese mothers perceive their children as an extension of themselves. This interdependence within the family and the community, as long as it is perceived as "theirs," is encouraged and perceived as positive. This is the manifestation of the concept of *amae* (Doi, 1973).

The combination of striving for *amae* and avoiding a sense of shame may also drive the Japanese immigrant families to seek help within "their" community, rather than from the social services. In Japanese culture, it is also very important to recognize that the concept of self/identity can be defined in terms of "the human relationships in which he finds himself, i.e. the group." (Doi, 1973, p. 134) The word, *jibun* can be translated as self and identity in Japanese. Doi (1973) explained that even though people in Japan frame their identity in terms of the group that they belong to, if the individual has blind loyalty toward the group and this prevents him/her from expressing their differences and discomfort, the one is considered as not having *jibun*.

Therefore, having self/identity does not mean to reject the group, but rather to maintain self/identity independently from the group to which one belongs and with respect to which one's identify is always where their identity is never connected by membership in the group (Doi, 1973). In the case of family violence and abuse, women may perceive family as who they are. On the other hand, their self/identity is negated to maintain the family relationship. This, in turn, creates "blind loyalty" and a state of *jibun ga nai* [lack of self]. As a result, when they have to go through divorce, it may cause them to loose their sense of identity. However, it is also possible to have a sense of self/identity independent from the group to which one belongs. The key is to help the victims of abuse and violence to establish their sense of self/identity independent from the group that they belong to, without separating from or denying the group or family to which they belong. This can be accomplished by empowerment, self-validation, discovering the meaning of their lives, and learning about self and family functions in case of abuse and violence.

REFERENCES

Abraham, M. (2000). *Speaking the unspeakable: Marital violence among South Asian immigrants in the United States*. New Brunswick, NJ: Rutgers University.

Adams, D. (1988). Treatment models of men who batter: A profeminist analysis. In K. Yllo & M. Bograd (Eds.), *Feminist perspective on wife abuse* (pp. 176-199). Newbury Park, CA: Sage.

American Psychiatric Association. (1994). *Diagnostic and statistical manual of mental disorders* (4th ed.). Washington, DC: Author.

Arias, I., & Pape, K. T. (1999). Psychological abuse: Implications for adjustment and commitment to leave violent partners. *Violence and Victims, 14*(1), 55-67.

Atkinson, D. R., Morten, G., & Sue, D. W. (1989). A minority identity development model. In D. R. Atkinson, G. Morten, & D. W. Sue (Eds.), *Counselling American minorities* (pp. 35-52). Dubuque, IA: W. C. Brown.

Avakame, E. F. (1998). Intergenerational transmission of violence, self-control, and conjugal violence: A comparative analysis of physical violence and psychological aggression. *Violence and Victims, 13*(3), 301-316.

Bartholomew, K., & Horowitz, L. M. (1991). Attachment styles among young adults: A test of a four-category model. *Journal of Personality and Social Psychology, 61*(2), 226-244.

Beck, A. T. (1999). *Prisoners of hate: The cognitive basis of anger, hostility, and violence.* New York: Harper Collins.

Berry, J. W. (1986). The acculturation process and refugee behavior. In C. L. Williams & J. Westermeyer (Eds.), *Refugee mental health in resettlement countries* (pp. 25-37). Washington: Hemisphere.

Berry, J. W., & Annis, R. C. (1974). Acculturative stress. *Journal of Cross-Cultural Psychology, 5*(4), 382-406.

Berry, J. W., Trimble, J. E., & Olmedo, E. L. (1986). Assessment of acculturation. In W. J. Lonner & J. W. Berry (Eds.), *Field methods in cross-cultural research.* (pp. 291-324). London: Sage.

Bowlby, J. (1973). *Attachment and loss* (Vol. 2). New York: Basic.

Briere, J., & Runtz, M. (1989). The trauma symptom checklist (TSC-33): Early data on a new scale. *Journal of Interpersonal Violence, 4*(2), 151-162.

Brislin, R. W. (1986). The working and translation of research instruments. In W. J. Lonner & J. W. Berry (Eds.), *Field methods in cross-cultural research* (pp. 137-164). Beverly Hills, CA: Sage.

Bronfenbrenner, U. (1979). *The ecology of human development: Experiments by nature and design,* Cambridge, MA: Harvard University.

Brownridge D. A., & Halli, S. S. (2001). Marital status as differentiating factor in Canadian women's coping with partner violence. *Journal of Comparative Family Studies, 32*(1), 117-125.

Chin, K. (1994). Out-of-town brides: International marriage and wife abuse among Chinese immigrants. *Journal of Comparative Family Studies, 25*(1), 53-69.

Choney, S. K., Berryhill-Paapke, E., & Robbins, R. R. (1995). The acculturation of American Indians: Developing frameworks for research and practice. In J. G. Ponterotto, J. M. Casas, et al. (Eds.), *Handbook of multicultural counseling* (pp. 73-92). Thousand Oaks, CA: Sage.

Church, A. T. (1982). Sojourner adjustment. *Psychological Bulletin, 91*(3), 335-338.

Cleary, P. D. (1987). Gender differences in stress-related disorders. In R. C. Barnett, L. Biener, & G. K. Baruch (Eds.), *Gender and stress.* New York: Free press.

Clow, D. R., Hutchins, D. E., & Vogler, D. E. (1990). Treatment for spousal-abuse males. In S. M. Stith, M. B. Williams, & K. Rosen (Eds.), *Violence hits home: Comprehensive treatment approaches to domestic violence* (pp. 66-82). New York: Springer.

Colaizzi, P. F. (1978). Psychological research as the phenomenologist views it. In R. S. Valle, & M. King (Eds.), *Existential-phenomenological alternatives for psychology* (pp. 48-71) New York: Oxford.

Coleman, K. H. (1980). Conjugal violence: What 33 men report. *Journal of Marital and Family Therapy, 6*(2), 207-213.

Conger, R. D., Elder Jr., G. H., Lorenz, F. O., Conger, K. J., Simons, R. L., Whitbeck, L. B., Huck, S., & Melby, J. N. (1990). Linking economic hardship to marital quality and instability. *Journal of Marriage and the Family, 52*(3), 643-656.

Cook, D. R., & Frantz-Cook, A. (1984). A systemic treatment approach to wife battering. *Journal of Marital and Family Therapy, 10*(1), 83-93.

Davidson, J. (1994). Issues in the diagnosis of posttraumatic stress disorder. In R. S. Pynoos (Ed.), *Posttraumatic stress disorder: A clinical review* (pp. 1-15). Lutherville, MD: Sidran.

The Department of Justice Canada (2005). *Spousal abuse: A fact sheet from the Department of Justice Canada.* Retrieved February 2005, from http://canada2.justice.gc.ca/en/ps/fm/spouseafs.html

Dobash, R. E., & Dobash, R. P. (1979). How theoretical definitions and perspectives affect research and policy. In E. J. Besharov (Ed.), *Family violence: Research and public policy issues* (pp. 108-129). Washington, DC: AEI.

Doi, T. (1973). *The anatomy of dependence.* Tokyo: Kodansha.

Dooley, D. G., & Catalano, R. (1984). The epidemiology of economic stress. *American Journal of Community Psychology, 12*(4), 387-409.

Dummett, M., & Dummett, A. (1982). The role of government in Britain's racial crisis. In C. Husband (Ed.), *Race in Britain.* London: Hutchinson.

Dutton, D. G. (1995). *The domestic assault: Psychological and criminal justice perspectives.* Vancouver, BC: The University of British Columbia.

Dutton, D. G. (1998). *The abusive personality: Violence and control in intimate relationships.* New York: Guilford.

Dutton, D. G., Saunders, K., Starzomski, A., & Bartholomew, K. (1994). Intimacy-anger and insecure attachment as precursors of abuse in intimate relationships. *Journal of Applied Social Psychology, 24*(15), 1367-1386.

Family violence situation paper. (1993, March). Family Violence Prevention Division, Social Service Programs Branch, Health and Welfare Canada, Government of Canada, Minister of Supply and Services Canada. Ottawa, Ontario.

Faris, R. E., & Dunham, H. W. (1960). *Mental disorders in urban areas.* New York: Hafner.

Fernández-Esquer, M. E., & McCloskey, L. A. (1999). Coping with partner abuse among Mexican American and Anglo women: Ethnic and socio-economic influences. *Violence and Victims, 14*(3), 293-310.

Fernando, S. (1984). Racism as a cause of depression. *International Journal of Social Psychiatry, 30*(1-2), 41-49.

Finkelhor, D. (1984). *Child sexual abuse,* London: Free.

Finn, J. (1985). The stresses and coping behavior of battered women. *The Journal of Contemporary Social Work,* 341-349.

Folkman, S., Lazarus, R. S., Gruen, R. J., & DeLongis, A. (1986). Appraisal, coping, health status, and psychological symptoms. *Journal of Personality and Social Psychology, 50*(3), 571-579.

Follingstad, D. R., Brennan, A. F., Hause, E. S., Polek, D. S., & Ruthledge, L. L. (1991). Factors moderating physical and psychological symptoms of battered women. *Journal of Family Violence, 6*(1), 81-95.

Furnham, A., & Bochner, S. (1986). *Culture shock: Psychological reactions to unfamiliar environments.* New York: Methuen.

Frankel-Howard, D. (1989). *Family violence: A review of theoretical and clinical literature.* The Minister of National Health and Welfare.

Frankl, V. E. (1959/1984). *Man's search for meaning.* New York: Washington Square.

Frankl, V. E. (1988). *The will to meaning: Foundations and applications of logotherapy.* New York: Meridian.

Frankl, V. E. (2000). *Man's search for ultimate meaning.* Cambridge, MA: Perseus.

Franklin, A. J., & Boyd-Franklin, N. (2000). Invisibility syndrome: A clinical model of the effects of racism on African-American males. *American Journal of Orthopsychiatry, 70*(1), 33-41.

Frieze, I. H. (1979). Perceptions of battered wives. In I. H. Frieze, D. Bar-Tal, & J. S. Carroll (Eds.), *New approaches to social problems* (pp. 79-108). San Francisco: Jossey-Bass.

Fry, P. S. (1994). Perfectionism, humor, and optimism as moderators of health outcomes and determinants of coping styles of women executives. *Genetic, Social, and General Psychology Monographs,* 213-245.

Ganley, A. L. (1989). Integrating feminist and social learning analyses of aggression: Creating multiple models for intervention with men who batter. In P. L. Caesar & L. K. Hamberger (Eds.), *Treating men who batter: Theory, practice, and programs* (pp. 195-235). New York: Springer.

Geffner, R., Rosenbaum, A., & Hughes, H. (1988). Research issues concerning family violence. In V. B. Van Hasselt, R. L. Morrison, A. S. Bellack, & M. Hersen (Eds.), *Handbook of family violence* (pp. 457-481). New York: Plenum.

Geller, J. A. (1992). *Breaking destructive patterns: Multiple strategies for treating partner abuse.* New York: Free.

Gelles, R. J. (1987). *Family violence.* Newbury Park, CA: Sage.

Gelles, R. J. (1990). Methodological issues in the study of family violence. In G. R. Patterson (Ed.), *Depression and aggression in family interaction: Advances in family research* (pp. 49-74). Hillsdale, NJ: Erlbaum.

Gelles, R. J., & Cornell, C. P. (1990). *Intimate violence in families.* Thousand Oaks, CA: Sage.

Gelles, R. J., & Straus, M. A. (1988). *Intimate violence.* New York: Simon and Schuster.

Giles-Sims, J. (1983). *Wife battering: A systems theory approach.* New York: Guilford.

Giorgi, A. (1971a). Phenomenology and experimental psychology: I. In A. Giorgi, W. F. Fischer, & R. Von Eckartsberg (Eds.), *Duquesne studies in phenomenological psychology: Volume I* (pp. 6-16). Pittsburgh, PA: Duquesne University.

Giorgi, A. (1971b). Phenomenology and experimental psychology: II. In A. Giorgi, W. F. Fischer, & R. Von Eckartsberg (Eds.), *Duquesne studies in phenomenological psychology: Volume I* (pp. 17-29). Pittsburgh, PA: Duquesne University.

Giorgi, A. (1975). An application of phenomenological method in psychology. In A. Giorgi, C. T. Fischer, & E. L. Murray (Eds.), *Duquesne studies in phenomenological psychology: Volume II* (pp. 72-79). Pittsburgh, PA: Duquesne University.

Hada, A. (1998). What did the survey, violence against women in Tokyo, discover? (Tokyo-to, Jyoseini taisuru boryoku, chyosa ha nanio akirakanishitaka), *Addiction and Family, 15*(3), 255-264.

Halford, K. W., Sanders, M. R., & Behrens, B. C. (2000). Repeating the errors of our parents? Family-of-origin spouse violence and observed conflict management in engaged couples. *Family Process, 39*(2), 219-235.

Harrell, S. P. (2000). A multidimensional conceptualization of racism-related stress: Implications for the well-being of people of color. *American Journal of Orthopsychiatry, 70*(1), 42-57.

Ho, C. K. (1990). An analysis of domestic violence in Asian American communities: A multicultural approach to counseling. *Women and Therapy, 9*(1), 129-150.

Hofeller, K. H. (1982). *Social, psychological and situational factors in wife abuse.* Palo Alto, CA: R & E Research.

Hotaling, G. T., Straus, M. A., & Lincoln, A. J. (1989). Intrafamily violence, and crime and violence outside the family. In L. Ohlin & M. Tonry (Eds.), *Family violence, crime and justice: A review of research, Vol. 11* (pp. 315-375). Chicago, IL: University of Chicago.

Hsu, F. L. K. (1970). *Americans and Chinese.* New York: Doubleday.

Huisman, K. A. (1996). Wife battering in Asian American communities: Identifying the service needs of an overlooked segment of the U.S. population. *Violence Against Women, 2*(3), 260-283.

Hutchison, I. W., & Hirschel, D. J. (2001). The effects of children's presence on woman abuse. *Violence and Victims, 16*(1), 3-17.

Ibrahim, F. A. (1985). Effectiveness in cross-cultural counselling and psychotherapy: A framework. *Psychotherapy, 22*(2), 321-323.

Ishiyama, F. I. (1989). Understanding foreign adolescents' difficulties in cross-cultural adjustment: A self-validation model. *Canadian Journal of School Psychology, 5*, 41-56.

Ishiyama, F. I. (1995). Culturally dislocated clients: Self-validation and cultural conflict issues and counselling implications. *Canadian Journal of Counselling, 29*(3), 262-275.

Ivey, A. E., Ivey, M. B. & Simek-Morgan, L. (1997). *Counseling and psychotherapy: A multicultural perspective.* Boston: Allyn and Bacon.

Kalmuss, D. (1984). The intergenerational transmission of marital aggression. *Journal of Marriage and the Family. 46*, 11-19.

Kelly, K. D. (1997). The family violence and woman abuse debate: Reviewing the literature, posing alternatives. In A. Sev'er (Ed.), *A cross-cultural exploration of wife abuse: Problems and prospects.* Lewiston, NY: Edwin Mellen.

Kerr, M. E., & Bowen, M. (1988). *Family evaluation: An approach based on Bowen theory.* New York: Norton.

Koenig, H. G., George, L. K., & Siegler, I. C. (1988). The use of religion and other emotion-regulating coping strategies among older adults. *The Gerontologist, 28*(3), 303-310.

Krishnan, S. P., Hilbert, J. C., Vanleeuwen, D., Kolia, R. (1997). Documenting domestic violence among ethnically diverse populations: Results from a preliminary study. *Family and Community Health, 20*(3), 32-48.

Kvale, S. (1983). The qualitative research interview: A phenomenological and a hermeneutical mode of understanding. *Journal of Phenomenological Psychology, 14*(2), 171-196.

Kvale, S. (1989). To validate is to question. In S. Kvale (Ed.), *Issues of validity in qualitative research* (pp. 73-92). Lund, Sweden: Studentlitteratur.

Kvale, S. (1994). Ten standard objections to qualitative research interviews. *Journal of Phenomenological Psychology, 25*(2), 147-173.

Lazarus, R. S., Coyne, J. C., & Folkman, S. (1982). Cognition, emotion, and motivation: The doctoring of Humpty-Dumpty. In R. W. J. Neufeld (Ed.), *Psychological stress and psychopathology.* New York: McGraw-Hill.

Lazarus, R. S., & Folkman, S. (1984). *Stress, appraisal, and coping.* New York: Springer.

Leonard, K. E., & Jacob, T. (1988). Alcohol, alcoholism, and family violence. In V. B. Van Hasselt, R. L. Morrison, A. S. Bellack, & M. Hersen (Eds.), *Handbook of family violence* (pp. 383-406). New York: Plenum.

Liem, R., & Liem, J. H. (1988). Psychological effects of unemployment on workers and their families. *Journal of Social Issues, 44*(4), 87-105.

MacLeod, L. (1980). *Wife battering in Canada: The vicious circle.* Ottawa, ON: Canadian Advisory Council on the Status of Women.

McGrath, A. (1991). *Roots that refresh: A celebration of reformation spirituality.* London: Hodder & Stoughton.

Mahler, M. (1971). A study of the separation-individuation process and its possible application to borderline phenomena in the psychoanalytic situation. *Psychoanaliytic Study of the Child, 26*, 403-424.

Margolin, G. (1988). Interpersonal and intrapersonal factors associated with marital violence. In G. T. Hotaling, D. Finkelhor, J. T. Kirkpatrick, & M. A. Straus (Eds.), *Family abuse and its consequences* (pp. 203-217). Newbury Park, CA: Sage.

Margolin, G., & Burman, B. (1993). Wife abuse versus marital violence: Different terminologies, explanations, and solutions. *Clinical Psychology Review, 13*, 59-73.

Margolin, G., Burman, B., & John, R. S. (1989). Home observations of married couples re-enacting naturalistic conflicts. *Behavioural Assessment, 11*(1), 101-118.

Martin, R. A., & Lefcourt, H. M. (1983). Sense of humor as a moderator of the relation between stressors and moods. *Journal of Personality and Social Psychology, 45*(6), 1313-1324.

Miles, M. B., & Huberman, A. M. (1994). *Qualitative data analysis*. Thousand Oaks, CA: Sage.

Ministry of Attorney General Police Services Division (1999). *Survey of spousal assaults reported to police in 1995 in British Columbia*.

Nazuna: Stop DV Toyama. (2000, August 1). [On-line]. Available: http://www.geocities.co.jp/HeartLand-Suzuran/3062/.

Nezu, A., Nezu, C. M., & Blissett, S. E. (1988). Sense of humor as a moderator of the relation between stressful events and psychological distress: A prospective analysis. *Journal of Personality and Social Psychology, 54*(3), 520-525.

Oberg, K. (1960). Cultural shock: Adjustment to new cultural environments. *Practical Anthropology, 7,* 177-182.

O'Brien, J. E. (1974). Violence in divorce-prone families. In S. K. Steinmetz & M. A. Straus (Eds.), *Violence in the family*, New York: Harper & Row.

Oldham, J., Clarkin, J., Appelbaum, A., Carr, A., Kernberg, P., Lotterman, A., & Haas, G. (1985). A self-report instrument for borderline personality organization. In T. H. McGlashan (Ed.), *The borderline: Current empirical research* (pp. 1-18). Washington, DC: American Psychiatric Press.

O'Leary, D. K. (1988). Physical aggression between spouses. In V. B. Van Hasselt, R. L. Morrison, A. S. Bellack, & M. Hersen (Eds.), *Handbook of Family Violence* (pp. 31-55). New York: Plenum.

Osborne, J. W. (1990). Some basic existential-phenomenological research methodology for counsellors. *Canadian Journal of Counselling, 24*(2), 79-91.

Outlaw, F. H. (1993). Stress and coping: The influence of racism on the cognitive appraisal processing of African Americans. *Issues in Mental Health Nursing, 14*, 399-409.

Padilla, A. M., Wagatsuma, Y., & Lindholm, K. J. (1985). Acculturation and personality as predictors of stress in Japanese and Japanese-Americans. *The Journal of Social Psychology, 125*(3), 295-305.

Papp, P., & Imber-Black, E. (1996). Family themes: Transmission and transformation. *Family Process, 35*(1), 5-20.

Pargament, K. I., Smith, B. W., Koenig, H. G., & Perez, L. (1998). Patterns of positive and negative religious coping with major life stressors. *Journal for the Scientific Study of Religion, 37*(4), 710-724.

Pedersen, P. B. (1991). Counseling international students. *The Counseling Psychologist, 19*(1), 10-58.

Pedersen, P. B. (1995). The culture-bound counsellor as an unintentional racist. *Canadian Journal of Counselling, 29*(3), 197-205.

Pedersen, P. B. (1997). *Culture-centered counselling interventions: Striving for accuracy*. Thousand Oaks, CA: Sage.

Pence, E., & Paymar, M. (1993). *Education groups for men who batter*. New York: Springer.

Perilla, J. L., Bakeman, R., & Norris, F. H. (1994). Culture and domestic violence: The ecology of abused Latinos. *Violence and Victims, 9*(4), 325-339.

Pilowsky, J. E. (1993). The courage to leave: An exploration of Spanish-speaking women victims of spousal abuse. *Canadian Journal of Community Mental Health, 12*(2), 15-29.

Polkinghorne, D. E. (1989). Phenomenological research methods. In R. S. Valle, & S. Halling (Ed.), *Existential-phenomenological perspectives in psychology: Exploring the breadth of human experience* (pp. 41-60). New York: Plenum.

Pressman, B. (1989). Power and ideological issues in intervening with assaulted women. In B. Pressman, G. Cameron, & M. Rothery (Eds.), *Intervening with assaulted women: Current theory, research, and practice* (pp. 21-46). Hillsdale, NJ: Erlbaum.

Reber, A. S. (1985). *Dictionary of psychology*. New York: Penguin.

Reker, G. T. (2000). Theoretical perspective, dimensions, and measurement of existential meaning. In G. T. Reker & K. Chamberlain (Eds.), *Exploring existential meaning: Optimizing human development across the life span* (pp. 39-55). Thousand Oaks, CA: Sage.

Rhee, S. (1997). Domestic violence in the Korean immigrant family. *Journal of Sociology and Social Welfare, 24*(1), 63-77.

Roberts, N., & Noller, P. (1998). The associations between adult attachment and couple violence: The role of communication patterns and relationship satisfaction. In J. A. Simpson & W. S. Rholes (Eds.), *Attachment theory and close relationships* (pp. 317-350). New York: Guilford.

Sakuta, K. (1964). *Haji no bunkasaiko*, Tokyo: Chikuma shobou.

Satir, V., Banmen, J., Gerber, J., & Gomori, M. (1991). *The Satir model: Family therapy and beyond*. Palo Alto, CA: Science and Behavior.

Scheier, M. F., Weintraub, J. K., & Carver, C. S. (1986). Coping with stress: Divergent strategies of optimists and pessimists. *Journal of Personality and Social Psychology, 51*(6), 1257-1264.

Seligman, M. E. P. (1992). *Helplessness: On development, depression and death.* New York: Freeman.

Seligman, M. E. P. (1998). *Learned optimism: How to change your mind and your life.* New York: Pocket.

Star, B. (1980). Patterns in family violence. In M. Elbow (Ed.), *Patterns in Family Violence* (pp. 5-12). New York: Family Service Association of America.

Stark, E., & Flitcraft, A. (1988). Violence among intimates: An epidemiological review. In V. B. Van Hasselt, R. L. Morrison, A. S. Bellack, & M. Hersen (Eds.), *Handbook of family violence* (pp. 293-317). New York: Plenum.

Stith, S. M., & Rosen, K. H. (1990). Overview of domestic violence. In S. M. Stith, M. B. Williams, & K. Rosen (Eds.), *Violence hits home: Comprehensive treatment approaches to domestic violence* (pp. 1-21). New York: Springer.

Straus, M. A. (1979). Measuring family conflict and violence: The conflict tactics scale. *Journal of Marriage and the Family, 41*, 75-88.

Straus, M. A., & Gelles, R. J. (1986). Societal change and change in family violence from 1975 to 1985 as revealed by two national surveys. *Journal of Marriage and the Family, 48*(3), 465-479.

Straus, M., Gelles, R., & Steinmetz, S. (1980). *Behind closed doors.* Garden City, NY: Doubleday.

Street, A. E., & Arias, I. (2001). Psychological abuse and posttraumatic stress disorder in battered women: Examining the roles of shame and guilt. *Violence and Victims, 16*(1), 65-78.

Sue, D. W., & Sue, D. (1990). *Counseling the culturally different.* New York: Wiley-Interscience.

Taft, R. (1977). Coping with unfamiliar cultures. In N. Watten (Ed.), *Studies in cross-cultural psychology Vol. 1* (pp. 121-153). London: Academic.

Tamura, T., & Lau, A. (1992). Connectedness versus separateness: Applicability of family therapy to Japanese families, *Family Process, 31*(4), 319-340.

Tatara, M. (1998). *Haji to iji.* Tokyo: Kohdansha.

Thomas, T. N. (1995). Acculturative stress in the adjustment of immigrant families. *Journal of Social Distress and the Homeless, 4*(2), 131-142.

Tolman, R. (1989). The development of a measure of psychological maltreatment of women by their male partners. *Violence and Victims, 4*(3), 159-177.

Utsy, S. O., Ponterotto, J., Reynolds, A. L., & Cancelli, A. A. (2000). Racial discrimination, coping, life satisfaction, and self-esteem among African Americans. *Journal of Counseling and Development, 78*(1), 72-80.

Valle, R. S., & King, M. (1978). An introduction to existential-phenomenological thought in psychology. In R. S. Valle & M. King (Ed.), *Existential-phenomenological alternatives for psychology* (pp. 3-17). New York: Oxford University.

Waldrop, D., Lightsey, Jr., O. R., Ethington, C. A., Woemmel, C. A., & Coke, A. L. (2001). Self-efficacy, optimism, health competence, and recovery from orthopedic surgery. *Journal of Counseling Psychology, 48*(2), 233-238.

Walker, L. E. (1984). *The battered woman syndrome.* New York: Springer.

Walker, L. E. (1986). Psychological causes of family violence. In Lystad, M. (Ed.), *Violence in the home: Interdisciplinary perspectives* (pp. 71-97). New York: Brunner/Mazel.

Wertz, F. J. (1986). The question of the reliability of psychological research. *Journal of Phenomenological Research, 17*, 181-205.

Westwood, M. J., & Ishiyama, F. I. (1991). Challenges in counseling immigrant clients: Understanding intercultural barriers to career adjustment. *Journal of Employment Counseling, 28*, 130-143.

Whitfield, L. C. (1991). *Co-dependence: Healing the human condition.* Deerfield Beach, Florida: Health Communications.

Wiebe, K. (1985). *Violence against immigrant women and children: An overview for community workers.* Vancouver, B.C.: Women Against Violence Against Women/Rape Crisis Centre.

Wong, P. T. P. (1993). Effective management of life stress: The resource-congruence model. *Stress Medicine, 9*(1), 51-60.

Wong, P. T. P. (1998a). Spirituality, meaning, and successful aging. In P. T. P. Wong, & P. S. Fry (Eds.), *The human quest for meaning: A handbook of psychological research and clinical applications* (pp. 359-394). Mahwah, NJ: Erlbaum.

Wong, P. T. P. (1998b). Meaning-centered counselling. In P. T. P. Wong, & P. S. Fry (Eds.), *The human quest for meaning: A handbook of psychological research and clinical applications* (pp. 395-435). Mahwah, NJ: Erlbaum.

Yoshihama, M., & Sorenson, S. B. (1994). Physical, sexual, and emotional abuse by male intimates: Experiences of women in Japan. *Violence and Victims, 9*(1), 63-77.

15

HOW VISIBLE MINORITY STUDENTS COPE WITH SUPERVISION STRESS

Lilian C. J. Wong

I. INTRODUCTION

Imagine yourself being a visible minority student in a foreign country. In addition to coping with academic demands and acculturation stress, you find yourself having to deal with a clinical supervisor "from hell". You can't find a better word to describe this supervisor, because she really creates hell in your life, with her racist attitudes, devastatingly unfair criticisms, and threats to expel you. Already sensitized to discrimination and fearful of the clinical supervision situation, now you are confronted with the worst nightmare of your life. Your academic career and professional future are all of a sudden collapsing before your very eyes. What do you do to save the day? How do you cope with your emotional trauma and your desperate situation? What can you do as a foreign student without the necessary resources to fight for academic survival and for justice?

In the stress and coping literature, little attention has been paid to supervision stress experienced by visible minority students, even though it is quite a common and stressful phenomenon. According to Kyle and Williams (2000), about 26% of psychology students in the American Psychological Association (APA) accredited programs identify themselves as racial or ethnic minorities. In addition, many of the racial or ethnic minorities are foreign students who have been uprooted from their own cultures. Given the presence of a large number of ethnic minority students in North America, how they cope with supervision stress is a phenomenon deserving research attention. The present study is part of a larger research project on cross-cultural supervision. I decided to focus on visible minorities, because their physical attributes make them easy targets for prejudice and discrimination.

Supervision stress cannot be simply treated as a case of interpersonal conflict, because of the vast power differential. Similarly, it cannot be treated as a daily hassle, because of the intense emotional impact and the potential harm to the supervisee's physical health and future career – the stakes cannot be higher from the perspective of students.

Lilian C. J. Wong, Trinity Western University & Meaning-Centered Counseling Institute, Inc.

When a minority student in a doctoral supervision seminar brought up the issue of difficulties faced by visible minority supervisees, her concerns were immediately dismissed by a White female student, who declared that "difficulties faced by visible minority counselors are similar to those faced by female counselors. It's very much the same as gender discrimination." Is that so? Let's consider the following cases:

1.1. Illustrative cases of supervision stress

A 55-year-old Asian-Canadian doctoral student, Brenda, who had a successful school-counseling career, was greeted with a strange look by her professor in her first class in an advanced counseling skills course. "Why are you here?" asked the professor. "I am a student in your class", answered Brenda, feeling puzzled by the question. Throughout the semester, the professor tried to ignore Brenda and did not call on her to present the weekly prepared assigned work, until one of the seven classmates reminded the professor that the visible minority student had not been given an opportunity to make her presentation.

In the following semester, Brenda happened to be assigned to this professor's internship group. Again, right from the start, Brenda was having problems. The professor delayed signing the supervision contract, and found excuses not to meet with Brenda for more than three weeks. Eventually after six weeks – in the middle of the semester, she suddenly informed Brenda that she would be expelled from internship for incompetence, without having given her any prior feedback that Brenda's counseling skills were not up to standard. This was a devastating blow to Brenda, because she had already established herself as an excellent counselor in the school system, and had received very positive evaluations from her other clinical supervisors. Brenda felt that her rights as a student had been violated, and she had been treated contrary to the ethical standards of supervision. She tried to appeal her case to the Department only to go through another six months of hell. Both her mental and physical health suffered greatly because of this traumatic experience. She wondered how many other visible minorities have experienced similar treatment.

Kim, a Korean student in a Counseling Psychology Program, had to repeat the basic counseling skills course, because of his language deficiency and apparent difficulty in demonstrating empathic reflections. With limited English vocabulary, he had difficulty communicating verbally with clients in practicum. His supervisor was worried that his clients might not return, but to his surprise, Kim's clients returned regularly. However, his supervisor was of the opinion that Kim spent too much time building relationships, and not enough time doing therapy. His main concern was Kim's limited vocabulary for reflecting feelings. He also considered Kim's approach too cognitive and too eager to give advice. In supervision, Kim politely acknowledged his professor's concerns. During group supervision, Kim tended to be reserved and quiet, and was also reluctant to do role-play. When the supervisor gave feedback on his counseling sessions in the group, Kim appeared painfully nervous. He felt ashamed and hopeless when his peers repeatedly brought up his expressive language difficulties at every group supervision session. He seriously considered quitting the program, doubting that he would ever make it as a counselor because of cultural and language barriers.

In another case, an internship supervisor was asked to take on Tim, a visible minority supervisee to her supervision group. The supervisor asked Tim to come to meet her group of interns. She then asked Tim to declare his approach to counseling. Tim replied that personally he liked the cognitive-behavioral approach, but he was willing to learn other approaches as well. However, after that initial meeting, the supervisor told Tim: "I am sorry that I cannot take you into my group. When I told the administrator that I would take you, I didn't know your theoretical framework of counseling. My group is totally Rogerian." This supervisor was also the professor of the ethics course; she should have known better, because it is unethical to deny any student's clinical supervision simply because they do not conform 100% to the supervisor's own theoretical approach. What was the real reason for rejecting Tim?

1.2. Lack of multicultural supervision competencies

The above vignettes are real situations with fictitious names. Many visible minority supervisees have reported negative experiences with clinical supervision and believed that their difficulties in supervision stemmed from just being visible minorities. Some White supervisors often assume that visible minority students will not make effective counselors because of language and cultural barriers. However, these cannot be the only problems. For example, in Brenda's case, her English cannot be distinguished from Euro-Canadians born in Canada, because she had been in Canada pretty well all her life.

Another explanation for the supervision stress experienced by visible minorities is the lack of multicultural supervision competencies on the part of the supervisors (Wong, 2000). Preliminary results (Wong & Wong, 2002) on supervision stress from supervisors' perspective are that supervisors are often unaware of the things that they have done in supervision that might have hindered their visible minority trainees. In fact, the supervisors interviewed had great difficulties recalling what they did or said that might have hindered supervisees' professional growth as counselors. Furthermore, unethical and harmful clinical supervision has been reported in recent literature (Ellis, 2001; Gray, Ladany, Walker, & Ancis, 2001; Nelson & Friedlander, 2001). A lack of multicultural supervision competencies simply compounds the problem and inflicts additional pain by blaming the supervisees' language deficits.

The cases cited above have alluded to the various kinds of unethical and harmful supervision experienced by visible minority students. In what ways do visible minority students experience difficulties that are unique to them? How do they cope with such problems? What constitutes bad and harmful supervision in working with visible minority students? These questions become increasingly pressing as more and more ethnic minority students are enrolled in graduate programs in counseling psychology.

2. THEORIES AND ORIENTATIONS OF CLINICAL SUPERVISION

Supervision is essential to counselor education and development (Carroll, 1996; Holloway, 1992; Stoltenberg & Delworth, 1987). Given the importance of supervision in preparing students for the counseling profession, there is now an ever-expanding literature on clinical supervision, especially on what constitutes effective supervision (Bernard & Goodyear, 1998; Holloway, 1995; Watkins, 1997; Worthington, 1987).

According to Hart (1982), "Clinical supervision is an ongoing educational process in which one person in the role of supervisor helps another person in the role of supervisee acquire appropriate professional behavior through an examination of supervisee's professional activities" (p. 12). Bernard and Goodyear (1998) identify two major goals for supervision: (a) teaching-learning, and (b) monitoring of client welfare. The teaching-learning objective is to develop students' clinical competencies needed for eventual licensure. At the same time, supervisors also have the responsibility to monitor the quality of client care provided by the supervisees and safeguard client's welfare. Evaluation is essential to both the teaching and monitoring functions. Similarly, Holloway (1995) emphasizes professional development as the main objective of supervision, but she also recognizes the importance of the supportive functions of supervision. She proposes that "The goal of supervision is the enhancement of the student's effective professional functioning, and the interpersonal nature of supervision provides an opportunity for the supervisee to be fully involved toward that end. In this way, the supervisee is empowered in the process of acquiring attitudes, skills, and knowledge for independent, effective professional practice" (p. 6). There is a consensus that the main objective of supervision is the development of clinical and professional competencies of supervisees. Closely related to this objective is the development of the student as a person, because the counselor's personal qualities and attitudes may be more important than clinical skills (Rogers, 1977, 1986).

2.1. A brief historical perspective of supervision research

The last twenty years have witnessed considerable increase in supervision research. Heppner and Roehlke (1984) observed that "although supervision has been extensively studied, there is still relatively little information about the specific variables that affect the actual supervision process" (p. 76).

Supervision has undergone changes over the past few decades. From a historical perspective, supervision research can be roughly grouped into five orientations: (a) behavior, (b) identity, (c) relationship, (d) development, and (e) person. These five orientations provide different perspectives of what needs to be emphasized in supervision.

2.1.1. Behavioral orientation

Initially, the emphasis of supervision research was on specific supervisory tasks, such as modeling, teaching clinical skills and giving evaluative feedback. Therefore, this behavioral emphasis may also be characterized as task-oriented.

Consistent with the Zeitgeist of behaviorism, researchers in supervision studied supervisory behaviors that could be readily operationalized. For example, Worthington and Roehlke (1979) measured the importance ratings of a wide range of supervisory behaviors. They found that supervisors considered giving feedback as the primary function of good supervision. In their study, supervisees perceived that good supervision depended on the following conditions: (a) that a personal and pleasant supervisor-supervisee relationship exists; (b) that supervisors provide relatively structured supervision sessions, especially during early sessions, and (c) that supervisors directly teach beginning counselors how to counsel and then encourage the new counselors to try out their new skills. Their finding of the discrepancy between supervisor and supervisee has considerable implications for both the research and practice of supervision.

2.1.2. Identity orientation

The second is "identity orientation". Ekstein and Wallerstein (1972) recognized the inadequacy of focusing on skills training during supervision. According to these authors, in order for students to become truly professional, they also need to learn from their supervisors a special quality related to practicing psychology, which Ekstein and Wallerstein (1972) referred to as a professional identity. This issue arose because as an emerging profession, competing with more established professionals, such as psychiatrists and the clergy, psychologists needed to have a clear sense of identity in terms of the professional specialty of their expertise and the value of their services.

This view is recently echoed by Bernard and Goodyear (1998) who emphasize that supervisors need to induce their supervisees into the profession by providing a role model and helping them develop a sense of professional identity. Therefore, the image, role model and professional associations of the supervisor are important considerations in supervisory training.

This aspect of supervision has been under-researched. What kind of experience during practicum and internship contributes to students' development of a professional identity? In what ways does the supervisor help or hinder professional identity development? These important questions remain largely unanswered.

2.1.3. Relationship orientation

The third stage of the evolution in supervision is relationship orientation (Heppner & Roehlke, 1984). The focus shifts to interpersonal relationship issues. A consensus has emerged that the goals of supervision can be best achieved through a good supervisor-supervisee relationship. One of the most consistent findings in supervision research is that a supporting, trusting relationship is critical to effective supervision (Heppner & Roehlke, 1984; Holloway, 1995; Hutt, Scott, & King, 1983; Ronnestad & Skovholt, 1993; Worthen & McNeill, 1996). The importance of having a good supervisor-supervisee relationship was summarized eloquently by Hunt (1986):

> It seems that whatever approach or method is used, in the end it is the quality of the relationship between supervisor and trainee therapist (or counselor) that determines whether supervision is effective or not... there needs to be a degree of warmth, trust and genuineness and respect between them in order to create a safe enough environment for supervision to take place. (p. 20)

Based on a review of the supervision literature, Carifio and Hess (1987) proposed that the ideal supervisor possesses good interpersonal skills (i.e., empathy and respect), and is generally supportive and non-critical. The ideal supervisor also possesses knowledge and experience, knows how to structure supervision, and provides an effective balance between direction and autonomy.

More recently, Watkins (1995a) reported that effective supervisors demonstrated support, empathy, and respect for supervisees, while engaging in teaching and conceptualizing, and encouraging self-assessment in the supervisees. Furthermore, effective supervisors are very explicit in goal setting, communicating expectations, and providing feedback. They know how to maintain a balance among "support, respect, skill, clarity and teaching/education" (p. 573).

2.1.4. Developmental orientation

The interactions between supervisors and supervisees are complex because of the multiple roles involved (Bernard, 1988). The supervisor-supervisee relationship is often fraught with tension and conflicts, due to differences in expectations, personality, counseling orientations, and cultural values (Holloway, 1995; Hunt, 1987; Vasquez, 1992). A major factor is the developmental changes in supervisees, because supervision needs and expectations may vary according to the different stages of counselor training (Holloway, 1987; Worthington, 1987).

Most of the recent supervision research has a developmental orientation. Ronnestad and Skovholt (1993) presented a comprehensive review on the characteristics of effective supervision for beginning and advanced graduate students. They pointed out that supervision of beginning level counselors is generally characterized by high levels of structure, a didactic orientation, and a skill focus. At this level, the supervisor often assumes the role of a teacher, because students want clear instructions and directions. However, even at this level, Worthington and Roehlke (1979) reported that students want their teachers to provide support and encouragement. Ronnestad and Skovholt (1993) observed that "the beginning student's vulnerability and anxiety make it important for the supervisor at this introductory level to create a relationship that is characterized by support and understanding" (p. 399).

At the advanced level, graduate students may experience considerable tension and anxiety for a different reason. They may feel quite confident in their basic counseling skills, but they also feel insecure and uncertain about their professional competence. Conflict with the supervisor is most likely to erupt at this stage. According to Moskowitz and Rupert (1983) (as cited in Ronnestad & Skovholt, 1993), about 39% of the doctoral students reported the experience of having a major conflict with a supervisor. These conflicts tend to result from (a) differences in personality styles, (b) differences in theoretical orientation or therapeutic approach, and/or (c) dissatisfaction with the style of supervision.

In view of the greater likelihood of conflict and dissatisfaction with supervision at the advanced level, the supervisor needs to be sensitive to the tension experienced by the advanced graduate students, to provide "clarifying feedback" to reduce their anxiety, and take on a more collegial and consultative role. "The supervisor needs to take responsibility to create, maintain, and monitor the relationship with her or his student" (Ronnestad & Skovholt, 1993, p. 403). They concluded that "the qualities of the supervisory relationship have an impact on learning at all levels of expertise. We know that the conditions of good counseling and therapy, such as empathy, respect, and a trusting and permissive attitude, have validity in supervision" (p. 401).

2.1.5. Person orientation

More recently, the supervision literature has begun to pay close attention to the personal qualities of the supervisor as well as the personal growth of the supervisee. There is no denial that what the supervisor does is important and how the supervisor relates to the supervisee is also important. But, from a person-orientation perspective, *being* is more important than *doing* and *relating*. Ultimately, the quality of supervision depends on the quality of the supervisor as a person (i.e., the supervisor's attitude, character, and core values). These qualities can affect both the nature of the relationship and the effectiveness of the supervisory behavior.

Recent research on the effectiveness of psychotherapy has discovered that the therapist as a person is a major factor (Lambert & Bergin, 1994; Metcalf, Thomas, Duncan, Miller, & Hubble, 1996). In other words, *who the therapist is* as a person may be more important than *what the therapist does* in bringing about positive outcomes. Therefore, Koss and Shiang (1994) have proposed that clinical training should focus on the development of the therapist as a person as much as skills development. This person-orientation of counselor training needs to begin with supervision, because the level of personal development of the supervisor may affect the personal development of the supervisee.

There is already some evidence that the supervisor as a person is an important contributing factor in effective supervision. For example, it has been demonstrated that positive attributes of the supervisor (expertness, attractiveness, and trustworthiness) were related to positive perceptions of the supervisory relationship (Heppner & Roehlke, 1984). Similarly, Allen, Szollos, and Williams (1986) found, according to doctoral students' opinions, what differentiated between good and bad supervision was trustworthiness and expertise of the supervisor. These authors also reported that another discriminator was the supervisor's emphasis on the personal growth of the supervisee; this finding suggests that person-orientation embraces a concern for the personal development of the supervisee.

In the Worthington and Roehlke's (1979) study, supervisors considered evaluation and giving feedback as the most important tasks in effective supervision. But, almost two decades later, in the Henderson, Cawyer and Watkins' (1997) study, supervision becomes much more person-oriented than task-oriented. These authors found that students also emphasized the importance of personal growth, such as the development of student confidence and autonomy.

According to this person-orientation, supervision or counseling is only as good as the people who practice it. Supervision that emphasizes good clinical skills, good supervisor relationships, and a professional identity may succeed in producing competent practitioners. But supervisors who are genuine, caring, empathic, trustworthy, and highly ethical are more likely to succeed in reproducing good counselors who are both competent and compassionate. At a recent international conference, three internationally renowned psychotherapists, Yalom (2000), Zeig (2000) and Spinelli (2000) all emphasized the importance of personal qualities of the therapists and the need for resolving personal issues. Research is needed to determine how the personal qualities of supervisors impact supervision effectiveness.

Together, the different dimensions of supervision provide a fairly complete picture of a good and competent clinical supervisor. Such a supervisor would do just fine with visible minority students, even if he or she has not been trained in multicultural supervision competencies. After all, caring, respect, and kindness speak a universal language, which every one can understand. Cross-cultural competencies become important, when supervisors do not have the necessary personal qualities or clinical competencies.

2.2. Cross cultural issues in supervision

None of the above orientations pays much attention to cross-cultural issues. While cross-cultural counseling has generated a great deal of interest and research (Atkinson, Morten, & Sue, 1993; Ivey, Ivey, & Simek-Morgan, 1997; Sue & Sue, 1990), cross-cultural supervision has received little attention as pointed out by Brown and Landrum-Brown (1995) and others (D'Andrea & Daniels, 1997; Stone, 1997).

Brown and Landrum-Brown (1995) reported that a high level of caution is needed in cross-cultural supervision, because racial minority supervisees tend to be sensitive to the abuse of power. Such sensitivity is understandable when there is an inherent power differential in the supervisory relationship (Williams & Haglin, 1995) and when there has been a history of discrimination (Sue & Sue, 1990).

Hunt (1987) recommended that racial and ethnic issues faced by minority trainees should be addressed within the supervisory relationship. Bernard and Goodyear (1998) pointed out that there is a need to prepare White middle-class faculty to work with minority counselor trainees. But there are very few published studies on the supervision of visible minority students.

Cook and Helms (1988) investigated the level of satisfaction with cross-cultural supervision in a survey of 225 African, Latino, Asian and Native-American trainees. The results showed that supervisors' unconditional liking for the trainees is related to their satisfaction with supervision. McNeill, Hom, and Perez (1995) acknowledged a dearth of information on the training needs of racial and ethnic minority trainees. After reviewing the relevant literature, these authors pointed out that:

> *Culturally diverse trainees are then faced with a struggle to assert their unique needs and make others aware of the multicultural implications of course material, counseling theories, and interventions. Most often, however, students are forced to attend to and accept this insensitivity for fear of repercussion because of the power differential between professor and student. (p. 253)*

McNeill et al. (1995) also pointed out that culture-specific communicational styles were often not recognized or accepted by Caucasian professors. They observed that visible minority students often experienced discrimination, isolation, and racism. Consequently, these students felt angry, confused, and discouraged, but chose not to disclose their feelings for fear of reprisal. They proposed that "it is incumbent on supervisors to take responsibility to create a supervisory relationship and environment in which these needs and issues are openly dealt with and met" (p. 255). They also proposed inclusion of multi-cultural curricula, peer support, and mentoring programs for minority trainees.

2.2.1. Ethical issues in cross-cultural supervision

Ethical issues become very important when the supervisor-supervisee relationship is complicated by cultural conflicts. Vasquez (1992) has made a significant contribution to our understanding of ethical responsibilities in cross-cultural supervision. Following Rest's (1984) model of moral development, Vasquez (1992) proposed that in the training setting, the supervisor has an obligation to provide professional and moral support for the supervisee to do what is morally right rather than what is expedient.

In addition to ethical considerations, developing clinical competence is another major responsibility of supervision. This obligation involves providing optimal experiences for the supervisees to gain competence in key areas of the profession, such as conceptualization, assessment, interventions, and the ability to work with clients from special populations. Vasquez (1992) pointed out the difficulty in cross-cultural situations:

This is a particular challenge for supervisors because most traditional training fails to teach how to apply the basic principles of counseling beyond the values and ethos of the majority culture. Society's cultural diversity and broad range of social classes provide a challenge for the ethical clinician to acknowledge and deal with potential barriers. (p. 198)

Still another important responsibility of the supervisor is to assess the personal functioning of supervisees. Vasquez (1992) stressed the importance of timely feedback and the imperative for supervisors to "set a climate of trust, openness, and responsibility so that supervisees feel able to engage in consultation and treatment-seeking behaviors" (p. 199). It is in the area of evaluation that conflicts in values and cultural assumptions are likely to erupt. In the absence of any objectively defined universal criteria of competence in counseling, good counseling practice according to a minority culture may be judged to be deficient from the perspective of the so called White middle-class Americans.

Vasquez (1992) recognized the potential for the abuse of power in the supervisor-supervisee relationship. Such abuse is more likely to happen when supervisors lack sensitivity to ethnic/minority cultures. Vasquez and McKinley (1982) recommended that in working with ethnic minority supervisees, it is important to be sensitive to their personal struggles to integrate their racial/ethnic identity with professional identity.

Vasquez (1992) reminded supervisors that they needed to recognize that the supervisees have similar rights to privacy, dignity and due process that clients have. A due process procedure should be available for the supervisees who feel that their rights and well-being have been violated by the supervisors. He concluded that "our effectiveness with supervisees, and indirectly with the clients of our supervisees, depends to a great extent on fulfilling our ethical responsibilities as clinical supervisors" (p. 201).

According to Sue and Sue (1990), counselors who are culturally skilled are aware of their own biases and are sensitive to the needs of their culturally different clients. Culturally skilled counselors also have a large repertoire of skills so that they can select culture-appropriate skills to help their clients. Corey, Corey, and Callanan (1998) also emphasized the importance of training in multicultural competencies.

By the same token, supervisors also need to be culturally skilled in order to be helpful to ethnic minority supervisees. Unfortunately, the importance of cross-cultural competence in supervision has not received the same kind of attention as issues related to gender or sexual orientation.

In sum, there is an urgent need for studying effective multicultural supervision for a variety of reasons. Firstly, an increasing number of graduate students in counseling psychology comes from different ethnic groups (Bernard & Goodyear, 1998; Kyle & Williams, 2000; Leong & Chou, 1996). Secondly, the possibility of misunderstanding, conflict, and discrimination is higher in cross-cultural situations because of cultural differences and language barriers (McNeill, Hom & Perez, 1995). Cross-cultural training may be able to reduce racism and discrimination in supervision. Thirdly, supervisors' lack of cross-cultural competencies may result in harm to visible minorities. Finally, multicultural supervision competencies are needed not only for ethnic minority students, but also for majority counselors. Wong & Wong (1999) point out that it is difficult for majority students to acquire multicultural counseling skills when their clinical supervisors do not possess cross-cultural competencies.

McNeill et al. (1995) have concluded that there is a lack of information on cross-cultural training of minority supervisees. In the area of cross-cultural supervision research, almost all published studies were done in the United States, focusing on African-Americans and Latin-Americans in a dominantly Caucasian society (e.g., Cook & Helms, 1988; McNeill, Hom, & Perez, 1995; Ladany, Brittan-Powell, & Pannu, 1997).

2.2.2. *Unethical and harmful supervision*

Lousy supervision (Magnuson, Wilcoxon, & Norem, 2000) due to immaturity, intolerance and incompetence, can be harmful to supervisees, because bad supervision cannot provide students with the necessary support and instructions needed for their professional development. Something worse than lousy supervision is unethical and harmful supervision, when a supervisor violates professional ethical codes and harms trainees as a result. The case of Brenda described earlier is an example of unethical and harmful supervision, which may be due to the supervisor's racial prejudice or some deep-seated unresolved personal issues. In recent years, researchers have begun to investigate unethical and harmful supervision.

The standards and ethical codes for counseling supervisors are intended to guard against unethical and harmful supervision (Disney & Stephens, 1995; Dye & Borders, 1990; Harrar, VandeCreek, & Knapp, 1990). Recently, Ellis (2001) sounded the bell of alarm about the dark side of supervision; he reported that between 30% and 46% of the supervisees developed unhealthy problems because of harmful, conflictual supervision. He also warned that we do not blame the victims by assuming that the fault lies with the supervisees rather than the supervisors or the department. Harmful supervision can be doubly damaging to visible minorities, who might have already been victimized by prior experiences of prejudice and discrimination. Remember Brenda! How can she and many like her survive the unethical and abusive behaviors of their supervisors, who are supposed to provide education and support? The present study investigated how they coped with the complex problems of supervision stress.

3. A CRITICAL INCIDENT STUDY

The present research adopted the critical incident methodology to study helpful and hindering incidents as experienced by visible minorities students. This chapter will focus on how they cope with supervision stress.

It is noteworthy that research on supervision has gradually moved from quantitative measures of supervisory behaviors (Worthington & Roehlke, 1979) to a phenomenological study of supervisees' subjective experiences (Hutt, Scott, & King, 1983; Worthen & McNeill, 1996). The Hutt et al. (1983) study examined both positive and negative experiences, while Worthen and McNeill (1996) only examined supervisees' experience of "good" supervision. Neither of these studies focused on the experience of visible minority supervisees.

In several studies, students were asked to identify critical incidents within the supervision setting that resulted in changes in the trainee's effectiveness as a counselor (Ellis, 1991; Heppner & Roehlke, 1984). Typically, trainees were asked to describe critical incidents in each supervision session. These studies focus exclusively on positive critical incidents taking place within a supervision session.

The present research is the first comprehensive study of both negative and positive experiences of visible minority students.

3.1. Methodology

This study was based on a modified version of Flanagan's (1954) Critical Incident Technique. The procedures followed closely Flanagan's (1954) direction that the objective be specified. This was accomplished both in explaining the research to participants during "orientation" and in the instruction given to participants prior to data collection. Participants were told: "The main objective of supervision is to develop supervisee's professional competence in the practice of counseling. Please describe specific incidents or examples of helpful and unhelpful supervision." Thus, the goal of supervision was clearly defined. Helpful and unhelpful incidents were defined with respect to the objective of developing professional competence in supervisees.

Secondly, I followed Flanagan's (1954) approach in defining critical incidents. Participants were told: "Think of a time when a supervisor has done or said something that you felt was an example of effective (ineffective) supervision. Please explain why you judge that to be a helpful (or unhelpful) incident." In the spirit of Flanagan's emphasis on objectivity, critical incidents were defined as what the supervisor actually did or said that had significantly impacted the task of supervision. The researcher continued to ask for additional examples until the participants were not able to think of any more helpful or unhelpful incidents.

Thirdly, I adopted the expanded critical incident method used by the University of British Columbia (U.B.C.) Counseling Psychology graduate students who had asked participants: What happened? What led up to it? What was the consequence or how did it turn out? Cochran (Lecture, 1996) suggested that such questions provided a fuller context of the incident. Participants were also asked: What did it mean to you? How did you feel about it? How did you cope with it? This additional semi-structured, open-ended interview component incorporated Herzberg, Mausner, and Snyderman's (1959) line of questioning. U.B.C.'s expanded Critical Incident Technique allows participants to freely talk about their experiences and feelings (Borgen & Amundson, 1996).

Fourthly, in the event of negative incidents, participants were asked to indicate what the short-term and long-term consequences were and how they managed to cope with them. Typically, when participants explained why they considered an incident as unhelpful, they naturally talked about the negative consequences and their coping efforts. The additional instruction was designed to have a complete account of the sequence of events emphasized by Herzberg et al. (1959).

Fifthly, all participants were asked to recommend, on the basis of their personal experiences, ways to improve supervision. This question was helpful because it empowered participants to have a positive closure on their supervision experience. It also allowed participants to process and integrate supervision experience and come up with some recommendations on how to provide good supervision to visible minority students. The open-ended interview component is important because it allows supervisees to fully share their experiences and express their opinions.

3.1.1. Recruitment of participants

Participants were recruited from universities in the Lower Mainland of British Columbia, Canada, using posters, personal contacts and through the word of mouth. Potential participants needed to meet the following qualifications: Member of a visible minority group, having had at least one year of supervision experience, and being able to articulate their supervision experience.

As a result, 19 females and six males were recruited. The average ages for females and males were 32 and 37 years, respectively. The majority of the participants came from the universities in the Lower Mainland. Three of the participants graduated from other provinces (Alberta and Ontario) and two from the United States. In terms of ethnic membership, there were 13 Chinese-Canadians, four Indo-Canadians, three First Nations, two Japanese-Canadians, one Afro-Canadian, one Korean-Canadian, and one Latin-Canadian. The 13 Chinese participants came from various parts of Asia, including Malaysia. In terms of levels of training, three were completing their Masters degree, 18 had graduated with their Masters, one was a doctoral candidate, and three had already obtained their Ph.D. degrees.

3.1.2. Procedure

All potential participants were first contacted by telephone and told about the purpose of the study, the nature of their participation, and they were assured of confidentiality and anonymity with respect to data collection and data analysis. The interviewer then made an appointment to meet with each participant at a time and place convenient to that individual. During the initial stage of the interview, the researcher provided an orientation of the study, answered whatever questions they might have and then asked them to sign the Consent Form. Then, the interviewer proceeded with the interview with a tape-recorder. At the end of the interview, the tape was transcribed verbatim and given an identification code.

Two graduate students from two different universities served as interviewers for two reasons. Firstly, based on my experience in a pilot study, some U.B.C. students were reluctant to disclose their supervision experience. The reason might be that they were concerned that some of the things they said about certain supervisors might get back to these supervisors. Their concerns would be lessened if they were interviewed by someone not connected with UBC. Secondly, having two interviewers might help minimize potential interviewer bias in qualitative research, which is vulnerable to this kind of bias.

3.2. Content analysis and results

3.2.1. Procedure for content analysis

The recorded interviews were coded and transcribed verbatim. The following procedure was employed to extract categories from the protocols:

1. The researcher read over several transcripts in order to get a sense of the scope and variety of the interview materials. This initial reading identified four clear sections, namely, positive incidents, negative incidents, outcomes of negative incidents, and recommendations. These sections closely parallel the questions of the interview (i.e., positive incidents, negative incidents, coping with negative incidents, and recommendations for change).

2. Both positive and negative incidents were identified by + or − respectively on the left margin of the transcript. Any specific incident was counted only once, even when the participant returned to the same incident several times in the course of the interview. In other words, the process of progressive elaboration seemed to be at work, when the participants returned to the same critical incident with more and more details. Two criteria were used to identify each critical incident: (a) the description of the incident was complete in the sense of having a beginning and an end, and (b) the incident was clearly related to supervision. It was worth noting that many critical incidents did not always consist of all three sequential components—what happened, what led up to it and what the consequences were. For example, a demeaning remark by a supervisor constituted a critical incident, but the participant could not recall what led up to that hurtful remark.

3. Each report of critical incident typically consisted of several meaning units, which were similar to Herzberg et al.'s (1959) thought units. A meaning unit may vary in length from one sentence or one paragraph, but it must contain a complete and clear idea marked by a transition in meaning (Aanstoos, 1983; Giorgi, 1975). The researcher identified each relevant meaning unit by bracketing it with a pencil. A meaning unit was considered relevant if it had a direct bearing on the phenomenon under investigation. Thus, any recollection of the supervision and related experiences would be considered relevant, while any comments on other matters, such as boy-friend-girl-friend issues, money matters, etc., would not be considered relevant. Such distinction is necessary, because in any open-ended interview situation, there is a tendency for participants to digress occasionally and talk about personal issues unrelated to the subject matter of the interview. "The end of this step is a series of meaning units still expressed in the subject's own everyday language" (Giorgi, 1997, p. 236).

4. A descriptor of each relevant meaning unit was created by the researcher and written on a 1" × 3" Post-it Note attached to the right margin of transcript as a tab. A descriptor could be a phrase or a sentence that accurately captures the meaning of the unit. "My supervisor validated me" would be an example.

5. A database of the relevant meaning units was created. Each meaning unit was entered under the appropriate Section (i.e., Positive Incidents, etc.) with its descriptor and code. For instance, "Vf1p3t" indicated that this meaning unit was taken from the interview of the first Female Visible Minority Student on the top section of Page 3. When there were more than 3 meaning units per page, a numerical value was used in the code. Thus, Vf1p6(4) indicated that it was the fourth meaning unit on Page 6 of Female participant 1. Such a procedure makes it possible for other researchers to check on validity of the coding in the proper context of the transcript.

6. In the process of describing meaning units, it soon became apparent that some descriptors were very similar in meaning. For example, "My supervisor was supportive and encouraging" was conceptually not different from "My supervisor validated me." Thus, these descriptors with highly similar meanings were merged

under a broader category "Supervisor was appreciative, accepting, supportive, encouraging, and validating." Such merging was an ongoing process.

Finally, themes were extracted from the descriptors following the procedure of Step 6. The main criterion for the final decision was that a theme must contain a distinct, psychological meaning and shared by several participants. Thus, "language difficulties and cultural barriers", "problem in getting a practicum site" and other difficulties related to minority status were all combined into the general theme of "Difficulties of being a visible ethnic minority." However, occasionally, a theme was experienced by only one or two individuals, but it had a clear and important psychological meaning; such themes were also retained. For example, some coping efforts were idiosyncratic and specific to a particular situation; therefore, the criterion of extracting relatively general theme was somewhat relaxed, resulting in many specific coping strategies.

3.2.2. Negative incidents and coping

A total of 380 meaning units were related to negative incidents in supervision. Fifteen themes were extracted from these meaning units, covering a wide range of negative experiences. The most common negative experience reported by 64% of the participants was "Difficulties of being a visible ethnic minority", which included such difficulties as securing a practicum site, being singled out for discrimination, etc. However, most of the negative experiences were directly related to the supervisors, such as "Supervisor was too controlling and insulting", "Supervisor lacked multicultural competencies", and "Supervisor was unprofessional, unethical and irresponsible." "Discrimination in the Department or Agency" was also a factor in supervision stress. Some of the other complaints were simply about bad supervision, such as failing to give feedback, or failing to provide a safe environment. The end result was that many supervisees (about 56%) complained about "Feeling worried, unsafe, confused, helpless and stressed out."

How did the participants cope with the various facets of supervision stress? In reporting negative incidents, almost invariably participants talked about how these incidents had negatively impacted them and how they tried to cope with the stressful situations. A total of 42 meaning units were related to coping efforts. Fifteen coping themes or strategies were extracted. Some of the coping strategies, such as "Sought support from friends, spouse and other students" were shared by many of the participants. However, some of the coping strategy, such as "Wrote down everything so that others may know" was reported by only one person.

The frequency and participation rate for each strategy are shown in Table 1. The fifteen coping themes were organized into four broader categories of coping strategies: Help seeking, Existential coping, Active coping and Emotional coping. Appendix A shows both definitions and examples for different coping strategies for each coping category.

The category of **Existential coping** refers to accepting a situation which one is powerless to change and creating a positive meaning in a negative situation (Wong, 1991, 1993; Chapter 11). **Help seeking** (Flett, Blankstein, Hicken, & Watson, 1995; Wong, 1993) refers to attempts to seek emotional and practical social support from a variety of sources; it also includes collective coping of having the family working together to resolve an issue. **Emotional coping** (Lazarus & Folkman, 1984) refers to various cognitive and defensive

Table 1. Categories and themes of coping

Categories (in bold) and themes (indented)	Participation[*]		Frequency[**]	
A. Help seeking	9	(36%)	15	(35.7%)
A1. Sought support from friends, spouse and other students	7	(28%)	8	(19.0%)
A2. Sought supervision from other sources	4	(16%)	5	(11.9%)
A3. Sought support from God	2	(8%)	2	(4.8%)
B. Existential coping	10	(40%)	13	(30.9%)
B1. Accepted what could not be changed	3	(12%)	3	(7.1%)
B2. Kept quiet	3	(12%)	5	(11.9%)
B3. Learned to put it all behind me	2	(8%)	2	(4.8%)
B4. Tried to make something positive of a negative experience	2	(8%)	3	(7.1%)
C. Active coping	6	(24%)	11	(26.2%)
C1. Counseled myself	3	(12%)	3	(7.1%)
C2. Learned more about the language and culture	3	(12%)	3	(7.1%)
C3. Changed my direction in research and counseling	1	(4%)	2	(4.8%)
C4. Confronting	1	(4%)	1	(2.4%)
C5. Switched to another program or supervisor	1	(4%)	1	(2.4%)
C6. Wrote down everything so that others may know	1	(4%)	1	(2.4%)
D. Emotional coping	2	(8%)	3	(7.2%)
D1. Became very defensive	1	(4%)	2	(4.8%)
D2. Concealed my anger	1	(4%)	1	(2.4%)

Note: [*]The number of participants reporting each category or theme is given in the Participation column, with the participation rate given in parenthesis. [**]The number of meaning units cited for each theme is given in the Frequency column, with the percentage of the total number of meaning units given in parenthesis.

efforts to manage one's feelings without actually solving the problem. **Active coping** includes both problem-focused coping (Lazarus & Folkman, 1984) and various active attempts to improve oneself, similar to the self-restructuring coping strategy (Chapter 11). Since most of the stressors in supervision are beyond one's control, it is not surprising that most of the coping strategies are not directed at confronting and solving the problem. Participants also realize that the Department and the University should also play a role to reduce supervision stress for visible minority students; their recommendations are shown in the next section.

3.2.3. Recommendations for change

A total of 88 meaning units were related to recommendations. Most of the comments were given in response to the question "In your opinion, what could be done to improve the quality of supervision for visible minority students?" However, occasionally, in the course of describing negative incidents, some participants spontaneously suggested ways to prevent the kind of problems they had experienced in supervision. Altogether, thirty-three categories were extracted. These specific recommendations can be grouped into four broad areas.

The first area addresses the need to improve the general quality of supervision. This area covers a number of specific recommendations, such as "Need better relationship and communication between supervisor and supervisee", "Supervisors need to provide more validation, encouragement and support" and "Supervisors need to provide specific and constructive feedback", and "Need to resolve conflict in an open and professional manner." Participants are smart enough to know that bad and incompetent supervision can cause a lot of grief and harm to all supervisees.

The second area refers to the need to improve multicultural competencies in supervision. This area is more directly related to the needs of ethnic minority students. For example, some participants suggested that some of the "assumptions and practices of Western model of counseling need to be questioned", because they may not be relevant in working with ethnic minorities or in some other cultures. It was also recommended that "supervisors need to be open-minded to alternative models of counseling" based on other cultures. Supervisors also need to better understand minority students. For example, one participant said, "Yes, being ESL (English as a Second Language), I already know I need to improve. Without them telling me, I know it. You don't need to point that out to me every single time." Another participant said, "You really have to understand how a visible minority student comes from. The family values, the core values they operate on...in some ethnic groups like aboriginal people, they will not speak. Something against authority? They are very silent. The silence doesn't mean they are not wanting help."

The third area recommends departmental changes in order to meet the needs of ethnic minority students in a multicultural society. There are several specific recommendations, such as "hire minority supervisors", "admit and help international students", "requires everyone to receive multicultural training". Most participants believed that with more multicultural competencies and sensitivity, supervisors would less likely harm visible minority students.

The fourth area recommends changes minority students need to make in order to do better in counseling training in the majority culture. They realize that they "need to be more self-confident and assertive". One participant said, "I am learning to be more assertive, because I'm still finding it frustrating following through on something that I don't really agree with." Some participants also recognized the "need to get organized and form an ethnic minority student group", believing that it would give them more voice in the department; this recommendation sounds like collective coping (Wong, 1993; Chapters 3 and 24).

Taken together, these recommendations resemble preventive coping (Wong, 1993, Chapter 11), because once implemented, the recommended changes will create a more positive supervision environment and reduce negative incidents for both visible minority students as well as graduate students in general. Some of the recommendations are directed towards visible minority students themselves, calling for personal improvement or self-restructuring, which is another form of preventive coping (Chapter 11.)

3.3. Coping with Supervision Stress

Negative incidents in supervision were often stressful and resulted in coping actions. Lazarus and Folkman (1984) defined stress as a "particular relationship between the person and the environment that is appraised by the person as taxing or exceeding his or her resources and endangering his or her well-being" (p. 19). Wong (1990) redefined stress as "problematic internal or external condition that creates tension/upset in the individual and calls for some form of coping" (p. 70), because some of the stress may stem from internal conditions, such as intrapsychic conflicts. In short, stress, whether it is external or internal, always requires some sort of coping efforts. The coping behaviors and recommended reported above represent the coping efforts of visible minority students in dealing with supervision stress.

After reading the entire transcripts of the interviews, one cannot help but sense the deep pains and agonies experienced by many of the participants. Often, they dwelled on the painful events, as if they were seeking some understanding and healing. Such rumination is typical of individuals who have been traumatized (Peterson & Moon, 1999). For some of the participants, their psychological pain is aggravated by the shattering of their assumptive world (Janoff-Bulman, 1999) – they were struggling with such questions: How could supervisors be so mean to their own supervisees? How could this happen in a Counseling Psychology Department, where students are constantly taught the importance of empathy and unconditional positive regard? There is also a sense of powerlessness and helplessness. What can a foreign student do to confront a powerful professor, when the department invariably comes to defend its own faculty? How many graduate students have the courage to stand up to their supervisors and run the risk of reprisal or even expulsion? How can visible minority students cope, when all the cards are stacked against them and the stressful situation is largely beyond their control?

In spite of the above bleak situation, there is also the evidence of resilience and heroism. Those who have been wounded and traumatized somehow have managed to survive and grow. As an epilogue to the study several years ago, all of the participants who endured the adversities have managed to complete their graduate training. I have observed that generally those who have survived the worst kind of abuse from supervisors are most likely to be devoted to advancing multicultural supervision competencies and protecting the well-being and rights of minority students. The present findings on the coping efforts of visible minority students shed light on both the nature of their supervision stress and their adjustment process. In order to facilitate discussion, their coping efforts are grouped into the following broad categories:

3.3.1. Help seeking

The most widely used coping strategy is help seeking with a 36% participation rate. However, some of the participants used more than one form of help seeking. For example, one may seek help from friends as well as pray to God for help.

The literature on help seeking and social support (Flett, Blankstein, Hicken & Watson, 1995) deals with both emotional, social support as well as practical, tangible help. According to Wong's (1993) Resource-Congruence model, when the stressor is appraised as controllable by self, one employs instrumental or problem-focused coping. However, when the stressor is appraised as beyond one's control, one resorts to others for both emotional support and tangible help. To the extent participants expressed feelings of powerlessness and helplessness in dealing with a controlling and powerful supervisor, help seeking would be an appropriate coping response.

Many participants sought emotional support from friends, spouse, and other students. Two of the participants also sought comfort and strength from God through prayers. Four participants sought practical help by seeking supervision from other sources when their own supervisor failed to provide adequate supervision.

It was noted that no participant sought help from Counseling Services or Administration. This observation is consistent with the literature that Asian Americans tend to seek informal help from their own social-support networks (Chou, 1988; Sue & Sue, 1990). Generally, Asian Americans have a less positive attitude towards counseling services than Whites (Lee & Mixson, 1995; Leong, Wagner, & Tata, 1995). There are many reasons for this phenomenon. One reason is that individuals from collectivistic cultures, such as Chinese or Japanese, do not want to seek help from strangers (Yeh et al., Chapter 3). There is also the reluctance to seek professional help from counselors, social workers, or psychologists; seeking professional help for distress is considered culturally inappropriate, because it may reflect negatively on one's character or family (Wong & Ujimoto, 1998; Yeh & Wang, 2000).

3.3.2. Existential coping

When a negative event shatters individuals' assumptions or overwhelms their coping resources, they not only ask "why" questions (Wong, 1991), but also resort to existential coping, which is basically consisted of two coping strategies: (a) Accept and endure what cannot be changed, and (b) Make something positive out of a negative event (Wong, 1993). The adaptive value of existential coping has been demonstrated by various authors (Carver and Scheier, 1999; Janoff-Bulman, 1999; Chapter 11).

The present findings provide some evidence of existential coping in terms of acceptance and endurance. Wong, Reker and Peacock (Chapter 11) have documented a wide array of evidence of the adaptive values of meaning-making and acceptance as coping strategies. The theme of "Accepted what could not be changed" refers to acceptance of all the unpleasant events one has encountered in the course of supervision training. The strategy of "Kept quiet" refers to forbearance, because of the perceived futility of appeal and fear of reprisal (Ladany, Hill, Corbett, & Nutt, 1996). Many graduate students just wanted to grin and bear until the ordeal is over. Here are two examples of existential coping; these two participants just wanted to accept and endure in order to survive.

"I think it's very Japanese side of me to accept it as it is...Just take it in and be submissive."

"I can't really say anything. I was just doing my time there...I just wanted to finish my program. I just wanted my internship hours to be finished. That's all my goal was for this internship."

Endurance or forbearance has long been recognized as an Oriental value (Chapter 3, Yue, 2001; Fukuhara, 1989). Forbearance involves a high degree of self-control and a high level of tolerance in the face of provocation. Such self-restraint is needed in a collectivistic culture in order to maintain social harmony. Another reason for such stoic display is that it may be very adaptive in situations of unrelenting suffering. Finally, acceptance and endurance are made easier, when one is willing to accept one's fate without complaints (Marsella, 1993). It is understandable why graduate students practice forbearance – there is very little they can do because of the vast power differential and fear of reprisal.

3.3.3. Active coping

This is similar to but broader than problem-focused coping (Lazarus & Folkman, 1984), because it also includes taking actions to improve oneself. Themes related to self-improvement include: "Counseled myself" and "Learned more about the language and culture". In one instance, the participant actually moved in with a Canadian family in order to improve her English and learn more about the Canadian culture. In another instance, the participant actually changed the direction of her dissertation research in order to learn more about cross-cultural supervision and counseling. With regard to self-counseling, one of the participants resorted to documenting her negative experience: "Wrote down everything so that others may know". This coping action has some thera-peutic benefits, because research has shown that writing about one's stressful event can be an effective coping strategy (Smyth & Pennebaker, 1999); furthermore, this intentional act of documentation has additional meaning, because she wanted to preserve a record so that one day she can tell her story for the benefit of other graduate students.

3.3.4. Emotional coping

Emotional coping refers to participants' attempts to manage their negative feelings of anger, resentment, worries, and fears. It is similar to but broader than the emotional-focused coping conceptualized by Lazarus and Folkman (1984). It includes defensiveness and anger management. Only two participants resorted to some form of emotional coping. "Became very defensive" can be counterproductive, because it would further confirm supervisor's neg-ative evaluation of the supervisee as someone being defensive and resistant to feedback.

3.3.5. Preventive and collective coping

The need for preventive and collective coping was expressed in a series of recom-mendations for the department to make changes and improve multicultural supervision competencies. These recommendations represent participants' desires for a better future for other visible minorities students through the collective efforts of the entire department. If their recommendations are implemented, supervisors would be less likely to inflict unnecessary pains and sufferings on their minority trainees. Most of the recommended changes require the collective efforts of departmental leadership and professional organi-zations. For example, very few professors would voluntarily take courses and receive train-ing in multicultural competencies, unless it is required by the department and accrediting agencies (Sue & Sue, 1990). There is also a need for due process and accountability to ensure that supervisors assume ethical and legal responsibilities towards ethnic minority supervisees because of their vulnerability to discrimination (Vasquez, 1992).

The needs for addressing multicultural issues and developing multicultural compe-tencies have been emphasized elsewhere (Fong & Lease, 1997; Gopaul-McHicol & Brice-Baker, 1998; Kaiser, 1997; Wong & Wong, 1999). Supervisors need to acquire these competencies in order to work effectively with ethnic minority students. Vasquez and McKinley (1982) emphasized that supervisors need to be more sensitive to the difficulties and struggles of ethnic minorities. Ladany et al. (1997) found that high levels of racial identity led to greater supervisor alliances. Constantine (1997) and Priest (1994) reported that some supervisors were reluctant to talk about racial, ethnic issues due to their own biases or lack of multicultural training. It is important to note that supervisors have the responsibility to address multicultural issues (Tyler, Brome, & Williams, 1991).

4. DISCUSSIONS AND CONCLUSION

This chapter has provided only an incomplete picture of supervision stress experienced by visible minority students. This issue has not received much attention from stress and coping researchers or cross-cultural psychologists. The training and supervisory needs of racial and ethnic minority students have been recognized (Garrett, 2001; Heppner & O'Brien, 1994; McNeill, Hom, & Perez, 1995;), but very little research has been done (Daniels, D'Andrea, & Kim, 1999).

Similarly, the coping strategies by ethnic minority students are also under-studied. Streets, Birum, Lighenberg, & Hunter (1998) studied how minority students coped with academic stress rather than supervision stress in counseling psychology. They reported that the majority of students employed seeking social support, planful problem-solving, self-control and positive reappraisal in coping with school-related stress. These coping strategies correspond to Help seeking, Active coping, and Existential coping respectively. Streets et al. (1998) defined positive reappraisal of problems in terms of "a deliberate effort to create a positive meaning by focusing on personal growth" (p. 8); this is essentially existential coping as defined by Wong (1993, chapter 11).

Given the increasing number of visible minority students in North America, supervision stress becomes an emerging area of research in its own right. In addition to the difficulties experienced by graduate students in clinical supervision, problems also exist in terms of thesis or dissertation supervision (Ho & Wong, 2005). We need to gain greater understanding of both the nature of supervision stress and effective coping strategies. More importantly, as recommended by the participants of the present study, we need positive changes in guidelines and procedures in order to safe guard students' rights and well-beings; such changes can only take place when the power that be at the departmental and university levels have the collective will to create a more positive learning environment for their graduate students. For many foreign students, their experiences in graduate schools will shape their attitudes and views of the host countries for years to come.

APPENDIX A

Definitions of Categories (in capitals) and Themes of Coping

(A) EXISTENTIAL COPING (accepting and enduring a situation which I am powerless to change).

(1) Accepted what could not be changed – Coping by accepting a difficult situation or own limitations.

"Perhaps accept myself in terms of issues around race and my own internalized races and all that kind of stuff."

"I think it's very Japanese side of me to accept it as it is...Just take it in and be submissive."

(2) Kept quiet – Coping by enduring the situation quietly.

"It meant that I've withdrawn more and more and got more disillusioned with counseling as a profession."

"I can't really say anything. I was just doing my time there...I just wanted to finish my program. I just wanted my internship hours to be finished. That's all my goal was for this internship."

(3) Learned to put it all behind me – Coping by trying to forget about the whole thing.

"But we managed to leave it behind and continue a very good relationship. I was able to let it go. I didn't sit down and think how unfair it was on her part."

(4) Tried to make something positive of a negative experience – Coping by creating a positive meaning in a negative situation.

"I tried to kind of take it more as a learning experience, as something I need to learn, and try not to get down on myself."

"I always have been able to find the positive out of the negative. But sometimes I also found a difference in that I try to avoid voicing the negative thing and I would feel good about myself."

(B) HELP SEEKING (seeking emotional and practical social support from various sources).

(5) Sought support from friends, spouse and other students – Coping through depending on others for emotional support.

"I was frustrated. I cried. I talked with my husband. He almost said he will go with me to the school to make the argument that they can't treat me like that. I said, No, you don't. I go by myself. All I need was for him to understand and support me. I have a place to cry. I really needed that."

"There were a couple of students in the class I did tell.... There were a few people who were very sympathetic".

(6) Sought support from God – Coping through praying to God.

"I definitely pray and depend on God."

(7) Sought supervision from other sources – Coping with inadequate supervision by seeking additional supervision from some other sources.

"I also actively pursue that. I wanted more supervision. When I didn't get it, I look for it."

"For myself, because I didn't find the supervision classes very helpful, I just sought other counselors or supervisors that I knew, either from different schools or just people I knew. I would go up to them and get more specific help from them. That was more useful".

(C) EMOTIONAL COPING (managing one's emotions and trying to feel better).

(8) Became very defensive – Coping with criticisms by becoming defensive.

"I found myself very defensive when people are talking to me of issues emphasizing more on emotions (in counseling)."

(9) Concealed my anger – Coping with my anger by keeping it under control.

"I think at first I was angry, but I don't think I showed it. I know myself. I am not a person good at showing my anger. I probably would just take it and be very angry with myself. I may be very sarcastic. That's the usual way I deal with difficulties.

(D) ACTIVE COPING (doing something about the situation or myself).

(10) Counseled myself – Coping by doing therapy on myself.

"Also I counseled my self, because I didn't know (what else to do.)"

"I know there are some things I need to go back in my own life and work on"

(11) Learned more about the language and culture – Coping with my language and cultural barriers by becoming more acculturated.

"We moved in with a Canadian family and lived there for years, basically everyday we would do everything together. That really helped a lot"

"Need to be strong and assertive (as Caucasians)."

(12) Changed my direction in research and counseling – Coping with my negative experience by doing something different in thesis research and counseling approach.

"After that I became very focused and changed my dissertation to the alternative approaches to counseling cross-culturally.... From that point I then started actually defining myself as a cross-cultural counselor, rather than a marriage or family counselor."

"I think I'll feel more comfortable doing that (becoming a multicultural counselor) than trying to perpetuate being a little white counselor".

(13) Confronting – Coping by confronting or challenging the supervisor.

"I tried approaching her directly on the number of sessions and that whole area. I didn't feel heard."

(14) Switched to another program or supervisor – Coping by switching to a better program or supervisor.

"I finally had to switch to a different university to take the course from a different department."

(15) Wrote down everything so that others may know – Coping with bad supervision by documenting everything.

"(She said): 'People do things sometimes that they know are not right, but you have to learn to let go and carry on.' I said I didn't want to be hurt. I want you to know everything that happened. I said I've written down everything that's happened the first term, but I haven't written down the second term. I am writing down and give to her. I want somebody to hear what happened."

REFERENCES

Aanstoos, C. M. (1983). The think aloud method in descriptive research. *Journal of Phenomenological Psychology, 14*, 243-266.

Allen, G. J., Szollos, S. J., & Williams, B. E. (1986). Doctoral students' comparative evaluations of best and worst psychotherapy supervision. *Professional Psychology: Research and Practice, 17*, 91-99.

Atkinson, D. R., Morten, G., & Sue, D. W. (Eds.). (1993). *Counseling American minorities: A cross-cultural perspective* (4th ed.). Dubuque, IA: Brown & Benchmark.

Bernard, J. M. (1988). Receiving and using supervision. In H. Hackney & L. S. Cormier (Eds.), *Counseling strategies and interventions* (3rd ed., pp.153-169). Englewood Cliffs, NJ: Prentice-Hall.

Bernard, J. M., & Goodyear, R. (1998). *Fundamentals of clinical supervision*. Boston: Allyn & Bacon.

Borgen, W., & Amundson, N. (1996). *The experience of unemployment*. Scarborough, ON: Nelson.

Brown, M. T., & Landrum-Brown, J. (1995). Counselor supervision: Cross cultural perspectives. In J. G. Ponterotto, J. M. Casas, L. A. Suzuki, & C. M. Alexander (Eds.), *Handbook of Multicultural Counseling* (pp. 263-286). Thousand Oaks, CA: Sage Publications.

Carifio, M. S., & Hess, A. K. (1987). Who is the ideal supervisor? *Professional Psychology: Research and Practice, 18*, 244-250.

Carroll, M. (1996). Counseling and supervision: Theory, skills, and practice. London: Cassell.

Carver, C. S., & Scheier, M. F. (1999). Stress, coping, and self-regulatory processes. In L. A. Pervin and O. P. John (Eds.), *Handbook of Personality* (2nd ed.) (pp. 553-575). New York: Guilford Press.

Chou, Y-J. (1988). Informal help-seeking behavior among Chinese Americans. *Dissertation Abstracts International, 48*(7-B): 2139.

Cook, D. A., & Helms, J. E. (1988). Visible racial/ethnic group supervisees' satisfaction with cross-cultural supervision as predicted by relationship characteristics. *Journal of Counseling Psychology, 35*, 268-274.

Constantine, M. G. (1997). Facilitating multicultural competency in counseling supervision: Operationalizing a practical framework. In D. B. Pope-Davis & H. L. K. Coleman (Eds.), *Multicultural counseling competencies: Assessment, education and training, and supervision* (pp. 310-324). Newbury Park, CA: Sage Publishers.

Corey, G., Corey, M. S., & Callanan, P. (1998). *Issues and ethics in the helping professions*. (5th Ed.) Pacific Grove, CA: Brooks/Cole Publishing.

Daniels, J., D'Andrea, M., & Kim, B. S. K. (1999). Assessing the barriers and changes of cross-cultural supervision: A case study. In M. H. Smaby (Ed.), *Counselor education and supervision, 38*(3), 191-203. Reno, NV: American Counseling Association.

D'Andrea, M., & Daniels, J. (1997). Multicultural counseling supervision: Central issues, theoretical considerations, and practical strategies. In D. B. Pope-David & H. L. K. Coleman (Eds.), *Multicultural counseling competencies: Assessment, education and training, and supervision* (pp.290-309). Thousand Oaks, CA: Sage.

Diseny, M. J., & Stephens, A. M. (1995). *Legal issues in clinical supervision* (Volume 10). Annapolis Jct., MD: American Counseling Association.

Dye, H. A., & Borders, L. D. (1990). Counseling supervisors: Standards for preparation and practice. *Journal of Counseling and Development, 69,* 27-32.

Ekstein, R., & Wallerstein, R. S. (1972). *The teaching and learning of psychotherapy* (2nd Ed.). New York: International Universities Press.

Ellis, M. V. (1991). Critical incidents in clinical supervision and in supervisor supervision: Assessing supervisory issues. *Journal of Counseling Psychology, 38,* 342-349.

Ellis, M. V. (2001). Harmful supervision, a cause for alarm: Comment on Gray et al. (2001) and Nelson and Friedlander (2001). *Journal of Counseling Psychology, 48*(4), 401-406l.

Flanagan, J. C. (1954). The critical incident technique. *Psychological Bulletin, 51,* 327-358.

Flett, G. L., Blankstein, K. R., Hicken, D. J., & Watson, M. S. (1995). Social support and help-seeking in daily hassles versus major life events stress. *Journal of Applied Social Psychology, 25,* 49-58.

Fong, M. L., & Lease, S. H. (1997). Cross-cultural supervision: Issues for the White supervisor. In D. B. Pope-David & H. L. K. Coleman (Eds.), *Multicultural counseling competencies: Assessment, education and training, and supervision* (pp.380-407). Thousand Oaks, CA: Sage.

Fukuhara, M. (1989). Counseling psychology in Japan. *Applied Psychology: An International Review, 38,* 409-422.

Garrett, M. T. (2001). Multicultural supervision: A paradigm of cultural responsiveness for supervisors. *Journal of Multicultural Counseling & Development, 29*(2), 147-158.

Gopaul-McNicol, S-A, & Brice-Baker, J. (1998). *Cross-cultural practice: Assessment, treatment, and training.* New York: John Wiley & Sons.

Giorgi, A. (1975). An application of phenomenological method in psychology. In A. Giorgi, C. F. Fischer, & E. L. Murray (Eds.), *Duquesne studies in phenomenological psychology, 2,* 82-103. Pittsburgh, PA: Duquesne University Press.

Giorgi, A. (1997). The theory, practice, and evaluation of the phenomenological method as a qualitative research procedure. *Journal of Phenomenological Psychology, 28,* 235-260.

Gray, L. A., Ladany, N., Walker, J. A., & Ancis, J. R. (2001). Psychotherapy trainees' experience of counterproductive events in supervision. *Journal of Counseling Psychology, 48,* 371-383.

Harrar, W. R., VandeCreek, L., & Knapp, S. (1990). Ethical and legal aspects of clinical supervision. *Professional Psychology: Research and Practice, 21,* 37-41.

Hart, G. M. (1982). *The process of clinical supervision.* Baltimore, MD: University Park Press.

Henderson, C. E., Cawyer, C. S., & Watkins, C. E. Jr. (1997). *A comparison of student and supervisor perceptions of effective practicum supervision.* Poster session presented at the annual meeting of the American Psychological Association, August, Chicago, IL.

Heppner, M. J., & O'Brien, K. M. (1994). Multicultural counselor training: Students' perceptions of helpful and hindering events. *Counselor Education & Supervision, 34*(1), 11-35.

Heppner, P. P., & Roehlke, H. J. (1984). Differences among supervisees at different levels of training: Implications for a developmental model of supervision. *Journal of Counseling Psychology, 31,* 76-90.

Herzberg, F., Mausner, B., & Snyderman, B. B. (1959). *The Motivation to Work* (2nd ed.). New York: John Wiley & Sons.

Ho, J. C. W., & Wong, L. C. J. (2005). *What helps and hinders thesis completion: A critical incident study.* Poster presentation at 113th Annual Convention of the American Psychological Association (APA), August 18-21, 2005. Washington, DC.

Holloway, E. L. (1987). Developmental models of supervision: Is it development? *Professional Psychology: Research and Practice, 18,* 209-216.

Holloway, E. L. (1992). Supervision: A way of teaching and learning. In S. D. Brown, & R. W. Lent (Eds.), *Handbook of counseling psychology* (pp. 177-214). New York: John Wiley & Sons.

Holloway, E. (1995). *Clinical supervision: A systems approach.* Thousand Oaks, CA: Sage.

Hunt, P. (1986). Supervision. *Marriage Guidance, Spring,* pp. 15-22.

Hunt, P. (1987). Black clients: Implications for supervision of trainees. *Psychotherapy: Theory, Research, and Practice, 24,* 114-119.

Hutt, C. H., Scott, J., & King, M. (1983). A phenomenological study of supervisees' positive and negative experiences in supervision. *Psychotherapy: Theory, Research and Practice, 20,* 118-123.

Ivey, A. E., Ivey, M. B., & Simek-Morgan, L. (1997). *Counseling and psychotherapy: A multicultural perspective* (4th ed.). Boston, MA: Allyn & Bacon.

Janoff-Bulman, R. (1999). Rebuilding shattered assumptions after traumatic life events. In C. R. Snyder (Ed.) *Coping: The psychology of what works.* (pp.305-323). New York: Oxford University Press.

Kaiser, T. L. (1997). *Supervisory relationship: Exploring the human element.* Pacific Grove, CA: Brooks/Cole.

Koss, M. P., & Shiang, J. (1994). Research on brief psychotherapy. In A. E. Bergin & S. L. Garfield (Eds.), *Handbook of psychotherapy and behavior change* (4th ed., pp. 664-700). New York: Wiley.

Kyle, T. M., & Williams, S. (2000). *Results of the 1998-1999 APA survey of graduate departments of psychology*. Washington, DC: American Psychological Association.

Ladany, N., Hill, C. E., Corbett, M. M., & Nutt, E. A. (1996). Nature, extent and importance of what psychotherapy trainees do not disclose to their supervisors. *Journal of Counseling Psychology, 43*, 10-24.

Ladany, N., Brittan-Powell, C. S., & Pannu, R. K. (1997). The influence of supervisory racial identity interaction and racial matching on the supervisory working alliance and supervisee multicultural competence. *Counselor Education and Supervision, 36*, 284-304.

Lambert, M. J., & Bergin, A. E. (1994). The effectiveness of psychotherapy. In A. E. Bergin & S. L. Garfield (Eds.), *Handbook of psychotherapy and behavior change* (4th ed., pp. 143-189). New York: Wiley.

Lazarus, R. S., & Folkman, S. (1984). *Stress, appraisal, and coping*. New York: Springer.

Lee, W. M. L., & Mixson, R. J. (1995). Asian and Caucasian client perceptions of the effectiveness of counseling. *Journal of Multicultural Counseling and Development, 23*, 48-56.

Leong, F. L. T., & Chou, E. L. (1996). Counseling international students. In P. B. Pedersen, J. G. Draguns, W. J. Lonner, & J. E. Trimble (Eds.). *Counseling across cultures* (4th ed., pp. 210-242). Thousand Oaks, CA: Sage.

Leong, F. L. T., Wagner, N. S., & Tata, S. P. (1995). Racial and ethnic variations in help-seeking attitudes. In J. G. Ponterotto, J. M. Casas, L. A. Suzuki, & C. M. Alexander (Eds.), *Handbook of multicultural counseling* (pp. 415-438). Thousand Oaks, CA: Sage.

Magnuson, S., Wilcoxon, S. A. & Norem, K. (2000). A profile of lousy supervision: Experienced counselors' perspectives. *Counselor Educationand Supervision, 39*, 189-202.

Marsella, A. (1993). Counseling and psychotherapy with Japanese Americans: Cross-cultural considerations. *American Journal of Orthopsychiatry, 63*, 200-208.

McNeill, B. W., Hom, K. L., & Perez, J. A. (1995). The training and supervisory needs of racial and ethnic minority students. *Journal of Multicultural Counseling and Development, 23*, 246-258.

Metcalf, L., Thomas, F. N., Duncan, B. L., Miller, S. D. & Hubble, M. A. (1996). What works in solution-focused brief therapy. In S. D. Miller, M. A. Hubble & B. L. Duncan (Eds.), *Handbook of solution-focused brief therapy* (pp. 335-349). San Francisco, CA: Jossey Bass.

Nelson, M. L., & Friedlander, M. L. (2001). A close look at conflictual supervisory relationships: The trainee's perspective. *Journal of Counseling Psychology, 48*, 384-395.

Peterson, C., & Moon, C. H. (1999). Coping with catastrophes and catastrophizing. In C. R. Snyder (Ed.) *Coping: The psychology of what works* (pp. 252-278). New York: Oxford University Press.

Priest, R. (1994). Minority supervisor and majority supervisee: Another perspective of clinical reality. *Counselor Education and Supervision, 34*, 152-158.

Rest, J. R. (1984). Research on moral development: Implications for training counseling psychologists. *The Counseling Psychologist, 12*, 19-29.

Rogers, C. (1977). *Carl Rogers on personal power: Inner strength and its revolutionary impact*. New York: Delacorte Press.

Rogers, C. (1986). Carl Rogers on the development of the person-centered approach. *Person-Centered Review, 1*, 257-259.

Ronnestad, M., & Skovholt, T. (1993). Supervision of beginning and advanced graduate students of counseling and psychotherapy. *Journal of Counseling and Development, 71*, 396-405.

Smyth, J. M., & Pennebaker, J. W. (1999). Sharing one's story: Translating emotional experiences into words as a coping tool. In C. R. Snyder (Ed.) *Coping: The psychology of what works* (pp.70-89). New York: Oxford University Press.

Spinelli, E. (2000, July). *Exploring the meaning of therapy from an existential standpoint*. Keynote address presented at the International Conference on Searching for Meaning in the New Millennium, Vancouver.

Stoltenberg, C. D., & Delworth, U. (1987). *Supervising counselors and therapists: A developmental approach*. San Francisco: Jossey-Bass.

Stone, G. L. (1997). Multiculturalism as a context for supervision: Perspectives, limitations, and implications. In D. B. Pope-Davis, & H. L. Coleman (Eds.), *Multicultural counseling competencies* (pp.290-310). Thousand Oaks, CA: Sage.

Streets, B. F., Birum, I. L., Lichtenberg, J. W., & Hunter, J. (1998). *Coping strategies used by ethnic minority graduate students in counseling psychology*. Presented at the annual convention of the American Psychological Association, August, 1998, San Francisco, CA.

Sue, D. W., & Sue, D. (1990). *Counseling the culturally different: Theory & practice* (3rd ed.). New York: John Wiley & Sons.

Tyler, F. B., Brome, D. R., & Williams, J. E. (1991). *Ethnic validity, ecology, and psychotherapy: A psychosocial competence model.* New York: Plenum.

Vasquez, M. J. T. (1992). Psychologist as clinical supervisor: Promoting ethical practice. *Professional Psychology: Research and practice, 23,* 196-202.

Vasquez, M. J. T., & McKinley, D. L. (1982). Supervision: A conceptual model-Reactions and an extension. *The Counseling Psychologist, 10,* 59-63.

Watkins, C. E., Jr. (1995a). Psychotherapy supervision in the 1990s: Some observations and reflections. *American Journal of Psychotherapy, 49,* 568-581.

Watkins, C. E., Jr. (1997). *Handbook of psychotherapy supervision.* New York: Wiley.

Williams, S., & Haglin, R. P. (1995). Issues in psychotherapy supervision between White supervisor and the Black supervisee. *The Clinical Supervisor, 13,* 39-61.

Wong, L. C. J. (2000). *What helps and what hinders in cross-cultural clinical supervision: A critical incident study.* Unpublished Ph.D. Dissertation, University of British Columbia, BC.

Wong, P. T. P. (1990). Measuring life stress. *Stress Medicine, 6,* 69-70.

Wong, P. T. P. (1991). Existential vs. causal attributions. In S. Zelen (Ed.) *Extensions and new models of attribution theory* (pp.84-125). New York: Springer-Verlag Publishers.

Wong, P. T. P. (1993). Effective management of life stress: The resource-congruence model. *Stress Medicine, 9,* 51-60.

Wong, P. T. P., & Ujimoto, K. V. (1998). The elderly Asian Americans: their stress coping, and well-being. In L. C. Lee & N. W. S. Zane (Eds.), *Handbook of Asian American Psychology* (pp. 165-209). Thousand Oaks, CA: Sage Publications.

Wong, P. T. P., & Wong, L. C. J. (1999). Assessing multicultural supervision competencies. In W. J. Lonner, D. L. Dinnel, D. K. Forgays, & S. A. Hayes. *Merging past, present and future in cross-cultural psychology: Selected papers from the XIVth International Congress of the International Association for Cross-cultural Psychology.* Lisse, The Netherlands: Swets & Zeitlinger Publishers.

Wong, L. C. J., & Wong, P. T. P. (2002). *What helps and what hinders in multicultural supervision: From the perspective of supervisors.* Roundtable discussion: Hot topics in Clinical Supervision and Training APA Convention, Chicago, August 25, 1998.

Worthen, V. E., & McNeill, B. W. (1996). A phenomenological investigation of "good" supervision events. *Journal of Counseling Psychology, 43,* 25-34.

Worthington, E. L., Jr. (1987). Changes in supervision as counselors and supervisors gain experience: A review. *Professional Psychology: Research and Practice, 18,* 189-208.

Worthington, E. L., Jr., & Roehlke, H. J. (1979). Effective supervision as perceived by beginning counselors in training. *Journal of Counseling Psychology, 26,* 64-73.

Yalom, I. D. (2000, July). *Tips for the practice of existential psychotherapy.* Keynote address presented at the International Conference on Searching for Meaning in the New Millennium, Vancouver.

Yeh, C. J., & Wang, Y-W. (2000). Asian American coping attitudes, sources, and practices: Implications for indigenous counseling strategies. *Journal of College Student Development, 41,* 94-103.

Yue, X. (2001). Culturally constructed coping among university students in Beijing. *Journal of Psychology in Chinese Societies, 2,* 119-137.

Zeig, J. K. (2000, July). *The "being" of meaning.* Keynote address presented at the International Conference on Searching for Meaning in the New Millennium, Vancouver.

16

PSYCHOLOGICAL SKILLS RELATED TO INTERCULTURAL ADJUSTMENT

David Matsumoto, Satoko Hirayama, and Jeffery A. LeRoux

1. INTRODUCTION

People from all corners of the globe migrate or sojourn to different cultures to work, study, and live, and in doing so face many issues in dealing with and adjusting to a new culture. Research has well documented the stresses, trials, and tribulations of sojourners and immigrants, and has identified the important affective, cognitive, and behavioral skills, abilities, and aptitudes that contribute to successful, and unsuccessful, sojourns. Despite this wealth of knowledge, however, the field has been relatively slow in identifying the core psychological components associated with positive intercultural adjustment. In this chapter, we report work from our laboratory spanning 17 studies on the development and validation of a new measure of intercultural adjustment – the Intercultural Adjustment Potential Scale (ICAPS) – that has helped us identify the psychological skills related to intercultural adjustment for highly functioning people around the world. The goal of this chapter is to introduce the reader to those skills. We begin by discussing the importance of intercultural adaptation and adjustment, and then review the literature identifying the factors that influence adjustment. We then discuss our theoretical approach to understanding adjustment, and describe the development and validation of our ICAPS measure. Finally we highlight the psychological skills that multiple studies have demonstrated are correlated with adjustment.

2. INTERCULTURAL ADAPTATION AND ADJUSTMENT

2.1. Comparing and Contrasting Adaptation and Adjustment

In our work we have found that it is important to make a distinction between adaptation and adjustment. Using Ward's approach, we believe that adaptation is based in the sociocultural domain (Ward, 2001), that is, it is the process of altering one's behavior to

David Matsumoto, San Francisco State University; Satoko Hirayama, Ochanomizu University; Jeffery A. LeRoux, San Francisco State University fit in with a changed environment or circumstances, or as a response to social pressure. One of the most well known models of adaptation, for instance, is Berry's (1994) analysis of the interaction styles for sojourners, immigrants, and refugees. In this model, four categories of interaction style are identified on the basis of the yes/no answers to two questions: (1) is it important to maintain my cultural identity and characteristics, and (2) do I value and want to maintain relationships with people of the host culture? Individuals who say yes to both are considered "integrators;" those who say no to both are "marginalizers." Those who say yes to the first and no to the second are "separators," while those who say no to the first and yes to the second are "assimilators." clearly these processes refer to behavioral changes made in response to different environments.

In contrast, we define adjustment as the subjective experiences that are associated with and result from attempts at adaptation, and that also motivate further adaptation. Adjustment, therefore, essentially refers to the general concept of well-being, which is an affective evaluation of one's life situation. In line with this definition, previous researchers have incorporated a wide range of outcome measures of adjustment, including self-awareness and self-esteem (Kamal & Maruyama, 1990), mood states (Stone Feinstein & Ward, 1990), and health status (Babiker, Cox, & Miller, 1980) (all cited in Ward, 2001). Other typical measures of adjustment involve other subjective experiential constructs that refer to well-being, such as anxiety, mood, depression, subjective well-being, satisfaction, and happiness.

Some writers have developed synthesizing strategies to integrate these specific approaches to the definitions of adaptation and adjustment in order to highlight a smaller number of features. For example, Brislin (1981) has identified three factors of adjustment, including (1) having successful relationships with people from other cultures; (2) feeling that interactions are warm, cordial, respectful, and cooperative; and (3) accomplishing tasks in an effective and efficient manner. Hammer, Gudykunst, and Wiseman (1978) focused on these factors, and also included the ability to manage psychological stress effectively. Black and Stephens (1989) identified general adjustment involving daily activities, interaction adjustment involving interpersonal relations, and work adjustment related to work and tasks.

Research on adjustment outcomes for various adaptation strategies further highlights the conceptual difference between the two concepts. For example, while it is often politically correct to suggest that Berry's strategy of integration produces the best adjustment outcomes, in fact that is not often the case (see reviews by Berry & Sam, 1997; Ward, 2001; Rudmin, 2003a, 2003b). It appears that people who engage in separation or assimilation adjust just as well to their life contexts as do people who integrate. Research is not as clear about marginalization. We would propose that marginalizers often feel well-adjusted, but that the people around them probably do not feel that they are.

2.2. Positive and Negative Adjustment

As alluded to above, adapting to a new culture can have both positive and negative adjustment outcomes. On one hand the positive consequences include gains in language competence; self-esteem, awareness, and health (Babiker et al., 1980; Kamal & Maruyama, 1990); self-confidence, positive mood, interpersonal relationships, and stress reduction (Matsumoto et al., 2001). Clearly when intercultural experiences go well, many individuals report evolving in many qualitative, positive ways so that they are fundamentally different, and better, individuals. These include the development of multicultural identities and multiple perspectives with which to engage the world.

On the other hand, the negative consequences include psychological and psychosomatic concerns (Shin & Abell, 1999); early return to one's home country (Montagliani & Giacalone, 1998); emotional distress (Furukawa & Shibayama, 1994); dysfunctional communication (Gao & Gudykunst, 1991; Okazaki-Luff, 1991); culture shock (Pederson, 1995); depression, anxiety, diminished school and work performance, and difficulties in interpersonal relationships (Matsumoto et al., 2001). In extreme cases negative adjustment results in antisocial behavior (gangs, substance abuse, crime) and even suicide. Fortunately all sojourners do not experience this wide range of psychological and physical health problems, but most have probably experienced *some* of these problems at some point in their sojourn.

One of the goals, therefore, of intercultural adaptation is to adopt an adaptation pattern that minimizes these stresses and negative adjustment outcomes, and maximizes positive ones.

3. FACTORS THAT PREDICT ADJUSTMENT

3.1. Previous Literature

There have been many attempts to identify the factors that influence intercultural adjustment (reviewed in Matsumoto, 1999; Matsumoto et al., 2001). Studies have identified a wide range of variables, such as knowledge, language proficiency, attitudes, previous experiences, levels of ethnocentrism, social support, cultural similarity, adventure, and self-construals. Among these, three factors have consistently emerged as leading contributors to adjustment: knowledge of host and home culture, ethnocentrism, and language proficiency. In fact it is precisely because of these factors that many intercultural training interventions involve language skill and knowledge training. The underlying assumption of such training is that if people can speak the language of the host culture, and if they know some basic facts about the host culture, they can adjust to life better. Likewise, if people can recognize the existence of ethnocentrism – how our own cultural upbringing contributed to how we interact with the world and with others – and can recognize that our viewpoint is one of many valid and legitimate views, they will have successful adjustments.

3.2. A New Way of Understanding Intercultural Adjustment Focused on Emotion

In our work, we have chosen to focus on the social psychology of adjustment through an analysis of intercultural encounters. Because of differences in language, nonverbal behaviors, values, norms, attitudes, rules, systems, and other manifestations of culture, intercultural adjustment is replete with conflict, frustration, and struggle. They are, in fact, inevitable because of cultural differences, at least on the level of manifest behaviors (despite possible cultural similarities in underlying psychological goals and intentions).

These conflict-arousing contexts are seeped with emotion, often negative. Once aroused, intercultural encounters can easily lead to negative experiences, frustrations, stereotypes, attitudes, and a host of other affective/cognitive outcomes that are not conducive to successful adaptation. Therefore, we believe one of the keys to successful intercultural adjustment is the ability to regulate one's emotions, and to not allow negative affect, which may be inevitable, to overcome oneself and color one's cognitions and motivations.

Our theoretical framework was informed by the literature on stress and coping. While this literature of course indicates that major life events – marriage, divorce, births and deaths – have consequences on well-being, research has also emphasized the cumulative effects of day-to-day events, both positive and negative, on well-being and relationships (DeLongis, Folkman, & Lazarus, 1988; Kanner, Coyne, Schaefer, & Lazarus, 1981). This literature has shown that daily hassles and uplifts can have major effects on people's physical and psychological health, that is, adjustment, that is similar to or even stronger than the effects of major life events. This notion is even more relevant in the intercultural context, where daily life is replete with daily hassles because of the new cultural context in which to adapt and adjust, the inherent ambiguity of new cultural systems and intercultural communication, and the inevitable conflict that arises because of differences. Emotions, therefore, play a major role in adaptation and adjustment, just as they play a major role in the stress and coping process.

Emotions, in fact, are a large part of our lives. Emotions color our experiences, giving them meaning and relevance for our well being. Sadness, anger, disgust, fear, frustration, shame, and guilt – while all negative and often unattractive to us, are all important in that when we feel these emotions, they tell us something important about ourselves and our relationships with other people, events, or situations. Happiness, joy, satisfaction, pleasure, and interest are also important emotions, in that they, too, give us important information about our relationships with others. Emotions are "read-out mechanisms" because they provide information to us about our status in relation to the world (Buck, 1984).

Emotions are also important because they motivate behaviors. Sadness and anger, for example, make us do something, just as happiness and joy reinforce behaviors. The father of modern day research and theory of emotion in psychology – Sylvan Tomkins – suggested that emotions *are* motivation and if you want to understand why people behave the way they do, you had to understand their emotions (Tomkins, 1962, 1963). For these reasons, it is only natural that we give more consideration to this most-important and deserving part of our lives. We thus turned our attention to developing a theoretical framework that incorporated emotion and its regulation in explaining and predicting intercultural adjustment.

Emotion regulation allows individuals to engage in clear thinking about intercultural incidents without retreating into psychological defenses. If sojourners do not have the ability to regulate or control their emotions, they will be unlikely to adjust well because they will be locked into their automatic or habitual ways of thinking and interacting with the world. Emotion regulation seems likely to be the gatekeeper skill for intercultural adjustment.

The ability to regulate emotions, however, alone is not sufficient. Once held in check, individuals must then engage in learning about the new culture, which requires them to analyze the cultural underpinnings of the context, and understand the intentions and behaviors that produced conflict in the first place from a different cultural perspective. In doing so, individuals may draw on the reservoirs of knowledge that previous research has shown to be important in predicting adjustment, such as knowledge of host and own culture, previous experience, and the like. Important aspects of this ability to learn a new culture are likely to include being free of over-attachment to previous ways of thinking that have worked in the past and a willingness to tolerate the ambiguity of not knowing or being able to predict the likely outcomes of one's actions. One also needs the openness and flexibility to call to mind and to consider alternatives that would have been inappropriate in previous social experience. A further necessity in adjusting to a new culture must be the monitoring of the behaviors and reactions of one's self and others around one's self. It may also be the case that conscious, critical thinking about intercultural incidents, the generation of rival hypotheses that explain conflict other than those from their own cultural framework and the creation of a new set of ideas about social interaction are critical to adjustment.

This model is inherently a growth model. By engaging in critical thinking about cultural differences and being open and flexible to new ways of thinking, one allows for one's ways of person perception to grow. One continually adds more complexity to one's method of interacting with diversity. All of this is possible, however, only when emotions are regulated and negative emotions do not get the best of oneself.

If, however, negative emotional reactions overwhelm, people cannot engage in critical thinking about those differences. Rather, they regress to a previous way of thinking that is rooted in ethnocentrism and stereotype. Instead of creating rival hypotheses that will stimulate growth in thinking, people instead only reinforce pre-existing, limited thinking. Openness and flexibility to new ideas is not even an option because these new ideas don't exist. Instead, there is only a regurgitation of stereotypes and ethnocentric attitudes. This is a non-growth model.

The four main ingredients to personal growth in relation to dealing with cultural differences, therefore, is emotion regulation, critical thinking, openness, and flexibility. Of these, emotion regulation is the gatekeeper of the growth process, because if one cannot put inevitable negative emotions in check, it is impossible to engage in what is clearly higher order thinking about cultural differences.

Our approach to understanding intercultural adjustment is based on a stress and coping approach, which appears to offer the broadest framework to understand this issue. According to Ward (2001), the factors that predict intercultural adjustment include life changes, cognitive appraisals of stress, coping styles, personality, social support, cultural identity, type of acculturating groups, perceived discrimination, acculturation strategies, and sociocultural adaptation. Because intercultural contact and change are significant life events that are inherently stressful, coping skills are required to deal with life in a new and different environment (Ward, 2001). Models of cross-cultural coping such as problem focused vs. emotion focused, engagement vs. avoidance, and primary vs. secondary control have provided ample evidence to predict adjustment.

To be sure, these psychological skills – emotion regulation, openness, flexibility, and critical thinking – have been described in the previous literature. To our knowledge, however, they have not been empirically compared nor integrated into a single set of dimensions that accounts for intercultural adjustment. The studies we describe below represent an attempt to create a more complete model of the psychology of intercultural adjustment.

4. THE ASSESSMENT OF PSYCHOLOGICAL SKILLS THEORETICALLY RELATED TO INTERCULTURAL ADJUSTMENT – THE INTERCULTURAL ADJUSTMENT POTENTIAL SCALE (ICAPS)

4.1. Development of the ICAPS

For years the field has struggled with the creation of valid and reliable individual difference measures that will predict intercultural adjustment, for various reasons. For one, when researchers focus on variables that are culture- or context-specific, such as knowledge of host culture, it is nearly impossible to generate a valid measure because it would necessitate the assessment of knowledge that is specific to different cultures, and would be based on the assumption that such knowledge existed and was applicable to all contexts within that culture. Such measures would border on the assessment of knowledge of cultural stereotypes.

Another factor that has hindered the development of valid and reliable individual difference measures has been a lack of consensus on the underlying psychological components that are important to adaptation. As mentioned above, while previous research has identified many variables that appear to be associated with successful adjustment, there is no coherent model that unifies these components into a comprehensive and understandable framework for predicting adaptation. The identification of several psychological variables as the keys to intercultural adaptation bypasses the problem of culture-specific knowledge, and views the *potential* for intercultural adjustment as a function of the psychological skills that individuals possess within them. In doing so, it does not rely on the knowledge or attitudes that sojourners or immigrants may have, or on the specific host culture in which they reside, or on language proficiency. Thus, the potential applicability of this approach is considerably larger than previous models that are tied to knowledge and attitudes.

Because there was no measure that could assess individual differences in the potential for intercultural adjustment based on the factors outlined above, we opted to create our own, resulting in the development of the Intercultural Adjustment Potential Scale – ICAPS. Our strategy was to embody the several factors previously suggested as being related to intercultural adjustment in a pool of items and then to empirically test which had the strongest ability to predict intercultural adjustment, rather than to decide on an a priori basis which items should be included.

We thus examined item content from a number of valid and reliable personality inventories assessing psychological constructs related to emotion regulation, critical thinking, openness/flexibility, interpersonal security, emotional commitment to traditional ways of thinking, tolerance of ambiguity, and empathy. These included the Eysenck Personality Inventory (EPI), the Beck Depression Inventory (BDI), the State-Trait Anxiety Inventory (STAI), the Bem Sex Role Inventory (BSRI), the original Minnesota Multiphasic Personality Inventory (MMPI) item pool, the California Personality Inventory (CPI), the NEO Personality Inventory (NEO-PI), the Big Five Personality Inventory (BFI), the California F-Scale, and the Interpersonal Reactivity Index. We created items based on the ideas gleaned from our examination of these scales, and also constructed our own items. This resulted in the initial development of 193 items.

One issue that arose early in this work was whether this test would be developed for any sojourner of any cultural background, or for those from a single culture. We opted for the latter, assuming that it would be more beneficial to create and validate a measure that has as high a predictive validity as possible for one cultural group, rather than develop a general measure at the sacrifice of predictive validity. The development of a culture-general measure would require the testing of people from multiple home cultures in multiple host cultures, which would be practically infeasible. If a culture-specific measure were created, however, it could serve as the baseline platform for similar method development in other cultures. Thus, we focused on Japanese sojourners and immigrants, because of the literature in the area and our own expertise with this culture.

Because we were concerned with the cross-cultural equivalence of the 193 items, to take into account that respondents might have different English language capabilities, and to remove any colloquialism and difficulty of wording, two researchers created the items, reviewing and modifying all items in terms of language and style, rendering the wording appropriate for Japanese students who might possess a limited selection of English idioms commonly in use. Two native Japanese research assistants then reviewed the new items, ensuring that they were understandable to native Japanese. Care was taken to exclude items that depended for their utility on a cultural value in which Japanese and U. S. culture differ. In all cases, items were written to adapt the cultural meaning of an item in the United States to the same cultural context from a Japanese perspective.

The final selection of items was based on their empirical ability to predict intercultural adjustment, rather than their theoretical potential for prediction. Items having little or nothing to do with intercultural adjustment were eliminated, even if elsewhere they reliably measured an aspect of an underlying psychological skill (e.g., openness) that was theoretically purported to be related to adjustment. Also, some items predicted adjustment better than others; thus, only items that predicted adjustment the best, according to empirical criteria, were retained. This resulted in a final pool of 55 items. To date we have conducted 17 studies documenting the reliability and validity of this 55-item ICAPS in predicting intercultural adjustment success. Table 1 shows a summary of the findings. The evidence demonstrates the unique contribution of the ICAPS to the field.

4.2. Validity Studies of the ICAPS

The first eight studies provided considerable evidence for the internal, temporal, and parallel forms reliability of the ICAPS-55; for its predictive ability with not only subjective indices of adjustment, but also using psychometrically standardized measures, peer ratings, and expert ratings based on interviews with the participants; for its convergent validity with a similar measure; for its construct validity with various personality scales; for its incremental validity; and for its external validity in predicting changes as a result of intercultural seminars, and in identifying experts who work in the intercultural field (Matsumoto et al., 2001).

Encouraged by our initial studies, we engaged in further testing of the ICAPS, interested in the boundaries of its predictive abilities (Matsumoto et al., 2003; Matsumoto, LeRoux, Bernhard, & Gray, 2004). In Studies 9 through 14, we were particularly interested in ascertaining whether the ICAPS could predict adjustment in Japanese non-student samples and for non-Japanese. The results of these studies replicated and considerably extended the findings reported previously by Matsumoto et al. (2001). ICAPS scores predicted adjustment in Japanese non-student samples in a variety of ways, including

Table 1. A Summary of Studies using the ICAPS

Study	Scientific Issue Being Tested	What was Accomplished	Participants	Citation
1	Item reduction; Predictive validity	The 193 items were correlated with indices of intercultural adjustment. The least important items were eliminated, resulting in a 153-item test.	Japanese international students	(Matsumoto et al., 2001)
2	Further item reduction; Predictive validity; Internal reliability	The items were correlated with indices of adjustment. The least important ones were eliminated, resulting in a 55-item test, which we call the ICAPS-55. Internal reliability of the final 55 items was established.	Japanese international students	
3	Temporal and parallel forms reliability	English and Japanese versions of the ICAPS-55 were found to be equivalent. Scores on the test were found to be consistent even after time has elapsed between administrations.	Japanese international students	
4	Predictive validity	The ICAPS-55 was correlated with a variety of measures of adjustment.	Japanese international students	
5	Construct validity; Discriminant validity; Incremental validity	The ICAPS-55 was correlated with a variety of personal and psychopathology measures.	American university students	(Matsumoto et al., 2001)
6	External validity	Changes in ICAPS-55 scores were associated with participation in an intercultural adjustment seminar.	Japanese exchange students	

Continued

7	Norming	Factor analyses of the ICAPS-55 confirmed the existence of the four primary factors of the psychological engine – ER, CT, OP, and FL.	Japanese and American students and non-students	
8	External validity	The ICAPS-55 was associated with a number of characteristics of this group of experts that differed from the norm data.	Japanese and non-Japanese intercultural counselors and consultants	
9	Predictive validity	The ICAPS-55 was correlated with a variety of measures of adjustment.	Japanese business persons and housewives	(Matsumoto et al., 2003)
10	External validity	Changes in the ICAPS-55 were associated with participation in an intercultural training seminar.	Japanese international students and full-time workers	
11	Predictive validity	The ICAPS-55 predicted marital and life satisfaction for the women in these marriages.	Japanese women in international marriages	
12	Predictive validity	The ICAPS-55 predicted culture shock, adjustment, and life satisfaction for these students even though the ICAPS was administered prior to their sojourn while the students were still in Japan.	Japanese international students	
13	Predictive validity	The ICAPS-55 predicted subjective adjustment for international sojourners from many different countries and cultures to the U.S. and Americans who have sojourned abroad.	Non-Japanese sojourners	(Matsumoto et al., 2003)

Table 1. A Summary of Studies using the ICAPS—cont'd

Study	Scientific Issue Being Tested	What was Accomplished	Participants	Citation
14	Predictive validity; Parallel forms reliability	The ICAPS-55 predicted subjective adjustment and life satisfaction in Spanish speaking immigrants and sojourners from Central and South America. English and Spanish versions of the test were found to be equivalent.	Central and South Americans	
15	Incremental validity	The ICAPS-55 predicted adjustment above and beyond that already accounted for by the big five personality dimensions.	American university students	(Matsumoto et al., 2004)
16	Convergent validity; Predictive validity; Incremental validity	The ICAPS-55 was correlated with a variety of personal and psychopathology measures, and predicted adjustment above and beyond that already accounted for by the CPI.	American university students	(Matsumoto et al., 2004)
17	Predictive validity	The ICAPS-55 predicted actual behaviors above and beyond that already predicted by emotion recognition.	American university students	

standardized measures of anxiety and depression, subjective indices of adjustment, satisfaction with life, and marital satisfaction. The ICAPS also predicted culture shock in Japanese student sojourners even when ICAPS was administered prior to these individual's leaving Japan, and subjective adjustment in a general immigrant sample, as well as in samples from India, Sweden, and Central and South America. Finally, the ICAPS predicted subjective adjustment and satisfaction with life in Americans who had sojourned abroad as well. Coupled with the eight studies described earlier, these findings lent strong and consistent support to the psychometric reliability and validity of the ICAPS to predict intercultural adjustment.

Most recently three additional studies (Studies 15 through 17) examined the personality and behavioral correlates of the ICAPS (Matsumoto et al., 2004). The findings from the studies provided strong evidence for the validity of the ICAPS scales to predict adjustment above and beyond that already predicted by personality. Furthermore, the ICAPS predicted actual behaviors above and beyond that already predicted by emotion recognition.

5. THE PSYCHOLOGICAL SKILLS UNDERLYING THE ICAPS

5.1. Validity with Adjustment

The ICAPS was originally validated using a total score summed across all 55 items. Factor analyses using normative data (n approximately 2,300, half of whom are non-U.S. born and raised) suggested that four factors underlay the ICAPS – Emotion Regulation (ER), Openness (OP), Flexibility (FL), and Critical Thinking (CT) (Matsumoto et al., 2001). These findings provided support for our theoretical formulation in which the importance of ER, OP, CT, and FL are the key psychological ingredients to intercultural adaptation. These skills were hypothesized as necessary in allowing immigrants and sojourners to cope with stress and conflict that are inevitable in intercultural sojourns, while at the same time allowing for personal growth in understanding, tolerance, and acceptance of cultural differences.

To obtain further support for the validity of these four psychological skills to predict adjustment, we created scores for each of these scales and computed correlations between them and various adjustment variables across the studies conducted to determine which psychological constructs predicted adjustment. Table 2 shows a summary of the findings. The first column indicates the ICAPS scales that were significantly associated with the adjustment measures described in the second column.

The findings demonstrated that individuals who scored high on the ICAPS scales had less adjustment problems in work, house work, spare time, and family domains; less somatic, cognitive, and behavioral anxiety; less depression; greater subjective well-being in their adjustment to the US or another country; greater subjective adjustment; higher dyadic adjustments in international marriage; higher life satisfaction; less psychopathology; less culture shock and homesickness; higher language scores; better grades; more tendency to work; higher income; and many of the skills that are useful to managers in solving the complex problems of running a business. The correlations with the various adjustment outcomes provided strong support for this conglomeration of skills to predict adjustment.

Table 2. Adjustment that are Predicted by the ICAPS Scales

ICAPS factor	Adjustment Scale	Citation
Emotion	**Social Adjustment Scale Self-Report (SAS-SR)** Work, House work, Spare time, Family	(Matsumoto et al., 2003)
Regulation	**Somatic, Cognitive, Behavioral Anxiety Scale (SCBAI)** Total score, Somatic, Cognitive, Behavioral **Beck Depression Inventory II (BDI-II)** **Subjective adjustment (SA)** **Personal Opinion Questionnaire (POQ)** **Dyadic Adjustment Scale (DAS)** Total score, Dyadic Consensus (DCON) **Satisfaction with Life Scale (SWLS)** **Measurement of Culture Shock (CS)** Total, Culture shock (CCS), Interpersonal stress items (IS) **Homesickness and Contentment Scale (HS)** **Language Score** Verbal communication skill, Text skill, Overall language skill **GPA** **Working or not Income**	
	Millon Clinical Multiaxial Inventory-II (MCMI-II) Avoidant, Compulsive, Dependent, Histrionic, Narcissistic, Schizoid, Delusional, Debasement, Anxiety, Alcohol Dependence, Self-Defeating, Schizotypal, Passive-Aggressive, Borderline, Thought Disorder, Somatoform, Paranoid, Major Depression, Dysthymia **In-Basket** Quality of Decision, Decisiveness, Written Communication, Delegation, Goal Setting, Initiative, Total Score	(Matsumoto et al., 2004)
Openness	**Somatic, Cognitive, Behavioral Anxiety Scale (SCBAI)** Cognitive **Beck Depression Inventory II (BDI-II)** **Subjective adjustment (SA)** **Dyadic Adjustment Scale (DAS)** Dyadic Satisfaction (DS) **Satisfaction with Life Scale (SWLS)** **Measurement of Culture Shock (CS)** Total, Culture shock (CCS) **Homesickness and Contentment Scale (HS)**	(Matsumoto et al., 2003)

Table 2. Adjustment that are Predicted by the ICAPS Scales—cont'd

ICAPS factor	Adjustment Scale	Citation
	Language Score	(Matsumoto
	Text skill	et al., 2003)
	Millon Clinical Multiaxial Inventory-II (MCMI-II)	(Matsumoto
	Aggressive, Avoidant, Schizoid, Delusional, Debasement, Anxiety, Schizotypal, Thought Disorder, Paranoid, Major Depression, Dysthymia	et al., 2004)
	In-Basket	
	Written Communication, Problem Analysis, Sensitivity, Initiative, Fact Finding, Total Score	
Flexibility	**Subjective adjustment (SA)**	(Matsumoto
	Personal Opinion Questionnaire (POQ)	et al., 2003)
	Dyadic Adjustment Scale (DAS)	
	Dyadic Satisfaction (DS), Affectional Expression (AE)	
	Satisfaction with Life Scale (SWLS)	
	Language Score	
	Text skill, Overall language skill	
	Income	
	Millon Clinical Multiaxial Inventory-II (MCMI-II)	(Matsumoto
	Compulsive, Dependent, Histrionic, Desirability, Bipolar Manic	et al., 2004)
Critical Thinking	**Social Adjustment Scale Self-Report (SAS-SR)**	(Matsumoto
	House work	et al., 2003)
	Dyadic Adjustment Scale (DAS)	
	Total score	
	Satisfaction with Life Scale (SWLS)	
	GPA	
	Working or not	
	Millon Clinical Multiaxial Inventory-II (MCMI-II)	(Matsumoto
	Aggressive, Antisocial, Histrionic, Narcissistic, Drug Dependence	et al., 2004)
	In-Basket	
	Sensitivity	

Conceptually we suggested that ER was a gatekeeper skill because it is necessary for people to manage inevitable intercultural conflict and that once emotions were regulated individuals could engage in critical thinking and assimilation of new cognitive schemas that aid in adjustment. Various outcomes across all studies supported this contention because, as shown in Table 2, ER predicted most of the adjustment measures relative to the other ICAPS scales. In addition, hierarchical multiple regressions indicated that ER accounted for most of the variance in various adjustment outcomes when entered first in the regression; the additional variance accounted for by OP, FL, and CT was always negligible (Matsumoto et al., 2003).

At the same time the strong findings for ER do not argue against the importance of OP, FL, and CT. Theoretically these skills make sense in understanding intercultural adjustment. Thinking out of the box and examining rival hypotheses to understand uncommon behavior, which is necessary in intercultural adjustment, cannot occur without CT. Assimilation of new cognitive schemas of the world cannot occur without OP and FL. That the empirical relationships of these factors to adjustment indices were not as strong as that for ER may be related to their factor order and lower proportion of variance accounted for relative to ER. Despite this fact these scales still emerged with significant betas in a number of the regression analyses including ER.

5.2. Personality Traits Associated with Intercultural Adjustment Potential

In our previous studies we also examined correlations between each of the ICAPS scores with personality dimensions (summarized in Table 3). The ICAPS scores converge with a number of personality dimensions. For example, correlations with the personality traits of the Five Factor Model (Matsumoto et al., 2004) indicated that ER was correlated with Neuroticism, which measures a person's inability to regulate emotion in a normal fashion (Costa & McCrae, 1992). OP was correlated with Openness because it was constructed to be similar to Openness as measured in tests of the big five dimensions of personality. FL was negatively correlated with Conscientiousness because persons in the high ranges of Conscientiousness are characterized by rigidity in behavior and thought.

The ICAPS scores were also correlated with other personality traits. ER was correlated with the social ascendancy scales of the CPI as those are indicators of positive social skills and abilities. ER was also correlated with CPI Realization as it is associated with success in life, and negatively with Internality because it measures a tendency to withdraw from active involvement with the social world. ER was also correlated with the normative behavior scales of the CPI as most of these scales are indicative of internal organization, which leads to successful coping with one's culture of origin. ER and CT were associated with CPI scales measuring achievement and ability as these are aspects of successful coping, and self application requiring self-discipline and the ability to think critically, which are aspects of what we believe those parts of ICAPS measure. Finally ER, OP, and CT were positively correlate with CPI Psychological Mindedness as it predicts the dispassionate ability to analyze social situations and the mental processes required to cope in general, control one's own emotions, an openness to the various attributes of self, others and unique situations, as well as a capacity to think critically. These correlations and those reported in Table 3 provide a fairly comprehensive picture of the personality skills related to intercultural adjustment.

Table 3. Personality Dimensions that are associated with the ICAPS Scales

ICAPS factor	Personality Scale	Citation
Emotion Regulation	**Big Five Inventory (BFI)** Extraversion, Agreeableness, Neuroticism **California Personality Inventory (CPI)** *Social Ascendancy* Dominance, Capacity for status, Sociability, Social presence, Self-acceptance, Independence, Empathy *Normative Behavior* Tolerance, Sense of well-being, Communality, Responsibility, Socialization, Self-control, Good impression *Achievement* Achievement via Independence, Intellectual efficiency, Achievement via conformance *Miscellaneous* Flexibility, Psychological mindedness, Femininity (–) *Factor Scores* Internality (–), Realization **Social Opinion Questionnaire (SOQ)** Altruism **Myers-Briggs Type Indicator (MBTI)** Sensing-Intuition, Extroversion-Introversion	(Matsumoto et al., 2004) (Matsumoto et al., 2004)
Flexibility	**Big Five Inventory (BFI)** Extraversion, Agreeableness, Conscientiousness, Openness **California aPersonality Inventory (CPI)** *Social Ascendancy* Dominance, Sociability, Social presence, Independence, Empathy *Normative Behavior* Sense of well-being, Socialization, Self-control, Good impression *Achievement* Achievement via conformance *Miscellaneous* Flexibility, Psychological mindedness, Femininity (–) *Factor Scores* Internality (–), Norm-favoring **Social Opinion Questionnaire (SOQ)** Altruism (–)	

Continued

Table 3. Personality Dimensions that are associated with the ICAPS Scales—cont'd

ICAPS factor	Personality Scale	Citation
Flexibility	**Myers-Briggs Type Indicator (MBTI)** Sensing-Intuition, Extroversion-Introversion, Thinking-Feeling **Big Five Inventory (BFI)** Extraversion (−), Agreeableness (−), Conscientiousness (−) **California Personality Inventory (CPI)** *Social Ascendancy* Capacity for status, Social presence, Self-acceptance, Empathy *Normative Behavior* Communality, Responsibility, Socialization, Self-control *Achievement* Achievement via conformance *Miscellaneous* Flexibility, Psychological mindedness, Femininity *Factor Scores* Norm-favoring	(Matsumoto et al., 2004)
Critical Thinking	**Myers-Briggs Type Indicator (MBTI)** Sensing-Intuition, Judging-Perceiving **Big Five Inventory (BFI)** Agreeableness **California Personality Inventory (CPI)** *Social Ascendancy* Capacity for status *Normative Behavior* Tolerance, Sense of well-being, Communality, Responsibility, Socialization, Self-control, Good impression *Achievement* Achievement via Independence, Intellectual efficiency, Achievement via conformance *Miscellaneous* Flexibility, Psychological mindedness, *Factor Scores* Internality, Norm-favoring, Realization **Social Opinion Questionnaire (SOQ)** Altruism **Myers-Briggs Type Indicator (MBTI)** Sensing-Intuition, Extroversion-Introversion, Thinking-Feeling	(Matsumoto et al., 2004)

Note: (−) indicates negative correlation.

5.3. Studies Using the ICAPS by Others

Findings documenting the validity of the ICAPS to predict adjustment have also been reported by other laboratories. For instance Savicki et al. (in press) investigated actual and potential intercultural adjustment using the ICAPS. His purpose was four fold: (1) To compare ICAPS and adjustment scores of study abroad students (SA) with those of students who stay at home (Home) at the beginning and the end of the study abroad semester; (2) To examine whether ICAPS scores of SA at pre-departure predict adjustment at the end of the foreign culture sojourn; (3) To examine whether ICAPS and personal adjustment scores of SA increase over their stay in a foreign culture; and (4) to examine whether ICAPS and personal adjustment are related to personality characteristics and preferred coping strategies.

A group of 19 students from an American university who studied abroad for three months (SA) were matched with 46 students who stayed in the U.S. during the same semester (Home). The groups were matched for age (19 to 25, with 83% in the 20-22 range), gender (54% women), and class standing (all juniors and seniors). They completed ICAPS, the Satisfaction with Life Scale (SWLS), a Five Factor Personality Questionnaire, the Life Orientation Test (LOT), and scales assessing Hope and Coping. SA students' voluntary participation was requested at four points in time: within one month prior to departure for their study abroad experience, during the beginning, middle, and end of the academic term of the study abroad experience.

The results indicated that the SA group was higher than Home students on ICAPS-55, ER, and SWLS at the beginning of the semester, and on ER, CT, and SWLS at the end of the semester (Savicki, Downing-Burnette, Heller, Binder, & Suntinger, in press). ICAPS-55 and ER predicted higher personal adjustment approximately four months later at the end of the academic term in the SA group (Savicki et al., in press). This finding supported the predictive validity of the ICAPS-55 score and the notion that ER may be a "gatekeeper" for intercultural adjustment potential (Matsumoto et al., 2001). As to the changes in the SA group, FL and SWLS increased at a statistically significant level between pre-departure and the end of the term (Savicki et al., in press).

Finally, a similar pattern of correlations appeared for the ICAPS-55 and ER with personality and coping variables (Savicki et al., in press). Those who had higher ICAPS-55 and ER scores were outgoing, open to new experiences, positive in outlook, and hopeful of one's abilities and of potential outcomes. In addition, they applied specific strategies of dealing with stress that focused on actively planning and carrying out actions to directly reduce stress, as well as developing a positive framework for stressful situations. They were also less anxious, less negative in their outlook, less likely to ignore or withdraw from unpleasant events in the foreign culture. These findings were especially important because they were generated by researchers outside of our laboratory, and they, too, demonstrated the significance of the ICAPS in intercultural adjustment.

6. CONCLUSION

In this chapter, we reported recent work from our laboratory spanning 17 studies on the development and validation of a new measure of intercultural adjustment – the ICAPS. Focusing initially on sojourners from Japan, our studies suggested that the ICAPS is a highly valid and reliable measure to predict adjustment success for students, businesspersons, housewives, and individuals involved in intercultural marriages. Further tests indicated its validity for predicting adjustment in sojourners from other cultures as well. These findings in toto lead us to believe that the psychological constructs identified by the ICAPS are applicable to predicting intercultural success for sojourners from many different cultures. Individuals with the potential to adjust to life well in another culture are good at regulating emotions, open and flexible to new experience, and able to think critically. The availability of the ICAPS, and other measures like it, promises to continue to make a significant contribution to intercultural relations for years to come, and its findings point to the importance of certain key psychological skills important for adjustment.

REFERENCES

Babiker, I.E., Cox, J.L., & Miller, P. (1980). The measurement of cultural distance and its relationship to medical consultations, symptomatology and examination of performance of overseas students at Edinburgh University. *Social Psychiatry, 15*, 109-116.

Berry, J. (1994). Acculturation and psychological adaptation. In A. M. Bouvy, F. J. R. v. d. Vijver, P. Boski & P. Schmitz (Ed.), *Journeys into cross-cultural psychology* (pp.129-141). Lisse, Netherlands: Swets and Zeitlinger.

Berry, J., & Sam, D. (1997). Acculturation and adaptation. In J. W. Berry, M. H. Segall & C. Kagitcibasi (Ed.), *Handbook of cross-cultural psychology, Vol 3: Social and behavioral applications*. Boston, MA: Allyn and Bacon.

Black, J.S., & Stephens, G.K. (1989). The influence of the spouse on American expatriate adjustment and intent to stay in Pacific Rim overseas assignments. *Journal of Management, 15*(529-544).

Brislin, R. (1981). *Cross-cultural encounters*. New York: Pergamon.

Buck, R.W. (1984). *The communication of emotion*. New York: Guilford Press.

Costa, P.T., & McCrae, R.R. (1992). *Revised Neo-Personality Inventory (NEO-PI-R) and Neo Five Factor Inventory (NEO-FFI)*. Odessa, FL: Psychological Assessment Resources.

DeLongis, A., Folkman, S., & Lazarus, R. (1988). The impact of daily stress on health and mood: Psychological and social resources as mediators. *Journal of Personality and Social Psychology, 54*(3), 486-495.

Furukawa, T., & Shibayama, T. (1994). Factors influencing adjustment of high school students in an international exchange program. *Journal of Nervous and Mental Disease, 182*(12), 709-714.

Gao, G., & Gudykunst, W. (1991). Uncertainty, anxiety, and adaptation. *International Journal of Intercultural Relations, 14*(3), 301-317.

Hammer, M., Gudykunst, W.B., & Wiseman, R.L. (1978). Dimensions of intercultural effectiveness: An exploratory study. *International Journal of Intercultural Relations, 2*, 382-393.

Kamal, A.A., & Maruyama, G. (1990). Cross-cultural contact and attitudes of Qatari students in the United States. *International Journal of Intercultural Relations, 14*, 123-134.

Kanner, A. D., Coyne, J. C., Schaefer, C., & Lazarus, R. (1981). Comparison of two modes of stress measurement: Daily hassles and uplifts versus major life events. *Journal of Behavioral Medicine, 4*, 1-39.

Matsumoto, D. (1999). *Nihonjin no Kokusai Tekiouryoku*. Tokyo: Hon no Tomosha.

Matsumoto, D., LeRoux, A.J., Bernhard, R., & Gray, H. (2004). Personality and behavioral correlates of intercultural adjustment potential. *International Journal of Intercultural Relations, 28*(3-4), 281-309.

Matsumoto, D., LeRoux, A.J., Iwamoto, M., Choi, J., Rogers, D., Tatani, H., & Uchida, H. (2003). The robustness of the intercultural adjustment potential scale (ICAPS): the search for a universal psychological engine of adjustment. *International Journal of Intercultural Relations, 27*, 543-562.

Matsumoto, D., LeRoux, J., Ratzlaff, C., Tatani, H., Uchida, H., Kim, C., & Araki, S. (2001). Development and validation of a measure of intercultural adjustment potential in Japanese sojourners: The Intercultural Adjustment Potential Scale (ICAPS). *International Journal of Intercultural Relations, 25*, 483-510.

Montagliani, A., & Giacalone, R.A. (1998). Impression management and cross-cultural adaptation. *Journal of Social Psychology, 138*(5), 598-608.

Okazaki-Luff, K. (1991). On the adjustment of Japanese sojourners: Beliefs, contentions, and empirical findings. *International Journal of Intercultural Relations, 15*(1), 85-102.

Pederson, P. (1995). *The five stages of culture shock: Critical incidents around the world.* Westwood, CT: Greenwood Press.

Rudmin, F.W. (2003a). Critical history of the acculturation psychology of assimilation, separation, integration, and marginalization. *Review of General Psychology, 7*(1), 3-37.

Rudmin, F.W. (2003b). "Critical history of the acculturation psychology of assimilation, separation, integration, and marginalization": Correction to Rudmin (2003). *Review of General Psychology, 7*(3), 250.

Savicki, V., Downing-Burnette, R., Heller, L., Binder, F., & Suntinger, W. (in press). Contrasts, changes, and correlates in actual and potential intercultural adjustment.

Shin, H., & Abell, N. (1999). The homesickness and contentment scale: Developing a culturally sensitive measure of adjustment for Asians. *Research on Social Work Practice, 9*(1), 45-60.

Stone Feinstein, E., & Ward, C. (1990). Loneliness and psychological adjustment of sojourners: New perspectives on culture shock. In D. M. Keats, D. Munro & L. Mann (Ed.), *Heterogeneity in cross-cultural psychology* (pp. 537-547). Lisse, Netherlands: Swets and Zeitlinger.

Tomkins, S.S. (1962). *Affect, imagery, and consciousness (Vol. 1: The positive affects).* New York: Springer.

Tomkins, S.S. (1963). *Affect, imagery, and consciousness (Vol. 2: The negative affects).* New York: Springer.

Ward, C. (2001). The A, B, Cs of Acculturation. In D. Matsumoto (Ed.), *Handbook of Culture and Psychology* (pp. 411-446). New York: Oxford University Press.

Section 4

Culture, Coping, and Resilience

17

HARDINESS CONSIDERED ACROSS CULTURES

Salvatore R. Maddi and Richard H. Harvey

1. INTRODUCTION

By now, hardiness has been established through much research to be a particular pattern of attitudes and skills that facilitates resilience under stressful circumstances (e.g., Maddi, 1994, 1999, 2002; Maddi & Khoshaba, 2005; Maddi & Kobasa, 1984). Hardiness appears to be the courage, motivation, and strategies to turn stressful circumstancs from potential disasters into growth opportunities instead. It is time now to consider whether the significance of hardiness differs, or needs to be interpreted differently across cultures.

2. CURRENT KNOWLEDGE ABOUT HARDINESS

In the 25 years since hardiness was discovered, there has been considerable theorizing and research concerning its role in maintaining or enhancing performance, conduct, stamina, and health under stressful circumstances. Issues have emerged and been resolved, results have accumulated, and progress has been made in assessment and training.

2.1. Discovery of hardiness

Hardiness was discovered in the 12-year, longitudinal study at Illinois Bell Telephone (IBT) that began in 1975 (Maddi & Kobasa, 1984). A representative sample of 450 managers was tested extensively, both psychologically and medically, every year, in anticipation of the expected federal deregulation of the telephone industry in order to stimulate more rapid telecommunications development. In 1981, the deregulation occurred, with cataclysmic stressful change that is still regarded as among the major upheavals in corporate history.

In the wake of the upheaval, two-thirds of the IBT sample fell apart. There were heart attacks, strokes, cancer, mental disorders, violence in the workplace, suicides, and divorces. In contrast, the other third of the sample not only survived, but also thrived.

Salvatore R. Maddi and Richard H. Harvey University of California, Irvine

These employees actually found the dramatic changes imposed by the deregulation to provide a needed context for their ingenuity, self-confidence, and creativity, in the process of turning the stresses into growth opportunities for themselves and the company. Their performance, conduct, stamina, and health flourished as it had not before the upheaval. It was the psychological differences between the resilient and non-resilient sub-samples, measured before the upheaval took place, that illuminated the attitudes and skills of hardiness.

2.2. Hardy attitudes and skills

In the IBT and later studies, the hardy attitudes have emerged as the 3Cs of commitment, control, and challenge (e.g., Maddi, 2002; Maddi & Kobasa, 1984). If you are strong in commitment, you want to stay involved with the people and events in your world, even when the going gets rough, because that seems to you the way to maintain and find meaning in your life. Pulling back into isolation and alienation seems like a mistake. If you are strong in control, you want to keep trying to influence the outcomes going on around you, even if that is difficult, because that keeps you involved in your life. Sinking into powerless and passivity is not an answer for you. If you are strong in challenge, you think of stress and change as inevitable, and an opportunity to grow by finding new avenues of meaning, and learning more about experience and life. Expecting easy comfort and security in an unchanging world seems naïve to you.

It is the interactive combination of commitment, control, and challenge that defines hardiness as the existential courage to face stressful circumstances openly and directly, and the motivation to do the hard work of dealing with them constructively (e.g., Khoshaba & Maddi, 2001; Maddi, 2002). Important in this constructive process is hardy, or transformational coping (Maddi & Kobasa, 1984), which involves interpreting each stressful circumstance that is encountered as a problem that needs to be solved by your ingenuity. This hardy coping is in contrast to addressing the stresses by the regressive coping approach (Maddi & Kobasa, 1984) of denying and avoiding, or the destructive coping approach (Maddi, 2004) of catastrophizing and striking out. Whatever short term relief these regressive or destructive approaches may bring, they are much less effective in the long run than is hardy coping (Khoshaba & Maddi, 2001).

Another hardy skill concerns interacting with significant others in a fashion that enhances one's sense of social support (Maddi & Kobasa, 1984; Khoshaba & Maddi, 2001). To do this, you must identify and resolve conflicts with significant others, and replace them with a pattern of giving and getting assistance and encouragement, while avoiding competition or overprotection. Clearly, conflicts and competition undermine the process whereby assistance and encouragement characterize the relationship. It is also true, though perhaps less obvious, that overprotection has an undermining effect, as its message to the person receiving it is that he/she is not capable of functioning effectively and needs others to do it instead.

The third set of hardy skills (Maddi & Kobasa, 1984; Khoshaba & Maddi, 2001) involve self-care aimed at maintaining a level of organismic arousal that is optimal for the hardy coping and social interaction efforts. This pattern of self-care includes hardy use of relaxation techniques, and nutrition and exercise patterns. The overall aim here is not to moderate weight as much as to ensure an optimal level of energy—not too high or too low—whereby the hard work of hardy coping and social interaction will be facilitated (Khoshaba & Maddi, 2001).

2.3. Early criticisms of hardy attitudes

The original measure of hardy attitudes that emerged from the IBT study, called the Personal Views Survey (PVS), was comprised of six available scales from other tests that seemed relevant to commitment, control, and challenge (cf., Maddi, 1997). It was this questionnaire that led to the early criticisms that hardiness (1) was not a unitary characteristic, as the challenge component was unrelated to the commitment and control components in some samples, and (2) was little more than the opposite of negative affectivity, or neuroticism (Funk & Houston, 1987; Hull, Van Treuren & Virnelli, 1987). As to the alleged non-unitary quality of hardy attitudes, the major difficulty emerged as due to one of the scales used to measure challenge. The items on this scale appeared to be interpreted differently by college students than by working adults, leading to a unitary measure in the latter population, but a non-unitary situation in the former population (cf., Maddi, 1997). As to the alleged redundancy of hardiness with negative affectivity, the problem appeared to be that several of the scales initially used to measure the former characteristic included only negatively worded items (cf., Maddi, 1997).

The original hardy attitudes measure was quickly supplanted by the Personal Views Survey, Second Edidtion (PVS II), and this seemed to ameliorate both problems (cf., Maddi, 1997). In particular, the PVS II included only items written specifically for relevance to hardiness (rather than incorporating scales already in use for other purposes), and used close to an equal number of positively and negatively worded items for the components of commitment, control, and challenge. As expected, the PVS II characteristically yields estimates of the three components that are positively interrelated in samples not only of working adults and college students, but even of high school students (e.g., Maddi & Hess, 1992; Maddi, Wadhwa & Haier, 1996).

Further, there are studies showing that the PVS II does not appear to be redundant with negative affectivity. For example, the pattern of negative relationships between hardy attitudes and the clinical scales of the Minnesota Multiphasic Personality Inventory persists even after controlling for a standard measure of negative affectivity (Maddi & Khoshaba, 1994). This suggests that though hardiness is indeed a measure of mental health, its measurement effectiveness in this regard does not depend on shared variance with negative affectivity. And, in a study (Maddi, Khoshaba, Harvey, Lu & Persico, 2001) involving the NEO-FFI (Costa & McCrae, 1989), hardiness is not only negatively related to neuroticism, but also positively related to all four of the other factors in the Five Factor Model. As these five factors are independent of each other, it would be difficult to conclude that hardiness is nothing more than a negative indicator of neuroticism or negative affectivity. Furthermore, in the attempt to use it as a predictor, the NEO-FFI explained only about one-third of the variance of hardiness, suggesting that the latter variable may be substantially unexplained by the Five Factor Model. Also, the findings of a recent methodological study (Sinclair & Tetrick, 2000) speak against both early criticisms by confirming that, commitment, control, and challenge, as expected, are best regarded as related subcomponents of a higher order hardiness factor, and that this factor is empirically distinct from negative affectivity or neuroticism.

2.4. Conceptual comparison with other relevant variables

At a conceptual level, there are other concepts in psychology that appear similar enough to hardiness to provoke some consideration at this point. Examples of such concepts are ego-strength (Barron, 1953), self-efficacy (Bandura, 1977, 1982, 1986), optimism (Scheirer & Carver, 1985; Seligman, 1991), resiliency (Jew, Green & Kroger, 1999), and religiousness (Bergin, 1983; Wallace & Forman, 1998). Suffice it to say that such considerations as self-confidence and self-esteem are too general, non-technical, and devoid of a place in systematic psychological theorizing to warrant discussion here. Self-confidence and self-esteem are arguably part of hardiness, ego-strength, self-efficacy and optimism, but are too general to make any specific contribution.

The terminology of ego-strength comes from psychoanalytic theory. In that theory, one's ego is strong if it helps in the process of defending against awareness of selfish desires by channeling them through behaviors that appear socially appropriate instead (cf., Maddi, 1969/1996). This is not, however, what the ego-strength concept came to mean in psychological research. Barron's (1953) Ego-Strength (Es) scale, which is part of the Minnesota Multiphasic Personality Inventory (Hathaway & McKinley, 1967), has been described as a coping process bringing "adaptational capacity" and "situational control" (Dahlstrom, Welsh, & Dahlstrom, 1975). As such, ego-strength should be relevant to dealing effectively with stresses, thus facilitating performance and health (Folkman & Lazarus, 1988). Thus, even though ego-strength is not very salient in psychological research these days, it is as a concept somewhat similar to hardiness.

Conceptually, self-efficacy derives primarily from behavioristic theory. According to Bandura (1977, 1982, 1986), self-efficacy is very specific, involving judgments made of one's capacity to efficaciously perform specific, particular tasks. Presumably, one's level of self-efficacy in a particular circumstance reflects prior relevant experiences with similar situations, rather than a generalized component of personality. As such, if there were to be measures to self-efficacy, they would have to be very specific to the task at hand, and thus reflect a "microanalytic methodology" (Bandura & Adams, 1977). This position expresses the behavioristic unwillingness to conceptualize anything as general as a personality disposition (Maddi, 1969/1996). Nonetheless, someone less behavioristic might wish to consider the sum of all the specific self-efficacies that exist in a person, and conceptualize this as his or her characteristic self-efficacy. Such a measure has actually been developed by Bernard, Hutchison, Lavin and Pennington (1996). Their measure (S-Ef) may be similar to the control component of hardiness, though it is conceptually unclear whether there is any similarity with the commitment and challenge components.

Also deriving from behaviorism is the concept of optimism, which is defined as the expectancy that in most situations one will be able to attain desired goals (Seligman, 1991). Once again, this expectancy level summarizes one's past experiences in interacting with particular tasks and stresses. Although hardiness is a much more elaborated concept (combining the components of commitment, control, and challenge), there is a similarity of this concept with optimism. After all, if hardiness leads one to have the courage and skills to deal effectively with stressful circumstances, that should result in general optimism. It may be, however, that optimism may verge for some people on naïve complacency. Fortunately, there are several optimism scales (Fibel & Hale, 1978; Carver, Schierer, & Weintraub, 1989) that can be compared to the hardiness measure.

Typically, resilience has been considered the act of surviving despite stressful circumstances (Bonanno, 2004), and has tended to emphasize youngsters. In this position, it has been assumed that there are various factors, notably social support and hardiness, that are pathways to resiliency (Bonanno, 2004). In this approach, resilience would be measured by continuing to function well despite traumatic disruptions, and the various pathways that facilitate this would be measured accordingly. But, some investigators have fallen into construing resiliency as a disposition helpful in functioning well under stress (Jew, Green & Kroger, 1999). This disposition is considered to incorporate as many as 12 attitudes and behavioral inclinations (Mrazek & Mrazek, 1987). There does not appear to be any particular, organized personality theory from which the 12 suggested components are derived. The enormous task of measuring dispositional resilience has been taken on by Jew, et al. (1999), whose four related studies have led to three overall factors, namely, future orientation, active skill acquisition, and independence/risk-taking, as the components of dispositional resiliency. These three factors related to other already applicable measures of stress-resistance (such as coping), and differentiated institutionalized from non-institutionalized adolescents. The items of this measure suggest some level of similarity with hardiness. If evidence of adequate reliability and validity accumulates for this index of dispositional resiliency, it will make sense to compare its predictive power to that of hardiness.

Lately, the emphasis of resiliency on maintaining health and performance under stress has been supplemented by the thought that traumatic events can actually deepen and enhance one's functioning. This extension is covered by the emphasis on post-traumatic growth (Aldwin & Levenson, 2004), and transformational coping (Aldwin, 1994). But, in these extensions, the emphasis on coping is much less specific than in hardiness theory. As to hardiness, transformational coping refers to a particular procedure of putting a stressful circumstance in perspective, deepening one's understanding of it, and then planning and implementing a plan of action that should be decisive in decreasing its stressfulness by turning it to advantage (Kobasa, et al., 1982; Maddi & Kobasa, 1984). In contrast, Aldwin's (1994) usage of the term "transformational coping" refers much more generally to somehow thriving rather than being undermined under stress.

Although not likely to be a personality disposition, religiousness is nonetheless a potentially important factor in dealing with stressful circumstances (Bergin, 1983; Wallace & Forman, 1998). Based on a belief in a God-figure and a credo concerning good versus bad values and actions that is given on high, religiousness has been shown to protect against painful emotions, while encouraging acceptable behaviors. As such, religiousness is considered a buffer against being undermined by difficult, stressful circumstances. But, by comparison with personality variables like hardiness, religiousness may lead to less flexible, adaptable behaviors, due to its basis in an all-powerful figure who dictates a given, unchangeable credo.

2.5. Empirical comparison of hardiness with other relevant variables

A particularly effective way to compare the empirical value of hardiness with these other concepts is comparative analysis (Maddi, 1969/1996). This approach involves pitting hardiness against one or more of the other concepts as independent variables in the attempt to explain mutually relevant dependent variables.

To date, such an analysis has been accomplished by comparing hardiness and optimism in their relative relationship to transformational and regressive coping (Maddi & Hightower, 1999). In the three studies involved, hardiness was measured by the PVS III, and optimism by the LOT (Scheier & Carver, 1985). The first study utilized an undergraduate sample, and the 15 scales from Carver, Scheier and Weintraub's (1989) COPE test as an index of coping style. The second study also involved an undergraduate sample, but coping was measured by Moos' Coping Response Inventory (1993). The sample in the third study comprised women who were about to receive biopsies in order to determine whether their breast lumps were malignant. Before the biopsy, they completed not only the PVS III and LOT, but also the COPE test. In all studies, hardiness and optimism (which showed an expected, moderately positive correlation) were entered into regression analyses as independent variables, and compared in their relationship to particular dependent variables. This approach purified hardiness and optimism of their shared variance, permitting conclusions as to which concept better relates to coping style.

In the first two studies, which involved the everyday stresses of student life, hardiness showed considerably more positive relationships to expressions of transformational coping and negative relationships to regressive coping (Maddi & Hightower, 1999), than did optimism. In the third study, which involved participants who were under great health stress, optimism increased in the number of its positive relationships to transformational coping styles, but still showed virtually no negative relationships to regressive coping styles (Maddi & Hightower, 1999). Nonetheless, by comparison to optimism, hardiness continued to show a slightly greater number of positive relationships to transformational coping, and a considerably greater number of negative relationships to regressive coping styles. Overall, hardiness emerged as a stronger predictor of effective coping than did optimism, suggesting that the latter concept may include not only a basis for trying harder but also for naïve complacency (Maddi & Hightower, 1999).

There is also a comparative analytic study (Maddi, Brow, Khoshaba, & Vaitkus, 2004) evaluating the relative power of hardiness and religiousness in minimizing depression and anger under stress. The sample was composed of US military officers at or above the rank of Colonel, who were attending a year of additional training at the War College. They completed the PVS III-R as to hardiness, the Duke Religiosity Index of religious spirituality and practice, the CED-D test of depression (Radloff, 1977) and the STAXI test of anger (Impara & Plake, 1998). As expected, hardiness and religiousness showed a small, but significant positive correlation. Regression analyses using hardiness and religiousness as independent variables (which purified each of the variance shared with the other), and depression and anger indices as dependent variables produced a pattern of results in which there were main effects for hardiness but not for religiousness. Specifically, hardiness was negatively related to depression and anger variables. There were also a few interaction effects which, when plotted, showed that only when hardiness is low did religiousness relate negatively to depression and anger. These results suggest that hardiness is more powerful than religiousness in protecting against painful emotions under stress. In this, it may be important that hardiness involves more flexibility and resourcefulness than the more tradition-based, unchangeable views in religiousness.

Unfortunately, there are not yet other comparative analytic studies of hardiness and other conceptually similar variables. The more typical approach is to study the interrelationships of these variables, and determine whether something further can be learned through factor analytic efforts. This approach was taken in the studies conducted by Bernard, et al. (1996). In the first study, they administered the personality measures of ego-strength, hardiness (an early version of the PSV utilized by Gentry and Kobasa, 1984), self-esteem, self-efficacy, optimism, and maladjustment to a sample of college students and adult volunteers. What emerged was a pattern of positive intercorrelations among the first five measures, and negative correlations with the sixth. Further, they conducted a factor analysis, which led to an emergent health promotion factor with two lower-order factors, which they labeled self-confidence and adjustment. Hardiness, along with ego-strength and maladjustment loaded on the lower-order adjustment factor. This suggests that hardiness is not merely the same as the self-confidence factor composed of self-esteem, self-efficacy, and optimism.

In the second study (Bernard, et al., 1996), a sample of undergraduates and adult volunteers were administered the same six personality measures, plus the NEO-FFI (Costa & McCrae, 1989) and the Crowne-Marlowe Social Desirability (SD) Scale (Crowne & Marlowe, 1964). The results showed a similar pattern of correlations among the six personality measures, plus a tendency for all of them to correlate positively with the SD scale, and either positively or negatively with the various factors of the NEO-FFI. The small, positive correlation obtained between hardiness and social-desirability in this study is inconsistent with the absence of relationship between these two variables shown in a study (Maddi, Harvey, Khoshaba, Lu, Persico & Brow, 2004) which utilized a later, more refined measure of hardiness. In the Bernard, et al (1996) study, the relationships shown by hardiness and the NEO-FFI involved not only a negative correlation with neuroticism, and but also a positive correlation with the other four factors. A similar pattern emerged in the study by Maddi, et al. (2002), and is one reason why hardiness, though expressive of adjustment and mental health, cannot be explained away as nothing more than the opposite of neuroticism.

In the third study (Bernard, et al., 1996), all six personality measures showed similar, and conceptually expected patterns of relationship with measures of stress, health status, and ways of coping in a sample of adult volunteers. The picture for hardiness is similar to that obtained in other studies (e.g., Maddi, 2002). In an attempt to further determine the overlap among personality measures, a fourth study was conducted (Bernard, et al., 1996). In this study, the samples from Studies 2 and 3 were combined, and factor analyses were performed on the 143 individual items of the ego-strength, hardiness, and maladjustment measures. One emerging factor was defined by the maladjustment scale, whereas the second factor consisted of ego-strength and hardiness items, and the third only of hardiness items. The authors point out that the second and third of these factors (i.e., without maladjustment items) have the same degree of association with the criterion measures of stress, health status, and coping as does the overall adjustment factor itself. This pattern suggests that the relationships of ego-strength and hardiness to criterion variables is not reflective of negative affectivity or neuroticism, and that ego-strength and hardiness are not merely the same thing.

In summary, the available findings suggest that hardiness, though understandably related to some similar positive psychology concepts, is not merely the same thing as these concepts, and may actually be a better predictor of effective coping with stressful circumstances. Needless to say, more comparative analytic studies are needed before this conclusion can shift from tentative to certain.

2.6. Our current measurement of hardiness

Our measurement of hardy attitudes has evolved even further over the years. The latest and best measure is the PVS III-R, which is composed of the 18 most reliable and valid items that have survived from the PVS II (Maddi & Khoshaba, 2001a). The commitment, control, and challenge components of hardiness are each measured by an equal number of positively and negatively worded items. Over many studies differing in stressfulness contexts and sample types, the PVS II and III-R have demonstrated adequate reliability, and both convergent and discriminant validity. The PVS III-R can be administered either in hard copy form or on the internet, and yields commitment, control, challenge, and total hardy attitudes scores. The individual scale scores for commitment, control, and challenge, and total hardiness are compared to norms for various demographic, work, and ethnic groups emerging from our extensive data base of more than 10,000 protocols. There is also a test manual (Maddi & Khoshaba, 2001a) that documents reliability and validity. By now, the PVS II and III-R have been translated into 16 European, Asian, and Middle Eastern languages. These translations are used around the world, to say nothing of the countries that use the original English versions.

We have also developed the HardiSurvey III-R, a 65-item questionnaire that adds to the PVS III-R measure of hardy attitudes indices of stress, strain, hardy (transformational) coping, regressive coping, hardy work support, and hardy family support (Maddi & Khoshaba, 2001b). Also administrable in either hard copy for or on the internet, this test yields not only scale scores for the variables just mentioned, but also combines them into stress vulnerability and stress resistance factors. Meant to be used in comprehensive assessment of the resiliency of individuals under stress, this test produces a detailed, personalized report that utilizes the norms from our database of more than 10,000 cases. Also available is a test manual (Maddi & Khoshaba, 2001b) that documents reliability and validity.

2.7. Other hardiness measures

As to the hardy attitudes, there are also other measures than our own in use. In particular, Bartone (1995), who was a member of our original research team in the IBT study, has done his own refining of the PVS over the years, in his research with military personnel under stress. The evolution has gone from a lengthy test (Bartone, Ursano, Wright, & Ingraham, 1989) to a shorter version (Bartone, 1995), called the Dispositional Resiliency Scale (DRS). This measure includes more positively than negatively worded items, which may lead to response biases influencing the overall score. In his emphasis on studying military personnel under stress, Bartone (2002) has obtained findings that are quite consistent in reliability and validity with those in the accumulated research utilizing the PVS in its various revisions. But, there has not been much emphasis yet on discriminant validation, such as demonstrating that the DRS measure is unrelated to socially desirable responding. Also, it is unclear at present how relevant the DRS is to non-military contexts.

From time to time, other investigators attempt development of their own hardiness measures. For example, Pollock and Duffy (1990) have offered a health-related hardiness scale intended to determine how patients respond to various illnesses. Similarly, Lang, Goulet and Amsel (2003) have put forward a 45-item hardiness scale considered relevant to evaluating how bereaved parents respond following the death of their fetus/infant. Conceptually, both scales follow from the assumption that hardiness is not a general feature of personality, but rather a specific inclination as to how to react in particular circumstances (as Bandura has done with his self-efficacy notion). To date, very little validity and reliability research has been done on these scales. Nor is it likely that they measure a general tendency toward courage in a large variety of circumstances, rather than just illness or death.

Structurally, these other hardiness scales include a predominance of positively worded items. Also, the wording of the items makes clear what the researcher is trying to find out about the person taking the test. This problem is furthered by the term "hardiness" being included in the title of the test. Thus, it will be all the more important in the validation process to determine not only convergent but also divergent validity, especially regarding such confounding tendencies as socially desirable responding. In contrast, the PVS II and III-R tend to disguise what the test is intended to reveal by more neutrally worded items that are balanced as to positive and negative wordings, and avoid reference to hardiness. Understandably, the PVS III-R shows independence of socially desirable responding (Maddi, et al., 2004).

2.8. Additional research on hardiness

Since the IBT longitudinal study, considerable ongoing research has tended to confirm that hardy attitudes maintain and enhance health under stressful circumstances. In these studies, the PVS II or III-R has been used to measure hardy attitudes, with the exception of some studies of military personnel, which have used the DRT. In a wide range of stressful contexts, ranging from life-threatening events of military combat and peace-keeping missions (e.g., Bartone, 1999), through the culture shock of immigration (e.g., Kuo & Tsai, 1986) or work missions abroad (e.g., Atella, 1989), to ongoing work or school pressures and demands (e.g., Maddi, 2002; Wedderburn, 1995), the buffering effect of hardy attitudes is shown in decreasing mental and physical illness symptoms, whether these be self-reported or more objectively measured.

Further, there is research showing that hardy attitudes lead to the maintenance and enhancement of performance under stress. Examples are the positive relationship between hardiness and subsequent (1) basketball performance among varsity players (Maddi & Hess, 1992), (2) success rates in officer training school for the Israeli military (Florian, Milkulincer & Taubman, 1995; Westman, 1990), (3) effective leadership behavior among West Point military cadets (Bartone & Snook, 1999), (4) retention rate among entering community college students (Lifton, Seay & Bushke, 2000), and (5) speed of recovery of baseline functioning following disruptive culture shock (Atella, 1989; Kuo & Tsai, 1986).

Supplementing the findings on health and performance exemplified above is research elaborating the construct validity of hardy attitudes. In an experiential sampling study (Maddi, 1999) in which participants were paged at random to comment on their ongoing activities, there was a positive relationship between hardiness and (1) involvement with others and events (commitment), (2) the sense that the activities had been chosen and could be influenced (control), and (3) the positive process of learning from what was going on (challenge). Findings of other studies are consistent with the hypothesis that hardy attitudes lead to beneficial health and performance effects by providing the courage and motivation needed to carry out hardy coping, social support, and self-care efforts (Maddi, 1986, 1994, 1997, 2002). For example, results show that hardy attitudes are related to the tendency to view stressful life events as more tolerable (Ghorbani, Watson & Morris, 2000;

Rhodewalt & Zone, 1989), cope transformationally with these events (Maddi, 1999; Maddi & Hightower, 1999), avoid excessive physiological arousal (Allred & Smith, 1989; Contrada, 1989), and pursue positive while avoiding negative health practices (Maddi, Wadhwa & Haier, 1996; Weibe & McCallum, 1986).

2.9. Hardiness training

Hardiness seems so important in resiliency under stress that the question arises as to whether it is inherited or learned. That it may be learnable was suggested by the finding using IBT data that, by comparison with the sub-sample that deteriorated under the deregulation upheaval, the sub-sample that survived and thrived described their early lives as stressful, but remembered being selected by their parents as the hope of the family, and as having taken on that role throughout their lives (Khoshaba & Maddi, 1999). The view that hardiness can be increased or decreased by life experiences does not signify that it must be other than a personality disposition. In all fully elaborated personality theories, there are some components that are present at birth, and others that develop through the interaction of the person with others and situations. There are many conceptualized personality dispositions (e.g., need for achievement, ego-strength, optimism, hardiness) that fit into this latter, developed category (cf., Maddi, 1969/1996).

There is by now a hardiness training procedure that was begun at IBT (Maddi, 1987) and has been substantially elaborated since then (Khoshaba & Maddi, 2001). Consistent with hardiness theory, this approach emphasizes assisting trainees in coping effectively with their stressful circumstances, interacting with others by giving and getting assistance and encouragement, engaging in self-care procedures that facilitate this coping and supportive interaction, and learning how to use the feedback obtained from these various efforts to deepen the hardy attitudes of commitment, control, and challenge (Khoshaba & Maddi, 2001). Evidence is accumulating that hardiness training is effective not only in increasing hardy attitudes, but also in enhancing performance, and decreasing illness symptoms for working adults (Maddi, 1987; Maddi, Kahn & Maddi, 1998) and college students (Maddi, Khoshaba, Jensen, Carter, Lu & Harvey, 2003).

3. THE CROSS CULTURAL SIGNIFICANCE OF HARDINESS

Now that hardiness is well established as a pattern of attitudes and skills that helps one remain resilient under stress, it is time to consider its significance across cultures. Conceptually, it would seem that hardiness is useful universally. After all, the stresses of personal development and every day life occur everywhere. Further, that we live in dramatically changing times imposes additional stresses on everyone in every culture.

3.1. Hardiness as conceptually universal

Conceptually, hardiness is based in existentialism (Maddi, 1978, 2002), which emphasizes that life's meaning is subjective, and is determined by the pattern of decisions people make on a moment-to-moment, day-to-day basis (Frankl, 1960; Kierkegaard, 1954).

Regardless of whether there is an absolute meaning in the world, all any of us know is what we construe as the result of our decisions. In this position, personal wisdom and development is dependent upon choosing the future (the path that is less familiar) rather than the past (holding on to one's already established ways of understanding). This is the case whether choices are our own doing, or are imposed on us by socio-environmental changes. But, the obstacle to regularly choosing the future is the ontological anxiety involved in the inherent stressfulness of the unpredictability and uncertainty that is involved (Kierkegaard, 1954). So, to tolerate anxiety in order to be able to continue to develop and deepen life's meaning by future-oriented decisions, one must have existential courage (Tillich, 1952).

Hardiness has been conceptualized and researched as this needed existential courage (Maddi, 1986/1996). In making future-oriented decisions despite the various stresses you are experiencing, you need to have the hardy attitudes of believing in the importance of staying involved with the people and events that are going on (commitment), trying to have an influence on outcomes (control), and searching to learn from your experiences all the while (challenge). After all, the absence of hardy attitudes will lead you to react to stressful circumstances by detachment and alienation, powerlessness and passivity, and a threatened yearning for easy comfort and security. Conceptually, therefore, the 3Cs of hardy attitudes should be helpful in courageously facing the uncertainty of experience.

In addition, the emphasis on the hardy skills of transformational coping, socially-supportive interactions, and self-care should also be helpful in managing the inevitable stresses of living. After all, the combination of hardy attitudes and skills leads toward solving problems, giving and getting assistance and encouragement, and maintaining optimal bodily arousal. In contrast, the absence of hardy attitudes and skills pushes one toward reacting to stresses by either denying and avoiding, or overreacting and striking out, and by self-indulgence rather than balance and moderation.

It seems likely that, in any demographic or culture, the hardy attitudes and skills would involve behavior patterns that are constructive in dealing with developmental or imposed stressful circumstances. In contrast, the behavior patterns resulting from non-hardy attitudes and skills would be disadvantageous in any demographic or culture. There may, of course, be particular ways in which hardiness will get expressed in differing demographics or cultures. But, hardiness is so basic to psychosocial wellbeing that it would be hard to conceptualize it as irrelevant or even a negative influence in some demographics or cultures.

To pursue this point a bit further, let us consider the conceptualization of living inherent in Buddhism and Daoism, which appear at first blush to be quite different from existentialism (Carr & Ivanhoe, 2000). On closer analysis, however, these positions are not really that different in implications for how people function (Abi-Hashem, 2000; Moeller & Stan, 2003). Buddhism assumes that if there is an absolute meaning to living, it is imperfectly or subjectively construed by individuals. Thus, the path to wisdom and development involves recognizing this imperfection and subjectivity, and attempting to rise above it by learning more through scrutinizing one's experiences. This is surprisingly similar to existentialism, which considers recognition that one constructs meaning, and that this meaning needs to change as experience accumulates. Although Buddhism does not explicitly emphasize courage, it does assume that there is strength in rising above the specifics of one's beliefs in the pursuit of greater wisdom. Buddhism and existentialism also share an emphasis on the wholeness of experience, rather than dichotomizing rationality and emotions (Moeller & Stan, 2003).

It is harder to determine whether the specific hardy attitudes and skills coordinate with or violate Buddhist assumptions. The emphasis of hardiness is on using one's beliefs and behaviors in staying involved with people and events, solving rather than being undermined by stressful circumstances, and continuing to learn from these experiences. There is little reason to believe that Buddhism and Daoism would advocate the opposite, namely, alienation, powerlessness, and easy comfort and security. Most probably, Buddhism and Daoism would be more likely to endorse hardy attitudes and behaviors than their opposite. This tentative conclusion is facilitated through recognition that the hardy attitudes include little of the egotism that you are better able to navigate life's problems than are those around you, and combine reason and emotions into wholistic outlooks that evolve over time.

3.2. The role of hardiness across demographics

As to demographics, let us consider sex, age, and socioeconomic status. First, let us compare males and females in their need for hardiness. It is, of course, easy to say that males need hardiness more than females, as the former sex seems traditionally more invested in the struggle for economic, social, and political success than does the latter sex. Even in our culture, however, this sexual distinction tells us little about how stressful is the life of the two sexes. Females certainly experience similar levels of stresses associated with the developmental process. As much as do males, females must, as children, learn to move around and communicate; as adolescents, struggle to find their own lives in terms of careers and relationships; in adulthood, build on or reverse earlier decisions and help others dependent on them to develop; and in old age, find a graceful though painful way of putting all their experiences together into a meaningful whole. There is little conceptual reason to believe that this developmental process is less or more stressful, or that hardiness plays a less important role in managing the stresses, for females than males. The same logic applies for stresses that are ongoing signs of changing times, rather than developmental givens, as there is little reason to believe that these changes affect one sex more than the other.

Nor is there reason to believe that some age categories are more or less stressful times than others. Regarding development, the particular nature of the stresses characteristic of childhood, adolescence, adulthood, and old age certainly differ. But, the level of stressfulness is not likely to differ across these age categories. For example, just learning how to locomote and communicate is likely to be as stressful for you as a child, due to limited cognitive capacities and experience, than is trying out what career is best for you in adolescence and adulthood. And, of course, the imposed stresses of changing times are very likely to find their way to your experience regardless of your age category.

The same appears true when socio-economic class is considered, though this is perhaps more problematic. It may well be argued, for example, that the economically poor lead more stressful lives than their financially advantaged counterparts. It may also be argued that people with minority status are more prone to experiencing stress than are their more socially advantaged counterparts. There is little question that the stresses of the developmental process and of changing times have quite an impact on minorities, especially if the situation is concatenated by discrimination. Nonetheless, whatever the level of stress is due to socio-economic differences, the role of hardiness is still similarly relevant to how well that stress will be turned to advantage.

It would appear that hardiness is similarly relevant to being resilient under stress across demographic differences. This does not mean, however, that there are not important demographic differences in the level of hardiness that is characteristically learned in the developmental process. It may be, for example, that females are less instilled with hardiness than males, at least in certain cultures. It is also quite possible that the learning conditions important to hardiness development are less consistently available the lower is one's socio-economic level. And, as hardiness development probably takes time to reach fruition, it is possible that younger people show less of this key to resilience than do adults.

3.3. The role of hardiness in individualistic and collectivistic cultures

Important in psychology these days is the comparison of lives within individualistic as opposed to collectivistic cultures. It is certainly worth considering whether there are differences across these two kinds of culture in the levels of stress experienced and of hardiness developed.

It might be argued that there is less stress on people in collectivistic than in individualistic cultures. After all, members of collectivistic cultures minimize the uncertainty of living through defining themselves in terms of their group more than do members of individualistic cultures. Developmentally, however, people in both types of culture have to figure out how to function and get along with each other. It may be that the content of the stresses is different across the two types of culture, but it is not completely certain that the level of developmentally induced stress is also different. And, it is also not so clear that the level of externally induced stress is characteristically different across these culture types. Indeed, it might even be argued that externally induced stresses have a greater disruptive impact on members of collectivistic cultures.

Nor is it clear that there is likely to be a difference in hardiness levels across individualistic and collectivistic cultures. After all, the hardy attitudes involve not only trying to have an influence on outcomes (control), and learning from your experience (challenge), but also staying involved with others and events going on around you (commitment). Further, the hardy skills of coping by solving problems, interacting by deepening patterns of assistance and encouragement, and engaging in self-care to maintain optimal arousal, seem as consistent with collectivistic as individualistic emphases in living. It seems that there is no clear conceptual basis for hypothesizing a difference in characteristic hardiness levels in people across these two types of culture.

Despite the position taken here, it may still be argued that hardiness differs in collectivistic and individualistic cultures. For example, collectivistic cultures appear to emphasize addressing stresses by endurance, patience, humility and flexibility. This may seem to downplay the control, and perhaps the challenge components of hardiness. But, it seems unlikely that one could manage the mental and action dispositions mentioned above, as stresses mount, without beliefs in the importance of controlling one's potentially disruptive emotional reactions, and of the challenge to a deepened understanding that will make one's approach meaningful. After all, endurance, patience, humility, and flexibility are hardly irrelevant reactions to stress in individualistic cultures. In these cultures, if one reacts by avoidance, impatience, egotism, or rigidity, one is not likely to be very successful in gaining the support and admiration of other people. In short, hardiness should not be construed as a naïve approach to getting ahead at the disregard and expense of those around us.

3.4. Preliminary findings

There appears no clear-cut conceptual basis for differentiating the relevance and role of hardiness across demographic variables and culture types. This does not mean, however, that there is no importance to seeking empirical answers to the universality or relativity of hardiness. At present, there are some preliminary findings that are available, though the emerging picture is not by any means complete.

In the original Illinois Bell study of working adults, there were no differences in hardiness observed across the demographic variables of age, sex, managerial rank, or ethnicity (Maddi & Kobasa, 1984). To date, the major source of relevant data is a study (Maddi, et al., 2004) of 1239 participants ranging in age from 17 to 85 years, socioeconomic status from lower to upper class, and education from high school to advanced degrees. The sample included 753 females (60.8%), and the breakdown of race was: Caucasian, 66.8%; Asian, 22.1%; and all others, 11.1%. All participants completed the HardiSurvey III-R, which measures hardy attitudes, hardy coping, hardy social support interactions, and stress. In the sample as a whole, the reliability and intercorrelation of these variables corresponded to what other research with this measure has shown.

Of particular relevance here are the relationships shown between hardiness and the relevant demographic and cultural variables that were available in this study. As to hardy attitudes, there is a positive relationship to age ($r = .20$, $p < .01$), and education ($r = .19$, $p < .01$), but no relationship with sex ($r = .07$, ns) or race ($r = .06$, ns). Stress was negatively related to hardy attitudes ($r = .10$, $p < .05$), but showed no differences across age, education, sex, or race. The relationships obtained between demographic variables and the hardiness components of commitment, control, and challenge follow the same pattern as those with total hardiness.

At this time, there are many studies of hardiness being carried out in various cultures around the world. The results of a few of these studies are already available. In particular, Kuo and Tsai (1986) reported that, in their sample of Asian immigrants to the U.S., the higher the hardiness level, the more rapid was the ability to cope effectively with the stress of culture-shock, and assimilate into the new society by finding jobs and friends. Similarly, hardiness was positively related to the psychological adaptation of married couples in a sample of Turkish immigrants in Canada (Ataca & Berry, 2002). Further, Lopez, Haigh and Burney (2004) have found that among Latin American immigrants in Australia, hardiness level was negatively related to the level of stress they reported experiencing. These results mirror those concerning U.S. citizens on a two-year work mission in China (Atella, 1989), wherein hardiness level was positively related to the speed at, and level to which their emotional state and performance rebounded after the initial culture shock.

Also relevant are two studies (Florian, et al., 1995; Westman, 1990) concerning Israeli military personnel entering officer-training school. Both studies showed that the higher the hardiness level, the greater the effectiveness in dealing with training stresses, and graduating successfully. These results are mirrored in a study (Bartone & Snook, 1999) showing that U.S. cadets at West Point Military Academy were more successful in leadership efforts the higher was their hardiness level at the beginning of training.

More complicated are the results of a study (Harris, 2004) comparing African American and Caucasian college students. It was found that the Caucasian subsample had a higher mean hardiness level than the African American subsample. Nonetheless, among the African Americans, hardiness was negatively related to use of drugs, tobacco, and alcohol, supporting previous evidence that hardiness leads to self-care (Weibe & McCallum, 1986). But, hardiness among the African Americans was positively related to personal distress reports of anger, stress, depression, and anxiety, which was the opposite result of that with Caucasians. Harris (2004) suggests that differences in cultural teachings may account for the racial differences found in the relationship of hardiness to personal distress. Perhaps African Americans in the US have a harder time believing that they can influence the societal outcomes going on around them, though, if they are hardy, they do think they can take care of their own health. One possible problem in this study may have been the use of the DRS to measure hardiness. This measure has been validated and used primarily on military samples, though Harris' sample was college students. Further, the DRS is composed primarily of positively-worded items, and there has not yet been sufficient study of its discriminant validity. Another possible problem with this study is that the challenge component of the hardiness measure was deleted, as it showed lower reliability than the other two. As hardiness is conceptualized as an emergent characteristic of the combination of all three Cs (Maddi, et al., 2004), deleting one of them is problematic. It would be helpful for there to be further study of African Americans with regard to stress management through coping and social support interactions.

In addition, there is a study (Ghorbani, et al., 2000) of Iranian business managers, showing that the higher their hardiness level, the better their performance and health despite stressful circumstances. These findings are similar to those obtained on U.S. business managers (e.g., Maddi & Kobasa, 1984; Maddi, 2002).

With one exception, the results of the studies mentioned here do not show cross-cultural differences in the role of hardiness as a facilitator of resilience and enhanced performance under stress. There may be mean differences in hardiness across races or societies, though there is not yet enough evidence to form definite conclusions. At the individual level, however, hardiness level appears to be a factor in resilience under stress across races and societies. Once again, this conclusion is tentative, as more relevant studies are needed.

4. CONCLUSION

There is certainly an accumulation of evidence indicating that hardiness is a key to transforming stressful circumstances from potential disasters into growth opportunities instead. As to the emerging question of whether there are demographic and cultural differences in the role of hardiness, there are only a few relevant findings at this time. Although these available findings suggest little or no demographic or cultural differences in the importance of hardiness in surviving and thriving under stress, much more work needs to be done before a firm conclusion can be reached.

REFERENCES

Abi-Hashem, N. (2000). Psychology, time, and culture. *American Psychologist, 55,* 342-343.

Aldwin, C. M. (1994). *Stress, coping, and development: An integrative perspective.* New York, NY: Guilford.

Aldwin, C. M. & Levenson, M. R. (2004). Posttraumatic growth: A developmentalperspective. *Psychological Inquiry, 15,* 19-92.

Allred, K. D., & Smith, T. W. (1989). The hardy personality: Cognitive and physiological responses to evaluative threat. *Journal of Personality and Social Psychology, 56,* 257-266.

Ataca, B. & Berry, J. W. (2002). Psychological, sociocultural, and marital adaptation of Turkish immigrant couples in Canada. *International Journal of Psychology, 37,*13-26.

Atella, M. (1989). *Crossing boundaries: Effectiveness and health among Western managers living in China.* Unpublished Ph.D. dissertation, University of Chicago.

Bandura, A. (1977). Self-efficacy: Toward a unifying theory of behavior change. *Psychological Review, 84,* 191-215.

Bandura, A. (1982). Self-efficacy mechanism in human agency. *American Psychologist, 37,* 122-147.

Bandura, A. (1986). *Social foundations of thought and action.* Englewood Cliffs, NJ: Prentice-Hall.

Bandura, A., Adams, N. E., & Beyer, J. (1977). Cognitive processes mediating behavioral change. *Journal of Personality and Social Psychology, 35,* 125-139.

Bonanno, G. A. (2004). Loss, trauma, and human resilience: Have we underestimated the human capacity to thrive after extremely aversive events? *American Psychologist, 59,* 20-28.

Barron, F. (1953). An ego strength scale which predicts response to psychotherapy. *Journal of Consulting Psychology, 17,* 327-333.

Bartone, P. T. (1999). Hardiness protects against war-related stress in army reserve forces. *Consulting Psychology Journal, 51,* 72-82.

Bartone, P. T. (2002). Hardiness as a resiliency resource under high stress conditions. In D. Paton, J. M. Violanti, & L. M. Smith (Eds.), *Promoting capabilities to manage posttraumatic stress.* Springfield, IL: Charles C. Thomas.

Bartone, P. T., & Snook, S. A. (1999, May). Cognitive and personality factors predict leader development in U.S. Army cadets. Paper presented at 35th International Applied Military Psychology Symposium (IAMPS), Florence, Italy.

Bergin, A. E. (1983). Religiosity and mental health: A critical reevaluation and meta-analysis. *Professional Psychology, 14,* 170-184.

Bernard, L. C., Hutchinson, S., Lavin, A., & Pennington, P. (1996). Ego-strength, hardiness, self-esteem, self-efficacy, optimism, and maladjustment: Health-related personality constructs and the "big five" model of personality. *Assessment, 3,* 115-131.

Carr, K. L. & Ivanhoe, P. J. (2000). *The sense of antirationalism: The religious thought of Zhuangzi and Kierkegaard.* New York, NY: Seven Bridges Press.

Carver, C. S., Scheier, M. F., & Weintraub, J. K. (1989). Assessing coping strategies: A theoretically-based approach. *Journal of Personality and Social Psychology, 56,* 267-283.

Contrada, R. J. (1989). Type A behavior, personality hardiness, and cardiovascular responses to stress. *Journal of Personality and Social Psychology, 57,* 895-903.

Costa, P. T., Jr., & McCrae, R. R. (1989). *NEO-PI/NEO-FFI manual supplement.* Odessa, FL: Psychological Assessment Resources.

Dahlstrom, W. G., Welsh, G. S., & Dahlstrom, L. E. (1975). *An MMPI workbook: Vol. II. Research applications.* Minneapolis, MN: University of Minnesota Press.

Fibel, B. & Hale, W. D. (1978). The Generalized Expectancy for Success Scale—a new measure. *Journal of Consulting and Clinical Psychology, 46,* 924-931.

Florian, V., Milkulincer, M., & Taubman, O. (1995). Does hardiness contribute to mental health during a stressful real life situation? The roles of appraisal and coping. *Journal of Personality and Social Psychology, 68,* 687-695.

Folkman, S. & Lazarus, R. S. (1988). *Manual for the Ways of Coping questionnaire.* Palo Alto, CA: Consulting Psychologists Press.

Frankl, V. (1960). *The doctor and the soul.* New York, NY: Knopf.

Funk, S. C., & Houston, B. K. (1987). A critical analysis of the hardiness scale's validity and utility. *Journal of Personality and Social Psychology, 53,* 572-578.

Gentry, W. D. & Kobasa, S. C. (1984). Social and psychological resources mediating stress-illness relationships in humans. In W. D. Gentry (Ed.), *Handbook of behavioral medicine* (pp. 87-116). New York: Guilford Press.

Ghorbani, N., Watson, P. J., & Morris, R. J. (2000). Personality, stress, and mental Health: Evidence of relationships in a sample of Iranian managers. *Personality and Individual Differences, 28,* 647-657.

Hathaway, S. R. & McKinley, J. C. (1967). *The Minnesota Multiphasic Personality Inventory manual-2.* New York, NY: Psychological Corporation.

Harris, S. M. (2004). The effect of health value and ethnicity on the relationship between hardiness and health behaviors. *Journal of Personality, 72,* 379-411.

Hull, J. G., Van Treuren, R. R., & Virnelli, S. (1987). Hardiness and health: A critique and alternative approach. *Journal of Personality and Social Psychology, 53,* 518-530.

Impara, J. C. & Plake, B. S. (Eds.), (1998). *The 13th mental measurement yearbook.* Lincoln, NB: University of Nebraska Press.

Jew, C. L., Green, K. E., & Kroger, J. (1999). Development and validation of a measure of resiliency. *Measurement and Evaluation in Counseling and Development, 32,* 748-774.

Khoshaba, D. M., & Maddi, S. R. (1999). Early experiences in hardiness development. *Consulting Psychology Journal, 51,* 106-116.

Khoshaba, D. M., & Maddi, S. R. (2001). *HardiTraining.* Newport Beach, CA: Hardiness Institute.

Kierkegaard, S. (1843, 1849/1954). *Fear and trembling and the sickness unto death.* Garden City, NY: Doubleday Anchor.

Kuo, W. H., & Tsai, Y. (1986). Social networking, hardiness, and immigrants' mental health. *Journal of Health and Social Behavior, 27,* 133-149.

Lang, A., Goulet, C., & Amsel, R. (2003). Lang and Goulet hardiness scale: Development and testing on bereaved parents following the death of their fetus/infant. *Death Studies, 27,* 851-880.

Lifton, D. E., Seay, S., & Bushke, A. (2000, Summer). Can student "hardiness" serve as an indicator or likely persistence to graduation? Baseline results from a longitudinal study. *Academic Exchange.*

Lopez, O., Haigh, C., & Burney, S. (2004). Relationship between hardiness and perceived stress in two generations of Latin American migrants. *Australian Psychologist, 39,* 238-243.

Maddi, S. R. (1969/96). *Personality theories: A comparative analysis.* (6th Ed.). Prospect Heights, IL: Waveland Press.

Maddi, S. R. (1970). The search for meaning. In M. Page (Ed.), *Nebraska symposium on motivation.* Lincoln, NB: University of Nebraska Press.

Maddi, S. R. (1978). Existential and individual psychologies. *Journal of Individual Psychology, 34,* 182-191.

Maddi, S. R. (1986/1996). Existential psychotherapy. In J. Garske & S. Lynn (Eds.), *Contemporary psychotherapy.* New York: Merrill Publishers.

Maddi, S. R. (1987). Hardiness training at Illinois Bell Telephone. In J. P. Opatz (Ed.). *Health promotion evaluation.* Stephens Point, WI: National Wellness Institute.

Maddi, S. R. (1994). The Hardiness Enhancing Lifestyle Program (HELP) for improving physical, mental, and social wellness. In C. Hooper (Ed.), *Wellness lecture series.* Oakland, CA: University of California/HealthNet.

Maddi, S. R. (1997). Personal Views Survey II: A measure of dispositional hardiness. In C. P. Zalaqauett & R. J. Woods (Eds.), *Evaluating stress: A book of resources.* New York, NY: University Press.

Maddi, S. R. (1999). The personality construct of hardiness, I: Effects on experiencing, coping, and strain. *Consulting Psychology Journal, 51,* 83-94.

Maddi, S. R. (2002). The story of hardiness: Twenty years of theorizing, research, and practice. *Consulting Psychology Journal, 54,* 173-185.

Maddi, S. R. (2004). Hardiness: An operationalization of existential courage. *Journal of Humanistic Psychology, 44,* 279-298.

Maddi, S. R. (2005). On hardiness and other pathways to resilience. *American Psychologist,* in press.

Maddi, S. R., & Hess, M. (1992). Hardiness and success in basketball. *International Journal of Sports Psychology, 23,* 360-368.

Maddi, S. R., & Hightower, M. (1999). Hardiness and optimism as expressed in coping patterns. *Consulting Psychology Journal, 51,* 95-105.

Maddi, S. R., & Khoshaba, D. M. (1994). Hardiness and mental health. *Journal of Personality Assessment, 63,* 265-274.

Maddi, S. R., & Khoshaba, D. M. (2001a). *Personal Views Survey III-R: Test development and internet instruction manual.* Newport Beach, CA: Hardiness Institute.

Maddi, S. R., & Khoshaba, D. M. (2001b). *Hardi Survey III-R: Test development and internet instruction manual.* Newport Beach, CA: Hardiness Institute.

Maddi, S. R., & Khoshaba, D. M. (2005). *Resilience at work: How to succeed no matter what life throws at you.* New York, NY: Amacom.

Maddi, S. R., & Kobasa, S. C. (1984). *The hardy executive: Health under stress.* Homewood, IL: Dow Jones-Irwin.

Maddi, S. R., Kahn, S., & Maddi, K. L. (1998). The effectiveness of hardiness training *Consulting Psychology Journal, 50,* 78-86.

Maddi, S. R., Wadhwa, P., & Haier, R. J. (1996). Relationship of hardiness to alcohol and drug use in adolescents. *American Journal of Drug and Alcohol Abuse, 22,* 247-257.

Maddi, S. R., Brow, M., Khoshaba, D. M., & Vaitkus, M. (2004). The relationship of hardiness and religiousness in depression and anger. *Consulting Psychology Journal,* in press.

Maddi, S. R., Khoshaba, D. M., Harvey, R. H., Lu, J. L., & Persico, M. (2001). The personality construct of hardiness, II: Relationships with comprehensive tests of personality and psychopathology. *Journal of Research in Personality, 36,* 72-85.

Maddi, S. R., Khoshaba, D. M., Jensen, K., Carter, E., Lu, J. L., & Harvey, R. H. (2002). Hardiness training for high risk undergraduates. *NACADA Journal, 22,* 45-55.

Maddi, S. R., Harvey, R. H., Khoshaba, D. M., Lu, J. L., Persico, M., & Brow, M. (2004). The personality construct of hardiness, III: Relationships with repression, innovativeness, authoritarianism, and performance. Submitted.

Moeller, H. & Stan, L. (2003). On Zhuangzi and Kierkegaard. *Philosophy East and West, 53,* 130-135.

Moos, R. H. (1993). *Coping Response Inventory.* Odessa, FL: Psychological Assessment Resources.

Mrazek, P. J. & Mrazek, D. (1987). Resilience in child maltreatment victims: A conceptual exploration. *Child Abuse and Neglect, 11,* 357-365.

Pollock, S. E. & Duffy, M. E. (1990). The Health-Related Hardiness Scale: Development and psychometric analysis. *Nursing Research, 39,* 218-222.

Radloff, L. S. (1977). The CED-D Scales: A self-report depression scale for research in the general population. *Applied Psychological Measurement, 3,* 385-401.

Rhodewalt, F., & Zone, J. B. (1989). Appraisal of life events, depression, and illness in hardy and nonhardy women. *Journal of Personality and Social Psychology, 56,* 81-88.

Seligman, M. E. P. (1991). *Learned optimism.* New York, NY: Alfred A. Knopf.

Sherman, A. C., Plante, T. G., Simonton, S., Adams, D. C., Harbison, C., & Burris, S. K. (2000). A multidimensional measure of religious involvement for cancer patients: The Duke Religious Index. *Support Care in Cancer, 8,* 102-109.

Sinclair, R. R., & Tertrick, L. E. (2000). Implications of item wording for hardiness structure, relation with neuroticism, and stress buffering. *Journal of Research in Personality, 34,* 1-25.

Tillich, P. (1952). *The courage to be.* New Haven, CT: Yale University Press. Wallace, J. M. Jr. & Forman, T. A. (1998). Religion's role in promoting health and reducing risk among American youth. *Health Education and Behavior, 25,* 721-741.

Weibe, D. J., & McCallum, D. M. (1986). Health practices and hardiness as mediators in the stress-illness relationship. *Health Psychology, 5,* 435-438.

Wedderburn, A. A. I. (1995). Men and women who like continuous shiftwork are more "hardy": But what does it mean? *Work and Stress, 9,* 206-210.

Westman, M. (1990). The relationship between stress and performance: The moderating effect of hardiness. *Human Performance, 3,* 141-155.

RESILIENCE AS A COPING MECHANISM:
A Common Story of Vietnamese Refugee Women

Tan Phan

1. INTRODUCTION

The boat was too small for three hundred people. I sat at the bottom of the boat with both legs curled up because there was no room for my legs. We could not stretch our arms. We could not walk on the boat to use the bathroom so we `did it' right where we were. People above me urinated and feced on my head, so my whole body was covered with human waste. Before the journey I had brought with me some gold, money and jewelry I hid in my waist-belt. I covered my face with engine oil because I heard about sea pirates... When we boarded the boat my husband wanted my space and gave me a better spot but I did not want it because I wanted my husband and my children to be more comfortable. Fortunately, the worst spot saved my life. I, therefore, still had the gold and jewelry. That's how we were able to buy food, medicine and goods to sell in the camps. That was how my children lived; they didn't die of hunger and sickness. (Minh, a participant in this study).

Such was the reality for the Vietnamese refugee mothers nearly twenty years ago. What has happened to these women and what are their stories and those of the next generation? These are research questions. In this chapter I examine the lives of Vietnamese refugee women who came from Vietnam, after the American war, escaped the Communist regime and arrived in Canada in the 1980s. One of the most striking issues emerged from my research had to deal with the many ways that the Vietnamese mothers participate in the academic achievement of their children.

Tan Phan San Diego State University

2. LITERATURE REVIEW

A growing literature focuses on the relative academic success of Vietnamese refugee children after their arrival in North America, in spite of their socioeconomic and language barriers (Caplan, Choy, & Whitmore, 1991; Caplan, Choy, & Whitmore, 1992). Much of this success is attributed to family practices that promote and provide opportunities for academic excellence. Unlike most contemporary research that focuses on psychological variables and factors that that are correlated with refugee children's successes, this chapter will discuss the important role that Vietnamese mothers, living in a community in the Canadian Maritimes, play in fostering academic resilience and coping with life stressors as such as language, cultural, and socioecomic obstacles of their children

The underlying concept of resiliency is the belief that some children emerge from highly stressful conditions as competent, well-adapted individuals. Masten, Garmezy, Tellegren, Pellegrini, Larkin, & Larsen (1988) define resiliency as an intrinsic human capability to recuperate from adversity, to restore stability of functioning. Others have added that this capacity is an experience that may develop in the context of the person-environment process over the lifespan (Egeland, Carlson, & Sroufe, 1993). Resiliency can be described as the capacity for successful adaptation, positive functioning, or competence (Garmezy, 1993) despite high-risk status, chronic stress, or following prolonged or severe trauma. Resilience is often operationalized as the positive end of the distribution of developmental outcomes in a sample of high-risk individuals (Rutter, 1979, 1987). Still others have described resilience more simply as normal development in spite of trying conditions (Fonagy, Steele, Higgitt, & Target, 1994). Risk and resiliency research is traditionally part of the field of developmental psychopathology. In other words, resilience is a construct that started off in the field of child and adolescent psychology, surfacing as the contrast of psychopathology (Masten, Best, & Garmezy, 1990). Topics of concern have included the roles of risk, vulnerability, competence, and protective factors. Each of these topics has been related to the onset and course of the development of psychopathology. Many of the contributions to the field of developmental psychopathology have been made by distinguished researchers in clinical psychology, psychiatry, and child development. These researchers provided early information documenting the occurrence of psychosocial resilience in various, at risk populations (Rolf, Masten, Cicchetti, Nuecheterlein, & Weintraub, 1990). Interest has grown in ways of characterizing the range and complexity of healthy or adaptive response to risk, as opposed to psychopathological behavior. A major factor contributing to this interest has been research dealing with children at risk due to a parent's mental disorder, parental divorce, or similar family stress. These risk studies have in common the finding that significant numbers of children are resilient and manifest highly adaptive behavior (e.g., Garmezy, 1990; 1985; Masten, Best, & Garmezy, 1990; Rutter, 1987). Consequently, investigators who have examined individuals at high risk have begun to characterize adaptation as resiliency (Garmezy, Masten, & Tellegen, 1984; Werner, 1992; Werner & Smith, 1982).

Garmezy's Project Competence program (Garmezy, Masten, & Tellegen, (1984) explored the ability of some children in Minnesota to adapt well in spite of highly disadvantageous life events. The project focused on the search for risk and protective factors for competence in middle childhood and adolescence, and manifestation of competence in children despite exposure to stressful life circumstances. In this project, 205 participants from predominantly lower- and middle-class families were recruited. Forty-five percent were from "intact" families and 28 percent of the final sample of children represented ethnic minorities.

The Life Events Questionnaire (LEQ), was sent to parents. To measure stress, parents were interviewed about major life events of the past two years. A second viewpoint, on family qualities, was drawn from interviews. The interviewers compiled a set of 30 Family Rating Scales at the conclusion of three home visits. Through rational classification and factor analysis, designed to tap global clinical impressions of the family, and the Family Rating Scales where the interviewer assessed the level of family stress exposure, most of which concerned perceived family qualities of family rules, discipline, mother-child relationship, factor analysis suggested that this instrument (Masten, Best, & Garmezy, 1990) measured three dimensions. The most salient factor, Parenting Quality, measured maternal competence in relation to parenting.

Based on their research and the gather work of others, Garmezy, Masten and Tellegen (1984) described three mathematical models of stress resistance, two of which detailed the potential processes by which personal characteristics or attributes and stress may have an influence on adjustment.

1. The compensatory model predicts that high exposure to stressors is likely to diminish levels of competence and that various personal attributes work to raise levels of competence in a simple additive mode. In other words, persons who possess a protective factor are higher in competence than those without the factor with the same levels of stress exposure.

2. The immunity vs. vulnerability (or "protective factor") model depicts the relationship between stress and personal attributes in predicting that adjustment is an interactive process in which the occurrence of a given factor intervenes as a protecting effect against the impact of increasing stress on adaptation.

Masten and colleagues (1988) added four more mathematical models of stress and competence to the above array; two of these models also depict the effect of personal attributes on the stress and competence relationship. The first model predicts that it is the presence of the attribute alone, not the level of stress, which determines the level of competence in a linear mode.

The second model illustrates that it is the level of stress exposure, not the absence of a protective characteristics that inversely impacts competence. An illustration of this model would be that children would demonstrate declining competence with increasing risk exposure regardless of differences in personal or environmental attributes. The collective effects model posits that small amounts of stress exposure will have minimal effects on competence but that a clustering of stress events will result in a curvilinear decrease in competence.

The last model, or vulnerability model, describes that the relationship between stress and personal attributes in predicting adjustment is an interactive one where the presence of a given factor aids high competence under low levels of stress but mediates a harmful effect on adaptation when stress raises. While this line of inquiry has provided important insights, its emphasis on individual abilities, traits, and psychological attributes is incompatible with an East-Asian emphasis on interdependence. Within the Vietnamese community resilience is not an individual construct (Phan, 1997; 2003). Rather, it is a reflection and result of family and community processes and patterns of participation. Many Vietnamese refugee families insist on the fundamental relatedness of individuals to each other, with the emphasis on sacrifice and harmonious interdependence (Markus & Kitayama, 1991). For many Vietnamese families, the importance of hard work and communalism is viewed as a personal responsibility, as well as an intergenerational commitment to family and community.

2.1. Purpose of the study

The purpose was to discover the ways in which Vietnamese families fostered academic resilience and provided protective factors that helped their children coping and achieving academic excellence and interpret the meanings of their descriptions, in order to gain a greater understanding of the events of their lives. The main purpose of this study was to learn how individuals coping and promote resilience and academic resilience for their children, given the material, cultural, race, and language impediments in which they live.

3. METHODS

3.1. Sampling strategies

I used purposeful, criterion-based sampling strategies (Glaser & Strauss, 1967; Patton, 1990; Strauss & Corbin, 1990, 1998; Taylor & Bogdan 1998). I started recruiting participants for this study by visiting Vietnamese community and Vietnamese cultural festivities and religious institutions. I also employed 'snowball' or 'chain sampling' (Patton, 1990). That is, before or at the end of each interview, I asked the participants if they would identify others that fit the study's selection criteria. I telephoned those who expressed interest, standardizing contacts by using the same information handout.

3.2. Participants

Ten Vietnamese women interviewed for this study were all grew up in Vietnam, and they were all mothers, with children living at home, except for one woman whose children lived with her ex-husband. Some of the women with teen-aged children asked me to talk to their children. The children were very cooperative and sincere. Thus, in my analysis, I included the information from the children as well. I interviewed the women during the evenings, mornings, and weekends, in their businesses, and in their homes. Most of the interviews lasted between two to three hours. To maintain confidentiality fictitious names were used. The women were Vietnamese refugees and came to Canada at different times after the Vietnam War (A.K.A. American War in Vietnam). The youngest parent participant was 30 and the oldest was 55. The families had annual incomes of $15,000 to $30,000.

3.3 Design and procedures

The data collection involved tape-recorded face-to-face interviews, and field and observation notes were recorded during these times. These semi-structured interviews consisted of open-ended questions designed to explore a few general topics. They were designed not only to gain information from the participants' own words but also to gain insight on how participants interpreted their world. Being Vietnamese myself enabled me to engage comfortably with the participants. I asked their permission to record the interviews by tape recorder so that I could engage in the informal conversations while maintaining eye contact without interruptions. The interviews with the parents examined the framing of their role through discussions of their academic expectations for their children, and explored the parents' current life, background information, reasons for leaving Vietnam, and their experiences of leaving Vietnam and coming to Canada.

After each interview, I transcribed the tape and translated it into English. Throughout this paper, extensive and lengthy quotes from the women's were used. In addition, some excerpts of the participants were included to give texture to the analytic conclusions and to provide samples of the kind of evidence upon which those conclusions are based. Furthermore, as is in common qualitative studies, rich detail about the participants, the process, and the analysis also invites readers to determine transferability of results (Creswell, 2002; Mertens, 1998; Patton, 1990; Taylor & Bogdan, 1998).

4. DATA ANALYSIS

I recognize that no method is completely neutral although some may get closer to the real story. Therefore, in this study, I proposed no formal hypothesis for testing (Strauss & Corbin, 1990, 1998). During the interviews, I let the concepts, explanations, and interpretations of those participating in the study become the data I analyzed (Strauss & Corbin, 1990). Data were analyzed throughout the study rather than relegating analysis to a period following the data collection. This type of analysis served two purposes: a) to make decisions in data collection and b) to identify emerging topics and recurring patterns. The data from each of these sources were analyzed through a process of analytic induction (Glaser & Strauss, 1967; Miles & Huberman, 1994; Strauss & Corbin, 1990, 1998) in which field notes and interview transcripts were compared to identify an initial set of coding categories based on emerging patterns in the data. Interpretations also included my observations at churches, temples, and social gatherings within Vietnamese communities. The interview transcriptions and studied in order to determine relevant themes.

5. RESULTS

5.1. Resilience and coping: Serving in silence

Traditional psychological research on resilience does not sufficiently investigate the role of socio-political contexts, history and culture in its analyses. As a lens of individualism has been applied to theories of resiliency and achievement in North American psychology, this lens has not helped me focus my inquiry because for Vietnamese resiliency means different things to different generations. The following analysis offers a different way of seeing resiliency from conventional assumptions and traditional empirical expressions (Phan, 1998).

Resiliency for Vietnamese parents in is the sacrifice and the struggle of the previous generations for the survival and the futures of their children (2003). For example, the life stories from the journeys and the refugee camps may be seen as examples of mothers' audacity and heroism, and such heroism has not been acknowledged by the media or by academic literature. From these mothers' stories, I contend that these are stories of survival and resilience. The mothers' coping and resilience is informed by the logic of their children's survival. For the women, survival has meant both physical sustenance and an emotionally connected relationship for their children's future academic success. The mothers' emphasis is on caring for their children (Gilligan, 1982). It is also often on forging connections (Markus and Kitayama, 1991), especially within family, church and community. Characteristically, the mothers' resilience is informed by values of nurture, connection, community, family, and endurance. Minh described her plight:

> *There were too many people and no sanitation. People died of diarrhea because we used the river for cooking and drinking; we also used the same river for bathing and washing...I went to the local market, we were allowed to go outside the camps to buy food and I bought food and brought it back to the camp and cooked and sold it to the refugees. I made a little bit of money and bought medicine for my children. I bought canned food and sold it at the camps. So my family was a little bit better off than other was refugees were. I grew vegetables and flowers so we had fresh vegetable and flowers every day. I had a little garden. Sometimes I went to the village to get my hair done.*

The very routine nature of their work, carried out with a stubborn, inexorable strength was the bedrock that gave meaning to life and served as the underpinning that made all else possible. Listen to Thuy:

> *We stayed in an uncultivated island. Every day I got up at 4:00 a.m., walked for five hours to reach the station where the Red Cross gave us rice and dried food. We didn't have anything to cook. Other women and I shared a big pot and we used empty cans for dishes and a big can for the pot. I grew vegetables and flowers too. In the morning, my husband and I hunted fish in the ocean. We lived like primitive people.*

Thoa added:

> *I went to the woods, picked up some wood and I made tables and chairs from it. I went down to the beach to gather lumber and so we built our 'house'. I picked up canvas bags which were washed to the shore and I made blankets...and clothes from it*

In this context, concerns such as gardens and home improvements were part of mothers' struggle for normalcy. They were part of a struggle to provide for their families and protect their children from the worst and most degrading features of internment.

5.2. The importance of academic success for their children

In Canada, the mothers, in this study, voiced the sentiment that "life here is hard, but I don't mind because it is good for our children. They can get educated here." The mothers in my study manifested their immeasurable devotion to their families in all aspects, from economy to emotion. To these mothers, their family life was valuable and important and must be protected and nurtured `by mothers', who had the abilities to create an emotionally supportive environment for others in the midst of poverty, language and cultural barriers.

The mothers, the first-generation Vietnamese who came here, generally do not understand much English. They are not familiar with the Canadian public school system, and most of the time they do not know what their children are going through. Thus, poor communication between parents and children often occurs in such an environment. Nevertheless, these mothers, while they were at home, devoted their time to their children, nurturing and comforting them. Money provides a better standard of living and more chance of moving up the ladder in society for their children. They contested the view that working mothers had a negative effect on children's performance and development. None of this detracted from their deep commitment to motherhood and their children.

Some of the children I talked to felt uncomfortable about the older generation's insistence on maintaining old customs and parochial habits. Some of the children felt that this was an impediment to breaking loose from their parents' cultural control. What these children yearned for was to lead an independent, modern, and Western life, free of the burden of their parents' Vietnameseness and overwhelming hopes for their children. Le Anh complained: "My children really resists it when I tell them to act like Vietnamese children try to take my children to the Vietnamese festivities. . . but they are very reluctant." The mothers tried very hard to communicate with their children and wanted to provide all the opportunities they could for them. To them, education was the most important issue for their children. But the children never understood that their mothers' lives were shaped by the facts of their difficult and deprived lives, resulting, in part, from the historical effects of refugee camps, immigration, and wars. The children sensed the intensity of their mothers' aspirations, desires, and hopes for their children. Minh's daughter revealed: "I know my mother wants me to do well in school, but I felt a great pressure from her. I just wanted to be left alone. I love her; I wanted to do well too. Sometimes I have to separate myself from her." These young people often felt a tremendous pressure to fulfill their parents' expectations. And Minh's son stated:

I love my parents dearly. I was very sad and worried when my father had open heart surgery. I could not eat or sleep. My mother was alone working in the business, so I helped her after school. I am happy when my parents are happy. I work hard in school and always do well because I want my parents to be happy. It seems education is very important to them. But you know, lots of the time I wonder why I am studying so hard. What is the meaning of it for myself? Sometimes I feel very depressed because I don't know what I should do to make myself happy, or as long as my parents are happy I am happy.

Despite the difficulties associated with working and not being understood by their children, all the mothers spoke with great warmth and affection about their children. They gained prestige and power through their children. A major source of compensation for the

Vietnamese mothers was that, despite the hardships and suffering they endured, their children were receiving a university education. With the traditional Confucian belief in the importance of education, "an untaught child is not a person", the mothers particularly emphasized supporting harmony to raise educated children. It was their hope that, with this cultural capital, the next generation would be able to compete equally with white Canadians.

The Vietnamese people see in Canada the promise of education and qualifications that will enable their children to earn a living in Canada. Ngoc and her husband came to Canada over 19 years ago. Their three children have done well at school and Ngoc is very pleased with their achievement. The mothers devoted their time every evening to coaching their children in schoolwork. All of their hopes and dreams for a better life have been transferred to their children.

It was clear from the interviews that education matters enormously to all the mothers; they felt that it held out a real possibility of something better for their children. All the mothers I interviewed expressed it as: "My children come first." They kept working until their children graduated from university. They arranged their work hours to fit around their children's school hours so that they could be there when needed. For the Vietnamese mothers, working had meaning precisely because it enabled them to provide for their children.

5.3. Family, cultural and community

In Canada, while the Vietnamese mothers' place in the home keeps them subordinate to men, it also helps them to play a special role in maintaining Vietnamese national identity. In the home, isolated from the dominant cultural influences, the mothers pass Vietnamese culture on to the next generation and the family is a bulwark against the atomizing effects of legal and political constraints. The family helps to maintain ethnic and Vietnamese culture. The common interests of family members are the children's education and the maintenance of family authority, with emphasis on the continuation of cultural traditions. Struggles within the family over the division of labor are kept minimal, because the struggles against the outside forces that might compromise the children's take precedence for the survival of the family. By transmitting folkways and language, socializing children into an alternative value system, and providing a base for self-identity and esteem, the family helps to maintain the Vietnamese culture. All the mothers in my study claimed, as Minh did: "I teach my children Confucian and Buddhist beliefs and the Vietnamese customs and traditions. We celebrate the lunar year and the first day of the month (full moon) from the lunar calendar." Confucianism emphasizes education (Chu, 1985); children are socialized to achieve academically, and dictate that women are also responsible for teaching their children dignity, morality and integrity, "an untaught child is not a person." Holding to these traditional values, the mothers in this study worked hard to educate their children in both formal academic and informal educational practices. As Hong relates:

Most Vietnamese women work at the factory or in their own businesses; they work all day, then they do the shopping and cook and clean. Before I came to work today, I washed the clothes, vacuumed the house and fixed dinner also I made breakfast and packed lunches for everyone in my house. Today my daughter has ballet lesson I have to take her. My son has piano lesson on Friday.

Hoa Tran discussed her long hours: "As soon as I get home from work, I go right into the kitchen and start cooking. While I am cooking with my hands, my mouth, and my eyes are with the boys: Do your spelling, do your math."

Several times a year, the Vietnamese Association in metro Halifax celebrates cultural festivities. Cultural celebrations thus generate a strong feeling of togetherness for the Vietnamese community. The structure of friendship of the women involved in the preparations for the festivities is very widespread across all age groups. The women volunteer their time to cook and prepare for the festivities. They make the Vietnamese traditional food and desserts and sell it at the festival. The money they make is put into the Society. From my observations, the mothers participated in these activities as their socialization with other mothers and also on competitive grounds with each other. They observed each other and competed with each other about their children's achievement. Although they lacked formal education and had limited experience with regard to achieving academic success, the Vietnamese women in the community often compensate by providing other critical support to their young members. The members in the community commonly use storytelling to maintain the Vietnamese language and culture (which highly values education), to express high expectations of their young at all times, to convey indirect and direct messages that encourage success, to communicate love, and to transmit hopes and dreams (Phan, in press).

Since the parents invested their lives, hopes and dreams in their children being successful in Canada, the children were their escalators to the top of the social ladder. The children felt a great obligation to fulfill the parents' wishes. These children were working extremely hard as well. They were expected to be the top in school, in music and in sport. Some children I talked to expressed that they often carry a great feeling of guilt if they do not do well. The Vietnamese parents also competed with each other about whose children won more scholarships, were best in computer or mathematics, whose children went to medical school and whose children dropped out of school. The Vietnamese children felt this great pressure from their parents. It is apparent that those who fulfill their obligation toward their parents' wishes will have better lives, achieving a more comparable status to the white Canadian than their parents have had. However, those who could not make it gave their parents both a great feeling of pain and a sense of embarrassment in the Vietnamese community.

6. CONCLUSION

In this study, using a qualitative research method I explored the cultural meaning way of how Vietnamese mothers fostered resilience to support their children's school learning. Despite the hardships and suffering these women had personally endured, their children were receiving an education and excelling scholastically. According to these women, the major reasons for the children's academic success were the extensive personal sacrifices parents made.

For Vietnamese children resiliency means academic scholarship after years of dedicated studies, and in spite of difficult social and economic circumstances (Phan, 2003; in press). On the other hand, resiliency for the mothers means sacrifice, hardship endured and about the protection of cultural integrity. The refugee mothers' endurance provides their children with a story of collective resiliency, of cultural values and traditions that are the collaborative threads that weave the Vietnamese students' identity. The mothers were in guiding and fostering resiliency in their children's development.

The mothers celebrate cultural traditions and part of their vision of the future is bound up with their commitment to their children. The way in which the children will break free of poverty and racial oppression is through education. They want their children to have opportunities to pursue education as a means to a life that would be more autonomous. They struggle to make sense of their lives and to ensure a future for their children. The mothers have preserved their cultural identity against the invasions and the demands of the mainstream white society, and passed this on to their children. They are also effective in highlighting many diverse, courageous, and ingenious forms of resilience. The strategies of coping used by the mothers in their daily lives have transformed their actions into more non-Western forms of resilience. Extended families and the families of friends form a wide base of female support in the mothers' lives. Although they gossip and compete with each other, the mothers also provide each other with mutual aid, working together, and cooperating among themselves to enrich their lives and to make it easier for them to achieve their ends. The mothers give support for each others to maintain the family harmony that, they believed, is critical to children's academic socialization.

Thus, for the Vietnamese, resilience, as a collective construct, is a process for weaving family, community, and generations together (Phan, 1997, 1998, 2003, 2004, 2005). After all, these struggles are for the benefit of their children.

REFERENCES

Caplan, N., Choy, M. & Whitmore, J. (1991). *Children of the boat people: A study of educational success.* The University of Michigan Press.

Caplan, N., Choy, M. & Whitmore, J. (February, 1992). Indochinese refugee families and academic achievement: The children of Southeast Asian boat people excel in the American school system. *The Scientific American,* 36-42.

Chu, G. (1985). The changing concept of self in contemporary China. In A. Marsella, G. De Vos, and F. L. Hsu Ed. *Culture and self.* London: Tavistock.

Creswell, J. (2002). *Educational Research: Planning, Conducting, and Evaluating Quantitative and Qualitative Research.* New Jersey: Prentice-Hall, Inc.

Egeland, B., Carson, E., & Sroufe, L.A. (1993). Resilience as process. *Development and Psychopathology,* 5, 517-528.

Fonagy, P., Steele, M., Steele, H., Higgitt, A., & Target, M. (1994). The Emanuel Miller Memorial Lecture 1992: The theory and practice of resilience. *Journal of Child Psychology and Psychiatry and Allied Disciplines,* 35, 231-257.

Garmezy, N. (1990). Resiliency and vulnerability to adverse developmental outcomes associated with poverty. *American Behavioral Scientist, 34* (4), 416-430.

Garmezy, N., Masten, A, & Tellegen, A. (1984). The study of stress and competence in children: A building block for developmental psychopathology. *Child Development, 55,* 97-111.

Gilligan, C. (1982). *In a different voice: Psychological theory and women's development.* Cambridge, MA: Harvard University Press

Glaser, B.G. & Strauss, A. L. (1967). *The discovery of grounded theory: Strategies for qualitative research.* New York: Aldine de Gruyter.

Masten, A. S., Best, K. M., & Garmezy, N. (1990). Resilience and development: Contributions from the study of children who overcome adversity. *Development and Psychopathology, 2,* 425-444.

Masten, A. S., Garmezy, N., Tellegren, A., Pellegrini, D.S., Larkin, K., & Larsen, A. (1988). Competence and stress in school children: The moderating effects of individual and family qualities. *Journal Child Psychology and Psychiatry, 29*(6), 745-764.

Markus, H. and Kitayama, S. (1991). Culture and the self: implications for cognition, emotion, and motivation". *Psychological Review,* 98, 2, 224-253.

Mertens, D. (1998). *Research methods in education and psychology: Integrating diversity with quantitative and qualitative approaches*. Thousand Oaks, CA: Sage.

Miles, M., & Huberman, A. (1994). *Qualitative data analysis: An expanded sourcebook* (2nd ed.). Newbury Park: Sage.

Patton, M. (1990). *Qualitative evaluation and research methods* (2nd ed.). Newbury Park: Sage.

Phan, T. (2003). Life in school: Narratives of resiliency among Vietnamese-Canadian youths. *Adolescence, 38*, 555-566.

Phan, T. (2004). A qualitative study of Vietnamese parental involvement and their high academic achieving children. *Journal of Authentic Learning, 1*, 51-61.

Phan, T. (In Press). Interdependent self: Self perceptions of Vietnamese American youths. *Adolescence*.

Phan, T. (2005, In Press). Parental involvement: Vietnamese-American parents use storytelling as academic socialization for their children. *Journal of Authentic Learning*.

Phan, T. (2005, in press). Interdependent self: Self-perceptions of Vietnamese-American Youths. *Adolescence*.

Phan, T. (April, 1998). Deconstructing psychological research on academic resiliency. Paper presented at American Educational Research Association (AERA) Annual Meeting in San Diego, CA.

Phan, T. (May, 1998). *La generation aprè-guerre: Des enquêtes socio-culturelles de la résistance académique parmi les jèunes Vietnamiens des quartiers du center-ville*. Paper presented at Canadian Society for the Study of Education (CSSE) Ottawa.

Phan, T. (March, 1997). *A Feminist perspective on ways of mothering that supports Vietnamese refugee children's academic socialization*. Paper presented at American Educational Research Association (AERA) Annual Meeting in Chicago, Ill.

Rolf, J. Masten, A.S., Cicchetti, D., Nuechterlein, K.H., & Weintraub, S. (Eds.) (1990). *Risk and Protective Factors in the Development of Psychopathology*. New York: Cambridge University Press.

Rutter, M. (1979). Protective factors in children,s response to stress and disadvantage. In M.W. Kent & J. E. Rolf (Eds.), *Primary prevention of psychopathology: Social Competence in Children* (Vol. 3). Hanover, New Hampshire: University Press of New England.

Rutter, M. (1987). Psychosocial resilience and protective mechanisms. *American Journal of Orthopsychiatry, 57*, 316-331.

Strauss, A. & Corbin, J. (1990). *Basics of qualitative research: Grounded theory procedures and techniques.*. Newbury Park, CA: Sage Publication.

Strauss, A. & Corbin, J. (1998). *Basics of qualitative research: Technique and procedures for developing grounded theory* (2nd ed.). Newbury Park, CA: Sage Publication.

Taylor, S. & Bogdan, R. (1998). *Introduction to qualitative research methods: A guidebook and resource* (3rd Ed.). New York: Springer.

Werner, E. E. (1992). The children of Kauai: Resiliency and recovery in adolescence and adulthood. *Journal of Adolescent Health, 13*, 262-268.

Werner, E.E., & Smith, R.S. (1982). *Vulnerable, But Invincible: A longitudinal Study of Resilient Children and Youth*. New York: McGraw Hill.

STRESS AND COPING AMONG ASIAN AMERICANS:
Lazarus and Folkman's Model and Beyond

Edward C. Chang, Michele M. Tugade, and Kiyoshi Asakawa

1. INTRODUCTION

In the present chapter, we consider theoretical, empirical, and methodological issues related to the study of how Asian Americans cope with stress. We begin by first acquainting readers with some of the cultural complexities associated with being Asian American. Then, we provide a brief overview of Lazarus and Folkman's (1984) stress and coping model, as well as other coping models, and examine relevant findings comparing Asian Americans and Caucasian Americans. Following this, we explore potential sources of these coping findings as a function of differences in stressful experiences encountered by Asian Americans compared to Caucasian Americans. Finally, we end by discussing two promising methodological approaches that may help researchers gain greater insights to understanding the coping process among Asian Americans, namely, the use of psychophysiological assessments and experience sampling method.

2. ASIAN AMERICANS: COLLECTIVISM AS A COMMON VALUE

In recent decades, scientists have learned a great deal about how individuals cope with stressful life situations. Unfortunately, despite the growth of minority populations, much of our knowledge continues to be based on studies of individuals from European backgrounds (e.g., Caucasian Americans). Accordingly, and given our own research interests, we focus on Asian Americans to see if and how their coping behaviors might differ from that of Caucasian Americans.

Just as it is inaccurate to say that all Caucasian Americans look or act the same, it is important to realize that Asian Americans represent a very diverse population. According to Uba (1994), one can enumerate as many as 25 distinct Asian American ethnic groups living in the United States. However, because these Asian American ethnic groups differ

University of Michigan; Vassar College; Hosei University

across a number of important dimensions (e.g., history, nationality, language, and cultural practices), some researchers have argued that the term Asian American itself is misleading if important differences are not considered between different ethnic groups. However, we do not explore the coping response of each Asian American ethnic group here. Presently, there is too little research on any specific Asian American ethnic group to warrant such an examination. In addition, while we believe that there are important differences that need to be illuminated within the Asian American population, we believe that there also are important shared Asian American attributes that go beyond inter-ethnic differences among Asian Americans.

In recent years, psychologists have begun to recognize how cultural differences influence human behavior. In particular, a growing number of psychologists have emphasized the usefulness of distinguishing between individualistic and collectivist cultures (Triandis, 1995). Noteworthy, Western cultures have been described as individualistic, with individuals seeking independence from others by attending to self-based needs and desires (Greenwald, 1980). In contrast, the focus in Eastern cultures has been on the individual in maintaining a fundamental relatedness with others (Markus & Kitayama, 1991). Hence, attending to others, harmonious interdependence, and fitting in not only are valued, but also often are expected.

According to Markus and Kitayama (1991), these Eastern and Western cultural differences not only promote two relatively distinct notions of the self, but they also differentiate the thoughts, feelings, and actions of individuals from such cultures. Indeed, given that much of the coping research has used Caucasian American research participants, one would expect different results with individuals from Eastern cultures (e.g., Asian Americans). Yet, an examination of how Asian Americans might differ in their coping behaviors from Caucasian Americans, however, also will likely depend on the specific coping model being considered. Hence, to obtain an appreciation of ethnic differences in coping strategies and styles, we will briefly look at the coping behaviors of Asian Americans across different coping models. We begin with one of the most popular and researched models of coping in the literature, namely, Lazarus and Folkman's (1984) stress and coping model.

2.1. Lazarus and Folkman's Stress and Coping Model

Based on Lazarus and Folkman's (1984) model, *coping* refers to the behavioral and cognitive efforts one uses to manage the internal and external demands of a stressful situation. Coping can be classified as being either problem-focused or emotion-focused in nature. *Problem-focused coping* involves activities that focus on directly changing elements of the stressful situation, whereas *emotion-focused coping* involves activities that focus more on modifying one's internal reactions resulting from the stressful situation. According to this view, coping is a dynamic process. Hence, coping responses have commonly been assessed for by situation-specific measures like the Ways of Coping Checklist (Folkman & Lazarus, 1980), which asks respondents to indicate the extent to which they used specific problem-focused or emotion-focused coping strategies in managing a recent stressful situation.

While several studies examining the structure of coping and of coping measures have provided some consensus for distinguishing between these two coping dimensions (Carver, Scheier, & Weintraub, 1989; Stone & Neale, 1984), other studies have highlighted the dimensions of approach and avoidance (Roth & Cohen, 1986; Suls & Fletcher, 1985).

According to Suls and Fletcher (1985), *approach* coping refers to the use of strategies that focus on both the source of stress and reactions to it, whereas *avoidant* coping refers to the use of strategies that place focus away from both the source of stress and reactions to it. However, approach and avoidance coping and problem-focused and emotion-focused coping need not reflect mutually exclusive coping classifications. In that regard, Tobin, Holroyd, Reynolds, and Wigal (1989) have conceptualized coping strategies so as to take into account all of these elements. They accomplished this through the development of the Coping Strategies Inventory (CSI), a multidimensional coping measure of both engaged (approach) and disengaged (avoidance) problem-focused, and emotion-focused coping strategies.

The CSI scales assess for eight different coping strategies. Problem Solving is associated with efforts to engage in specific problem solving steps (e.g., "I made a plan of action and followed it"). Cognitive Restructuring involves efforts to think about the stressful situation in a more positive manner (e.g., "I looked at things in a different light and tried to make the best of what was available"). Express Emotions tap efforts to deal with stress by expressing one's emotions (e.g., "I let my emotions go"), similar to Freud's notion of catharsis. Social Support involves efforts to obtain emotional support from others (e.g., "I talked to someone about how I was feeling"). These four scales measure engaged and more adaptive coping efforts.

In addition, Problem Avoidance is associated with efforts to not deal with the problem situation at hand (e.g., "I wished that the situation would go away or somehow be over with"). Wishful Thinking involves efforts to think that a stressful situation simply will resolve itself (e.g., "I hoped a miracle would happen"). Self-Criticism gets at an excessive preoccupation with one's lack of ability to deal with the situation (e.g., "I criticized myself for what happened"). Social Withdrawal taps efforts to distance oneself from the problem and from others who might be able to help with the problem (e.g., "I avoided my family and friends"). These four scales represent disengaged and more maladaptive coping efforts.

Based on the view that Asian and Caucasian Americans are guided by two differing notions of the self (viz., interdependent versus independent), cultural differences might be expected to emerge in coping strategies. In that regard, the results comparing mean differences between the two ethnic groups on each of the CSI coping strategies as reported in Chang (2001) are presented in Table 1. As the table indicates, the two ethnic groups were not found to be significantly different in their use of different coping strategies to deal with a stressful situation. There were two exceptions, however. Namely, Asian Americans reported higher scores on Problem Avoidance and Social Withdrawal than did Caucasian Americans. This demonstrates that cultural differences in coping among Asian and Caucasian Americans indeed exist, at least for some coping strategies.

2.2. Epstein's Experiential Coping Model

Beyond Lazarus and Folkman's (1984) model, Epstein (1973, 1990) has proposed a model of coping that involves the way people generally respond to their external environments based on past experiences. In Epstein's (1990) Cognitive-Experiential Self-Theory or CEST, personality is composed of three relatively distinct conceptual systems, one that is rational, experiential, and, one that is associationist. According to CEST, the operations

Table 1. Mean Ethnic Differences Between Asian and Caucasian Americans on the Coping Strategies Inventory (CSI)

	Ethnic group		
CSI Scale	Asian	Caucasian	p
Problem Solving	27.07 (6.51)	26.16 (6.14)	ns
Cognitive Restructuring	27.04 (6.47)	27.47 (6.68)	ns
Express Emotions	23.87 (7.00)	25.18 (8.19)	ns
Social Support	27.24 (6.55)	29.04 (7.57)	ns
Problem Avoidance	21.91 (5.41)	18.82 (5.41)	<.01
Wishful Thinking	26.22 (6.92)	25.84 (8.78)	ns
Self-Criticism	22.80 (7.19)	20.00 (9.88)	ns
Social Withdrawal	22.82 (6.26)	18.16 (6.13)	<.001

Note: For Asian Americans, $n = 45$; for Caucasian Americans, $n = 49$. Numbers in parentheses are standard deviations. From "A look at the coping strategies and styles of Asian Americans: Similar and different?," by E. C. Chang, 2001, in C. R. Snyder (Ed.), *Coping with stress: Effective people and processes* (pp. 222-239). New York: Oxford University Press. Reprinted by permission of Oxford University Press.

of the experiential system plays a prominent role in facilitating effective coping with environmental stressors. Based on past experiences, one key response to the environment is to maintain a balance of pleasure over pain. When people feel good, they continue those activities which promote such feelings. In contrast, when people feel bad, they discontinue any causative related activities. In this manner, the experiential system is believed to be involved with the maintenance and promotion of positive well being.

To measure attributes of this experiential system, Epstein and Meier (1989) developed the Constructive Thinking Inventory (CTI). The CTI was developed to tap constructive and destructive thought patterns emerging from past experiences. Unlike the focus on particular coping strategies for specific stressful situations in the CSI (Tobin et al., 1989), the CTI focuses on trait-like ways of thinking and coping. Based on recent studies conducted by Epstein and his associates (Epstein, 1992; Epstein & Katz, 1992; Epstein & Meier, 1989), it appears that individuals who express greater constructive thinking (e.g., "I look at challenges not as something to fear, but as an opportunity to test myself and learn") are better able to cope with stressful situations than those who express greater destructive thinking (e.g., "I spend much more time mentally rehearsing my failures than remembering my successes"). Hence, if cultural differences influence how Asian and Caucasian Americans experience their worlds, then their experiential systems (as measured by the CTI) should be relatively distinct.

As before, Chang (2001) also examined potential coping differences between Asian and Caucasian Americans using a version of the CTI tapping three constructive and four destructive thinking styles. Global Constructive Thinking involves elements from all of the other CTI scales, except Naive Optimism (described below). In general, higher scores on the global scale reflect greater constructive thinking ability. Both the Behavioral

Coping and Emotional Coping scales are believed to tap distinct constructive dimensions of coping, similar to Lazarus and Folkman's (1984) distinction between problem-focused and emotion-focused coping, respectively. Emotional Coping refers to the tendency to not take things personally, not to be sensitive to disapproval, and not to worry excessively about failure (e.g., "If I said something foolish when I spoke up in a group, I would chalk it up to experience and not worry about it"). Behavioral Coping is associated with the tendency to think in ways that promote effective action (e.g., "When I realize I have made a mistake, I usually take immediate action to correct it").

In contrast, four scales reflect destructive dimensions of coping. Categorical Thinking involves the tendency to think in overly rigid and extreme ways (e.g., "There are two kinds of people in this world, winners and losers"). Superstitious Thinking refers to beliefs in personal superstitions (e.g., "I sometimes think that if I want something to happen too badly, it will keep from happening"). Esoteric Thinking is associated with beliefs related to matters such as astrology and ghosts (e.g., "I believe the moon or the stars can affect people's thinking"). Naive Optimism involves gross overgeneralizations following positive outcomes (e.g., "When something good happens to me, I feel that more good things are likely to follow").

Findings as reported in Chang (2001) for the CTI are presented in Table 2. As the table shows, Asian compared to Caucasian Americans reported lower scores on Global Constructive Thinking and on Emotional Coping. Alternatively, Asian compared to Caucasian Americans reported higher scores on Superstitious Thinking, Categorical Thinking, Esoteric Thinking, and on Naïve Optimism. Unlike the findings for the CSI, these results clearly indicate that there are significant normative differences between the two ethnic groups across the different experientially-based coping styles identified by Epstein and his colleagues.

Table 2. Mean Ethnic Differences Between Asian and Caucasian Americans on the Constructive Thinking Inventory (CTI)

CTI Scale	Ethnic group		
	Asian	Caucasian	p
Global Constructive Thinking	92.08 (15.92)	98.17 (17.01)	<.05
Emotional Coping	73.39 (17.29)	79.18 (16.42)	<.05
Behavioral Coping	50.36 (6.70)	52.16 (7.05)	ns
Superstitious Thinking	20.23 (5.40)	17.36 (4.69)	<.001
Categorical Thinking	46.19 (7.62)	43.38 (7.89)	<.05
Esoteric Thinking	38.66 (7.11)	35.63 (9.59)	<.05
Naive Optimism	53.56 (6.68)	51.03 (6.04)	<.01

Note: For Asian Americans, $n = 64$; for Caucasian Americans, $n = 175$. Numbers in parentheses are standard deviations. From "A look at the coping strategies and styles of Asian Americans: Similar and different?," by E. C. Chang, 2001, in C. R. Snyder (Ed.), *Coping with stress: Effective people and processes* (pp. 222-239). New York: Oxford University Press. Reprinted by permission of Oxford University Press.

2.3. D'Zurilla's Social Problem Solving Coping Model

Beyond the two previously discussed coping models, there is also the social problem solving coping model presented by D'Zurilla and his associates (D'Zurilla, 1986; D'Zurilla & Nezu, 1990). According to D'Zurilla and Nezu (1990), *social problem solving* refers to problem solving as it occurs in the real world. More specifically, it is defined as the self-generated cognitive-affective-behavioral process by which a person attempts to discover effective ways of coping with daily problematic situations. Thus, stressful situations are synonymous with problems in living, and they require some sort of coping action. The importance of this multi-faceted construct has been consistently documented in recent years when researchers have found a significant link between problem-solving deficits and maladjustment (D'Zurilla, 1986; Nezu, Nezu, & Perri, 1989). Moreover, in a growing number of studies examining suicidal risk in college populations, investigators have shown repeatedly that problem-solving also are significantly associated with greater hopelessness and suicide ideation (Chang, 1998; D'Zurilla, Chang, Nottingham, & Faccini, 1998).

According to D'Zurilla and his associates (Chang, D'Zurilla, & Sanna, 2004; D'Zurilla & Chang, 1995; D'Zurilla & Maydeu-Olivares, 1995; D'Zurilla, Nezu, & Maydeu-Olivares, 2002), social problem solving has been found to reflect five relatively distinct dimensions as measured by the Social Problem Solving Inventory-Revised (SPSI-R). Accordingly, the SPSI-R is composed of five scales. Positive Problem Orientation involves constructive ways of thinking about a problem (e.g., "When I have a problem, I usually believe that there is a solution for it"). Negative Problem Orientation taps destructive ways of thinking about a problem as well as the negative emotions that are associated with it (e.g., "I usually feel threatened and afraid when I have an important problem to solve"). Rational Problem Solving Style reflects the deliberate and systematic use of problem-solving skills to deal with a problem (e.g., "Before I try to think of a solution to a problem, I usually set a specific goal that makes clear exactly what I want to accomplish"). Implusivity/Carelessness Style involves problem solving efforts that are acted upon impulsively, and without much deliberation (e.g., "When I am attempting to solve a problem, I usually go with the first good idea that comes to mind"). Avoidance Style gets at efforts to procrastinate and take little action in dealing with the problem at hand (e.g., "I usually go out of my way to avoid having to deal with problems in my life"). Of these dimensions, only Positive Problem Orientation and Rational Problem Solving are believed to reflect positive or adaptive problem solving dimensions.

Table 3 shows results comparing differences between Asian and Caucasian Americans across these five SPSI-R scales as reported in Chang (2001). As the table shows, there was only one significant difference found between Asian and Caucasian Americans. Namely, Asian Americans, compared to Caucasian Americans, reported greater Impulsivity/Carelessness Style scores.

Although significant mean differences were not always found across the three coping measures reviewed here, significant differences were found on all but one coping dimension measured by the CTI. Insofar that constructive and destructive coping styles are influenced by experience (Epstein, 1990), one might ask what types of experiences might differentiate Asian from Caucasian Americans. In that regard, several factors may be considered.

Table 3. Mean Ethnic Differences Between Asian and Caucasian Americans on the Social Problem Solving Inventory-Revised (SPSI-R)

	Ethnic group		
SPSI-R scale	Asian	Caucasian	p
Positive Problem Orientation	12.16 (3.82)	11.78 (3.41)	ns
Negative Problem Orientation	19.78 (7.81)	17.43 (7.60)	ns
Rational Problem Solving Style	46.60 (11.43)	45.47 (14.11)	ns
Impulsivity/Carelessness Style	16.98 (7.54)	12.76 (6.97)	<.01
Avoidance Style	11.06 (5.15)	9.20 (5.70)	ns

Note: For Asian Americans, $n = 45$; for Caucasian Americans, $n = 49$. Numbers in parentheses are standard deviations. From "A look at the coping strategies and styles of Asian Americans: Similar and different?," by E. C. Chang, 2001, in C. R. Snyder (Ed.), *Coping with stress: Effective people and processes* (pp. 222-239). New York: Oxford University Press. Reprinted by permission of Oxford University Press.

3. SOURCES OF DIFFERENCES IN THE EXPERIENCE OF ASIAN COMPARED TO CAUCASIAN AMERICANS

Given the unique pressures associated with ethnic minority status in the United States, considerable evidence points to increased vulnerability to stress in ethnic minorities. Ethnic minorities often differ on coping because they have distinct notions about who they are as a member of an ethnic group, what is "right" to do as a member of their ethnic group, and how other people will treat them because of their ethnic group identity. Abe and Zane (1990) for example, found greater levels of psychological distress among foreign-born Asian American students than among Caucasian American students. Interestingly, these differences were evident even when demographic, personality, and response-style variables were controlled. These findings are consistent with early reports of greater nervousness, loneliness, and anxiety among Chinese American and Japanese American students (Sue & Frank, 1973; Sue & Kirk, 1973). More recently, researchers have explored other sources of stress for Asian Americans including: being labeled as a model minority, ethnic identity, and stress related to the acculturation process.

Among ethnic minority groups, the case of Asian Americans is interesting because one could argue that as a group, Asian Americans are not a minority *per se* because they are not viewed as underrepresented in academic or economic domains (e.g., Raspberry, 1994). Moreover, Asian Americans appear to be socially integrated. For instance, rates of intermarriage are higher among Asian Americans than they are among other ethnic minority groups (Fugita & O'Brien, 1985; Kitano, Yeung, Chai, & Hatanaka, 1984). Nonetheless, Asian Americans carry the label *model minority*. This very label suggests that Asians are not viewed simply as an indistinguishable part of the mainstream even though there is much overlap between Asian and American values of achievement and Asian American attainment of educational, occupational, and income markers of success (Chan, 1991; Fugita & O'Brien, 1985; Lee, 1996; Osajima, 1995; Takaki, 1993). Thus, rather than being labeled successful Americans, Asian Americans are dubbed the model minority. Some Asian Americans may view being a model minority positively; that is, one is viewed as a model, as an example for imitation or emulation. On the other hand, the term may be viewed as a means of keeping this group outside of social boundaries, maintaining the minority status and not allowing Asians into mainstream society.

Not surprisingly, the persistent model minority image of Asian Americans as highly successful, upwardly mobile, well-educated, and relatively well-adjusted can also be can also be a source of stress. The strong emphasis on education and high academic standards, along with a cultural emphasis on filial obligations, conformity, and respect for authority (Kitano, 1969; Sue & Wagner, 1973) may place Asian Americans at risk for problems with achievement (Pang, 1991) as well as social and emotional adjustment (Kitano, 1969; Sue & Zane, 1985).

Finally, stresses can also arise from the acculturation process for Asian Americans, a group with indigenous collectivist values residing in a highly individualistic nation. Considerable evidence suggests, for instance, that Asian Americans attempt to separate from the family in accordance with Western norms of becoming an individuated and self-reliant person. However, they also experience a pull in the opposite direction, toward loyalty to the norms of family cohesion, interdependency, and identification to the Asian culture. Thus, internal and external conflicts arise from the dynamic struggles with opposing value systems in which breaking away from the family's belief structures may evoke turmoil and guilt over the failure to comply with one's internalized obligations to the family (e.g., Lieber, Chin, Nihira, & Mink, 2001; Ownbey & Horridge, 1998).

4. FUTURE METHODOLOGICAL DIRECTIONS FOR STUDYING THE COPING BEHAVIORS OF ASIAN AMERICANS

In this chapter, our goal was to provide a preliminary examination of the coping behaviors of Asian Americans compared to Caucasian Americans. However, to obtain a better understanding of how Asian Americans cope, it may also be worth discussing methodological approaches that go beyond the use of self-report instruments because any single measure of coping, on its own, is incomplete.

In cultural studies using self-report measures, for instance, it is difficult to know whether differences between cultures reflect real differences in experience, differences in cultural rules regarding the disclosure of emotional states, or both. In addition, it is unclear whether different cultural beliefs and values regarding emotions and coping will translate into tangible differences in physiological responding. Thus, to more-fully understand the phenomena unfolding when one copes with a stressful experience, it is useful to utilize multiple methods of investigation including self-report, behavioral, and psychophysiological measures. Here, we focus on two promising methods which may offer additional insights to the coping process for Asian Americans. These involve the use of psychophysiological assessments and ecological sampling methods (ESM).

4.1. Using Psychophysiological Assessments to Examine Coping in Asian Americans

While a full discussion of all psychophysiological modes of measurement is beyond the scope of this chapter (see Cacioppo & Tassinary, 2000, for a review of psychophysiological methods), we will direct our discussion to those focusing on autonomic nervous system (ANS) activity. Among the most-widely used indices to measure ANS activation include those that measure electrodermal activity, respiratory activity, and cardiovascular activity. Of these, the broadest set of measures index cardiovascular activity (e.g., heart rate, diastolic and systolic blood pressure, see Obrist, 1981). Like every other major physiological subdivision of the body, the cardiovascular system is one of complexity and many responsibilities. The heart muscles and the blood vessels work together to meet the ever-changing demands of our organs and to serve as a network of supply of oxygen and nutrients, as well as provide communication within the body.

In early psychophysiological research, measurements of the cardiovascular system were often taken as indices of arousal. Since those early beginnings, however, researchers have moved on to examine various patterning of cardiovascular responses in different emotional states. Studies on stress and coping that use psychophysiological methods, for instance, have examined a variety of phenomena, including how individual differences in personality account for physiological consequences related to coping (e.g., Type A personalities, Hinton, 1988; hostility, Fredrickson et al., 2000; hardiness, Wiebe, 1991), the relations between emotion regulation and physiological reactivity and recovery (e.g., Fredrickson & Levenson, 1998; Fredrickson, Mancuso, Branigan, & Tugade, 2000; Gross & Levenson, 1993, 1997; Tugade & Fredrickson, 2004), the role of cognitive appraisals on physiological responses to stress (e.g., Tomaka, Blascovich, Kibler, & Ernst, 1997), and finally, cultural similarities and differences in physiological responding. The latter area of study (i.e., cultural studies), is perhaps the least examined area of psychophysiological study. Moreover, such studies arenotably sparse in their focus on Asian cultures.

Of the studies that have focused on psychophysiological responding among Asian cultures, an area that has received much interest centers on the individualism/collectivism paradigm. Cultural ideologies of individualism and collectivism are intertwined with notions about emotional expression and control. For instance, ethnographic proscriptions suggest that members of most Asian cultures believe more in the importance of moderating or controlling one's emotions compared to more individualistic, Caucasian Americans. As such, these cultural notions suggest that psychophysiological differences between Asian and Caucasian cultures are worth exploring.

Some studies have found compelling evidence for greater emotional moderation among members of Asian cultures compared to Caucasian cultures, while others have not. Furthermore, the pattern of cultural differences can vary as a function of the aspect of emotion being measured (e.g., subjective, physiological), which underscores the importance of multi-measure analyses. For instance, Levenson, Ekman, Heider, and Friesen (1992) examined the emotional responses of the Minangkabau of West Sumatra, a culture with strong proscriptions against public displays of negative emotion. Particiapants in this study were Minangkabau and Caucasian American males and females. Continuous measures of ANS activation were collected from participants as they took part in a Directed Facial Action (DFA) task, wherein they were asked to contract their facial muscles in configurations that, when coded, are thought to correspond to different affective experiences. After each facial configuration was made, participants provided self-reports of their subjective experiences of emotion. Levenson and colleagues found that, in terms of self-report measures, the Minangkabau reported less intense emotions, compared to Caucasian Americans. This finding is consistent with cultural stereotypes, indicating greater emotional moderation among Asian cultures. Interestingly, while there were cultural differences in self-reported experiences of emotion, there were no evident cultural differences in ANS activation.

Most of the early studies on cultural differences in physiological activation have only examined the interplay between culture and physiological indices of coping in relatively nonsocial contexts (cf., Tsai & Levenson, 1997). Accordingly, Tsai and Levenson (1997) compared physiological and self-reported, subjective, responses of emotion of Asian American and Caucasian American dating couples as they described the greatest conflict in their relationship. As in previous research, the authors found minimal cultural differences at the level of physiological responding. However, self-reports of emotional experiences corroborated cultural notions about emotion modulation: Compared to Caucasian Americans, Asian Americans reported less intense emotions.

Together, these studies highlight the need to further explore coping and Asian Americans through a psychophysiological lens. A particularly interesting future area of research might be to extend research beyond exploring how Asian Americans and Caucasian Americans differ in their *magnitudes* of physiological activation (e.g., arousal levels), to investigation how they might differ in their *durations* of physiological responding (e.g., how quickly they physiologically recover from the reactivity generated by certain stressors). This area of inquiry is particularly important in coping research, because considerable evidence indicates that sympathetic arousal occasioned by negative emotional states for extended periods of time is related to the onset of cardiovascular disease, such as coronary heart disease and essential hypertension (for reviews, see Anderson, 1989; Blascovich & Katkin, 1993; Krantz & Manuck, 1984; Williams, Haney, Lee, Kong, Blumenthal, & Whalen, 1980). Because this area of research has been relatively understudied, it would be fruitful to explore the relations between ethnographic proscriptions of emotion control and modulation and durations of physiological activation, in addition to different levels of arousal.

4.2. Using The Experience Sampling Method to Assess for Coping in Asian Americans

Another innovative approach to study the stress and coping process that goes beyond the use of conventional self-reports involve ecological sampling methods. These methods provide information about "phenomenological" aspects of the coping process and of behavior that often cannot be captured by typical self-report research instruments. The Experience Sampling Method (ESM) is one of such methods.

To provide a brief overview, the ESM has been developed to capture the subjective experiences of people interacting in their natural environments. It allows researchers to repeatedly measure a participant's everyday activities, thoughts, and accompanying psychological states in natural settings (Csikszentmihalyi & Larson, 1987; Csikszentmihalyi, Larson, & Prescott, 1977; Feldman Barrett, & Barrett, 2001; Larson & Csikszentmihalyi, 1983). In a typical ESM study, participants carry a pre-programmed signaling wristwatch, an electronic pager, or a personal digital assistant (PDA), which signals them at random times during a random or specific period of time (determined by the researcher) from early morning to 11 P.M. or later, over several weeks. In most cases, participants are signaled up to 10 times daily, and whenever signaled, they complete self-report forms (either on the PDA or on paper). At the signal, participants report their activities, location, thoughts, and companions, and rate their state of consciousness at the moment on various numerical scales, regarding how happy they are, how well they are concentrating, how strongly they are motivated, how high their self-esteem is, and so on. The reliability and validity of the ESM have been demonstrated in a growing body of literature (e.g., Conner, Tugade, & Feldman Barrett, 2004; Csikszentmihalyi & Larson, 1987; Feldman Barrett, 2004; Hormuth, 1986; Moneta & Csikszentmihalyi, 1996). Considering its procedural and phenomenologically oriented aspects, the ESM is a unique and innovative method which makes it possible to "bridge the precision of paper-and-pencil measurement and the ecological validity of on-site observational techniques" (Csikszentmihalyi et al., 1993, p. 49).

To date a number of studies have used the ESM to illuminate subjective experiences of people in their daily lives. However, only a few studies have specifically examined the phenomenology of Asian Americans' everyday life experiences by using the method. One ESM study by Asakawa and Csikszentmihalyi (1998b) compared the studying habits of Asian American and Caucasian American adolescents and found that Asian Americans had greater positive experiences than Caucasian Americans when studying. Figure 1 shows Asian and Caucasian groups' average "z" scores of happiness, enjoyment, feeling good about themselves, activeness, unself-consciousness (level of not being self-conscious), and perceived control of the situation when they were studying. The value "zero" for average "z" score for each experiential variable indicates the weekly average of each group. Thus, for example, if the variable "happy" is positive for Asian Americans when studying, it means that Asian Americans feel happier when studying than they feel on average during the ESM week. According to the results in Figure 1, when studying, Asian American adolescents were significantly happier, felt more enjoyment, felt better about themselves, and felt more in control than Caucasian American adolescents. Asian American adolescents also tended to be less self-conscious than their Caucasian American counterparts when studying. Thus, these findings clearly show that the Asian American adolescents had relatively more positive experiences than their Caucasian American counterparts when they were studying.

The ESM analysis described above focused on the subjective experiences of adolescents in a specific situation. However, the ESM can also allow researchers to examine situational and temporal changes of respondents' experiences. In that regard, Asakawa and Csikszentmihalyi (1998a) found interesting patterns of experience change observed as the levels of Asian and Caucasian American adolescents' perceptions of importance for their future goals changed from low to high across time. Figure 2 shows the two groups' average "z" scores on the five dimensions of experience in the two situations – one is where the perceived importance to their future goals was high (higher than the weekly average) and the other is where the perceived importance to their future goals was low (lower than the weekly average). The results indicate that when perceived future importance was low, Asian American adolescents were less happy, felt less enjoyment, felt worse about themselves, less active, and more self-conscious than their weekly average, while when their perception of future importance was high, Asian American adolescents were happier, felt more enjoyment, felt better about themselves, were more active, and less self-conscious than their weekly average. Moreover, the level of Asian American adolescents' experience

Figure 1. Quality of experience while studying
~ = marginal significance. $^*p < .05.$ $^{**}p < .01.$
Source: Adapted from Asakawa and Csikszentmihalyi (1998b).

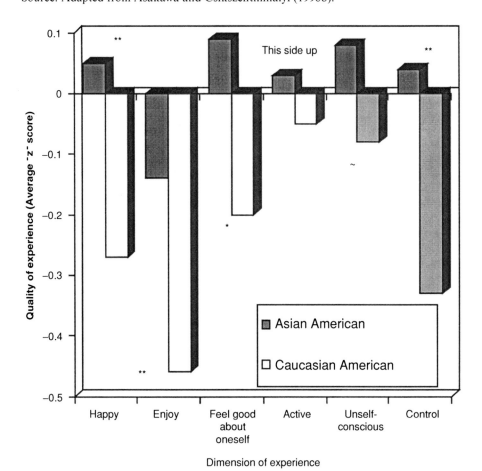

changed dramatically from negative to positive as their perception of future importance changed from low to high.

Interestingly, it seems that Caucasian American adolescents' quality of experience in the same situations is quite different. When their perception of future importance was low, they were happier, felt more enjoyment, and were less self-conscious, but felt worse about themselves and less active than their weekly average. When their perception of future importance was high, they were feeling better about themselves and more active, but they were less happy, felt less enjoyment, and were more self-conscious than their weekly average.

To date a few ESM studies have been conducted to examine Asian Americans' experiences in an attempt to explore the reasons for their high academic attainments (Asakawa, 2001; Asakawa & Csikszentmihalyi, 1998a, 1998b, 2000). While the number of

Figure 2. Quality of experience related to importance to future goals.

Note: ANCOVA with

A: Future importance (High vs. Low)

B: Ethnicity (Asian vs. Caucasian) as factors.

Happy   A × B, $p < .01$

Enjoy   A × B, $p < .01$

Feel good about oneself   A × B, $p < .05$; A, $p < .001$

Active   A × B, marginal significance; A, $p < .001$

Unself-conscious   A × B, $p < .05$

Source: Adapted from Asakawa and Csikszentmihalyi (1998b).

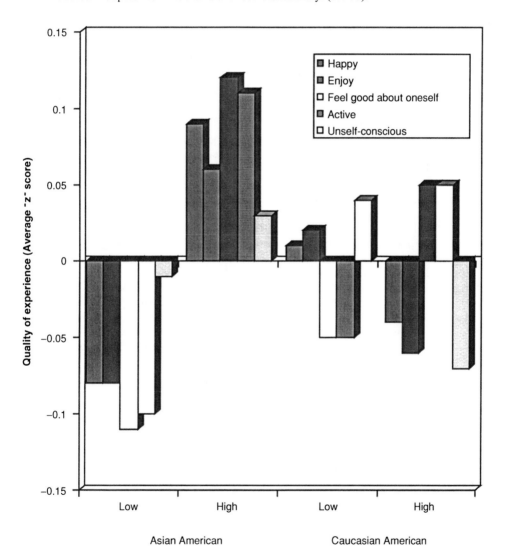

ESM studies focusing on Asian Americans is scarce, those studies that do exist have certainly provided insightful information about Asian Americans' academic success from a phenomenological perspective. How then can we use this innovative research technique of the ESM to assess for coping in Asian Americans? As mentioned previously, the most unique aspect of the ESM is that it captures situational and temporal details of experiences. Accordingly, this method allows researchers to examine an individual's coping strategies, coping process, and accompanying psychological states in his or her natural settings across time. For example, the ESM would allow researchers to identify specific stressful events as they naturally unfold for Asian Americans, to identify specific coping behaviors or activities Asian Americans engage in, to determine the places and people Asian Americans go to when experiencing stress, and to also clarify changes in the thoughts and feelings experienced by Asian Americans after they encounter a stressful situation. Thus, the ESM would be able to tap both the external (i.e., activities, location, and companions) and the internal (i.e., thoughts, and psychological states) dimensions of Asian American's experience in their on-going coping process.

CONCLUSION

In conclusion, it is clear to us there is much that remains to be understood about the stress and coping experience of Asian Americans as a whole. Indeed, beyond the coping models discussed in the present chapter, there are a number of alternative and novel models of coping that can and should also be examined in future studies of Asian Americans. For example, Wong (1993; Wong & Ujimoto, 1998; see also Hobfoll, 2001) has proposed that a variety of coping strategies may be used by individuals from different cultural groups to effectively deal with stressful experiences as long as appropriate resources are available to them to meet new challenges and threats. Similarly, findings from some studies show that beyond differences in coping practices among Asian Americans, there may be differences in coping sources sought (e.g., seeking familial and social resources over professional resources; Yeh & Wang, 2000). In sum, it is clear to us that researchers will be most likely be able to obtain a rich understanding of how Asian Americans cope with stress by considering varied methodologies and theoretical models. And because Asian Americans do not represent a singular collective, the use of different methodologies and theoretical frameworks may also help identify important stress and coping differences between the many Asian American ethnic groups.

REFERENCES

Abe, J. S., & Zane, N. W. S. (1990). Psychological maladjustment among Asian and White American college students: Controlling for confounds. *Journal of Counseling Psychology, 37*, 437-444.

Anderson, N. B. (1989). Racial differences in stress-induced cardiovascular reactivity and hypertension: Current status and substantive issues. *Psychological Bulletin, 105*, 89-105.

Asakawa, K. (2001). Family socialization practices and their effects on the internalization of educational values for Asian and White American adolescents. *Applied Developmental Science, 5*, 184-194.

Asakawa, K., & Csikszentmihalyi, M. (1998a). The quality of experience of Asian American adolescents in activities related to future goals. *Journal of Youth and Adolescence, 27*, 141-163.

Asakawa, K., & Csikszentmihalyi, M. (1998b). The quality of experience of Asian American adolescents in academic activities: An exploration of educational achievement. *Journal of Research on Adolescence, 8*, 241-262.

Asakawa, K., & Csikszentmihalyi, M. (2000). Feelings of connectedness and internalization of values in Asian American adolescents. *Journal of Youth and Adolescence*, *29*, 121-145.

Blascovich, J., & Katkin, E. S. (1993). *Cardiovascular reactivity to psychological stress and disease*. Washington, DC: American Psychological Association.

Cacioppo, J. T., Tassinary, L. G., & Bernston, G. G. (Eds.). (2000). *Handbook of psychophysiology*. New York: Cambridge University Press.

Carver, C. S., Scheier, M. F., & Weintraub, J. K. (1989). Assessing coping strategies: A theoretically based approach. *Journal of Personality and Social Psychology*, *56*, 267-283.

Chang, E. C. (1998). Cultural differences, perfectionism, and suicidal risk: Does social problem solving still matter? *Cognitive Therapy and Research*, *22*, 237-254.

Chang, E. C. (2001). A look at the coping strategies and styles of Asian Americans: Similar and different? In C. R. Snyder (Ed.), *Coping with stress: Effective people and processes* (pp. 222-239). New York: Oxford University Press.

Chang, E. C., D'Zurilla, T. J., & Sanna, L. J. (Eds.). (2004). *Social problem solving: Theory, research, and training*. Washington, DC: American Psychological Association.

Conner, T., Tugade, M. M., & Barrett, L. F. (2004). Ecological momentary assessment. In N. Anderson (Ed.), *Encyclopedia of health and behavior* (pp. 291-292). Thousand Oaks, CA: Sage.

Csikszentmihalyi, M., & Larson, R. (1987). Validity and reliability of experience-sampling method. *Journal of Nervous and Mental Diseases*, *175*, 526-536.

Csikszentmihalyi, M., Larson, R., & Prescott, S. (1977). The ecology of adolescent activity and experience. *Journal of Youth and Adolescence*, *6*, 281-294.

Csikszentmihalyi, M., Rathunde, K., & Whalen, S. (1993). *Talented teenagers: The roots of success and failure*. New York: Cambridge University Press.

D'Zurilla, T. J. (1986). *Problem-solving therapy: A social competence approach to clinical intervention*. New York: Springer.

D'Zurilla, T. J., & Chang, E. C. (1995). The relations between social problem solving and coping. *Cognitive Therapy and Research*, *19*, 549-564.

D'Zurilla, T. J., Chang, E. C., Nottingham, E. J., IV, & Faccini, L. (1998). Social problem-solving deficits and hopelessness, depression, and suicidal risk in college students and psychiatric inpatients. *Journal of Clinical Psychology*, *54*, 1-17.

D'Zurilla, T. J., & Maydeu-Olivares, A. (1995). Conceptual and methodological issues in social problem-solving assessment. *Behavior Therapy*, *26*, 409-432.

D'Zurilla, T. J., & Nezu, A. M. (1990). Development and preliminary evaluation of the Social Problem-Solving Inventory (SPSI). *Psychological Assessment*, *2*, 156-163.

D'Zurilla, T. J., Nezu, A. M., & Maydeu-Olivares, A. (2002). *Manual for the Social Problem-Solving Inventory-Revised*. North Tonawanda, NY: Multi-Health Systems.

Epstein, S. (1973). The self-concept revisited, or a theory of a theory. *American Psychologist*, *28*, 404-416.

Epstein, S. (1990). Cognitive-experiential self-theory. In L. A. Previn (Ed.), *Handbook of personality: Theory and research* (pp.165-192). New York: Guilford Press.

Epstein, S. (1992). Coping ability, negative self-evaluation, and overgeneralization: Experiment and theory. *Journal of Personality and Social Psychology*, *62*, 826-836.

Epstein, S., & Katz, L. (1992). Coping ability, stress, productive load, and symptoms. *Journal of Personality and Social Psychology*, *62*, 813-825.

Epstein, S., & Meier, P. (1989). Constructive thinking: A broad coping variable with specific components. *Journal of Personality and Social Psychology*, *57*, 332-350.

Feldman Barrett, L., & Barrett, D. J. (2001). An introduction to computerized experience sampling in psychology. *Social Science Computer Review*, *19*, 175-185.

Folkman, S., & Lazarus, R. S. (1985). If it changes it must be a process: Study of emotion and coping during three stages of a college examination. *Journal of Personality and Social Psychology*, *48*, 150-170.

Feldman Barrett, L. (2004). Feelings or words? Understanding the content in self-report ratings of emotional experience. *Journal of Personality and Social Psychology*, *87*, 266-281.

Fredrickson, B. L., & Levenson, R. W. (1998). Positive emotions speed recovery from the cardiovascular sequelae of negative emotions. *Cognition and Emotion*, *12*, 191-220.

Fredrickson, B. L., Mancuso, R. A., Branigan, C., & Tugade, M. M. (2000). The undoing effect of positive emotions. *Motivation and Emotion*, *24*, 237-258.

Fredrickson, B. L., Maynard, K. E., Helms, M. J., Haney, T. L., Siegler, I. C., & Barefoot, J. C. (2000). Hostility predicts magnitude and duration of blood pressure response to anger. *Journal of Behavioral Medicine*, *23*, 229-243.

Fugita, S. S., & O'Brien, D. J. (1985). Structural assimilation, ethnic group membership, and political participation among Japanese Americans: A research note. *Social Forces, 63*, 986-995.

Greenwald, A. G. (1980). The totalitarian ego: Fabrication and revision of personal history. *American Psychologist, 35*, 603-618.

Gross, J. J., & Levenson, R. W. (1993). Emotional suppression: Physiology, self-report, and expressive behavior. *Journal of Personality and Social Psychology, 64*, 970-986.

Gross, J. J., & Levenson, R. W. (1997). Hiding feelings: The acute effects of inhibiting negative and positive emotion. *Journal of Abnormal Psychology, 106*, 95-103.

Hinton, J. W. (1988). The psychophysiology of stress and personal coping styles. In H. L. Wagner (Ed.), *Social psychophysiology and emotion: Theory and clinical applications* (pp. 175-195). New York: John Wiley & Sons.

Hobfoll, S. E. (2001). The influence of culture, community, and the nested-self in the stress process: Advancing conservation of resources theory. *Applied Psychology: An International Review, 50*, 337-370.

Hormuth, W. E. (1986). The sampling of experience in situation. *Journal of Personality, 54*, 262-293.

Kitano, H. H. (1969). *Japanese Americans: The evolution of a subculture.* Englewood Cliffs, NJ: Prentice-Hall.

Kitano, H. H., Yeung, W., Chai, L., & Hatanaka, H. (1984). Asian-American interracial marriage. *Journal of Marriage and the Family, 46*, 179-190.

Krantz, D. S., & Mauck, S. B. (1984). Acute psychophysiologic reactivity and risk for cardiovascular disease: A review and methodological critique. *Psychological Bulletin, 96*, 435-464.

Larson, R., & Csikszentmihalyi, M. (1983). The experience sampling method. In D. W. Fiske, and H. T. Reis (Ed.), *Naturalistic approaches to studying social interaction* (pp. 41-56). San Francisco: Jossey-Bass.

Lazarus, R. S., & Folkman, S. (1984). *Stress, appraisal, and coping.* New York: Springer.

Lee, E. (1996). Asian American families: An overview. In M. McGoldrick & J. Giordano (Eds.), *Ethnicity and family therapy* (pp. 227-248). New York: The Guilford Press.

Levenson, R. W., Ekman, P., Heider, K., & Friesen, W. V. (1992). Emotion and autonomic nervous system activity in the Minangkabau of West Sumatra. *Journal of Personality and Social Psychology, 62*, 972-988.

Lieber, E., Chin, D., Nihira, K., & Mink, I. T. (2001). Holding on and letting go: Identity and acculturation among Chinese immigrants. *Cultural Diversity and Ethnic Minority Psychology, 7*, 247-261.

Markus, H. R., & Kitayama, S. (1991). Culture and the self: Implications for cognition, emotion, and motivation. *Psychological Review, 98*, 224-253.

Moneta, G. B., & Csikszentmihalyi, M. (1996). The effect of perceived challenges and skills on the quality of subjective experience. *Journal of Personality, 64*, 275-310.

Nezu, A. M., Nezu, C. M., Perri, M. G. (1989). *Problem-solving therapy for depression: Theory, research, and clinical guidelines.* New York: Wiley.

Ownbey, S. F., & Horridge, P. E. (1998). The Suinn-Lew Asian Self-Identity Acculturation Scale: Test with a non-student, Asian-American sample. *Social Behavior and Personality, 26*, 57-86.

Orbist, P. A. (1981). *Cardiovascular psychophysiology: A perspective.* New York: Plenum Press.

Osajima, K. (1995). Racial politics and the invisibility of Asian Americans in higher education. *Educational Foundations, 9*, 35-53.

Pang, V. (1991). The relationship of text anxiety and math achievement to parental values in Asian-American and European-American middle school students. *Journal of Research and Development in Education, 24*, 1-10.

Phinney, J. (1996). When we talk about American ethnic groups, what do we mean? *American Psychologist, 51*, 918-927.

Roth, S., & Cohen, L. (1986). Approach, avoidance, and coping with stress. *American Psychologist, 41*, 813-819.

Stone, A. A., & Neale, J. M. (1984). New measure of daily coping: Development and preliminary results. *Journal of Personality and Social Psychology, 46*, 892-906.

Sue, D. W., & Frank, A. C. (1973). A typological approach to the psychological study of Chinese and Japanese American college males. *Journal of Social Issues, 29*, 129-148.

Sue, D. W., & Kirk, B. A. (1973). Differential characteristics of Japanese-American and Chinese-American college students. *Journal of Counseling Psychology, 20*, 142-148

Sue, S., & Zane, N. (1985). Academic achievement and socioemotional adjustment among Chinese university students. *Journal of Counseling Psychology, 32*, 570-579.

Suls, J., & Fletcher, B. (1985). The relative efficacy of avoidant and non-avoidant coping strategies: A meta-analysis. *Health Psychology, 4*, 249-288.

Takaki, R. (1993). *A different mirror: A history of multicultural America*. Boston, MA: Clearinghouse.

Tweed, R. G., White, K., & Lehman, D. R. (2004). Culture, stress, and coping: Internally- and externally-targeted control strategies of European Canadians, East Asian Canadians, and Japanese. *Journal of Cross-Cultural Psychology, 35*, 652-668.

Tobin, L. D., Holroyd, K. A., Reynolds, R. V., & Wigal, J. K. (1989). The hierarchical factor structure of the Coping Strategies Inventory. *Cognitive Therapy and Research, 13*, 343-361.

Tomaka, J., Blascovich, J., Kibler, J., & Ernst, J. M. (1997). Cognitive and physiological antecedents of threat and challenge appraisal. *Journal of Personality and Social Psychology, 73*, 63-72.

Triandis, H. C. (1995). *Individualism and collectivism*. Boulder, CO: Westview Press.

Tsai, J. L., & Levenson, R. W. (1997). Cultural influences of emotional responding: Chinese American and European American dating couples during interpersonal conflict. *Journal of Cross-Cultural Psychology, 28*, 600-625.

Tugade, M. M. & Fredrickson, B. L. (2004). Resilient individuals use positive emotions to bounce back from negative emotional experiences. *Journal of Personality and Social Psychology, 86*, 320-333.

Uba, L. (1994). *Asian Americans: Personality patterns, identity, and mental health*. New York: Guilford Press.

Wiebe, D. J. (1991). Hardiness and stress moderation: A test of proposed mechanisms. *Journal of Personality and Social Psychology, 60*, 89-99.

Williams, R.B., Haney, L.T., Lee, K.L., Kong, Y., Blumenthal, J., & Whalen, R. (1980). Type A behavior, hostility, and coronary atherosclerosis. *Psychosomatic Medicine, 42*, 539-549.

Wong, P. T. P. (1993). Effective management of life stress: The resource-congruence model. *Stress Medicine, 9*, 51-60.

Wong, P. T. P., & Ujimoto, K. V. (1998). The elderly: Their stress, coping, and mental health. In L. C. Lee & N. W. S. Zane (Eds.), *Handbook of Asian American psychology* (pp. 165-209). Thousand Oaks, CA: Sage Publications.

Yeh, C., & Wang, Y. W. (2000). Asian American coping attitudes, sources, and practices: Implications for indigenous counseling strategies. *Journal of College Student Development, 41*, 94-103.

AUTHOR'S NOTE

The first author would like to acknowledge Chang Suk-Choon and Tae Myung-Sook for their encouragement and support throughout this project.

Correspondence concerning this work should be sent to Edward C. Chang, Department of Psychology, University of Michigan, 525 East University Avenue, Ann Arbor, MI 48109. Electronic mail may be sent to changec@umich.edu.

THE AGONY, SILENT GRIEF, AND DEEP FRUSTRATION OF MANY COMMUNITIES IN THE MIDDLE EAST:
Challenges for Coping and Survival

Naji Abi-Hashem

1. INTRODUCTION

The Middle East is a vast area with a rich history and heritage. The majority of its people are friendly, content, and hospitable; they are also pleasant, non-aggressive, non-political, and non-radical. Many parts of the Middle East and the Arabic-Islamic world are peaceful and tranquil and life appears easy and meaningful. However, several areas in the region have been marked for generations by conflict, turmoil, and wars. Internal instability and external interference have contributed to the major troubles and chronic disorders, which in turn have resulted in substantial agony, lingering trauma, deep frustration, and communal suffering to multitude of people of all backgrounds, ages and walks of life.

The Middle East is the birthplace of ancient civilizations and prominent world religions. Its major cities are the vibrant places where tradition, customs, faith, and values meet with modern lifestyles and diverse societies and worldviews. Social appropriateness is emphasized in speech, behavior, and appearance. Titles and compliments are important. The respect of the elderly is imperative. Both immediate and extended families are the primary places where social roles are institutionalized and one's identity is formed and maintained. The concept of "shame" is a powerful dynamic in communal and familial life because it affects interactions and shapes the majority of public behaviors and personal conducts.

Religious identity is an important ingredient in the fabric of the Middle Eastern societies and mentalities. Actually one's religious sect or affiliation, such as Sunnii, Shiitte, Eastern Orthodox, Maronite, Latin, Greek Catholic, Jewish, or Druze is written on their personal identification card in most countries and provinces

The outside observer will immediately notice several major characteristics of any society in the Arabic-Islamic world: 1) a strong family bond, 2) a strong sense of community and belongingness, 3) a strong social identity, 4) a strong fondness of the historical

Naji Abi-Hashem, Independent Scholar & Associate with Venture International heritage, and 5) a strong rootedness in the land. Community is a very significant factor and a powerful organizing principle in the life of the people in the Middle East. People are aware of its presence and function as if it has a personality of its own. The concept of community is different from the concept of society at large. It is the lively molecule of culture or nation. Like culture, community is difficult to explain or define. It is best felt, lived, and experienced.

Therefore, when wars break out, they can be devastating, not only to individuals, but also to families, societies, and cultures. Arms conflicts severely disturb the community spirit and the sense of rootedness in the land. They destroy the continuity between generations and the precious cultural characteristics of people. Besides the social-historical consequences of war, there are significant psychological-emotional consequences. Exposure to extreme violence, severe stress, multiple losses, constant fear of death, and war tragedies, can have a long lasting damaging effects on young, middle-aged, or older people alike. Research studies have shown that some of the victims who were exposed to the stress of war will never completely recover (Green, Lindy, & Grace, 1988; Hobfoll et al., 1991; Silver & Wortman, 1980).

According to Carballo et al (2004, ¶ 1), recently there has been a real concern about the impact of war on people: "The twentieth century has seen an increased concern for the implications of war for civilian populations, and more attention has been given to psychosocial impacts of uprooting and displacement." Acute and chronic traumas, severe family disruptions and separations coupled with multiple losses of place, national identity, personal health, home environment, close friends and relatives can have a serious negative impact on the psychosocial and spiritual well-being of the people.

Following any given ethno-political conflict or war, family reunification, house reconstruction, and basic survival skills have become of utmost importance to humanitarian agencies and crisis intervention care-teams. The *war-victims*, who eventually become *war-survivors*, have to reconstruct their mental, physical, and emotional lives and to relearn how to navigate life's essential demands anew, while carrying within them the many scars of the tragedy and pain.

Social struggles, political instabilities, economic hardships, religious tensions, confusion of norms, the rise of extremism, polarization of values, clash of cultures and ideologies, apprehension of the future conditions, lack of trust in leaderships, are vividly present in many parts of the Middle East, even within the Israeli society itself. The constant threat, fear, fighting, bombing, kidnapping, killing, exploding, shelling, invading, sounds of sirens, guerrilla warfare, scenes of shattered buildings, burned cars, twisted debris and glasses filling the streets, and sight of blood and physical injuries become heavily imprinted on people's unconscious mind and regulate their actions and reactions. All that is compounded by sudden and multiple moves under danger and by the harsh living conditions inflicted upon them. In addition, the lack of basic services like water, food, electricity, medicine, transportation, and telecommunication (phone, radio, TV), in addition to the ethnic segregation and demographic shift of major groups and population, have been causing a lot of social disintegration, family disruption, mental disorientation, emotional disconnection, cultural disharmony, and existential crisis.

Given the above bleak picture of war-torn areas of the Middle East, the phrase *stress and coping* seems hardly adequate to capture the lingering trauma and prolonged suffering that people have to endure in such highly troubled places. The agony and grief are usually so intense, pervasive, and chronic that they can only be described as deep suffering. The challenge for psychologists is to understand how people cope with such prolonged agony and suffering. In the following sections, we will examine more closely the trying situations in the Middle East and the people's various patterns of coping.

1.1. The Case of Lebanon: A Personal Account

I was born and raised in Lebanon. I left Beirut in the early eighties, when I was 30 years old, and came to the US as a student to pursue further education in Cultural Studies, Theology, Psychology and Counseling. Therefore, I witnessed most of the civil wars and devastations, which started in the late seventies and persisted on and off, and in different locations around Beirut, to the early nineties. Presently, I go back home each year for at least two months trying to help in any way possible by making myself available to the community at large. There are so many needs and opportunities for service. I am often humbled by the acceptance and respect I receive from educators, community leaders, pastors, and healthcare professionals alike; not to mention the joy, warmth, and reward I always experience as a result of my walking along them and being part of their lives.

The fact that Lebanon is not in the daily news anymore does not mean that all its troubles have disappeared or deep psychosocial wounds have healed. This tiny nation has endured a tremendous hardship and still is suffering on many levels. The aftermath of all the violence, injuries, losses, and traumas are still alive and clearly evident to the sensitive and professional eye. Lebanese people are known for their remarkable resiliency, survival skills, and social bonding. They attempted to bounce back after each crushing tragedy and devastating experience. However, the price has been very costly as the agony continues.

A whole generation was born and grew up in that violent, unstable, tense, and dangerous environment. For example, all my nine nieces and nephews were born during the troubled years. To them, and thousands like them of the same generation, the normal world of their childhood included explosions, shelling, blocked roads, fear of invasions, stories of wars, scenes of deaths, interrupted school life, no electricity for weeks, limited amount of water, little or no toys to play with, staying in shelters of basements for many long nights, being uprooted several times, and worries about what kind of a future was waiting for them as they grow up.

In Beirut, the Lebanese people have suffered from such political unrest for more than 15 years, and the tragedy continues. We have other people's wars on our land. The media always reported that Moslems and Christians were fighting while the real issues were pure political, mainly caused by outside interferences. Lebanese have lived together for centuries and they sincerely want to be left alone. Many wonder, where were the nations of the world and where were the superpowers when Lebanon was invaded several times and Beirut was under constant shelling for months? Both Israel and Syria have violated Lebanon have had strategic and economical interests in Lebanon. Our destiny at this point is still vulnerable and unclear. That deeply hurts our national psyche. The Lebanese people were always proud of their accomplishments and high standard of living, rich history, cultural uniqueness, and leadership role in the region. Although they are part of the Arabic world, they, especially the Christian community, consider themselves more European in nature than Arabic (Nydell, 1987). Israel had the green light to create the so-called security zone in South Lebanon. Syria had the green light to take over East Beirut and the presidential palace and thus exercise control over all Lebanon, with heavy military and secret intelligence presence, in return for its participation in the so-called "allied forces" during the first Gulf War. Radical groups and Shiite or other Iranian backed groups (like the controversial Hozballah) are strongly present, armed, and active both in West Beirut and in South Lebanon, resisting Israel on the one hand and, on the other hand, reinforcing their ideological, cultural, and religious stand. Lebanon appears to be lost on the bargaining table of the Middle Eastern crisis and the ambiguous international agendas and politics (cf. Abi-Hashem, 1992b; 1999d). Filled with hopelessness, anguish, grief, and desperation, the Lebanese people, especially from the Christian community, are presently migrating in great numbers. They cope by leaving their homeland.

Not all the countries in the Middle East have oil or are financially rich. Some are still developing like Egypt, Syria, and Jordan. Some are wealthy and well established like United Arab Emirates. Lebanon, for example, was a leading country in the whole region in terms of finances, education, tourism, and income per capita, though it has no oil, deserts, or camels. It was the most free and democratic country in the whole region. For decades it was called the Switzerland of the Middle East. Not anymore! Unfortunately, small nations often pay the price of regional struggles and become victims of world politics. Lebanon now has significantly deteriorated and disintegrated and the Lebanese people still deeply grieve the loss of their accomplishments, uniqueness and most probably their country. With the winds of change and unpredictable politics in the region, we are afraid that our beautiful country would become another Cyprus or perhaps a second Palestine. It is losing its role as a leading nation, its mosaic cultures, its freedom of press and religion, its historic heritage, and its strategic place in the world.

Lebanon currently is caught between two opposing countries and in the midst of intensive regional conflicts. Lebanon's neighbors alternate frequently from being friendly to being aggressively intrusive into its affairs and territories. As it is usually the case in other parts of the world, surrounding countries, local powers, and far away superpowers have used many opportunities to manipulate Lebanon and to split its people, its balance, and its affairs over the last two decades and, mostly, they succeeded well (cf. Abi-Hashem, 1992b; 1999d).

When I personally hear or read about the agony of another country–like what happened in Kosovo and Yugoslavia and what is happening now in Iraq, Palestine-Israel, Sudan, and other places, I cannot help but take in these events seriously in a sad and sober mood. I could relate deeply because I have been there! Over the last few decades, I have experienced the severe agonies of my own people, while with them or apart from them following their suffering from a distance. How do I cope with my agonies and frustrations? I feel better when I feel their pain. I pray for them, and help whenever I can with any resources available. I also keep a close observation on and a keen interest in the new developments both in Lebanon and the whole Middle East region.

2. COPING WITH ETHNOPOLITICAL CONFLICTS AND WARS

Normally, during any kind of civil unrest, political turmoil, or military conflict, life can become unbearable and psychological problems multiply. Hobfoll et al., (1991, ¶ 4) has provided a comprehensive description of the negative effects of war on mental health:

*Some individuals will react in a more severe fashion, but they may be only a small per-
centage of those who were involved in the conflict. If the stress has become traumatic
and individuals develop full-blown posttraumatic stress disorder (PTSD), they are
likely to continue to react to current stimuli that are reminiscent of the original trauma
with psychological and physiological reactions appropriate only to the traumatic event.
If this occurs, one can expect to see (a) nightmares, (b) intrusive daytime images and
bodily sensation related to the traumatic experience, (c) excessive physiological star-
tle, (d) extreme anxiety states alternating with numbing and anhedonia, (e) difficulty
modulating arousal in general and anger in particular, and (f) dissociative reactions.*

It is important to note that war-related events may exacerbate former vulnerabilities
and reawaken unresolved matters. Normally, people who have had previous exposure to
wars with experiences of severe traumas, or who have had a history of psychological disturbances or psychopathology of any sort, are at higher risks than the other segments of
population. However, the mere presence of risk factors do not necessarily lead to negative
psychological outcome, social disturbances, or psychosomatic symptoms. According to
Hobfoll et al. (1991), there are two major factors that put people at risk as a result of the
stress of war: First, the greater the threat of loss or the actual loss to which they are
exposed, the greater their level of risk (threat to life being primary). Second, the fewer coping resources people have, the more likely they will be overwhelmed by their losses.
According to a number of specialists and researchers (cf. Abi-Hashem, 1999a, 1999c,
1999e; Worden, 1991), the outcomes usually depend on many additional factors such as:

- Circumstances surrounding the fighting, conflicts, and war troubles
- Emotional stability of the survivors
- Support systems available to the family or group during and after the crisis
- Age and gender of each individual involved
- Personality traits and the pre-existing conditions
- Severity of the conflictual trauma in terms of its timing, magnitude, and duration
- Problem solving skills, educational level, and financial abilities of the victims
- Availability of alternative options and opportunities
- Group experience in handling previous war traumas and tragedies
- Cultural background and tradition in the life of the survivors
- Practicing common rituals and customs
- Spiritual faith and the degree of existential hope

2.1. Relevant empirical findings

In a research study on the effect of the first Gulf War on the burnout and well-being
of civilians, Melamed (1992) found that the war impacted primarily the younger generation those below age 45. The danger of war would give rise to burnout or exacerbate similar preexisting symptoms. Burnout, normally associated with occupational stressors,
represents the chronic depletion of coping resources following prolonged exposure to
emotionally charged demands. It is manifested by symptoms of emotional, physical, and
cognitive exhaustion. The impact of the war was mediated by threat appraisal, as indicated by worry and apprehension. Worry was positively associated with pre-war burnout,
and negatively with age and education. Melamed concluded that the war accelerated the
depletion of coping resources.

Gavrilovic et al. (2003) studied the coping strategies used by civilians during the air attacks in Yugoslavia in the year 1999. Symptoms of intrusion and avoidance were assessed, as well as general psychological symptoms. Coping strategies included: walking and sport, leisure activities, talking and gathering, humor, avoidance, philosophical approach, getting information, business and work, and substance abuse. Among a large group of medical students, those who used dominantly 'talking and gathering' had the highest score on intrusion, and the ones that mostly used 'leisure activities' had the lowest score on intrusion. However, there were significant gender differences in coping style. The authors concluded that the type of coping strategies used during the air attacks may contribute to the level of intrusive symptoms even one year later. Longitudinal and prospective studies are still needed to draw definite conclusions on causal relationships between coping strategies and the level of posttraumatic stress.

Punamaki (1990) examined the relationships between political change, personal factors, and the psychological stress process among 40 West Bank Palestinian women. The women were interviewed both in spring 1982 and in autumn 1985. The stress process in question usually consisted of the exposure to stressful life events, the way that women perceived the severity of stress (worry), and appraisal of their own resources to cope with it (locus of control). The results showed that the Palestinian women had more personal and political worries and showed more personal helplessness (external locus of control) after the Lebanon war in 1985 than in 1982. The results further showed that women have employed less avoidance and retreat, and less denial in their coping style. Younger women expressed more political worries and initiative (internal locus of control) on the Palestinian issue but women with many children had fewer political concerns and more personal worries.

2.2. When Both Grief and Trauma are Predominately Present

Although any significant loss could have some elements of both trauma and grief, not all losses are traumatic (e.g., the gradual and peaceful death of a loved one) nor all traumas are grief-stricken (e.g., shaking by a major explosion or watching a sudden terrifying event). However, traumatic stress and bereavement can clearly overlap. Therefore, when both elements are strongly present, their impact on the survivors is deeper and greater. The combined symptoms become intensify, further impairing the emotional conditions of the person, family, or group. Consequently, the steps leading toward resolution, healing, and recovery become long, demanding, and complicated. That is especially true when there is no break in the cycle of stress and despair or when the circumstances for personal reflection, communal mourning, or emotional survival are limited and psychologically unfavorable.

Prolonged and unresolved grief can have strong negative consequences on individuals, families, groups, communities, and even nations. Severe and extended mourning affects the emotional, mental, physical, and spiritual conditions of the bereaved. It affects their mood, functioning, outlook, stability, and relationships. Any focused treatment approach or counseling method must target the twin goals of trauma mastery and grief resolution (Abi-Hashem, 1999a, 1999c; Meichenbaum, 1994; Rando, 1996). Similarly, Stroebe, Schut, and Stroebe (1998) suggested "the dual model of coping" when therapy approaches ought to address both, the manifestation of grief from the major losses and the severe stress from the traumatic events.

When examining the sociological outcomes of the civil war in Beirut, Khalaf (as quoted in Oweini, 1996), observed the following dynamics: "the prevailing state of demoralization and humiliation of Lebanese civilians, decadence of social and public values, proclivity for violence, compromise of patriotic values, embracement of territoriality and self-interest, reconfiguration of social classes, and prevalence of a culture of dishonesty and profiteering" (Oweini, 1996, Review of literature, ¶ 5).

Similarly, Durakovia-Belko, Kulenovia, and Dapia (2003) examined the risk and protective factors of postwar adjustment among adolescents who have been exposed to war traumas in Bosnia. The results indicated that dimensions of war traumas, individual characteristics, cognitive appraisals, and coping mechanisms played a significant role in determining who will have more serious PTSD symptoms. The dimensions of war-traumas also were significantly correlated with depressive symptoms. Common risk factors for more serious depression and PTSD symptoms in postwar adjustment were both female gender and low optimism, while the strongest predictor of posttraumatic stress reactions (PTSR) was trauma experience in the category of loss.

Many people in the troubled areas of the Middle East have suffered and continue to suffer from all types of losses, which often result in chronic cases of unresolved grief and complicated bereavement. Losses are being experienced on many levels: Individual and communal, sudden and gradual, real and symbolic, private and public, existential and material, etc. Past and present losses are compounded by the apprehension of the "unknown" and the anticipation of certain future losses, causing a phenomenon known as *anticipatory grief*. This normally happens when all surrounding events give no sign of hope, relief, or possible ending of the conflict in-sight but rather a continued deterioration. The idea, that any devastating conflict or war injury could be justified or satisfactorily explained, is usually essential to inspire any victimized person cope with the war anguish and its aftermath. However, the more people perceive that the war as meaningless or endless, the worse they will feel and eventually become.

For example, Lebanese people have suffered from all kinds of losses through the 15 years of serious troubles on their land (cf. Farhood, 1993). Likewise, many common people in the state of Israel, the majority of people in the Palestinians territories, and presently scores of Iraqi people have been experiencing the heavy combination of trauma and grief. There is hardly any family that has remained untouched or unaffected by one or more kinds of severe losses. Survivors must endure a host of symptoms and agonies ranging from mild to severe depending on the degree of exposure or closeness to the impacting event. They struggle with prolonged traumatic residuals and many grief reactions. My own mother is a case in point. She barely survived a major shelling in the apartment building in Beirut in the early 90s when she was there alone in our family house at night. That explosion threw her on the floor almost paralyzed among the rubbles, unable to move for hours, until the neighbors came in and helped her out during a cold and dark winter night. Subsequently, she never recovered from that powerful shock. She has been anxious, fearful, vulnerable, and physically weak ever since, all that was compounded by the grief of seeing her two sons (including myself) migrating to a different country and her two daughters (and grand-children) moving far away with their families. She found herself living and sleeping alone in the house. Similarly, millions of victims have to live with the unfortunate consequences of devastating wars and strong urban conflicts. They may never be able to master their traumas or resolve their grief and perhaps never to experience any significant relief for years to come (Abi-Hashem, 1999a; Prigerson, 1997; Rando, 1993; Worden, 1991). Some deeply affected individuals try to medicate themselves to numb the pain and sense of terror. Others are more fortunate because they benefit from the social support, warmth, and network available around them in the community and from the closeness of friends and family members who care enough to prevent them from suffering alone. Therefore at times, deeply affected survivors respond well to these natural therapeutic resources, which are beautifully imbedded in their own society and culture.

2.3. Unhealthy Coping in Time of War

There are certain unproductive methods of coping that, in most cases, lead to negative consequences. Some survivors who were affected by war can easily fall into apathy and despair. That tendency is hard to resist even for previously high functioning individuals. Observing the gradual deterioration and constant devastation of their daily situation often cause them to experience agony over their accumulated losses and the disappearance of the normal aspects of their sustainable life.

Some people respond with prolonged avoidance and hesitation to face emerging difficulties. Absence of action can further lead into immobilization and mental paralysis. Of course, war related shocks and stressors can result in psychological numbness and marked helplessness. Individuals have to make a constant effort to remain active and alert and to break the emotional passivity. This is very difficult to achieve especially when every thing around the survivors is bleak, dark, hopeless, and violent with no end in sight. People often become confused and drift into negative cycles of coping. They may become ineffective and totally incapacitated in facing their problems and suffer from lack of necessary skills for adequate mastery over the environment. Prolonged social isolation is also another maladaptive avenue for coping. In troubled times, most people tend to gravitate around each other and create circles of friends or units of community where they can share, talk, eat, belong, discuss, gain insight, give and receive nurture, and stay in realistic perspective. However, some tend to isolate, not only the loners by nature, but those who easily become seriously anxious when hearing the local news or hear of local tragedies, so they shut themselves off. Others become embarrassed due to their physical injury or material losses so they do not want to mix. Yet, others isolate because they are threatened by the idea of joining a tiny cell of people or by being too close in proximity, suddenly losing their personal space. They cut down social appearance and participation (like attending religious services, personal visitations, or community meetings even when organized under severe conditions). They tend to deal with their fear, loss, uncertainty, and the unknown quite alone. Usually, their isolation is reluctantly broken when a disaster hits close to home and they are obliged to evacuate or share their residence with others.

Blaming and lashing out is another common response to the stress of war. High irritation, deep frustration, stored anger, and low tolerance are very common. Lack of proper sleep, inability to make good decisions, living in crowded places, the presence of constant danger, the endless wait for an end to conflict and full resolution, etc., are all strong factors generating angry or aggressive behaviors. Obviously, this can harm the loved ones around them and build tension in all relationships. Some people blame others (near or far, loved ones or enemies, local or government officials, etc.) or blame themselves for the conditions they ended up experiencing. Many deeply regret decisions they had made at certain points. At times, survivors have to make a last minute or a split second decision without adequate knowledge or resources. Therefore, they struggle with guilt and self-blame which can further demoralize and paralyze them and compound their negative coping style.

According to Hobfoll et al. (1991), cynicism, excessive pessimism, and drug and alcohol use/abuse are yet another set of unhealthy coping mechanisms. Pessimism about the present and the future are often displayed by many who are caught in what seems to be an endless conflict or war in order to keep their expectations extremely low and to protect themselves from being greatly disappointed in the future. This is a protective measure used by bereaved or low tolerance individuals who already have experienced major disappointments or losses. Cynicism and pessimism are powerful and can lead people to believe that the worst is inevitable, no matter what they do or what happens, amplifying every problem into a catastrophe and insurmountable crisis. Eventually, pessimistic individuals drive others away, including potential supporters, in a time when they need help most.

An easy way to find solace for war related stress and personal problems is through drugs and alcohol use. Chemical and substance abuse is a very common avenue for coping during social conflicts and wars. "Small amounts of chemicals may aid individuals by limiting very intense emotions, especially during initial periods of distress. However, prolonged usage or use of large amounts of illicit or prescriptive drugs or alcohol can be very destructive" (Hobfoll et al., 1991, Negative coping pathways, ¶ 6). In many countries, legal drugs are easily obtained from regular pharmacies without prescription. Illegal drugs are often the focus in this regard and become available as the society's infrastructure breaks down and the black market flourishes. Of course, some drugs of abuse are both dangerous and habit forming and represent a warning sign even in small dosages. Most people who use chemicals and substances during wartime find themselves addicted and continue the abuse even after the situation calms down and life returns to some kind of normal functioning.

3. TRAUMA, SUFFERING, AND AGONY IN THE MIDDLE EAST

3.1. The Agony of the Common People in Iraq

The Iraqi people have been suffering, struggling, and paying high prices for the last several decades. Constantly they have tried to adapt and readapt to new painful realities and harsh conditions. They have been through a long armed conflict and deadly war with Iran. Then they endured merciless sanctions that devastated their lives, emotional stability, country's economy, and children's health and survival. All of this was happening under an irony rule of an internal system of government that was mainly oppressive and intimidating. According to Lorieux (1993), just two years after the beginning of the United Nations economic embargo against Iraq, the Iraqis already became increasingly worse off. Only few elites, the favorites of the regime, were actually spared. In addition, the embargo bred injustice among the people of the land and alienated its various communities. It created more tension and competition between the north, the south, and the central parts further dividing the country. "Sanctions killed an estimated 5,000 children under the age of 5 each month, and left 25 per cent of all Iraqi children irreparably damaged by chronic malnutrition"

(Skeet, 2003a). Since the early 90's, the U.S. and the U.K. maintained a policy, through the United Nations, of severe and continuous sanctions, which resulted at the end in killing a total of 1.5 million people. Later, those superpowers reinforced a no-fly zone, which squeezed, paralyzed, and further aggravated that country. Even when an U.N panel sought to ease the suffering of the Iraqi people by highlighting their misery and deteriorated condition, the panel expected the United States would oppose their planned recommendation (Miller, 1999). "The U.S. and U.K. deflected all blame for the terrible suffering in Iraq. It was Saddam's fault, they insisted, because he would not abide by their directives and dismantle his weapons of mass destruction so that the sanctions could be lifted" (Skeet, 2003a). The average Iraqis became the first and only victims of the endless embargo.

Again recently, it is hard to imagine what they have gone through since the beginning of the second Gulf War directly targeting their country. They were already depleted by internal oppression and external isolation. They felt greatly abandoned by all the nations of the world, both near and far, who were either silent or indifferent. Iraqi people were already under the burden of their internal regime and feeling the scars of the long extended sanctions, which left them in severe psychosocial pain and geopolitical isolation, let alone material deprivation. And most recently, it is indeed hard to imagine how they felt when their cities and towns began to be bombarded from the air, the land, and the sea by Western superpowers. They were not consulted about the invasion nor prepared to handle its aftermath—which is still unfolding almost daily as more casualties, destruction, and devastation are occurring. Most probably, the majority of the Iraqi people are now feeling confused, vulnerable, and grieving over their many losses, both actual and symbolic. They are struggling with many daily explosions, serious threats, daily fear of venturing out beyond necessary limits (rather staying at home or shelters at night), and a host of radical extremists, imported strangers, zealous militias, and western foreign armies in their towns and on their streets. Iraqis, of all walks of life, are experiencing an existential loss and a deep national grief especially after they watched their country disintegrated and their long-term president and many government leaders captured and placed in custody in a humiliating way. They feel the humiliation as their proud country is being occupied, and their treasured homeland being thrown into utter chaos.

During the early phases of this second Gulf War, many regional and international humanitarian agencies began planning for relief and medical operations (which is also another irony of modern wars; one party plans for attack and use of military force, the other plans for rescue and relief following the aggressive aftermath and devastation). Most cities and towns were paralyzed and in deep shock. Lack of the usual basic services like electricity, water, fuel, communication, etc., was greatly compounded by the massive displacement and internal migration of people who tried to escaped harm and fire-power by running from one place to another without any sense of plan or direction. Kapp (2003) reported that these huge relief operations were facing both political controversy and physical risks. These programs to assist Iraqis were inadequate due to the immense difficulties on the ground and the deep psychological trauma and mental confusion facing the people. Sadly, more recent reports from the United Nations in Geneva are showing that malnutrition among Iraqi children is still acute and in fact increasing, almost similar to some hard-hit African countries. "Overall, more than a quarter of Iraqi children don't get enough to eat ... Acute malnutrition rates among Iraqi children under five rose last year from 4% to 7.7% ... The war in Iraq and its aftermath have almost doubled [these] rates ... Acute malnutrition signifies that a child is actually wasting away" (Fowler, 2005, p. 1). The report also indicates that an estimate of 100,000 additional victims have died (than normally would have died under sanctions) since the beginning of this war, most of them are women and children.

3.2. The Agony of the Common People in Palestine

The majority of the Palestinian people have been displaced and scattered. Families have been broken and spread around the world. Since the establishment of the state of Israel, and the intense dispute over that land, most native Palestinians have migrated or simply were forced out of their neighborhoods to become refugees in another country. Several hundreds thousands of them went to neighboring countries and to the Gulf area. Jordan and Lebanon hosted the majority of Palestinians as they settled in refugee camps, temporarily, on the hope of returning, some day. . . and that day never came. The older generation has been dying in exile and the younger is melting within the hosting societies. The common Palestinians have been grieving the loss of their nationality, heritage, and homeland. The country of Palestine remains only a memory and a symbol in the minds of people, its original citizens. It is an abstract country with no visible borders or ID cards. Scattered Palestinians feel like nomads. Many are well established in businesses and academia while others are still struggling socially and economically. The ones left in the occupied territories are caught between some defused politics and crippled leadership on one hand and religiously radical and strong angry militant groups on the other hand. They have a love-hate relationship with both of these classes and as feel they need to face the larger threat of the Israeli occupation and repression. The first group tries to preserve their identity while the second tries to express their accumulated frustration and aggression. Yet, the common majority of people seem to want an end of violence and confrontation, and, like their Israeli counterparts, want to actually co-exist and live in peace and tranquility.

Miller (1991) indicated that the effects of the first Gulf War on the scattered Palestinians is hard to measure. At least a quarter of a million have fled Kuwait and Iraq since the beginning of the crisis. Miller reported that more than 200,000 Palestinians working in Saudi Arabia and the Persian Gulf have been methodically replaced by Asians, Egyptians, and other nationalities. "Mostly, the war has deepened the despair of Palestinians–everywhere ... and has compounded the daily suffering of the 1.7 million Palestinians in the occupied territories ... With world attention diverted by the Gulf crisis, Israel seemed to step up its repression of the Palestinians, despite official denials" (pp. 13, 32). At the same time, the Gulf War widened the divisions among Palestinians, "splitting them openly for the first time, not just ideologically but geographically and economically" (p. 13).

Some critics believe that Israel's goal recently has been to weaken or disintegrate the Palestinian entity and national presence. Obviously, Israel is freely expanding into Palestinian territory, randomly closing their roads, schools, and factories, frequently controlling their resources, and constantly putting high pressure on their daily livelihood. Israeli government fully knows that these measures deeply aggravate the Palestinians therefore many of them will leave the occupied land while some others tend to act in hysteric desperation, which in turn gives Israel a green light to exercise on them further corporate restriction and punishment—and the cycle continues. Consequently, Israeli political and military leaders justify their own aggression against Palestinians as legitimate defense or necessary retaliation, and in post 9-11 era, as a legitimate war against terrorism. Paradoxically, both the Palestinians and the Israelis have had similar tragic history. They both have been mistreated and misplaced and by now have identical mental and emotional scars, needs, and injuries. Both are acting out of their basic fears, hurts, and anger. They keep persecuting each other and massively projecting on each other. They have so much in common yet they are so different in their developmental stages. They share the same ground and face the same destiny; yet, they desire to eliminate each other. While the radical wing in Palestine may be fueled by an ideological-political Jihad, the radical Jewish wing may be fueled by their holy war and orthodox zeal. However, they both forget that it is so easy for the one who has been oppressed and abused to eventually become the very one who abuses and victimizes others in return (cf. Abi-Hashem, 2004).

A local observer for the United Nations' Committee on Inalienable Rights of the Palestinian People (2002, ¶ 6-7), following a two year cycle of horrific violence, said that the situation in the occupied Palestinian territories, including Jerusalem, "was one marred daily by the incessant bloody Israeli military campaign being waged against the Palestinian people and the Palestinian leadership since 28 September 2000. For over 16 months now, the Palestinian people under Israeli occupation had suffered countless violations of their human rights, war crimes and State terrorism." According to (Behrman, 2001), some Palestinians feel they are refugees in their own land. According to Dwairy (1998), who is a Christian Palestinian psychologist living and working in Israel, "If Arabs are the people most misunderstood by the West, Palestinians Arabs are the most misunderstood Arab people. Political conflicts and historical events have dehumanized them and overshadowed their national tragedy, culture, and other human aspects of their lives ... Publications about Arabs in English ... that make the connection between Arab mental health and sociopolitical issues are very rare" (p. xvii).

Humanitarian agents, social workers, and pro-Palestinian groups in the area feel that the average Palestinian people are feeling oppressed and depressed. The fear, anger, grief, and trauma are well entrenched in their psyche, spreading wide instability and despair also into their future. Unfortunately, there is no Palestinian Ghandi, no Israeli Martin Luther King, in sight or over the horizon, waiting to emerge (Steele, 2002). People on both sides of the fence are very depleted and disillusioned. However, the moderate Arab minds believe that most Israelis still have a human heart and a glimpse of hope in the midst of a long dark history and, ultimately, the people of Israel will appreciate a peaceful struggle in the name of good will and humanity.

3.3. The Agony of the Common People in Israel

The most devastating events and traumatic experiences the people of Israel have endured in recent years, no doubt, are related to the unexpected violent intrusions of suicide bombers. Regardless of the reasons behind the attacks and the sociopolitical climate building to their executions, humans acting as bomb explosives become the most horrifying and damaging events to the mind, body, and soul of the recipients. Definitely, the psychological impact on the masses exceeds the physical injuries and destructions they cause. They are also designed to install tremendous fears, major doubts, crippling insecurities, and terrifying anxieties in all dwellers. Since the bombers act suddenly and self sacrificially, it is hard to predict, detect, or fight them, even with the most advanced technology, because human bombers are using their ultimate weapon, themselves, with determined and convicting faith. Such advanced tactics are deeply shaking the nation's conscience and the government confidence as well.

Since the establishment of the state of Israel, tension has been building in the area as the equilibrium of space and power has been shifted. Many local communities have been living on nervous edge and in constant turmoil. Although Israel was founded as a Jewish state, the majority of its population seems to be non-political and non-religious for that matter. Israeli society at large is secular and extremely diverse and, on many levels, quite divided. Some citizens who migrated from wealthy and western countries appear to have the higher echelon, while others who are viewed as less fortunate, less sophisticated, and less cultured, face many struggles and feel like second class citizens. Certainly, the most powerful groups and ehthnopolitical parties are ruling the country and determining its behaviors. These include the influential entities strongly present in the military, business, academia, religion, and politics. On the ideological-theological end, the ultra-conservative Jewish groups have a great say in shaping the direction of the government and its future decisions. However, the majority of people in the land of Israel, like elsewhere in the Middle East, are non-aggressive, non-political, quite friendly and easygoing. Many soldiers dread going on missions or engage in fighting as well. They sincerely have no aggressive ambitions or militant mind (like many of their counterparts in Palestine and other Arabic nations) but just want to live in tranquility and harmony with their neighbors. They represent the silent majority, the moderate class, and the peace-loving people. Even voting for leaders in Israel is agonizing, at many times, because the choices are polarized. So voters normally try to make the less evil choice when sorting the agendas of the old guards. Unfortunately, their voice is not as heard as the radical minorities, which are capable of making a lot noise, greatly influencing the political machine. Therefore, the silent and peaceful majority is constantly torn and paying the highest price of agony, injuries, and deaths.

There are many civic and religious figures in Israel today who are really tired of the cycle of violence and death. They are worried about the moral decline and degree of hate in Israel toward all Arabs and Palestinians. They are diligently working for peace and human rights and fervently denouncing mistreatment and violence on all sides. Sacks (as quoted in "Israel set on tragic path," 2002, ¶ 3, 4), the chief Rabbi in Great Britain, said, "There is no question that this kind of prolonged conflict, together with the absence of hope, generates hatreds and insensitivities that in the long run are corrupting to a culture ... It is forcing Israel into postures that are incompatible ... with our deepest ideals." He said that he is profoundly shocked by the escalation of the destructive measures and sent an unprecedented warning to Israel to remain in harmony with its historic values and moral role.

Peacemakers are reaching out to moderate leaders and constituencies across the divide lines both within and outside the borders. According to Saperstein (2002, ¶ 4), who is the director of the Religious Action Center of Reform Judaism, stated in a public address in Washington DC, "Just as ... courageous religious leaders recognize the need to denounce publicly the violence terrorizing the people in the Middle East, so must we condemn the acts that seek to destroy the work of those who have taken us this far. Leaders like Anwar Sadat and Yitchak Rabin gave their lives in the pursuit of peace. Their mission of peace is incomplete and it is our responsibility to ensure that it is finished."

Following each major suicide bombing, the survivors and the general people feel utter devastation and intense anger as they sink into deep anguish. Since September 2000, Israel has been through one terror attack after another. The impact of these tragedies upon the

Israeli society is enormous. Rabbi Kadosh (as quoted in Wagner & Brimmer, n.d., ¶ 1, 2) spoke to the friends and family of a young lady killed in a bus bomb: "We are tired of crying, tired of mourning, tired of sorrow.' People on both sides of the fence have clearly reached marked levels of exhaustion." Ascherman said (as reported by Hill, 2005, ¶ 15), "it seems what we are doing is beating our heads against the wall. We do have to say very clearly that the occupation must end [and] we should always have the wisdom and the courage to tip the scales in the right direction." Similarly, Saperstein (2002, ¶ 8) added, "Israeli and Palestinian parents who had lost children in the conflict... brought a message that should be heard throughout the world. The words of Salama Temeiza, a Palestinian who suffered the loss of his son, resonate especially loudly at this critical juncture. He told us, 'Palestinians and Israelis want to live together... We want reconciliation... We want to work for justice, peace, equal rights for both sides.' Although it feels like eons, it was not long ago that, as did so many Israelis and Palestinians, we as Jews, Christians, and Muslims, sat together, united in the quest for peace. Despite our differences, we stand together today to begin the process of renewing that vision. Mr. Temeiza closed his remarks by saying, 'We don't want other families to taste what we taste.' It is our urgent responsibility to ensure that his wish is granted."

3.4. The Deep Frustration of Many Communities in the Arab-Muslim World

Depending on their location and their proximity to the green lines or conflicts zones, many people in the Middle East and North Africa are feeling, to a different degree, the turmoil of global events and regional instabilities. Some are experiencing the heat of the so-called "war on terrorism" which is perceived by many as a "cultural war" and an indirect attack on their heritage, traditions, and ways of life. Others are feeling targeted as the object of an ideological campaign aiming to change their country's regime or government. Still others feel directly stereotyped and labeled as fanatics just because they are Arabs or Muslims (or combination), especially if traveling abroad or dealing with the West. In general, there is a universal feeling of uneasiness about the turn of events, uncertainty of what may come next, and a fear of the unknown looming over their homeland.

The intellectuals and moderate elements of the Arabic-Islamic societies are quite frustrated with some of their own rigid governments, angry with the few active radical groups among them, which are flourishing and gaining power, and with the skewed, imbalanced, and confusing world politics. They feel that the notion of being a national Arabic or a devote Muslim has been quite distorted, or rather hijacked, by both the Western media and the radical-fanatic Islamic groups. These moderate elements find themselves engaged in an unavoidable fight to clarify the meaning of their national identity and to promote a reasonable version of Islam.

There are several sensitive matters currently present in the vast Near East area that could be rather explosive in nature. Each of them seems to be the desire of many governments or powerful nations both far and near. Analysts and observers believe that each of these trophies may cause a potential war in the future as regional and global superpowers have their eyes on them and closely watching their development: Land, both the precious and the strategic; Oil, desperately needed by industrial nations, rightly called the black gold; Water, increasingly scarce yet badly needed as the future lifeline for many deserts and dry areas; Warm and rich beaches of the gulf and the red sea, a dream outlet for northern powers, etc. "During the last few decades, there has been a constant tension in many parts of the Middle East between the forces of traditionalism and those of modernism.

These opposing trends and conflicting polarities are becoming increasingly pronounced as manifested by the rise of radical and fundamentalist groups on one hand and the secular and materialist groups on the other" (Abi-Hashem, 2004, p. 70).

Certain Middle Easterners communities are careful to preserve what is left of their cultural heritage and religious traditions, fearing all may be lost or eroded soon. Others, mostly the young and educated, who live in more restricted area, are increasingly longing for more freedom and relief from the old-held regimes. They view their own Muslim societies as lacking the average freedom for religious and political expression found elsewhere. Obviously, the leaders of such nations are trying to be true to their own social heritage and religious beliefs. They fear the corruption that may come with great social flexibility and openness. Thus, it is not surprising that many groups, communities, and branches of governments, are real frustrated with each other, with themselves, with their neighbors, and with the West in general. They are frustrated with themselves for not being able to move beyond a certain point of dysfunction, for having leaders who are not accountable, for cultural and political denial, and for being unable to rise above a certain level of stagnation and deal with the old myth of a pan-Arab mentality or pan-Muslim brotherhood. They are angry with the radical groups and fundamental factions (including zealous clergy) flourishing in their midst or being imported from outside their borders, constantly promoting fanaticism and radicalism which is foreign to their socio-cultural and religious peaceful heritage. Therefore, these actively concerned and moderate groups are trying to fight for the soul of Islam, for the value of being a Muslim, and for the honor and dignity of being a culturally Arabic and nationally a Middle Easterner.

During the first Gulf war, Ibrahim (1991) described that resulting crisis as deepening the Arab wounds, further agonizing the soul-searching in the Arab-Islamic states, heightening the contrast between the poor and the rich, and widening the mental and emotional confusion throughout the Middle East "over who is right and who is wrong, what the fighting is all about, and even how to define victory ... But without consensus on what direction the region should take in the postwar era, or who should lead it, the forces of change could simply translate into renewed chaos" (p. 1, 2). In addition, many people and groups are finding themselves confused about the campaign on terrorism, caught in the middle of the winds of politics, pushed and pressed by radical powers on either side, alienated and humiliated by the global media stereotypes, wanting peace and tranquility, just to be left alone, yet, as a silent majority, their voices are still not heard.

Mallat (2005, ¶ 3-4) wrote about 'White Arabism' as a new phenomenon. He explained the reasons why moderate Arabs have failed to stand up and speak up:

> For the past 20 years, so-called Arab civil society has been slowly denting the status quo. Initially, questions were defensive and focused on human rights, while participants in human rights gatherings were incapable of mustering the courage needed to name those leaders responsible for all kinds of violations ... In part this was understandable, and the level of repression meted out against dissidents was uniquely high: Scores of dissenters were brutally assassinated, thrown in jail and tortured, while the usual 'higher national interest' argument was put forward whereby Arab liberals saw their reform efforts condemned ... As time passed, however, the connection between brutality at home and the inability to stand up to ... rhetoric became increasingly apparent: From the condemnation of the Arab record in general ... particulars of repression were linked to people at the helm of power in every single Arab country. Local Arab democrats are still hesitant to accuse the emirs and kings in the

Gulf, but the taboos have fallen in the Levant and North Africa: [presidents] are being openly challenged, and the perceived weakness of the hard-liners [even] in Israel, leading to the withdrawal from settlements in Gaza and the West Bank, will accelerate the trend of decoupling Arab domestic reform from the fig leaf.

Many in the West are currently asking an important question: Why are so many people angry with the West? Although some reasons may be sentimental, illogical, ideological, or unrealistic, other reasons are quite legitimate, historical, profound, and realistic. They must not be dismissed but rather be taken into serious consideration. Many analysts, both actually in the East and in the West, believe that some political and religious leaders or groups in the Arabic-Islamic world are becoming more hostile toward the West in general and the United States in particular due to the following reasons: a) Cultural and moral invasion, b) Economic and geopolitical exploitation, c) Political and imperialistic manipulation, and d) Unilateral and military expansion (cf. Abi-Hashem, 2004). With all the good intentions, technological assistance, friendly gestures, academic exchanges, and humanitarian help, which the West and the USA provide to the developing world, there are also a lot of political inconsistencies, relational biases, material greed, arrogant attitudes, unhealthy products, moral corruption, military dominance, religious insensitivity, etc. These negative perceptions have brought grievances to many Arabic-Islamic societies, resulting in negative reactions and even serious threats from many groups. Unfortunately, the radical and jihadist groups are capitalizing on those factors to incite hate and mobilize attacks against the West and its allies. Consequently, these radical groups are victimizing more people and contaminating the global climate by disturbing all international relations and peaceful living.

4. CHALLENGES FOR COPING AND SURVIVAL

4.1. Current Coping Patterns in the Middle East

In this section we will describe some healthy and unhealthy coping styles, behaviors, maneuvers, and strategies that are being utilized on regular basis in order to survive the severe stress of ethnopolitical wars and manage the hardships of living in conflict zones. At the same time, we will describe some obstacles, barriers, and hindrances that have been preventing people from recovery, healing, and restoration even into a baseline of functioning and well being.

Typically, after each devastating event or an intensely dark phase of the ongoing conflict, local people usually experience deep agony and intense feelings of misery and hopelessness. They seem to go into phases of demoralization, disheartening, and community paralysis. Besides what has been mentioned elsewhere in this chapter about the negatives consequences of long-term exposure to severe conflicts and about the unhealthy ways of coping with the mounting pressures, it is worth noting here that it is hard to predict exactly how people would react or respond to every new developing situation.

4.1.1. Negative coping patterns

However, based on my personal observation, experience, interviews, and readings, people living in conflict zones tend to display some of the following negative behaviors: general low tolerance, impatience, being on edge, venting anger and frustration on each other, feeling caged, crippled, immobilized, or tied down against their will (like something is dying on the inside), becoming pushy and irritable, apathetic and pessimistic, highly nervous and scared, losing temper easily while driving, doing business, standing in line, at the store, or at the bank, in school or at home, etc. Also it is not uncommon to hear yelling, shouting, complaining, and cursing in public, even from ladies (young or old from all backgrounds–an unusual behavior for ladies, non-existent prior to war conditions). With the increase of stressful events and ongoing conflicts, and the decrease of financial resources and income, many people become tight with their money, greedy, self-protective, dishonest, and manipulative. Consequently, this phenomenon feeds into the decline in civility and cultural values like being polite and considerate to others or showing great hospitality to neighbors and relatives. As few elite groups become "nouveau riche" in wartimes, due to their quickly accumulated wealth (e.g., raising prices of basic goods), the majority of people become significantly poor as the middle class of their society rapidly disappears. Therefore, cheating, steeling, heavy smoking, drug use and alcohol abuse, acting out sexually and becoming materialistic, greedy, hedonistic, numb to danger and death, indifferent to the misery of others, showing high level of self-centeredness and preservation, dependence on pain killers and tranquilizers, all become prevalent signs. In addition, being involved in crime, joining gangs or non-political militias that would take advantage of the social deterioration and would break into shops, homes, banks, etc., or kidnaps wealthy individuals (or their children) demanding high ransom for their release. We have seen such destructive practice occurred in Beirut in the past and now it is happening in the large cities of Iraq. Such anti-social behaviors could occur in any society when its norms and infrastructure collapse. Such negative coping patterns from addiction to lawlessness are counterproductive to the extent that they create rather than solve social and psychological problems.

4.1.2. Leaving homeland and facing acculturation stress

Another way of coping is by leaving, escaping, and migrating to another part of the country (which causes a major demographic shift in the country's population) or to another country all together, especially by those who are able and can afford to travel (which causes a significant void among the young, educated, and established class, referred to as business or "brain drainage"). Some people escape because they feel increasingly upset and hopeless with the ongoing conflict (the so-called fed up syndrome), while others look for work elsewhere to support their families back home. There are many others who are forced to leave due to persecution and mistreatment.

Migration or asylum to foreign countries provides an escape from the pressures and agonies related to conflicts or wars, but it also presents a new set of psychosocial challenges. These Arab and Muslim immigrants have to learn to function in a totally different environment, and to adopt a new language, mindset, and lifestyle. They miss home yet closely follow the news from home. At the same time, they try to be productive in a foreign system, while dealing with unresolved emotional residuals of their losses and traumas, worrying about the safety of loved ones left behind, etc. In order to cope with the new external and internal stressors, many displaced survivors tend to split their minds and loyalty by distancing themselves from their painful past. Many, fully immerse themselves in the new settings to the extent of minimizing their background. They even become critical of their own country, roots, and heritage.

4.1.3. Positive coping skills

For those remaining in conflict zones, a significant healing factor is normally found in the amount of social support the individual receives. In cases where the extended family can pull together or the friends remain loyal, the survivor is more likely to adjust well regardless of the intensity of the tragedy experienced. Another helpful factor is the ability to make sense of what has happened to them. When people in conflict zones cannot explain their tragedies, or when no one else around them can help them make sense of that tragedy, then they would feel frozen in time. Therefore, some form of grief counseling is needed to facilitate their healing and better coping and functioning.

Social gatherings of family members and friends and eating meals together are a powerful therapeutic means to cope with the agony and despair of war. Hosts normally go to a great extent to prepare elaborate meals even though they have limited resources. They may borrow money or promise the shop owner to pay later in order to provide enjoyable meals and great hospitality and to honor their guests real well. Preparing for such gathering can reinforce communal bond and alleviate anxiety and depression; eating together can also give a certain feeling of bliss, comfort, and solidarity.

Individuals and families really do help and care for each other during war conflicts and intense crises. If one falls into severe despair or depression, or if one becomes totally exhausted and depleted, others would quickly rally around him/her supporting, encouraging, challenging, uplifting until he/she feels stronger and bounces back to a better mood and functioning. So, people take turn in encouraging each other. The stronger uplifts the weak, with each person realizing that his/her turn in feeling down maybe next and will definitely need the close watch and the caring entourage of others. Various kinds of social support and collective coping play a big part in helping individuals cope and survive war stress.

Other forms of positive coping include dancing at home or in large halls with Arabic music, group singing of folk music, observing and celebrating religious feasts of all types and faiths, playing cards and familiar games, and evening group visitations (Sahraat)–almost every night just for any reason or no reason at all. Outdoors activities include playing sports, picnics and road trips, strolling on roads and seashores, gathering to discuss the issues of the day, working on a common neighborhood project, visiting worship places, attending services and public prayers, planning teaching activities to neighborhood children who are constantly missing school, etc. Such natural and creative activities provide an emotional release and positive distraction from the daily worries and dark news of wartime conditions.

At the level of community service, many ways of helping each other also take place. Getting involved in the work of humanitarian agencies (like the Red Cross and Red Crescent), in local political party or office, in religious charities and ministries, or in mental health and mentoring services are all examples of the multiple ways people mobilize their efforts to help each other. If basic services are interrupted, inaccessible, or nonexisting, friends and neighbors would gather quickly, form a team or a committee, and recruit other volunteer to assist them. Thus, they begin solving local problems and delivering crucial services, such as gathering and burning garbage, distributing bread, water, medicine, candles, batteries, and providing night watch for the streets to stop intruders and crimes. In addition, they engage in fund raising efforts, check on the elderly and the sick, volunteer at a local clinic, school, hospital, church, mosque, bakery, or newly established reservoir of water, etc. All of that happens spontaneously in an effort to raise moral, spread a sense of stability, and care for the needy, lonely, and desolate.

The most prevalent custom of coping in the Middle East is the old time habit of visiting friends, relatives, acquaintances, and neighbors. During the war troubles these practices actually intensify as if they become the lifeline of any struggling community. No one is left to suffer alone! Spending long hours or frequent night-stays together, recreating in a tribal atmosphere, and helping the heavyhearted forget their agonies and the harsh realities of living a life in constant danger. That type of communal gathering substantially nurtures the group's soul and mind and gives them a sense of calm, assurance, and warmth. Thus they can endure the dangers, face the unknown, and navigate through the endless pressures and traumas of war.

Many people, of all ages and background, who are suffering from the impact of war stress and tragedies become chronically damaged and emotionally handicapped, but many others bounce back rather quickly and become innovative in their responses and coping style. What contributes to their resilience? The Lebanese people are a case in point. Generally, they show a high degree of survival skills, emotional resiliency, and stress tolerance in the face of the devastating civil war. They have endured daily fighting and random shelling that took place in their streets and around their homes. Many have become creative in launching new personal businesses, in repairing their houses and buildings, in finding ways to make money by buying and selling various needed items in the midst of severe economic stagnation and dangerous streets. Some ventured out of their sealed neighborhoods and discovered back roads, away from the militia controlled areas, to travel back and forth or in and out the city or even the country. In sum, rebuilding, planning ahead, being innovative and creative, forming support groups, socializing, etc., are some of the positive ways employed by conflict zone survivors to cope with the dark side of life and with the crippling anguish of wars.

4.1.4. Additional observations of negative and positive coping

Arabs and Muslims in Middle East have used both positive and negative coping strategies to help themselves survive crises and deal with the painful and discouraging conditions of war. Some strategies, such as committing horrific violence or participating in suicide bombings, are purely negative, because they make lives worse and inflict further hatred, fears, and miseries. According to Wong's (1995) frustration theory, frustration and pain tend to evoke aggression as a part of the instinctive fight-or-flight coping mechanisms. However, when aggression fails to attain the desired goal, both animals and human beings tend to explore alternative ways of coping, and eventually explore alternative goals when they face prolonged frustration and repeated setbacks. Indeed, many people in the Middle East have developed creative and innovative ways of coping with the chronic problems of living in a war zone; their creative coping may be considered transformative coping (see Chapters 1&11), because they have the effects of increasing resources and creating at least a psychologically healthier way of living under constant danger.

Some people cope by leaving their war-torn country. They are tired of putting their lives on hold, subjecting their lives to daily threat, and having to deal with their intense feelings of despair, anguish, and fear. Of course, some victims passively wait until the conditions become favorable before acting constructively while others apt to take risks suddenly in spite of the deteriorating situation. Those who act obviously have more external and internal resources than those who remain passive. Personality is another factor that might mediate the different coping reactions. Oweini (1996, Results, ¶ 31), who conducted a study among war-stressed university students, have the following observation:

Just as certain personality traits foster effective adaptation to extreme conditions, other traits are detrimental to the individual and produce maladaptive coping. Being emotional indecisive, angry, withdrawing, and nervous were cited as factors that interfered with adaptive coping. However, it is clear that those negative traits were offset by the more positive, more adaptive personality characteristics that most of the group possessed.

Furthermore, Oweini explained that both males and females, who lived under severe conditions, reported personality traits like being cool-tempered, sociable, optimistic, resilient, in control, adaptable, patient, unwavering, forgetful, resourceful, indifferent, and humorous. These traits played a key role in helping them withstand the stress of war and reflected, to a certain extent, some of the cultural aspects of the Arab character and the general societal expectations. "Being brave and tough in the face of grief and strain, being resilient, patient, in control and tolerating as much stress and pain as possible are integral aspects of the experience of the. . . people who are accustomed to hardships brought forth by persecution, repeated invasions and prolonged occupations" (¶ 27).

Friedman (as quoted in Oweini, 1996, Review, ¶ 8) wrote in his memoirs, as a war correspondent to the New York Times in Beirut and Jerusalem, that he was perplexed by the ability of the Lebanese people to endure the ongoing hardships of the civil war. "Friedman identified five interrelated coping patterns of the Lebanese: (1) developing emotional shields, (2) rationalizing dangerous events using probability and inferences, (3) perceiving the environment selectively, (4) maintaining a sense of detachment vis-a-vis the war; and finally, (5) channeling energy into productive activity."

4.2. Children Coping with the High Stress and Devastation of War

Children are often the silent victims of war tragedies and traumas. A great deal of attention should be given to their unspoken needs. A common misperception about children is that they are not affected by war stress like adults. But children are aware of the horrors going on around them. Their well-being and survival should not be taken for granted. Although some children show outstanding resiliency and inner strength, many others suffer greatly and become highly vulnerable and victimized. Hobfoll et al. (1991, Children special needs, ¶ 1) emphasized the importance of taking a developmental perspective:

A knowledge of developmental differences and the social world of children is paramount to successful prevention and early intervention work with children. Children are less likely than adults to speak directly about their problems or even to know they are having them. . . Children are also vulnerable because they have less experience coping with stressful events. Lack of prior experience may lead them to exaggerate their problems and prevent them from seeing light at the end."

Regarding the children and the youth living in troubled areas, Stichick (2001, ¶ 1) emphasized that it is undeniable that the impact of war on children is a significant matter that deserves continued efforts in research and intervention:

It is time for a shift in paradigms; instead of focusing solely on exposure to traumatic events and defining pathology per dominant diagnostic criteria, it is essential that research turn to examining the effect of chronic stressors and exploring how certain mechanisms may be protective or act to moderate the psychosocial impact of war on children. The role of such protective mechanisms must be examined for differences by development and gender and by cultural context and the nature of the conflict situation itself.

Stichick (2001) further argued that any investigation should target the health and psychosocial well-being of war-affected children. The programs that serve these children must attend to the restoration of their basic needs, find adequate sources of support, and integrate any relevant cultural practices of healing. "The coping efforts of young people and their families and the creation of more positive roles for youth also must be explored. Addressing these fundamental issues in research and programming will go a long way in fostering new opportunities for peace, healing, and the promotion of mental health and well-being for war-affected children in modern times" (Stichick, 2001, ¶ 1).

The stress and struggles of children usually emerge out in their eating and sleep patterns, relationships with parents, siblings, and peers, mental faculties, school work, physical health, emotional stability, and overall mood and functioning (cf. Abi-Hashem, 1992a). The specific coping patterns that are effective for younger or older adults need to be adjusted for children to meet their age-appropriate level of functioning and comprehension. According to Hobfoll et al. (1991, Children special needs, ¶ 2), the following suggestions apply specifically to highly distressed children who are subject to war conflicts and violence (see also Green & Kocijan-Hercigonja, 1998; Punamaki, R-L., 1997):

- Parents and caregivers should be encouraged to listen in a nonjudgmental fashion to children's concerns, feelings, thoughts, and ideas about the conflict and war.
- Adults should provide warmth and reassurance to children, without minimizing their concerns. Children need to feel that there is a safe haven provided by strong adults.
- Adults should not impose their fears or burdens on children. This does not mean that children should be entirely sheltered from family difficulties, but neither should they be made to feel that it is up to them to shoulder responsibilities that are beyond their developmental capability.
- Children need accurate information about what has happened and why, information that is appropriate to their developmental stage. This explanation should be provided to them before, during, and after the stressful events. Children also need to know why certain behaviors are required of them. Examples of what is expected and not expected of them should be clearly shown to children. Sometimes rehearsal of each behavior is appropriate in order to help them build it in their repertoire. It should not be assumed that children do see the "dark side" of life and current events. Given that they have seen horrible scenes on television or have overheard

serious discussions, it is incumbent on adults to help children work through the meaning and significance of these disturbing events through discussion, support, and care. In cases of severe trauma, professional help is recommended, provided that such treatment is available and affordable.

- Children's reactions will often mirror the reactions of their parents. This is a double-edged sword. If their parents are combating tension and stress effectively, the children will gain a sense that they can too overcome their difficulties. If, however, their parents are not adjusting properly, their children develop a sense of hopelessness and view problems are insurmountable. It is critical that parents see that, seeking help and support for themselves when they needed it, would be the best therapy for them and their troubled children alike.

- As with adults, children should be involved in helpful behaviors. By being part of the solution in their own classrooms, families, and communities, children will develop an enhanced sense of mastery and control over their lives and cope more effectively with war crises and other stressful events.

5. CHALLENGES FOR MENTAL HEALTH PROFESSIONALS

5.1. Treatment of War Trauma, Loss, and Grief: A Culturally Challenging Task

When dealing with the aftermath of wars and conflict tragedies, it is essential to move beyond the concept of individual trauma into the concept of *social trauma* and beyond personal grief into *collective grief*. The impact of war injury normally extends beyond the individual into the larger community, the social matrix, and the global region. Such impact psychologically affects a whole field of the social mind and national psyche. Interestingly enough, in the midst of any war or conflict zone and following any major attack or invasion (e.g., September 11, 2001 in the USA) the whole nation responds, feels, acts, and reacts similar to an *individual Self*. Virtually, there are parallel characteristics to "trauma responses" and "grief reactions" between a single person and a large community. The concept of social trauma may be new to many researchers and to the body of literature but it is quite important to take into consideration when planning for intervention and treatment, especially across cultural barriers. Psychological symptoms are not limited only to individuals, are not humanly isolated, and do not occur in a socio-cultural vacuum. They are a communal phenomenon, are existential in nature, and are the direct result of living in a local conflict zone. Actually, they are the manifestation of the ethno-political forces and dynamics, well integrated within the cultural environment and religious dimensions of the people. Therefore, applying culturally sensitive approaches is absolutely crucial for the success of any mediations and interventions instead of merely relying on clinical methods developed in the West that, in part or in whole, prove to be unhelpful or irrelevant to many other societies including the various Middle Eastern communities and subcultures (cf. Abi-Hashem, 1997, 1998, 1999b; Marsella & Christopher, 2004; Summerfield, 1995).

The most conventional ways of handling the aftermath of traumas and losses have been already outlined by a number of theorists and clinicians (cf. Meichenbaum, 1994; Rando, 1993; Worden, 1991) and the research on these related topics continues. However, there are rich resources of dealing with the different agonies of life found in the books and teachings of prominent philosophers, theologians, and mentors of all faiths. Spiritual wisdom and sacred writings hold many therapeutic keys to health and healing that modern psychology and social sciences, and even medicine, are discovering just recently. Generally speaking, most people in Eastern and African cultures have different views of the world, the existing reality, and the human nature compared to their Western counterparts. They assign different meaning to time, hardship, contentment, future, pain, despair, and death. Majority of them have a strong belief in the concepts of fate and destiny and in the afterlife of eternity. They elevate the place of faith, tradition, values, mentors, elders, and wise persons. They also assign special meaning to self, others, even children, and they encourage a total surrender to the sovereign purpose and ultimate will of God.

Prolonged and unresolved grief can have strong negative consequences on individuals, families, groups, communities, and nations. Severe and extended mourning affects the emotional, mental, physical, and spiritual condition of the bereaved. It affects their mood, functioning, outlook, stability, and relationships. Any focused treatment approach or counseling intervention must target the twin goals of trauma mastery and grief resolution (Abi-Hashem, 1999a, 1999c; Meichenbaum, 1994; Rando, 1996). Similarly, Stroebe, Schut, and Stroebe (1998) suggested "the dual model of coping" when therapy approaches ought to address both, the severe stress from the traumatic events and the manifestation of grief from the major losses. When planning any type of care to help the survivors, it is essential to find out the surrounding events and cultural context of the disturbances and mobilize the many resources available to these troubled people within their family and community, both the natural and professional ones.

Normally, reactions to traumas range from mild and short-term symptoms to severe and long-term crippling symptoms. In terms of trauma therapy, victims need safe connections and warm support, help in recounting their experiences, skills for stress management and tension reduction, better self observation and awareness, rational reframing of their automatic responses, redefining the meaning of their trauma(s), moving from a victim to a survivor mentality, encouragement to reach out to others in caring service, developing a positive attitude, setting new objectives and goals, etc. (Abi-Hashem, 1999c; Meichenbaum, 1994). In terms of grief therapy, bereaved people need help in these gradual recovery steps: a) to admit fully that the loss has taken place indeed and it is irreversible and unfortunately final (reversing the negative coping of denial), b) to express all range of deep thoughts, memories, and emotions both the pleasant and unpleasant (undoing suppression), c) to release the lost (object, idea, person, etc.) and let go of them by setting free and saying repeated goodbyes using any ritual or experiential technique possible (undoing the dynamic of clinging), and d) to reinvest the psychological energy, consumed earlier in unsuccessful resolution of grief, into new endeavors, people, goals, and relationships (reversing the condition of stagnation) (Abi-Hashem, 1999a; Worden, 1991). In attempting to plan or conduct grief counseling with people across cultures, is it important to use appropriate methods and give sensitive suggestions to the bereaved individuals or families, integrating their local customs and religious rituals in facilitate the mourning and eventual recovery.

5.2. The Contribution of Mental Health Professionals and Counselors

Following any kind of disaster, experienced counselors and caregivers can make a great contribution by sharing their talents and seasoned skills. Most importantly, they can provide encouragement and support by their presence in time of need and by walking along the hurting and struggling in the midst of their trauma and pain. At times, it is necessary to interact through translators among very simple people and under rough living conditions. In such cases, patience, flexibility, and adaptation are absolutely essential. Listening and learning, reaching out and being available, sharing and empowering, etc., all can be very therapeutic to the victims and survivors if done in a spirit of humility and genuine care, and not in an attitude of personal detachment or professional superiority.

Hobfoll et al. (1991) emphasized that mental health professionals have a clear responsibility to concern ourselves with the psychological welfare of those people affected by war conflicts and combat, including the combatants themselves, their loved ones, and the nation as a whole. There is much we can do to prevent psychological distress after the war and many of these interventions can truly limit the negative emotional and social sequelae that often emerge following war tragedies and disturbances.

Based on his work in many troubled areas, Saul (as quoted in Collins, 2005, ¶ 2) believed that "when entire communities experience trauma, providing one-on-one therapy is neither practical nor useful." Saul argued that large-scale disasters normally push therapists to think in broader terms and force them to develop models mobilizing the community's own resources and healing capacities. Creating peer-support networks and forums and helping people come together and connect to each other will allow them to take collective action and rise above the devastation.

The following are some basic recommendations, suggestions, and therapeutic guidelines designed to help counselors, educators, caregivers, therapists, and ministers to effectively serve across the cultures especially among the Middle Easterners who represent various backgrounds, social classes, affiliations, mindsets, and religions (cf. Abi-Hashem, 1999b):

- Be open to learn about the values, norms, faith, customs, and traditions of the people.
- Find the common grounds and build solid bridges. Earning trust and confidence of the community will increase your effectiveness as a caregiver.
- Indicate your willingness to learn about their lives and appreciate their heritage at the same time as you offer to help, support, and serve them.
- Acknowledge the obvious differences between you and the survivors. Gently ask if they have any concerns about relating to you or working with you.
- If they belong to an ethnic or religious minority, acknowledge the reality of their situation and possible hardship they may be facing, especially if they are sheltered in an unfriendly country or they have migrated to the West as refugees.
- Try to find out the family's or individual's degree of trauma, mourning, and bereavement as well as the level of acculturation within the new society or environment.
- Apply appropriate Grief & Bereavement Counseling, Critical Incident Debriefing Techniques, or Trauma Mastery Approaches (or combination of these) according to the need, especially following a major crisis, war disaster, civil unrest, significant loss, or horrifying act.
- Do not be afraid of silence! Be careful not to interpret politeness, slow disclosure, repetition, indirectiveness, low expressiveness, and minimum eye contact as defensiveness, high resistances, or emotional disturbances.

- Make an effort to be sensitive in your comments, clear in your instructions, and relevant in your interpretations and psychological feedback.
- Avoid generalization! Do not label or classify, e.g., "You Arab people ... All practicing Muslims can be fanatic ... You poor women living in a men-dominated society ... Middle Eastern cultures are still primitive ... etc." These comments can be stereotyping, alienating, and quite damaging.
- Inquire gently! Allow enough time, and be patient. Do not demand information or put pressure on them to quickly and completely describe their heritage, struggles, habits, pain, or needs.
- Watch the non-verbal dimensions. Listen to the signals, cues, and style of communication. Do not impose on them your ideas, solutions, values, or personal preferences.
- Be faithful to what you learn from them. They internally expect you to remember and honor their personal history and delicate information they already have share with you.
- Allow yourself to grow and change as a result of such cultural discoveries and experiences. Appreciate the depth and richness of these life-changing encounters.

6. CONCLUSION

6.1. Future Directions for Research and Intervention

More substantial research studies and adequate surveys are much needed to understand the coping strategies and mental and emotional dynamics among the various Middle Eastern communities. These approaches should be very appropriate and based on comprehensive observation, deep knowledge, new conceptual frameworks, evaluative thinking, careful design, and friendly manners. Any research team should include experts who are intimately familiar with the Middle East in general and with the country or region of the Arabic-Islamic world in particular where the research is being targeted. All attempts to understand and study any Middle Eastern society must be culturally sensitive and psychosocially relevant. Insensitive approaches or literally translated questionnaires from Western sources, are misleading and confusing both to the participants and the researchers alike and may completely miss their purpose and goals.

In addition, a new paradigm should be developed with collaboration among the concerned international community, including the United Nations, combining resources and expertise to help nations and societies at large to cope and recover well. Thus far, the focus of research and intervention has been largely targeted toward the small unit of society (individuals, couples, families) but not toward the whole community, town, society, or nation. Normally, nations act and react, grieve and rejoice, and show weakness and resiliency just like individuals or small group units, as if they have a mind and a soul on their own. We have seen this phenomenon clearly around the events of 9-11 in the United States. Lustig et al. (2004, ¶ 1) pointed out, "More research is needed on interventions, specifically on efficacy and cultural relevance. Interventions that have an impact on multiple ecological levels need further development and evaluation."

In my opinion, any research study, academic approach, or clinical intervention (even humanitarian service) to be conducted in the Middle East or in the Arabic-Islamic world, should take the following guidelines into serious consideration. Even though the location and the population determine, to a large degree, the content and the approach of any investigation or study, in general, all research attempts in the Middle East need to reflect the following basic qualities:

- Non-western in nature. Must be culturally sensitive and quite relevant to the Eastern mentality. Although many concepts and approaches in psychology, counseling, and social sciences are global and universal in their meaning and applications, many others are not. They need adaptation, modification, alteration, and complete change and, at times, omission all together.
- Non-pathological in orientation Trying to detect not only the malfunctions and disorders but also the strength and health of the people. Able to detect the inter-generational wisdom, communal support, and resiliency that keep them surviving and to find their hidden sources of hope, innovation, and endurance.
- Non-individualistic but collective. To focus on the familial and communal aspects and dynamics of the large group and not be exclusively limited to individuals. Western psychology and psychotherapy have been traditionally intrapsychic in nature. Shift of paradigm is necessary in non-Western societies.
- Non-superficial but philosophical in nature. Able to detect and focus on the existential depth, rooted agony, accumulated grief, and communal injuries. At the same time, able to detect the resiliency, strengths, and sources of tolerance. It is important to keep in mind that most people in developing countries have a different view of *time* and of *hardship* than people in developed or Western countries.
- Non-diagnostic but comprehensive in its coverage. Focusing on the global picture rather than trying to isolate one single DSM-IV criteria or diagnosis at a time. That is too limiting and artificial (e.g., targeting one type of Anxiety or Depression or PSTD) but rather remaining open-ended and looking for the underlying clusters, features, and syndromes. Most people, even in western societies, do not fit under one single diagnosis of the DSM-IV (which is based on Western context anyway). Must fit a combination and an integration of many disturbances and diagnoses. Thus, the challenge is to capture their human experiences and global conditions rather than focus on only one small segment or slice of the psycho-social picture.
- Non-secular but spiritual. Communal heritage, spiritual faith, and religious affiliation are vital parts of any Middle Eastern group-identity and social function. Many are culturally religious while others are spiritually dedicated and very active in their faith. So, mentioning God and faith are important and can be an appropriate indicator of their conditions. Even at times including some theological and religious themes or questions would be very revealing and helpful.
- Non-literal but meaning oriented. Not mono-linguistic either! Many educated people, especially in large towns and cities, are fluent in more than one language. Therefore, it would be appropriate to use some terminologies in English or French in adjunction to the Arabic terms so that the meaning is clearer and well integrated.
- Non-provincial or materialistic but broad in its scope and worldview. That means non-linear or non-mechanical but circular in its approach to reality and thinking mode. Should be concerned, not only with details, pieces, or fragments, but also with the larger reality, broad situation, and global picture. Virtually for the Eastern mind the *whole* is more important than the *parts*.

- Non-intrusive but respectful. Avoiding embarrassing and hot topics or too private and revealing conversations (like detailed sexual information and inventories) and also non-provocative (describe your *anger* at your father or mother. . . Report about your *guilt* and *shame*).
- Non-artificial but realistic. Avoid presenting a quick fix or an easy solution for their struggles, pain, and problems. Most people in developing countries are able to tolerate psychic agony and physical pain much more than their Western counterparts.

There is need to help create centers for mental health and emotional rehabilitation in different parts of the Middle East. This can be accomplished by volunteering time from experienced practitioners in more developed societies who possess cultural insight and sensitivity and can afford the time and resources. Also by designing literature for the public and training programs for the local nationals who already are engaged in caregiving and counseling, even on a generic or informal levels, such as community elders, religious leaders and clergy, school and university teachers, healthcare providers, parents and mentors, etc. For example, Cardozo et al. (2004) conducted a survey in Afganistan and have found that, given the prevalence rates of symptoms of depression, anxiety, and PTSD were high, presently there is a pressing need for donors and health care planners to address this current lack of mental health services, resources, facilities, and trained professionals in that war torn country.

6.2. A Closing Word

Given the intensive, chronic, and pervasive stressors present in many communities in the Middle East, how do people in those areas cope and survive? We have tried to describe and document their living conditions, deep agony, grief, and frustration they have and continue to experience. It seems to me that *suffering* is a more accurate term than *stress* to describe what these dear people have to cope with (see Chapter 1) on daily or weekly basis. We can no longer conceptualize stress as an isolated encounter, which is appraised as more than one's coping resources, because they have to deal with is a huge constellations of external stressful events, constant threats, and intense internal agonies, similar to what Wong (1993) referred to as self-perpetuated emotional stress. They have to cope with all the external and internal demands all at once, because they are all inter-related. In addition to coping with personal suffering, they also have to cope with collective suffering as a people with a common heritage and national identity; they feel the pressure, agony, and worries when their own community and their own people suffer together as they face a bleak and an uncertain future.

Based on the intensive and extensive nature of their suffering, the various coping models developed in the West are basically inadequate for many reasons. First of all, the problems they face are beyond individuals and extend to their community, nation, region, and the world. Therefore, all the coping strategies from an individualistic perspective are not enough. What is needed is more than an individualistic approach or mere community coping, it is the collective richness and vast resources from all the stakeholders in the region and from around the world. The prolonged ethnopolitical conflicts in the Middle East demand the cooperative efforts of the United Nations and all other major powers. Wong's (1993) resource-congruence model is quite relevant. What we need is to collaboratively work together to increase the resources, greatly needed, in order to decrease the global sense of deprivation, poverty, injustice, and frustration. The objective is to increase the sense of efficacy and well-being of suffering and disadvantage people. Wong's emphasis on congruence is so relevant. Terrorism or military might cannot solve or resolve any problem or ethnopolitical conflict, because they are not congruent with the nature of the crisis. If the problem is social, like chronic poverty or injustice, violence would not be the appropriate intervention to address these issues. We need a new taxonomy of coping that encompassed all the various strategies and approaches available, which in turn are needed to adequately help resolve such global issues of poverty, human rights, and world peace (see Chapter 11).

In conclusion, I would like to encourage caregivers, educators, and mental health providers of all professions to volunteer time and effort in serving the many hurting people who are caught in war crises and still are suffering from multiple trauma, losses, and grief. To be able to engage effectively in those settings, one definitely needs a balanced mindset and worldview, cultural understanding and sensitivity, a heart full of compassion, and a creative mind that is flexible and adaptable to each new situation. Volunteering our time and using our talents in international service can be very rewarding and enriching to us and greatly appreciated by the people on the ground who normally become very grateful for any little help they can receive. In this way, we will bridge the gaps, increase friendliness and understanding, and bring some healing and restoration to many agonizing minds and souls. Hopefully, our little contribution can make this troubled world a better place to live, less torn by conflicts and wars, and, ultimately, a healthier environment and a peaceful home.

REFERENCES

Abi-Hashem, N. (1992a). *The reactions of children and adolescents to the death of a parent.* Unpublished doctoral dissertation. Biola University, La Mirada, California.

Abi-Hashem, N. (1992b). The impact of the Gulf War on the churches in the Middle East: A socio-cultural and spiritual analysis. *Pastoral Psychology, 41* (1), 4-26.

Abi-Hashem, N. (1997). Reflections on "International Perspectives in Psychology." *American Psychologist, 52* (5), 569-570.

Abi-Hashem, N. (1998). Returning to the fountains. *American Psychologist, 53* (1), 63-64.

Abi-Hashem, N. (1999a). Grief, loss, and bereavement: An overview. *Journal of Psychology and Christianity, 18* (4), 309-329.

Abi-Hashem, N. (1999b). Cross-cultural psychology. In D.G. Benner & P.C. Hill (Eds.), *Baker encyclopedia of psychology and counseling* (2nd ed., pp. 294-298). Grand Rapids, MI: Baker.

Abi-Hashem, N. (1999c). Trauma. In D.G. Benner & P.C. Hill (Eds.), *Baker encyclopedia of psychology and counseling* (2nd ed., pp. 1229-1230). Grand Rapids, MI: Baker.

Abi-Hashem, N. (1999d, Fall-Winter). Ethnopolitical conflicts: A Lebanese perspective. *International Psychology Reporter: APA Division 52 Newsletter, 3* (2, 3), 29-31.

Abi-Hashem, N. (1999e). Loss of function. In D.G. Benner & P.C. Hill (Eds.), *Baker encyclopedia of psychology and counseling* (2nd ed., p.705). Grand Rapids, MI: Baker.

Abi-Hashem, N. (2004). Peace and war in the Middle East: A psychopolitical and sociocultural perspective. In F. M. Moghaddam and A. J. Marsella (Eds.), *Understanding terrorism: Psychosocial roots, consequences, and interventions* (pp. 69-89). Washington DC: American Psychological Association Press.

At the gates of Baghdad. (2003, April 5). *Economist, 366* (8318), 11, 2p, 1c.

Behrman, S. (2001, September 22). The diary of a people's agony. *Socialist Worker Online.* Retrieved March 13, 2005 from http://www.socialistworker.co.uk/article.php4?article_id=1493

Carballo, M., Smajkic, A., Zeric, D., Dzidowska, M., Gebre-Medhin, J., & Van Halem, J. (2004). Mental health and coping in a war situation: The case of Bosnia [Electronic version]. *Journal of Biosocial Science, 36* (4), 463-477.

Cardozo, B.L., Bilukha, O.O., Crawford, C.A., Shaikh, I., Wolfe, M.I., Gerber. M.L., & Anderson, M. (2004, August). Mental health, social functioning, and disability in postwar Afghanistan. *JAMA: The journal of the American Medical Association, 292* (5), 575-84.

Cohen, R. (2004, May 18). A region in agony [Opinion]. *The Washington Post.* Retrieved March 13, 2005 from http://www.washingtonpost.com/wp-dyn/articles/A34783-2004May17.html

Collins, G. R. (2005, February 10). Surviving major disasters. *Gary R. Collins Newsletter* [Letter 126]. Retrieved from http://www.garyrcollins.com/archive.jcm?id=146

Committee on inalienable rights of the Palestinian people. (2002, February 12). *United Nations: Press Release.* Retrieved March 14, 2005 from http://www.unhchr.ch/huricane/huricane.nsf/0/BC85DF14A3CF71CFC1256B5F002B5C7A?opendocument

Durakovia-Belko, E., Kulenovia, A., & Dapia, R. (2003). Determinants of posttraumatic adjustment in adolescents from Sarajevo who experienced war. *Journal of clinical psychology, 59* (1), pp. 27-40.

Dwairy, M. (1998). *Cross-cultural counseling: The Arab-Palestinian case.* New York: The Haworth Press.

Eckersall, F. (2002, March 29). Twin town agony [Guest opinions]. *The Bournemouth Echo.* Retrieved from http://www.jewishcomment.com/cgibin/news.cgi?id=12&command=shownews&newsid=227

Farhood, L., Zurayk, H., Chaya, M., Saadeh, F., Meshefedjian, G., & Sidani, T. (1993). The impact of war on the physical and mental health of the family: The Lebanese experience. *Social Science and Medicine 36,* 1555-1567.

Findley, P. (1993, July/August). Israeli exercise in mischief-making. *Washington Report on Middle East Affairs.* Retrieved March 13, 2005 from http://www.washington-report.org/backissues/0793/9307009.htm

Friedman, T.L. (2005, March 3). Brave, young and Muslim [Op-Ed]. *The New York Times.* Retrieved from http://www.nytimes.com/2005/03/03/opinion/03friedman.html?n=Top%2fOpinion%2fEditorials%20and%20Op%2dEd%2fOp%2dEd%2fColumnists%2fThomas%20L%20Friedman

Fowler, J. (Ed.). (2005, March 3). More Iraqis suffer now [Special report]. Retrieved April 4, 2005 from http://www.news24.com/News24/World/Iraq/0,6119,2-10-1460_1683149,00.html

Gavrilovic, J., Lecic-Tosevski, D., Dimic, S., Pejovic-Milovancevic, M., Knezevic, G., & Priebe, S. (2003). Coping strategies in civilians during air attacks [Electronic version]. *Social Psychiatry & Psychiatric Epidemiology, 38* (3), 128-33.

Green A. H, & Kocijan-Hercigonja, D. (1998). Stress and coping in children traumatized by war. *Journal of the American Academy of Psychoanalysis, 26* (4), 585-597.

Green, B.L., Lindy, J.D., & Grace, M.C. (1988). Long term coping with combat stress. *Journal of Traumatic Stress, 1,* 399-412.

Hill, T.R. (2005, February 17). Israeli rabbi works for peace, yet understands the need to feel safe. *Presbyterian News Service.* Retrieved from http://www.pcusa.org/pcnews/2005/05100.htm

Hobfoll, S.E., Spielberger, C.D., Breznitz, S., Figley, C., Folkman, S., Lepper-Green, B, Meichenbaum, D., Milgram, N.A., Sandler, I., Sarason, I., & van der Kolk, B. (1991). war-related stress: Addressing the stress of war and other traumatic events [electronic version]. *American Psychologist, 46* (8), 848-855.

Ibrahim, Y. M. (1991, February 3). In the Mid-east, a fear that war is only the beginning. *The New York Times: The Week in Review,* pp. 1-2.

Israel set on tragic path, says chief rabbi. (2002 August 27). *Peace Movement Aotearoa.* Retrieved from http://www.converge.org.nz/pma/cra0824.htm

Kapp, C. (2003). Relief crisis unfolds as Iraq war progresses. *Lancet, 361* (9363), 1103, 1c.

Lorieux, C. (1993, January). Sanctions and suffering in Iraq [Electronic version]. *World Press Review, 40* (1), 50, 1bw.

Lustig, S.L., Kia-Keating, M., Knight, W.G., Geltman, P., Ellis, H., Kinzie, J.D., Keane, T., & Saxe, G.N. (2004). Review of child and adolescent refugee mental health [Electronic version]. *Journal of the American Academy of Child and Adolescent Psychiatry, 43* (1), 24-36.

Mallat, C. (2005, March 08). A new 'White Arabism' would help generate liberal societies. *The Daily Star* [Commentary]. Retreived from http://www.dailystar.com.lb/article.asp?edition_id=10&categ_id=5&article_id=13229

Marsella, A.J., & Christopher, M.A. (2004). Ethnocultural considerations in disasters: An overview of research, issues, and directions. *Psychiatric Clinics of North America, 27* (30), 521-539.

Meichenbaum, D. (1994). *A clinical handbook/practical therapist manual for assessing and treating adults with PTSD.* Waterloo, Ontario: Institute Press.

Melamed, K.T. (1992). The Gulf *War* and its impact on burnout and well-being of working civilians [Electronic version]. *Psychological medicine, 22* (4), 987-995.

Miller, J. (1991, July 21). Nowhere to go: The Palestinians after the War. *The New York Times Magazine*, pp. 13, 32.

Miller, J. (1999, March 31). U.N. panel seeks to ease suffering of Iraq's people. *New York Times, 148* (51478), p. A6.

Nydell, M. K. (1987). *Understanding Arabs: A guide for Westerners*. Yarmouth, ME: Intercultural.

Oweini, A. (1996). Stress and coping: The experience of students at the American University of Beirut during the Lebanese civil war [Electronic version]. *Arab Studies Quarterly, 18* (1), 69-91.

Prigerson, H.G., Shear, M.K., Friank, E., & Beery, L.C. (1997). Traumatic grief: A case of loss-induced trauma. *American Journal of Psychiatry, 154*, 1003-1009.

Punamaki, R.L. (1990). Impact of political change on the psychological stress process among West Bank Palestinian women [Electronic version]. *Medicine and War, 6* (3), 169-181.

Punamaki, R-L. (1997). The visible invisible: Psychological reality of war children. *Peace & Conflict; 3* (3), 311-314.

Rando, T.A. (1993). *Treatment of complicated mourning*. Champaign, IL: Research Press.

Rando, T.A. (1996). On treating those bereaved by sudden, unanticipated death. *In Session: Psychotherapy in Practice, 2*, 49-71.

Silver, R., & Wortman, C.B. (1980). Coping with undesirable life events. In J. Garber & M.E.P. Seligman (Eds.), *Human helplessness* (pp. 279-375). San Diego, CA: Academic.

Skeet, J. (2003a, December 16). Sanctions killed 1.5 million: The plight of Iraq. [Letter to the editor] [Electronic version]. *Toronto Star*, p. A27.

Skeet, J. (2003b, March 9). Too much suffering in Iraq: A view of the world on the brink of war [Editorial] [Electronic version]. *Toronto Star*, p. A12.

Sorrows of war (2003, April 5) [Electronic version]. *Christian Century, 120* (7), 5.

Saperstein, D. (2002, March 26). Statement of Rabbi David Saperstein, Director, Religious Action Center of Reform Judaism on the Alexandria Declaration. Retrieved from http://rac.org/Articles/index.cfm?id=543&pge_prg_id=4368

Steele, J. (2002, August 29-September 4). Dare to dream in Jerusalem. *The Guardian Weekly*, p. 14.

Stichick, T. (2001). The psychosocial impact of armed conflict on children: Rethinking traditional paradigms in research and intervention [Electronic version]. *Child and adolescent psychiatric clinics of North America, 10* (4), 797-814.

Stroebe, M.S., Schut, H., & Sroebe, W. (1998). Trauma and grief: A comparative analysis. In J.H. Harvey (Ed.), *Perspectives on loss: A sourcebook* (pp. 81-96). Philadelphia, PA: Bruner/Mazel.

Summerfield, D. (1995). Addressing human response to war and atrocity: Major challenges in research and practices and the limitations of Western psychiatric models. In J. Kleber, C. Figley, P. Berthold and R. Gersons, *Beyond Trauma: Cultural and Social Dynamics* (pp. 17-29). New York , NY: Plenum Press.

Wagner, C,H, & Brimmer, R. (n.d.). We are tired of crying! *Bridges of Peace*. Retrieved February 24, 2005 from http://www.bridgesforpeace.com/publications/dispatch/generaltopics/Article-0.html

Watkins, J. (n.d.). Is it a 'just' war? Retrieved February 02, 2005 from http://www.gospelcom.net/watkins/just-war.htm

Wilson, S. (2004, July 14). Afternoon of mixed emotions: Sight of Saddam Hussein brings sadness, joy, relief to Baghdad street. *The Washington Post*, p. A 11.

Wong, P.T. P. (1993). Effective management of life stress: The resource-congruence model. *Stress Medicine, 9*, 51-60.

Worden, J.W. (1991). Grief counseling and grief therapy: A handbook for the mental health practitioner (2nd ed.). New York, NY: Springer.

21

STRESS, CULTURE, AND RACIAL SOCIALIZATION:
Making an Impact

Micah L. McCreary, Jera Nelson Cunningham, Kathleen M.
Ingram, and John E. Fife

1. INTRODUCTION

As counseling psychologists, we approach the topic of coping and socialization from a perspective that attempts to address mental health issues by examining social relevance and contextual influences. We come from a tradition that promotes and seeks remedial, preventive and educational advancement for our consumers (Whiteley, 1984).

We approach the writing of this chapter on stress, socialization and coping skills among African American families from a resiliency perspective. Moreover, we discuss the challenges imposed on these resiliency models by the context and experiences of African Americans. We also explore the coping mechanisms that researchers have suggested lead to resiliency in general and in African American families specifically. This is followed by a discussion of our theoretical understanding of culture and the stress process, and the potential mechanisms for coping with stress, particularly racially-oriented stressors, employed by African American families that can lead to resiliency in their children. Finally, we present an applied program of acculturation and stress, via "The IMPACT Programs," a family-based psychoeducational intervention which explores the effect of racial socialization and identity on African American children's adjustment.

2. TRADITIONAL MODELS OF RESILIENCY

James Garbarino (1999) defined resilience as the ability to bounce back and overcome adversity. He suggested that some youth possess qualities that make them resilient, while others are nurtured in an environment that teaches them to be resilient. Garbarino further mentioned a number of psychological, behavioral, social, and spiritual anchors that under-lie components of resilience in children and youth. Some of these anchors are a strong parental attachment (Garbarino, 1999), the capacity to actively respond to stressful events

All authors are affiliated with Virginia Commonwealth University.

rather than passively react to them (Garbarino, 1999; Losel & Bliesener, 1990), intellectual ability or cognitive competence (Garbarino, 1999; Losel & Bliesener, 1990), authentic self-esteem (Garbarino, 1999; Losel & Bliesener, 1990), constructive coping strategies (Garbarino, 1999), and an ability to seek constructive and appropriate social support from non-family members (Garbarino, 1999; Losel & Bliesener, 1990).

Researchers have found other general, non-ethnic specific, resiliency factors in children, such as temperament (Hetherington, Stanley-Hagan, & Anderson, 1989; Rutter, 1987; Werner, 1986; Werner & Smith, 1982), parental monitoring of children's activities (Yoshikawa, 1994), emotional understanding and emotional regulation (Smith, 2001), parental warmth and control (Losel & Bliesener, 1990), self-efficacy (Losel & Bliesener, 1990), acute stressors as opposed to chronic stressors (Davidson & Smith, 1990), parental attitudes (Holden & Edwards, 1989), and child future-orientation (Garbarino, 1999; Wyman et al., 1992; Wyman, Cowen, Work, & Kerley, 1993). Over the last decade, scientific literature and research on resilience has found that temperament is a moderator affecting the relation between numerous aspects of parenting and child outcomes (Rutter, 1987). For example, temperament has been shown to be a resiliency factor when there is a high level of psychosocial stress and poor parenting (Werner, 1986; Werner & Smith, 1982) or when children experience divorce and remarriage of their parents (Hetherington et al., 1989).

Although some of the universal resiliency factors apply to children in general, there are studies examining resilience in African American children that have direct application to African American parenting and socialization. African American parents' level of adolescent monitoring was positively associated with youths' self-efficacy (Spencer et al., 1996). Parental monitoring was seen by the adolescents as hassles, but these "hassles" included parental encouragement, instilling values, and pushing the adolescent to achieve. Spencer et al. (1996) labeled a positive perception of parental hassles (monitoring) as a positive, reactive coping method that is linked to academic performance. Spencer and colleagues (1996) found that parental monitoring increased as adolescents reported more stressful life events. For African American adolescent girls, predictors of taking responsibility for learning were high perceived self-efficacy, high-stress life events, high home/family monitoring, and a lack of pressure for adolescent independence (Spencer et al., 1996). For boys, predictors of academic responsibility were high perceived self-efficacy, high home/family monitoring, and high-stress life events (Spencer et al., 1996). Regardless of gender, adolescents' increased levels of perceived self-efficacy and stressful life events led to increased levels of taking responsibility for their academic achievement (Spencer et al., 1996). In essence, Spencer et al. (1996) found that African American adolescents appear to be motivated by parental encouragement to take responsibility for their schooling seriously. In addition, Yoshikawa (1994) found that lack of parental supervision with children was a predictor of child delinquency.

While some skills taught by parents of families that are related to resilience are culture-specific for African American children, other traits or skills seem to be more universal for leading to child competencies. One study of 36 low-income and middle-class African American preschoolers focused on emotional understanding and emotional regulation as predictors of peer acceptance (Smith, 2001). This was a 6-month longitudinal study for which teachers completed behavioral and social measures and for which children participated in interviews and provided sociometric ratings. Smith (2001) found that children who were well-liked had greater emotional understanding, better emotional regulation (ability to delay gratification), thought more empathetically, and were less aggressive and hostile. These findings are similar to those from Caucasian and middle-class families but are important to study in African American children.

For a Black, inner-city, low-income sample, parent attitudes had more effect on children's academic performance than most demographic variables (Holden & Edwards, 1989). Parents' educational expectations for children and parents' satisfaction with the quality of children's education were significant predictors of children's math and reading achievement, teacher-rated social adjustment and competence, and teacher-rated problem behavior, even after controlling for parent education, marital status, gender, lunch subsidy, number of children in the family, parent employment, grade retentions, and preschool with follow-up intervention (Holden & Edwards, 1989). Parent behavior toward children's school did not predict academic outcomes or mediate attitudes about school, which suggests that family interventions targeting family functioning and academic performance should focus on parent attitudes and expectations (Holden & Edwards, 1989).

Another powerful resiliency anchor mentioned by Garbarino (1999) is the power of being future-oriented. John Wideman (1984) tells the story of overcoming or surrendering to the influences of the environment in his book, *Brothers and Keepers*. Regarding resiliency, Wideman wrestles with his resiliency and his brother's vulnerability and clearly presents a treatise on the power of being future-oriented and the dangers of utilizing terminal thinking. Wideman discusses his ability to overcome adversity, while theorizing about the stress and sadness that resulted in his brother's hopelessness for the future, and eventual criminal activities. Wideman did and his brother did not display the internal qualities that anchor resiliency. The younger brother of John Wideman surrendered to the hopeless, racist, sexist, and "classist" zeitgeist that facilitates the disenfranchisement experienced by many African Americans.

We suggest that resiliency anchors are conveyed to children by parents and other social agents through the process of socialization. By socialization we are referring to the process through which ideas about what one should do (prescriptions) and ideas about what one should not do (prohibitions) are transmitted to family members (McClintock, 1972). Currently, investigators are examining the socialization process of parenting. Parents socialize their children as they teach them the skills necessary to survive in the world and become active functioning members of society (Harrison, Wilson, Pine, Chan, & Buriel, 1990). This process involves learning a set of rules, beliefs, values, and attitudes for living (Westman, Brackney, & Bylski, 1992). The family is generally regarded as the first and most important socializing agent for the child (Demo & Hughes, 1990; Wilson, Kohn, Curry-El, & Hinton, 1995). A strong family provides goals, values, and structure for the developing child. Families that do not intentionally socialize their children may leave them more vulnerable to stress and poor adjustment.

3. TOWARD A MULTICULTURAL MODEL OF STRESS AND CULTURE

It is quite evident that each of the aforementioned stress and resilience factors is important. Our research at Virginia Commonwealth University has focused on the factors of family socialization and enhancement of self-efficacy and self-esteem. We are also keenly interested in investigating the manner in which the family and community provide a stable emotional environment and relationship, social support, and positive parenting practices and cultural messages. Our community interventions have sought to address these factors through a series of workshops and experiences that foster active coping, goal-oriented behaviors, and supportive educational climates that incorporate cultural factors.

This was our position when we proposed the multicultural model of the stress process in 1991 (Slavin, Rainer, McCreary, & Gowda). In that paper, we suggested a model of the stress process that incorporated cultural and ethnicity factors in an explicit way. We expanded and annotated a version of the Lazarus and Folkman (1984) model systematically, incorporating what we had learned from the literature on multicultural psychology and from our work with minority adolescents. The five major components of the model were the: (1) occurrence of a potentially stressful event, (2) primary cognitive appraisal of the event, (3) secondary cognitive appraisal of the event, (4) implementation of a coping strategy, and (5) physical and mental health outcomes. In our 1991 article, we highlighted aspects of culture and experiences that could be incorporated into explorations of stress with cultural groups. For example, we hypothesized that for African Americans exposure to environmental stressors related to racism and poverty, racial identity development and obtainment, and culturally prescribed coping strategies such as spirituality and extended family were relevant variables that would add to the predictive abilities of the standard stress model.

In a follow-up study of the multicultural model of the stress process, McCreary, Slavin, and Berry (1996) investigated the predictive ability of the Lazarus and Folkman (1984) model. We took the five major components of the Lazarus and Folkman model of stress, which is considered to be cyclical and interactive, and incorporated into the model a cognitive and affective variable that we proposed would aide our understanding and investigation into the stress process among African American adolescents.

From the survey results of 297 African American adolescents attending a Baptist-church sponsored retreat, we learned that perceived stress and perceived social support were positive predictors of psychosocial outcomes and emotional support from family and friends in a sample of adolescents (McCreary et al., 1996). The study also indicated that the predictive ability of the stress model was strengthened by the inclusion of the racial identity and cultural variables.

This research paradigm and perspective has been further substantiated by the research of Gorman-Smith and colleagues (2000), Pinderhughes and colleagues (2000) and others (O'Conner, Brooks-Gunn, & Graber, 2000) who all found that people's responses to stressful experiences vary in relation to ethnic and cultural differences. Recently, Tolan, Gorman-Smith, and Henry (2004) reported about a family-focused preventive intervention called SAFEChildren, which addresses issues of social support within families and which was delivered as a multiple-family group intervention for a number of families. In the study, 57.5% of the sample self-identified as Hispanic and 42.5% as African American. We suggest that the family-focused SAFEChildren intervention is a cultural specific and culturally sensitive intervention because it uses an intervention the researchers have found effective and preferred by ethnic minorities in America.

Thus, in attempting to study stress and social support among African Americans, researchers have validated our 1991 proposition which was that researchers, teachers, and clinicians must modify their models of stress and coping to reflect the unique cultural and social circumstances of different ethnic groups. We believe that it is critical and relevant to integrate culture into our stress and coping models.

4. CULTURE OR RACE-SPECIFIC FACTORS THAT ARE RELATED TO RESILIENCE

A study of family functioning and adolescent outcomes with urban African American and Mexican American families showed that African American families tended to be more task-oriented and higher functioning as a family unit than Mexican American families, but that African American families tended to be less emotion-focused in their interactions than other ethnic groups (Gorman-Smith et al., 2000). If African American families are more task-oriented than emotion-oriented, this may have an impact on the way African American parents socialize their children about emotions and how to cope with emotion-laden racial events. This also is important for how interventions are developed for African American families.

There are qualities of African American families that are unique to that cultural group that might provide for more resiliency in children. Mandura and Murray (2000) pointed out factors other than parental marital status that may impact African American children's competence, such as economic strain, neighborhood context, level of family functioning, and the presence or absence of extended kin. The functioning of the family including extended family and religious beliefs might be two important strengths of African American families. A questionnaire and focus group study of low-income mothers from different ethnic backgrounds (African American, Euro-American, English-speaking Latinas, and Spanish-speaking Latinas) found that the ways in which families coped with economic hardship and the effects of economic deprivation differed by ethnic group (Gomel, Tinsley, Parke, & Clark, 1998). While economic hardship negatively impacted family relationships in all four ethnic groups, the experiences related to low-income status that Caucasian families experience cannot be applied blindly to other ethnic groups because their experiences of economic deprivation are likely different (Gomel et al., 1998). Other recommended areas of study for African American families came from a theoretical article by Randolph, Koblinsky, and Roberts (1996). They cited the importance of examining African American parents' adaptive childrearing strategies when living in violent neighborhoods, such as restricting play, keeping children inside the home, and using prayer, that might be different than those strategies of middle-class Caucasian families (Randolph et al., 1996).

The African worldview is based on a holistic conception of human condition. In the African worldview the human being is conceived as being a series of interlocking systems. This idea of interdependence and interrelatedness extends to the entire universe. In this universe, the Supreme Being is above all. Human beings are next in the hierarchy, followed by animals, plants and inanimate objects in descending order (White & Parham, 1990). African spiritual traditions have historically held a central place in African American communalism (Mbiti, 1990) and were vital to survival during the time of slavery. The African worldview has persisted in the lives of many African Americans because it provided familiar patterns of beliefs about the supernatural and collective survival, and this allowed early African Americans to establish a sense of meaning about the world around them. As it was in Africa, so has spirituality and religion been at the center of African American community life and folk experience. Spirituality has been identified by a number of researchers and scholars as a fundamental attribute of African American personality. In essence, for people of African descent, spirituality significantly contributes to those assumptions about self, others, and self-world relationships. Consequently, religion has been identified as a key coping mechanism for many African American families. One of the ways that religion is a coping mechanism for many African Americans is the view of a God who is for the oppressed. Cone (1986) argues that African American religiosity is thematically and existentially concerned with the issues of oppression, freedom, hope and justice. In addition to these thematic concerns, African American religions have developed specific visions of the relationship between humans and God and the mission of believers (Cone, 1986; Lincoln, 1990). In Muslim and African American Christian traditions God, Christ, and Allah are seen as champions of the oppressed, and as symbols of victory over oppression. By envisioning Christ and God as usurpers, religious African Americans remind themselves and each other of the prospect of "making a way out of no way" (Cone, 1986; Lincoln, 1990).

In African American culture, religious attendance and celebration is an important type of ritual. Church attendance and involvement in the African American culture then can be viewed as a ritual that may provide tremendous stability for the African American family and community. For families who attend weekly services together, it is a reminder that there is a supreme being that is in control of all things, and that support is available in the midst of the trials of life. African American youth must become adults in a period of many societal challenges and limitations. Nobles (1986) suggests that African American families are responsible for creating and maintaining three senses in African American youth; the sense of history, the sense of family, and the sense of an ultimate supreme power or God. The sense of the ultimate Supreme Being will assist African American children to realize that there is a power and a will that is greater than them, and that they are connected to this Supreme Being. This belief in a connection to a supreme being is meant to assist African Americans in recognizing that their potential is limitless despite the limitations presented by their environment and by society.

5. RACISM AS A SPECIAL STRESSOR EXPERIENCED BY AFRICAN AMERICAN FAMILIES

Being a member of an ethnic minority group can increase the number of stressors with which families must cope. Families may have to handle racial discrimination or racism and other social barriers that may be due to one's skin color or ethnic background. Child development in this context may be different from the highly researched developmental trajectory for majority group children. A review of recent work suggests that parenting styles and family function do differ by ethnic group. Some of these differences are due to social contexts in which these families interact, and the differences are frequently related to resilience (Luthar, 1999).

Recently, Dr. Micah L. McCreary was taking his 10-year-old daughter to school. They were late and so instead of walking together down the path to her school, she ran ahead and he followed. A woman driving by saw this encounter and presumed that "some pervert was chasing a girl through the woods." Dr. McCreary's license plate numbers were taken, the police were called, and the matter was investigated. We have talked about this experience with parents at the school and among ourselves as a research team. We all agree that we are glad the woman passing by was concerned about the well-being of Dr. McCreary's daughter. Yet, we all wonder if she would have come to a different conclusion about what she saw if the male adult was not African American.

We truly will never know what underlying factors affected the woman's perspective, but we do know the added stress that this caused Dr. McCreary and his family. We also know that since arriving in Virginia in 1983, this is the third time that Dr. McCreary had been approached by the police for "being Black."

This experience of race-related stress is not the exclusive property of Dr. McCreary. Many studies found that racial discrimination led to higher stress levels and poorer mental health. A sample of adult African Americans reported frequencies and stress associated with various forms of racism and discrimination. Almost every participant (98%) reported experiencing some form of discrimination in the past year (Landrine & Klonoff, 1996). The most common racist event experienced by participants was being discriminated against by strangers and by people in service jobs (83% each). Being discriminated against by institutions (64%) and by people in the helping profession (55%) was common, as was being called racist names (50%). Being picked on, hit, shoved, or threatened with harm happened to one third of the sample. More than a third of the participants indicated they had to take extreme steps in response to a racist event in the past year, such as quitting a job or filing a lawsuit (Landrine & Klonoff, 1996). Almost two thirds of the sample expressed intense anger about a racist act that was directed toward them (Landrine & Klonoff, 1996). Participants rated most of the racist events in the past year as at least somewhat stressful and many of the racist events were rated as extremely stressful (walking around feeling angry about an event, being called racist names, wanting to tell people off for being racist but not saying anything, getting into arguments about racism, being discriminated against by institutions, and being suspected/accused of wrongdoing) (Landrine & Klonoff, 1996). There were no gender differences in the frequency or stress appraisal of racist events (Landrine & Klonoff, 1996). This study is a demonstration of the level of discrimination and thus resulting stress that a majority of African Americans experience on a regular basis.

Another study of African Americans found that racial events were related to poorer mental health. Fischer and Shaw (1999) found that the majority of African American college students reported being treated unfairly by people in service jobs or by strangers because they were Black. For African American college students, racist event perceptions were related to poorer general mental health for students depending on parental racial socialization messages (Fischer & Shaw, 1999). Again the study found negative effects of racial discrimination for African Americans.

Not only is racial discrimination related to higher levels of stress, it is also connected with other psychological difficulties and mental health. The more racial discrimination participants experienced in the past year, the more somatic symptoms and feelings of low self worth participants reported (Landrine & Klonoff, 1996). Participants who had high scores on psychiatric symptoms reported experiencing more racism than participants who had low scores and also reported the events as more stressful than did the participants with few symptoms (Landrine & Klonoff, 1996). For these participants, experiences of discrimination were related to poorer mental health and self-esteem.

The type of cultural beliefs and practices that people held influenced the impact of racist events. For people who held traditional African American beliefs and values, more frequent racist events were reported and the resulting stress was rated as more intense than for African Americans who had acculturated into mainstream America (Landrine & Klonoff, 1996). Possible reasons for this relationship could be that people who hold these beliefs may isolate themselves from the mainstream and surround themselves with others who share their experiences and cultural mistrust and may not have other positive experiences with members of the mainstream or other cultural groups to counter experiences of discrimination. African Americans who are more acculturated may not actually experience less discrimination, but have more experiences that balance the negative ones, so they do not rate these alienating experiences as stressful as people who are not involved in or acculturated to the mainstream culture. Another study found similar results when surveying African American adults over the telephone about race-related factors and satisfaction with life (Broman, 1997). African Americans who experienced discrimination reported less life satisfaction, while those who attended predominantly White schools (not dependent on the number of White friends) reported more life satisfaction (Broman, 1997). Income level was not related to racial composition of participants' schools. This study may again support the notion that students who attend predominately White schools and are presumably more acculturated into the mainstream culture may have positive and healing experiences to buffer negative or racist encounters, which would allow them to feel more positive about themselves and their lives and reduce stress levels. It also could be that African American students who attend primarily White schools do not view their race as an important issue and focus more on personal attributes than collective or group identity.

6. COPING AND RESILIENCE

One important variable that can promote resilience is coping, which has been described as efforts to enact or mobilize characteristics and resources in response to stress (Compas, Connor-Smith, Saltzman, Thomsen, & Wadsworth, 2001). A number of studies have examined the types of coping strategies that African American children and adolescents use to deal with stress (e.g., Clark, Novak, & Dupree, 2002; Scott, 2003a), and have provided useful information about how particular coping behaviors are associated with factors such as parenting practices. However, only a few studies have investigated the potential link between coping strategies and resilience among African American children and adolescents.

Steward et al. (1998) examined factors associated with resilience among urban African American adolescents in their first year of high school. Overall psychological adjustment was assessed by the extent to which the adolescents' positive affect exceeded their negative affect. Students with the highest level of psychological adjustment tended to use family-oriented coping strategies (e.g., talking with parents or siblings about problems, sharing activities with family, and going along with parents' requests and rules) and tended to use humor to minimize problems. Students who tended to use relaxation activities to cope with day-to-day stressors reported lower levels of overall adjustment. As Steward et al. noted, these findings suggest that parenting skills training can make an important contribution to resilience among African American adolescents by helping to strengthen families, thereby providing a stable source of support upon which adolescents can rely.

In another study that assessed the coping strategy of seeking social support from family members, Allison, Belgrave, Butler, Edwards, and Plybon (2003) examined resources associated with positive school outcomes among urban African American adolescent girls who ranged in age from 11 to 14 years. The researchers assessed the extent to which the girls sought support from parents and from other adults (e.g., ministers, mentors, adult friends, and other adult relatives) when the girls encountered problems. Seeking support from parents was associated with higher school self-efficacy, after controlling for socioeconomic status. The coping strategy of seeking support from other adults was not significantly associated with school self-efficacy or self-reported grades. However, a significant interaction effect was found between neighborhood cohesion and seeking support from other adults. Specifically, among girls who reported high levels of seeking support from other adults, grades increased as neighborhood cohesion increased. These findings point to the importance of understanding how contextual factors may influence the choice of coping strategies, which in turn may have an impact on school outcomes.

Whereas other studies of coping and resilience among African American adolescents have focused on urban samples, Markstrom, Marshall, and Tyron (2000) studied African American adolescents from a rural, low-income region in West Virginia. In this sample of 10th graders, problem-focused coping was positively correlated with resiliency, as assessed by a measure of ego strength. In contrast, wishful thinking and avoidant coping were inversely associated with ego strength. The researchers assessed students' perceptions of support that was available from family and friends, but did not measure the coping strategy of seeking social support. Somewhat surprisingly, neither source of support was significantly associated with ego strength when entered into the same regression equation as problem-focused coping, wishful thinking, and avoidance coping. Markstrom et al. speculated that social support may influence resilience indirectly, by leading to greater use of problem-focused coping. Thus, if support is available, then African American adolescents may perceive that they have sufficient resources for attempting to use an active coping strategy of problem solving to deal with a stressor.

Rather than studying stressors in general, Utsey, Ponterotto, Reynolds, and Cancelli (2000) investigated coping strategies African Americans use to deal with the specific stressor of racism. African American college students were asked to indicate which coping strategies they used in response to a racist event they encountered in the past year. Gender differences emerged in the choice of coping behaviors for dealing with racism. Females reported having used the strategy of seeking social support significantly more than men did. In examining the link between coping and resilience, Utsey et al. found that the use of avoidant coping to deal with the racist event was negatively associated with both life satisfaction and self-esteem. Neither problem-solving coping nor seeking social support was significantly associated with either indicator of well-being. In addition, seeking social support was positively correlated with race-related stress. Utsey et al. noted that in many instances in which African Americans encounter racism (e.g., as part of widely accepted cultural practices in American society), seeking social support may be the only viable coping strategy. Given the pervasiveness of racist events and their negative consequences for mental and physical health (Landrine & Klonoff, 1996), it is important to continue to identify effective strategies for coping with racism and to determine the best ways of teaching those strategies to African American children and adolescents.

In a longitudinal study, McCubbin et al. (1999) examined the association between coping and resilience in a sample of at-risk African American youth with an average age of 15 who participated in a residential treatment program for young offenders. Increases in the coping strategy of directing efforts at spirituality and personal development and decreases in coping behaviors related to incendiary communication and tension management (e.g., behaviors that exacerbate interpersonal conflicts, and cognitive strategies that make the issue larger than it is) were significant predictors of successful program completion. In addition, this same pattern of change in the two coping strategies was significantly associated with successful post-treatment adaptation 12 months later. When considered together, changes in youth coping and changes in coping of the family unit yielded the highest accuracy rate in predicting successful program outcomes. Coping strategies of the family unit as a group included affirming the family's confidence in its ability to handle major problems, seeking professional and spiritual guidance, and seeking support from relatives and friends. These findings suggest that family members and the coping strategies they use as a group can play an important role in fostering resilience among African American adolescents. Therefore, McCubbin et al. suggested that when designing interventions, it is important to consider ways of strengthening the coping repertoire of the family as well as the individual adolescent.

In addition to studies of African American children and adolescents that have examined the relationship between coping and positive outcomes, several studies have investigated the association between coping and distress. Myers and Thompson (2000) studied violence exposure in a sample of African American adolescents ranging in age from 14 to 19 years. The researchers examined two types of coping strategies: active coping (ventilating feelings, problem solving, engaging in demanding activities, seeking spiritual support, and avoiding problems) and calming or soothing ways of coping (relaxing, seeking diversion, investing in close relationships, and being humorous). There was a significant inverse correlation between active coping and symptoms of posttraumatic stress disorder (PTSD). Thus, adolescents who reported using more active coping strategies to deal with stressors reported fewer PTSD symptoms. Although females engaged in more calming coping strategies than males did, calming coping strategies were not significantly associated with symptoms of PTSD. Finally, life events served as an important predictor of active coping. As the number of negative life events increased, active coping decreased. As Myers and Thompson noted, it is important to consider contextual factors that may influence an adolescent's ability to enact effective coping behaviors. Therefore, to teach effective coping skills to African American adolescents, it seems important to help the adolescents recognize that the accumulation of recent stressful events may interfere with the ability to engage in active coping. It might make sense to teach adolescents that when they believe active coping would be the most effective response but are having difficulty enacting that strategy, it can be useful to seek support from a parent or other adult first.

In a longitudinal study, Steele et al. (1999) examined the association between coping and distress in a sample of urban African American children who ranged in age from 6 to 11 years. Results indicated that the children's reported use of avoidant and emotion-focused coping did not change over three points in time (baseline, 12-14 months later, and 18-20 months after baseline). The proportion of emotion-focused coping was significantly associated cross-sectionally with child-reported aggressive behavior and depressive symptoms at all three time points, and with mother-reported externalizing and internalizing behavior at Time 2. In addition, the proportion of emotion-focused coping at Time 1 was significantly associated with child-reported aggressive behavior and depressive symptoms at Time 2; the same pattern was found between Times 2 and 3. In contrast, the proportion of avoidant coping was not significantly related to behavior problems cross-sectionally or longitudinally. In discussing the link between emotion-focused coping and behavior problems, Steele et al. noted that emotion-focused strategies may be effective for short-term stressors but may be ineffective in dealing with the distress associated with chronic stressors. Thus, it seems that children and adolescents should be taught to evaluate the effectiveness of the strategy they have chosen to respond to a particular stressor and to be flexible about changing their strategy, especially if the stressor is chronic or long-term.

Finally, two studies examined whether coping serves as an intervening variable in the relationship between stress and distress. Grant et al. (2000) investigated coping as a potential moderator of the association between stressful life experiences and psychological symptoms in a sample of 6th though 8th grade urban African American adolescents. Avoidant coping was the only coping strategy to demonstrate a protective influence. Specifically, avoidant coping appeared to buffer the effects of stress on externalizing symptoms for boys, but not for girls. In supplemental analyses focusing on specific subtypes of stressful life events, both avoidant coping and social support-seeking coping appeared to amplify, rather than diminish, the relation between daily hassles and internalizing symptoms for girls. According to Grant et al., these findings suggest that the protective effects of a particular coping strategy may depend, in part, on characteristics of the individual and the context of the stressor. In a study of inner-city African American adolescents ranging in age from 10 to 14 years, Dempsey (2002) found that negative coping strategies (e.g., ignoring the problem, crying, hitting or fighting, and screaming or yelling) mediated the association between exposure to community violence and distress. Thus, increased exposure to violence was associated with increased use of negative coping, which, in turn, was associated with increased symptoms of PTSD, depression, and anxiety. In contrast, positive coping strategies (e.g., thinking about how to solve the problem, seeking guidance from an adult, and taking deep breaths to calm oneself down) were not significantly inversely related to distress. Dempsey observed that it may be naïve to simply teach children and adolescents to replace negative coping strategies with positive ones, and that there is much to be learned about how other factors such as family characteristics may influence the relationship between violence exposure and psychological outcomes.

Additional research is needed to understand how coping is associated with resilience among African American children and adolescents. For example, longitudinal studies would help to identify how different types of coping might predict resilience over time. In addition, it would be useful to include culture-specific measures of coping, such as the Africultural Coping Systems Inventory (Utsey, Adams, & Bolden, 2000). Taken together, existing studies of coping and resilience suggest that it is inadvisable to use a "one size fits all" approach when attempting to teach effective coping strategies to African American children and adolescents. Interventions should be designed to teach children and adolescents a variety of coping strategies and to teach them decision making skills for choosing the strategy that is most likely to be effective in a particular situation, taking into account factors such as personal characteristics, available resources, the timing, and the nature of the stressor. Family-based psychoeducational interventions might be particularly effective, given that parents and family seem to play an important role in fostering adaptive coping among African American children and adolescents (Allison et al., 2003; McCubbin et al. 1999; Steward et al., 1998).

7. RACIAL SOCIALIZATION AND IDENTITY AS COPING RESOURCES

African American parents socialize or parent somewhat differently than other ethnic groups (Allen, 1985). For example, Allen (1985) found that African American parents rated ambition and obedience as the most important goals, while Caucasian American parents rated honesty and happiness as the most important goals. Pinderhughes (1982) also found ethnic differences in child-rearing values. She stated that Caucasian American parents emphasize independence, achievement, material assets, and planning. African American parents emphasize sharing, obedience to authority, and spirituality. Ogbu (1981, 1985) argued that child-rearing practices and coping strategies and goals cannot be separated from the environmental resources and opportunity structures. Parents socialize their children according to the strategies that have been effective. From this research it appears that psychoeducational interventions with African American families must incorporate and utilize culturally relevant techniques and practices in order to be successful. Two important and related cultural variables for families to teach and instill in children are racial socialization and racial identity.

7.1. Racial Socialization

Racial socialization is the process by which parents teach children important messages about their racial or ethnic group. Results from a study using a nationally representative cross-section of African American adults indicated that two thirds of Black parents act on or talk about aspects of race as they are raising their children (Thornton, Chatters, Taylor, & Allen, 1990). Parents who are married are more likely to socialize their children about race than are those parents who have never married (Thornton et al., 1990). Some studies have found that older (Caughy, O'Campo, Randolph, & Nickerson, 2002; Thornton et al., 1990), more educated (Caughy et al., 2002; Thornton et al., 1990), and female caregivers are more likely to teach their children about their race than are younger, less educated parents or men (Thornton et al., 1990), although other studies with school-age children found no relation between racial socialization and education or income (Cunningham & Kliewer, 2005; Frabutt et al., 2002).

Where families live seems to affect the racial socialization messages that parents impart to their children. Parents in the Northeast are more likely to racially socialize their children than are parents in the South (Thornton et al., 1990). Mothers are more likely to teach about race when the families live in neighborhoods that are diverse (half Black residents) as opposed to all Black neighborhoods (Thornton et al., 1990). This may be because race becomes more salient in diverse neighborhoods than when everyone is of the same race. It would make sense that different lessons are needed for survival in different neighborhoods and communities. Children living in diverse communities need skills to interact with people who are different from themselves and need support to explore those differences and cope with challenging racial events. While the racial or ethnic composition of the neighborhood may affect race-related messages, there is no evidence to support the relation between the quality of the neighborhood and racial socialization. Racial socialization messages were not related to perceived neighborhood safety with adolescents from diverse neighborhoods (Miller & MacIntosh, 1999) or to perceived safety or crime statistics for low-income, inner-city families living in primarily African American neighborhoods (Cunningham & Kliewer, 2005).

Regardless of where African American families live, they are still likely to experience some form of discrimination. Research has found that racial socialization messages appear to be related to families' experiences with discrimination. Frequency of race-related socialization was positively correlated with parental perceptions of racially discriminatory acts against their children (Hughes & Johnson, 2001). Similarly, adolescents reported more racial socialization messages if family members had experienced racism (Stevenson, Cameron, Davis, & Herrero-Taylor, 2002).

7.1.1. Racial Socialization Messages

There are different messages that parents impart when teaching their children about race. Interview studies have examined the type of messages related to race that African American parents were trying to teach their children (Cunningham & Kliewer, 2005; Marshall, 1995; Parham & Williams, 1993; Thornton et al., 1990). In a nationally-representative sample of African American adults with children, the most common racial socialization message given by parents was the importance of work ethic and achievement (22%) (Thornton et al., 1990). The next most common racial socialization message was that of racial or ethnic pride (17%), and the third most mentioned race-related messages were teaching about Black heritage and historical traditions (Thornton et al., 1990). Overall, about half of parents' racial socialization message pertained directly to race or ethnicity and the other half pertained to hard work, self-development, equality, religion, or other personal qualities (Thornton et al., 1990).

Parham and Williams (1993) conducted a retrospective study in California with adult African Americans regarding racial socialization messages they received from their parents. The participants were born and raised in various areas of the United States. A little over a third of participants were raised to feel good about being Black, while almost half of the participants did not receive any positive racial messages while growing up (messages were either neutral or negative) (Parham & Williams, 1993). More than a quarter of the sample were raised to believe that all people were equal, regardless of the color of their skin, and a fifth of the sample hardly ever heard or discussed race or racial attitudes with their families (Parham & Williams, 1993).

Interestingly, when middle-class African American parents of school-age children were asked what their most important parenting goals were, only 2% listed development of ethnic identity, yet when asked directly about teaching about ethnicity while raising their children, 89% of parents indicated it was important (Marshall, 1995). It is interesting to note that all of the African American children in this sample attended primarily White public schools (Marshall, 1995). The following racial socialization messages were given by the parents in this study when asked what they are teaching their children about their race: universal values (i.e., equality and self-development) (31%), racial pride (30%), racial barriers (14%), and physical attributes (8%) (Marshall, 1995). Nearly one fifth of the parents stated they are not teaching their children anything about race or ethnicity (Marshall, 1995). The findings from this study seem to be consistent with other studies of racial socialization messages. Most parents in this study listed one message they were trying to convey. In a recent study of low-income, inner-city African American families with school-age children, parents were asked what they were teaching their children about their race. Cunningham and Kliewer (2005) found that the most common race-related messages that parents conveyed to their children were acceptance of mainstream culture and equality (74%), racial pride (58%), how to cope with discrimination (45%), appreciation of Black legacy and history (26%), reliance on spirituality (20%), and preparation for/awareness of discrimination (19%).

7.1.2. General Racial Socialization and Outcomes

The various types of racial socialization messages that parents impart to their children are associated with a variety of outcomes—both adaptive and maladaptive. In studies that examined racial socialization messages in general (did not categorize racial messages or included all racial socialization messages together), results have been mixed. Positive outcomes associated with general race-related messages include more advanced ethnic identity (Marshall, 1995; Stevenson, 1995), less sadness for girls (Stevenson, Reed, Bodison, & Bishop, 1997), less helplessness for girls (Stevenson et al., 1997), and increased self-worth (Murry & Brody, 2002).

Racial socialization messages in general were found to have a protective effect when considering levels of discrimination and mental health (Fischer & Shaw, 1999). African American college students participated in studies that questioned them about their experiences with racial discrimination and racial socialization and also asked about mental health (Fischer & Shaw, 1999). The majority of participants (65%) were raised in primarily African American neighborhoods, another 21% were raised in mostly non-African American neighborhoods, and the other 14% in neighborhoods that were about half African American. Generally, racial socialization was not associated with mental health or self-esteem (Fischer & Shaw, 1999). For a college student sample, racist event perceptions were related to poorer general mental health for students with low levels of racial socialization (Fischer & Shaw, 1999). Students who did not receive many intentional messages about their race from their families appeared to internalize the negative messages they received from others due to their race. African American children who have received racial socialization messages from their families were protected from the negative effects of racism and discrimination on their mental health. Racial socialization experiences from one's family moderated the link between racist events and overall mental health, although racial socialization beliefs did not moderate the link. The difference between racial socialization experiences and beliefs is significant because until one encounters a situation in which one's beliefs are challenged or confirmed, the beliefs may not be based in reality. Self-esteem did not mediate the relationship between perceptions of racist events and mental health (Fischer & Shaw, 1999). Thus, it seems that helping children making sense out of real-world racial events is an important component of racial socialization—building a child's self-esteem or promoting certain beliefs without being able to apply those beliefs to experience does not appear to provide a buffer for children experiencing racism.

General racial socialization messages were also related to some poorer outcomes. The more racial socialization messages that parents provided, the lower children's reading grades (Marshall, 1995), the less self-esteem adolescent girls felt (Stevenson, 1995), the more stress reported (Miller & MacIntosh, 1999), and the more perceived racial discrimination (Miller & MacIntosh, 1999). Some of these findings may be due to the fact that the more parents teach children about their race and what type of unfair treatment they might experience because of their race, the more those children and adolescents might be aware of and feel bad about racial discrimination directed toward themselves or family members.

7.1.3. Specific Racial Socialization Messages and Outcomes

Some types of racial socialization messages are related to better outcomes for children and adolescents than others. While some racial socialization messages are related to primarily positive results, others are related to mixed or negative results.

Racial pride messages from caregivers were associated with primarily positive adjustment or family dynamics. Parents who provided African American preschoolers with messages about being proud of their race also were more affectionate with their children, allowed more child self-expression, provided cognitive enrichment materials to their children, monitored children's television viewing, and used more reasoning discipline with their children (Caughy et al., 2002). The preschoolers who received racial pride messages had fewer behavior problems (Caughy et al., 2002). Similarly, adolescents who had received racial pride messages (along with appreciation of Black legacy/heritage) also experienced less unprovoked anger and less anger suppression (Stevenson et al., 1997) than those adolescents who did not receive such messages. African American adolescents who attended Black parochial school had higher peer self-esteem if they received more racial pride messages from their parents (Constantine & Blackmon, 2002). Adults felt closer to other Blacks if they had received racial pride (and appreciation of Black legacy/heritage) messages while growing up compared to those who received mainstream or mistrusting other racial group messages from parents (Demo & Hughes, 1990). On one hand, racial pride messages appear to be given in conjunction with other positive parenting skills and to be associated with better child or adolescent behavior and better feelings about others and getting along with others. On the other hand, racial pride messages were also related to higher intensity of situational anger and fewer ways of expressing anger in adolescents (Stevenson et al., 1997). Given that adolescents who received racial pride messages had less unprovoked anger and less holding anger inside but more intense anger in specific situations and fewer modes of anger expression (Stevenson et al., 1997), it may be that children who encounter a racial event get upset about it, tell other people about it, and then feel better because they expressed their feelings and reactions to the event. Another study found that parental racial pride identity was associated with decreased child self-regulation (Murry & Brody, 2002). There may be some link between parental messages regarding racial pride and child or adolescent difficulty dealing with anger or other strong emotions. It may be that in the face of discrimination, youth have difficulty reconciling their positive view of themselves and their race when someone is treating them poorly due to their race.

Both racial pride and appreciation of Black heritage and legacy are similar in that they promote positive feelings regarding African Americans. Several of the studies above (Stevenson et al., 1997; Demo & Hughes, 1990) combined these two racial socialization messages in their study. In addition to those studies, Cunningham and Kliewer (2005) found that parents who promoted Black heritage and legacy also had better communication with their children and used more active coping than parents who did not provide positive race-related message to their children. Another study found that promoting Black culture in concrete ways by displaying African American art, pictures, artifacts, etc. (Africentric home environment) was related to better factual knowledge and better problem-solving skills for preschool boys (Caughy et al., 2002). It appears that promoting Black heritage and culture is primarily associated with better outcomes for children and adolescents and provides youth with a positive home environment. Parents can also teach about cultural heritage by emphasizing the history and relations from a larger family context. Stevenson and colleagues (1997) found that racial socialization messages regarding the importance of extended family were associated with decreased anger control for girls and increased anger control for boys. It is unclear whether these findings are related to the quality of actual family relationships in adolescents' lives or whether the emphasis on extended family has different implications for boys and girls. For boys, receiving messages about the importance of family is connected with better anger regulation, while it is connected with poorer anger regulation for girls. It could be that African American women play a strong role in family relationships and female family members have more conflict as they interface with other strong women. It could be that boys receive additional support from extended family and may be exposed to male role models who may not be available in the immediate family.

Another positive race-related concept that African American caregivers teach their children is spirituality. Spirituality can include deriving meaning about the world and people; acknowledging a creator who has made people the way they are; relying on a power greater than oneself; relying on spirituality, church, or God for support and survival; praying; anticipating heaven or freedom from oppression, etc. Parents who gave more spirituality messages to their children also were more affectionate with their children, permitted child self-expression, provided cognitive enrichment to children, monitored television viewing, and disciplined using reasoning (Caughy et al., 2002). Another study looking at parental predictors of racial socialization messages found that parents who taught their children reliance on spirituality were more emotionally competent (themselves and in coaching their children about emotions), had better parent-child communication on a video discussion task, and used more active coping themselves in situations beyond their control (Cunningham & Kliewer, 2005). Caughy and her colleagues (2002) found that parents who provided spirituality racial socialization and were involved with their children had preschoolers with fewer behavior problems.

Besides teaching children about positive aspects of their race, many African American parents also teach their children about possible negative effects of their race in American society. Some parents teach their children to be aware of potential racism, discrimination, or bias. When African American parents prepared their school-age children for unfair treatment due to their race, these children had higher levels of racial identity exploration compared to children who had received messages regarding ethnic pride/heritage or promotion of mistrust toward other racial groups (Hughes & Johnson, 2001). Children who were prepared for discrimination also seem to consider who they are in relation to others in society.

Going beyond making youth aware of possible discrimination, some parents provide messages about how to cope with racism or unfair treatment. Parents who provided moderate messages about how children could cope with discrimination were also more involved with their children's lives versus parents with high levels of proactive responses to discrimination (Frabutt et al., 2002). In addition, these parents who provided moderate proactive messages displayed more warmth and communication on parent-child tasks and reported higher levels of monitoring their children than did parents who provided low or high levels of proactive messages (Frabutt et al., 2002). Similarly, parents who taught their children how to cope with discrimination showed higher levels of affection toward their children, allowed children more self-expression, and provided cognitively enriching materials for their children (Caughy et al., 2002). This research seems to indicate that preparing children for discrimination and providing them some tools to cope with unfair treatment is also related to other ways parents are raising and socializing their children to be competent. In a study of middle- to upper-class African American adolescents who attended private parochial schools, racial socialization messages regarding coping with discrimination were related to adolescents' increased use of self-reliant and problem-solving strategies in response to discrimination (Scott, 2003b). It appears that these adolescents were able to employ the racial socialization messages received from their parents in order to effectively cope with discrimination.

Parents can take their racial socialization messages beyond preparation for and coping with discrimination. Some parents teach their children to mistrust people from other racial groups. When parents promoted mistrust, children reported more unfair treatment by their peers (Hughes & Johnson, 2001), less inter-racial contact during adolescence and adulthood (Demo & Hughes, 1990), and fewer behavior problems (Caughy et al., 2002). It makes sense that children and adolescents would want to avoid people they expect will treat them badly.

Racial socialization messages concerned with integrating in the mainstream culture, the importance of mainstream values, and/or messages about equality are considered mainstream racial socialization messages. If youth received only racial socialization messages related to mainstream culture, adolescents attending a Black parochial school had lower academic self-esteem (Constantine & Blackmon, 2002). Similarly, adolescents who received and believed in the idea of racelessness had higher levels of self-efficacy (Arroyo & Zigler, 1995), but also had higher levels of anxiety and depression (Arroyo & Zigler, 1995), higher perceived stress (Miller & MacIntosh, 1999), and less identification with African Americans as a group (Arroyo & Zigler, 1995). The racial socialization messages about achievement appear to make adolescents feel like they can accomplish what they set out to do, but this message also has been related to more internalizing behaviors and stress, as well as feeling disconnected from their collective racial group.

There are more positive outcomes related to racial socialization as a whole than negative ones. Some specific racial socialization messages appear to have more beneficial effects on children and adolescents than others. In addition, the family environment and the larger community in which the youth interacts likely affect the usefulness of particular racial socialization messages. Several studies found that older children receive more racial socialization messages than younger children and this may be due to the type of experiences that youth have had. Some parents may not teach their children about racial issues or discrimination until children have experienced some race-related conflict or situation. Overall these studies seem to point to the importance of including positive aspects of race along with other messages about how to live in society and cope with discrimination. Racial socialization messages related to racial and cultural pride (including appreciation of heritage and legacy) and spirituality appear to have the most positive research findings. Children who feel good about who they are and where they came from are likely to be able to handle discrimination or difficult circumstances (e.g., poverty or violence) more adaptively if they feel good about themselves and have been prepared to cope with unfair treatment. Receiving emotional support from family or friends is likely also important for buffering the effects of negative life experiences or difficulties. Thus, parents who are able to provide a loving home environment and talk with their children about life events are facilitating their children's ability to cope. For example, a study by Cunningham and Kliewer (2005) found that particular combinations of racial socialization messages were connected to better adjustment for children. That study found that children who received racial socialization messages related only to mainstream values and racial pride (without any teaching about discriminatory treatment, how to cope with difficult race-related experiences, reliance on spirituality, or how to view those who discriminate) and who felt less acceptance from their caregivers had less hope for their future than children who received more comprehensive racial socialization messages or who felt accepted and loved by their caregiver (Cunningham & Kliewer, 2005). Racial socialization is a complex process and like many other aspects of child development, living in contexts that facilitate growth and resilience (e.g., nurturing and structured family environment, safe neighborhood, having basic needs met) complements the messages children receive from parents and allow youth to cope better with difficulties related to their race.

7.2. Racial Identity

Racial identity is another important resource that can contribute to resilience in African American youth. African American adolescents participated in a study of racial socialization and identity as protective factors of urban stress (Miller & MacIntosh, 1999). The study found that as daily urban hassles increased, collective self-esteem and ethnic identity decreased (Miller & MacIntosh, 1999). Collective self-esteem is the way one feels about their ethnic group and the degree to which they feel affiliated with their ethnic group. The results of this study seem to indicate that as adolescents have to deal with more environmental stressors, the less they have time to develop their ethnic identity and the less positive they may feel about their ethnicity. Stress affected both adolescents' sense of identity, as well as school engagement. The safer adolescents rated their neighborhoods, the more they participated in school activities and the fewer days of school they missed (Miller & MacIntosh, 1999). The higher adolescents' collective self-esteem, the more school activities in which they participated, the higher GPA they had, and fewer days of school missed (Miller & MacIntosh, 1999). Ethnic identity appeared to buffer the effects of a stressful urban environment—adolescents who have a weak ethnic identity are more likely to have urban hassles interfere with their academic performance (Miller & MacIntosh, 1999).

Parham and Williams' (1993) retrospective study regarding racial socialization messages with adult African Americans is relevant to the study of racial identity, as well as racial socialization. Again, Parham and Williams conducted the study with participants who were born and raised in various areas of the United States. Participants who were born in the East or South had higher levels of racial identity than their counterparts born in the West (Parham & Williams, 1993). Another factor associated with racial identity is education. Participants who were more educated had lower Immersion attitudes. Immersion attitudes refer to the level of involvement in organizations and activities that are predominately comprised of members of one's own ethnic group. More educated participants may have been less likely to reject mainstream American values without experiencing a racial event. When they do have such an experience, they do not have the psychological and social resources to cope with the situation and would not necessarily turn to support from the African American community. Another possible explanation is that the more educated participants have already dealt with racist events and may have a broad support network toward which to turn when encountering difficult circumstances, not just ethnic-affiliated groups. Income level also affected racial identity, in that people with higher income levels were rated higher on the Pre-Encounter stage and lower on the Internalization stage (Parham & Williams, 1993). This seems to indicate that African Americans with more financial resources have not grappled with racial identity and what it means to be African American. It could also mean that those people with more money do not associate themselves with other African Americans as a collective group, but rather operate from a more individualistic perspective (consistent with mainstream values and beliefs).

One way to view race is to essentially ignore cultural backgrounds and differences and focus on everyone being equal as human beings. This concept is called racelessness. Arroyo and Zigler (1995) conducted a study to test a measure of the construct of racelessness, which has been associated with high-achieving African American adolescents. In the first part of the study, a racially mixed group of adolescents participated (63% African American, 33% Caucasian, 1% Hispanic, and <1% Asian). Racelessness was associated with higher achievement, regardless of ethnicity (Arroyo & Zigler, 1995). High achievers, both African American and Caucasian, reported feeling more alienated and regulating their behaviors while with peers more than low achieving students (Arroyo & Zigler, 1995). These students feel different from others and may diminish the importance of achievement while with their peers in order to be accepted.

In the second part of the study, which looked at associations with racelessness, 60% of the participants were African American, 40% were Caucasian, and all adolescents attended the same public high school (Arroyo & Zigler, 1995). The more students endorsed racelessness, the more anxiety and depression they reported, but also the more self-efficacy they felt on the achievement attitudes of the racelessness scale (Arroyo & Zigler, 1995). A complex relationship between raceless attitudes emerged for African American students: When African Americans endorsed racelessness, they were more likely to accept racial stereotypes about their race and then use impression management to affect others' perceptions of them (Arroyo & Zigler, 1995). These students might try to counter racial stereotypes by presenting themselves as not fitting with those racial generalizations. Those African American youth who agreed with racial stereotypes applied to their racial group had less positive impressions of their racial group (collective self-esteem) and did not identity with their race as much as those who had lower racelessness scores (Arroyo & Zigler, 1995). These adolescents tended to view themselves as individuals rather than as part of a larger racial group. Collective self-esteem and self-efficacy were related differently for African American and Caucasian youth. For African Americans, identity aspects of the collective self-esteem scale were related to self-efficacy, while membership aspects of the collective self-esteem scale were related to self-efficacy for Caucasians (Arroyo & Zigler, 1995). The more African Americans identified with their racial group, the more effective they felt. The more Caucasians felt accepted by their racial group, the more effective they felt.

For African American adults, close interpersonal relationships with friends and family members were related to a positive view of Blacks as a group, more inter-racial contact, and higher SES (Demo & Hughes, 1990). This means that the more positive contact African American have with important members of their racial and family group, the more positive their view of all African Americans and the more they interact with people from diverse groups. This shows the importance of family influences on offspring's view of their race and the way they interact with others from different racial groups.

8. IMPACT PROGRAMS: DOING THE RESEARCH AND APPLING THE LESSONS

Parenting is an arduous and often stressful task. Parenting "while Black" can be even more stressful. As a result, we have directed our counseling, community, and research endeavors to ameliorating as much of the parental stress and culture-related parental stress as possible. To accomplish this task we have developed "The IMPACT Programs" (IMPACT)[1]. IMPACT is a family, school, community, and university based collaboration that provides culturally enhanced psychoeducational programs to children ages 6 to 11 and their parents. IMPACT has been conducted with faith-based communities, schools, substance abusing families, and community organizations. We also have shared a partnership with Richmond Behavioral Health Authority, the primary agency responsible for assessment of Richmond residents with substance abuse problems, several Richmond City Public Schools, Virginia Commonwealth University's Department of Psychology, and Spring Creek Baptist Church.

IMPACT is an acronym for "I Must Parent According to Cultural Teachings; I Must Pause Analyze, Chill and Take Action; Improving Mentoring, Preparing, and Cultivating Talent." The overall goal of IMPACT is to further implement, conduct and evaluate a culturally congruent family-based program for reducing behavioral, emotional, social, and cognitive problems among children and parents. The intervention strategies are based on the assumption that developing strong families and ethnic and parenting values will promote resiliency and prosocial behaviors among children of substance abusing parents.

The components comprising the IMPACT programs are three-fold. There are components that are specifically designed for the children, for the parents, and for both child and parent. There also are mental health benefits to families involved with "The IMPACT Programs."

8.1. Child Service Components

8.1.1. Child Psychoeducational Sessions

These sessions have been designed to improve children's outcomes through a culturally congruent psychoeducational group that is designed to enhance parent-child relationships, promote appropriate ways of handling anger, reduce child aggression, increase communication skills, decision making skills, and conflict resolution skills.

8.1.2. Values Education

This component has been developed to reinforce healthy cultural values and behaviors. We have used the seven principles of Kwanzaa (guidelines for healthy living for African Americans), which are taught and applied throughout the Rites sessions along with the eighth principal, Heshema, meaning respect. We have also used a Christian Education and Vacation Bible School curriculum to reinforce the values of unity, love, cooperation, healthy relationships, and respect. We have found from focus groups with staff and discussion with participants that the seven principles of Kwanzaa and the spiritual principles of Christian Education are entirely compatible.

8.1.3. After School Tutoring and Educational Support

This component has been implemented to assist the children with age appropriate learning objectives and homework. We now use a two-year rotation of Math and English. We also used weekly trips to the library to reinforce the importance and skills of reading.

8.1.4. *Martial Arts and Athletic Activities*

These activities have been incorporated into the program to support and encourage discipline of the mind, body and spirit. We have discovered that combining physical activity, Martial Arts and athletic activities, with lessons on discipline, responsibility, and being a respectful citizen has helped our students internalize the IMPACT program in such a way that students stop us years after participating in the program and testify how much they enjoyed the program. I (Dr. McCreary) still recall the night in a counseling session with a young student, that after reaching an impasse, I ended the session and told the young man that I was going to my marital arts class. He asked if he could go. I consulted with his mother and they accompanied me to the class. I will never forget how this resistant young man began to listen and apply my counsel as I trained him in the marital arts. In addition, our martial arts and athletic activities component of the program has helped children develop more appropriate ways of dealing with anger and aggressive behaviors.

8.2. Parent Service Components

8.2.1. *Parent Psychoeducational Sessions*

This component was designed to complement the child psychoeducational sessions and seek to help parents identify the needs of the family. The specific areas include: developing an interest in your child, developing a mission of parenting and mastering a parenting style that balances love and limits, accepting parental responsibility, and being committed to parenting. Parents are also welcome to participate in the martial arts classes.

8.3. Family Service Components

8.3.1. *Family Celebrations and Trip*

Throughout the program families participate in ceremonies such as the African naming ceremony and the rites of separation ceremony. There are also ceremonies to begin and end the program. In addition, family field trips that promote learning of cultural heritage are planned.

8.4. Research on IMPACT

In an initial evaluation of IMPACT, McCreary, Belgrave, and Allison (2001) studied 80 parents and children who participated in the intervention group and 60 participants in the comparison group who completed the questionnaire at baseline. Observations by the evaluation team revealed a great deal of enthusiasm and interest. Parents seemed to be especially pleased with the communal approach and the integration of their comments and concerns in the session's topic for the day. They welcomed discussions of parenting issues unique to their circumstances, including ways in which they could be more effective parents. Intervention staff members were well trained and receptive to the needs of the group. It also was of interest to note that the older and perhaps more secure parents helped parents who were younger and in more need of parenting support. The principal investigator, Dr. McCreary, modeled a communal and a holistic approach where discussions and lessons learned are not hierarchical but based on the expertise of all group members.

Children were equally excited about the program and always pleased to come to the sessions. They were especially excited about the Martial Arts component and developed much self-confidence and competence through this activity. They enjoyed seeing the student interveners and bonded with them.

A series of analysis of covariances were computed to test for differences between the treatment and the comparison group after controlling for baseline scores. McCreary et al. (2001) found that parents in the intervention group ($M = 3.89$, $SD = .71$) reported higher access to support than parents in the comparison group ($M = 3.43$, $SD = .90$), $F(1, 85) = 6.78$, $p < .05$. There was a significant difference in perception of neighborhood risk, controlling for baseline scores, $F(1, 81) = 3.81$, $p < .05$, with parents in the treatment group perceiving less risk ($M = 2.25$, $SD = .55$) than those in the control group ($M = 2.45$, $SD = .50$). McCreary et al. (2001) also found a significant difference in the number of substances used at exit, controlling for number of substances used at baseline, $F(1, 83) = 3.97$, $p < .05$, with parents in the treatment group reporting a lower number of drugs used ($M = 6.71$, $SD = 1.49$) than parents in the comparison group ($M = 7.49$, $SD = 1.37$). Additional evaluation data on IMPACT revealed that parenting stress and children's adjustment were strongly related, and that the association between parent stress and children's adjustment was mediated by maternal responsiveness and monitoring. McCreary et al. (2001) also found that high parenting stress was related to elevated levels of depression and aggression among children. Also, findings revealed that mothers with high parenting stress engaged in lower levels of monitoring. In addition, Kilgour and McCreary (2002) found that as the stress level of parents in the program increased, their substance use also increased, and that social support buffered the association between stress and substance use.

For the children in the McCreary et al. (2001) study, there was a significant effect for cognitive development at exit, controlling for baseline scores, $F(1, 92) = 5.06$, $p < .05$, with children in the treatment group having higher cognitive growth ($M = 3.61$, $SD = .48$) than children in the comparison group ($M = 3.36$, $SD = .57$). There also was a significant effect at follow-up for peer acceptance, after controlling for baseline scores, $F(1, 70) = 7.26$, $p < .05$, with children in the treatment group having higher peer acceptance ($M = 3.56$, $SD = .47$) than those in the comparison group ($M = 3.16$, $SD = .73$).

Results from these evaluations must be viewed in context and interpreted with caution. Unfortunately, there were several significant issues that we believe affected implementation, design and results from the study. In chronological order, these issues were: (1) the program had to be redesigned from a University-based program to a school-based delivery program; (2) Virginia Commonwealth University (VCU) was placed on human subject suspension during the project; (3) the program had to be redesigned a second time into a summer day treatment program; and (4) the program was redesigned again back to an after-school program.

However, a number of lessons were learned during this challenging grant project. First, we learned the importance of maintaining staff morale and garnering respect and commitment from the intervention staff. Second, we learned the value of training a skilled undergraduate and graduate student team and coupling them with skilled members of the community who have existing, ongoing relationships with the population being served. Third, we learned that engaging parents in intervention programs is very difficult, but can be accomplished with the aide of community experts. Fourth, we learned the importance of institutionalizing the project in the community and working with the community on matters of transportation, advertising, and community involvement (McCreary et al., 2001)

9. SUMMARY AND CONCLUSIONS

Working effectively with families of color in America around issues of mental health, cultural trust and mistrust, and stress and coping, particularly African American families, is not a simple matter. Effective prevention, intervention, and community consultation within the framework of stress, socialization, and coping skills must begin with an understanding of traditional resiliency among families of color. Then, mental health professionals must apply this understanding of resiliency to the specific context and experiences of African Americans. In this chapter, we explored some of the coping mechanisms and resources that researchers have suggested lead to resiliency in African American families. We further discussed the potential mechanisms that African American families employ with their children for coping with racially-oriented stressors.

We agree with sociologist, Orlando Patterson (1997), who suggested that the situation of African Americans has greatly progressed since the 1950s. However, racial, ethnic, and cultural situations continue to exist that foster resentment within African Americans and between Caucasian Americans and African Americans. For example, Whaley (2001) conducted a meta-analysis of cultural mistrust among African Americans and their attitudes and behaviors toward mental health services and found that younger African Americans are more mistrusting than their older counterparts. This finding elevates the importance of younger African Americans possessing healthy coping mechanisms, such as social support, healthy family relationships, and positive peers. It further suggests the need to develop culturally specific coping mechanisms such as positive racial awareness, racial identity, and group identity. We suggest that parents, mental health professionals, and other social agents utilize racial socialization to enhance the race-specific coping strategies among African American children and youth.

Finally, we presented the framework for our family-based psychoeducational intervention, "The IMPACT Programs," which incorporate racial socialization and identity development into family training programs for people of color. We are currently conducting the programs in churches, communities, and group homes. The program has adolescent, child, family, and staff development components, and seeks to empower families and communities to build relationships that allow them to function in healthy ways. As issues of race, ethnicity, and culture continue to surface as important concerns among African American families, mental health professionals who seek to facilitate the well-being of these families will need to broaden their healing practices to include issues of race, ethnicity, and culture.

REFERENCES

Allen, W. R. (1985). Race, income, and family dynamics: A study of adolescent male socialization processes and outcomes. M. B. Spencer, G. K. Brookins, & W. R. Allen (Eds.), *Beginnings: The social and affective development of Black children,* (pp. 273-292). Hillsdale, NJ: Erlbaum.

Allison, K. W., Belgrave, F. Z., Butler, D., Edwards, L., & Plybon, L. E. (2003). Examining the link between neighborhood cohesion and school outcomes: The role of support coping among African American adolescent girls. *Journal of Black Psychology, 29,* 393-407.

Arroyo, C. G., & Zigler, E. (1995). Racial identity, academic achievement, and the psychological well-being of economically disadvantaged adolescents. *Journal of Personality and Social Psychology, 69,* 903-914.

Broman, C. L. (1997). Race-related factors and life satisfaction among African Americans. *Journal of Black Psychology, 23,* 36-49.

Caughy, M. O., O'Campo, P. J., Randolph, S. M., & Nickerson, K. (2002). The influence of racial socialization practices on the cognitive and behavioral competence of African American preschoolers. *Child Development, 73,* 1611-1625.

Clark, R., Novak, J. D., & Dupree, D. (2002). Relationship of perceived parenting practices to anger regulation and coping strategies in African-American adolescents. *Journal of Adolescence, 25,* 373-384.

Compas, B. E., Connor-Smith, J. K., Saltzman, H., Thomsen, A. H., & Wadsworth, M. E. (2001). Coping with stress during childhood and adolescence: Problems, progress, and potential in theory and research. *Psychological Bulletin, 127,* 87-127.

Cone, J. H. (1986). Speaking *the truth: Ecumenism, liberation and Black theology.* Grand Rapids, MI: W. B. Eerdmans.

Constantine, M. G., & Blackmon, S. M. (2002). Black adolescents' racial socialization experiences: Their relations to home, school, and peer self-esteem. *Journal of Black Studies, 32,* 322-335.

Cunningham, J. N., & Kliewer, W. (2005). Racial socialization in African American families: Links with caregiver, child, and neighborhood qualities. Manuscript submitted for publication.

Davidson, J., & Smith, R. (1990). Traumatic experiences in psychiatric outpatients. *Journal of Traumatic Stress, 3,* 459-475.

Demo, D. H., & Hughes, M. (1990). Socialization and racial identity among Black Americans. *Social Psychology Quarterly, 53,* 364-374.

Dempsey, M. (2002). Negative coping as mediator in the relation between violence and outcomes: Inner-city African American youth. *American Journal of Orthopsychiatry, 72,* 102-109.

Fischer, A. R., & Shaw, C. M. (1999). African Americans' mental health and perceptions of racist discrimination: The moderating effects of racial socialization experiences and self-esteem. *Journal of Counseling Psychology, 46,* 395-407.

Frabutt, J. M., Walker, A. M., & MacKinnon-Lewis, C. (2002). Racial socialization messages and the quality of mother/child interactions in African American Families. *Journal of Early Adolescence, 22,* 200-217.

Garbarino, J. (1999). *Lost boys: Why our sons turn violent and how we can save them.* New York: The Free Press.

Gomel, J. N., Tinsley, B. J., Parke, R. D., & Clark, K. M. (1998). The effects of economic hardship on family relationships among African American, Latino, and Euro-American families. *Journal of Family Issues, 19,* 436-467.

Gorman-Smith, D., Tolan, P. H., Henry, D. B., & Florsheim, P. (2000). Patterns of family functioning and adolescent outcomes among urban African American and Mexican American families. *Journal of Family Psychology,14,* 436-457.

Grant, K. E., O'Koon, J. H., Davis, T. H., Roache, N. A., Poindexter, L. M., Armstrong, M. L., Minden, J. A., & McIntosh, J. M. (2000). Protective factors affecting low-income urban African American youth exposed to stress. *Journal of Early Adolescence, 20,* 388-417.

Harrison, A. O., Wilson, M. N., Pine, C. J., Chan, S. Q., & Buriel, R. (1990). Family ecologies ofethnic minority children. *Child Development, 61,* 347-362.

Hetherington, E. M., Stanley-Hagan, M., & Anderson, E. R. (1989). Marital transitions: A child's perspective. *American Psychologist, 44,* 303-312.

Holden, G. W., & Edwards, L. A. (1989). Parental attitudes toward child rearing: Instruments, issues, and implications. *Psychological Bulletin, 106,* 29-58.

Hughes, D., & Johnson, D. (2001). Correlates in children's experiences of parents' racial socialization behaviors. *Journal of Marriage and Family, 63,* 981-995.

Kilgour, J. M., & McCreary, M. L. (2002). *Stress and social support among African American substance abusing mothers.* Unpublished manuscript, Virginia Commonwealth University.

Landrine, H., & Klonoff, E. A. (1996). The Schedule of Racist Events: A measure of racial discrimination and a study of its negative physical and mental health consequences. *Journal of Black Psychology, 22,* 144-168.

Lazarus, R. S., & Folkman, S. (1984). *Stress, appraisal, and coping.* New York: Springer.

Lincoln, C. E. (1990). *The Black church in the African American experience.* Durham, NC: Duke University Press.

Losel, F., & Bliesener, T. (1990). Resilience in adolescence: A study on the generalizability of protective factors. In K. Hurrelmann & F. Losel (Eds.), *Health hazards in adolescence* (pp. 299-329). Berlin, Germany: Walter de Gruyter.

Luthar, S. S. (1999). *Developmental clinical psychology and psychiatry series: Vol 41. Poverty and children's adjustment.* Thousand Oaks, CA: Sage.

Mandura, J., & Murray, C. B. (2000). Effects of parental marital status, income, and family functioning on African American adolescent self-esteem. *Journal of Family Psychology, 14,* 475-490.

Markstrom, C. A., Marshall, S. K., & Tyron, R. J. (2000). Resiliency, social support, and coping in rural low-income Appalachian adolescents from two racial groups. *Journal of Adolescence, 23,* 693-703.

Marshall, S. (1995). Ethnic socialization of African American children: Implications for parenting, identity development, and academic achievement. *Journal of Youth and Adolescence, 24,* 377-396.

Mbiti, J. S., (1990). *African religions and philosophy* (2nd ed.). Oxford, England: Heinemann.

McClintock, C. G. (1972). Social motivation: A set of propositions. *Behavioral Science, 17,* 438-454.

McCreary, M. L., Belgrave, F. Z., & Allison, K. W. (2001). *Final project report for Project IMPACT: A family based psychoeducational prevention project for substance abusing families.* Virginia Commonwealth University.

McCreary, M. L., Slavin, L. A., & Berry E. J. (1996). Predicting problem-behavior and self-esteem among African-American adolescents. *Journal of Adolescent Research, 11,* 217-236.

McCubbin, H. I., Fleming, W. M., Thompson, A. I., Neitman, P., Elver, K. M., & Savas, S. A. (1999). Resiliency and coping in "at risk" African-American youth and their families. In H. I. McCubbin (Series Ed.) & H. I. McCubbin, E. A. Thompson, A. I. Thompson, & J. A. Futrell (Vol. Eds.), *Resiliency in families series: Resiliency in African-American families* (pp. 287-328). Thousand Oaks, CA: Sage.

Miller, D. B., & MacIntosh, R. (1999). Promoting resilience in urban African American adolescents: Racial socialization and identity as protective factors. *Social Work Research, 23,* 159-169.

Murry, V. M., & Brody, G. H. (2002). Racial socialization processes in single-mother families: Linking maternal racial identity, parenting, and racial socialization in rural, single-mother families with child self-worth and self-regulation. In H. P. McAdoo (Ed.), *Black children: Social, educational, and parental environments.* Thousand Oaks, CA: Sage.

Myers, M. A., & Thompson, V. L. S. (2000). The impact of violence exposure on African American youth in context. *Youth & Society, 32,* 253-267.

Nobles, W. (1986). *African psychology: Toward its reclamation, reascension, and revitalization.* Oakland, CA: The Institute for the Advanced Study of Black Family Life and Culture.

O'Conner, L. A., Brooks-Gunn, J., & Graber, J. (2000). Black and White girls' racial preferences in media and peer choices and the role of socialization for Black girls. *Journal of Family Psychology, 14,* 510-521.

Ogbu, J. U. (1981). Origins of human competence: A cultural-ecological perspective. *Child Development, 52,* 413-429.

Ogbu, J. U. (1985). A cultural ecology of competence among inner-city Blacks. In M. B. Spencer, G. K. Brookins, & W. R. Allen (Eds.), *Beginnings: The social and affective development of Black children* (pp. 45-66). Hillsdale, NJ: Erlbaum.

Parham, T. A., & Williams, P. T. (1993). The relationship of demographic and background factors to racial identity attitudes. *Journal of Black Psychology, 19,* 7-24.

Patterson, O. (1997). *The ordeal of integration: Progress and resentment in America's "racial" crisis.* New York: Civitas.

Pinderhughes, E. E. (1982). Afro-American families and the victim system. In M. McGoldrick, J. K. Pearce, & J. Giordano (Eds.), *Ethnicity and family therapy* (pp. 108-122). NY: Guilford.

Pinderhughes, E. E., Dodge, K. A., Bates, J. E., Petit, G. S., & Zelli, A. (2000). Discipline responses: Influences of parents' socioeconomic status, ethnicity, beliefs about parenting, stress, and cognitive-emotional processes. *Journal of Family Psychology, 14,* 380-400.

Randolph, S. M., Koblinsky, S. A., & Roberts, D. D. (1996). Studying the role of family and school in the development of African American preschoolers in violent neighborhoods. *Journal of Negro Education, 65,* 282-294.

Rutter, M. (1987). Psychosocial resilience and protective mechanisms. *American Journal of Orthopsychiatry, 57,* 316-331.

Scott, L. D. (2003a). Correlates of coping with perceived discriminatory experiences among African American adolescents. *Journal of Adolescence, 27,* 123-127.

Scott, L. D. (2003b). The relation of racial identity and racial socialization to coping with discrimination among African American adolescents. *Journal of Black Studies, 33,* 520-538.

Slavin, L. A., Rainer, K. L., McCreary, M. L., & Gowda, K. K. (1991). Toward a multicultural model of the stress process. *Journal of Counseling and Development, 70,* 156-163.

Smith, M. (2001). Social and emotional competencies: Contributions to young African American children's peer acceptance. *Early Education and Development, 12,* 49-72.

Spencer, M. B., Dupree, D., Swanson, D. P., & Cunningham, M. (1996). Parental monitoring and adolescents' sense of responsibility for their own learning: An examination of sex differences. *Journal of Negro Education, 65,* 30-43.

Steele, R. G., Forehand, R., Armistead, L., Morse, E., Simon, P., & Clark, L. (1999). Coping strategies and behavior problems of urban African-American children: Concurrent and longitudinal relationships. *American Journal of Orthopsychiatry, 69,* 182-193.

Stevenson, H. C. (1995). Relationship of adolescent perceptions of racial socialization to racial identity. *Journal of Black Psychology, 21,* 49-70.

Stevenson, H. C., Cameron, R., Davis, G. Y., & Herrero-Taylor, T. (2002). Development of the Teenager Experience of Racial Socialization Scale: Correlates of race-related socialization frequency from the perspective of Black youth. *Journal of Black Psychology, 28,* 84-106.

Stevenson, H. C., Reed, J., Bodison, P., & Bishop, A. (1997). Racism stress management: Racial socialization beliefs and the experience of depression and anger in African American youth. *Youth and Society, 29,* 197-222.

Steward, R. J., Jo, H. I., Murray, D., Fitzgerald, W., Neil, D., Fear, F., & Hill, M. (1998). Psychological adjustment and coping styles of urban African American high school students. *Journal of Multicultural Counseling and Development, 26,* 70-82.

Thornton, M. C., Chatters, L. M., Taylor, R. J., & Allen, W. R. (1990). Sociodemographic and environmental correlates of racial socialization by Black parents. *Child Development, 61,* 401-409.

Tolan, P. H., Gorman-Smith, D., & Henry D. B. (2004). Supporting families in a high-risk setting: Proximal effects of the SAFEChildren Preventive Intervention. *Journal of Consulting and Clinical Psychology, 72,* 855-869.

Utsey, S. O., Adams, E. P., & Bolden, M. (2000). Development and initial validation of the Africultural Coping Systems Inventory. *Journal of Black Psychology, 26,* 194-215.

Utsey, S. O., Ponterotto, J. G., Reynolds, A. L., & Cancelli, A. A. (2000). Racial discrimination, coping, life satisfaction, and self-esteem among African Americans. *Journal of Counseling and Development, 78,* 72-80.

Werner, E. E. (1986). Resilient offspring of alcoholics: A longitudinal study from birth to age 18. *Journal of Studies on Alcohol, 47,* 34-40.

Werner, E. E., & Smith, R. S. (1982). *Vulnerable, but invincible: A longitudinal study of resilient children and youth.* New York: McGraw-Hill.

Westman, A. S., Brackney, B. E., & Bylski, N. C. (1992). Religious beliefs are socialized in the same way as are other beliefs. *Psychological Reports, 70,* 1107-1110.

Whaley, A. L. (2001). Cultural mistrust and mental health services for African Americans: A review and meta-analysis. *The Counseling Psychologist, 29,* 513-531.

White, J. L., & Parham, T. A. (1990). *The psychology of Blacks: An African-American perspective* (2nd ed.). Englewood Cliffs, NJ: Prentice-Hall.

Whiteley, J. M. (1984). A historical perspective on the development of counseling psychology as a profession. In S.D. Brown & R.W. Lent (Eds.), *Handbook of counseling psychology* (pp. 3-55). New York: Wiley.

Wideman, J. E. (1984). *Brothers and keepers.* New York: Penguin.

Wilson, M. N., Kohn, L. P., Curry-El, J., & Hinton, I. D. (1995). The influence of family structure characteristics on the child-rearing behaviors of African American mothers. *Journal of Black Psychology, 21,* 450-462.

Wyman, P. A., Cowen, E. L., Work, W. C., & Kerley, J. H. (1993). The role of children's future expectations in self-esteem functioning and adjustment to life stress: A prospective study of urban at-risk children. *Development and Psychopathology, 5,* 649-661.

Wyman, P. A., Cowen, E. L., Work, W. C., Raoof, A., Gribble, P. A., Parker, G. R., & Wannon, M. (1992). Interviews with children who experienced major life stress: Family and child attributes that predict resilient outcomes. *Journal of the American Academy of Child and Adolescent Psychiatry, 31,* 904-910.

Yoshikawa, H. (1994). Prevention as cumulative protection: Effects of early family support and education on chronic delinquency and its risks. *Psychological Bulletin, 115,* 28-54.

AUTHOR'S NOTE

Micah L. McCreary is now a member of both the Department of Psychology and the Provost Staff in Academic Affairs at Virginia Commonwealth University. Jera Nelson Cunningham is now at St. Joseph's Villa, Richmond, Virginia. John E. Fife is now with the Division of Addiction Psychiatry in the Department of Psychiatry, Virginia Commonwealth University.

We would like to acknowledge our grant (80-249) from the U.S. Department of Health and Human Services, Substance Abuse and Mental Health Services Administration, Center for Substance Abuse Prevention, which provided support for the writing of this chapter.

Send correspondence to Micah L. McCreary, Ph.D., Virginia Commonwealth University, 808, P.O. Box 842018, Richmond, VA 23284-2018. Email: mccreary@vcu.edu

FOOTNOTE

Although "The IMPACT Programs" are the "brain child" of Micah L. McCreary, he would like to express his gratitude to Faye Belgrave, Kevin Allison, Susan Nicholson, Toni Harris, and Famebridge Gray, as well as other VCU faculty colleagues and graduate students, for their efforts in the development of "The IMPACT Programs."

ADJUSTMENT AND COPING IN ABORIGINAL PEOPLE

Roderick McCormick and Paul T. P. Wong

1. INTRODUCTION

Many therapists who have worked with Aboriginal clients remark on how resilient Aboriginal people seem to be. Despite having experienced incredible levels of trauma, losses etc., most Aboriginal people are still able to function well and are able to lead reasonably healthy lives. Some of them even flourish in spite of their difficult personal and collective histories. These observations raise interesting questions for both therapists and researchers: What are coping strategies, models, and practices employed by the Aboriginal people to account for their resiliency?

This chapter will provide a brief history of discrimination and abuse of Aboriginal people in Canada as the necessary backdrop for their resilience. We report empirical findings on practices, which contribute to healing and assist Aboriginal peoples in leading healthy lives. We then discuss how such lessons are related to the larger literature of effective coping and resilience. Throughout the chapter we use the inclusive term "Aboriginal". This term is interchangeable with the terms "Native", " Metis", "Indian" or "First Nations", and refers to the same people.

2. HISTORICAL BACKGROUND

In order to understand resiliency amongst Aboriginal peoples in Canada it is first necessary to understand some of the history of Aboriginal peoples since their first contact with European settlers. Since space does not permit a lengthy review, we will limit this section to the last two centuries and merely provide a few of the relevant highlights.

The 1800s saw the involuntary replacement of traditional Aboriginal governments with the Indian Act. Many traditional ceremonies were outlawed, such as the sundance ceremony and the potlatch ceremony. Indian Reserves or holding compounds were created and Aboriginal people had their traditional lands seized and the people were relocated to these reserves. Government policy also dictated that all Aboriginal children were to be

University of British Columbia; Trinity Western University

taken from their families and placed in residential schools run by the government and then later by the churches. Aboriginal people were prohibited from voting, attending university, owning land, entering a public bar, etc. unless they were willing to give up their Indian status. Diseases brought by European immigrants killed almost 90 % of all Aboriginal people in Canada. In some cases they were intentionally exposed to diseases, such as smallpox and tuberculosis. The 1900's saw the reduction of the small amounts of land in Indian reserves reduced to 1/3 of 1% of the total land base. Indian people were granted the right to vote in 1960. The residential schools continued to operate until 1984 when the last one was shut down.

3. INDIAN RESIDENTIAL SCHOOLS

These schools were put in place in an effort to assimilate Aboriginal people as part of the government solution to the "Indian problem". Canada's first Prime Minister Sir John A. McDonald believed that the "Indian savages" had to be civilized and that the most effective way was by taking the children away from their home and families. An underlying goal was to assimilate the Indians so that they would not have to be compensated for their lands that were taken. Learning from experienced colonizers e.g., England, the Indian Residential Schools were built modeled on the British Prison system so that children could then be forcibly removed from their homes and placed in these institutions for their entire childhood. This policy and these schools remained in place in Canada for over 100 years (1861-1984). Despite the fact that the government used the students for manual labor, they still found that they could save even more money if they let the churches run the schools. With the churches now running the schools on much smaller budgets an added goal was added to the mandate of the residential schools. They were to not only civilize the savages but to Christianize them as well. Unfortunately this was not all that occurred in the residential schools. At present in Canada there are tens of thousands of lawsuits currently before the courts against the Canadian government and churches amounting to billions of dollars claimed in damages for the physical and sexual abuses that occurred to Aboriginal children in the residential schools. Extensive documentation has revealed that in addition to rampant physical and sexual abuse more than seven generations of Aboriginal people were subjected to traumas in the schools, such as medical experiments, forced sterilization, elimination of their language and cultural practices, starvation, emotional torture etc. Historians have found that Adolf Hitler was so impressed by the residential schools in North America that they provided the inspiration for the Nazi concentration camps used in addressing the "Jewish Problem".

4. EFFECTS ON ABORIGINAL PEOPLE

Over a century of government and church attempts at cultural genocide have taken their toll on Aboriginal people in both Canada and the United States. The negative effects of physical, emotional, and sexual abuse that occurred in Residential Schools are often insidious and intergenerational. Choney, Berryhill-Paapke, and Robbins (1995) conclude that "one of the most blatant examples of threat to personal integrity is the forced acculturation, racism, and discrimination continually experienced by tribal people in the

United States. The product of these actions may be thought of as intergenerational PTSD" (p. 80). Similarly, Green (1997) observes that negative impact of past injustices is still evident in some First Nations communities in British Columbia:

In essence, this oppression through the installation of reserves, residential schools, and the `big scoop' (apprehension and adoption procedures of First Nations into non-First Nations homes) has resulted in over three times the provincial suicide rate, and alcohol-related deaths which were over six and a half times the national average. (p. 22)

McCormick (2000) attributes the widespread problem of alcoholism in B.C.'s First Nations communities to dislocation and forced assimilation: "The devastating effects of these attempts at cultural genocide have revealed to Aboriginal people the strong link between cultural dislocation and sickness. Alcohol abuse has simply been one symptom of that sickness" (p. 28).

Despite the negative impact of over a century of abuse, many Aboriginal people remain resilient and there are grounds for optimism for Canadian First Nations communities (Ponting & Voyageur, 2001). There are many indications that they will survive as independent nations and they will be able to manage their own lives in a healthy way. Education, counseling, and research can all contribute to this progress.

5. TRAUMA AND RESIDENTIAL SCHOOL SURVIVORS

For the thousands of Aboriginal people abused in Canadian residential schools their experience has been one of trauma. Judith Herman (1992) in her landmark book: Trauma and Recovery, states that trauma undermines the basic sense of trust that is normally established in the first few years of life as well as leaving the victim with a sense of abandonment, alienation, and disconnection which will effect all future relationships. The sexual and physical abuse experienced by Aboriginal people who attended residential schools inevitably led to experiences of trauma for the vast majority of victims. As most attendees were held captive and subjected to this abuse for up to 12 years, the trauma is even more severe. In cases such as this where victims have been held captives for prolonged periods of time, Herman (1992) states that all of the psychological structures will be broken down so that the victims cannot assume their former identity. According to Krugman (1997) childhood trauma will be incorporated into the pattern of family life in the next generation, unless it has been repaired. If the childrens interpersonal boundaries are violated and they are not provided with adequate care and protection then they are likely to adopt coping mechanisms, such as isolation, dissociation, hyper sexuality, hyper aggression, and sensation seeking. These maladaptive ways of coping can make them abusive or exploitive mates or parents when they grow up (Krugman, 1997).

Duran and Duran (1995) add to our understanding of the effects of trauma on Aboriginal peoples with the concept of "internalized oppression" arising from the abuses of colonization and the residential schools. In this phenomenon the victim loses all power and attempts to take on the power of the oppressor. This leads to self-hatred, which can either be internalized or externalized. If internalized it can lead to alcoholism or suicide and if externalized to physical or sexual abuse of others.

A similar explanation is provided by Freire (1993) who states that these experiences can lead to lateral sexual and physical abuse. Lateral violence is the result of being abused by an oppressor who is deemed all-powerful. Since retaliation against the oppressor is not possible, the rage and anger are directed to those closest in the form of sexual, emotional, and physical abuse. These terms: internalized oppression, lateral violence, and Post Traumatic Stress Disorder (PTSD) have recently been utilized in the context of the residential school legacy in an attempt to understand the damages done and their long lasting effects. According to Krugman (1997), the impact of posttraumatic stress on the family will likely result in either constriction leading to enmeshment, avoidance leading to disengagement, or impulsive behavior leading to chaos. Adult survivors of childhood sexual abuse may also experience: depression (Browne and Finkelhor, 1986a); anxiety (Hall and Lloyd, 1989); dissociation (Landecker, 1992); and eating disorders (Browne and Finkelhor, 1986b).

6. RESEARCH ON ABORIGINAL RESILENCE

Most of the research concerning Aboriginal peoples' health has focused on problems and pathology. This trend has perpetuated the disempowerment of Aboriginal peoples. In order to understand resiliency it must be researched. However, not all victims of residential schools developed adjustment problems.In fact, many survivors are able to overcome a history of abuse against them as individuals as well as a people. Some of them have even become better and stronger persons, demonstrating what may be called post-traumatic growth.

Very little research has been conducted on Aboriginal resiliency until very recently. There are only a few studies that focus on the positive psychology of Aboriginal resilience. McEvoy and Daniluk (1995) examined the experiences of Aboriginal women survivors of sexual abuse. Their research revealed six themes that represented the experiences of participants as they lived with and tried to make sense of their history of childhood sexual abuse. Those themes were: A sense of shame and guilt, a sense of acute vulnerability, a sense of internal fragmentation, a sense of invalidation and cultural shame, a need to make sense of the abuse, and the experience of reintegration. Thus meaning-making and meaning-reconstruction play a role in their survival.

According to McCormick (1995, 1996, 1997a, 1997b, 1997c, 2000), resiliency in Aboriginal peoples can also be attributed to several cultural and spiritual factors. In one such study, McCormick (1995) examined what factors facilitated healing for Aboriginal people in British Columbia. Although there was some mention of Western healing approaches in the results, the majority of the themes reflected the strength of traditional approaches to healing. Through interviews with 50 participants, 437 critical incidents were elicited reporting what facilitated healing for Aboriginal people of British Columbia. In this study, the 437 critical incidents were placed into 14 categories that were found to be reasonably reliable. These categories are: participation in ceremony, expression of emotion, learning from a role model, establishing a connection with nature, exercise, involvement in challenging activities, establishing a social connection, gaining an understanding of the problem, establishing a spiritual connection, obtaining help/support from others, self care, setting goals, anchoring self in tradition, and helping others. These categories were organized into four divisions: separating from an unhealthy life, obtaining social support and resources, experiencing a healthy life, and living a healthy life.

A preliminary examination of the healing outcomes for Aboriginal people was thought to invoke empowerment, cleansing, balance, discipline, and belonging. Distinct themes in Aboriginal healing were also developed as a result of analyzing narrative accounts of participants. These themes are: a broad spectrum of healing resources are available to Aboriginal people; Aboriginal people have a different way of seeing the world which has to be understood before effective counseling services can be provided; Aboriginal people expect that whatever is healing should help them attain and/or maintain balance; self transcendence followed by connectedness is a common route to healing for Aboriginal people, and Aboriginal people act as agents for their own healing.

A few years ago, McCormick was involved in another study conducted in partnership with the Association of BC First Nations Treatment Program Directors (ABCFNTP) and the NECHI Centre, and Aboriginal Healing Foundation (2002). The purpose of the study was to examine what practices helped Aboriginal Residential School survivors and their children who experienced physical or sexual abuse. Through interviews with 87 First Nations adults, 790 critical incidents were elicited concerning what facilitated or hindered healing in this population. The 790 critical incidents were organized into 39 facilitating categories and seven hindering categories. Many of the categories identified by participants in this study are identical to categories found in the study conducted by McCormick (1995). There were however, a few new categories identified that add to what we know about Aboriginal resiliency. A description of a number of these healing categories from both studies will be described here to illustrate the unique nature of Aboriginal healing.

6.1. Balance

Most Aboriginal cultures have a teaching about balance. In order to live a healthy life a person should try to keep the physical, mental, emotional, and spiritual dimensions of self in balance. The Aboriginal Medicine Wheel model illustrates that these four dimensions are all equal and all part of a larger whole. It is thought that people will become ill if they live life in an unbalanced way (Medicine Eagle, 1989). Traditional Aboriginal healing always incorporates all four dimensions in healing as it is difficult to isolate any one aspect (Primeaux, 1977). This philosophy of healing is described in a report on Aboriginal health and healing in Canada. Throughout the history of Aboriginal people-the definition of health evolved around the whole being of each person-the physical, emotional, mental, and spiritual aspects of a person being in balance and harmony with each other as well as with the environment and other beings. This has clashed with the Western medical model which, until very recently, has perpetuated the concept of health as being 'the absence of disease' (Favel-King, 1993, p. 125).

6.2. Interconnectedness

Another important Aboriginal teaching that pertains to health and resiliency is that of connectedness. Interconnectedness can be viewed as the individual's connection to the world outside the self. Practically, this means to become connected or reconnected to friends, family, spirituality, community, nature, and culture. Aboriginal mental health researchers have continuously stressed the collective orientation of Aboriginal people

(Trimble & Hayes, 1984; Lafromboise, Trimble, & Mohatt, 1990). This philosophy is well described by Ross (1992) when he states that interconnectedness means:

> *That we are not alone, nor can we go it alone. We are here not to assert our domin-*
> *ion or to rise above the rest, but to make a contribution to the rest. The successful*
> *man is the one who understands his role as the conduit of sustenance for all compo-*
> *nents of creation and who dedicates his efforts towards maintaining harmony and*
> *balance within all creation. (p. 182).*

Interconnectedness is prevalent throughout most Aboriginal cultures and has been aptly described as a series of relationships, starting with the family, that reaches further and further out so that it encompasses the universe (Epes-Brown, 1989). The emphasis on interconnectedness is often in conflict with the modern Western emphasis on individuality. Some Aboriginal people even see mental illness as a result of excessively individualistic behavior that is best treated by utilizing the power of the community (Lafromboise, 1988). Katz and Rolde (1981) found that the goal of traditional Aboriginal healing was not to strengthen the client's ego as in non-Aboriginal counseling, but to encourage the client to transcend the ego by considering himself or herself as imbedded in and expressive of community. Like family therapy, systems therapy, and community psychiatry, Aboriginal healing promotes the idea of bringing together many forces to best utilize the powers that promote health (Hammerschlag, 1988). Traditional Aboriginal ceremonies such as the Vision Quest and Sweat Lodge reinforce adherence to cultural values and help to remind people of the importance of keeping family and community networks strong (Lafromboise et al., 1990).

6.3. Spirituality

Spirituality plays an important role in the resiliency of Aboriginal people. Aboriginal worldview does not separate spirituality from healing as it is seen as an integral part of the process (Couture, 1996; Halfe, 1993; Duran & Duran, 1995). It is thought that in times of need, the Aboriginal person will turn to the Great Spirit, which is perceived everywhere (Dugan, 1985). Aboriginal healers often consider somatic illness, depression, anxiety, and alcoholism as having originated from spirit illness (Halfe, 1993, Hammerschlag, 1988). Spirituality takes on such an important role in healing that it is seen as the essence of healing for many Aboriginal people (Medicine Eagle, 1989, Hammerschlag, 1988, Torrey, 1986). Many of the Aboriginal healing ceremonies emphasize the spiritual aspect of healing. In the Vision Quest ceremony the Aboriginal person makes contact with his or her spiritual identity (Hodgson & Kothare, 1990). The Medicine Wheel symbolized by the circle also represents spiritual ties that bind human beings to one another and to the natural world (Bell, 1991). Examples of spiritual connection found in this study encompassed prayer, attending church services, and other forms of connection and communication with the Creator, Great Spirit, and/or God. Spirituality was highlighted as an important component in Residential School healing. Many participants mentioned the need to transform their negative childhood experience with the church into a positive experience with spirituality. Related to their spirituality, participants reported experiencing healing dreams and visions; such experiences led to increase self-awareness, guidance, and inspiration for participants.

6.4. Traditional Healing

Healing ceremonies are not a uniquely Aboriginal invention but they are a method of healing that have been used by Aboriginal peoples for thousands of years. Mental health professionals who have worked with Aboriginal people have found that ritual and ceremony allow Aboriginal people to give expression to personal experience while at the same time connecting people with their community (Hammerschlag, 1993). Ceremonies such as the Spirit dances, the Sweatlodge, and the Pipe ceremonies are tools to maintain and deepen the individual's sense of connectedness to all things (Ross, 1992). The Vision Quest ceremony is said to help the participant to realize the vastness of the universe, and by enabling the person to transcend himself, to realize ultimately his oneness with nature (McGaa, 1989). Although there has not been empirical research conducted on the efficacy of traditional healing ceremonies, such as those mentioned, anecdotal evidence exists within the literature to attest to their effectiveness in healing (Torrey, 1972; Jilek, 1982; Hammerschlag, 1988). Examples of healing ceremonies from the authors' research ranged from the Sweat Lodge Ceremony to the Pipe Ceremony. Certain ceremonies such as the Sweat Lodge Ceremony were mentioned numerous times. The Sweat Lodge Ceremony, for example, is often considered to be a cleansing or re-birthing ceremony. Elements of this ceremony, such as the darkness and the drumbeat are likened to the experience of being in the womb of Mother Earth. The process of sweating can represent the intermingling of the participant's life fluids with that of mother earth's. Powerful images such as these help to facilitate healing for those who participate in the Sweat Lodge Ceremony and other Aboriginal ceremonies.

In addition to these ceremonies, traditional healer, medicine man, or medicine woman also play a role in contributing to healing. These healers employ a range of techniques from prayer to healing touch.

6.4.1. Treatment/Healing Centers

These 'treatment/healing centers' provide a safe and supportive environment, which is essential for healing. The educational function of these centers was also very important. Sharing with others and being able to tell one's story was another important function of the centers. Important teachings at the centers as reported by participants were learning about: grieving, boundaries, co-dependency, shame, abandonment, and expressing emotions. As a result of attending these centers participants reported a higher level of self-awareness, self-esteem, empowerment, cleansing, and connectedness.

Participants also benefited from support groups in their healing journey. Examples range from AA groups, ACOA, talking circles to Drum groups. Support groups facilitated connectedness, self-awareness, and empowerment.

6.5. Tradition/Culture

Some Aboriginal people believe that not maintaining one's cultural values and community respect is one of the reasons for psychological and physical problems (Lafromboise, Trimble, & Mohatt, 1990). It is therefore thought that one of the roles of therapy for traditional Aboriginal society has been to reaffirm cultural values. A culturally sensitive counseling framework for Aboriginal people must therefore include the theme of the importance of personal and cultural identity (Anderson, 1993). In a study of traditional healing with Aboriginal women who were victims of sexual abuse, Heibron and Guttman (2000) found that adhering to Aboriginal culture was integral to the healing process. In similar studies traditional Aboriginal healing methods were found to promote cohesiveness and inner strength within Aboriginal communities by reinforcing cultural values (Lafromboise, Trimble & Mohatt, 1990). Culture and traditional teachings play a significant role in Aboriginal resiliency. According to Duran (1995) the most effective models of treatment are those that incorporate traditional Aboriginal thinking and practice. By focusing on Aboriginal knowledge, initiatives for Aboriginal health can reflect the wisdom of those who stand to benefit from them (RCAP, 1996).

The teaching of traditional culture has been found to be a successful way to facilitate healing in Aboriginal people. In one Aboriginal community, it was possible to reduce dramatically the teen suicide rate by having tribal elders teach traditional culture to the teens in a group setting (Neligh, 1990). By providing Aboriginal people with culture through stories and shared cultural activities, elders were able to provide community members with guidance, direction, and self understanding (Halfe, 1993). This incorporation of self, or identity with traditional ideology also provides Aboriginal people with strength for coping in the mainstream environment (Axelson, 1985). This movement towards reconnecting with cultural beliefs, tradition, and ceremony as a way of overcoming problems has been referred to as "retraditionalization" (Lafromboise et al., 1990).

Critics of traditional Aboriginal healing approaches argue that the traditional ways have been lost. Certainly, there is evidence that some of the old ways of healing have been largely forgotten. Colonialism was responsible for the rapid erosion of indigenous medicine, including herbalism and forms of spiritual healing (Warry, 2000). Other factors contributing to the erosion of traditional healing ways were Indian Act amendments forbidding traditional healing ceremonies sponsored by Aboriginal agents and Missionaries who were afraid that Christian farmers might be converted. Fortunately, Aboriginal healing practices like Aboriginal cultures have themselves been eroded but are not lost.

Participants have indicated their attempt to be better connected with their culture; they want to learn about and accept their identity as an Aboriginal person. Through methods such as being given an Indian name, or through learning about their family history, participants reported increased sense of belonging, self-acceptance, and confidence. Learning to accept themselves includes owning up their own feelings and loving themselves the way they are. Self-acceptance resulted in increased self-esteem, empowerment, and a sense of authenticity or genuineness.

6.6. Family and Community

Resiliency can also be attributed to the healing power of family and community. For traditional Aboriginal people, healing is often in the form of a community sanctioned and community run cleansing ceremony that involves the whole community (Ross, 1992; Torrey, 1972). According to a traditional Aboriginal view, a person's psychological welfare must be considered in the context of the community (Trimble & Hayes, 1984). Similarly, therapy for Aboriginal people should encourage the client to transcend himself or herself by conceptualizing the self as being imbedded in and expressive of community (Katz &

Rolde, 1981). For Aboriginal people there exists a focus on family and community responsibility for the emotional, mental, physical, and spiritual health of one another (Ross, 1992). Traditional healing methods have generalized therapeutic benefits because they often include the participation of family and community members which increases the social support of the individual (Renfrey, 1992). Guilmet and Whited (1987) also found that the extended family was of paramount importance to most Aboriginal clients in terms of emotional support. One approach that utilizes family and community members in healing is called "Network therapy". The network approach utilizes family, friends, and relatives as a network and social support system to help the person in need (Lafromboise, Trimble, & Mohatt, 1990; Redhorse, 1982). Neligh (1990) describes network therapy as the grand opera of psychotherapy, because the therapist draws forth from the group the definition of the problem in terms satisfactory to all and facilitates the solution of the problem in terms satisfactory to all.

Related to the importance of family and community, participants experienced healing from learning about the intergenerational nature of Residential School damage to people, self, and relations. Participants became aware of intergenerational PTSD, and family patterns of alcoholism and abuse. This awareness led to relief of shame, anger, guilt, increased self-awareness, and motivation to change.

6.7. Identifying and Expressing Emotions

This category included the expression of feelings and emotions through varying channels such as talking, crying, and screaming. Participants also utilized many creative ways to get feelings out, such as by listening to music or exercising. Several participants mentioned the significance of keeping this emotional dimension of themselves in balance through the expression of emotion. By learning how to identify and express emotion, participants were able to build up their emotional dimension. In learning how to express emotions in an appropriate manner, participants reported that they gained strength and balance in this aspect of their lives. Anger towards an abuser, for example, could be expressed in an effective, nondestructive manner and not turned inwards against oneself. This is a large category and indicates both the need and tremendous healing benefit derived from expression of emotion.

6.8. Role Models/Mentors

In this category the participant obtained guidance, instruction or example from someone whom he or she had established as a role model or mentor. Examples ranged from learning from others who were successfully coping with similar problems, to following the example of leaders or relatives. Participants often felt inspired or motivated as a result of having role models/mentors.

6.9. Establishing a Connection with Nature

This category includes being in or with nature and in using the natural world for self-healing. This category does not focus on spiritual connection but on the many ways that nature is used. For many Aboriginal people, there is a spiritual connection that exists between nature and humans, in that humans are seen as part of nature. All of creation is seen as being equal and part of the whole, and is therefore equal in the eyes of the Creator. Connection with nature was sometimes seen as getting back to creation and the Creator. Many of the incidents obtained could overlap with "Establishing a spiritual connection" but were chosen because they specifically dealt with nature. Examples ranged from the use of water in healing to the healing benefits of being in the forest amongst trees. Nature helped participants to feel relaxed, cleansed, calmed, and stronger.

To illustrate the often unique nature of Aboriginal resiliency the research category of `connection to nature' will be discussed. The relationship that Aboriginal people have with nature is often different than the relationship between nature and non-aboriginal people. Aboriginal people see nature as an essential and equal element of creation and therefore an important source of guidance and assistance. Mainstream psychological thought and practice reinforces the separation of the psyche from nature. This leads to people disregarding nature as a means of healing. Aboriginal people believe that there is a spiritual connection that exists between nature and humans because humans are seen as part of nature. All of creation is seen as being equal and part of the whole, and is therefore equal in the eyes of the Creator. Among many aboriginal people human beings are considered frail and require the guidance and assistance of the natural and spiritual world. Connection to nature can cause humans to feel something much larger, less lonely, feeling grounded, and secure. The following examples are taken from various studies conducted by McCormick to illustrate how nature can lead to resiliency. These excerpts are in the words of the participants and have not been edited for grammar.

6.9.1. Wind Example

The wind is very healing. I stand up on a hill or mountain and I just hold my arms out so it's just me and the wind and there is nothing between us and I feel free. That's a great feeling and it's healing. If there is nothing between me and the sky except for the wind then I feel very free and peaceful and there is nothing bothering me, it's just me and nature

6.9.2. Water Example

I have used water to cleanse myself emotionally and spiritually too. I wash my hands, my eyes, and ears and I ask for wisdom and to listen, and hear things, and see things clearly. This is a technique that I was taught as a child and I have used it to heal myself.

6.9.3. Mountain Example

Mountains have helped me. One time I was really anxious in remembering the sexual abuse I had experienced as a kid. I was at my Dads house and feeling sad, and I looked out the window at this snow-capped mountain. It was beautiful and it was solid, and it had been there a long, long time. At different times of the year it looks different, sometimes it is mostly snow and other times it is mostly green. That helped me that day to think about that mountain that was put there by the creator. Sometimes we are given a huge problem to deal with for a reason. Without seeing that mountain I don't think I would have survived that day. I wanted to be like that Mountain. The mountain will always be there it doesn't go anywhere but it changes how it looks. It has strength and beauty. The problem I have with those memories will always be there but some days it will look a lot better than other days. I am learning to be like that mountain.

7. COPING AND RESILIENCE

The above has provided a sketchy picture of Aboriginal people's unique ways of coping with trauma and achieving healing. For example, their connectedness with nature and their healing ceremonies have been found beneficial in their recovery process. Water, for example, was used in healing through ritual cleansing, by drinking it and bathing with it, water was used as a metaphor to teach people the path to healing; even the sounds of water were healing. Elders in their communities know these ways of using water, wind, and rocks etc. and can teach them to others. These are effective and legitimate ways of healing and deserve to be given the recognition and credibility they deserve.

In addition to culture-specific ways of coping, the Aboriginal people also employ coping strategies widely used by non-native people. For example, their attempt to seeking healing through identifying and expressing emotions is similar to coping strategy of Active Emotion; Wong, Reker and Peacock (Chapter 11) have demonstrated the various adaptive functions of this coping method. Aboriginal people's emphasis on interconnectiveness, family, and community is similar to other collectivistic cultures, which favor collective coping (Wong, 1993; Wong & Ujimoto, 1998) and collectivistic coping (Yeh, et al., Chapter 3). Their spirituality is similar to the various forms of spiritual coping employed in other cultures (Klaassen, et al., Chapter 6). Wong has emphasized both acceptance and meaning-making as the two major types of existential coping (Wong, 1993; Chapter 11). Clearly, Aboriginal people attempt to make sense of what has happened to them (McEvoy & Daniluk, 1995).

What we have learned is that the Aboriginal people are able to put their unique, indigenous stamp on coping strategies that are also employed by non-natives. For example, their concept of collective coping and interconnectiveness encompasses nature. There spiritual healing includes a unique set of healing ceremonies.

8. TRAGIC OPTIMISM AND POST-TRAUMATIC GROWTH

The goal of healing is more than survival and recovery – it needs to aim at personal growth. Earlier, we pointed out that in spite of their collective history and personal experience of abuse, some Aboriginal people are leading healthy and productive lives. Their resilience is similar to what has been considered as post-traumatic growth or PTG (Tedeschi & Calhoun, 1995) or stress-related growth (Park, Cohen, & Murch, 1996). It would be helpful to both Aboriginal people and other trauma survivors, if we can identify factors contributing to PTG. Among other things, Tedeschi and Calhoun (1995; 2004) have emphasized the importance of effective coping responses, social support, religiosity, wisdom, and personality characteristic. Taylor's (1983) cognitive adaptation theory emphasizes the importance of mastery and meaning. Maddi's hardiness model (Maddi, et al., Chapter 17) is based on understanding of existential courage:

The combined hardy attitudes of commitment, control, and challenge constitute the best available operationalization of existential courage. The hardy attitudes struc- ture how you think about your interaction with the world around you and provide motivation to do difficult things. When they occur together, the three C's of hardy attitudes facilitate awareness that you formulate life's meaning for yourself by the decisions you make and that choosing the future regularly, despite the anxiety of uncertainty, leads to the most vibrant life. (Maddi, 2002)

Wong's (1993) resource-congruence model emphasizes on the importance of having sufficient coping resources and matching coping response with the nature of the stressor and the cultural context (Wong, et al., Chapter 11). All the above models incorporate some elements of Aboriginal ways of coping with trauma. However, we propose that the tragic optimism model (Wong, 2001; Wong & McDonald, 2002), which was based on Viktor Frankl's (1985) construct of tragic optimism, seems to be most compatible with Aboriginal people's history and experiences. It is through the devastating and dehuman- izing experiences in Nazi concentration camps that Dr. Frankl developed logotherapy and tragic optimism. Wong (2001) has extended Frankl's concept into the five-factor model of tragic optimism (TO). We will briefly describe these five factors and show their relevance to PTSD. The accent of this model is enduring hope – the kind of hope that can endure a history of abuse and the worse kind of traumatic experiences. We propose that hope is the key to recovery and resilience. All the helpful cultural practices and coping methods would not be adequate without the hope that one can survive and thrive against the odds. Therefore, it is important to examine the presence of any elements of enduring hope in the Aboriginal ways of coping and healing.

8.1. Acceptance of What Cannot Be Changed

Acceptance is the first step towards developing enduring hope. It involves:(1) Recognizing that suffering is an inevitable part of life; (2) Accepting the fact that what has been done in the past cannot be undone; (3) Accepting one's own identity and one's own limitations and all the misfortunes that have come one's way; and (4) Accepting that bad things do happen to good people. The movement among Aboriginal people towards self- acceptance has played a big part in their healing. By confronting and accepting the painful past and the difficult present, one is embarking on the journey of healing and growth. It is interesting to note that one of the major dimensions of mental health and happiness (Ryff & Keys, 1995; Wong, 1998, 2001a) is a healthy sense of reality. However, the bene- fits of acceptance may be dependent on the concomitant presence of positive beliefs and attitudes, such as Affirmation.

8.2. Affirmation of the Meaning and Value of Life

Affirmation represents the first positive step towards coping with traumas and rebuilding shattered assumptions. It is the turning point from the negative affect of accept- ing the harsh realities towards a more positive affect in affirming the intrinsic values of life. Affirmation states that there is something inherently good and meaningful in this life that is worth fighting for, no matter how bleak and hopeless the situation. Affirmation of the meaning and value of life is the turning point from despair to optimism (Wong, 2001, 2002). Frankl (1985) affirms that positive meanings can be discovered and life is worth living under all circumstances. Suffering with meaning makes suffering more bearable. Affirmation with acceptance will lead to the task of restoring meaning and hope in a shattered world. It will mean undertaking the difficult task of attributing new meanings to traumatic events and future goals. The reconstruction of one's assumptive world will never be the same as its former world (Janoff-Bulman, 1992).

When Aboriginal people affirm the values of their own tradition and culture, when they affirm the values of education and the possibility for a meaningful and healthy life, they will have a powerful motivation to move forward in spite of all the negative experiences they have endured.

8.3. Courage to Face Adversity

It takes courage to move forward. It takes courage to face an uncertain future and many obstacles. Courage to face adversity is the defiant human spirit or heroism that empowers one to move forward in spite of fears and failures. Frankl (1985) considers the defiant human spirit as a magical medicine chest, because when there are no cures and no solutions, a courageous attitude to face suffering and a positive, affirmative attitude to face the future can contribute to the healing of both psychological and physical pains.

8.4. Self-transcendence

Self-transcendence involves not only the attitude of transcending past traumas, present circumstances, but also the expression of this attitude in actions. The human capacity to transcend painful memories and difficult present circumstances provides the basis for freedom and creativity in developing a meaningful future. It can be very therapeutic when counselors encourage clients to shift from their self-absorption and self-pity to helping others who are worse off. The belief that one is serving a higher cause can also imbue life with meaning (Wong, 1998). Self-Transcendence is demonstrated, whenever we embrace suffering for the benefit of others (Frankl, 1985). Most religions espouse spiritual growth through transcending self-interests and serving a higher purpose (Richards & Bergin; 1997, 2000). McCormick (1996) also emphasizes the value of self-transcendence in counseling Aboriginal people.

8.5. Faith in God and Others

Finally, undergirding Frankl's tragic optimism is his faith in God, the source of ultimate meaning and love. It is this belief that enabled him to affirm that meaning can be found in the most horrible situations. It is this faith that enabled him to project himself into the future with hope even when everything all around him was so full of gloom and despair. Faith represents the only positive expectation in an otherwise hopeless situation (Wong, 2001). Tillich (1958) notes that such hope comes not from oneself but from an ultimate higher power. Trusting in others becomes critical when one does not have theistic beliefs

(Erikson, 1964; Capps, 1995; Conners, Toscova, & Tonigan, 1999). Capps (1995) stresses that without trust, one would not dare hope at all.

Faith in God and others is the ultimate source for affirmation and courage (Wong, 2002). Depending on one's faith tradition, God may be conceptualized as Nature, Higher Power or Spiritual force. When everything else has failed, faith becomes the only flicker of hope in an otherwise dark tunnel. Much more has been achieved by faith the world ever knew. A simple faith in God has given people the courage and hope to survive impossible situations. The recent survival story of the miners in Philadelphia is a case in point (Goodell, 2002). They credit their survival to faith in God and faith in their rescuers. The belief that man's adversity is God's opportunity often serves as the ray of light found in the darkness of tragedy. In many movie classics (i.e., Star Wars, The Lord of Rings, etc.), whether it is faith in the "force" or trust in the fellowship of the companions, their heroes ultimately secure hope beyond themselves and triumph over the opposition. As a result, counselors need to look for openings to encourage their clients to explore spirituality and faith, regardless of their religious orientations, as an added resource for coping with adversities and traumas beyond their control. Since Aboriginal people are spiritually oriented, McCormick (1996) has emphasized spiritual faith and meaning in Aboriginal counseling.

8.6. Empirical Evidence

Wong and his graduate students have carried out a series of studies on the relationship between tragic optimism and post-traumatic growth. Leung, Steinfort, & Vroon (2003) present the initial evidence of reliability and validity of the Life Attitude Scale (LAS) developed to measure TO; they demonstrated that the LAS was positively correlated with measurements of hope, meaning and spirituality; more importantly, they found that the LAS was a significant predictor of post-traumatic growth.

In another study, Lynn Dumerton (2004), compared a sample of Aboriginal people from British Columbia, Canada and a comparable predominantly Euro-Canadian sample based on those who attended a 5-day Choices Personal Growth Seminar. The original Choices Seminar was designed by Dr. Phil McCraw, Dr. Joe McGraw and Thelma Box. The present Choices Personal Growth Seminar was run by Thelma Box on a regular basis in Canada and was very popular with Aboriginal people in British Columbia and Alberta. Through this seminar, participants learn to make changes in their lives through acceptance and empowerment; the Choices Seminar implicitly taught several concepts which are consistent with Wong's model of tragic optimism. Attendees who volunteered to participate in the present study were given a package of questionnaires prior to and after the seminar. Results confirmed our hypothesis that the Aboriginal sample indeed experienced more traumas and had significantly higher TO as measured by the LAS; furthermore, both groups showed a significant increase in TO on Time 2 after completing the Choices Seminar, suggesting that the five components of TO can be learned not only through the experience of having overcome past traumas, but also through learning from Choices Seminar.

9. CONCLUSIONS

According to Wong and McDonald (2002), incorporating the five components of Tragic Optimism into clinical practices can help clients to maintain hope and recover even in the most adverse circumstances. As Frankl's personal triumph over the suffering in Nazi death camps attested that none of the horrible atrocities and dehumanizing deprivation inflicted upon him can strip him of his dignity and hope in the meaning and value of life. Frankl also notes that an inner strength of a genuine faith is crucial to human vitality.

The incorporating tragic optimism into one's worldview means more than the adaptation of a new set of strategies so to better cope with life or re-authorize one's life story. TO can be developed through experience and learning. Participating in workshops like the Choices Seminar and reading life stories of others who have overcome great tragedies can stimulate the development of tragic optimism – the only kind of enduring hope. Learning from the elders, sages, and spiritual leaders can also give them wisdoms in facing the tragedies of life. Counseling can also facilitate the development of TO, because a competent counselor can provide a safe and supportive environment for the clients to confront their troubled life circumstances and muster the necessary courage to discover and restore meaning and purpose for their future. A counselor equipped with the existential model of optimism can be more effective in addressing such issues as acceptance, affirmation, and courage in order to facilitate the restoration of shattered assumptions and the regaining of hope.

Generally, enduring can be very adaptive. In going about the everyday ordinary business, enduring hope liberates us to cultivate a greater appreciation of life, enlarge our capacity for hope and happiness, and live a more meaningful and fulfilling life. In face of tragedies and traumas, tragic optimism powers up our positive attitude to embrace life in the presence of fear and despair. The present chapter has indicated the adaptive function of acceptance, affirmation, courage, self-transcendence, and faith, which are imbedded in many of the values and practices of Aboriginal people.

REFERENCES

Aboriginal Healing Foundation (2002). Therapeutic safety in healing: Facilitation of healing for Aboriginal school survivors. Ottawa: Aboriginal Healing Foundation.

Anderson, B. M. (1993). *Aboriginal counselling and healing processes*. Unpublished master's thesis, University of British Columbia, Vancouver, B.C.

Axelson, J. (1985). *Counseling and development in a multicultural society*. Monterey: Brooks Cole.

Bell, J. (1991, January-February). To find a Cure. *Arctic Circle*. pp 14-19.

Browne, A., & Finkelhor, D. (1986a). Impact of child abuse: A review of the research. *Psychological Bulletin*, 99(1):66-77.

Browne, A., & Finkelhor, D. (1986b). Initial and long-term effects: A review of the research. In D. Finkelhor (Ed.). *A sourcebook on childhood sexual abuse* (pp.143-198). Beverly Hills: Sage Publications.

Capps, D. (1995). *Agents of hope: A pastoral psychology*. Minneapolis, MN: Fortress.

Choney, S., Berryhill-Paapke, E., & Robbins, R. (1995). The acculturation of American Indians: Developing frameworks for research and practice. In J. G. Ponterotto, J. M. Casas, A. Suzuki, & C. M. Alexander (Eds.), *Handbook of multicultural counselling* (pp. 73-92). London: Sage Publications.

Connors, G. Toscova, R. T., & Tonigan, J. S. (1999). In W. R. Miller (Ed.) *Integrating spirituality into treatment*. Washington, DC: American Psychological Association.

Couture, J. (1996). The role of Native elders: Emergent issues. In D. Long & O. Dickason (Eds.) *Visions of the heart: Canadian Aboriginal issues* (pp. 41-56). Toronto: Harcourt Brace.

Dugan, K. M. (1985). *The Vision Quest of the Plains Indians: Its Spiritual Significance*. Lewiston, NY. : Edwin Mellin Press.

DuMerton, C. L. (2004). *Thesis: Tragic optimism and choices: The Life attitudes scale with a First Nations Sample*. Unpublished MA thesis, Trinity Western University, Langley BC.

Duran, E., & Duran, B. (1995). *Native American Post Colonial Psychology*. New York: SUNY Press.

Epes-Brown, J. (1989). Becoming part of it. In D. M. Dooling & P. Jordan-Smith (Eds.), *I became part of it: Sacred dimensions in Native American life*. (pp. 9-20). San Francisco: Harper.

Erikson, E. H. (1964). *Human strength and the cycle of generations: Insight and responsibility*. NY: Norton.

Favel-King, A. (1993). The treaty right to health. In The Path to Healing: Report of the National Round table on Aboriginal health and Social Issues.

Frankl, V. (1985). *Man's search for meaning: Revised and updated*. NY: Washington Square.

Freire, P. (1993). *Pedagogy of the oppressed*. New York: Continuum.

Goodell, J. (Ed.) (2002). *Our story: 77 hours that tested our friendship and our faith*. NY: Hyperion.

Green, H. (1997). May I walk in reality. *Guidance and Counseling, 12*(2), 22-27.

Guilmet, G. M., & Whited, D. L. (1987). Cultural lessons for clinical mental health practice: The Puyallup tribal community. *American Indian and Alaskan Native mental health research*, 1(2), 1-141.

Halfe, L. (1993). Native Healing. *Cognica*, 26(1), 21-27.

Hall, L., & Lloyd, S. (1989). *Surviving childhood sexual abuse: A handbook for helping women challenge their past*. New York: The Palmer Press.

Hammerschlag, C. (1993). *Theft of the spirit: A journey to spiritual healing with Native Americans*. New York: Simon & Schuster

Hammerschlag, C.A. (1988). *The dancing healers: A doctor's journey of healing with Native Americans*. San Francisco: Harper & Row.

Heilbron C.L., & Guttman, M.A.J. (2000). Traditional Healing methods with First Nations women in group counselling. *Canadian Journal of counselling*, 34 (1), 3-13.

Herman, J. L. (1992). *Trauma and recovery*. New York: Basic Books.

Hodgson, J. & Kothare, J. (1990) *Native spirituality and the church in Canada*. Toronto: Anglican Book center.

Janoff-Bulman,R. (1992). *Shattered assumptions: Towards a new psychology of trauma*. NY: Maxwell Macmillan International

Jilek, W. (1982). *Indian healing: Shamanic ceremonialism in the Pacific Northwest today*. Surrey: Hancock House.

Katz, R., & Rolde, E. (1981). Community Alternatives to psychotherapy. *Psychotherapy, Theory, Research and Practice, 18*, 365-374.

Krugman, R. D. (1997). *The battered child (5th ed.)*. Chicago: University of Chicago Press.

Lafromboise, T. (1988). Cultural and cognitive considerations in prevention of American Indian adolescent suicide. *Journal of Adolescence, 11*(2), 139-153.

Lafromboise, T., Trimble, J., & Mohatt, G. (1990). Counseling Intervention and American Indian Tradition: An Integrative Approach. *The Counseling Psychologist, 18*, 628-654.

Landecker, H. (1992). The role of childhood sexual abuse in the etiology of borderline personality disorder: considerations for diagnosis and treatment. *Psychotherapy, 29*(2): 234-242.

Leung, M., Steinfort, T., & Vroon, E. J. (2003). *Life attitudes scale: Development and validation of a measurement of the construct of tragic optimism*. Unpublished MA thesis, Trinity Western University, Langley BC.

Maddi, S. R. (2002). The Story of Hardiness: Twenty Years of Theorizing, Research, and Practice. *Consulting Psychology Journal, 54*(3), 173-185.

McCormick, R. M. (1995). The facilitation of healing for the First Nations people of British Columbia (monograph). *Canadian Journal of Native Education, 21*(2), 251-319.

McCormick, R. M. (1996). Culturally appropriate means and ends of counselling as described by the First Nations people of British Columbia. *International Journal for the Advancement of Counselling, 18*(3), 163-172.

McCormick, R. M. (1997a). First Nations Counsellor training: Strengthening the circle. *Canadian Journal of Community Mental Health, 16*(2).91-100

McCormick, R. M. (1997b). Healing through interdependence: the role of connecting in First Nations healing practices. *Canadian Journal of Counselling, 31* (3), 172-184.

McCormick,R. M. (1997c). An integration of healing wisdom: The vision quest ceremony from an attachment theory perspective. *Guidance and Counselling, 12*(2), 18-22.

McCormick, R. M. (2000). Aboriginal traditions in the treatment of substance abuse: Let only the good spirits guide you. *Canadian Journal of Counselling, 34*(1), 25-32.

McEvoy, M., & Daniluk, J. (1995) Wounds to the soul: The experiences of Aboriginal women survivors of sexual abuse. *Canadian psychologist, 36*, 221-235

McGaa, E. (1989). *Mother Earth Spirituality: Native American paths to healing ourselves and our world*. San Francisco: Harper & Row.

Medicine Eagle, B. (1989). The Circle of Healing. In R. Carlson & J. Brugh. (Eds.), *Healers on Healing* (pp. 58-62).

Nechi Institute on Drug Education and Research Centre (1992). *The eagle has landed: Data base study of Nechi participants-1974-1991*. Edmonton: Author.

Neligh, G. (1990). Mental health programs for American Indians: Their logic, structure and function. *American Indian and Alaskan Native Mental Health Research*, Vol. 3, monograph 3, 1-280.

O'Neil, J. D. (1993). Aboriginal health policy for the next century; A discussion paper for the Royal Commission for Aboriginal Peoples (RCAP).

Park, C. L., Cohen, L. H., & Murch, R. L. (1996). Assessment and prediction of stress-related growth. *Journal of Personality, 64*(1), 71-105.

Ponting, J. R., & Voyageur, C. J. (2001). Challenging the deficit paradigm: Grounds for optimism among First Nations in Canada. *Canadian Journal of Native Studies, 21*(2), 275-307.

Primeaux, M.H. (1977). American Indian Health Care Practices: A Cross cultural perspective. *Nursing Clinics of North America, 12*, 55-65.

Redhorse, Y. (1982). A cultural network model: Perspectives for adolescent services and para professional training. In S. Manson (Ed). *New directions in prevention among American Indian and Alaskan Native communities*. (pp.173-185). Portland, OR: Center for American Indian and Alaskan native Research.

Renfrey, G. S. (1992). Cognitive-Behavior therapy and the Native American client. *Behavior Therapy, 23*, 321-340.

Report of the Royal Commission on Aboriginal Peoples (1996) *Volume 3: Gathering Strength*. Ottawa, Canada: Ministry of Supply and Services.

Richards, P. S. & Bergins, A. E. (1997). *A spiritual strategy for counseling and psychotherapy*. Washington, DC: American Psychological Association.

Richards, P. S., & Bergins, A.E. (Eds.) (2000). *Handbook of psychotherapy and religious diversity*. Washington, DC: American Psychological Association.

Ross, R. (1992). *Dancing with a ghost: Exploring Indian reality*. Markham: Octopus.

Ryff, C. D., & Keyes, C. L. M. (1995). The structure of psychological well-being revisited. *Journal of Personality and Social Psychology, 69*, 719-727.

Taylor, S. E. (1983). Adjustment to threatening events: A theory of cognitive adaptation. *American Psychologist, 38*, 1161-1172.

Tedeschi, R. G., & Calhoun, L. G. (1995). *Trauma & transformation: Growing in the aftermath of suffering*. Thousand Oaks, CA: Sage Publications.

Tedeschi, R. G., & Calhoun, L. G. (2004). Posttraumatic growth: Conceptual foundations and empirical evidence. *Psychological Inquiry, 15*, 1-18.

Tillich, P. (1958). *The dynamics of faith*. New York: Harper Collins.

Torrey, E. F. (1986). *Witchdoctors and psychiatrists: The common roots of psychotherapy and its future*. NY: Harper Row.

Torrey, E. F. (1972). *The Mind game: Witch doctors and psychiatrists*. New York: Emerson Hall

Trimble, J. E., & Hayes, S. (1984). Mental Health Intervention in the Psychosocial contexts of American Indian Communities. In W. O'Conner & B. Lubin (Eds.), *Ecological Approaches to clinical and community psychology*, (pp. 293-321). New York: Wiley

Warry, W. (2000). *Unfinished dreams: Community healing and the reality of Aboriginal self-government*. Toronto: University of Toronto Press.

Wong, P. T. P. (1993). Effective management of life stress: The resource-congruence model. *Stress Medicine, 9*, 51-60.

Wong, P. T. P. (1998). Meaning-centered counselling. In P. T. P. Wong & P. S. Fry (Eds.) *The human quest for meaning: A handbook of psychological research and clinical application* (pp. 395-435). Mahwah, NJ: Lawrence Erlbaum Associates.

Wong, P. T. P. (2001a). Tragic optimism, realistic pessimism, and mature happiness: An existential model. Paper presented at the Positive Psychology Summit, Washington, DC, October 2001.

Wong, P. T. P. (2002). Triumph over terror: Lessons from logotherapy and positive psychology, Part 1. Retrieved August 14,2002 from http://www.meaning.ca/articles/presidents_column/print_copy/triumph_terror_part 1_feb02.htm

Wong, P. T. P., & Ujimoto, K. V. (1998). The elderly Asian Americans: Their stress, coping, and well-being. In L. C. Lee & N. W. S. Zane (Eds.), Handbook of Asian American Psychology, (pp. 165-209). Thousand Oaks, CA: Sage Publications.

Wong, P. T. P., & McDonald, M. J. (2002). Tragic optimism and personal meaning in counselling victims of abuse. *Sciences Pastorales, 20*, 231-249.

Section 5

Occupational Stress

TOWARDS AN UNDERSTANDING OF OCCUPATIONAL STRESS AMONG ASIAN AMERICANS

Frederick T. L. Leong and Dwight Tolliver

1. INTRODUCTION

Despite considerable research demonstrating the adverse effects of stress in the workplace, there is a surprising dearth of both theoretical and empirical literature on occupational stress among Asian Americans. Our purpose in this chapter is to remedy that situation by reviewing both the literature directly related to occupational stress as well as the literature on stress in general to serve as a framework for stimulating more research in this neglected area. To achieve this purpose, we will use the theoretical model of occupational stress developed by Osipow and Spokane (1987) as the framework for analyzing the extant literature.

In order to understand stress among Asian Americans, it seems important to begin with an overview of the mental health of Asian Americans in order to provide a context for our discussion. For this, we will turn to a recent review of that literature by Lee, Lei, & Sue, (2001). In their review of research regarding mental health of Asian Americans, they found that the prevalence rates of depression, somatization, and posttraumatic stress disorder (PTSD) among Asian Americans are at least as high as those for White Americans, and, in many cases, higher rates. More importantly, they went on to observe that stressors associated with the process and experiences of immigration make recent immigrants primary candidates for developing anxiety symptoms. According to Lee, et al. (2001), the refugee migrations of the 1970s and 1980s, in which Asian immigrants and refugees were exposed to life-threatening, traumatic events, have been found to produce the higher rates of PTSD, depression, and anxiety among these sub-groups. Hence there are particular subgroups of Asian Americans that have experienced higher levels of stress and therefore are at considerable higher risk for developing stress related mental health problems.

But what of occupational stress among Asian Americans? Unfortunately, there are only a handful of relevant articles in the psychological literature. Owing to this dearth in the literature, there is the accompanying lack of theoretical models and theories with

Frederick T. L. Leong and Dwight Tolliver, University of Tennessee at Knoxville respect to the experience and impact of occupational stress among Asian Americans in the workplace. For this chapter, we propose to use the theoretical model of occupational stress developed by Osipow and Spokane (1987) to guide our literature review. We hope that this review will encourage other investigators to begin examining occupational stress among Asian Americans using this model and establishing linkages between the various factors reviewed in this chapter.

2. OSIPOW & SPOKANE'S MODEL OF OCCUPATIONAL STRESS

2.1. Stress, Strain, & Coping

This section will be devoted to an overview of the occupational stress model proposed by Osipow and Spokane in 1987 to serve as the foundation for our review. The original model and measurement was released in 1981 and revised in 1983, 1987, and 1998. In order to understand the conceptual model more thoroughly, the key contributors to this model must be mentioned; however, detailing all of the other models and contributions is beyond the scope of this section. Osipow and Spokane (1987) extended credit to French (1976) and Schuler (1979) for their contributions to the stress-strain relationship on individuals in the work environment. They also recognized Lazarus, Averill, and Opton (1981) and Roskies and Lazarus (1980) for their work on coping skills and for their contribution to the perception of stress by an individual in the workplace. In Osipow (1991), credit was also extended to Hans Selye (1976) for his idea that responses to stress may be undesirable even though all stress is not necessarily undesirable. These models, ideas, and contributions converged to form a model based on the dynamic relationship between stress, strain, and coping on individuals in the work environment.

The conceptual model developed by Osipow and Spokane (1987) contains the following three overarching domains: perceived occupational stress, experienced personal strain, and coping resources. The model viewed these domains as separate but related. In Osipow (1991), an explanation is given to elucidate the meaning of separate but related. In this explanation, the model proposes a system in which the work environment assigns roles to individuals that potentially create the perception of stress, individuals then use their resources to resolve or cope with these stresses, and the success of these methods in combination with the intensity of the stress as well as a number of personal variables interact to produce a level of strain. In other words, the stress-strain relationship is mediated by coping resources. The conceptual model was subsequently followed by a way to measure the three overarching domains.

2.2. Occupational Stress Inventory

The measurement for Osipow and Spokane's (1987) conceptual model serves as a natural and logical extension of their model. The Occupational Stress Inventory (OSI) is this instrument, which comprises the Occupational Roles Questionnaire (ORQ), Personal Strain Questionnaire (PSQ), and Personal Resources Questionnaire (PRQ). Osipow (1987) delineated six stress-inducing work roles (role overload, role insufficiency, role ambiguity, role boundary, responsibility, and physical environment) that result in four sets of strains (psychological, physical, interpersonal, and vocational), which are mediated by four sets of coping behaviors/resources (self-care behavior, social support systems, cognitive skills, and recreational activities). The entire assessment consists of 140 questions with 60 questions relating to ORQ and 40 each to measure PSQ and PRQ.

A review from Dorn (1991) reveals a desire for the clinical relatedness of the OSI with respects to direct counseling interventions. Dorn (1991) posed four questions relating to the OSI being used in a predictive manner, the amount of time that coping resources can curtail the effects of the stress and strain, the differences within organizations that affect individual scores, and the integration of the OSI into an assessment package. In Osipow (1991), we find responses to these queries. In these responses, Osipow (1991) suggests that variables such as employee turnover may be more effectively measured by job satisfaction and ability instruments; however, the OSI is continuing to evolve and variables such as employee turnover and issues with the adjustment to work are being studied. In the validation section, we present a study that attempted to look at the topic of employee turnover. In regards to the coping resources staving off the effects of stress and strain, Osipow (1991) argues that social support appears durable but, given the complex nature of social support, more research may need to be completed to understand the long-term effects of this personal resource.

With respects to Dorn's (1991) final two queries, one of the more intriguing aspects of Osipow and Spokane's (1987) conceptual model is that it was intended to be generic and to apply across occupational field and levels (Osipow, 1991; Spokane & Ferrara, 2001). Even though the conceptual model has to bear some universal qualities, it certainly does not mean that all occupations, organizations, and individuals within an organization are the same. Furthermore, the organization becomes the population when the OSI is administered in a particular organization. The meaning of the OSI for one organization engaged in the service of crisis counseling where the professionals work primarily with suicidal clients is different from an organization engaged in the business of manufacturing aluminum siding where the workers are primarily working on assembly lines packaging a product. Osipow (1991) states differences in environmental stress "can be inferred by aggregating Occupational Role Questionnaire scores ... across individuals in the organization." (p. 332).

Taking the analysis even further, there are many different roles within an organization that would need to be analyzed and treated differently. For example, a payroll supervisor may need to be treated differently in regards to OSI scores than a traveling salesperson within that same organization. There are certainly some universal qualities to stress, coping, and strain; however, there are also role specific qualities to the dynamic nature of the stress-strain-coping interaction. Considerations would also need to be made for the values, beliefs, and structure of the organization. Organizations operate and function differently, and, ultimately, any organization is comprised of individuals who bring their unique personalities, values, and beliefs into the organization. Osipow (1991) suggests that the utilization of the OSI by counselors working with an organization would vary by counselor while interacting with different organizations.

As we link acculturation with occupational behavior among Asian Americans later in this chapter, we find possible support for the dynamic role that different organizations play in the outcomes of stress within a cultural context. Therefore, the proactive nature of how organizations view employees and the process by which a particular organization attempts to utilize the OSI serves an important role. By analyzing the different departments, different ethnic groups, different levels of work roles, and different individuals at the organizational level, these organizations would have the ability to respond to inherent issues within the organization and be more informed about locating a good person-environment fit among job applicants.

2.3. Validation of the OSI & Empirical Research

A complete and thorough analysis of the validation of the scales is beyond the scope of this contribution. Instead a summary of the phases of validation and two recent studies that utilized the OSI are presented. In Spokane and Ferrara (2001), four distinct but overlapping phases of validation were discussed. *Initial psychometric validation* includes an examination of the internal consistency, item-scale inter-correlations, and test-retest reliability. *Model confirmation* includes confirmatory factor analyses and tests of the OSI model examining relationships between stress, strain, and coping as predicted by the model. *Construct validation* refers to studies of the relationship of the OSI scales and subscales to other measures and constructs in order to establish a nomological net of their meaning. This included an examination of gender differences as well as replications across occupational samples for confirmation of the generic nature of the scales. *Utility of functional validation* refers to including studies of the effects of interventions employing the OSI, and the use of the OSI as an outcome measure in other practical applications.

Layne, Hohenshil, and Singh (2004) studied the stress-strain-coping model in relation to the turnover intentions of rehabilitation counselors. The study used the OSI-R and an individual data form, which gathered information on age, gender, ethnicity, certification status, years in the profession, practice setting, hours worked, and number of clients on caseload. The study also adapted a turnover intention model into a four-question turnover intention scale that was added to the individual data form. The participants indicated that they were full-time practicing rehabilitation counselors and the total number of subjects tested totaled 174.

Layne et al. (2004) found that in this study, stress has a positive, direct effect on turnover intentions. The study also found that coping has a significantly direct effect on strain, stress has a direct effect on strain and coping, and age, experience, and number of clients on caseload did not affect turnover intentions. However, the number of clients on a caseload did affect coping resources. The study hypothesized that coping and strain would have a statistically significant effect on turnover intentions, as the study cited has been found in other studies, but this was not found in this study. For our purposes, the OSI displayed validity, model confirmation in particular, in testing the stress-strain-coping interaction. It also led us to discovering more about Dorn's (1991) review, which posed the question about how the OSI can be used in a predictive manner.

The next study was selected for review because it displays another dynamic relationship of Osipow and Spokane's (1987) stress-strain-coping model. Promecene and Monga (2003) studied occupational stress among Obstetricans/Gynecologists. The participants were 69 obstetricians/gynecologists residing in Houston, Texas. The OSI was the only instrument used in this study. Promecene and Monga (2003) found that 32% of the participants scored high in at least one scale of the ORQ and 32% scored moderately high in at least two of the ORQ scales. Role responsibility showed the highest stress scores. The interesting part of this study is that, given these relatively high perceived stress scores, psychological strain was reported as low. Only 7% scored high on at least one scale of the PSQ and 13% scored moderately high in two of the PSQ scales.

Therefore, if Osipow and Spokane's (1987) model measures what it purports to measure then the coping resources must be reported as high in order to mediate the stress-strain relationship. This is exactly what the study found. The study found 9% of the participants reported low levels of coping on at least one scale of the PRQ and 22% scored moderately low in two of the scales. The relatively high, perceived stress of the participants in this profession was offset by higher levels of personal resources, which led to lower levels of reported psychological strain.

2.4. Relevance of the Osipow and Spokane's Model for Asian Americans?

Our focus is on the vocational behaviors of Asian Americans. How do Asian Americans fit into this model? The research on occupation stress in relation to ethnic minorities in the United States is lacking depth and some understanding. The integration of Osipow and Spokane's (1987) model with Asian Americans borrows largely from the convergence of universal, cultural, and individual elements along with the dynamic nature of the stress-strain-coping interaction. It is our goal to garner these resources in order to accommodate the unique worldviews of Asian Americans along with striving to find a voice for Asian Americans in the workplace. Before attempting an integration of the Asian American stress literature into the Osipow and Spokane model, it would be useful to first review the general stress literature among Asian Americans.

3. STRESS AMONG ASIAN AMERICANS

As pointed out by Lee, Lei, & Sue, (2001), given that a significant portion of Asian Americans are recent immigrants and refugees, a significant amount of the mental health problems experienced by this population are likely to be related to their immigrant and refugee status and subsequent adjustment in this country. Therefore, an understanding of the nature and experience of the stress among Asian Americans must take into account their acculturation process and the associated acculturative stress. Similarly, a complete understanding of stress among Asian Americans also requires a review of racism-related stress. While we may not have the consistent empirical data yet, it would be logical to assume that these and other stress factors for Asian Americans will also impact them in their work place and serve as sources of occupational stress as outlined in the Osipow and Spokane model (1987).

3.1. Acculturation Process

Our discussion on the acculturation process is limited and generic due to the scope of our topic. There are many advances, both quantitatively and qualitatively, on the topic of acculturation. This discussion is relegated to an overview of an acculturation model, a popular procedure that attempts to measure acculturation, acculturative stress, bicultural stress, and linking the acculturation process to occupational stress among Asian Americans.

Berry's (1980) model of acculturation outlines the choice or acculturative strategy that takes place during a cross-cultural encounter. Berry's (1980) model is multidimensional in that individuals of the non-dominant culture have to decide the extent to which they will value and maintain their traditional culture and the extent to which they will embrace the host culture. The model can consequently be viewed as a 2×2 matrix that examines the extent to which ethnic minorities maintain their traditional culture and/or the extent to which they embrace the host culture. These two questions, hypothetically, lead to four different identities. If individuals maintain their traditional culture as well as embracing the host culture, Berry (1980) labels them as integrationists. If individuals maintain their traditional culture but reject the values and beliefs of the host country, Berry calls them separationists. The next group would be the individuals who give up their Asian culture but who strongly adhere to the American culture. Asian Americans favoring this acculturative strategy would be called assimilationists. The final group would be Asian Americans who reject both cultures. According to Berry (1980), they would be considered marginalists.

3.2. Measuring Acculturation

The Suinn-Lew Asian Self-Identity Acculturation Scale (SL-ASIA; Suinn, Ahuna, & Khoo, 1992) is the most widely used measurement of acculturation among Asian Americans. The instrument comprises 21 multiple-choice questions, which assesses language use, ethnic identity, personal preferences, and friendships (Zane & Mak, 2003). According to Leong (2001), the SL-ASIA has served as the operationalization of Sue and Sue's (1971) ethnic identity model and Berry's (1980) acculturation model. Leong (2001) also mentions that the SL-ASIA is not an ideal operationalization of Berry's model because it does not measure marginalist individuals and consists of linear rather than orthogonal conception of the acculturation process; however, despite the problems (Ponterotto, Baluch, & Carielle, 1998; Suinn et al., 1992), the SL-ASIA has a supporting body of literature regarding its psychometric properties.

3.3. Acculturative Stress

Roysircar and Maestas (2002) define acculturative stress as "a specific kind of stress directly related to the process of acculturation and can be distinguished from general life stress and hassles". This has been reported to involve the acculturation adaptation process of first generation immigrants. Acculturative stress may be mediated by the nature of the migration (e.g., forced vs. voluntary), the receptiveness of the host society, and the degree of similarity between the traditional culture and the host culture (Berry, 1997; Berry & Annis, 1974, Berry & Kim, 1988; Berry, Kim, Minde, & Mok, 1987).

This is an extremely dynamic process because the interactions of the host culture with the non-dominant culture have to be evaluated on different levels, which can occur at the individual, group, institution, national, or universal levels (Leong & Tang, 2002; Leong, 1996; Berry, 2003). As our discussion moves towards a cultural accommodation approach with respects to Asian Americans in the workplace, the importance of this concept will hopefully emerge with greater emphasis.

Specific stressors that have been identified for first generation immigrants include learning a new language, redefining role expectations (e.g., gender, work), rebuilding social networks, and integrating the values and norms of the host society (Padilla, Wagatsuma, & Lindholm, 1985; Nicholson, 1997). Padilla et al.'s (1985) study of first generation, second generation, and third/later generation Japanese Americans attending college found that first generation Japanese Americans experienced greater stress and lower self-esteem. Padilla et al. (1985) intimated that this new environment might lead to stress, which may be manifested by psychological discomfort, poor self-concept, helplessness, and a feeling of loss.

It was also mentioned earlier that the nature of the migration might affect acculturative stress. Nicholson (1997) and Westermeyer, Neider, and Vang (1984) studied Southeast Asian refugees who, for some, were forced to leave their homelands against their will and who either witnessed or were victims of politically provoked torture and trauma. The studies showed persistent mental health concerns that resulted from a combination of pre- and post-emigration stressors. This study displays a more enhanced view of acculturative stress. This group of individuals has a greater obstacle to overcome and the long-term psychological distress implicated in these studies appears to support this theory.

3.4. Bicultural Stress

Biculturalism (Roysircar & Maestas, 2002) refers to ethnic minorities' experience of inheriting two different cultural traditions. The resulting stress can be viewed as the battle to mediate or negotiate between two contrasting value systems. The stress is created by the conflicts that arise out of their bicultural socialization (De Anda, 1984). Roysircar and Maestas (2002) presented an integrative model of acculturation and ethnic identity that shows their multidirectional interfaces with mediating variables, stress, and coping strategies. The bicultural stressors identified in the model were cultural alienation, cultural confusion, cultural conflict, and bicultural conflict while mediating variables, such as generational status, characteristics of the ethnic group, physical appearance, and conflicts with parents over values, behaviors, and family roles were identified.

Bicultural stress has been differentiated from acculturative stress empirically by studying first generation Asian Americans with second/third generation Asian Americans. Padilla et al. (1985) found that second/third generation students reported less stress and higher self-esteem than first generation Asian Americans; however, second generation students reported lower self-esteem when compared with third generation students. Biculturalism refers to second and later generation Asian Americans in most of the literature yet differences are noticed when generational status is dissected even further. The assumption is that bicultural stress lessens over generations, or, at a minimum, serves as a mediating variable with regards to stress. While second generation individuals negotiate between their bicultural socialization, it appears that their struggle creates a less distressed, more integrated effect on their children with respects to the two cultural traditions. Padilla et al. (1985) suggests that second generation Asian Americans "may be in transition from traditional values held by the parents to those held by third/later generation individuals." (p. 304).

3.5. Linking Acculturation to Vocational Behavior

There is a dearth of research linking acculturation to vocational behavior with respects to Asian Americans. In Leong and Chou (1994), we found explicitly stated hypotheses that attempts to add to our understanding of the vocational psychology of Asian Americans. These hypotheses were formed in order to be tested in future research. The purpose of this section is to discuss the integrated model discussed by Leong and Chou (1994) and to present a test of that model in subsequent research.

Leong and Chou (1994) began their analysis by linking career development with acculturation. Leong and Tata (1990) examined the relation between level of acculturation and work values among Chinese American fifth and sixth graders. The students ranked money and task satisfaction as their most important values while object orientation (making and handling things) and solitude (not working closely with others) were ranked as their least important work values. Also, students who were more highly acculturated valued self-realization more than those who were less acculturated. Leong and Chou (1994) interpreted these findings as showing cultural differences between individualism (White American) and collectivism (Asian). Leong and Tata (1990) concluded that "persons from individualistic cultures are therefore more likely to view occupational choice as a personal matter and an opportunity for self-expression and self-actualization (i.e., self-realization), whereas those from collectivistic cultures may view the same choice in the context of potential contributions and obligations to the group" (p. 211).

Leong and Chou (1994) presented an integrated model of racial and ethnic identity, which borrows from acculturation models, and ethnic identity models. For our purposes, these models converge to give a picture of acculturation that looks similar to Berry's (1980) model. Leong and Chou (1994) proceeded to make the argument that the status of Asian Americans in the acculturation process serves as moderators with the experiencing of the American opportunity structure and career development. This has also been noted previously in our discussion on acculturative and bicultural stress with regards to overall mental health functioning of Asian Americans.

Leong and Chou (1994) included a discussion on each of the following issues relevant to the career behavior and/or development of Asian Americans in the workplace: occupational segregation and stereotyping, occupational discrimination, work attitudes and occupational choice/interest, career maturity and occupational aspirations/expectations, and occupational prestige and mobility. Each topic is explored in depth while making assertions that connect vocational behaviors with acculturation. For example, Leong and Chou (1994) discussed occupational mobility in terms of opportunities being more difficult for ethnic minorities. They then proposed that assimilationists and integrationists would find it easier to move upwardly as compared to separationists, and they wondered whether assimilationists would be at more of an advantage as compared to integrationists.

In Leong (2001), we find a test of these hypotheses and formulations. The hypothesis that Asian Americans with lower levels of acculturation would experience higher levels of occupational stress and lower levels of job satisfaction was tested. The participants were 39 Asian Americans at two major companies who attended career development workshops. One of the companies was a high-tech government, engineering contractor with 24 of the participants. The second company was a Fortune 500 household product company with 15 participants.

The participants completed the SL-ASIA, the OSI, Brayfield and Rothe's (1951) Job Satisfaction Inventory (JSI), and Super, Thompson, and Lindeman's (1988) Adult Career Concerns Inventory (ACCI). The results indicated that, for both companies, high acculturation level (assimilationist or integrationist identity) was positively correlated with job satisfaction. Low acculturation levels (separationist identity) were associated with higher levels of occupational stress for the Fortune 500 company but not for the engineering company. High acculturation identities in the engineering firm were positively correlated with two measures of stressors, role ambiguity and responsibility, and two out of four measures of strain, psychological and physical. In the Fortune 500 company, low acculturation identities experienced higher levels of role insufficiency (stressor), and psychological, interpersonal, and physical strains.

The findings in study 1 generally support Leong and Chou's (1994) hypothesized relationship between acculturation and occupational stress and job satisfaction. Higher levels of acculturation were positively correlated with job satisfaction; however, the relationship between acculturation and occupational stress varied across the two companies. Leong (2001) hypothesized that the type of stressors and strains experienced seemed to interact with the type of organizations in which the participants worked.

In study 2, the participants were from the same Fortune 500 company; however, they were from a different division. There were 17 Asian Americans in this study. The SL-ASIA and OSI were used in this study as well as supervisor performance ratings for each participant. High acculturation identities among Asian American were significantly, positively correlated with receiving higher performance ratings. These findings supported Leong and Chou's (1994) hypothesis that acculturation seems to be related to occupational stereotyping and discrimination as evidenced by the perception that highly acculturated Asian American workers are better workers.

3.6. Racism-Related Stress

Racism is characterized by the subordination of a racial/ethnic group with relatively little social power by a group with more power (Liang, Li, & Kim; 2004). Racism manifests itself on various levels, such as discriminatory laws, race hate groups, racial stereotyping, and racial discrimination (Liang, Li, & Kim; 2004). Asian Americans have been subjected to racism; however, there is a dearth of empirical studies to validate the effects of racism with respect to them. The strains of racism-related stress have been studied primarily with African Americans. These studies have indicated an inverse relationship between stress and life satisfaction and self-esteem as well as a positive relationship between racism and physiological stress (Liang, Li, & Kim; 2004).

Liang, Li, and Kim (2004) attempted to develop a measure of racism-related stress for Asian-Americans. Liang, Li, & Kim (2004) noted that there are measurements for racism-related stress for African Americans and Asian American Vietnam Veterans but no measurements are geared primarily for the racism-related stress faced by the average Asian American in our society. For example, Utsey, Chae, Brown, and Kelly (2002) studied racism-related stress among African Americans, Asian Americans, and Latino Americans by using a measurement that was designed specifically for African Americans in race-related situations. The study undoubtedly found that African Americans experienced higher levels of race-related stress when compared with Asian Americans and Latino

Americans. However, this finding is potentially limited with respects to Asian Americans and Latino Americans. Therefore, the Asian American Racism-Related Stress Inventory (AARRSI) was developed to solicit future studies on the effects, prevalence, and magnitude of racism-related on, specifically, the Asian American community.

Liang, Li, and Kim (2004) were successful in developing a measurement that displayed concurrent and discriminant validity. The measurement comprises a three-factor structure, which includes the prevalence of racism against Asian Americans throughout U.S. history (Socio-Historical Racism), the stereotypes about Asian Americans being perpetuated by our society (General Racism), and the view by other Americans that Asian Americans are perpetual foreigners (Perpetual Foreigner Racism). The study was not successful in finding a link between the AARRSI and some other measurements that attempt to measure general life stressors. For example, the AARRSI was not correlated with a measurement designed to assess minority college student status stress.

Liang, Li, and Kim (2004) speculated that racism-related stress is different from general life stress in that it may be more difficult to recognize, label, and eliminate. The hypothesis is that Asian Americans are considered honorary Whites and non Whites at the same time, which may enhance and account for the barrier of detecting racism-related stress. More research is needed in this area to help explain the unique aspects of racism-related stress as well as the effects of racism and the personal resources needed to stave off the deleterious effects of racism. However, the establishment of the AARRSI is a pleasant initial step in this process.

While we do not have the space to provide an in-depth analysis of the topic, a clear example of the racism-related stress would be that of the internment related stress experienced by the Japanese Americans during the second World War. Nagata (1990), in her study investigating the cross-generational impact of the World War II American internment of Japanese-Americans on the children of those who were incarcerated, found that little communication had occurred between the Sansei and their parents about the internment. More importantly, she found that Sansei participants whose parents had been interned reported being less secure about their rights in the US, having a greater preference for affiliation with other Japanese-Americans, and more strongly favoring monetary redress for those who were interned than Sansei whose parents had not been interned.

4. VARIOUS FORMS OF STRAINS FROM STRESS

In the Osipow and Spokane model of occupational stress (1987), stressors can lead to four different types of strains, including psychological strains, physical health strains, vocational strains, and interpersonal strains. For our present purposes, we will focus only on psychological strains for Asian Americans and its various manifestations.

Kinzie's (2001) review of the literature for Southeast Asian refugees provides an excellent example of the types of strains experienced by many Asian refugees and immigrants in general. Given the differences in language, culture, and expectations of treatment as well as their experience of massive psychological trauma, the disruption of an individual's life and sense of security, many Asian immigrants and refugees may indeed be suffering the symptoms of PTSD or the less severe version of post traumatic stress syndrome in their workplaces.

Nicholson's (1997) study of stressors among Southeast Asian refugees is an example of the pervasiveness of the strains created by migration-related stress. Using path analysis, Nicholson (1997) examined the direct and indirect effects of a series of pre-emigration and post-emigration factors on mental health status among 447 Southeast Asian refugees. Relying on bicultural interviewers who administered a cross-sectional survey to a stratified sample of community residents (Cambodian, Vietnamese, Laotian, and Hmong), Nicholson found that 40% of subjects suffered from depression, 35% from anxiety, and 14% from posttraumatic stress disorder (PTSD). One pre-emigration factor, experienced trauma, and two post-emigration factors, degree of current stress and perceived health, directly affected all mental health outcomes. Furthermore, it was found that current stress, which measured the degree of stress created by acculturative tasks such as learning a new language, seeking employment, rebuilding social supports, and redefining roles, was the strongest overall predictor of mental health.

Related to PTSD, some research has found that the experience of this disorder appears to be similar across ethnic groups. For example, Sack, Seeley, and Clarke (1997) sought to determine whether the factor structure of the posttraumatic stress disorder (PTSD) syndrome in Cambodian refugee youth resembles earlier reported factor studies in Caucasian samples. Using a sample of 194 Khmer refugees (aged 13-25 yrs) who reported prior significant trauma and who were administered the PTSD module of the Diagnostic Interview for Children and Adolescents, they found the following four factors: arousal, avoidance, intrusion, and numbing. A confirmatory factor analysis yielded a good fit for the 4-factor solution and the factor solution resembled those found in earlier studies on traumatized Caucasian and African-American adults. The investigators concluded that "these results lend credibility to the veracity of this diagnosis with refugee samples".

One common manifestation of psychological strain created by stressors is the development of substance abuse. In a chapter on the relationships between acculturation, psychological distress, and alcohol use, Gong, Takeuchi, Agbayani Siewert, & Tacata, (2003) examined how acculturation, ethnic identity, and religiosity may influence psychological distress (PD) and alcohol dependence (AD) among Filipino American immigrants. Using data collected from the Filipino American Epidemiological Study (1,796 respondents aged 18-65 yrs), they found that the developmental context of immigration and the time spent in the US had strong implications for lowering indicators of ethnic identity. AD was inversely affected by age during immigration. When controlling for other demographic and acculturation variables, analyses revealed that ethnic identity was an especially significant variable in predicting PD. Other findings indicated that ethnic identity and religiosity partially mediated the effect of age during immigration on AD. Finally, the results also suggested that age during immigration has direct and indirect effects on AD. Thus it appears that ethnic identity and religiosity are significant factors in reducing the risk of AD.

In another article related to substance misuse, Erickson D'Avanzo, (1997) reviewed studies on Southeast Asians (SAs) who migrated to the US during 1975-1977 and 1978-1980. According to Erickson D'Avanzo, (1997), many of these refugees were ill-prepared for life in the US and found the transition to be difficult and stressful. The combined stressors that these refugee groups had to face put them at high risk for substance misuse. However, it was noted that there is sparse and conflicting information relative to the use of substances by these groups due to the absence of national prevalence data. There were also differences in substance use (mainly alcohol) among more acculturated versus less acculturated Asian Pacifics. For example, prevalence rates for alcohol consumption by Japanese and Korean men appear similar to their American counterparts. On the other hand, the use of psychoactive drugs, alcohol, and opium for either relief of physical pain or psychological problems occurs in the SA community. Finally, Erickson D'Avanzo, (1997) concluded that there is a critical shortage of culturally-appropriate treatment and intervention programs for SAs who misuse drugs.

Another common manifestation of psychological strain is suicide. Based on a qualitative approach with a group of Asian American female college students, Chung (2003) examined the cultural nuances underlying the emotional distresses and motivation of the suicidal behavior of this particular group. It was found that several Asian cultural values and norms may have accentuated their distress and contributed to the suicidal potential. The culturally-relevant issues, as well as implications for assessment and interventions with these Asian American female students who sought treatment were highlighted in the article.

In another study examining the relationship between acculturation and suicide among the Chinese in Taiwan, Lee, Chang, and Cheng, (2002) conducted psychological autopsy interviews for consecutive suicides from two native Taiwanese groups. The Taiwan Aboriginal Acculturation Scale was used to measure the extent of acculturation. They found that a lower degree of social assimilation was significantly associated with a higher risk of suicide in the Atayal and the male groups. In multivariable regression analysis, a significant effect of low social assimilation on the risk of suicide was found in Atayal and in men, even after controlling for the effects of depressive episode and emotionally unstable personality disorder. According to the investigators, it appears that for the native Taiwanese, the stress from rapid acculturation into the main Chinese society is crucial to their mental health. Thus, there seems to be a link between acculturative stress, psychological distress, and suicide.

The studies reviewed in this section demonstrates that there are both culture-general and culture-specific stressors for Asians and Asian Americans. These stressors in turn can create psychological strains and the various manifestations of those strains such as PTSD, substance abuse, and suicide. While the studies are suggestive, more rigorous research is clearly needed to establish the linkages more firmly and conclusive. Furthermore, studies are needed to determine how these stressors and strains may actually manifest themselves in the workplace for Asian Americans.

5. COPING WITH STRESS AMONG ASIAN AMERICANS

The conceptual model by Osipow and Spokane (1987) is based on the dynamic relationship between stress, strain, and coping. The OSI measures the personal resources of an individual. In theory and through validation, the coping resources have served as mediators to the effects of stress, known as strain. Osipow and Spokane (1987) measure these personal resources through four categories, which are as follows: recreation, self-care, social supports, and rational/cognitive.

Recreation refers to the extent to which individuals take advantage of their leisure time by engaging in activities that they enjoy or find relaxing (Osipow & Spokane, 1987). An individual who scores high in this category would be reporting a clear boundary between his or her personal and professional lives as well as being actively engaged in many activities outside of work. A prerequisite for being engaged in activities outside of work entails having these hobbies and community activities at their disposal. Self-care refers to an individual's exercise, sleep, eating, and relaxation behaviors (Osipow & Spokane, 1987). A high score in this category would most likely demonstrate a physically healthy individual who takes pride in his or her physical health.

Social supports refer to the types of personal relationships an individual has outside of work. The OSI (1987) does not ask about the number of friends. The inventory is more concerned about the emotional connection of, at least, one personal relationship. For example, is that person sympathetic to work concerns and emotionally available to you? Rational/cognitive refers to being problem-focused with problems, and having a systematic approach to working through problems (Osipow & Spokane, 1987). This category also comprises other important factors, such as individuals being flexible with their work schedule, establishing and following priorities, and the ability to leave work at work.

5.1. Other Measurements

The rationale for this discussion is due to the lack of published research that compares an Asian American population with Caucasian Americans with respects to the personal resources scale of the OSI. There has been, however, research that uses other coping instruments, which directly compares Asian Americans with Caucasian Americans. These other measurements will be presented in the hopes of synthesizing their findings with the OSI. This should not be viewed as a limitation of the OSI since the OSI's populations are organizations. Most research on differences in stress, strain, and coping among ethnic minorities is completed at the college student population. In Chang (2001), we find a summary of these different instruments and a comparison of Asian Americans and Caucasian Americans with respects to each instrument.

5.2. Coping Strategies Inventory

The first instrument is the Coping Strategies Inventory (CSI; Tobin, Holroyd, Reynolds, & Wigal, 1989). The CSI measures eight coping strategies, which are as follows: problem solving, cognitive restructuring, express emotions, social support, problem avoidance, wishful thinking, self-criticism, and social withdrawal. Chang (2001) summarized a study of 45 Asian Americans and 49 Caucasian Americans attending a large public university in the northeast. Chang (2001) found that Asian Americans differed from Caucasian Americans on two of the scales. Asian Americans utilized problem avoidance and social withdrawal coping strategies more often than Caucasian Americans, as measured by comparing the mean scores of the two groups. This was statistically significant at .01 and .001, respectively.

The other scales showed no significant difference among means between the two groups. Therefore, the findings indicate that there are two scales that differ; however, the study also looked at outcomes. Problem avoidance did not correlate to lower levels of life satisfaction or depressive symptoms, and social withdrawal correlated with greater depressive symptoms for Asian Americans.

In comparison with the PRQ of the OSI, it would appear that problem solving, cognitive restructuring, expressing emotions, and social support would compare favorably with the rational/cognitive and social support scales of the PRQ. Obviously, research would need to validate this assumption. The PRQ adds the recreation and self-care measures to the analysis. The PRQ seems more comprehensive than looking just at different coping strategies because it looks into the structure of an individual's world along with personal strategies of coping. It essentially asks the question, "Is your life structured in a manner that allows or gives you the opportunity to cope with stress, and, if so, are your individual responses to perceived stress rationale and healthy"?

5.3. Constructive Thinking Inventory

The second instrument is the Constructive Thinking Inventory (CTI; Epstein & Meier, 1989). The CTI measures seven coping styles, which are as follows: global constructive thinking, emotional coping, behavioral coping, superstitious coping, categorical thinking, esoteric thinking, and naïve optimism. Chang (2001) summarized a study of 64 Asian Americans and 175 Caucasian Americans attending a large public university in the northeast. The findings indicated that Asian Americans differed significantly on all coping styles except for behavioral coping. Asian Americans reported lower global constructive thinking, emotional coping, and greater superstitious thinking, categorical thinking, esoteric thinking, and naïve optimism when means were compared to Caucasian Americans.

In this study, higher scores on the global constructive thinking, emotional coping, and behavioral coping led to greater life satisfaction and lower depressive symptoms for both groups (Chang, 2001). The significantly lower scores for Asian Americans on the global thinking and emotional coping styles did predict less life satisfaction and more depressive symptoms; however, the model predicts that the four other coping styles would also predict these outcomes (superstitions, categorical thinking, esoteric thinking, and naïve optimism). The significantly lower scores from the Asian Americans in these categories did not predict less life satisfaction or greater depressive symptoms.

The PRQ of the OSI would probably not correlate well with this model, especially the final four categories. The CTI does not appear to possess much cultural validity but, it is still interesting to observe the different coping styles of Asian Americans as compared to Caucasian Americans. Asian Americans have attributed successful coping to luck and have demonstrated more internal locus-of-control (acceptance as a coping style) (Kawanishi, 1995) when faced with stress; however, this does not necessarily equate to poorer psychological and/or physical strains.

5.4. The Social Problem Solving Inventory-Revised

The third and final instrument is the Social Problem Solving Inventory-Revised (SPSI-R; D'Zurilla, Nezu, Maydeu-Olivares, 2002). The SPSI-R measures five problem solving styles, which are as follows: positive problem orientation, negative problem orientation, rational problem solving style, impulsivity/carelessness style, and avoidance style. Chang (2001) indicates that the study only noted a significant difference with the impulsivity/carelessness Style. Asian Americans reported the use of this problem solving style to a greater degree as compared with Caucasian Americans. The model predicted that this problem solving style would lead to less life satisfaction and more depressive symptoms but this was not supported in the study.

5.5. Primary/Secondary Control and Self-Construal

Lam and Zane (2004) studied ethnic differences in coping with interpersonal stressors. The participants were 79 Asian Americans and 79 White Americans from a Southern California University. The instruments included a measure to assess primary and secondary control, and a measure to assess self-construal. The study found that Asian Americans oriented themselves more towards secondary control while White Americans were more oriented to primary control. However, the study also differentiated between the behaviors of and goals of coping styles across ethnicity. The results indicated that both Asian and White Americans preferred primary control coping goals. Some other important findings in the study were that an independent self-construal fully accounted for the White-Asian ethnic difference in primary control and an interdependent self-construal only partially accounted for the difference for the White-Asian ethnic difference in secondary control.

Lam and Zane (2004) speculated that other important factors might be contributing to this partial mediating effect in regards to ethnic difference in secondary control among the Asian American participants. One proposed factor was the minority status of Asian Americans. The use of secondary control seems adaptive in this sense since the premise behind primary control entails changing an aspect of the environment. With minority status, the reality of oppression and discrimination may lead to adopting a coping style that leads to a change within the individual not the environment. In other words, Asian Americans may view primary control as unattainable (Lam & Zane, 2004).

5.6. Ethnic Identity as a Protective Factor

Lee (2003) conducted a study that examined the resilience of Asian American college students with respects to the role of ethnic identity and other-group orientation. Study 1 participants were 91 Asian American undergraduate students from a large, public university in Texas. The instruments used were an ethnic identity measure, a racial tension scale, a self-esteem scale, a social connectedness scale, and a sense of community scale. Study 2 participants included 67 Asian American students of Indian descent. For our purposes, the only difference between this study was the use of a perceived personal ethnic discrimination instrument. The studies focus on discrimination as a psychological stressor and the idea of ethnic identity as a protective factor. Discrimination and stress were attended to earlier; therefore, the analysis of this particular study will cover the possible coping behavior/strategy with respects to ethnic identity as a protective factor.

Lee's (2003) rationale for this study arose out of the lack of empirical data on ethnic identity and other-group orientation serving as protective factors in terms of shielding ethnic minorities from the perceived threat of discrimination. The study indicated that ethnic identity and other-group orientation correlated positively with psychological well being. Contrary to the initial hypothesis, however, findings did not indicate that ethnic identity and other-group orientation moderated or mediated the negative psychological effects of minority group discrimination or personal ethnic discrimination. This study is included here because ethnic identity and other-group orientation has been thought of as a coping strategy for Asian Americans. Lee (2003) suggests that other specific coping strategies contribute to the resiliency of Asian Americans when faced with discrimination.

5.7. Coping Strategies and Psychological Strain

Bjorck, Cuthbertson, Thurman, and Lee (2001) conducted a study to assess coping strategies, stress and coping appraisal, and psychological distress among Korean Americans, Filipino Americans, and White Americans. The participants were 86 White Americans, 93 Korean Americans, and 49 Filipino Americans. It should also be noted that 32% of the Asian Americans in this study were born in the United States. The measurements used were an assessment of coping behaviors, a depression index, an anxiety inventory, and a single-item coping efficacy scale. In regards to measuring stress appraisal, the study also asked each participant to write a brief description of his/her most stressful situation experienced in the past week. The participants then rated that situation with respects to degree of threat, challenge, and loss.

The findings indicated that Korean American participants appraised events as greater losses than Caucasian Americans while both Korean and Filipino Americans appraised events as greater challenges than Caucasian Americans (Bjorck et al., 2001). The study also found that Korean and Filipino Americans reported more passive coping behaviors, such as accepting responsibility, religious coping, distancing, and escape-avoidance; however, the Filipino American participants reported more problem-solving coping behaviors than both Caucasian and Korean Americans. The passive coping behaviors were also related to lower scores on the depression index.

Bjorck et al. (2001) speculated that the Eastern values of accepting fate and submitting to authority are important factors in appraising events as losses that one must accept. This worldview is opposed by the Western emphasis on an independent self-construal, which, theoretically, led to the Caucasian participants' likelihood of attempting to change a situation or eliminating the need for a loss appraisal. An interesting finding in the study was that the Asian American participants reported greater use of all of the coping behaviors in comparison with Caucasian Americans. This finding highlights a significant limitation of the study and a call for more research on coping differences among Asian Americans.

5.8. Final Thoughts on Ethnic Differences in Coping

The challenge of discussing ethnic differences in coping is many. Studies have found and indicated several disparate meanings and studies comparing ethnic differences in coping are few. The CTI found significant differences between Asian Americans and Caucasian Americans among all but one of their scales while Bjorck et al. (2001) found that Asian Americans reported greater use of all of the coping behaviors that were involved in their study. Lam and Zane (2004) found that Asian Americans preferred primary control coping behaviors even though the study indicated that they use secondary control. Osipow and Spokane (1987), under the normative data section, noted that data of ethnic background was not available. There are many questions that have arisen in regards to coping behaviors among Asian Americans. As we move toward a cultural accommodation approach to ethnic minorities, a greater understanding of Asian Americans at the group level with respects to coping behaviors will be needed.

6. CONCLUSION

Owing to the dearth of literature, this chapter has been more about how the stress literature on Asian Americans can help us understand and conduct future research on occupational stress than about occupational stress directly. Nevertheless we felt that this is an important and neglected topic that needs attention. In an attempt to stimulate more direct research on this topic we have used the theoretical framework of occupational stress developed by Osipow and Spokane (1987) to guide us in this review. Using the framework, we have examined some of the relevant Asian Americans literature related to stress, strains and coping resources.

REFERENCES

Berry, J. W. (1980). Acculturation as varieties of adaptation. In A. M. Padilla (Ed.), *Acculturation: Theory, models, and some new findings* (pp. 9-25). Boulder, CO: Westview Press.

Berry, J. W. (1997). Immigration, acculturation, and adaptation. *Applied Psychology: An International Review, 46,* 5-34.

Berry, J. W. (2003). Conceptual approaches to acculturation. In K. M. Chun, P. B. Organista, & G. Marin (Eds.), *Acculturation: Advances in theory, measurement, and applied research* (pp. 17-37). Washington, DC: American Psychological Association.

Berry, J. W., & Annis, R. C. (1974). Acculturation stress: The role of ecology, culture, and differentiation. *Journal of Cross-Cultural Psychology, 5,* 382-406.

Berry, J. W., & Kim, U. (1988). Acculturation and mental health. In P. R. Dasen, J. W. Berry, & N. Sartorius (Eds.), *Health and Cross-Cultural Psychology: Towards Application* (pp. 207-236). Newbury Park, CA: Sage.

Berry, J. W., Kim, U., Minde, T., & Mok, D. (1987). Comparative studies of acculturative stress. *International Migration Review, 21,* 491-511.

Bjorck, J. P., Cuthbertson, W., Thurman, J. W., & Lee, Y. S. (2001). Ethnicity, coping, and distress among Korean Americans, Filipino Americans, and Caucasian Americans. *Journal of Social Psychology, 141*(4), 421-442.

Brayfield, A. H., & Rothe, H. F. (1951). An index of job satisfaction. *Journal of Applied Psychology, 35,* 307-311.

Chang, E. C. (2001). A look at the coping strategies and styles of Asian Americans: Similar and different? In C. R. Snyder (Ed.) (2001), *Coping with stress: Effective people and processes.* (pp. 222-239). London: Oxford University Press.

Chung, I. W. (2003). Examining suicidal behavior of Asian American female college students: Implications for practice. *Journal of College Student Psychotherapy, 18*(2), 31-47.

De Anda, D. (1984). Bicultural socialization: Factors affecting the minority experience. *Social Work, 29,* 101-107.

Dorn, F.J. (1991). The Occupational Stress Inventory: A picture worth a thousand words about work. *Journal of Counseling and Development, 70*(2), 328-329.

D'Zurilla, T. J., Nezu, A. M., & Maydeu-Olivares, A. (2004). Social problem solving: Theory and assessment. In T. J. D'Zurilla et-al., & E. C. Chang (Eds.), *Social problem solving: Theory, research, and training* (pp. 11-27). Washington, DC, US: American Psychological Association.

Erickson D'Avanzo, C. (1997). Southeast Asians: Asian-Pacific Americans at risk for substance misuse. *Substance Use and Misuse, 32*(7-8), 829-848.

Epstein, S., & Meier, P. (1989). Constructive thinking: A broad coping variable with specific components. *Journal of Personality and Social Psychology, 57*, 332-350.

French, J. R. P. (1976, September). *Job demands and worker health.* Presented at American Psychological Association Symposium, Washington, DC.

Gong, F., Takeuchi, D. T., Agbayani S. P., & Tacata, L. (2003). Acculturation, psychological distress, and alcohol use: Investigating the effects of ethnic identity and religiosity. In K.M. Chun et al. (Eds.), *Acculturation: Advances in theory, measurement, and applied research* (pp. 189-206). Washington, DC: American Psychological Association.

Kawanishi, Y. (1995). The effects of culture on beliefs about stress and coping: Causal attribution of Anglo-American and Japanese persons. *Journal of Contemporary Psychotherapy, 25*(1), 49-60.

Kinzie, J. (2001). The Southeast Asian refugee: The legacy of severe trauma. In J. Streltzer & W. S. Tseng (Eds.) (2001), *Culture and psychotherapy: A guide to clinical practice* (pp. 173 191). Washington, DC, US: American Psychiatric Publishing, Inc.

Lam, A. G., & Zane, N. W. S. (2004). Ethnic Differences in Coping with Interpersonal Stressors: A Test of Self-Construals as Cultural Mediators. *Journal of Cross Cultural Psychology, 35*(4), 446-459.

Layne, C. M., Hohenshil, T. H., & Singh, K. (2004). The relationship of occupational stress, psychological strain, and coping resources to the turnover intentions of rehabilitation counselors. *Rehabilitation Counseling Bulletin, 48*(1), 19-30.

Lazarus, R. B., Averill, J. R., & Opton, E. M., Jr. (1981). The psychology of coping: Issues of research and assessment. In G. V. Coehlo, D. A. Hamburg, & J. E. Adams (Eds.), *Coping and adaptation* (pp. 249-315). New York: Basic Books.

Lee, C. S., Chang, J. C., & Cheng, A. T. A. (2002). Acculturation and suicide: A case-control psychological autopsy study. *Psychological Medicine, 32*(1), 133-141.

Lee, J., Lei, A., & Sue, S. (2001). The current state of mental health research on Asian Americans. *Journal of Human Behavior in the Social Environment, 3*(3-4), 159-178.

Lee, R. M. (2003). Do ethnic identity and other-group orientation protect against discrimination for Asian Americans? *Journal of Counseling Psychology, 50*(2), 133-141.

Leong, F. T. L. (1996). Toward an integrative model for cross-cultural counseling and psychotherapy. *Applied and Preventive Psychology, 5*, 189-209.

Leong, F. T. L. (2001). The role of acculturation in the career adjustment of Asian American workers: A test of Leong and Chou's (1994) formulations. *Cultural Diversity and Ethnic Minority Psychology, 7*(3), 262-273.

Leong, F. T. L. & Chou E. L. (1994). The role of ethnic identity and acculturation in the vocational behavior of Asian Americans: An integrative review. *Journal of Vocational Behavior, 44*, 155-172.

Leong, F. T. L., & Tang, M. (2002). A cultural accommodation approach to career assessment with Asian Americans. In S. Okazaki, K. S. Kurasaki, & S. Sue (Eds.), *Asian American mental health: Assessment theories and methods* (pp.77 94). New York: Kluwer Academic/Plenum Publishers.

Leong, F. T. L., & Tata, S. P. (1990). Sex and acculturation differences in occupational values among Chinese-American children. *Journal of Counseling Psychology, 37*(2), 208-212.

Liang, C. T. H., Li, L. C., & Kim, B. S. K. (2004). The Asian American Racism-Related Stress Inventory: Development, Factor Analysis, Reliability, and Validity. *Journal of Counseling Psychology, 51*(1), 103-114.

Nagata, D. K. (1990). The Japanese American internment: Exploring the transgenerational consequences of traumatic stress. *Journal of Traumatic Stress, 3*(1), 47-69.

Nicholson, B. L. (1997). The influence of pre-emigration and postemigration stressors on mental health: A study of Southeast Asian refugees. *Social Work Research, 21*(1), 19-31.

Osipow, S. H. (1991). Developing instruments for use in counseling. Journal of Counseling and Development, *70*, 322-326.

Osipow, S. H., & Spokane, A. R. (1981). *Occupational Stress Inventory: Manual-research version.* Odessa, FL.: Psychological Assessment Resources.

Osipow, S. H., & Spokane, A.R. (1987). *Occupational Stress Inventory: Manual-research version.* Odessa, FL.: Psychological Assessment Resources.

Padilla, A. M., Wagatsuma, Y., & Lindholm, K. J. (1985). Acculturation and personality as predictors of stress in Japanese and Japanese-Americans. *Journal of Social Psychology, 125*(3), 295-305.

Ponterotto, J. G., Baluch, S., & Carielli, D. (1998). The Suinn-Lew Asian Self-Identity Acculturation Scale (SL-ASIA): Critique and research recommendations. *Measurement and Evaluation in Counseling and Development, 31*, 109-124.

Promecene, P. A., & Monga, M. (2003). Occupational stress among obstetrician/gynecologists. *Southern Medical Journal, 96*(12), 1187-1189.

Roskies, E., & Lazarus, R. S. (1980). Coping theory and the teaching of coping skills. In P. O. Davidson & S. M. Davidson (Eds.), *Behavioral Medicine: Changing health lifestyles* (pp. 38-69). New York: Bruner Mazel.

Roysircar, G., & Maestas, M. L. (2002). Assessing acculturation and cultural variables. In S. Okazaki, K. S. Kurasaki, et al. (Eds.) (2002), *Asian American mental health: Assessment theories and methods* (pp.77-94). New York, NY, US: Kluwer Academic/Plenum Publishers.

Sack, W. H., Seeley, J. R., & Clarke, G. N. (1997). Does PTSD transcend cultural barriers? A study from the Khmer Adolescent refugee project. *Journal of the American Academy of Child and Adolescent Psychiatry, 36*(1), 49-54.

Schuler, R. S. (1979). *Definitions and conceptualizations of stress in organizations* (Working Paper 79-50). Columbus: Ohio State University, College of Administrative Science.

Selye, H. (1976). *The stress of life* (rev. ed.). New York: McGraw-Hill.

Spokane, A. R. & Ferrara, D. (2001). Samuel H. Osipow's contributions to occupational mental health and the assessment of stress: The Occupational Stress Inventory. In F. T. L. Leong & A. Barak (Eds.), *Contemporary models in vocational behavior: A volume in honor of Samuel H. Osipow* (pp. 79-96). Mahwah, NJ: Erlbaum.

Suinn, R. M., Ahuna, C., & Khoo, G. (1992). The Suinn-Lew Asian Self-Identity Acculturation Scale: Concurrent and factorial validation. *Educational and Psychological Measurement, 52*, 1041-1046.

Sue, S., & Sue, D. W. (1971). Chinese American personality and mental health. *Ameriasia Journal, 1*, 36-49.

Super, D. E., Thompson, A. S., & Lindeman, R. H. (1988). *The Adult Career Concerns Inventory*. Palo Alton, CA: Counseling Psychologist Press.

Tobin, L. D., Holroyd, K. A., Reynolds, R. V., & Wigal, J. K. (1989). The hierarchical factor structure of the coping strategies inventory. *Cognitive Therapy and Research, 13*, 343-361.

Utsey, S. O., Chae, M. H., Brown, C. F., & Kelly, D. (2002). Effect of ethnic group membership on ethnic identity, race-related stress and quality of life. *Cultural Diversity and Ethnic Minority Psychology, 8*(4), 366-377.

Westermeyer, J., Neider, J., & Vang, T. F. (1984). Acculturation and mental health: A study of Hmong refugees at 1.5 and 3.5 year postmigration. *Social Sciences Medicine, 18*, 87-93.

Zane, N., & Mak, W. (2003). Major approaches to the measurement of acculturation among ethnic minority populations: A content analysis and an alternative empirical strategy. In K. M. Chun, P. B. Organista, & G. Marin (Eds.), *Acculturation: Advances in theory, measurement, and applied research* (pp. 39-60). Washington, DC: American Psychological Association.

24

A MULTICULTURAL PERSPECTIVE ON WORK-RELATED STRESS:
Development of a Collective Coping Scale

Dan Zhang and Bonita C. Long

1. INTRODUCTION

With the increase in ethnic diversity in today's workplace, culturally specific influences on work-related stress and coping have recently garnered attention (James, 1994; Marsella, 1994; Chan, 2001; Siu et al., 2002). This diversity is reflected in the influx of skilled Chinese professionals working in countries outside of China (Employment and Immigration Canada, 1990; Mak, 1991; Hwang et al., 2002). Despite this shift in employment patterns, few researchers have examined Chinese professionals' ways of coping with occupational stress–a situation that is partly due to the lack of availability of a culturally sensitive coping measure. Thus, our goal is to describe the initial development of a coping scale that focuses on collective coping strategies reflecting Chinese cultural values.

Results from cross-cultural research indicate that cultural values influence people's perceptions of stress (McCrae, 1984; Ting-Toomey, 1985; Leung, 1988), the appraisal of stress (Chiu and Kosinski, Jr., 1995; Roseman and Dhawan, 1995; Aycan and Berry, 1996), and coping behaviors (Wong et al., 1992; Yue, 1993; Cross, 1995; Scherer et al., 2000). Two cultural dimensions that have been posited as having a strong influence on work behaviors are individualism and collectivism (e.g., Hofstede, 1980; Kagitcibasi, 1987; Triandis, 1995). People who hold individualistic values are more likely to attach importance to individual achievement, whereas people who hold collectivistic values are more likely to find being different from one's in-group distressing. In general, the dominant cultures in the United States, Canada, and Australia are individualistic; in contrast, Chinese, Japanese, and Korean cultures have been recognized as collectivistic (Hofstede, 1980).

Greater ethnic diversity in the workplace highlights the importance of understanding how employees cope with workplace stress in cross-cultural settings. In addition to experiencing work stressors common to all employees (e.g., work overload, lack of control, time pressure), attempts to adapt to a different cultural environment bring additional stressors (Marsella, 1987; Pinderhughes, 1989; Bhagat et al., 1994). Interactions with a

---

Dan Zhang, Kwantlen University College; Bonita C. Long, University of British Columbia

new culture may result in employee distress because of the organization's ambivalence toward differences (James, 1994) and conflicts between cultural values (Aldwin and Greenberger, 1987; Bond, 1988). People from different cultures may view group productivity and personal achievement differently (Kahn and Byosiere, 1991; Marsella et al., 1998). For example, Chinese collectivistic values emphasize loyalty to one's organization–a moral commitment involving all employees (Yang, 1986; Chao, 1990). Thus, for Chinese workers who have strong collectivistic values, loyalty is inspired by conscience, is duty-bound, and constitutes a strong motivation for joint effort and task involvement. Such employees tend to work hard and are unlikely to refuse work assignments even if they are beyond their ability (Chiu and Kosinski, 1995). As a result, distress and frustration may increase due to work overload or because of an inability to do the work (Chiu and Kosinski, 1995).

Overseas Chinese workers may also experience work-related pressures due to expectations of their in-groups (i.e., family, close friends, and immediate community). For example, great emphasis is placed on the anticipated reactions of others in deciding what to do in an encounter to a certain extent, Chinese people who hold strong collectivistic values may fear "losing face" to their in-group when they cannot meet expected standards (Ho, 1986). Lack of English language competency (Aycan and Berry, 1996) and local work experience (Cumming et al., 1989) are also common obstacles faced by overseas Chinese workers. As a consequence, their qualifications may not be fully recognized, especially in certain professions (e.g., counseling, law, teaching) where spoken and written English is required (Mak, 1991). Mastering the English language usually takes a long time. Thus obtaining appropriate work experience may be difficult for overseas workers struggling for professional acceptance.

Although attention has been focused on investigating the conceptual structure of individualism and collectivism (e.g., Singelis, 1994; Triandis, 1995), collective forms of coping have not been systematically studied and remain at a descriptive level (Bond, 1985; Kashima and Triandis, 1986; Yang, 1986; Wong, 1993). To date, the coping measures that have been developed focus predominantly on individual coping efforts and largely ignore collective approaches (e.g., Lazarus and Folkman, 1984).

1.1. Background Theory of Stress and Coping

Lazarus and Folkman's (1984) stress and coping framework is the most frequently applied theoretical approach to psychosocial stress, and has been widely used to investigate variation in responses to workplace stress (e.g., Long et al., 1992; Terry et al., 1996; Portello and Long, 2001), as well as other types of stress. According to Lazarus and Folkman (1984), psychological stress is defined as a relationship between the person and the environment in which demands exceed the person's resources, and hinder his or her well-being. Moreover, coping strategies are "constantly changing cognitions and behavioral efforts to manage specific internal and external demands that are appraised as exceeding the resources of the person" (Lazarus and Folkman, 1984, p. 141). Lazarus and his colleagues identified two coping functions: (a) managing the person/environment relationship that is the source of stress (problem-focused coping), and (b) regulating one's emotional response to stress (emotion-focused coping). However, Tobin et al. (1989) identified two higher order coping factors–engagement coping (active efforts aimed at managing both problem- and emotion-focused aspects of the stressful event) and disengagement coping (thoughts and behaviors that focus attention away from the stressful event), which subsumes both problem- and emotion-focused coping (cf. Kahn, 1990; Long et al., 1992). We expected collective coping to be distinct from engagement and disengagement coping, and to serve a third coping function.

1.2. Collective Coping Strategies

Empirical evidence indicates that, in general, members of individualistic cultures prefer open and active ways of coping with stress, such as direct self-expression and confronting others (e.g., Oettingen et al., 1994). In contrast, members of collectivistic cultures favor indirect approaches that include avoidance, control of internal expectations, and emphasize group cohesion as a means of coping (Bond et al., 1985; Kashima and Triandis, 1986; Yang, 1986).

Cross-cultural research has indicated that interdependence is one of the most significant characteristics of collectivistic cultures, and that maintaining harmony and conforming to group norms are common ways of handling conflicts among individuals (Kashima and Triandis, 1986; Yamaguchi, 1990; Kirkbride et al., 1991).

Within a collectivistic culture there is a greater emphasis on the views, needs, and goals of in-groups, rather than of individuals. The in-group usually defines social norms and duties. Moreover, people have greater readiness to co-operate and to expect assistance from in-group members (Triandis and Marin, 1983; Bond, 1985; Kuo, 2002). Collectivistic values and beliefs are reflected in greater interdependence, with the group as the basic unit for survival. Thus, individuals contribute to group activities, which in turn, reinforce cultural collectivism and reward the individual with a sense of belonging and support (Krause et al., 1989; Singelis and Brown, 1995). For example, in a conflict situation, one should make a great effort to confirm one's personal opinions with the general views of the in-group, and to adjust oneself to fit the group and environmental needs, rather than trying to change others' views or the environment (Ho and Chiu, 1994; Leung, 1996).

Thus, collective coping strategies are construed as activities that function to orient attention to in-group members. Collective coping strategies are expected to be consistent with collectivistic characteristics that emphasize group effort and the use of togetherness as strength (e.g., Kashima and Triandis, 1986; Yang, 1986; Lockett, 1988). Kirkbride et al. (1991) posited that in stressful situations, collectivism has a tendency to locate the importance of the events or issues in relation to an in-group, organization, or even society at large. For example, when conflicts arise, individuals who hold collectivistic values determine whether other members of their group have been or can be involved. If so, the individual would discuss the issue with the in-group and ask for help. At the same time, research also indicates that collectivists are encouraged to take responsibility together, and very often the entire in-group is held responsible for both the positive or negative actions of its individual members, especially in conflict situations (Ho and Chiu, 1994; Han and Park, 1995).

Thus, collective coping strategies focus on the group dynamics of pulling together and rallying behind the individual to provide a solution to the problem. Successful coping may depend not only on an individual's efforts to resolve the stressful event, but also on strengthening relationships as well as drawing on relationships within one's social-cultural in-group. As described by Ho and Chiu (1994) "one's business is also the business of the group; and friends should be concerned with each other's personal matters" (p. 139). There is a popular saying within the Chinese culture, "unity is strength." Thus, co-operative efforts toward achieving collective goals are emphasized more than individual competitiveness (Ho, 1986), and being loyal, making a commitment to collective goals, helping others, and strengthening the unity of in-groups are collectivistic ways of coping with workplace stressors (Tu, 1984).

Of note, Wong (1993) has differentiated between collective coping and social support. He posited that what makes collective coping unique is that the group, such as a family, takes on a family member's problem as their own, and together they find a solution to the problem. This is quite different from an individual who uses his or her own effort to garner social support based on personal relationships. As Wong (1993) noted, "collective is more than receiving social support, it means the concerted effort involving all members of a group to tackle the same problem" (p. 57). Although a measure of relationship-focused coping (i.e., empathic and support provision in interpersonal relationships) was recently developed by O'Brien and DeLongis (1996) and may capture some collective coping behaviors, items on this measure do not reflect coping strategies aimed at reducing stress levels by using group connections.

1.3. Coping Resources and Outcomes

According to Lazarus and Folkman (1984), coping resources are relatively stable characteristics of the person's disposition and social environment, and may be drawn upon when developing coping responses. Coping resources that may be related to collective coping include Chinese cultural values, one's sense of self-efficacy, and perceptions of social support. Because cross-cultural studies have found that Chinese values influence an individual's ways of coping (Yue, 1993; Chiu and Kosinski, 1994; Liang and Bogat, 1994), we expected that individuals who hold strong Chinese values would use more collective coping because they would be motivated to strengthen group task involvement and joint coping efforts, and would work towards achieving collective goals and the common good (Chiu and Kosinski, 1995). Moreover, general self-efficacy (i.e., a broad and stable sense of personal agency or competence developed through one's past experiences in dealing effectively with a variety of stressful situation, Jerusalem and Schwarzer, 1992), as opposed to situation-specific self-efficacy (Bandura, 1992) has been associated with greater use of proactive coping (Long et al., 1992; Zhang and Schwarzer, 1995; Yue, 1996). Although general self-efficacy is an individual attribute, individuals with greater general self-efficacy hold high expectations and contribute greater effort and commitment in dealing with stressors in general (Jerusalem and Schwarzer, 1992). Thus, we expected that individual's with greater self-efficacy would use more collective coping strategies as well as proactive (i.e., engagement coping strategies) in managing workplace stressors. Although social support is not conceived as being the same as collective coping, because individuals who are more satisfied with social support (e.g., information and emotional assistance) from colleagues, friends, and family are more likely to rely on others and be concerned about what others think (Cohen and Wills, 1985), we expected that they would use more collective coping in managing work-related stress.

In summary, the purpose of the present study was to develop a valid and reliable coping instrument that reflects a collective coping function. As the first step in this process, we generated collective coping items and examined the validity of the new scale.

2. METHOD

2.1. Design and Procedure

The development of the collective coping measure was a three-phase approach and is part of a larger study on workplace stress and coping (Zhang, 1999). Phase 1 involved the use of focus groups and item generation methods to conceptualize the collective coping construct and develop initial items. In Phase 2, the items were administered to a sample of overseas Chinese professionals, and exploratory analyses were conducted. During Phase 3, we examined the convergent and predictive validity of the scale. All questionnaires (or items) used in the study were written in English to preserve response consistency and every item was translated into Chinese, and then back translated into English.

2.2. Phase 1: Focus Groups and Scale Development

Focus group discussions (via e-mail) provided an opportunity for 20 ($n = 17$ men; $n = 3$ women) overseas Chinese professionals to describe their workplace stress and coping strategies. All participants of the focus group were working in Canada or the United States, and they were recruited through postings on e-mail networks. Ninety-three percent had graduate degrees and the participants were from occupations such as professor (36%), researcher (36%), technician (21%), and research assistant (7%). Length of stay overseas ranged from 1 to 12 years ($M = 7.07$; $SD = 2.78$).

Although each participant had access to the e-mail network, and returned informed consent forms, no group list was formed and personal e-mail addresses were not displayed. To maintain confidentiality, e-mail messages were sent directly to the first author, who removed the address of the sender, and then distributed the message to all participants. In turn, participants responded to each other's comments by first sending their responses to the first author, who continued to distribute the responses to all participants until the discussion ended. Each person responded to the questions: What are some of the stressful things that are difficult when you work in an overseas environment? What are some of the ways you dealt with your difficulties? All e-mail messages were printed, omitting the name and e-mail address of each participant. This text was content analysed for type of coping strategy. The content analysis followed several steps. First, the texts were read and re-read, and then open codes were identified for each coping strategy. Next, open codes were grouped and regrouped into categories according to the constant comparison method (Glaser and Strauss, 1967). Nine coping themes were identified (see Table 1).

A total of 18 collective coping items were developed. Eleven items were developed from the results of the content analysis of the focus group text, some of which were also based on modifications of items found in the coping research literature that reflected these themes. In addition, seven items were drawn from other coping instruments. Four items were from the Ways of Coping (WOC) instrument (Folkman et al., 1986) and the Chinese

Table 1. Coping Themes and Sample Quotes from E-Mail Focus Group

Theme	Sample Quotes
Theme 1 Working harder: This theme centers on overseas Chinese major coping mechanism	"I know I need to readjust myself, so simply to work harder and to learn more. We have overcome many hardships in the past even if in China. We know how to do better jobs, and We believe that hard work always pay back."
Theme 2 Active efforts: Theme 2 includes coping with stressful aspects of work by taking an active role in learning social skills, adapting, and familiarizing oneself with the local culture.	"I found the willingness to readjust myself is very important and necessary." "I found familiarity with the pop-culture (TV show literature, or just everyday life) helped a lot. I tried to join conversation with my co-workers. I found that good ideas are not often easy to be understood but tidy neat presentation would certainly give a better impression." "I learned how to communicate with my supervisor and my colleagues. Once I talk more and join their water-cooler conversations, hallway gatherings, and lunch table triages, in other words, once I started to "fit in," the workplace became a much likable environment."
Theme 3 Find commonality: This theme represents overseas Chinese cognitive action of looking for similarities rather than differences in terms of work environment, work values, and relationships.	"I do not like to exaggerate the differences because problems are everywhere the same. I see other people (such as Italian, Irish, Jewish, Arab, Eastern Indian) may have the same feelings as we do." "Good value judgments are equally important and useful in the Western society. I found there are so many things in common, such as people's attitude to work, relationship, love, family, and friends, maybe not all but in general." "There are people's common behaviors in the new world and the old one. Once you know them, they are not really much different with those in China or any other places."

Theme 4
Pride in being Chinese and making a home in Canada: Theme 4 includes overseas Chinese positive self image and their active involvement in the society.

"We should feel proud about our background that include our special experiences in China and Chinese culture. It is nothing wrong to be a new comer in Canada. I view Canada as my home. The home feeling provides me the most strong confidence on myself in my working place and in the society."

"Canada promotes multiculturalism, even if I am a Chinese in origin, I know I am a real Canadian, not because I can speak the language, but I pay my tax, most importantly, involve in and contribute to the society."

Theme 5
Confidence in one's intelligence and prepared to take risks: This theme reflects overseas Chinese positive view about their educational background and skills.

"I believe we are group of intelligent people who could struggle and made so far from where we come from."

"I believe the education background, skills and work experiences have made and will make us confident to deal with stressful situations."

"I am a hard worker, I come here prepared to take risks, I know things are difficult, but I will make the best I can anyway."

Theme 6
Seeking support:
This theme includes making new friends with other overseas Chinese as well as local people.

"Very often at workplace, we Chinese stick together because we know how we feel and we usually have better advice to each other."

"Discussions can ease our stress. I also got many support from local people. Our colleagues, bosses, and people we deal with are generous. I feel that they know how to respect something that is totally new in their experiences. You can make friends with them without losing your dignity."

Theme 7
Negative view and avoidance: This theme involves overseas Chinese passive ways of coping with their difficulties.

"In general, I do not think that out of China town Canadian society really has a large interest in us other than to attract money and educated people for this country."

Continued

Table 1. Coping Themes and Sample Quotes from E-Mail Focus Group—cont'd

Theme	Sample Quotes
	"Maybe I am wrong, I still feel the origins of English and French as well as Germans get the most cultural respect here." "I don't want talk about it because it makes me feel down. I may have to leave here."
Theme 8 Blame and doubt about oneself: This theme is comprised of personal beliefs that they are not doing a good job.	"Certainly there are problems with my knowledge and language, I need to do more or learn more so that I can stand at the same level as other Canadians." "I still regret that I could not make enough local friends here in Canada. I don't know if I could ever do the work the same as native Canadians."
Theme 9 Thinking positively about future: This theme reflects overseas Chinese positive views about their future	"Compared to where I come from (the time I arrived Canada), I see the differences, I think we were able to do things better in the long run."

Ways of Coping Questionnaire (Chan, 1994). These items were modified by replacing the word someone with the phrase someone from my group of people. Finally, the highest loading three items from O'Brien and DeLongis's (1996) Relationship-focused Coping Scale were also included (the other person was replaced with the phrase the other people in my group). These 18 items include the domains of seeking support from one's in-group (e.g., emphasizing interpersonal relationships), conforming to one's group norms, and using group action to cope.

Next, we assessed the clarity and face validity of the 18 collective coping items. Through an e-mail network, 23 (8 women and 15 men) overseas Chinese professionals working in Canada (91%) and the United States (9%) completed the coping items, and other questionnaires used in the larger study. Respondents ranged in age from 27 to 50 years (M = 34.58; SD = 5.09). The average length of time participants lived overseas was 5.72 years (SD = 2.82). The sample consisted of researchers (44%), teachers (13%), accountants (9%), managers (4%), counsellors (4%), professors (4%), lawyers (4%), engineers (4%), and other professionals (14%). Coping items were responded to on a 4-point scale indicating the extent to which they used each item (0 = *not used or does not apply* to 3 = *used a great deal*). The item means ranged from 1.10 to 1.85 (*SD*s ranged from 0.60 to 1.08). Correlations ranged from 0.25 to 0.76 among the items, with one exception (r = 0.96). These two highly correlated items were combined into one: Shared my feelings and experiences in order to help others in my group deal with similar problems, because sharing "feelings" and "experiences" may be viewed as identical. Due to low endorsement, the item, Tried to find a solution by using Chinese email networks, was also deleted. No further changes were made to refine the remaining 17 items (see Table 2).

2.3. Phase 2: Exploratory Factor Analysis

2.3.1. Participants

The sample used for the main analysis (Phase 2 and 3) consisted of 228 overseas Chinese professionals (100 women and 128 men). The participants ranged in age from 19 to 61 years (M = 32.61, SD = 6.66). Sixty-four percent were married, 25% were single, and 7% either were divorced, widowed, or did not specify. Fifty-two percent had no children, 32% had one child, and 16% had two or more children. Eighty-one percent were either living with their immediate family (62%), friends (17%), or roommates (2%). The average length of time living overseas was 5.95 years (SD = 5.32). Approximately 47% reported their annual family income as 29,000 or less Canadian dollars, 27% between 30,000 and 59,000, and 26% above 60,000. The majority of participants were born in the People's Republic of China (93%) and the remaining born in Hong Kong (3%), Taiwan (2%), Indonesia (1%), and Singapore (1%). Ninety-six percent had a post-secondary education, and 98% reported that English was their second language. More than half indicated that they were fluent (55%), very fluent (23%), or functional (22%) in English. The sample consisted of researchers (47%), engineers (13%), teachers (7%), managers (7%), lecturers (6%), professors (5%), and other professionals (15%). The majority of participants were working in North America (United States, 48%; Canada, 34%), some were in Australia (5%), and the remainder were employed in Sweden, Finland, United Kingdom, or Germany.

Table 2. Sources and Loadings of Initial Collective Coping Items

Coping Item	Loading	Source
1. Talked to someone from my group of people about the situation.	.47	Changed "someone" to "someone from my group of people." Item from WOC (Folkman et al., 1986). Item loaded on Seeking Support and Ventilation factor in Chan's (1994) Chinese Ways of Coping model. Item from Carver et al. (1989) "I talked to someone to find out more about the situation," loaded on Seeking Social Support for Instrumental Reason factor.
2. Tried to avoid arguing with people in my group to maintain harmony.	.50	Item from Yamaguchi (1990) "Avoiding arguments with one's group even though one strongly disagrees with other group members" and "Maintaining harmony in one's group," on Collectivism Scale. Item from Singelis and Brown (1995) "It is important for me to maintain harmony within my group" and "Even when I strongly disagree with group members, I avoid an argument," on Interdependence and Self-Construal Scales.
3. Talked to someone from my group of people about how I was feeling.	.51	Changed "someone" to "someone from my group of people." Item from WOC I (Folkman et al., 1986). Item loaded on the Disengagement Coping factor in Long et al. (1992). Item loaded on Seeking Support and relation factors in Chan (1994).
4. Tried to understand the problem by determining whether it is a common issue at my workplace.[a]	.61	Based on Ho and Chiu's (1994) collectivism that "One's business is also the business of the group."
5. Tried to find out how important the problem is for my group.[a]	.73	Based on research by Kirkbride et al. (1991) on Chinese conflict preferences and negotiating behavior (e.g., "Collectivist position .... in problem situation...there may be a tendency to locate the issue in terms of its importance for the group, organizational unit, or even society at large" p. 367).
6. Spoke out for the benefit of my group.[a]	.65	Based on research by Ho and Chiu (1994) on collectivism that "One's business is also the business of the group."

Item	Loading	Notes
7. Tried to confirm that my feelings were similar to those of other people in my group.[a]	.66	Based on collectivism theory (Ho and Chiu, 1994) "Conformity to society or group norms, compliance, and harmony." Based on Singelis and Brown's (1995) item "It is important for me to maintain harmony within my group."
8. Tried to find out if my reactions to the problem were acceptable to others in my group.[a]	.74	See item 7.
9. Followed the ways that other people in my group dealt with similar problems.[a]	.63	See item 7.
10. Shared my feelings and experiences to help others in my group who have similar problems.[a]	.64	See item 7.
11. Tried to make others in my group get involved in order to solve the problem.[a]	.61	Based on Ho and Chiu's (1994) notion on collectivism that "Friends should be concerned with each other's personal matters," One's business is also the business of the group;" "Do things together;" "Collective efforts are superior;" and "Unity is strength.
12. Tried to find a solution by using Chinese e-mail networks.[a]	.36	Item developed from FG pilot study.
13. Talked to someone from my group who could do something concrete about the problem.[a]	.59	Changed "someone" to "someone from my group of people" WOC (Folkman et al., 1986). "Talked the problem over with my colleagues, item loaded on Engagement Coping in Long et al. (1994). Item loaded on Seeking Support and Ventilation factor in Chan (1994).
14. Asked a respected relative/friend for advice.	.55	Item from WOC (Folkman et al., 1986). Loaded on Seeking Support and Ventilation factor in Chan (1994). Item from Hui (1988) "I can count on my relatives for help if I find myself in any kind of trouble," loaded on "Kin" Collectivism.

Continued

Table 2. Sources and Loadings of Initial Collective Coping Items—cont'd

Coping Item	Loading	Source
15. Tried to understand the other person's concerns.	.63	Item from O'Brien (1992) Relationship-Focused Coping.
16. Tried to understand how other people in my group felt.	.71	Item from O'Brien (1992) Relationship-Focused Coping (changed "the other person" to "the other person in group").
17. Tried to figure out what would make other people in my group feel better.	.67	Item from O'Brien (1992) Relationship-Focused Coping (changed "the other person" to "the other person in my group").

Note: [a]Items identified in E-mail Focus Group (FG) Discussion. WOC = Ways of Coping (Folkman, S., Lazarus. R. S., Dunkel-Schetter, C., DeLongis, A., and Gruen, R. J., 1986). WCC = Ways of Coping Checklist (Lazarus, R. S. and Folkman, S., 1984).

2.3.2. Procedures

Volunteers were recruited through e-mail networks. A letter of invitation was posted on multiple networks (e.g., provincial, state, regional, country, and World Wide Web sites). Information about the voluntary nature of participation and confidentiality was explained in the posting. No personal e-mail addresses or any other personal information was available in the public sites and no identifying information remained on the questionnaires once they were received for analysis.

An informed consent and three sets of questionnaires (distributed 2 weeks apart) were sent via e-mail to each participate in order to examine a work-related stress and coping model (Zhang, 1999). Only the measures used here are reported. In order to assess convergent and predictive validity, participants were administered a number of relevant measures 2 weeks before and 2 weeks after coping was assessed (Time 1 and 3). At Time 1, participants completed coping resources questionnaires: Chinese cultural values (Chinese Culture Connection, 1987), general self-efficacy (adapted by Zhang and Schwarzer, 1995), social support satisfaction (Sarason et al., 1987), and work support (after Short and Johnston, 1997). Baseline measures of job satisfaction (Hoppock Job Satisfaction Scale; McNichols et al., 1978), somatization (SCLO-90-R Somatization Subscale; Derogatis, 1983), and depression (Center for Epidemiological Studies Depression Scale; Radloff, 1977) were also completed. Two weeks later (at Time 2) participants recorded a workplace stressful incident that had occurred in the past 2 weeks and indicated how they appraised and coped with it. Two weeks later (at Time 3) job satisfaction, somatization, and depression were again assessed.

2.4. Data Analysis

In order to define the structure of the Collective Coping Scale, first maximum likelihood analysis was performed on the 17-item scale. Next, in order to determine whether there were any higher order structures, the Collective Coping Scale was combined with two additional coping scales that represented the coping functions of engagement and disengagement coping (25 items). These scales were based on empirical work on the occupational stress and coping efforts of Canadian professionals (Long et al., 1992). For all items, participants responded to a 4-point scale indicating the extent to which they used each item ($0 = $ *not used or does not apply* to $3 = $ *used a great deal*). The higher the coping score is, the greater the usage of the coping strategy.

Because previous research generally finds that individuals use a wide variety of coping strategies, rather than one particular set of strategies to the exclusion of others, it was expected that the coping subscales would be intercorrelated. Thus, maximum likelihood with Oblimin rotation was considered to be an appropriate method of extracting factors and was used in the present study. A three-factor solution was identified a priori (collective, engagement, and disengagement coping), and a minimal loading of 0.40 was utilized as the criterion for inclusion of an item under the factor it was proposed to measure.

We tested convergent validity of the newly developed scale by examining the correlations between coping resources (Chinese values, self-efficacy, and social support) assessed at Time 1 and the collective coping scale. Predictive validity was tested by examining the correlations between the collective coping scale and changes in well being, such as depression, somatic symptoms, and job satisfaction. Change in well being was ana-lyzed using the residuals from the simple regression of the Time 3 outcome measures on Time 1 measures (job satisfaction, somatic symptoms, and depression symptoms).

3. RESULTS

3.1. Psychometric Characteristics

The results of the initial maximum likelihood analysis, with the number of factors set to be extracted at one, provided support for a single collective coping factor that accounted for 41% of the total variance. All items but one (0.37) loaded greater than 0.40 on a single factor (see Table 2 for factor loadings).

The second analysis (maximum likelihood with Oblimin rotation), with the number of factors set to be extracted at three, revealed eigenvalues ranging from 0.19 to 0.69, and accounted for 38% of the total variance. Items were first checked for low endorsement–no items were removed on this basis. Nine items were deleted due to low loadings, and were deleted one at a time. The final analysis on the remaining 33 coping items supported the expected three-factor solution, namely, Collective, Engagement, and Disengagement Coping ($\chi^2 = 882.79$, $df = 403$, $p <0.001$). Factor 1 accounted for 40% of the variance of the model and included 13 items reflecting collective coping strategies. Because collective coping items loaded separately (loadings greater than 0.50), there is initial support for the existence of a new collective coping dimension of coping. Factor 2 accounted for 33% of the variance and consisted of 11 engagement coping strategies. Factor 3 accounted for 27% of the variance and consisted of 9 disengagement coping strategies. The Engagement and Disengagement coping factors resembled previous factor analysis results (e.g., Tobin et al, 1989; Long et al, 1992; Portello and Long, 2001) and yielded clear and interpretable results on both concep-tual and empirical grounds. Means, standard deviations, and item factor loadings of the Collective, Engagement, and Disengagement subscales are presented in Table 3. Item-analy-sis further supported this three-factor solution and indicated acceptable internal consistency for collective, engagement, and disengagement coping (Cronbach's alpha = 0.90, 0.78, 0.70, respectively). The interscale correlations, calculated from the raw score item totals for each subscale, were positive and moderate. Collective coping positively correlated with Engagement (0.48) and Disengagement Coping (0.36), Engagement and Disengagement Coping correlated (0.41). The factors showed no evidence of multicollinearity, as evidenced by the relatively moderate correlations among them. They can therefore be treated as meas-ures of reasonably distinct psychological characteristics in multivariate analyses and in other types of research, and constitute a multifaceted coping skills construct. Finally, mean levels did not statistically differ for men and women on the Collective Coping Scale, $F < 1$, or Engagement and Disengagement coping scales, both $F < 1$.

3.2. Phase 3: Validation Study

Zero-order correlations revealed small but statistically significant positive relation-ships between Chinese cultural values and the Collective Coping Scale ($r = 0.19$, $p <0.01$) and work support and the Collective Coping Scale ($r = 0.20$, $p <0.01$). Consistent with

Table 3. Three Factor Coping Scale: Means, *SD*s, and Item Factor Loadings

Factor	*M*	*SD*	Loading	Item
Collective Coping (13 items)	17.22	8.72	.75	Shared my feelings and experiences in order to help others in my group who have similar problems. (35)
			.73	Tried to confirm that my feelings were similar to those of other people in my group. (32)
			.70	Tried to get other people in the group get involved in order to solve the problem. (36)
			.69	Talked to someone from my group who could do something concrete about the problem. (38)
			.68	Talked to someone from my group of people about how I was feeling. (28)
			.67	Tried to find out if my reactions to the problem were acceptable to others in my group. (33)
			.64	Tried to find out how important the problem is for my group. (30)
			.64	Talked to someone from my group of people about the situation. (26)
			.63	Spoke out for the benefit of my group. (31)
			.62	Followed the ways that other people in my group dealt with similar problems. (34)
			.53	Asked a respected relative/friend for advice. (39)
			.53	Tried to understand how the other people in my group felt. (41)
			.50	Tried to understand the problem by determining whether it is a common issue at my workplace. (29)
Engagement Coping (11 items)	18.83	6.19	.63	Made a promise to myself that things would be different next time. (17)
			.58	Tried to see things from another perspective. (25)
			.58	Criticized or lectured myself. (13)
			.54	Realized I brought the problem on myself. (5)
			.53	Increased my efforts to make things work. (14)
			.48	Rediscovered what is important in life. (15)
			.47	Changed or grew as a person in a good way. (9)

Continued

Table 3. Three Factor Coping Scale: Means, SDs, and Item Factor Loadings

Factor	M	SD	Loading	Item
			.47	Made a plan of action and followed it. (20)
			.46	Prepared for the worst. (23)
			.45	Tried to keep my feelings to myself. (12)
			.45	Went over in my mind what to say or do. (22)
Disengage-ment	9.22	4.67		
Coping (9 items)			.59	Didn't let it get to me; refused to think about it too much. (3)
			.58	Refused to get too serious about the situation; tried to laugh about it. (2)
			.53	Went on as if nothing had happened. (16)
			.49	Kept others from knowing how bad things were. (10)
			.48	Expressed anger to the person who caused the problem. (6)
			.46	Hoped a miracle would happen. (7)
			.43	Had fantasies about how things might turn out. (19)
			.41	Waited to see what would happen before acting. (24)
			.40	Wished the situation would go away or somehow be over with. (18)

Note: The number in the parentheses ( ) after each coping item corresponds to the question on the 33-item coping questionnaire.

previously studies (eg., Chan, 1994), this pattern of results provides some evidence for convergent validity. However, there was no relationship between general self-efficacy ($r = -0.02$, ns) or social support satisfaction ($r = 0.04$, ns) and collective coping.

Regarding the predictive validity of the Collective Coping Scale, change in job satisfaction, somatization, and depression (over 4 weeks) did not significantly correlate with collective coping, indicating that work-specific collective coping strategies were not associated with changes in global psychological distress or well being for Chinese professionals. [Note, disengagement coping scores, however, did correlate significantly with a reduction in job satisfaction ($r = -0.20$, $p < 0.01$), and an increase in somatization ($r = 0.13$, $p < 0.05$) and depression ($r = 0.32$, $p < 0.01$), and are consistent with the results of other studies (e.g., Long et al., 1992; Terry et al., 1996; Portello and Long, 2001).

In order to determine whether gender might affect these results, we examined the men's ($n = 128$) and women's ($n = 100$) data separately. For the women's group only, collective coping significantly predicted an increase in depressive symptoms ($r = 0.20$, $p < 0.05$) over the 4 weeks. However, it is important to note that the mean scores on the Collective Coping Scale did not differ statistically for men and women ($F < 1$; $M = 17.27$; $SD = 8.18$; $M = 17.17$; $SD = 9.41$, respectively). Thus, there is weak support for predictive validity of the Collective Coping Scale but only for Chinese professional women.

4. DISCUSSION

The present study provides an initial step in the development of the Collective Coping Scale. Collective coping is defined as activities that orient attention to relationships with in-group members and the maintenance of interpersonal relationships with the goal of managing work-related stress. Collective coping strategies include seeking support from one's in-group (e.g., Talked to someone from my group of people about how I was feeling), conforming to one's in-group norms (e.g., Tried to confirm one's feelings with people in the group), and using group action to cope (e.g. Tried to get other people in the group to get involved in order to solve the problem). The Collective Coping Scale has good internal consistency. Although the intercorrelations among the three coping dimensions (Collective, Engagement, and Disengagement coping) are relatively moderate, these findings are not surprising when one considers the fact that most coping subscales are interrelated because individuals tend to engage in a number of coping strategies, rather than in one particular form of coping (Folkman and Lazarus, 1980; Folkman et al., 1986). The factors also provide evidence of construct validity–collective items were distinct from engagement and disengagement items and support the independence of a third coping function–collective coping. Thus, in addition to the use of engagement and disengagement coping, when confronted with work-related stressors, overseas Chinese employees may also attempt to maintain in-group relationships through collective coping.

We found some evidence of convergent validity. The greater the belief in Chinese values and the more work support Chinese professionals experienced, the more collective forms of coping were used when encountering stressful situations at work. This finding supports the notion that Chinese values (i.e., Confucian task completion and hard work) contribute to the collective strategies individuals draw on to manage stressful events (Yang, 1986; Chan, 1989; Yue, 1993). It is important to note that the Chinese people are not a homogeneous group. For example, Chinese born in the People's Republic of China,

Hong Kong, Taiwan, or North America differentially endorse traditional Chinese values. However, in the present study, 93% of the participants were born in the People's Republic of China and thus were more likely to hold similar beliefs. Moreover, an examination of our descriptive data revealed that the mean of the Chinese values scale was slightly higher ($M = 6.2$, $SD = 0.75$; $M = 5.3$, $SD = 0.59$, respectively) than for managers (men and women, $N = 150$) employed in the People's Republic of China (Ralston et al., 1992). These findings support our expectation that the overseas Chinese professionals in the present study retained their Chinese values.

Perceptions of support from fellow workers and supervisors also have an important influence on collective coping and reflect the collectivistic values of group effort as a means of problem solving (Bond et al., 1984; Stipek et al., 1989; Yue, 1993; Scherer et al., 2000). It appears that the perceived quality of interpersonal relationships and the avail- ability of co-workers, colleagues, and supervisors plays a role in determining whether col- lective coping strategies are used to cope with work-related stress.

Unexpectedly, the coping resources, general self-efficacy and social support satisfac- tion, were not associated with collective coping. General self-efficacy refers to the stable sense of personal agency or competence developed through one's past experience in deal- ing effectively with a variety of stressful situations. We used the Chinese version of the General Self-efficacy Scale (Zhang and Schwarzer, 1995), which has been found to relate negatively to test anxiety (Yue, 1996). It is probably not surprising that this individualis- tic construct was not associated with an increase in collective coping strategies, suggest- ing that our original hypothesis was ill-conceived. Satisfaction with social support has been hypothesized as bolstering an individual's perceived ability to cope with stress (Cohen and Wills, 1985), and previous research has found evidence for the stress-buffer- ing effect of satisfaction with social support on the psychological adjustment of Chinese students (Liang and Bogat, 1994). However, to our knowledge no study has found direct effects of satisfaction with social support on coping strategy use for Chinese profession- als. We can surmise that since the Chinese professionals in the present study were focused on occupational stress, satisfaction with more general, rather than work sources of social support (e.g., family members), did not enhance collective coping strategies aimed at a work-related stressors. Perhaps if we had assessed the participants' satisfaction with col- lective forms of social support (i.e., actively sharing and supporting members of the in- group; Johnson, 1989), the expected relationships may have emerged. In the present study, the participants had the opportunity to access family support as the majority of the participants lived with their immediate family (62%) and another 17% lived with friends.

There was little evidence of predictive validity for the Collective Coping Scale. Changes over 4 weeks in job satisfaction, somatization, and depression were not associ- ated with collective coping. This lack of a direct relationship between collective coping and change in these outcomes was unexpected and it may be that there are other collec- tive coping strategies that could be included in a measure of collective coping. Conversely, according to the resource-congruence model developed by Wong (1993; Wong & Ujimoto, 1998), collective coping would not predict greater job satisfaction if there was a lack of congruence between the practice of collective coping by Chinese professionals and the highly individualistic corporate culture in western organizations. Thus, further research is needed to explore the usefulness of the resource-congruence model, and the Collective Coping Scale's content and construct validity.

We did find a small but statistically significant relationship between Chinese professional women's greater use of collective coping strategies and an increase in depression over the month ($r = 0.20$, $p < 0.05$). These results may be due to the type of stressors the women experienced. In the present study, the men reported stressors such as working longer hours and work overload more frequently than the women, and women reported encountering more unfair treatment by co-workers and colleagues more frequently than the men. Moreover, demographic information revealed that the Chinese professional men and women were employed in similar occupations before going overseas; but once employed overseas, men were more likely employed in the natural science field and women were more likely employed in the social science field. Thus, future research would benefit from examining the effectiveness of collective coping strategies for different types of stressors; as well as the role of structural differences between men and women (e.g., level of power or influence in the workplace) and work task differences in the coping process. Future research also needs to examine whether there is a match or congruence between collective coping and corporate culture. If the corporate culture is cooperative rather than competitive, then collective coping may be effective.

As far as we are aware, this is the first study to focus on the development of a measure of occupational collective coping. This measure is still at an early stage of development and is far from complete. Although the present study focused on Chinese professionals working overseas, maintaining close connections with an in-group may be an important form of coping, regardless of cultural orientation. Coping that serves the function of maintaining interpersonal relations (i.e., asking for help from others, maintaining harmony, and conforming to one's in-group) may be used by individuals from both collectivistic and individualistic cultures (Kashima and Triandis, 1986; Yamaguchi, 1990; Kirkbride et al., 1991; Ho and Chiu, 1994). As such, the Collective Coping Scale should be examined with other cultural groups and within different cultural settings. Conversely, it is likely that Chinese overseas professionals hold both collectivistic and individualistic values (e.g., Wong & Sproule, 1984) and use multiple forms of coping. Thus, the relative use of engagement, disengagement, and collective coping should be explored for both work and non-work stressors. Finally, the lack of association between collective coping and changes in psychological well being (depression, somatic symptoms, and job satisfaction) found in this study suggests that the relationships among collective coping and these outcomes may be more complex than first thought. Thus, the development of a valid and reliable instrument that adequately reflects the full range and function of collective coping strategies requires continued study.

REFERENCES

Aldwin, C. M., and Greenberger, E. (1987). Cultural differences in the prediction of depression. *American Journal of Community Psychiatry* 15:789-813.
Aycan, Z., and Berry, J. W. (1996). Impact of employment-related experiences on immigrants' psychological well-being and adaptation to Canada. *Canadian Journal of Behavioural Science* 28:240-251.
Bandura, A. (1992). *Social Functions of Thought and Action: A Social Cognitive Theory.* Prentice Hall, Englewood Cliffs, NJ.
Bhagat, R. S., O'Driscoll, M. P., Babakus, E., Frey, L., Chokkar, J., Ninokumar, B. H., Pate, L. E., Ryder, P. A., Fernandez, M. J. G., Ford, Jr., D. L., and Mahanyele, M. (1994). Organizational stress and coping in seven national contexts: A cross-cultural investigation. In: Keita G. P. and Hurrell, J. J. Jr. (eds.), *Job stress in a Changing Workforce.* American Psychological Association, Washington, DC, pp. 93-105.

Bond, M. H. (1985). Language as a carrier of ethnic stereotypes in Hong Kong. *Journal of Social Psychology* 125:53-62.

Bond, M. H. (1988). Finding universal dimension of individual variation in multi-cultural studies of values: The Research and Chinese value surveys. *Journal of Personality and Social Psychology* 55:1009-1015.

Bond, M. H., Chiu, C. K., and Wan, K. C. (1984). When modesty fails: The social impact of group-effacing attributions following success or failure. *European Journal of Social Psychology* 14:335-338.

Bond, M. H., Wan, K. C., Leung, K., and Giacalone, R. A. (1985). How are responses to verbal insult related to cultural collectivism and power distance? *Journal of Cross-Cultural Psychology* 16:111-127.

Carver, C. S., Scheier, M. F., and Weintraub, J. K. (1989). Assessing coping strategies: A theoretically based approach. *Journal of Personality and Social Psychology* 56:267-283.

Chan, D. W. (1989). Personality and adjustment correlations of locus of control among Hong Kong Chinese. *Journal of Personality Assessment* 53:145-160.

Chan, D. W. (1994). The Chinese Ways of Coping Questionnaire: Assessing coping in secondary school teachers and students in Hong Kong. *Psychological Assessment* 6:108-116.

Chan, D. W. (2001). Dimensionality and correlates of problem solving: The use of the Problem Solving Inventory in the Chinese context. *Behaviour Research and Therapy* 39:859-875.

Chao, Y. T. (1990). Culture and work organization: The Chinese case. *International Journal of Psychology* 25:583-592.

Chinese Culture Connection (1987). Chinese values and the search for culture-free dimensions of culture. *Journal of Cross-Cultural Psychology* 13:186-200.

Chiu, R. K., and Kosinski, Jr., F. A. (1994). Is Chinese conflict-handling behavior influenced by Chinese values? *Social Behavior and Personality* 22:81-90.

Chiu, R. K., and Kosinski, Jr., F. A. (1995). Chinese cultural collectivism and work-related stress: Implications for employment counselors. *Journal of Employment Counseling* 32:96-110.

Cohen, S., and Wills, T. A. (1985). Stress, social support, and buffering hypothesis. *Psychological Bulletin* 98:310-357.

Cross, S. E. (1995). Self-construes, coping, and stress in cross-cultural adaptation. *Journal of Cross-Cultural Psychology* 26:673-697.

Cumming, P. A., Lee, E. L., and Oreopulos, D. G. (1989). *Access! Task Force on Access to Professions and Trades in Ontario*. Ministry of Citizenship, Toronto, ON.

Derogatis, L. R. (1983). *SCL-90-R: Administration, Scoring and Procedures manual-II*. Clinical Psychometric Research, Towson, MD.

Employment and Immigration Canada (1990). *Managing Immigration: A Framework for the 1990s*. Government Publications, Ottawa, ON.

Folkman, S., and Lazarus, R. S. (1980). An analysis of coping in a middle-aged community sample. *Journal of Health and Social Behavior* 21:219-239.

Folkman, S., Lazarus, R. S., Dunkel-Schetter, C., DeLongis, A., and Gruen, R. J. (1986). The dynamics of a stressful encounter: Cognitive appraisal, coping, and encounter outcomes. *Journal of Personality and Social Psychology* 50:571-579.

Glaser, B. G., and Strauss, A. I. (1967). *The Constant Comparative Method of Qualitative Analysis*. Aldine, Hawthorne, NY.

Han, G., and Park, B. (1995). Children's choice in conflict: Application of the theory of individualism-collectivism. *Journal of Cross-cultural Psychology* 26:298-313.

Ho, D. Y. F. (1986). Chinese patterns of socialization: A critical review. In: Bond M. H. (ed.), *The Psychology of the Chinese People*. Oxford University Press, Hong Kong, pp. 1-37.

Ho, D. Y., and Chiu, C. Y. (1994). Component ideas of individualism, collectivism, and social organization: An application in the study of Chinese culture. In: Kim, U., Triandis, H. C., Kagitcibasi, C., Choi, S. C., and Yoon, G. (eds.), *Individualism and Collectivism*. Sage, Thousand Oaks, CA, pp. 137-156.

Hofstede, G. H. (1980). *Culture's Consequences: International Differences in Work-related Values*. Sage, Beverly Hills, CA.

Hui, C. H. (1988). Measurement of individualism-collectivism. *Journal of Research in Personality* 22:17-36.

Hwang, C., Scherer, R. F., Wu, Y., Hwang, C-H., and Li, J. (2002). A comparison of coping factors in western and non-western cultures. *Psychological Reports* 90:466-476.

James, K. (1994). Social identity, work stress, and minority workers' health. In: Keita, G. P., and Hurrell, J.J. Jr. (eds.), *Job Stress in a Changing Workforce*. American Psychology Association, Washington, DC, pp. 127-145.

Jerusalem, M., and Schwarzer, R. (1992). Self-efficacy as a resource factor in stress appraisal processes. In R. Schwarzer (ed.), *Self-efficacy: Thought Control of Action*. Hemisphere, Washington, DC, pp. 195-214.

Johnson J. V. (1989). Collective control: Strategies for survival in the workplace. *International Journal of Health Services.* 9:469-80.

Kagitcibasi, C. (1987). Individual and group loyalties: Are they compatible? In: Kagitcibasi, C. (ed.), *Growth in Cross-cultural Psychology* Swets & Zeitlinger, Netherlands, pp. 94-104.

Kahn, W. A. (1990). Psychological conditions of personal engagement and disengagement at work. *Academy of Management Journal,* 4:841-870.

Kahn, R. L., and Byosiere, P. (1991). Stress in organizations. In: M. Dunnette and L. Hongh (eds.), *Handbook of Industrial and Organizational Psychology,* Volume 3, 2nd ed. Counseling Psychologists Press, Palo Alta, CA, pp. 571-650.

Kashima, Y., and Triandis, H. C. (1986). The self-serving bias in attributions as a coping strategy: A cross-cultural study. *Journal of Cross-Cultural Psychology* 17:83-98.

Kirkbride, P. S., Tang, S. F., and Westwood, R. I. (1991). Chinese conflict preferences and negotiating behavior: Cultural and psychological influences. *Organization Studies* 12:365-386.

Krause, N., Liang, J., and Yatomi, N. (1989). Satisfaction with social support and depressive symptoms: A panel analysis. *Psychology and Aging* 4:88-97.

Kuo, C-H. B. (2002). *Correlates of coping of three Chinese adolescent cohorts in Toronto, Canada: Acculturation and acculturative stress (Ontario).* University of Nebraska, Lincoln, NB (unpublished dissertation).

Lazarus, R. S., and Folkman, S. (1984). *Stress, Appraisal, and Coping.* Springer, New York.

Leung, K. (1988). Some determinations of conflict avoidance. *Journal of Cross-cultural Psychology* 19:125-136.

Leung, K. (1996). The role of beliefs in Chinese culture. In: Bond, M. H. (ed.), *The Handbook of Chinese Psychology.* Oxford University Press, New York, pp. 247-262.

Liang, B., and Bogat, G. A. (1994). Culture, control, and coping: New perspectives on social support. *American Journal of Community Psychology* 22:123-147.

Lockett, M. (1988). Culture and problems of Chinese management. *Organization Studies* 4:497-510.

Long, B. C., Kahn, S. E., and Schutz, R. W. (1992). Causal model of stress and coping: Women in management. *Journal of Counseling Psychology* 39:227-239.

Mak, A. S. (1991). From elites to strangers: Employment coping styles of new Hong Kong immigrants. *Journal of Employment Counseling* 28:144-156.

Marsella, A. J. (1987). The measurement of depressive experience and disorders across cultures. In: Massella, A. J., Hirschfeld, R., and Katz, M. (eds.), *The Measurement of Depression.* Guilford Press, New York, pp. 376-398.

Marsella, A. J. (1994). Work and well-being in an ethnoculturally pluralistic society: Conceptual and methodological issues. In: Keita, G. P., and Hurrell, J.J. Jr. (eds.), *Job Stress in a Changing Workforce* American Psychology Association, Washington, DC, pp. 127-145.

Marsella, A. J., Oliviera, J., Plummer, M., and Crabbe, K. (1998). Native Hawaiian concepts of culture, mind, and well-being. In: McCubbin, H., Thompson, A., and Thompson E. (eds.), *Stress and Resiliency in Racial Minority Families in the United States.* Sage, Thousand Oaks, CA, pp. 93-113.

McCrae, R. (1984). Situational determinants of coping responses: Loss, threat and challenge. *Journal of Personality and Social Psychology* 46:919-928.

McNichols, C., Stahl, M., and Manley, T. (1978). A validation of Hoppock's Job Satisfaction Measure. *Academy of Management Journal* 21:737-742.

O'Brien, T. B. (1992). *The role of personality and situation factors in three modes of coping: Emotion-focused, problem-focused, and relationship-focused* University of British Columbia, Vancouver, BC, Canada (unpublished thesis).

O'Brien, T. B., and DeLongis, A. (1996). The interactional context of problem-, emotion-, and relationship-focused coping: The role of the big five personality factors. *Journal of Personality* 64:775-813.

Oettingen, G., Little, T. D., Lindenberger, U., and Baltes, P. B. (1994). Causality, agency, and control beliefs in East versus West Berlin children: A natural experiment on the role of context. *Journal of Personality and Social Psychology* 66: 579-595.

Pinderhughes, E. (1989). *Understanding Race, Ethnicity, and Power.* Free Press, New York.

Portello, J. Y., and Long, B. C. (2001). Appraisals and coping with workplace interpersonal stress: A model for women managers. *Journal of Counseling Psychology* 48:144-156.

Radloff, L. S. (1977). The CES-D Scales: A self-report depression scale for research in the general population. *Applied Psychological Measurement* 1:385-401.

Ralston, D. A., Gustason, D. J., Elsass, P.M., Cheung, F. M., and Terpstra, R. H. (1992). Eastern values: A comparison of managers in the United States, Hong Kong, and the People's Republic of China. *Journal of Applied Psychology* 77:664-671.

Roseman, I. J., and Dhawan, N. (1995). Cultural differences and cross-cultural similarity in appraisal and emotional responses. *Journal of Cross-Cultural Psychology* 26:23-48.

Sarason, I. G., Sarason, B. R., Shearin, E. N., and Pierce, G. R. (1987). A brief measure of social support: Practical and theoretical implications. *Journal of Social and Personal Relationships* 4:497-510.

Scherer, R. F., Hwang, C-E., Yan, W., and Li, J. (2000). The dimensionality of coping among Chinese health care workers. *Journal of Social Psychology* 140:317-327.

Singelis, T. M. (1994). The measurement of independent and interdependent self-construals. *Personality and Social Psychology Bulletin* 20:580-591.

Singelis, T. M., and Brown W. J. (1995). Culture, self, and collectivist communication linking culture to individual behavior. *Human Communication Research* 21:354-389.

Siu, O-L., Spector, P. E., Cooper, C. L., Lu, L., and Yu, S. (2002). Managerial stress in greater China: The direct and moderator effects of coping strategies and work locus of control. *Applied Psychology: An International Review* 51:608-632.

Short, K. H., and Johnston, C. (1997). Stress, maternal distress, and children's adjustment following immigration: The buffering role of social support. *Journal of Counseling and Clinical Psychology* 65:494-503.

Stipek, D., Weiner, B., and Li, K. (1989). Testing some attribution-emotion relations in the People's Republic of China. *Journal of Personality and Social Psychology* 56:109-116.

Terry, D., Callan, V. J., and Sartori. G. (1996). Employee adjustment to an organizational merger: Stress, coping and intergroup differences. *Stress Medicine* 12:105-122.

Ting-Toomey, S. (1985). Toward a theory of cognitive and culture. In: Gudy Kunst, W., Stewart, L., & Tnig-Foney, S. (eds.), *Communication, Culture, and Organizational Process*. Sage, Beverly Hills, CA, pp. 71-86.

Tobin, D. L., Holroyd, K. A., Reynolds, R. V., and Wigal, J. K. (1989). The hierarchical factor structure of the coping strategies inventory. *Cognitive Therapy and Research* 13:343-361.

Triandis, H. C. (1989). The self and social behavior in different cultural contexts. *Psychological Review* 26:506-520.

Triandis, H. C. (1995). *Individualism and Collectivism*. Westview, Boulder, CO.

Triandis, H. C., and Marin, G. (1983). Ethic plus emic versus pseudoetic: A test of a basic assumption of contemporary cross-cultural psychology. *Journal of Cross-Cultural Psychology* 14:489-500.

Tu, W. M. (1984). *Confucian Ethics Today: The Singapore Challenge*. Federal Publication, Manila.

Wong, C. L., Tjosvold, D., and Lee, F. (1992). Managing conflict in a diverse work force–A Chinese perspective in North America. *Small Group Research* 23:302-321.

Wong, P. T. P. (1993). Effective management of life stress: The resource-congruence model. *Stress Medicine* 9:51-60.

Wong, P. T. P., and Ujimoto, K. V. (1998). The elderly: Their stress, coping, and mental health. In: Lee, L. C., & Zane, N. W. S. (eds.), *Handbook of Asian American Psychology*. Sage, Thousand Oaks, CA, pp. 165-209.

Wong, P. T. P., and Sproule, C. F. (1984). Attributional analysis of locus of control and the Trent Attributional Profile (TAP). In: Lefcourt, H. (ed.), *Research with the Locus of Control Construct: Volume 3: Limitations and Extensions*. Academic Press, New York, pp. 309-360.

Yamaguchi, S. (1990). *Personality and cognitive correlates of collectivism among the Japanese: Validation of collectivism scale*. University of Tokyo, Department of Social Psychology, Tokyo, Japan (unpublished paper).

Yang, K. S. (1986). Chinese personality and its change. In: Bond, M. H. (ed.), *The Psychology of the Chinese People*. Oxford University Press, Hong Kong, pp. 71-86.

Yue, X. D. (1993). *Coping with psychological stress through Confucian self-cultivation and Taoist self-transcendence*. Harvard University, Cambridge, MA (unpublished dissertation).

Yue, X. D. (1996). Test anxiety and self-efficacy: Levels and relationship among secondary school students in Hong Kong. *Psychologia* 39:193-202.

Zhang, D. (1999). *Culture, workplace stress, and coping: A study of overseas Chinese professionals*. University of British Columbia, Vancouver, B, C., Canada (unpublished dissertation).

Zhang, J. X., and Schwarzer, R. (1995). Measuring optimistic self-beliefs: A Chinese adaptation of the General Self-Efficacy Scale. *Psychologia* 38:174-181.

Conclusion

25

KNOWLEDGE GAPS ABOUT STRESS AND COPING IN A MULTICULTURAL CONTEXT

Paul B. Pedersen

1. INTRODUCTION

While everyone agrees that stress and coping are culture-mediated there are knowledge gaps about exactly how culture influences stress and/or coping. Since all behaviors are learned and displayed in a cultural context we can expect that cultural context to influence the experiences of stress and coping. Wong, Wong, & Scott (this volume) point out that even the construct of stress may be culturally biased, because the magnitude and the scale of problems experienced in some parts of African and Asian, such as the AIDS epidemic and the tsunami, cannot be adequately understood as merely stressors, such as life events and daily hassles. In fact Prof. Chen (this volume) in Taiwan argues that suffering is more accurate than stress in describing the painful experiences Asians have to endure.

By the same token, Abi-Hashem (this volume) uses such terms as agony, deep frustration and anxiety to describe the experiences of many communities in the Middle East, because of terrorism, occupation, etc. Naji Abi Hashem (this volume) describes how the global trauma of stressors and the inadequacy of coping resources describes many aspects of life as examples of culture shock. We need to go beyond the fact that culture shapes stress and coping, but go the next step of exploring how to modify and expand the basic concepts of stress and coping. Wong (1993) has already suggested additional terms for stress and coping from a multicultural perspective.

Several authors in this volume (Chen; Chun, Moos, & Cronkite; Yeh, Kwong-Arora, & Wu) have proposed new ways of looking at stress and coping. Thus, new theoretical developments and research methodologies are needed to expand our understanding of the stress and coping process. The previous chapters review most if not all that we know about stress and coping in a multicultural context they also demonstrate knowledge gaps where future research will be required. A "knowledge gap" is a research question for which we do not yet have the answer. This chapter will attempt to identify some of those knowledge gaps.

Paul B. Pedersen, University of Hawaii

2. THE CONTROVERSY ABOUT CULTURE SHOCK:

Culture shock is a profoundly personal encounter with persons or situations from a different culture resulting in stress and requiring a high level of coping facility. While I agree with Berry (this volume) that acculturative stress is a more accurate term to describe the experience, the term "culture shock" remains the more commonly used description. The experience of culture shock will not be the same for any two persons or for the same person at two points in time. Kalvero Oberg (1958) introduced the concept "culture shock" to describe anxiety resulting from losing one's sense of when and how to "do the right thing". This adjustment process involves a nonspecific state of uncertainty, where the persons do not know what others expect of them or what they can expect of the others with emotional, psychological, behavioral, cognitive and physiological consequences.

The most frequently cited indicators of culture shock include the absence of familiar cues about how to behave, the reinterpretation of familiar values about what is good, an emotional disorientation ranging from anxiety to uncontrollable rage, a nostalgic idealization of how things used to be, a sense of helplessness in the new setting and a feeling that the discomfort will never go away. Variations on the culture shock label with similar characteristics have included culture fatigue, language shock, role shock, and pervasive ambiguity. Any new situation such as a new job, divorce, graduation, being fired, being arrested, cancer, or radical change involves some adjustment of role and identity might result in culture shock.

The early research on culture shock compared it to a "disease" which resulted in disability and which could be cured with the right treatment. Culture shock was described as a "stress reaction" resulting from disorientation regarding values, norms and expectations resulting from change and adaptation and a "deficit" of resources for an appropriate response. Gudykunst and Hammer (1988) emphasized uncertainty reduction as an essential deficit resulting in culture shock. "The reduction of uncertainty and anxiety is a function of stereotypes, favorable contact, shared networks, intergroup attitudes, cultural identity, cultural similarity, second language competence, and knowledge of the host culture (p.132)" Stephen and Stephen (1992) link culture shock to fear of negative psychological consequences such as loss of control or frustration, negative behavioral consequences through exploitation or derogation, negative evaluations or stereotyping by out-group members, and negative evaluations or rejection by in-group members for having contact with out-groups.

Other recent research on culture shock has emphasized the "growth" or "educational" model. The experience of acculturative stress is not entirely negative, but may include a positive and creative force to stimulate, motivate and enhance long-term change. People develop skills and abilities through culture shock which may not otherwise be available. Acculturative stress is not necessarily a negative process. Kealey (1988) found that many persons who were successful abroad had experienced intense culture shock. Culture shock is a learning experience which can lead to greater self awareness and personal growth.

Furnham and Bochner (1986) highlight the potentially positive consequences of culture shock, advocating a skill-learning response to the culture shock experience. These skills may include language learning, turn taking in conversation, learning rules of communication, knowing the protocol of politeness, identifying communication styles and learning appropriate nonverbal behaviors. Learning appropriate skills will enhance multicultural competence and increase the likelihood of success in the host culture. These skills include (1) knowing the rules for interpersonal communication, (2) accommodating the effect of biological factors, demographic characteristics and geopolitical conditions, and (3) understanding the characteristics of their own culture from the host culture viewpoint. Culture shock may be viewed as a specialized form of learning and educational growth, combining a social skills model with a culture-learning model to increase the potentially positive consequence of multicultural contact.

Culture shock has at least six identifying features: cue problems, value discrepancies, an emotional core, a set of typical symptoms, adjustment mechanisms, and a pattern of emergence over time. When the cues or messages we receive in another culture are confusing, it is usually because familiar cues we've learned to depend on are missing, important cues are there but not recognized as important, or the same cue has a different meaning in the new culture. Many of the problems in culture shock involve learning to deal with new cues. Each culture values its own "familiar" behaviors, attitudes, ideas, and values which define the meaning of good, desirable, beautiful, and valuable Although the visitor does not need to discard familiar values, it is necessary to recognize alternative value systems in order to adapt to a new cultural system.

Those experiencing or anticipating culture shock can reduce the negative effect of culture shock in a variety of ways. *First*, the visitor needs to recognize that transition problems are usual and normal in the stress of adjusting to a strange new setting. The visitor can be helped to recognize, understand, and accept the effects of adjustments in the context of a host culture support system.

Second, the maintenance of personal integrity and self-esteem becomes a primary goal. The visitor often experiences a loss of status in the new culture where the language, customs, and procedures are strange or unfamiliar. the visitor will need reassurance and support to maintain a healthy self-image.

Third, time must be allowed for the adjustment to take place without pressure or urgency. Persons adjust at their own rate, and recognize that their reconciliation with the host culture, although painful, will enhance their future effectiveness.

Fourth, recognizing the patterns of adjustment will help the visitor make progress in developing new skills and insights. Depression and a sense of failure will be recognized as a stage of the adjustment process and not as a permanent feature of the new experience.

Fifth, labeling the symptoms of culture shock will help the visitor interpret emotional responses to stress in the adjustment process.

Sixth, being well adjusted at home does not ensure an easy adjustment in a foreign culture. In some cases visitors uncomfortable "back home" may find it easy to adjust to a foreign culture. In extreme cases of maladjustment visitors are more likely to carry their "back home" problems with them into the new culture. With existing measures it is difficult to predict a hard or easy adjustment for most individuals.

Seventh, although culture shock cannot be prevented, preparation for transition can ease the stress of adjustment. Preparation might include language study, learning about the host culture, simulating situations to be encountered, and spending time with nationals from the host culture. In all instances the development of a support system is essential to helping the visitor reconstruct an appropriate identity or role in the new culture.

Knowledge gaps

The culture shock construct is a loosely defined category of behavior which has heuristic value but which is defined differently by those researching the phenomenon. Some knowledge gaps are: (1) What are the specific conditions that define culture shock? (2) At what point does any stressful situation become an example of culture shock? (3) Does culture shock proceed through stages or not? (4) What are the underlying causes of culture shock? (5) What are the positive effects of culture shock? (6) What are the long/short term negative effects of culture shock? (7) How can culture shock be prevented?

3. DEFINING "CULTURE"

The terms used to describe a culture-centered perspective are themselves confusing. Cross-cultural has typically involved a comparison of Western and non-Western approaches or the modification of Western approaches to fit non-Western contexts. The problem of comparison is one side always appears stronger than the other. Trans-cultural is another term which attempts to be ultimately inclusive. The problem is that culture then becomes an abstraction. Intercultural is another favorite especially in the communications literature. The problem is it implies a relationship between just two cultural perspectives. Multicultural has emerged as the favorite but that term is now so politically loaded that it inspires instant controversy. Indigenous is gaining popularity but it is uniquely focused on home-grown perspectives that are typically isolated from outside influences. I prefer the term culture-centered, where cultural perspectives are central to the generic application of psychological sciences.

Chun, Moos and Cronkite (this volume) describe "culture" as one of the most important neglected contexts for coping research. The multicultural perspective seeks to provide a conceptual framework that recognizes the complex diversity of a plural society while, at the same time, suggesting bridges of shared concern that bind culturally different persons to one another. The ultimate outcome may be a multicultural theory, as Segall, Dasan, Berry, and Poortinga (1990) suggested. "There may well come a time when we will no longer speak of cross cultural psychology as such. The basic premise of this field—that to understand human behavior, we must study it in its sociocultural context—may become so widely accepted that all psychology will be inherently cultural" (p. 352). During the last 20 years, multiculturism has become recognized as a powerful force, not just for understanding exotic groups but also for understanding ourselves and those with whom we work.

By defining culture broadly, to include within-group demographic variables (e.g., age, sex, place of residence), status variables (e.g., social, educational, economic), and affiliations (formal and informal), as well as ethnographic variables such as nationality, ethnicity, language, and religion, the construct "multicultural" becomes generic to all relationships. The narrow definition of culture has limited multiculturalism to what might more appropriately be called "multi-ethnic" or "multi-national" relationships between groups with a shared sociocultural heritage that includes similarities of religion, history, and common ancestry. Ethnicity and nationality are important to individual and familial identity as one subset of culture, but the construct of culture—broadly defined—goes beyond national and ethnic boundaries. Persons from the same ethnic or nationality group may still experience cultural differences. Not all Blacks have the same experience, nor do all Asians, nor all American Indians, nor all Hispanics, nor all women, nor all old people, nor all disabled persons. No particular group is unimodal in its perspective. Therefore, the broad and inclusive definition of culture is particularly important in preparing to deal with the complex differences among and between people from every cultural group.

Just as differentiation and integration are complementary processes, so are the emic (culture specific) and etic (culture general) perspectives necessarily interrelated. The terms *emic* and *etic* were borrowed from "phonemic" and "phonetic" analysis in linguistics describing the rules of language to imply a separation of general from specific aspects. Even Pike (1966), in his original conceptualization of this dichotomy, suggested that the two elements not be treated as a rigid dichotomy but as a way of presenting the same data from two viewpoints. Although research on the usefulness of emic and etic categories has been extensive, the notion of a "culture free" (universal) etic has been just as elusive as the notion of a "culture pure" (totally isolated) emic.

There is a strong argument against the broad definition of culture. Triandis, Bontempo, Leung, and Hui (1990) distinguished between cultural, demographic, and personal constructs. Cultural constructs are those shared by persons speaking a particular dialect; living in the same geographical location during the same time; and sharing norms, roles, values, and associations, and ways of categorizing experience described as a "subjective culture" (Triandis, 1972). This view contends that demographic level constructs deal with these same topics but are shared only by particular demographic groups within a culture, such as men and women or old and young. Personal level constructs belong to still another category of individual differences and cannot be meaningfully interpreted with reference to demographic or cultural membership.

Likewise, Lee (1991) and Locke (1990) made a persuasive argument against the broad definition of culture. They argued that the term *multicultural* is in imminent danger of becoming so inclusive as to be almost meaningless. The broad definition includes all constituent groups that perceive themselves as being disenfranchised in some fashion. This has resulted in diffusing the coherent conceptual framework of multiculturalism in training, teaching, and research, confusing cultural and individual differences.

The distinction between individual differences and cultural differences is real and important. The cultural identities to which we belong are no more or less important than is our individual identity. Skin color at birth is an individual difference, but what that skin color has come to mean since birth is cultural. Although culture has traditionally been defined as a multigenerational phenomenon, the broad definition of culture suggests that cultural identities and culturally significant shared beliefs may develop in a contemporary horizontal as well as vertical historical time frame and still be distinguished from individual differences.

Another application of the broad inclusive definition of culture is "cultural psychology," which presumes that every sociocultural environment depends for its existence and identity on the way human beings give it meaning and are in turn changed in response to that sociocultural environment. Cultural psychology studies the ways cultural traditions and social practices regulate, express, and transform people in patterned ways. "Cultural psychology is the study of the ways subject and object, self and other, psyche and culture, person and context, figure and ground, practitioner and practice live together, require each other, and dynamically, dialectically and jointly make each other up" (Shweder, Mahapatra & Miller, 1990, p. 1).

Knowledge gaps

There is a great deal of disagreement about the definition of culture as a construct resulting in a great many knowledge gaps. (1) Should culture be defined broadly or narrowly? (2) How do you differentiate individual from cultural differences? (3) How can a culture-centered approach help to manage stress and enhance coping? (4) What are the implications of cultural psychology for understanding stress and coping? (5) Is culture an example of a self-generating dynamic system in the mode of chaos theory?

4. ACHIEVING A HEALTHY "BALANCE"

Theoretically achieving a healthy balance is an important point. Western psychologists tend to adopt a linear, "either/or" way of thinking while many cultures depend on a "both/and" alternative way of thinking. Thus, individuals are either internal or external, happy or sad. However, the oriental ways of thinking is more dialectic and paradoxical. It is not either this or that but both these and those. Chen's (this volume) chapters on Taoism and Buddhism, and Hong Seock Lee (this volume) present a biosocioexistential model are all relevant to the argument for a healthy balance.

Cognitive balance is a search for consistency in an otherwise volatile situation and has traditionally been achieved by changing, ignoring, differentiating or transcending inconsistencies to avoid dissonance. However, there are more complicated definitions of balance demonstrated through a tolerance for inconsistency and dissonance where differences are not resolved but are managed in a dynamic, ever-changing balance.

In a more complicated and asymmetrical definition of dynamic balance, the task may be to find meaning in both pleasure and pain rather than to always seeking to resolve conflict in favor of increased pleasure. Social change in this context is perceived as a continuous and not an episodic process. Balance as a construct seeks to reflect the complex and sometimes asymmetrical metaphors of organic systems in holistic health. Problems, pain, and otherwise negative aspects of our experience may also provide necessary resources for the dark side of healthy functioning, in an ecological analysis of the psychological process.

In many non-Westernized systems there is less emphasis on separating the person from the presenting problem than in Western cultures. Chen (this volume) has three chapters describing the balance between suffering and happiness, the healing qualities of Taoism and other Asian perspectives relevant to stress and coping. There is less of a tendency to locate the problem inside the isolated individual but rather to relate that individual's difficulty to other persons or even to the cosmos. Balance describes a condition of order and dynamic design in a context where all elements, pain *as well as* pleasure, serve a useful and necessary function. The non-Western emphasis is typically more holistic in acknowledging the reciprocal interaction of persons and environments in both their positive and negative aspects.

Success is achieved indirectly as a by-product of harmonious two-directional balance rather than directly through a more simplistic one-directional alternative. In a one-directional approach the goal is to make people feel more pleasure, less pain; more happiness and less sadness; more positive and less negative. In the two-directional alternative the goal is to help people find meaning in *both* pleasure and pain; *both* happiness and sadness; *both* negative and positive experience. In the Judeo-Christian tradition God not only tolerates the devil's presence but actually created demonic as well as angelic forces in a balance of alternatives. Maddi (this volume) discusses the construct of "hardiness" as a form of balance as does Phan in discussing "resiliency."

Balance as a construct involves the identification of different or even conflicting culturally learned perspectives without necessarily resolving that difference or dissonance in favor of either viewpoint. Healthy functioning in a multicultural or pluralistic context may require a person to simultaneously maintain multiple, conflicting and culturally learned roles without the opportunity to resolve the resulting dissonance.

Knowledge gaps:

In many cultures the construct "balance" is used to describe a condition of health for the individual and society. This perspective reveals numerous knowledge gaps, particularly in Western cultures. (1) How would you define asymmetrical balance as distinguished from the more familiar notion of symmetrical balance? (2) How would a "two-directional" perspective of stress and coping differ from a "one-directional" perspective? (3) How can non-Western perspectives of balance be incorporated into Western cultures? (4) How can a condition of balance be achieved in a stressful situation. (5) How can a condition of balance enhance the coping process?

5. MEASUREMENT PROBLEMS

Both R. G. Tweed and A. DeLongis, (this volume) and Sanchez, Spector, & Cooper (this volume) have identified methodological and measurement issues in cross-cultural stress research. It has been so inconvenient to attend to complicated cultural—not to mention multicultural—confounding variables in research methodology that many of our well-intentioned colleagues have chosen to ignore culture and "pretend" that these differences will, at least in aggregate data, cancel one another out to provide a one-size-fits-all solution to the measurement problems. This convenient short-cut has done us, our subjects and the general public a profound disservice.

A less convenient alternative is to isolate and account for culturally learned biases that influence the research process. It is worth mentioning that the more fundamental problem is cultural biases in the theory that informs the development of a psychological measurement. For example, by following a culture-sensitive resource-congruence mode, Wong, Reker & Peacock (this volume) are able to develop a coping inventory which includes coping strategies seldom studied in America (i.e. existential coping and acceptance). Similarly, Yeh et al. (this volume) and Zhang & Long (this volume) have developed scales to measure collective coping, which has also been ignored in American stress research.

Miller (1999) examined the self-interest motive and the self-confirming role of assuming self-interest in textbook psychology. "It is proposed that a norm exists in Western cultures that specifies self-interest both is and ought to be a powerful determinant of behavior. This norm influences people's actions and opinions as well as the accounts they give for their actions and opinions. In particular, it leads people to act and speak as though they care more about the material self-interest than they do" (p. 1053). The theory of self-interest has led to a psychological norm of self-interest fostering a powerful descriptive and prescriptive expectation in Western society.

A report by the Basic Behavioral Science Task Force (1996) of the National Advisory Mental Health Council (NAMHC) documents the extent of cultural, encapsulation of mental health services. First, anthropological and cross-cultural research has demonstrated that cultural beliefs influence the diagnosis and treatment of mental illness. Second the diagnosis of mental illness differs across cultures. Third, research has revealed differences in how individuals express symptoms in different cultural contexts. Fourth, culturally biased variations in diagnosis vary according to the diagnostic categories relevant to the majority population. Fifth, most providers come from a majority culture whereas most clients are members of minority cultures. If the standard practices of mental health services are themselves encapsulated, as suggested by the NAMHC report, then these cultural biases will certainly influence the practical applications of psychology through counseling and therapy.

The presence of cultural bias in psychology requires that all research studies address external validity issues for the populations being researched, that different research approaches be used as appropriate to each population and that the psychological implications of a population's ethno-cultural belief system be considered in making comparisons across cultures (S. Sue, 1999). While there has been much attention to internal validity in psychological research there has been less emphasis on external validity. External validity is the extent to which one can generalize the results of research. "The lack of internal validity does not allow causal inferences to be made without some degree of convincingness or credibility. The lack of external validity may render findings meaningless with the actual population of interest" (p. 1072). The greater the emphasis on internal validity the more psychological research will be dominated by majority-dominant culture values.

Lewis-Fernandez and Kleinman (1994) have identified three culture-bound assumptions about mental health and illness based on North American values. The first assumption is the egocentricity of the self where individuals are seen as self-contained and autonomous units whose behavior is determined by a unique configuration of internal attributes. The second assumption is the mind-body dualism, which divides psychopathology into organic disorders and psychological problems. The third assumption is the view of culture as an arbitrary superimposition on the otherwise "knowable biological reality."

Western cultures are likewise described by Berry et al (1993) as more "ideocentric" emphasizing competition, self-confidence and freedom, compared to collectivistic cultures that are more allocentric, emphasizing communal responsibility, social usefulness and the acceptance of authority. These Westernized beliefs grew out of a naturalistic understanding of the physical world from the Age of Enlightenment in Europe. This Westernized psychological perspective has conventionally defined standards for ethics, competence and other professional psychological issues.

Wrenn (1962) first introduced the concept of cultural encapsulation. This perspective assumes five basic identifying features. First, reality is defined according to one set of cultural assumptions. Second, people become insensitive to cultural variations among individuals and assume their own view is the only right one. Third, assumptions are not dependent on reasonable proof or rational consistency but are believed true, regardless of evidence to the contrary. Fourth, solutions are sought in technique-oriented strategies and quick or simple remedies. Fifth, everyone is judged from the viewpoint of one's self-reference criteria without regard for the other person's separate cultural context. The encapsulation has not diminished over time.

The former President of the American Psychological Association, George Albee (1994) describe how completely psychology in the United States has been encapsulated in the last hundred years. "Most of the early leaders in psychology embraced ideological views that stressed the natural superiority of a white male patriarchy, the acceptance of Social Darwinism, the inferiority of women and of the brunette races. Calvinism stressed economic success as the hallmark of salvation and psychology concurred. Anti-semitism and homophobia were standard. Eugenics spokesmen urged the elimination of the unfit and inferior and opposed welfare programs, decent wages and safe working conditions" (p. 22). These views continue to be held today, although sometimes in more subtle forms.

Perhaps the most urgent example of cultural encapsulation requiring our attention is the bias in psychological tests and measures. Samuda (1998) reviews the issues and consequences of cultural bias in testing American minorities. Dana (1998) takes an even broader perspective in reviewing the controversies of cultural identity in the process of accurate assessment of clients from different cultural groups using different approaches. Sanchez, Spector and Coooper (this volume) focus on methodological issues which create measurement problems. Tteed (this volume)and DeLong (this volume) discuss problems in uses of rating scales for cross cultural research. On the positive side Lee (this volume) presents an interesting approach to measurement based on personality theory. Matsumoto, Hirayama and LeRony (this volume) present results from their ICAPS study where they managed measurement problems effectively. Zhang and Long (this volume) have developed a measure for collective coping. Chang and Tugade and Asakawa (this volume) also present a promising approach from studying Asian Amerricans.

Cultural bias in the use of tests and measures is likely to result in overdiagnosis, underdiagnosis or misdiagnosis. Although it is generally accepted that these biases exist in the tests and measures on which psychologists depend (Paniagua, 1994, in press; Dana, 1993), this does not necessarily mean that those tests and measures can not or should not be used.

The search for culture free or even culture fair tests has failed. Such a test would need to demonstrate content, semantic, technical, criterion and conceptual equivalence across cultures. Escobar (1993) points out that no test or assessment can fulfill these five criteria effectively. We are left with the need to interpret culturally biased tests and measures so that the resulting data can be understood accurately and meaningfully across cultures.

Knowledge gaps:

The constructs of stress and coping in a multicultural context have eluded precise measurement because of their complexity. (1) How does the self-interest bias continue to influence research about stress and coping? (2) Are all tests culturally biased toward the cultural context in which those tests were constructed? (3) Why have we neglected external validity in our research about stress and coping in multicultural contexts? (4) To what extent can measures that assume an individualistic perspective be used in collectivistic cultures? (5) Does our perspective on stress and coping continue to be culturally encapsulated?

6. RELIGIOUS AND SPIRITUAL RESOURCES

My more traditional Chinese students tell me that the counselor of first resort for them is to go inside themselves and learn from remembered Confucian sayings learned in childhood from their parents. This inside-the-person resource applies to many—perhaps most—people of the world who depend first and foremost on spiritual and religious resources for counseling. These alternatives to talk therapy become extremely important in several ways. First, it is important for counselors with a more secular orientation to recognize the importance of spiritual resources for their more religious clients. Second, these inner resources provide an important resource that can be mobilized. Third, —in terms of numbers—talk therapy is actually the more exotic form of counseling in a world where the vast majority depend on spiritual and religious meaning for healthy functioning. Klassen, McDonald and James (this volume) present an excellent discussion of religious and spiritual coping mechanisms. Tweed and Gideon-Conway III (this volume) discuss culturally influenced beliefs around the world.

"Contrary to science, in religion the preexistence of a singular core of truth is not agreed to be discoverable through some regulated means by its seekers. There is little doubt that religionists believe that there is such a truth. Freedom of religion, however, permits as many "core truths" and searches for these as there are observers. Everyone is entitled to his or her own religious or private beliefs, without any necessary proof or methods to demonstrate these but science is a group concensus, moderated and regulated by experts (Weiss, 1995, p. 544)."

When everything seems to be changing in a personal or social perspective what are the things that don't change? These unchanging elements act as a hinge on the door of change. The changing process can only occur relative to these unchanging elements. These unchanging elements are essentially "religious". There is a considerable literature on how religion inhibits change and on how religion is irrelevant to change (Bellah, 1965). Religion also facilitates change by providing a point of traditional reference through which change may occur and this suggests how religion can be viewed as the basis for counseling.

Worthington (1989) suggests five reasons to consider the implications of religion in their understanding of development and intervention. First, a high percentage of the population identifies itself as religious. Second, Many people who are undergoing emotional crises spontaneously consider religion in their deliberations about their problem. Third, many clients are reluctant to bring up their religious considerations because of their perception that therapy is an essentially secular process. Fourth, In general, therapists are not as religiously oriented as their clients. Fifth, As a result of being less religiously oriented than their clients, many therapists are not as well informed about religion as might be appropriate.

Psychological theories have incorporated religious factors in theories of personal transition, coping, stress management, and cognitive behavioral theories. Fowler (1981) provides a seven stage example for measuring faith, with (0) undifferentiated faith, (1) intuitive-projective faith, (2) mythic-literal faith, (3) synthetic-conventional faith (4) individuative-reflective faith, (5) paradoxical-consolidative faith and (6) universalizing faith. Other psychological theories address religion as well. Alport's development of religious sentiments and Jung's individuation provide several examples. Religious and spiritual factors influence individual behavior in several ways. First, religious commitment and involvement influences a person's behavior. Second, religious and spiritual factors can be important to the context. Third, religious or spiritual explanations of a specific event may trigger a person's attributions.

Worthington (1989) describes psychological issues in judging the quantity, type and quality of religious information. (1) How formal should the assessment be? (2) To what degree is the content of a person's faith to be assessed versus the process of "faithing?" (3) How is religion involved in the life of the client? (4) How mature is the client in his or her religious life as well as in his or her cognitive moral and socio-emotional life? (5) To what degree, if any, is the client's religion related to the diagnosis? (6) To what degree is the client's religion involved in the etiology of the problem? (7) Is religion part of the client's identity? (8) Is the counselor competent to deal with a client's religious and spiritual concerns? There has been little research on the outcomes of religious counseling or dynamic spiritual factors in a client's evolving perspective.

Knowledge gaps:

Religious and spiritual resources have been largely neglected in the research on stress and coping, probably in an attempt to protect scientific objectivity. Consumers however are much more likely to recognize the value of religious and spiritual resources. (1) How is "prayer" useful in managing stress and enhancing coping? (2) How can intra-psychological healing resources like meditation be mobilized through religious and/or spiritual means? (3) Do religious and spiritual resources define a truth beyond science? (4) Does religion and spirituality enhance change, inhibit change or is it irrelevant to change? (5) Why has religion and spirituality been such a neglected resource among providers more than among consumers in managing stress and enhancing coping?

7. THE MULTICULTURAL FAMILY CONTEXT

Family systems therapy has emphasized the importance of context for a long time, recognizing that a family member's problems may (1) serve an important function for the family, (2) be a consequence of the family's transitional difficulty and/or (3) be a symptom of dysfunctional patterns learned in the family context. The family member client is part of a living context are essential features. The family system itself is the primary unit of treatment and not the identified patient (Goldenberg and Goldenberg, 1995). Cunningham, McCcreary and Ingram (this volume) demonstrate the importance of family for the Afrrican American community. Padilla and Borero (this volume) point out thee effect of accultural stress for Hispanic families

All families – given differences of age, gender and life style – are bicultural to a greater or lesser extent, but not all families are willing or able to deal with their contrasting cultural contexts. When the families' cultural contexts include ethnocultural differences however, bicultural factors become more obvious and are more likely to attract our attention. Both the traditional family model—where the individual served the family—and more modernized models—where the family is expected to serve the individual—have broken down in a confusion of bi-cultural and multi-cultural alternatives. Takano (this volume) discuss how culture shapes spousal violence in Japanese cultures for example. "Different cultures had differing ways of understanding "appropriate" family organization, values, communication and behavior. Although the family perspective had revolutionized the individual view of the client by taking family context into account, it now needed to understand its own unit of analysis (i.e., the family) in light of an even larger context: culture (Gushue, and Sciarra, 1995, p. 588).

Traditionally the family has served four functions: (1) provided and regulated affectional needs for intimacy and social-sexual relations, (2) provided care and rearing of the young, (3) provided units of economic cooperation and (4) enculturated members into society. These same "common-ground" functions are expressed very differently in different cultures requiring care-givers to understand each cultural context from its own culture-centered perspective.

Increased multicultural contact has resulted in increased conflict, especially for bicultural families. The nuclear family is experiencing internal conflict from a variety of sources. (1) More working mothers are experiencing frustration and guilt for separating themselves from home and family. (2) Conflict in redefining shared responsibility between husband and wife has increased. (3) More wives are seeking careers outside the home. (4) Increased pressure from media-driven idealized family and parenting models leads to a sense of failure. (5) Otherwise successful families – as defined by family members – are experiencing painful separation from increased mobility when children leave or family members are displaced. (6) Increased conflict in legal obligations toward one another by husbands, wives and children has complicated family relationships. The tensions and stress of modern society has resulted in a variety of adaptations. Axelson (1993) describes some of the alternatives which have been invented by multicultural and/or bicultural families.

1. Single parent families of either a father or mother with children have increased among divorced, never-married, separated and widowed persons. Temporary single parent families might also occur due to military service, employment conditions or other non-voluntary separation of parents and children.

2. Blended families are reconstituted by the remarriage of a divorced man and/or divorced woman including children from one or both partner. This family alternative is on the increase since most divorced persons remarry.

3. Extended families or joint families including relatives or in-laws who share the nuclear family household or may live nearby and interact as a single family unit. Members of the extended family may be single, abandoned, legally separated, divorced or widowed as well as inter-generational.

4. Augmented families may include non-relatives who share the household with a nuclear family as roomers, boarders, friends, transients or long-term guests.

5. A "non-family shared household" consisting of two or more unrelated persons living together has developed to meet personal financial and social needs in modernized, mobile and frequently fragmented societies.

6. Non-family households living alone by choice or circumstance provide another alternative on the increase, particularly among the elderly and dispossessed.

7. Persons or families who are homeless due to financial or political conditions have also increased in frequency as an accepted alternative and chronic condition of modern society.

Healthy families have traditionally been identified as expressing emotions freely and openly with each member having a right to be her or his unique self with an equal or fair division of labor, egalitarian role relationships and with the nuclear family as the primary concern. In care-giving to bicultural families the main goal is usually to achieve harmony, treating all members of the family together and perceiving the family itself as the corporate client requiring the provider to help the family modify relationships and communication patterns in some way. Not all cultures value these characteristics in the same way and a more broadly defined list of criteria is required for bicultural families.

The communication approach to family counseling presumes that problems are a result of bad communication. Communication in the bicultural family is especially complicated, involving roles, relationships and power levels that change over time. The methods ,as well as the content,of communication in different cultures will also be significantly different. The culture-centered provider needs to monitor several different "languages" of communication, each one conveying its own uniquely cultural content. The structural approach to family counseling emphasizes the interlocking roles of family members. Bicultural families are constantly changing, structuring and restructuring themselves according to each new crisis. The structural approach defines boundaries, creates alliances, identifies patterns and structures. Problems are regarded as "boundary disputes" which are particularly frequent in bicultural families (Sue & Sue, 1990).

Knowledge gaps

In most cultures the family is the primary building block in a society. Family relationships are typically a primary resource for managing stress, but this raises many unanswered questions. (1) How do you define "family" in Western and non-Western cultures? (2) How might the family contribute to creating stressful conditions as well as coping with that stress? (3) What is the direction of change for modern families? (4) What are the consequences of a strong/weak family identity? (5) Can an individual "invent" a family from among non-blood relative peers? (6) What are the typical communication problems in a family context?

8. DEFINITIONS OF IDENTITY AND "SELF"

Identity is developed in a cultural context. Belonging to a cultural group means accepting the beliefs and symbols of that group as having meaning and importance in a profoundly personal sense. Identity includes personal elements such as one's name, social connections such as family and cultural connections such as ones nationality and ethnicity. This combined description of identity has also been referred to as our personality. As we become more aware of how ethnographic, demographic , status and formal/informal affiliations have shaped our lives we become more intentional in developing our own multicultural awareness. We become more aware of our cultural identity through contact with persons from other cultures who are different from ourselves and we see ourselves in contrast. Cultural identity is complicated. Sometimes within-group differences seem to exceed between-group differences as we track the complex and dynamic salience of our own cultural self-identity across situations and times. Yeh, Arora and Wu (this volume) discuss a new collectivistic model for coping.

Oetting and Beauvais (1991) developed a theory of cultural identification that does not polarize cultures but instead acknowledges the simultaneous multiplicity of coexisting identities in each of us. This "orthogonal" model recognizes that increased identification with one culture does not require decreased identification with other cultures. We can belong to many different cultures at the same time.

The five most frequently used alternative models of cultural identity are less complex but are also less adequate. The *dominant majority* model simply imposes a dominant culture on all minority groups, regardless of the consequences. The *transitional* model presumes a movement toward the dominant culture as an appropriate adjustment. The *alienation* model seeks to avoid stress from anomie by assisting persons in transition to make successful adjustments. The *multidimensional* model presumes transition on several dimensions at the same time with different degrees of change on each dimension. The *bicultural* model presumes that one can adapt to one new culture without losing contact with an earlier culture. The *orthogonal* model, however, suggests that adapting simultaneously to any one culture is independent from adapting to many other cultures, providing an unlimited combination of patterns that combine the preceding five alternative models as each being partially true.

The orthogonal model presumes a higher level of complexity and a more comprehensive inclusion of cultural identities. The orthogonal model offers several advantages.

1. Cultural groups may exist in association with one another without isolating themselves or competing with one another.
2. Minority cultures need not be eliminated or absorbed in order to coexist with the dominant majority culture.
3. A permanent multicultural society may be possible that is multifaceted and multidimensional without becoming a melting pot imposed by the dominant culture or anarchy and chaos imposed by the different competing cultural minorities.
4. Conflicts of value and belief do not present insurmountable barriers but may be combined in a realistic pluralism. While some primary values and beliefs of each cultural group can not be compromised, other secondary values and beliefs can be adapted and modified to fit a changing society.
5. Cultural conflict may become a positive rather than a negative force from the perspective of shared common-ground expectations, even when the culturally learned behaviors of minorities are perceived to be different and seemingly hostile to the dominant culture.
6. Members of minority groups may be less inclined toward militancy when their survival is not threatened. Personal and social advancement requires an environment that is safe enough that people can take risks with one another. Without safety no one will take the risk. Without risk, little or no learning occurs.
7. Interaction between minority and majority cultures may be less destructive for all parties. The orthogonal model describes a "win-win" outcome for conflict among culturally different peoples.
8. There are economic advantages of releasing resources previously consumed by cultural conflict. Imposed and enforced harmony is expensive and frequently ineffective in the long range. Voluntary harmony promotes the best interests of everyone if it can be achieved through willing cooperation.
9. There are already models of orthogonal relationships in healthy bicultural and multicultural individuals or social units. These models have appeared briefly but have then usually been overcome by the need for power by a dominant majority

or the need to protect special interests by a hostile minority. Pluralism is neither easy to achieve nor simple to maintain. However, alternative political systems are likely to be more expensive in the long term.

While Erikson (1968) emphasized the importance of autonomy and initiative development during the childhood years in his classic model of identity, it is also true that his psychosocial concepts defined the individual self in the context of a community's values, norms and social roles. While Erikson's model favors the individualistic worldview and perhaps the more masculine roles, the notion of a "separated self" is now being replaced with a notion of "self-in-relationship," where the sense of self reflects the relationships between people.

The individualized self, rooted in individualism of the Western world, is being overtaken by a more familial self, typical of the global majority, as best described by Clifford Geertz (1975). "The Western conception of the person as a bounded, unique, more or less integrated motivational and cognitive universe, a dynamic center of awareness, emotion, judgment and action organized into a distinctive whole and set contrastively both against other such wholes and against a social and natural background is, however incorrigible it may seem to us, a rather peculiar idea within the context of the world's cultures (p. 48)." The more corporate notion of a relational self is integrated into the orthogonal perspective.

Theories of self identity frequently fail to take into account the significance of social identification in the definition of self. Social identities are self-definitions that are more inclusive than the individuated self concept. The orthogonal self identity becomes a link between the individual self or selves and the social context in which that individual self or selves exist. The sociocultural context guides the definition of self in several ways (Markus & Kitayama, 1991). One way is through independent self-construal, where the self is perceived as a separate identity with internal characteristics that are stable across situations regardless of context. This perspective is typical of the more individualistic cultures. An alternative way more typical of collectivistic societies connect their notion of self to societal roles and relationshps. This interdependent self construal is relationship centered, requiring conformity and seeking harmony over personal goals. This interdependent self depends more on context than internal attributes.

Kagitcibasi (1996) characterizes Western psychology as affirming the separated self as a healthy prototype basic to the prescriptive nature of applied psychology. When this expresses itself as selfishness, self-centeredness and a lack of social commitment, psychology becomes more a part of the social problems for non-Western cultures than part of the solution. The individualistic Western cultural ethos favored by American psychology draws a clear and narrow boundary between the self and non-self, contrary to the construal of self in many non-Western cultures. However, since American psychology has a dominant position and is self contained, the individualistic perspective is often assumed to be universal. The linking of the social with the individual perspective is essential to the development of multicultural awareness.

Knowledge gaps:

The construct of self-identity is one of the features that characterizes humans. It is ironic that there is, none the less, so much disagreement and confusion regarding the definition of self across cultures. (1) What is the definition of the self? (2) How does one's self identity change? (3) What are the boundaries of the self in a socio-cultural context? (4) What are the advantages of the orthogonal definition of self for managing stress? (5) Is the notion of "relational self" relevant and appropriate for understanding stress and coping across cultures?

9. CONCLUSION

The survey of research on stress and coping across cultures helps identify both what we already know and what we do not yet know. These knowledge gaps were classified into seven categories including culture shock controversies, defining culture, achieving a healthy balance, measurement problems, religious and spiritual resources, the multicultural family context and defining the self. Each of these knowledge gap categories are mentioned by one or more chapters of this volume.

By reviewing these unanswered question the directions of future research can be identified more clearly. The field is defined as much by what we do not yet know as it is by what we know. The research on stress and coping is a vital and dynamic movement producing more and more urgently needed findings. The utility of this book will depend on the new research stimulated by these findings.

REFERENCES

Axelson, J.A. (1993). Counseling and development in a multicultural society. Pacific Grove CA: Brooks Cole.

Albee, G.W. (1994). The sins of the fathers: Sexism, racism and ethnocentrism in psychology. International Psychologist, 35 (1) 22.

Basic Behavioral Science Task Force of the National Advisory Mental Health Council (1996). Basic behavioral science research for mental health: Sociocultural and environmental processes. American Psychologist, 51, 722-731.

Bellah, R.N. (1965). Religion and progress in modern Asia. New York: Free Press.

Berry, J.W., Poortinga Y.H., Segall, M.H., & Dasen, P.J. (1992). Cross cultural psychology: Research and applications. Cambridge, England: Cambridge University Press.

Dana, R.H. (1993). Multicultural assessment perspectives for professional psychology. Boston: Allyn & Bacon.

Dana, R.H. (1998). Understanding cultural identity in intervention and assessment. Thousand Oaks, CA: Sage.

Erikson, E.H. (1968). Identity: Youth and crisis New York: Norton.

Escobar, J.I. (1993). Psychiatric epidemiology. In A.C.Gaw (Ed.) Culture, ethnicity and mental health (pp.43-73) Washington D.C.: American Psychiatric Press.

Furnham, A., & Bochner, S. (1986). Culture shock: Psychological reactions to unfamiliar environment. London: Methuen.

Geertz, C. (1975). On the nature of anthropological understanding. American Scientist, 63, 329-338.

Goldenbeerg, H. & Goldenberg, I. (1995). Family therapy. In R.J. Corsini & D.Wedding (Eds.) Current psychotherapies (pp. 356-385) Itasca, Il: F.E.Peacock.

Gudykunst, W.B., & Hammer, M.R. (1988). Strangers and hosts: An uncertainty reduction based theory of intercultural adaptation. In Y.Y. Kim & W.B. Gudykunst (Eds.) Cross-cultural adaptation: Current approaches (pp. 106-139). Newbury Park, CA: Sage.

Gushue, G.V., & Sciarra, D.T. (1995). Culture and families: A multidimensional approach. In J.G.Ponterotto, J.M. Casas, L.A. Suzuki, & C.M. Alexander (Eds.) Handbook of multicultural counseling (pp. 586-606) Thousand Oaks, Newbury Park, CA: Sage.

Kagitcibasi, C. (1996). Family and human development across cultures. Mahwah, NJ: Erlbaum.

Kealey, D.J. (1988). Explaining and predicting cross-cultural adjustment and effectiveness: A study of Canadian technical advisors overseas. Unpublished doctoral dissertation, Dept of Psychology, Queens University, Kingston, Ontario, Canada.

Lee, C.C. (1997). Promise and pitfalls of multicultural counseling. In C.C.Lee (Ed.) Multicultural issues in counseling: New approaches to diversity, Second Edition, (pp. 3-13). Alexandria VA: American Counseling Association.

Lewis-Fernandez, R., & Kleinman, A. (1994). Culture, personality and psychopathology. Journal of Abnormal Pssychology, *103*, 67-71.

Locke, D.C. (1990). A not so provincial view of multicultural counseling. Counselor Education and Supervision, *30*, 18-25.

Miller, J. (1994). Cultural diversity in the morality of caring: Individually oriented versus duty-based interpersonal moral codes. Cross-Cultural Research, *28*, (1) 3-39.

Oberg, K. (1958). Culture shock and the problems of adjustment to new cultural environments. Washington, DC. U.S. Department of State.

Oetting, E.R., & Beauvais, F. (1991). Orthogonal cultural identification theory: Te cultural identification of minority adolescents. International Journal of the Addictions *25*, 655-685.

Paniagua, F.A. (1994). Assessing and treating culturally diverse clients: A practical guide. Thousand Oaks, CA: SAGE.

Pike, R. (1966). Language in relation to a united theory of the structure of human behavior. The Hague, The Netherlands: Mouton.

Samuda, R.J. (1998). Psychological testing of American minorities: Issues and consequences (2nd edition) Thousand Oaks, CA: Sage.

Segall, M.H., Dasen, P.R., Berry, J.W., & Poortinga, Y.H. (1990). Human behavior in global perspective: An introduction to cross-cultural psychology. New York: Pergamon Press.

Stephen, C.W., & Stephen, W.G. (1992). Reduciing intercultural anxiety through intercultural contact. International Journal of Intercultural Relations, *16*, 89-106.

Shweder, R.A., Mahapatra, M., & Miller, J.A. (1990). Culture and moral development. In Cultural psychology: Essays on comparative human development (pp 130-204) New York: Cambridge University Press.

Sue, S. (1998). In search of cultural competencies in psychology and counseling. American Psychologists, *53*, 440-448.

Triandis, H.C., Bontempo R., Leung, K., & Hui, C.H. (1990). A method for determining cultural, demographic and person constructs. Journal of Cross-Cultural Psychology, *21*, 302-318.

Triandis, H.C. (1972). The analysis of subjective culture. New York: Wiley.

Weiss, A.S. (1995). Can religion be used as a science in psychotherapy? American Psychologist, *50*, (7) 543-544.

Worthington E.L. (1989). Religious faith across the life span. The Counseling Psychologist *17* (4) 555-612.

Wrenn, C.G. (1962). The culturally encapsulated counselor. Harvard Educational Review, *32*, 444-449.

Author Index

Subject Index

Breinigsville, PA USA
01 February 2011
254599BV00007B/21/P